HORROR

HORROR

A Connoisseur's Guide to Literature and Film

Leonard Wolf

Facts On File
New York • Oxford

Horror: A Connoisseur's Guide to Literature and Film

Library of Congress Cataloging-in-Publication Data

Wolf, Leonard.
    Horror : a connoisseur's guide to literature and film / Leonard
Wolf.
      p. cm.
    Bibliography: p.
    Includes index.
    ISBN 0-8160-1274-1
    1. Horror tales—History and criticism. 2. Horror tales—
Bibliography. 3. Horror films—History and criticism. 4. Horror
films—Bibliography. I. Title.
PN3435.W6 1988
809.3'872—dc19   88-11126
                                        CIP

ISBN 0-8160-1274-1 (HC)
ISBN 0-8160-2197-X (PB)

Printed in the United States of America

10 9 8 7 6 5 4 3 2 1

The author graciously acknowledges the Film Stills Archive of the Museum of Modern Art
(New York) for use of the photographs on the following pages: 23, 27, 34, 40, 44, 54, 89, 95,
111, 113 (top), 115, 119, 121 (top), 130, 144, 152, 153, 156, 173, 201, 219, 222, 235.

The author is grateful to the collection of David Del Valle for use of the photographs on
pages: 15, 26, 46, 48, 58, 81, 90, 104, 128, 129, 160, 167, 177, 178, 189, 214, 230, 232
(both).

CONTENTS

To E. F. Bleiler,
master editor and pioneer scholar
of the literature of fear.

ACKNOWLEDGMENTS

A labor of love can be, nevertheless, a labor, and my task has been frequently eased by the help I have had from some very generous people. Let me thank them here.

I have had two invaluable research associates, William Nylen who helped me with texts and Maitland McDonagh who worked with me on film. Her vast film experience and her shrewd critical estimates have been especially helpful.

David Del Valle, that great storehouse of horror film lore, has been a frequent consultant as well as a tenacious film and film stills finder.

Thanks must also go to the librarians at The New York Public Library, The Museum of Modern Art and Columbia University without whose help I might have floundered.

Finally, I want to thank John Thornton and David Laskin, my editors at Facts On File, who have made of patience a creative art. I have been well served by their tact, lucidity and judgment.

INTRODUCTION

There's never too much of a good, truly disquieting thing.

—*San Francisco Chronicle*

We do not think of fear as attractive. Anyone looking into the muzzle of a .38 caliber pistol, or coughing in the smoke of a theater fire, or hearing the sound of lake ice cracking underfoot, knows that the taste of fear in moments when we are helpless and in danger is anything but delicious. And yet, there is an admirable thriftiness in human nature that prompts us to make even of fear a source of pleasure. Because in its grip we feel vividly alive. Our hair stands on end, our blood courses swiftly, our eyes turn preternaturally keen. Instead of being creatures weighed down by the perplexities of civilization, we become simply creatures, attentive, focused, and intent on staying alive.

Think for a moment of the array of sports and diversions in which the excitement for the participants comes from risking their lives: tightrope walkers, bullfighters, skiers, hang-glider pilots, parachute jumpers, rodeo riders, motorcycle and automobile racers, mountain climbers. In such ventures, the pleasure, for the participants, comes not only from mastering the skills they need to avoid death but also from the pleased awareness of just how close the call has really been.

So much, then, for the active thrill seekers. But there are also the spectators at thrill-seeker diversions, who prefer to appreciate fear passively without actually risking its dangers. They watch the tightrope walkers, the downhill racers, the lion tamers with divided attention: first, admiring skill, but also, though few dare confess it, anticipating the possibility that something may go wrong.

Aficionados of horror literature (and film) share that same vicarious pleasure but they are two removes away from the experience they seek. They neither do the dangerous thing nor watch it really being done. Instead, horror literature aficionados are consumers of imitation. Passive as sports spectators, they content themselves with "as if" experiences. As if they had met the saber-toothed tiger; as if they had dreamed the atrocious dream or encountered the mad killer in an alley. Their delight in fear is little distant from the pleasure people experience in funhouses where skeletons shriek, maniacs yell, ghosts howl, gorillas pounce, crocodiles yawn and dragons, to the scream of sirens, spew flame. In both instances "as if" is the name of the game. For both sports spectators and horror aficionados, the joy they seek is to be frightened in a safe place.

The beauty of horror literature—and my reader should understand that I am treating film here as a form of literature whose text is not read, but screened—the beauty of this literature is that it comes with its own consolation. At the most intense moment, when the hair on our heads is standing up, when we know we cannot endure the nightmare for another second, the reassuring certainties come. First, that it is happening to someone else. Second, that in any event we are safe: it is only a book; it is only a movie. In the scary book or film we get to experience the blessed nightmare, the one from which we can wake at will.

Horror literature can do more than frighten us in a safe place. At its best, it provides us with images that speak to our subconscious because they resonate with myth. In the pages of horror fiction and in the shadow plays of film we see gathered, as if in a sort of game reserve, all the impossible creatures that, in our dreams, represent the panoply of our fears. In horror literature, we find the vast troop of uncreatures—the shape-shifters and the mixed-up beasts, lamias and manticores, part-lion and part-woman; part-lion and part-man; part-woman and part-serpent. There too stalk the creatures that our guilts and secret hungers invent: the sexually ravenous 50-foot woman; the incubi and succubi for whose attentions we may secretly long.

Horror literature touches the nerve of paranoia that many of us cherish by confirming our suspicion that there is a "they" or an "it" or a "he" or a "she" that is out to get us. In horror fictions there are all kinds of evidence that the universe is badly made or ruled by forces other than those we have so far acknowledged. In the grip of horror literature, we find ourselves assuming what Lovecraft has called "a subtle attitude of awed listening as if for the beating of black wings or the scratching of outside shapes and entities on the known universe's utmost rim."

In this book, the reader will find a partial record of my own listening. Let me say at once that the entries that follow do not constitute a list of the best stories and films ever made. Then, why were they chosen? For three reasons: historical spread, thematic variety and fun. I have tried, as I made my selections, to keep in mind that my readers are connoisseurs, people who have, or are acquiring, a wide and an instructed experience of horror literature. But there is no connoisseur worthy of the name who is not also having fun.

A word about fun. Thomas Hoving, the editor of *The Connoisseur Magazine*, asks, as he is about to launch into an enthusiastic appreciation of *Cobra*, a truly wretched Sylvester Stallone film, "How can you maintain an appreciation for quality if you don't—sometimes—probe to the nadir?" Having uttered that high-minded excuse, Hoving then makes it very clear that he has had a high old time watching *Cobra*, particularly scenes in which

> Cobra and his girl wipe out the "psychos," who die in a magnificent choreography of somersaults, *pliés*, and *pas de deux*, accompanied by great "unghh's," "aieee's," and groans . . . The slaughter is so clean and unaffecting that you cannot take it seriously except as modern dance.

There really is no reason for me to claim that I read or watch some of the awful stuff that comes my way because I want to sharpen my critical faculties. The truth is that I have an "awful tooth" the way some people have a sweet tooth. I'm fond of novels like *Varney the Vampire* and films like *The Attack of the 50-Foot Woman* for their own squalid, raunchy, low-down sake.

But, like Hamlet, I can tell a hawk from a handsaw. I know a wretched novel or film when I see one. If I have included some of them here it is either because, like *Attack of the Crab Monsters*, the work is a distillation of the absolutely awful or, more likely, because I have been drawn by some glimmer in it of the unusual.

Let me pursue the question of quality for a few moments more. Horror literature (text and film) suffers from a curious disability that, if I am to be clear about it, requires me to talk briefly about the Aristotelian definition of dramatic tragedy. Aristotle, it will be remembered, says that the protagonist of a tragedy must be a great good man who falls from a high place because of some fatal flaw in his character and that the story of that fall must engender pity and terror in the spectators and then purge them of those feelings through their participation in his story.

My point is that the horror writer sets for himself only half the tragic writer's goal: He or she is intent on producing terror only. As a result, horror literature, the pitiless genre, tends to focus on plot, not character. It is the genre in which "What?" is a more important question than "Who?"

Let me illustrate the point. In Poe's "The Pit and the Pendulum," what fascinates us is the narrator's situation, not

Edgar Allan Poe

his personality. For all intents and purposes he is a man without qualities. It does not matter that we do not know his name. If anyone else were to take his place in the story it would make no difference. What is important is that he is part of a design whose elements are the lethal pendulum, the heated and enclosing walls, the pit and the rats. It is that design that we will remember long after we have forgotten the narrator.

And it is this apparent lack of three-dimensional people that has served the critics as an excuse to treat horror literature as a déclassé genre.

But even if it is true that Ambrosio, the villain of Matthew Lewis's *The Monk*, is merely an emblem of superb wickedness, that Eric, the hideously scarred phantom in *The Phantom of the Opera*, stands for The-Anguish-of-the-Ugly-Doomed-Never-To-Be-Loved-By-Beauty, and that all the characters in *Dracula* are either two-dimensional, vapid or absurd—what then? Does that prove that we have an inferior literature?

The answer, it seems to me, is that we need a more inclusive definition of greatness. We need to see that horror literature is essentially symbolic. Like fairy tales, like myths of every kind, it has less to do with individuals than with archetypes. When horror writers succeed, as Bram Stoker does in *Dracula* or as a team of writers, James A. Creelman and Ruth Rose did with *King Kong*, readers and audiences recognize that, as Arthur Machen puts it, they are acquiring symbolic knowledge of the most awful, most secret forces that lie at the heart of all things; forces before which the souls of men must wither and die and blacken.

There is a great scene in H. Rider Haggard's *She* that illustrates the point. Ayesha, the novel's heroine, who for 2,000 years has been able to retain her youth and beauty because she had passed through an immortalizing flame, steps into it again to demonstrate to Kallikrates/Leo, the man she loves and whom she wants to make immortal, that the flame will do him no harm. But this time something is wrong.

"Look! look! look!" shrieked Job . . . she's shrivelling up! . . .

True enough—I faint even as I write it in the living presence of that terrible recollection—Ayesha was shrivelling up; the golden snake that had encircled her gracious form slipped over her hips and to the ground. Smaller and smaller she grew; her skin changed colour, and in place of the perfect whiteness of its lustre it turned dirty brown and yellow, like to an old piece of withered parchment. She felt at her head: the delicate hand was nothing but a claw now, a human talon resembling that of a badly preserved Egyptian mummy. Then she seemed to understand what kind of change was passing over her, and she shrieked—ah she shrieked!—Ayesha rolled upon the floor and shrieked.

Smaller she grew, and smaller yet, till she was no larger than a monkey. Now the skin had puckered into a million wrinkles, and on her shapeless face was the stamp of unutterable age.

If we remember that earlier on, as she stepped into the flame, "No angel out of heaven could have worn a greater loveliness," we understand what has happened. Angels may be permitted immortality. But a mortal immortal, a contradiction in terms, is finally a monster that nature will inevitably spurn.

Allegory, then, or the reassertion of archetypal design, or the restatement of myth, or the salvaging of our dream life are the goals of the horror writer. When the goals are achieved we get a literature that brings pity in by the back door, fulfilling thereby Algernon Blackwood's requirement that it "enact forgiveness that will outlive us."

We turn now to a somewhat troubling theme, the role of women in the literature of horror.

From its beginnings as a distinct literary genre in England, Gothic literature, as the horror fictions came to be called, extracted all the fear that it could from the imbalance of power that is implicit in the relationship between men and women. In the standard plot of a Gothic novel, a young, beautiful and sensitive female protagonist found herself being pursued through many pages and through such dreadful places as dismal forests, ruined castles or corpse-filled charnel vaults, by a tall, dark, usually Italian male whose intent was only too obvious.

Implied sexual violence against women was the animating element in all of these fictions. Rape and incest were the commonest threats, though sadism not infrequently hovered nearby. In Ann Radcliffe's great novels, both rape and incest are imminent but never accomplished. In Matthew Lewis' *The Monk*, the villain Ambrosio commits brother-sister incest, rape and matricide.

What is especially interesting about the early history of this genre of fiction, at the end of the 18th and well into the 19th centuries, is that women were not only its chief audience but also its primary authors. Beyond Ann Radcliffe, who towers over the rest, there are Charlotte Dacre, Ann Doherty, Ann Fuller, Sarah Greene, Mary Ann Hanway, Isabella Kelly, Sophia Lee, Anna Maria Mackenzie, Eliza Parsons, Mary Pilkington, Mary-Anne Radcliffe, Regina Maria Roche and Eleanor Sleath. Finally there is the astonishing Mary Shelley who, at the age of 17, by abandoning the Gothic formula enlarged the horror novel's scope in *Frankenstein*.

The appeal of Gothic fiction for women in the late 18th and throughout the 19th centuries suggests that, whether reading or writing these fictions, women saw in them stylized images of the repressions hemming in their lives. In the details of the novels, in which pursuit and violation of the self were elaborated, they recognized the objectification of their own bodies.

Horror literature generally goes beyond the narrow focus of sexuality in Gothic fiction to open up a range of sexual behavior, or the projections of sexual fantasy or fear, that is pretty nearly endless.

Even a brief list of well-known fictions and films will demonstrate the point. In Mary Shelley's novel *Frankenstein* (1817) we see what violence can result when, in "a workshop of filthy creation," a man eight feet tall and horribly ugly is born fully developed, with all of a man's instincts and no conceivable way to fulfill them. Sheridan Le Fanu's vampire tale "Carmilla" (1872) is an early and delicate treatment of lesbianism. In Robert Louis Stevenson's novelette, *Doctor Jekyll and Mr. Hyde* (1886), though sexuality is singularly absent, it is precisely that absence that makes us suspect what sort of unacknowledged urge has prompted the well-bred, confirmed bachelor Jekyll to create the potion that releases the untrammeled Hyde. And certainly the various film versions of the story have hastened to make explicit the story's erotic implications.

If we turn to Bram Stoker's novel *Dracula* we find a fiction whose central metaphor, blood drinking, is so redolent with sexuality that it occasionally verges on the downright pornographic. And it is not hard to see why. In the novel and on the screen the blood-drinking episodes, which a reader soon learns to "read" as an intimate exchange of forbidden body fluids, have the soft serenity of a romantic love scene.

It is in films like *King Kong* (1933) and *The Creature From the Black Lagoon* (1954) that we find ourselves confronting the embarrassment of bestialism. Because, after all, what are such films about except the impossibility of the union of Beauty with the Beast. In the fairy tale, Beauty learns to kiss the Beast and thereby turns him into a prince, but in the Kong and Creature films, in which we take our pleasure from fearing the worst, it is not a simple kiss that is at stake.

In metamorphosis films like *The Wolf Man* (1941) and *Cat People* (1942), sexuality is seen as an uncontrollable force that, when it seizes us, reverses the upward climb of evolution, turning us once more into the beasts we were. The image of *The Wolf Man* speaks with special power to adolescent boys for whom the sudden appearance of hair on their bodies coincides with the onset of strange new longings, and one guesses that newly adolescent girls respond with similar understanding to the gentle heroine of *Cat People* who becomes a snarling (but still beautiful) black panther when sexually aroused.

Here, given the drift of the paragraphs above, a word of caution is needed. Pervasive as sexual themes are in horror literature, they are not always and forever at its center. Classic ghost stories, for instance, are likely to be sexless, though there are exceptions here and there, such as Henry James's "The Turn of the Screw."

The images of fear in horror literature come in an infinite variety, but no one image has the same impact on all of horror's readers. This was borne in upon me once again not long ago when in a literary spoof by Arthur Conan Doyle called "A Literary Mosaic" I read the following description of Jedediah Anchorstock, a sailor aboard a British man-of-war called *The Lightning*:

> The most striking peculiarity of this individual was, however, that in his boyhood some evil minded person had tattooed eyes all over his countenance with such marvelous skill that it was difficult at a short distance to pick out his real ones among so many counterfeits. (*The Best Supernatural Tales of Arthur Conan Doyle*, p. 177)

What was for Doyle a piece of lightweight absurdity I found terrifying in the extreme because I am scared when bad things happen to eyes. I was never comfortable with the myth of Argus who, according to Ovid, had a hundred eyes. I squirmed at the story of Polyphemus who had but a single eye in his forehead, and in the fairy tale of Little One-eye, Little Two-eyes and Little Three-eyes, I wanted the little monsters to win.

Eyes, then, are one of my idiosyncrasies. I am drawn, too, to stories of doubles ("William Wilson"), ventriloquists' dummies ("The Rival Dummy") and dolls ("The Doll"), which, because they all involve duplication, imitation or confusion of identity I find enormously threatening. Doubles are scary because they put one's very existence into question: "Which of them is me?" As for dolls, surely anyone who has ever stared into the fixity of a doll's blue eyes must have seen in them as I do the malevolent will to be alive glowing beneath the paint. As for ventriloquists' dummies, they are a byword for spiritual vampirism, as, forgetting who animates them, they steal the minds or souls of their ventriloquists.

Beyond the images of fear that appeal to me personally, there are others that appear so frequently in horror literature that it is possible to categorize them as follows:

1. Featured creatures: animals, real or imagined. We have had cats, "The Black Cat" (1843); dogs, *Cujo* (1981); rats, *Willard* (1970); ants, *Them* (1954); and flies, *The Fly* (1958 and 1986).
2. Mad killers or mad machines on the loose: *Psycho* (1959), *Peeping Tom* (1959), "I Have No Mouth and I Must Scream" (1967), *Alien* (1979), *Demon Seed* (1977),
3. Shifting shapes: *Dracula* (1931), *The Werewolf* (1956), *The Incredible Shrinking Man* (1957), *The Attack of the 50-Foot Woman* (1958), "The Curse of Yig" (1929).
4. Homemade people: *The Golem* (1920), *Frankenstein* (1817), *The Island of Doctor Moreau* (1896).
5. Invaders from . . . : *The Thing* (1951), *The Blob* (1958), *Alien* (1979).
6. The spawn of hell: *The Monk* (1976), *The Abbot of Montserrat* (1826), *Daughters of Darkness* (1971).
7. Ghosts or malevolent spirits: "The Horla" (1886), "Afterward" (1902), *The Curse of the Demon* (1956).
8. Mad, bad scientists: *Dr. Jekyll and Mr. Hyde* (1886), *The Great God Pan* (1894), *Scanners* (1981), *Screamers* (1981).
9. Horrid children: *Village of the Damned* (1960), *The Other*, novel and film (1971, 1972).
10. Comic horror: *Abbott and Costello Meet Frankenstein* (1948), *The Little Shop of Horrors* (1960), Dahl's "The Visitors" (1974).

At first glance one would suppose that comic horror would be a contradiction in terms and yet on consideration it is clear that both comedy and horror are forms of distortion. Each of the genres exploits warp, exaggeration, disproportion, the sense that something has gone wrong. In comic writing the distortion is meant to produce laughter while in horror writing it produces fear. The two forms are, however, linked to each other by a curious law of balances. With only a very small tilt, comedy can turn into horror—or vice versa. What produces the tilt is an increase or a decrease in the sympathy we feel for the characters. The more we care for protagonists who are in danger, the more horror we experience watching them. On the other hand, if we have been made to see them as objects, we are quite capable of laughing at them in their predicament.

We all understand how this works from our experience in childhood when we laughed at scenes in animated cartoons in which characters were flattened by steamrollers, exploded by sticks of dynamite and sawn apart by whirling saws. We laughed because Daffy Duck or the Road Runner were only people-like objects who had no home address, no life to get on with. As two-dimensional beings they had an immortality that kept us from ever worrying that they might die and so we laughed at the distortions that were their adventures.

A more complicated example of how comedy and horror are linked is to be found in Edgar Allan Poe's short story, "Berenice" (1835), where the narrator is a neurasthenic who is given to seizures of monomania. He marries his dying cousin Berenice, who is given to seizures of epilepsy. The narrator tells us that, in the early stages of Berenice's illness, he developed a fixation on her teeth. When Berenice dies of an epileptic seizure and is laid in her grave we are engulfed in horror as we learn that, while in a trance, the narrator has visited Berenice's grave where something happened that caused a shriek to be heard and "a search in the direction of the sound . . . [and the discovery] of a disfigured body enshrouded, yet still breathing, still palpitating, still alive."

Had the story stopped there we would still be well and truly horrified because we would have known, or guessed, how the narrator's fixation on teeth has affected the "disfigured body" of the still living Berenice. But Poe, in a great miscalculation, shifts all of our attention away from Berenice to the little box that once belonged to the family physician.

> With a shriek I bounded to the table, and grasped the box . . . But I could not force it open; and in my tremor it slipped from my hands, and fell heavily, and burst into pieces; and from it, with a rattling sound, there rolled out some instruments of dental surgery, intermingled with thirty-two small,

white and ivory-looking substances that were scattered to and fro about the floor.

It is, I submit, the "thirty-two small, white and ivory-looking substances" coupled with the coy avoidance of the word "teeth" that, by completing the objectification of Berenice, elicits the impermissible laughter that now wells up in one's throat.

We have similar moments in horror movies. In *Scanners* (1981), for instance, where the special effects people have created the illusion that we are seeing someone's head exploding on camera, what happens is that the explosion steals all humanity from the scene and we find ourselves laughing. And when, some years later, George A. Romero, profiting by still further advances in technology, made exploding heads a staple of *Dawn of the Dead* (1979) and *Day of the Dead* (1985) it became apparent very soon that we were watching a new kind of slapstick.

If, now, we want an example of how the comic can turn horrid let us turn to Roald Dahl's story "The Visitor." Here Dahl, the wickedest horror writer of our age, gives us a first person narrator who, in the tradition of the sexual conquistador, brags of his triumphs for page after page. At no time does Dahl give his readers a clue that he has anything but a wittily erotic tale to tell. It is only as we come to the very end of the story, when we hear death's secret exhalation at almost the same moment in which the protagonist is preening himself on his latest bedroom triumph, that the tribute of laughter we were about to pay the fiction turns to a horrified gasp.

In the discussion that follows and in four or five of the entries to come sharp-eyed readers will catch echoes of phrases and paragraphs that have appeared in some of my earlier work on the subject of fear literature. In those books and in discussions with my students at San Francisco State University and at The New School in New York I have found it useful to suggest that there are two great categories of horror writing: Horror From Without and Horror From Within. The first, and by far the largest as well as historically the oldest and most traditional category is Horror From Without. A good example of the formula that animates such fictions is in the film *The Most Dangerous Game*, where we have a sympathetic man being pursued by someone who means to kill him. The formula is the same in Gothic fiction except that there the person being pursued is a young woman and the harm intended is sexual. In all cases of Horror From Without, readers see the pursuer as evil, and the person pursued as good.

One of the givens about Horror From Without is that both the protagonists and the antagonists in the fictions know precisely who they are. Even when, in their adventures, they are transformed into toads or pigs or geese, they never have any doubts that they are princes or princesses who will one day become themselves again. As for the villains of such tales, there is nothing ambiguous about them. They are defined as villains and they behave villainously (or, in the case of animals, brutally). The hero or the heroine's problem is to escape the villain or to destroy him.

With the end of the 19th century, as we entered the Age of Introspection, a new category of fiction appeared: Horror From Within. In a short story like "Axolotl" by Julio Cortazar, the disaster the tale illustrates is the consequence of something transpiring in the protagonist's mind. The new danger is confusion of identity rather than physical destruction. In Charlotte Perkins Gilman's *The Yellow Wall Paper* (1899), the protagonist's enemy is her own paralysis which makes her unable to resist the destructive love of her too attentive husband, while in Kipling's "The Mark of the Beast" (1891) Fleete's personal guilt works with ancient superstition to achieve his destruction. And in Ben Hecht's "The Rival Dummy," there is no pursuing enemy except the protagonist himself.

Works that fit the category Horror Form Without can be divided once again into two groups: natural and supernatural. Natural includes those works in which the physical laws of the universe govern the plot. In supernatural horror, the laws of nature are suspended or ignored. Bizarre though Mary Shelley's *Frankenstein* is, it is nevertheless firmly grounded in the real world. Neither Victor nor the Creature have supernatural powers. Bram Stoker's *Dracula,* on the other hand, depends upon our willingness to believe that Dracula, being a creature of Satan, has supernatural powers lent to him by the Enemy of All Mankind. Among Gothic novelists, Ann Radcliffe, though she loved to hint at the supernatural, always ended her fictions by retreating safely into the world of reason, while Matthew Lewis, in *The Monk*, gives Ambrosio access to supernatural powers with help from Satan.

Let me suggest two further distinctions that may be helpful in dealing with horror literature: wet and dry. The terms as I use them have to do with the quantity and the kinds of violence the author feels we must be shown and can apply either to style, to content or to an author's vision. Wet writers, as one may guess, are unwilling to spare us any gore, while dry writers, like the classical Greeks, are more reticent and keep their scenes of violence offstage.

Readers who are addicted to reruns or who are old enough to remember the horror films of the twenties, thirties and forties will have noticed how "dry" the earlier films were. For instance, in Tod Browning's 1931 *Dracula,* when Dr. Van Helsing, at the climax of the film, is about to destroy Count Dracula by driving a stake through his heart, he picks up a piece of splintered wood and goes offscreen to look for his enemy. A moment later and from offscreen we hear a groan that tells us the deed is done. But in 1957, in *The Horror of Dracula,* a history-making Hammer Films production from England, when a young female vampire is about to be staked in her coffin, the camera comes in close and we watch the truly monstrous stake being positioned above her lovely breast. Then, as the hammer strikes the stake, there is a gush of Technicolor blood, straight up into the camera's eye. Since 1957 films have become many times wetter.

Among writers, H. P. Lovecraft is the quintessentially "wet" writer. Robert Bloch, despite the famous shower scene in *Psycho* (1960), is dry. Poe, though he is not given to self-indulgence about anatomical detail, imagines such scabrous tales, and tells them at so high a pitch as to seem "wet." D. H. Lawrence's "The Rocking Horse Winner" is dry. In film, the 1958 *The Fly* is dry, while the 1986 version is wet.

Which brings us to the newest and wettest film genre of all, the Splatter Films, which are always and only wet. If the goal of the mainstream horror film is to give its viewers pleasure by rousing fear, the sub-genre, the splatter film, seeks to give pleasure by driving its viewers to the very edge of loathing. To that end, and with the help of special effects undreamed of until the end of the 1950s, the viewer is given closely filmed decapitations, disembowllings, flayings. Murders are committed with chainsaws, electric drills, augurs, axes, timber saws. Rape scenes, torture scenes and cannibalism are filmed in such unsparing detail that one quite understands the impulse to deplore the whole venture or to conclude that the phenomenon of the splatter films is one more sign of the decay of civilization.

I am not myself very fond of the genre, though here and there, as the reader will discover, I have found notable moments even in the worst of them.

But it would be a mistake to think that the recent interest in the pornography of pain is an entirely new phenomenon. Leaving to one side the long history of blood sports, like the ancient gladiatorial games, bullfighting, bearbaiting, cockfighting, we see that literature too has had its bloodsoaked genres. In the age of Nero there was Senecan tragedy. The 16th- and 17th-century English revenge tragedies, borrowing from Seneca, put a rich variety of horror on the stage, as we see if we look briefly at Shakespeare's *Titus Andronicus.* There, in a stage direction that opens Scene 4, Act V, we read ''Enter the Empress's Sons [Demetrius and Chiron] with Lavinia, her hands cut off, and her tongue cut out, and ravish'd.'' Later in the play, Lavinia, her uncle Marcus and her father Titus, who was tricked into allowing one of his hands to be cut off, thinking it would save the lives of his two sons, leave the stage in a melancholy procession with Titus carrying one head, Marcus another and poor handless Lavinia carrying her father's lopped off hand between her teeth.

I am by no means suggesting that contemporary splatter films are on a par with either Seneca or Shakespeare. My point is simply that more people are and have been fascinated by the deplorable than is dreamed of in our philosophy. I suspect that the recent resurgence of interest in splatter movies has less to do with the decline of taste than with the sudden leap forward in the technology available to film studio special effects crews. The toys are new; the effects are new and it is more than likely that, for another decade or two, there will continue to be audiences who go to splatter movies out of simple curiosity to see what new illusion of gore has been cooked up this time.

One thing more and I have done. I have said nothing in this book about Godzilla films simply because, no matter how hard I try, I get bored watching the fire-breather smashing up Tokyo and its semblances with his tail. This, despite the fact that in two Godzilla movies I have come upon a couple of memorable moments. One is in *Godzilla vs. the Thing* (1964), featuring a pair of diminutive, melodic twins who speak in unison. The other is in *King Kong vs. Godzilla* (1962) where there is a crazy sequence in which both Godzilla and King Kong, suspended by hot air balloons, are seen floating through the air.

No. On second thought, there is a Godzilla film that a horror connoisseur will love. It is the greatest 30-second movie ever made and is called *Bambi Meets Godzilla.* Here, in a not quite professionally drawn, animated cartoon, we see a saccharine Bambi tripping along through a forest glade until he (she or it) meets Godzilla. What happens next, depending on how you feel about Bambi, is either just right or a terrible pity. In any case, a tiny classic has been perpetrated.

THE ABBEY OF ST. ASAPH   Novel

Mrs. Isabella Kelly

Great Britain

1795, London, Minerva Press; reprinted 1977, New York, Arno.

This charming, swiftly paced Gothic fiction is written in candid imitation of Ann Radcliffe. It is, nevertheless, a Gothic novel with a difference. The story, involving two generations of intricate interrelationships among members of the nobility, the middle class and the English peasantry, is too complex to be briefly summarized. It will be enough to say that there is a nobleman, Sir Eldred Trevallion, whose estate has been usurped and who, for 17 years, is a prisoner in the ruins of the Abbey of St. Asaph; there is a nearby family, the Montagues, whose fate is closely tied to that of the Trevallions; and there is the beautiful Jennet Apneu, a young peasant woman (or supposed peasant woman) who, because she appears too refined to be truly a peasant, turns out (predictably) not to be one.

For about two-thirds of its length, the characters in the novel perform a sort of gavotte as they approach or recede from the possibility of marriage. Understanding gives way to misunderstanding, would-be lovers please, offend or disturb each other. Finally, in the last third of the narrative, the tale turns roundly and soundly Gothic: the terrified Jennet, moving through the ruins of the Abbey of St. Asaph, comes upon a ghost that breathes sulfur and a chattering skull that moves of its own accord. She comes, too, upon the imprisoned Sir Eldred Trevallion, believed by everyone (including the reader) to have been dead for the past 17 years.

Eventually, all the misunderstandings are cleared up, the wicked are chastised and the good, as in all proper bourgeois fiction, are rewarded with both love and money. Unfortunately, because she is following in the footsteps of Ann Radcliffe, Mrs. Kelly is at pains to explain that the supernatural events we have seen are in fact not supernatural at all. Each of them has some logical explanation that, while it illuminates our intelligence, works against the air of mystery that is the source of the power in Gothic fiction.

Beyond its quite shivery scenes of fear, *The Abbey of St. Asaph* is distinguished by its tempestuous domestic scenes and its exuberant plotting. It has, too, that delightfully heady mixture of elegance and primordial passion that is the hallmark of Radcliffe's fiction. But beyond all this, there is in Mrs. Kelly's novel a realism that one does not find easily in Radcliffe. Mrs. Kelly's families and her heroine behave like possible people, as if Henry Fielding had been responsible for shaping her sensibility while to Ann Radcliffe she owed her diction and the imbroglios of her plot.

THE ABBOT OF MONTSERRAT   Novel

William Child Green

Great Britain

1826, London, A.K. Newman; reprinted 1977, New York, Arno.

All of the machinery of Gothic fiction is skilfully deployed in this early 19th-century novel: a dreary ruin, a wild tempest, a virgin of impeccable sensibility threatened by a lustful monk, a mountain fastness that harbors robbers, a pool of blood and a crucifix of skulls, a virulent demon modeled on the one Matthew Lewis turns loose in *The Monk* and coincidences so amazing that they call all the laws of probability into question.

There are two stories intertwined here. First there is the tale of the lovers Fernandez de Leon and Isabel de Gracey who are the grown children of feuding families. Then there is the story of the lustful as well as ambitious monk Obando who, having by murder achieved the title of Abbot of Montserrat, falls in love with Isabel and then calls on the demon Zatanai to help him gratify his wicked desires.

It is the conception and description of Zatanai that makes *The Abbot of Montserrat* a distinctive Gothic fiction. He has a fine and wicked vitality. Green describes him answering Obando's summons:

Slowly, and as if with a sullen kind of unwillingness, did the yellow-scaled Zatanai appear . . . At first the burning gleam was alone visible; anon the form of the fiend might have been traced therein, still gathering in intensity and brightness, although not so fast as it had hitherto arrived at its completion: at length the hues grew fiercer—the variable scales became distinguishable in all their fiery lustre and transparence; the head upreared its horrible glowing crest—the visage grew distinct, and the perfect demon stood before him.

And when Zatanai speaks he uses the fine old cadences of a fiend who knows his own mind. To his disciple he says, ''I speak not to thee in parables, Obando, nor in parables will be answered. If there is aught pertaining to our compact of which thou wouldst complain, speak it with perspicuity—Zatanai will attend to thee.''

Green, for the most part, narrates his plot in a lively manner. His romantic characters (Isabel and Fernandez), like most protagonists of Gothic ficiton, are cardboard cutouts of sweet decency who, of course, are destined to have each other at the story's end. And, like Montague Summers, the great Gothic scholar, we regret the vapid explanation of the Pool of Blood, which, for much of the fiction, we really thought was supernatural. But the vibrantly wicked Obando and the even wickeder Zatanai are the real reasons for reading *The Abbot of Montserrat*.

ABBOT AND COSTELLO MEET FRANKENSTEIN   Film

(Alternate release titles: **MEET THE GHOSTS; THE BRAIN OF FRANKENSTEIN**)
1948 (B&W)   U.S.A.   83 min.
Production Company: Universal International; *Director:* Charles T. Barton; *Producer:* Robert Arthur; *Screenplay:* Robert Lees, Frederic Rinaldo, John Grant; *Photography:* Charles Van Enger; *Special Effects:* David S. Horsley; *Music:* Frank Skinner.
Cast: Bud Abbott, Lou Costello, Bela Lugosi (Dracula), Lon Chaney, Jr. (The Wolf Man), Glenn Strange (The Frankenstein Creature), Lenore Aubert (Sandra Mornay), Vincent Price (The Invisible Man)

Abbott and Costello made up the hardiest comedy team that was ever turned loose on the classic monsters of the screen. Before their careers were over this phenomenal pair of zanies would meet Dr. Jekyll, Mr. Hyde and The Mummy as well as the creatures they encounter here in the most inventive and energetic—as well as the funniest—of their adventures. In *Abbott and Costello Meet Frankenstein* they meet not only the Frankenstein Creature, but Dracula, the Wolf Man and (if you can call it a meeting) the Invisible Man.

The slender plot has Dracula intent on putting Lou Costel-

Abbott and Costello meet a bevy of monsters. © Universal Pictures lo's brain into the skull of the Frankenstein Creature. Lon Chaney, Jr., again plays the woebegone Wolf Man. A typical exchange between the funny men and monster goes: The Wolf Man: ''You don't understand—when the moon rises, I turn into a wolf!'' To which Lou Costello replies, ''You and fifty million other guys.''

Abbott and Costello Meet Frankenstein has over the years become a sort of icon for terror film aficionados. A critic as cerebral as James Twitchell calls it ''Universal's scariest movie . . .'' (*Dreadful Pleasures*, p. 313). Perhaps its quality derives from the unforced enthusiasm (and sheer silliness) with which the comedians collide with the monsters. Or from the film's shrewd juggling of fear with laughter.

THE ABOMINABLE DOCTOR PHIBES   Film
1971   (C)   U.S.A.   94 min.
Production Company: American International; *Director:* Robert Fuest; *Producer:* Louis M. Heyward, Ron Dunas; *Screenplay:* James Whiton, William Goldstein; *Photography:* Norman Warwick; *Special Effects:* George Blackwell; *Music:* Basil Kirchen, Jack Nathan.
Cast: Vincent Price (Dr. Anton Phibes), Joseph Cotten (Dr. Vesalius), Hugh Griffith (rabbi), Terry-Thomas (Dr. Longstreet), Virginia North (Vulnavia), Aubrey Woods (Goldsmith).

Though David Pirie calls this film ''the worst horror film made in England since 1945'' (*A Heritage of Horror,* p. 175), a good deal can actually be said in its favor.

Made in 1971 when the word ''camp'' was still reasonably fresh, *The Abominable Doctor Phibes* is campy to the hilt. Still, it is a very imaginative, very controlled and highly stylized film in which, after the first few moments, nobody would dream of looking for probable events. It is all utterly improbable and yet so devilishly ingenious as it develops the story of the brilliant and vindictive Doctor Phibes, who lost his face and his wife as the result of an automobile accident. Phibes, who blames his wife's death on the incompetence of the surgical team that operated on her, has, like Hercules, a certain number of vengeful acts to accomplish as he destroys the doctors. But he has no interest in any ordinary vengeance. He designs each of his murders to exemplify one of the plagues that God, at Moses' instigation, sent to punish the Eyptians when the Israelites were slaves there. And so the surgeons die by locusts, rats, frogs and so on. Before each of the murders, we get glimpses of the exquisite and always totally silent Vulnavia (Virginia North) playing her violin. Phibes' final act of vengeance is especially intricate and cruel, involving, as it does, surgery on the 10-year-old son of one of the surgeons. The doctor must remove a key from the boy's chest in order to prevent his son from being destroyed

Vincent Price (left) and Joseph Cotten in **The Abominable Dr. Phibes.** © American International Pictures

by acid contained in a alembic poised above him that is timed to tilt within a very few minutes. The scene is filled with shiny glass tubes and a truly desperate sense of urgency.

Throughout, Vincent Price, in really top form, speaks Phibes's lines with all the bravura of a 19th-century actor reveling in bombast for its own sake. And as each task of murder is accomplished, we see Phibes exulting as he plays a grand theater organ while an orchestra of life-sized puppets accompanies him.

Dr. Phibes Rises Again appeared in 1972, but it is a pale imitation of the original. This time, Phibes goes to Egypt on a quest for the waters of life that flow in a rarely surfacing stream. His intent, with the help, once again, of the still silent and still beautiful Vulnavia, is to revive his wife and to live with her forever in his retreat at the bottom of a pyramid. He is bothered by a number of people, British detectives as well as various bad guys, and especially by the wicked, and wildly miscast, Robert Quarry. There are the usual number of Phibesean deaths and then the grand and vengeful organist suffers certain setbacks that bring the film to a close.

AFTERWARD   Short Story
Edith Wharton
U.S.A.
1910, in *Tales of Men and Ghosts,* New York, Scribner; reprinted 1983 in *Roald Dahl's Book of Ghost Stories,* New York, Farrar, Straus & Giroux.

"Afterward" is a ghost story that, employing a refined and elegant prose style that owes much to Henry James, manages to expose just how much of "nature red in tooth and claw" was involved in the business ethics that made possible the great 19th-century American fortunes.

Mary and Ned Boyne are a couple of Americans who for 14 years have "endured . . . the soul-deadening ugliness of a Middle Western town . . ." until a triumphant business deal makes them, in a single stroke, wealthy enough to realize their ambition to live in cultivated retirement in England while Ned writes his long-planned book on the "Economic Basis of Culture." After some searching, they find Lyng, the house of their dreams, in Dorsetshire. Among its other old world charms, the house is said to be haunted, but in rather a curious fashion. When Mary asks, "Is there a ghost at Lyng?" she is told, 'Oh, there is one, of course, but you'll never know it . . . not till afterward, at any rate."

For a while, that seems to dispose of the ghost question and Mary and Ned live contentedly in the fine old house until one day, when they both catch a glimpse of a stranger on their grounds who, when Ned goes to greet him, seems to have vanished utterly. Later, they receive a newspaper clipping that informs them that a man named Bob Elwell has brought suit against Ned in connection with the Blue Star Mine, the spectacular business transaction that made Ned rich; but when Elwell dies a few months after a botched suicide attempt, the suit lapses. When Mary asks if everything is now all right, Ned, reassuring her, says "I give you my word it was never righter!"

It turns out that he is catastrophically mistaken, as we learn when we come to the chilling climax of the story in which a ghost does indeed make its appearance and we get a glimpse of what the gentle Ned's commercial ethics were like: "It's

the kind of thing that happens every day in business," says a colleague of Ned's, "I guess it's what the scientists call the survival of the fittest . . ."

"Afterward" is a polished, finely crafted, leisurely ghost story, perhaps the only one ever written in which a ghost takes a hand in the progress of evolution.

ALIEN   Film
1979   (C)   U.S.A.   116 min.
Production Company: 20th Century-Fox; *Director:* Ridley Scott; *Producer:* Gordon Carroll, David Giler and Walter Hill; *Screenplay:* Dan O'Bannon (from a story by Dan O'Bannon and Ronald Shusett); *Photography:* Derek Vanlint; *Editor:* Terry Rawlings; *Special Effects:* Brian Johnson, Nick Allder, Denys Ayling, Carlo Rambaldi (Alien head effects); Alien design by H.R. Giger; *Music:* Jerry Goldsmith.
Cast: Tom Skerritt (Dallas), Sigourney Weaver (Ripley), Veronica Cartwright (Lambert), Harry Dean Stanton (Brett), John Hurt (Kane), Ian Holm (Ash), Yaphet Kotto (Parker).

The spaceship *Nostromo* ("Our Man"—a not too subtle borrowing from Joseph Conrad) lands on a barren planet from which it has intercepted radio signals. An exploration team comes upon what looks like the shell of a vast spacecraft; they enter the structure and one of the party, examining what seem to be egg pods, is suddenly attacked by a furiously squirming organism which then attaches itself to him. The afflicted man is brought back to his own spacecraft where an implanted life form bursts quite literally from him onto the screen.

From here on, *Alien* becomes a horror-in-an-enclosed-space story as the people on the *Nostromo* try to find and destroy the nearly unkillable and continually growing thing that infests their ship. For viewers, the search is made splendidly awful because of the film's imaginative special effects. The ship itself is conceived as an inhuman high-tech structure—a perfect background for a primordial confrontation between quite ordinary men and women and a life form that, on any showing, is better prepared to survive than they are.

Ridley Scott, the director, paces his film tightly. The creature becomes ever more sinister as it eludes the crew and takes on the ever-larger dimensions of a deadly-toothed cross between a very wet reptile and the vilest insect ever imagined. The rivalry among the crew who fight over pay and prestige, and the free market profit-making mentality of the corporation that has sponsored the expedition, make a neat counterpoint to the crew's epic struggle for survival.

At its best, *Alien* is altogether harrowing. At its worst—like every great work it has a few bad moments—it depicts the damage done by the alien to human tissue all too graphically. The filmmaker's elaborate attentiveness to minority representation on the crew, while politically correct, seems condescending. But all that to one side, if maximum startle and maximum fear are what one goes to scary movies for, *Alien* is a masterpiece in its genre.

ALIENS   Film
1986   (C)   U.S.A.   137 min.
Production Company: Brandywine/20th Century-Fox; *Director:* James Cameron; *Producer:* Gale Anne Hurd; *Screenplay:* James Cameron; Story by James Cameron, David Giler and

Walter Hill, based on characters created by Dan O'Bannon and Ronald Shusett; **Photography:** Adrian Biddle; **Editor:** Ray Lovejoy; **Special Effects:** Alien effects created by Stan Winston; Certain special visual effects created by L. A. Effects Group, Inc.; **Music:** James Horner.
Cast: Sigourney Weaver (Ripley), Carrie Henn (Newt), Michael Biehn (Corporal Hicks), Paul Reiser (Burke), Lance Henriksen (Bishop), Bill Paxton (Private Hudson), William Hope (Lieutenant Gorman), Jenette Goldstein (Private Vasquez).

What Sylvester Stallone did in *Rambo* for the waning self-confidence of men who would still like to believe in the macho ethic, Sigourney Weaver's performance in *Aliens* should do for the growing self-confidence of women who have long suspected that they could outclass men.

As *Aliens* begins, we find Ripley, whom we last saw as a tenacious and quick-witted survivor in *Alien*, being brought out of the long suspended-animation in which she journeyed away from LB-426, the barren planet on which the *Alien* saga began.

Ripley, who is well over 90 years old (she spent 57 years homeward bound, not counting the years spent outward bound), is in great shape. Still, she is reluctant to go back to LB-426 until the sly-tongued, corporate dastard, Burke, appealing to her hatred of her old enemies, persuades her to join a "seek-and-destroy" Marine Corps mission against the aliens who, it appears, have attacked a colony of humans on the ill-fated planet.

Back on LB-426, there is soon hell to pay as the film's grandeur unfolds. We have already seen marvelously crafted high-tech sets on a space station and in the space ship carrying the crew to its destination. Almost as an aside, we see and admire machinery whose use we will only later understand. And again, as in *Alien*, there is a poignant contrast between the gadgetry and the frail humans who operate it.

But it is the battle, immediate, sustained, tenacious, audacious (on both sides) between the aliens and the humans that rivets our attention. The creatures are vibrant, horrid, wet, wily and ever present. The people have to fight not only their enemies but also flaws in their own, or each other's characters. Writers Cameron, Giler and Hill have added to all this a 10-year-old girl, the colony's lone survivor who, in the context of what the aliens look like, is bizarrely named Newt.

The film becomes an instant allegory in which manhood and womanhood are tested. It has to be said at once that manhood in this film is, by and large, a dismal failure. Womanhood (and human surrogate motherhood) is a signal success. It may not be too much to say that as the film ends we get the filmmakers' visionary portrait of the family of the future: Ripley, a gunslinging, grenade throwing, machine wielding, competent and fiercely loving, powerful mommy; one thumbs-up, courageous little girl child; and a vague paternal presence patched together out of a couple of feckless men and one half of a splendidly reliable android.

There is one other, related dimension to the film. The epic final battle in which Ripley confronts the alien Queen Mother in her brooder cavern is couched as a battle between females: "Get away from her, you bitch," says Ripley, defending Newt as she faces a hydra-featured Queen Mother hovering over

her brood. For the viewer, there is no choice between the two faces of motherhood. We root for our species, but it is hard not to notice that the Queen Mother has, if not justice, at least instinct on her side.

Alien was a triumphant film. *Aliens,* violating the law of sequels, is a colossal triumph.

ALRAUNE   Novel
Hanns Heinz Ewers
Germany
1929, New York, John Day (tr. S. Guy Endore); reprinted 1976, New York, Arno.

Alraune (the name means "mandrake root") is an exquisite horror fiction that is profoundly indebted to Baudelaire and to Huysmans for its braiding of the sensual and the deadly. The book is redolent of wine and roses, of sun-warmed damask, of limpid pools and flower-strewn couches of love. Always, there hovers over it a breath of spring in which one still feels the chill of winter—the hint of death lurking nearby.

Ewers writes a dispassionate prose that, by tightly buttoning the horrors he describes, makes them appear unbearable. Incest in one barely disguised form or another is the book's primary theme and homosexual hunger is a close second.

Alraune, the protagonist of Ewers' masterpiece, is a wonder child, the creation of an amoral, rich and ugly German scientist and entrepreneur named Professor Jacob ten Brinken who has been experimenting with artificial insemination. The professor's nephew, Frank Braun, a young student, is intrigued by the macabre folklore of the mandrake root as a fertility symbol, and prods his uncle to perform an experiment: to create a human life by fertilizing the ovum of an erotically insatiable prostitute, Alma Raune, with the semen ejaculated by Noerisson, a rapist-murderer, at the moment of his execution.

Alraune, the girl born of this artificial insemination, is raised by Professor ten Brinken as his own daughter. From the moment of her birth, her life proves deadly to others. The physician who operates on the infant to correct a condition known as *Atresia Vaginalis* (the narrowing of the vagina) dies of an infection contracted when he is scratched by Alraune's tiny fingernail. As the beautiful child grows, she is perceived as the source, if not invariably the direct agent, of a variety of evils. At her school, small creatures, pets or wild animals are abominably tortured by innocent children whom Alraune has mysteriously egged on.

As she grows older and more beautiful, men and women fall in love with her and she, by subtle suggestion and manipulation, contrives their destruction. But always, there is no way to blame her. She remains (or appears to remain) an innocent bystander. Finally, her creator, Professor ten Brinken, a brilliant, heartless, suave and unsavory old lecher, more than 60 years older than his ward, falls madly, if ambiguously, in love with her. The result is one more suicide—and Alraune is left an heiress, with Frank Braun designated as her guardian.

The narrative of the love affair between Frank Braun, who conceived the idea of Alraune, and the flesh and blood Alraune, contains some of the most compelling erotic writing in contemporary terror fiction. The atmosphere of their affair is at once cloying, suffocating, and deliciously sensual. At

The bowl and the dice.

times when the evil force of which Alraune is a distillation manifests itself in their embraces they achieve moments of the most corrosive ghastliness. Then human ecstasy turns vampiric and love approaches crime.

Before the book ends, we are given a lovely and eerie scene in which Alraune, meaning to forecast the future, rattles the dice made from her father's vertebrae in a bowl made of her mother's skull.

ALRAUNE
Film

1930 (1934 in U.S.A.) B&W Germany 103 min.
Production Company: U.F.A.; *Director:* Richard Oswald; *Producer:* Erich Pommer; *Screenplay:* Charlie Roellinghoff, Richard Weisbock; *Photography:* Guenther Krampf.
Cast: Brigitte Helm (Alraune), Albert Basserman (Geheimrat ten Brinken), Harald Paulsen, Kaethe Haack, Bernhard Goetzke.

This film version of the Hanns Heinz Ewers novel *Alraune* has aged well over the decades since it was released in the U.S. in 1934. While it presents the plot of the novel in rather a clipped fashion it retains a considerable amount of Ewers' horrified sensuality. Director Richard Oswald conveys this quality more by the way he lets the camera linger over the heavily carved, dark wooden interiors than by anything the characters do.

Brigitte Helm's Alraune is generally more vixenish than erotic, but Albert Basserman performs masterfully the role of the corrupt scientist who, at the instigation of his nephew Frank Braun, creates Alraune by artificially inseminating Germany's most lascivious prostitute with the sperm of the country's most vicious criminal.

As in the novel, Alraune is responsible for the deaths of the men who, one after the other, fall under her spell. Curiously enough, except for the scene in which we see her urging the family chauffeur to drive faster and faster until he cracks up

the car and himself, we never know quite what it is she does to produce the string of disasters. In the novel, they happen simply because she is a distillation of evil toward whom evil events naturally gravitate.

This "Alraune," with all of its flaws (and even without English subtitles), is a fine and gratifying film.

THE AMBER WITCH
Novel

Wilhelm Meinhold
Germany
1843, Berlin, Duncker & Humblot; reprinted in E. F. Bleiler's (ed.) *Five Victorian Ghost Novels*, 1971, New York, Dover.

This very long short story, or very short novel, is a masterpiece that is not nearly as well known as it ought to be. It purports to be an account by a Protestant parson on the island of Userow in the Baltic Sea of the tribulations endured by his daughter, Maria Schweidler, a young woman who, because she rejects the sexual advances of the sheriff of Userow, is accused of being a witch. It is an accusation that, for all sorts of very carefully developed reasons, falls on fertile ground. Maria is arrested, brought before a tribunal, threatened with torture and finally condemned to be executed.

Meinhold gives the story the form of an extensive, quasi-legal deposition of the events that preceded and then resulted from the accusation of witchcraft. His tale has the ruminative pace of a gentle country parson who, as he tells the story, scrupulously orders his memories even as he is unable to hide his torment. The details of the plot against Maria are so minutely and so elaborately given that the story, when it was first published, was believed to be an authentic account of a witch trial written by an historical personage who lived in the seventeenth century, the time when the events took place.

What makes this fiction so remarkable is not its plot but the poignancy of its prose. While reading it we have the illusion that we are hearing the voice of a narrator whose sense of language has been steeped in the rhythms of theological discourse as well as illuminated by his devoted reading in the Latin classics. His pious and meticulous account of the fiendish plot against his daughter's life does two things: It sets the story firmly in the very midst of the real world and it touches his circumstantial tale with a subtle but pervading irony. Though the tale comes to a nearly perfect fairytale ending, its theme is profoundly tragic: Without the intervention of God, impotent innocence confronting wicked power is invariably doomed.

AN AMERICAN WEREWOLF IN LONDON   Film
1981   (C)   Great Britain   97 min.
Production Company: Poly Gram Pictures-Lycanthropy Films/Universal; *Director:* John Landis; *Producer:* George Folsey, Jr.; *Screenplay:* John Landis; *Photography:* Robert Paynter; *Editor:* Malcolm Campbell; *Special Effects:* (Makeup) Rick Baker; *Music:* Creedence Clearwater Revival, Elmer Bernstein.
Cast: David Naughton (David Kessler), Jenny Agutter (Nurse Alex Price), Griffin Dunne (Jack Goodman), Brian Glover (chess player), John Woodvine (Dr. Hirsch).

The quippy horror film, which ought to be a contradiction in terms, is very much in evidence in the eighties of this century. It's as if filmmakers had concluded that the youthful audiences for which, by and large, scary films are made, have become so sophisticated they must have crackling one-liners to go along with their gore. If one must have such anomalies, then *An American Werewolf in London* is one of the best of the lot, because it does not, finally, sacrifice authentic moments of fear for the sake of mere quips, and because it takes the folklore (and the filmlore) of the werewolf seriously.

The story in brief: A couple of young Americans doing a walking tour in the north of England on a night of the full moon encounter a werewolf. In the melee that follows, one of the young men, Jack Goodman, is killed, the other, David Kessler, is wounded. It is not long before David, who is warned of what will happen by the ghost of his friend, begins to show the classic signs of the werewolf. In the hospital where he has been taken to be treated for his wounds, he complicates his situation by falling in love with his nurse. What follows, despite the subdominant comic wit of the film's script writers, is as grisly as can be.

A few scenes in *An American Werewolf in London* are so moving, and so apt, that they give this otherwise sometimes-bumpy film more than a touch of class. One scene is when David sits in a film viewing booth of a porno house and takes counsel with the ghastly shade of his friend Jack. The second is the masterful and touching scene when David, in an interval between werewolf seizures, knowing that he is doomed to die, or worse, makes a collect call from a streetcorner phone booth in London to his suburban American home only to get his self-engrossed little sister on the phone. His efforts to impose the proper tone of loving, deathbed farewell on a conversation with his bubble gum-generation sister ought to have won David Naughton, who played the role, an Oscar. As it was, Rick Baker, who designed the makeup for the werewolf transitions, did indeed get one for special effects.

THE AMOROUS GHOST   Short Story
Enid Bagnold
Great Britain
1921, in Ethel Dell's (ed.) *Rosa Mundi,* New York, Burt; reprinted 1966 in Kurt Singer's (ed.) *The Gothic Reader,* New York, Ace.

Here is a tiny story so utterly unimposing, so simple and direct that one is entirely deceived into thinking that its unalarming prose style cannot possibly lead to anything truly dreadful.

What is there to be afraid of? The owner of a plain white house, Mr. Templeton, discovers that his housemaids have given notice after finding, strewn about his bedroom, various female undergarments that do not belong to his wife. And he, himself, two nights ago

> had seen the two hands hanging idly over the back of the chair as though an unseen owner were kneeling in the seat.

Then, on another night, he sees not only a hand but also "the tip of a mound of fair hair . . ." after which the hand (or something) deposits a bundle on the back of a chair. That bundle turns out to be a pair of stays. Then Templeton believes that he has caught glimpses of a woman "Undressing . . . washing."

If that was the extent of the ghostly visitor's activities, we would have a modestly amusing little tale. Because that is not all, what we have is a short, sharp tale with an utterly convincing and atrocious climax.

AMOUR DURE   Short Story
Vernon Lee (pseudonym of Violet Paget)
Great Britain
1890, in *Hauntings,* London, Heinemann; reprinted 1974 in Montague Summers' (ed.) *The Supernatural Omnibus* (1st, 1931), New York, Causeway.

In his introduction to *The Supernatural Omnibus,* Montague Summers, that most crotchety of all critics, says of Vernon Lee that "even Le Fanu and M.R. James cannot be ranked above the genius of this lady." This time, Summers is absolutely right. Vernon Lee is a past master in the high manner of terror tale writing and in "Amour Dure" we see her at her regal best: Wielding a prose style of singular grace and fluency, she infuses her 19th-century tale with the aura of the Italian Renaissance. What is more wonderful still is that her story, despite the richness of its color, texture and design, nevertheless leaves us with the sense of gaping horror that is the proper goal of the terror tale.

"Amour Dure" has a first person narrator, Spiridion Trepka, a 24-year-old scholar who has been employed to write a history of Urbania, a village in the Italian Apennines. In the course of his researches, he comes upon the story of Medea, a beautiful 16th-century woman whose "history and character remind one of that of Bianca Cappello, and at the same time of Lucrezia Borgia." Hers was the sort of beauty that stirred love in the hearts of many men and where she bestowed her love, the men died.

The roster of her victims included young Pico to whom she was married when she was 14. Then the Duke of Stimigliano. Then the groom who at her instigation killed the Duke. Still later there was the Duke Guidalfonso II who gave her refuge when she fled the vengeance of Stimigliano's kinsmen. Guidalfonso not only protected her, he also actually married the 19-year-old Medea when his own wife, neglected by him, pined away and died. Guidalfonso in turn died "suddenly and mysteriously." Later, other men infatuated by her beauty died while doing her bidding, even when she was in prison. So powerful was her effect on men that Duke Robert, her captor, who was able to resist her because he never set eyes on her, insisted that "only women . . . should be employed for the deed" of strangling Medea.

This much of the story of "Amour Dure" purports to be 16th-century history. The rest of our tale tells what happens to the young Polish researcher Spiridion who, like Medea's other victims, becomes so enthralled by what he has read about her that he finds it perfectly natural to serve the 300-year-dead Medea in accomplishing her last, and dreadful, design. By that time, he is thoroughly under her spell:

> The possession of a woman like Medea is a happiness too great for a mortal man; . . . And only death, the willingness to pay for such happiness by death, can at all make a man worthy of being her lover; he must be willing to love and suffer and die. This is the meaning of her device—'Amour Dure—Dure Amour'. . . . it is a constant and cruel love.

For the romantic young Pole, death is a trivial impediment to such happiness as he imagines the ghost of Medea will give him. Though he asks whether the others who loved her and died—"Pico, the Groom, Stimigliano, Oliverotto, Frangipani, Prinzivalle degli Ordelaffi"—will be there, he dismisses the question in loverlike fashion: "But she shall love me best—" and moves on to his doom.

ANCIENT SORCERIES   Short Story
Algernon Blackwood
Great Britain
1908, in *John Silence, Physician Extraordinary*, London, Eveleigh Nash; reprinted 1973 in E. F. Bleiler's (ed.) *Best Ghost Stories of Algernon Blackwood*, New York, Dover.

We get most of the story of "Ancient Sorceries" as it is told by "commonplace little [Arthur] Vezin, who was fore-ordained to live and die according to scale."

Arthur Vezin, "a timid, gentle, delicate soul," returning from a vacation in northern France, is mildly irritated by the chatter of a crowd of Bretons on his train. Though he is warned to beware "because of the cats and of sleep," he impulsively leaves his compartment when the train stops in a mountain village in France; he takes a room in a hotel there. Vezin says that "This was the beginning apparently of an adventure somewhere deep within me, in a region I could not check or measure, and a feeling of alarm mingled itself with my wonder . . ."

Once registered in the hotel, Vezin finds himself transported back to a time in which he and all the inhabitants of the village were members of a Satan-worshipping witches' coven; by means of a salve they rubbed on their bodies, they were able to transform themselves into cats.

The whole affair is suffused with the rank and yet gorgeous perfume of wild and forbidden sexuality as Vezin is led further and deeper into the adventure by the lithe and beautiful Lise, the daughter of the huge, yet graceful proprietress of his inn. With her he hears the ancient cry, "Anoint and away! Anoint and away . . . To the Dance that never

dies! To the sweet and fearful fantasy of evil." When the adventure is all over, the erotic ebullience gives way to loathing, but for Vezin, a 40-year-old bachelor who has been made to stare at aspects of himself he did not know existed, the experience may have proved fatal.

"Ancient Sorceries" owes a debt to Hawthorne's "Young Goodman Brown," but Blackwood's story is more immediately sensual. What he does best is to create the illusion of a sinister secret town all of whose inhabitants, intent on the worship of evil, move with the agility of cats. At the same time, he dilutes the horror of his tale by introducing the suggestion that Vezin's experience is the result of "subliminal uprushes of memory [which] can be exceedingly painful, and sometimes exceedingly dangerous." The fantasies induced by the fascination and the fear of sex, as they assault a timid and rigid mind, animate the tale sufficiently. We prefer the "sweet and fearful fantasy of evil" and can do without the lame science.

THE APPARITION   Short Story
Guy de Maupassant
France
1883, in *Le Gaulois*; reprinted 1975 in *Complete Short Stories of Guy de Maupassant*, New York, Hanover House.

Victor, a young French army officer stationed at Rouen, meets a down-at-heels former comrade in arms who desperately implores him to go to a certain dreary chateau and to bring back from it a diary that he will find there. Victor, to ease his friend's mind, goes to the chateau and finds the diary, but while he is looking at it, a woman appears before him. A woman with very long hair which she begs Victor to comb for her. Victor describes the experience: "I took the comb from her hand and lifted that long hair. That hair that gave me the feeling of awful cold . . . Of handling snakes. I handled that icy hair; I twisted it; I braided it; I bound it and unbound it . . . ."

The woman in the dreary house is, of course, a ghost, and she tells Victor that his friend Jacques murdered her by strangling her with her own hair when he discovered, by reading her diary, that her love for him had turned to hatred.

When Victor brings the diary back to his friend Jacques, he finds that the ghost has already exacted her revenge.

"The Apparition" is an icy, urgent and grim tale that moves with a strangely exhilarated pace and gives us glimpses of interior squalor we would rather not know about.

For other chilling hair stories, see Helen Addam's poem "I Love My Love" and "The Black Hair" episode in the film *Kwaidan*.

THE ASH TREE   Short Story
M.R. James
Great Britain
1904, in *Ghost Stories of an Antiquary*, London, Edward Arnold; collection reprinted 1971, New York, Dover.

In "The Ash Tree," as elsewhere, M.R. James creates tension by the contrast between his scholarly, detached tone and the glimpses he gives us of the terrifyingly inchoate, and here nauseating, forces that inhabit our world with us. Close and neutral as his descriptions appear to be, they are nevertheless disturbingly sensuous, as when the murderous creatures of this tale, having done their fatal business, leave their victim: "There! something drops off the bed with a soft plump, like a kitten . . ."

In this story, set in the last years of the 17th century, in Castringham in eastern England, James tells of a woman named Mrs. Mothersole who was tried and executed for being a witch. The chief witness against her was the local squire, Sir Matthew Fell, the owner of Castringham Hall. His testimony was that he had seen her gathering twigs from the ash tree that overlooked his bedroom window.

Before Mrs. Mothersole died "in a poysonous rage," she promised Sir Matthew that "there will be guests at the Hall." One morning, not many weeks later, Sir Matthew was found dead, his body black and swollen. And for 50 years thereafter, the ash tree exerted a malevolent influence over cattle and wild animals that came near it.

When Matthew Fell's grandson, who has long nurtured suspicions about the ash tree, chooses to sleep in the bedroom where his grandfather died, he too is found black and swollen, and stone dead. When, later that day, a cat disappears into the tree and shrieks so appallingly that women faint, the tree is subjected to close investigation, in the course of which a gardener's lantern that has fallen into the tree's hollow trunk sets it on fire. The flames drive out the tree's grisly inhabitants, their round bodies all covered with fire.

> This, five or six times; then a similar ball leapt into the air and fell on the grass, where after a moment it lay still. The Bishop went as near as he dared to it, and saw—what but the remains of an enormous spider, veinous and seared. And, as the fire burned lower down, more terrible bodies like this began to break out from the trunk, and it was seen that these were covered with greyish hair.

While M.R. James attends to matters like plot and characterization meticulously, it is the interplay between the sedate and civil tone of the narrator, and the sense of texture and sight—the way things feel to the fingers and are glimpsed in the corner of the eye—that is the hallmark of his fiction. What he does best is conjure up spiders with veinous bodies covered with greying hair. Hair alone would be bad enough. It is the greying hair that makes us stifle an unwary scream.

ATTACK OF THE CRAB MONSTERS   Film
1957   (B&W)   U.S.A.   70 min.
Production Company: Allied Artists; **Director:** Roger Corman; **Producer:** Roger Corman; **Screenplay:** Charles Griffith; **Photography:** Floyd Crosby; **Editor:** Charles Gross, Jr.; **Music:** Ronald Stein.
Cast: Richard Garland (Dale Drawer), Pamela Duncan (Martha Hunter), Russell Johnson (Hank Chapman), Leslie Bradley (Dr. Karl Weigand), Richard Cutting (Dr. James Carson).

Attack is a post-atomic bomb "creatures" film, interesting now for that reason and because it is a neat example of the Roger Corman quickie style. Plot, not characterization, was always the focus of a Corman film, and here the plot was meant to be frequently shocking. The shocks have not aged well since the fifties, but the Corman kinky verve is still there.

The story concerns a team of government scientists who come to a Pacific island to investigate the disappearance of a previous team. The island is shaken by earthquakes and tidal waves, and one by one, members of the team disappear or are lured to their deaths by the voices of lost team members who call to them during the night.

The island is preternaturally quiet; nothing but seagulls and land crabs are visible. Eventually, the enemy is discerned: the island is being destroyed, and its inhabitants being killed, by a highly intelligent new species of giant land crab produced by atomic radiation. These crabs, after ingesting human prey, acquired human brain power and the capacity to project human voices.

This bodes ill for humankind until the dwindling force of scientists learns that the crabs can be destroyed by electric power. In a climactic scene, the last, and pregnant, giant crab is destroyed by a self-sacrificing Hank who topples a high tension power on to the sad-eyed arthropod. "He died to save us," says Martha to her fiance, Dale.

ATTACK OF THE 50-FT. WOMAN   Film
1958   (B&W)   U.S.A.   65 min.
Production Company: Allied Artists; **Director:** Nathan Hertz; **Producer:** Bernard Woolner; **Screenplay:** Mark Hanna; **Photography:** Jacques Marquette; **Music:** Ronald Stein.
Cast: Allison Hayes, William Hudson, Yvette Vickers, Roy Gordon, Ken Terrell.

Donald Willis in his *Checklist* characterizes this film as "really rotten" and Carlos Clarens asks, "Who can claim such devotion to film research as to have sat through . . .

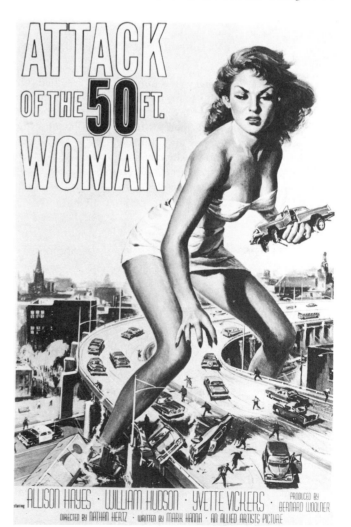

Poster art.

'The Attack of the Fifty Foot Woman?' " A fair question, because the film, short as it is, is punishingly slow. It comes close to being a negligible movie except that it encapsulates in its story line two quite powerful elements: the classic theme of metamorphosis *and* a quite moving, and startling, image of modern marital distress.

A rich woman is taken by her cad of a husband into the desert and left there to die. She is affected by the radiation incident upon the arrival of an outer-space visitor. Brought back to town by rescuers, she begins to grow. When she has reached the 50-foot height, she goes off to avenge herself on her unfaithful husband. "I know where my husband is; he's with that woman . . ." she cries as, with a flick of her wrist, she tears up the honkytonk in which her husband and his floozy are dancing. The scene bears comparison with King Kong's mute search among the skyscrapers of New York for his vanished Fay Wray, and is, in its context, as unforgettable.

ATTACK OF THE KILLER TOMATOES   Film
1978   (C)   U.S.A.   87 min.
Production Company: Four Square Productions; *Director:* John De Bello; *Producer:* Steve Peace and John De Bello; *Screenplay:* C.J. Dillon, Steve Peace and John De Bello; *Photography:* John K. Culley; *Music:* Gordon Goodman and Paul Sundfor.
Cast: David Miller (Mason Dixon), Cindy Charles (housewife), Joe Price (Detective 1), Wayne Cyphert (husband), George Wilson (Jim Richardson), Sharon Taylor (Lois Fairchild).

Attack of the Killer Tomatoes is a one-line joke stretched out for 87 minutes. The film is meant to be a spoof on horror films, and particularly on "Invasion of . . ." and "Attack of . . ." films, but after five minutes of tomatoes bobbing up and down and growling as the filmmakers try to keep their ridiculous joke entertaining, the amusement stops abruptly.

As the film ends we get a second—and very tiny—blip of humor as we learn that a sequel, *The Attack of the Killer Carrots*, is on somebody's drawing board. With good luck, it will stay there.

THE AUTOPSY   Short Story
Michael Shea
U.S.A.
December 1980 in *The Magazine of Fantasy and Science Fiction*; reprinted 1985 in *A Treasury of American Horror Stories*, New York, Bonanza.

The 57-year-old Doctor Williams, dying of cancer, is called on to perform autopsies of 10 people killed in an explosion in a tiny Colorado town. The deaths have occurred after a period of time in which seven local people had vanished within the space of seven weeks. That mystery is complicated by the discovery of the body parts of a man named Dougherty whose remains have been severely drained of blood. The doctor learns from the sheriff that the investigation of that murder was abruptly terminated when the chief suspect, a man named either Allen or Sykes, fled from the police into the local mine where he and the nine other victims were killed in an explosion.

Methodically, the doctor examines each of the bodies and

slowly begins to understand that one of them, the one belonging to Joe Allen, may not be what we call dead at all. And with that understanding comes proof. The body of Joe Allen suddenly stands before the doctor and out of its mouth come the words, "Please. Help me."

The voice that speaks thus out of Joe Allen is that of an extraterrestrial, and the mine accident was his contrivance to prevent discovery of his presence. The doctor's problem: What to do about what he now knows? The dialogue and the stratagems that the doctor and the alien play out against each other are the substance of the rest of the story. The absolute horror of the tale comes when we watch Allen's animated, though rotting, corpse perform surgery that will link the cancer-ridden living body of the doctor with its own.

The alien tells us, however, that it is more than gross feeding that will take place between himself, the alien parasite, and his host, the doctor: "It is not mere blood that feeds this lust I feel to tenant you . . ." says the creature. "My truest feast lies in compelling you to feed in that way and in the utter deformation of your will this will involve."

The creature, avid to be a parasite of thought as well as flesh, is outwitted by the dying doctor in the simplest and most logical fashion. By the time that happens our admiration for Shea's patient and graceful craftsmanship comes close to being overwhelming. Shea, who was a 1983 winner of the World Fantasy Award, ought surely to be better known.

THE AWAKENING   Film
1980   (C)   Great Britain   100 min.
Production Company: Solofilm/Orion; *Director:* Mike Newell; *Producer:* Robert Solo; *Screenplay:* Allan Scott, Chris Bryant, Clive Exton; *Photography:* Jack Cardiff; *Editor:* Terry Rawlings; **Special Effects:** John Stears; *Music:* Claude Bolling.
Cast: Charlton Heston (Matthew Corbek), Susannah York (Jane Turner), Jill Townsend (Anne Corbeck), Stephanie Zimbalist (Margaret Corbeck).

The Awakening, a comparatively recent addition to the mummy film genre, is based loosely on one of Bram Stoker's less readable novels, *The Jewel of the Seven Stars*. The film has been considerably modernized with the imposition of an incest theme onto its post-Victorian source.

In the story as we now have it, an archaeologist named Corbek, aided by his attractive young assistant, Janie, discovers the tomb of Kara, an Egyptian princess, at the very same instant that his wife, Annie, is giving birth to their daughter Margaret in a Cairo hospital.

Eighteen years later, Corbek is living in England with his second wife, his amiable former assistant, Janie. Meanwhile, in Cairo, the embalmed body of Kara is giving out signals that reach both London and the United States. In answer to the mysterious summons, Margaret leaves her mother in America and flies to London. From there she and her father go to Egypt where they visit Kara's tomb. There, the father and daughter are suddenly aware that there is an incestuous passion developing between them. They become unconscious collaborators with the dead Kara who has plans to come to life again. In Egypt and in London, a number of people die in furtherance of the wicked, dead princess's plans.

The Awakening is an expensive, beautifully photographed

production that, despite the interest added by the incest theme, does not really improve on Stoker's ineffective novel.

AXOLOTL   Short Story
Julio Cortazár
Argentina
1963, in *End of the Game and Other Stories,* New York, Pantheon.

The opening paragraph of "Axolotl" is as laconic and arresting as the opening sentence of Kafka's "Metamorphosis." Cortazár writes: "There was a time when I thought a great deal about the axolotls. I went to see them in the aquarium at the Jardin des Plantes and stayed for hours watching them, observing their immobility, their faint movements. Now I am an Axolotl."

The axolotls, the narrator tells us, are

a species of salamander of the genus Abystoma. That they were Mexican I knew already by looking at them and their little pink Aztec faces and the placard at the top of the tank . . . [they are] capable of living on dry land during the periods of drought, and continuing their life under water when the rainy season came.

And what is wonderful, and horrifying, about the story is the way that Cortazár's prose imitates the drift of sympathy the narrator feels with these creatures who have arrived at a minimum relationship with their environment and how we ourselves drift into sympathy for the dry transformation that takes place at the story's end. What that climax reveals is "a hell that has no 'otherness.' "

There is neither blood nor violence in this tale. What there is is a perfect objectification of that most tempting of human temptations this side of suicide: inconsequential consciousness, apathy as a passionate idea.

B

BASKET CASE
Film

1982   (C)   U.S.A.   89 min.

Production Company: Ievins/Henelotter; *Director:* Frank Henenlotter; *Producer:* Edgar Ievins; *Screenplay:* Frank Henenlotter; *Photography:* Bruce Torbet; *Music:* Gus Russo.

Cast: Kevin Van Hentenryck (Duane Bradley), Terri Susan Smith (his girlfriend).

Here is one of those sad, sad, inexpensive, grimy movies whose central idea is so morbid, and whose execution is so deplorable that one can only wish it had never been made or at least that one could somehow manage to forget it. But the awful truth is that this sleazily made and revolting study of brotherly love has images that are so bizarre and suffuses them with so much sincerity that it compels attention from the most unwilling viewer.

It is instructive, if one can stand it, to see this film in conjunction with Brian de Palma's *The Sisters.* Where de Palma transforms the misfortune of separated Siamese twin sisters into a frequently delicate and complex tragedy, Frank Henenlotter uses a similar story involving the separation of Siamese twin brothers as an excuse for his camera to get as close as it can to deformity.

Henenlotter's story, briefly: When Duane Bradley was born an incompletely developed twin brother was found attached to his torso. Duane and his sibling, named Belial, are cared for together until their father has the deformity surgically removed, wrapped in plastic and thrown into a garbage pail from which Duane, whose psychic bond to his brother is intense, rescues him.

The rest of the film chronicles the adventures of Belial and Duane. Duane, obedient to his vengeful and bloodthirsty brother whom he keeps in wicker basket, takes vengeance first on their father and then on the three doctors who performed the separating surgery. Belial, as unsightly a construct as was ever devised by a special effects man, finally turns on Duane and the resolution of that conflict brings the film mercifully to its end.

Filmgoers who have seen buzz saws threatening the lives of ingenues in the melodramas of the twenties and thirties may feel a touch of nostalgia in the scene in which such a buzz saw cuts Duane's father neatly in two. As very black humor goes, it is a scene worth a chuckle or two. Beyond that, this film's only other ahievement is to impress us with how dangerous it can be simply to be born.

THE BECKONING FAIR ONE
Short Story

Oliver Onions

Great Britain

1911, in *Widdershins,* London, Secker; collection reprinted 1979, New York, Dover.

Algernon Blackwood, himself a master of the scary tale, called "The Beckoning Fair One" the best ghost story in English.

As in other truly fine horror fictions like Henry James' "The Turn of the Screw," Le Fanu's "Green Tea" and de Maupassant's "The Horla," the ghost, or the thing that is doing the haunting, is intricately and intimately intertwined with the victim's character and psyche. That is to say, the victim is at least half responsible for the appearance or the persistence of whatever is haunting him. In "The Beckoning Fair One," Oliver Onions links the psychological dislocation of his protagonist, Paul Oleron, to the needs and hungers of his ghostly companion in such a seamless fashion that the reader is hard put to know whether Oleron brings his calamity down upon himself or whether it is the work of the ghostly woman who is "the unknown conumerator of his abode."

Paul Oleron, a writer of serious, if unremunerative fiction, is in the midst of his most important novel just as he chooses to move into an old house in a shabby quarter of London. Elsie Bengough, a fellow writer and old friend who, no doubt, would welcome Paul's falling in love with her, has a premonition that the house will not be good for him and tells him so.

And, indeed, something about the house works on his psyche in such a way that the 15 chapters of his new book, *Romilly,* chapters Elsie and others have admired, now seem ineffectual and dreary and he decides to rewrite his book completely. But as the months pass, it becomes clear that he is not writing; and that there is a female, ghostly presence in the house that has cast an intensely erotic spell over him. He becomes increasingly and intensely reclusive. He has food and other necessities delivered to him so that he can avoid any occasion for leaving the house. And always he is keenly attuned to a persistently recurring sound: the silken hiss of a brush moving through a woman's long hair.

That woman, or her ghostly presence, becomes the malevolent third angle of an erotic triangle with Oleron and Elsie. And what Onions does breathtakingly well is to make us feel the ghost's erotic presence like a rare, and vaguely sick, perfume.

Once the love triangle is established, the story moves with all deliberate speed to its crushing conclusion. Onions, keeping the few events that make up Oleron's life clearly in the foreground of his tale, also manages to probe into the hidden wounds that, for many artists, are the source of their creativity. With great patience and superb skill, he chronicles Oleron's long decline into a sweet, slow-motion apathy whose sweetest climax finally is death.

Any writer, anyone at all who has ever suffered from a block to his or her creativity, will understand the exquisite inertia to which Oleron succumbs. It is the void misperceived as passion down which one drifts with eyes wide open and a grateful surrender of the will.

BEDLAM   Film

1946 (B&W) U.S.A. 79 min.
Production Company: RKO; *Director:* Mark Robson; *Producer:* Val Lewton; *Screenplay:* Carlos Keith (Val Lewton), Mark Robson; *Photography:* Nicholas Musuraca; *Editor:* Lyle Boyer; *Special Effects:* Vernon L. Walker; *Music:* Roy Webb. *Cast:* Boris Karloff (Master Sims), Anna Lee (Nell Bowen), Billy House (Lord Mortimer), Richard Fraser (Hannay).

The time is 1761. The place, London. The mood about what you would expect from a Val Lewton film, especially one that takes its inspiration from a Hogarth print.

Nell Bowen, a sprightly young "friend" of a London nobleman, becomes involved in the dismal lives of the inmates of Bethlehem Hospital (Bedlam). She pities them and falls in love with a Quaker brickmason who teaches her the beauties of truth and social conscience. Boris Karloff is the heavy, playing the role of the Apothecary General, in charge of the Bedlam madhouse. The Apothecary General is cruel to his charges on principle. When Nell Bowen (as a result of some murky plotting) is incarcerated in Bedlam, he looks forward to getting some luscious vengeance but, with the help of the inmates to whom Nell has been kind, he gets his comeuppance and the otherwise honest Quaker bricklayer is taught to be judiciously, if a bit immorally, silent about the wicked tyrant's fate.

This is not one of Val Lewton's best films. The plotting, as has been suggested, is sometimes murky. But visually it has its rich moments. There is the rebellion in the madhouse, always an anxiety provoking idea; and then there is the

Boris Karloff as Master Sims in **Bedlam.** © RKO Pictures

camera work, especially the interplay between the events on the screeen and the Hogarthian world that inspired the film. If we add a literate script, an otherwise somewhat unfocused production acquires distinction of a sort.

THE BEGGAR WOMAN OF   Short Story
LUCARNO

Heinrich von Kleist
Germany
1810, in *Erzählungen;* reprinted 1978 in *The Marquise of O. and Other Stories,* trans. and ed. by David Luke and Nigel Reeves, New York, Penguin.

Kleist, whose mind and whose fiction can be labyrinthian, gives us here a tiny but jewel-like tale that is utterly unsparing in the brief glimpse it gives us of the way, in Kleist's view, the moral universe is arranged.

There are really only three characters in the story: an Italian marquis and his wife, the marquise, who live in a castle in northern Italy, and an old beggar woman, who one day is given permission by the marquise to lie down for a rest on a bundle of straw in the corner of a room. When the marquis, returned from his hunting, wants to put his stick in its usual corner and finds the old woman lying there, he orders her rudely to

remove herself behind the stove. As she rose, the woman's crutch slipped on the polished floor and she fell, dangerously injuring the lower part of her back, as although she did manage with indescribable difficulty to get to her feet and to cross the room from one side to the other in the direction indicated, she collapsed moaning and gasping behind the stove and expired.

That, then—the death of the old woman and the manner of it—are the events on which the story turns. The marquis' arrogant rudeness turns out to have been one of those gestures that sets destiny in motion. Years later, when the marquis wants to sell the castle, a prospective buyer who is spending the night in the room in which the old woman died, flees from the room and babbles that it is haunted.

When the marquis and his wife investigate they find that their guest was telling the truth. Night after night in that room there is a ghostly reenactment of the torment and the death of the old woman. Now it is the marquis and his wife who are tormented until finally the story ends with the marquis, ''weary of his life,'' devoting himself to the destruction of his line.

The tone of Kleist's 1810 story, its bare bleakness, its grinding inevitability, make it read like a Beckett play—or, like a grown-up fairy tale that, leached of all wonder, asserts the grim moral that your own interior goblin will get you if you don't watch out.

BIANCA'S HANDS   Short Story
Theodore Sturgeon
U.S.A.
1947, in *Argosy* (U.K.); reprinted 1985 in Barry N. Malzberg and Martin H. Greenberg's (eds.) *Great Tales of Horror and the Supernatural*, Secaucus, N.J., Castle.

This eerie tale works because Sturgeon has managed to combine nausea and eroticism in an amazingly tight balance. ''Bianca,'' we are told ''was squat and small with dank hair and rotten teeth.'' She is, moreover, an imbecile, and yet when young Ran sees her (or, better, when he catches sight of her amazingly beautiful hands) he is overwhelmed by them and is determined to attach his life to Bianca's at whatever cost.

The story alternates between the lyric and the loathesome as, with an amazing economy of means, Sturgeon constructs a truly creepy allegory of erotic fixation. Ran, despite Bianca's obvious and debilitating imbecility, unerstands that the hands he has fallen in love with are inhabited by an entire being altogether different from her; a being that is graceful, dynamic and sensuous.

Caught up in this compulsive fascination, Ran marries Bianca for the sake of the hands to which, unfortunately, the monstrous rest of her is attached. And when, on the nuptial night, the monster and the beautiful hands act together for one murderous moment, Ran does not find excessive the price he has to pay for his strange love.

BILLY THE KID VERSUS DRACULA   Film
1965 (C) U.S.A. 84 min.
Production Company: Circle; *Director:* William Beaudine; *Producer:* Carroll Case; *Screenplay:* Carl Hittleman; *Photography:* Lothrop Worth; *Editor:* Roy Livingston; *Special Effects:* Cinema Research Corporation; *Music:* Raoul Kraushaar.
Cast: John Carradine (Dracula), Chuck Courtney (Billy the Kid), Melinda Plowman (Betty Bentley), Virginia Christine (Eva Oster), Olive Carey (Doc), Harry Carey, Jr. (Ben), Marjorie Bennett (Mrs. Bentley).

There is something wonderfully carefree and vigorous about the way Hollywood ties together mythologies that have nothing to do with each other. Here we get the lore of the vampire and the lore of the American West uneasily, albeit pleasingly, linked.

In 1965, when *Billy the Kid versus Dracula* was made, John Carradine's eyes had deep pouches under them; but despite the fact that he was then the oldest actor who had ever played Dracula, Carradine's hypnotic stare burned out of the screen.

It is not quite clear why Dracula has come to Texas, but there he is, irritating Billy the Kid who loves the ingenue Betty and resents her interest in her too-fascinating foreign uncle, Count Dracula. Billy is helped in his combat with ancient evil by a wide-eyed German-accented couple named Oster who want to avenge their daughter's death at the fangs of the vampire. Even more helpful is ''Doc,'' a tough-talking, homespun, self-taught Annie Oakley sort of country doctor who has just enough German to read a book on vampires which she just happens to have with her out there in Texas. This ''female backwoods pill slinger,'' examining the wounds in Betty's throat, says, ''If I didn't know better, I'd say it was a vampire. I been reading up on that stuff. It's pretty spooky.''

Indeed, the situation is so spooky that it flusters the local sheriff, to whom ''Doc'' indignantly says, ''Somebody's got to go save the child . . . if you won't, then Billy must.'' Billy does, first emptying his sixgun at the vampire, without effect, and finally driving a stake through Carradine's heart, with surprising results. The vampire crumbles to dust even as a bat that represents him flutters to earth and dies. Meanwhile, Betty is restored to herself, justifying ''Doc's'' diagnosis that ''the spell is broken. She's going to be all right.'' Billy, his arm around the wan young woman says, ''Come on, honey. We're going home.''

The reason that this essentially foolish film is so engaging is that Carradine in his red-lined cloak plays the role of Dracula with dignity and flair despite the campiness of the film's script and despite the film writer's unforgiveable intrusion of a scene in which we learn that at least one of the vampire's victims is a sheep.

William Beaudine, who in this film retained his sense of humor and his sense of proportion, also made *Jesse James Meets Frankenstein's Daughter* (1966). That effort, though once again a fusion of old world with new world mythologies, is so ludicrous that even when it is seen it cannot be believed.

THE BIRD WITH THE CRYSTAL   Film
PLUMAGE
1970 (C) Italy-Germany 98 min.
Production Company: Seda Spettacoli (Rome) and C.C.C. Film (Berlin); *Director:* Dario Argento; *Producer:* Salvatore Argento; **Screenplay:** Dario Argento; *Photography:* Vittorio Storraro; *Editor:* Franco Fraticelli; *Music:* Ennio Morricone.
Cast: Tony Musante (Sam Dalmas), Suzy Kendall (Julia), Eva Renzi (Monica Ranieri), Entico Maria Salerno (Inspector Morrosini), Mario Adorf (Berto Castaldi), Renato Romano (Dover), Umberto Raho (Alberto Ranieri).

Roger Greenspan, reviewing *The Bird With the Crystal Plumage* for the *The New York Times*, observed that ''Like almost everything else in the film, the title is wonderfully fancy and eighty per cent irrelevant.'' Even 80 percent may be too high an estimate, but it hardly matters if the lyric title serves to entice viewers to this first rate murder mystery-cum-horror film.

As *The Bird . . .* begins, the screen shows us Roman newspapers headlining a new, mysterious homicide, the third within a month. Then we meet young Sam Dalmas, an American writer who, with his girlfriend Julia, has been living in Rome, supporting himself as best he can with hack work. Now, with the proceeds from his latest assignment, he is getting ready to go back to the States. Then fate steps in.

As he is walking one evening past a lighted art gallery, he sees a man and a woman struggling over a knife. The woman falls, the man jumps down a low staircase and makes his escape. Dalmas, horrified, tries to get to the wounded woman and, in one of the best photographed sequences in the film, proves unable to reach her. His desperate lunges against impassive plate glass, his inability either to hear what the pleading woman is calling to him or to be heard as he tries to reassure her is a horrifying vignette and serves as a presage of the horrors yet to come.

In the event, Monica Ranieri, the victim of that attack, is only lightly wounded, but Dalmas, as a material witness, is detained by the police who then confiscate his passport to prevent him from leaving the city. Meanwhile, there are more killings and Dalmas finds himself ineluctably drawn into the search for the killer, despite Julia's warning, ''Isn't it slightly ridiculous and rather dangerous to play detective . . . This thing is beginning to turn into an obsession.''

That it is dangerous he learns quickly enough when attacks are made on his own life, but the obsession grows because he is convinced that he saw something on the night of the attack which, if he could only remember it, would help him—and the police—solve the mystery.

One clue Dalmas follows up is the identity of a painter one of whose paintings was sold by the killer's first victim. The sequence in which Dalmas visits the antisocial painter who has bricked up all the doors and windows of his house and who lives and paints in an attic where he raises plump cats on which he dines makes for very welcome comic relief.

Finally, Carlo, one of Dalmas' friends, solves the mystery of a strange background noise that can be heard on a tape recording Dalmas has made of the killer's voice. It is the call of the Bird With the Crystal Plumage, a rare Siberian bird one specimen of which lives in the zoo. From that moment on, the film moves to its doubly surprising climax with helter-skelter speed.

Dargento, who, like De Palma, is constantly being compared to Alfred Hitchcock, has, I think, an imagination that is considerably more intricate and sensuous. He likes strange, angular shots—his temptation is to disorient his viewers with familiar images made suddenly unfamiliar: plate glass windows, rooftops, long corridors, doorways. In addition, he has a keen ear for the noises in the ordinary world that can be employed to sound sinister: breathing, the clicking of doors, snatches of someone singing, the breaking of glass. The result is that, though he works with a plot no more intricate than murder mysteries usually require, he achieves an atmosphere far more horrifying than one either expects or gets in the usual whodunnit. What it all adds up to in *The Bird With the*

Crystal Plumage is typical Dargento fare: a complicated and brutal story imaginatively filmed to create as much tension as possible.

THE BIRDS   Short Story
Daphne du Maurier
Great Britain
1952, in *Kiss Me Again, Stranger,* Garden City, N.Y., Doubleday; collection reprinted 1972, New York, Avon.

Though it is the basis for the Alfred Hitchcock film of the same name, Daphne du Maurier's story bears no resemblance to the film aside from the presence of malevolent birds.

Her perfectly focused, spare and sinister tale of the malign indifference of the universe to the human species begins laconically enough: ''On December the third the wind changed overnight and it was winter.'' Almost at once we meet Nat Hocken, a disabled World War II veteran who works as a handyman and who, watching the winter movement of the birds on the sea-girt peninsula where he lives, notices how, this year, the birds are particularly restless. When Nat observes that there are many more birds than usual, a farmer replies that they are more daring, too. ''It will be a hard winter,'' says the farmer. ''That's why the birds are restless.''

That very night, Nat, hearing a tapping at his bedroom window, opens it and is attacked by a bird that draws blood from his knuckles with its beak. That relatively mild bloodletting marks the beginning of the nightmare in which, to the accompaniment of flapping wings and piercing cries, an entire universe of birds, ''robins, finches, blue tits, larks and bramblings,'' mounts its attack against all humankind.

Later, protecting one of his children, Nat battles a hostile flock of small local birds and kills more than 50 of them. At the beach, where he has gone to bury the little bodies, he becomes aware that there are tens upon tens of thousands of gulls riding the waves off shore. Back home, he learns from the radio that bird attacks have been reported all over the British Isles, and he understands that a grave disaster is in the making. He sets about turning his home into a fortress that he hopes will be impregnable to the birds' attacks, which, when they come, are continuous, sustained and cruel.

As Nat in his barricaded house listens to the ''tearing sound of splintering wood,'' he wonders ''how many million years of memory were stored in those little brains, behind the stabbing beaks, the piercing eyes, now giving them this instinct to destroy mankind with all the deft precision of machines.'' We, for our part, may find ourselves wondering whether du Maurier, remembering the Lufwaffe making its daily raids on England in World War II, is telling us that there may be another as yet unimagined enemy hidden in nature (or in human nature) that is waiting for a particular change in the wind to take to its wings and strike.

THE BIRDS   Film
1963   (C)   U.S.A.   119 min.
Production Company: Universal Pictures; ***Director:*** Alfred Hitchcock; ***Producer:*** Alfred Hitchcock; ***Screenplay:*** Evan Hunter; ***Photography:*** Robert Burks; ***Editor:*** George Tomasini; ***Special Effects:*** Lawrence A. Hampton; ***Sound Consultant:*** Bernard Herrmann; ***Bird Trainer:*** Ray Berwick.
Cast: Rod Taylor (Mitch), Tippi Hedren (Melanie), Jessica

Tandy (Lydia, Mitch's mother), Suzanne Pleshette (Annie), Ethel Griffies (Kathy).

There are a couple of reasons why this quite tedious, nearly inert film must be included here. First, there are the two or three stunningly staged scenes that capture, even if only for a moment, something of the terror that is to be found in the Daphne du Maurier short story on which the film is based. Second, Alfred Hitchcock directed this venture, and it is instructive to see how even this master can nod.

Evan Hunter's screenplay has almost nothing to do with the du Maurier story except for the premise of an unprovoked attack by birds against people. Hunter invents a love story in which Mitch, a young Bodega Bay criminal lawyer, meets and is drawn to Melanie, the sleek, elegantly coiffed, and very wealthy daughter of a San Francisco newspaper publisher. Melanie, resounding to Mitch, finds an excuse to go to Bodega Bay where he is staying with his mother, Lydia, and his sister, Kathy. Annie, Mitch's former lover, now only a friend, is a dark woman of considerable pulchritude who, to be near Mitch, teaches school in Bodega Bay. Kathy, Mitch's 12-year-old sister, is in the plot so that audiences will have a child to worry about when the dangerous action begins.

That action, the attack by the birds, seems to have been endlessly delayed while Mitch accepts or ignores or abuses or courts the devotion of the four females in his life, all of whom, including the child Kathy, are impeccably groomed. Their hair especially seems to have been so doted on that even in the battle scenes with the birds, hardly a strand of anyone's hair is so much as mussed.

We never learn why the birds attack, though one hysterical local woman blames it all on Melanie, whose arrival in Bodega Bay coincides with the first attack. Whatever the reason, once the birds in their thousands mount their assault against mankind, the filmgoer begins to get a bit of the kind of excitement for which he or she goes to an Alfred Hitchcock movie. The best of the battle scenes involves an attack on a group of schoolchildren and later a swooping attack by hundreds of birds on Melanie in the attic of Mitch's family home. Brilliantly enough, Hitchcock has her battling the birds in silence, so that all we hear is the frantic fluttering of wings. Brilliant, too, are the moments when the camera stares at a door that is being slowly shredded by the frenzied hammering of beaks and bills.

Except for these brilliant scenes, *The Birds* is, for the most part, a mindless venture. And it is never more mindless than at the very end when, after we have seen how the birds can cut their way through solid wooden doors, Mitch, in the course of an unexplained truce in the destruction, drives his loved ones away in a canvas-topped convertible while the inscrutable birds look on.

THE BLACK CAT
Film
(Alternate release titles: **HOUSE OF DOOM, THE VANISHING BODY**)
1934 (B&W) U.S.A. 65 min.
Production Company: Universal; *Director:* Edgar G. Ulmer; *Producer:* Carl Laemmle, Jr., E.M. Asher; *Screenplay:* Peter Ruric; *Photography:* John Mescall; *Musical Director:* Heinz Roemheld.
Cast: Bela Lugosi (Dr. Vitus Verdegast), Boris Karloff (Hjal-

Bella Lugosi and Jacqueline Wells in **The Black Cat.**

mar Poelzig), David Manners (Peter Allison), Herman Bing (car steward), Jacqueline Wells (Jean Allison), Lucille Lund (Karen Poelzig).

There is no connection, whatever the screen credits may say, between this film and Edgar Allan Poe's story of the same name—unless the black cat that runs across the set once or twice is a sufficient link.

Hjalmar Poelzig, played by Boris Karloff, a sometime architect, and onetime traitor during World War I, is now a high priest of a satanic cult who has built himself a retreat in a mysterious corner of Hungary. To his strangely beautiful house (a gorgeous imitation of the best of Bauhaus) come Dr. Vitus Verdegast, played by Bela Lugosi, and a couple of innocent young Americans on their honeymoon who have made a wrong turn that has brought them to Poelzig's den of European iniquity. Poelzig and Verdegast, it develops, are ancient enemies. Long ago, Poelzig ran off with Verdegast's wife. That wife, now dead, lies embalmed in Poelzig's marvelously imagined cellar while Poelzig lives upstairs as the husband of Verdegast's daughter.

Verdegast is soon aware that Poelzig has his eyes on the young American woman. The doctor and his archenemy engage for a while in a well-bred struggle (that includes a lovely chess game) in which the lives of the Americans are at stake. Poelzig wants to sacrifice the young woman to Satan. Verdegast, moved more by hatred of Poelzig than any rush of affection for the American woman, does what he can to save her and her bumbling husband. As the film ends, it becomes, as Carlos Clarens says, "a contrived catalogue of satanism, necrophilia, sadism, and murder." Curiously enough, despite an on-camera scene in which Verdegast is about to flay Poelzig, there is almost no visible violence. Even pistols popping off sound harmless.

And yet *The Black Cat* is a gem of a film. Individual scenes feel like the museum exhibit of a stylish, if brooding, photographer. The sets, rather like grown-up and smoother versions of the sets in *The Cabinet of Dr. Caligari,* are a continuous delight to the eye.

And Karloff and Lugosi have never been better. They play their roles with high-style irony, as if they were aware of the film's strange, and perhaps unintentional subtext: a kind of psycho-political allegory of the helplessness of American innocence in the presence of European evil. The young Americans, David Manners and Jacqueline Wells, whenever they are on camera, appear hopelessly outclassed. They are uncultivated, uncouth and unaware. By contrast, when our two arch-villains appear, one senses the presence of deeply civilized and profoundly corrupt, ancient and secret forces struggling with each other. The fact that the Americans are saved at the end has nothing to do with either their merit or skill.

BLACK MAGIC: A TALE OF THE RISE AND FALL OF ANTICHRIST

Novel

Marjorie Bowen
Great Britain
1909, London, Alston Rivers

Black Magic is a most congenial tale of Satanism that gratifies our suppressed taste for trappings and high style rhetoric at the same time that it gives us an effective, if not truly profound, study of a supremely wicked man. It has, for a novel published early in this century, a surprisingly contemporary look.

In its opening chapter, we meet three young people, Dirk Rensewoude, a sculptor who is interested in the occult, Balthazar of Courtrai, an extremely handsome "knight-at-arms," and Thierry of Dendermonde, a student who, like Dirk Rensewoude, is fascinated by the forbidden sciences. The astonishing careers of these three men form the substance of the novel even as the complex and ambiguous love-hate relationship between Dirk and Thierry serves as the thread that binds all other elements together.

Dirk, who is a direct literary descendant of Matthew Lewis' Ambrosio in *The Monk,* looms before us finally as a towering figure of evil. Starting as a lowly sculptor who has only a bare acquaintance with the arcana of Satanism, he becomes an adept sorcerer who makes use of spells and conjurations to further a career in wickedness with the goal of achieving the Papacy. Dirk's contrivances turn Balthazar first into the Emperor of Germany, and then into the Emperor of the West. But all the while, Dirk's goal is to lift Thierry to the heights of power that he, Dirk, has reached. Eventually, he succeeds, but by then the cost to all the characters in the book is appalling.

Subvert homosexual and overt heterosexual lusts are the source of the novel's considerable energy. Dirk's passion for Thierry, Thierry's passion for Jacobea, Jacobea's lust for her steward Sebastian, and Ysabeau's lust for Balthazar form an erotic chain of personal, political and religious disasters. Add to all this several imps, demons and other deplorable beings from the precincts of hell, as well as scenes of uninhibited pageantry in which rubies and diamonds, incense-laden air, silks, satins, and masked mysterious figures play their parts, and what you get is a merrily seething and entirely satisfying post-Gothic fiction.

Black Magic is marred to some degree by Marjorie Bowen's decision to let her characters speak a fake medieval English, relying on archaisms like "varlet," "certes" and "mayhap" that frequently pass over into bombast. At its best, however, the inflated prose allows her characters to posture in the grand manner. Dirk says, "Aye, I will be emperor . . . though the world I rule rot about me, though ghouls and fiends make my imperial train—I will join hands with Anti-Christ to see if there be a God or no."

Finally, *Black Magic* is a tour de force of plotting: The reader does not even begin to guess, until the last several pages of the novel, just what the real truth is about Dirk. The letter he leaves behind is a triumph of ambiguity: "If I be a devil I go whence I came, if a man I lived as one and die as one, if woman I have known Love, conquered it and by it have been vanquished. Whatsoever I am I perish on the heights, but I do not descend from them . . ."

THE BLACK ROOM

Film

1935 (B&W) U.S.A. 75 min.
Production Company: Columbia; *Director:* Roy William Neill; *Producer:* Robert North; *Screenplay:* Henry Meyers, Arthur Strawn; *Photography:* Al Sigler.
Cast: Boris Karloff (Anton/Gregor), Marian Marsh (Thea Hessel), Robert Allen (Lt. Lussan), Thurston Hall (Colonel Hessel), Katherine deMille (Mascha).

The Black Room is one of those films whose charm lies in its simplicity and its predictability. Watching it is a little like hearing a favorite old tale being retold for the thousandth time.

Identical twin noblemen, bad Gregor and good Anton (who has a paralyzed right arm), have been separated to avoid the fulfillment of a family curse that predicts that the younger brother will kill the elder and bring about the downfall of their line. Now they are reunited when Anton is lured back to the family castle after Gregor has assured him that he has walled up the Black Room in which the prophecy is supposed to be fulfilled.

But it is all a ruse. Gregor, who is hated by the populace for his depredations among their women, senses that he is about to be deposed and has sent for Anton as part of an ingenious plot. First, he announces to a rebellious mob that he plans to give over the estate to Anton while he, Gregor, leaves the country. Once the mob is appeased by this promise Gregor takes Anton into the Black Room. There he throws him into the pit into which he has regularly thrown his women victims once he has finished with them. Then, affecting a paralyzed arm as he pretends to be the popular Anton, he woos the beautiful Thea and rules his now pacified populace. Thea, it should be said, loves the handsome and faithful Lt. Lussan, but for reasons of state she agrees to marry the false Anton.

Vile Gregor's plot seems to be succeeding. Then, on the day of his marriage to Thea, when the priest asks, "If there be any here who see an impediment to this marriage, let him speak now . . ." the dead Anton's dog, a great Dane plunges through the crowd in the church and attacks Gregor who fends him off with his supposedly paralyzed arm. The crowd, perceiving that they have been duped, chase Gregor from the church, and he rushes back to his castle to take refuge in the Black Room where, of course, the dog, the villagers and his doom find him.

There are several things to be grateful for in this fine old chestnut of a film. First there is Karloff's dual performance. He handles the good brother/bad brother roles with a marvelous sense of irony. When he is the wicked Gregor, the sneer on his lips seems grafted there. When he is the decent and lovable Anton, his frank and open smile marks him as a friend to the world. In addition to Karloff's performance, we have richly romantic sets and scenes, one in particular of a fascinating Eastern rite marriage ceremony. Finally we have Roy William Neill's astute direction, which avoids disturbing the fairy tale charm of the story. The result is a fine costume piece with plenty of ingenious action and an old fashioned, dependable moral.

BLACK SABBATH   Film
1964 (C)   Italy-France   99 min.
Production Company: Galatea Films/Emmepi Cinematografica/Societe Cinematographique Lyre; **Director:** Mario Bava; **Producer:** Paolo Mercuri; **Screenplay:** Mario Bava, Marcello Fondata, Alberto Bevilacqua; **Photography:** Ubaldo Terzano; **Editor:** Mario Serandrei; **Music:** Roberto Nicolosi; Les Baxter.
Cast: Michele Mercier (Rosy), Mark Damon (Vladimir), Susie Anderson (Sdenye), Lydia Alfonsi (Mary), Boris Karloff (Gorca), Jacqueline Soussard (nurse).

Black Sabbath is an anthology film comprising three tales each of which has an utterly unimportant introduction spoken by Boris Karloff. The first and second of the tales are satisfactory without being remarkable; the third is a chilling, nightmarish, utterly persuasive vampire tale that is in a class all by itself.

The first of the tales is based on a Chekhov story, "The Drop of Water." Here, an unscrupulous and alcoholic nurse who has been called in to lay out the body of one of her patients, a spiritualist who died in the course of a seance, steals the dead woman's ring. The dead woman's face, by the way, is frozen into a mask of terror so appalling that it can hardly be matched by the combined action of the rest of the episode, which in any case is pretty predictable. The sequence is made sinister by Mario Bava's imaginative use of a buzzing fly, dripping water and the slyly casual presence of a cat.

"The Telephone," the second episode, is based on a short story by Howard Snyder. Here we have Rosy, a beautiful but unscrupulous and expensive prostitute who receives sinister phone calls from a man named Frank who once left a young woman named Mary for Rosy's sake. Rosy appeals to Mary for help and Mary comes to spend the night with her. There, Frank mistakenly kills Mary and is killed in his turn by Rosy. The sequence has a supernatural ending that, after the two deaths, is hardly frightening at all.

Black Sabbath's final episode, "The Verdelaks," based on a story by Alexey Tolstoy, is the one that makes the film worth while.

All of this episode's action is filmed on sets of such eery inertness that one often has the feeling that everything is taking place in slow motion. First, we see a young nobleman named Vladimir riding through a bizarre terrain on his way to Jassy. He comes upon a horse ridden by the splendidly dressed, headless body of a man who has a dagger sticking out of his back.

Vladimir leads the horse to a lonely house where he meets five members of the same family, two men, two women and a little boy. Vladimir learns that the headless body is that of a bandit named Aly Beg and that the dagger that killed him belongs to Gorca, the father of the family, who went into the hills five days ago. Vladimir learns, too, that there is some

danger that their father, may return as a verdelak, a vampire.

When the wounded Gorca, magnificently played by Karloff, returns, his behavior is at first ambiguous, but his true nature is revealed very soon as, one after the other, he vampirizes his sons, his daughter-in-law and his grandson. Nor is that all. In fact, things get very much worse by the time the tale comes to its end. The image of the vampirized child returned from the grave, standing outside the family home, knocking to be admitted and crying, "Mother, let me in. I'm cold. Mother, let me in," tears at one's vitals—until the inevitable happens. It is a scene almost as horrifying as the later one in which beautiful Sdenye, herself now a vampire, takes her first victim as the camera swings to the gloating faces of three generations of vampires (including the little one) pressing against the glass.

Black Sabbath, while it can not match the director's much more powerful *Black Sunday* (1960), is worth watching as a sort of sequential display of Mario Bava's directorial skills. In the first two episodes he is clearly warming up, but he is fully engaged and at his best when he comes at last to the verdelaks. There Alexey Tolstoy's story is transformed into a dense film metaphor of the vampiric implications of family life. No one else, with the exception of Anne Rice in her *Interview With the Vampire* (1976), has developed those implications quite so pointedly.

BLACK SUNDAY   Film
(Alternate release titles: **LA MASCHERA DEL DEMONIO, REVENGE OF THE VAMPIRE, THE DEMON'S MASK, HOUSE OF FRIGHT**)
1960 (CC)   Italy   83 min.
Production Company: Galatea/Jolly-American International; **Director:** Mario Bava; **Producer:** Massimo di Rita; **Screenplay:** Ennio de Concini, Mario Bava, Marcello Coscai; **Photography:** Ubaldo Terzano, Mario Bava; **Editor:** Mario Serandrei (original) and Salvatore Billitteri (U.S. version); **Music:** Roberto Nicolosi; Les Baxter (U.S. version).
Cast: Barbara Steele (Princess Asa & Katia), John Richardson (Dr. Kubayan), Ivo Garrani (Prince), Andre Checchi (Dr. Andreus), Arturo Dominci (Javutich), Enrico Olivieri (Constantin).

Black Sunday is partly engaging Grand Guignol, partly a love-and-horror story, and partly an elaborate exercise in startling ways to spill blood on camera. But it has imaginative tracking shots into and around crypts and cemeteries and occasional moments of high elegance, as if the opulence of a Hammer film had been fused with the pseudo-lyricism of Roger Corman's Poe films.

Two hundred years ago, Princess Asa Vajda, the high priestess of a satanic cult, and her serf Javutich are burned at the stake for witchcraft by Asa's brother, the Grand Inquisitor. As the flames lap round her she cries, "It's I who renounce you. In the name of Satan, I place a curse upon you. . . . My revenge will strike down you and your accursed house. . . . I shall return to torment and to destroy throughout the nights of time . . ."

Then a cruel, spiked mask is hammered onto her face, the flames leap up and . . . that should have been the end of the witch. But a Satan-induced deluge puts out the flames and

Princess Asa is laid to rest in the family crypt. Her serf and colleague in evil, Javutich, is buried in unhallowed ground.

Now, 200 years later, our tale properly begins with two Moldavian doctors, Dr. Kubayan and his younger colleague, Dr. Andreus, who are on their way to a medical convention somewhere near "Milgorod." As they pass through the present Prince Vajda's domain, Dr. Kubayan inadvertently resuscitates the vampire Princess Asa with a few drops of his blood. She embarks immediately on her campaign of vengeance against her family's descendants who now include the Princess Katia (also played by Barbara Steele), Katia's father the prince, and her brother Constantin.

The vampire princess also contrives to reanimate her serf Javutich and together they wreak considerable vampire havoc on the family. Parenthetically, the young doctor Andreus and Princess Katia fall in love.

What makes this slightly clumsy classic work is the authority given to the variety of folk traditions that inform it: the tradition of Black Sunday; the perennial battle between satanic and Christian forces; and the whole lore of vampirism as Bram Stoker and Hollywood have recreated it for us.

But beyond that, the film's heavy-footedness is offset by the skilful use of every Gothic cliche in the book: thunder and lightning, secret passages, slamming doors, ground fog, bombastic curses, hypnotic gazes ("Look into my eyes. I can bring you pleasure mortals cannot know."). And of course and forever, pretty maidens in desperate danger.

BLACULA   Film

1972   (C)   U.S.A.   92 min.

Production Company: American International; **Director:** William Crain; **Producer:** Joseph T. Naar; **Screenplay:** Joan Torres, Raymond Koenig; **Photography:** John M. Stevens; **Editor:** Allan Jacobs; **Special Effects:** Roger George; **Music:** Gene Page.

Cast: William Marshall (Mumawalde/Blacula), Vonetta McGee (Tina), Denise Nicholas (Michelle), Gordon Pinsent (Lt. Peters), Thalmus Rasulala (Gordon Thomas), Emily Yancy (Nancy).

Blacula, despite its title and a mostly black cast, makes no effort to shed any light on black and white tensions. There are, it is true, three moments when these are briefly touched upon: an opening scene in 1815 Transylvania in which we see Count Dracula being frostily chastised for ogling the black Prince Mumawalde's wife, Luva; later, in Los Angeles, we hear a casual reference to Black Panther political activity; finally, a black undertaker comments ironically that he does not get to work on white bodies. Beyond those glancing references, *Blacula,* unlike its inferior sequel, *Scream, Blacula, Scream* (1972), is innocent of political or sociological significance.

As *Blacula* opens, we see Count Dracula entertaining the black African, Prince Mumawalde, who has come to Transylvania to enlist Dracula's help against the slave trade. However, Dracula turns out to be a lustful racist who turns Mumawalde into a vampire:

> I put the curse of suffering on you. I will damn you to a living hell . . . a hunger for human blood. I curse you with my name. You shall be Blacula.

Poster art.

We cut to 1972 and Dracula's castle, where a couple of gay American antique dealers, Billy, who is white, and Bobby, who is black, buy up all the furniture in the castle and ship it to Los Angeles. Included in the deal, of course, is Mumawalde's inhabited coffin.

In Los Angeles, Mumawalde rises as Blacula. In his vampire mode, he has very shaggy eyebrows, a sharp widow's peak, Emperor Franz Joseph sideburns, and fangs. On social occasions, his eyebrows are normal, the sideburns disappear and he wears a handsome cloak (silver-lined, not red) and formal wear of some sort.

Once out of his coffin, he goes right to work drinking blood. Soon the trail of his victims is causing anxiety to the Los Angeles Police Department, but most particularly to Dr. Gordon Thomas, a black physician who works for the Scientific Investigation Division.

Thomas catches on very quickly that there is a vampire loose in Los Angeles. With the help of his lover, Michelle, he learns who that vampire is. But by then, to their dismay, Michelle's sister, Tina, has fallen in love with Mumawalde who has convinced her that she is the reincarnation of his dead wife, Luva.

There is a final, bloody confrontation scene in an underground chemical factory in which scores of policemen battle unavailingly against the unkillable vampire who simply wants a few quiet moments in which to give Tina, who is at his side, the gift of immortality. When ''the only reason I have for living'' is taken from him, he chooses the means of his own destruction.

Blacula is very far from being a great film. Its plot is utterly banal; most of the characters, black and white, are stamped out of the same old Hollywood cookie cutter; finally, it absolutely passes up its opportunity to say anything meaningful about race relations in America.

And yet, the film has stature because of William Marshall's complex performance as Prince Mumawalde/Blacula. Marshall dominates the film in the same way that Frank Langella dominates John Badham's 1979 *Dracula*. Marshall is so unforgettable in the dignity, dimension and grandeur he gives to the role of the reluctant vampire that one wonders why he has not become a major figure in mainstream film.

THE BLOB   Film
1958   (C)   U.S.A.   85 min.
Production Company: Tonylyn Productions/Paramount; *Director:* Irwin S. Yeaworth Jr.; *Producer:* Jack Harris; *Screenplay:* Theodore Simonson, Kate Phillips; *Photography:* Thomas

Spalding; *Editor:* Alfred Hillman; *Special Effects:* Bart Sloane; *Music:* Ralph Carmichael.
Cast: Steve McQueen (Steve), Aneta Corseaut (Jane), Earl Rowe (police lieutenant), Olin Howlin (old man), Steven Chase (Doctor Hallen), John Benson (Sgt. Burt).

The Blob has become something of a classic of simplemindedness.

A couple of ''nice'' teenagers are necking in the feckless way of the fifties, which means that he wants to, and she wants to but both of them know that after panting and wrestling for a while the answer will be no. They see a falling star. A while later, an unlikable old farmer pokes at a coruscated cylinder and cracks it open. What he gets is a crimson slime on the end of his stick. That slime is our first introduction to the blob, a formless, ever-growing, Jello-like mass that, presumably, is the life form that has arrived from outer space with the falling star. The blob, we soon learn, is a strawberry-colored, viscous appetite that seems quite capable of engorging the world.

For a long time, this Jello-on-the-march seems invincible. It engulfs the farmer who found it, then various other people. Dr. Hallen, the film's doctor-in-residence, says that ''it is a

Poster art.

parasite that assimilates flesh.'' But he, like everyone else, is powerless to stop it. Finally, someone makes the accidental discovery that the spray from an ordinary fire extinguisher, though it will not kill the blob, will render it inert. And so the film ends, with the ground well prepared for a sequel, which inevitably followed.

One wonders why the memory of *The Blob* still lingers on, and the twofold answer seems to be that: (a) it is almost a perfect fossil of what Hollywood (and the slick magazines of that day) imagined teenage life in the fifties was like; and (b) it helped to establish early the formula for successful American scary movies—that is, to create a plot in which a number of attractive male and female high school students are exposed, or actually succumb, to great danger. In short, beam sex and violence at school audiences and the cash registers will ring. In this film both the sex and the violence are pretty bland.

BLOOD OF DRACULA'S CASTLE   Film
1969 (C) U.S.A. 84 min.
Production Company: Crown International; *Director:* Al Adamson; *Producer:* Al Adamson; *Screenplay:* Rex Carlton; *Photography:* Laszlo Kovacs; *Editor:* Ewing Brown, Peter Perry; *Music:* Lincoln Mayorage.
Cast: John Carradine (George), Paula Raymond (Countess Townsend/Countess Dracula), Alex d'Arcy (Count Townsend/Count Dracula), Robert Dix (Johnny), Gene O'Shane (Glen Cannon), Barbara Bishop (Liz Arden).

Four years after his appearance in *Billy the Kid Versus Dracula*, John Carradine shows up here playing an evil, moon-worshipping, murderous, but otherwise quite normal butler to the Count and Countess Dracula who live in Falcon Rock, a Spanish-style house on the dunes somewhere near San Diego. The elegant Draculas have a cellar in which are chained a number of pretty girls from whose veins the loyal butler taps the daily cocktail that keeps his employers alive. Carradine brings it to them in champagne glasses, saying, ''I think you'll enjoy this—type double-o-positive. The type is rare.''

''Beautiful,'' says the count, after an appreciative sip.

''Pure?'' asks the connoisseur countess.

''Oh, that is too much to hope for,'' replies the count.

The film, part spoof of the vampire genre and part earnest soft porn, turns on the conflict between the vampire count and countess and a young couple named Cannon who have inherited Falcon Rock. The script writers and the director do better with their soft porn and with individual scenes of violence than they do with the vampire tradition, but it is John Carradine's austere and sinister presence that makes buoyant a film that without him would have sunk without a trace.

BLOOD SIMPLE   Film
1984 (C) U.S.A. 96 min.
Production Company: Circle Releasing Corp.; *Director:* Joel Coen; *Producer:* Ethan Coen; *Screenplay:* Joel and Ethan Coen; *Photography:* Barry Sonnenfeld; *Editor:* Roderick Jaynes and Don Wiegmann; *Special Effects:* Loren Bivens; *Music:* Carter Burwell.
Cast: John Getz (Ray), Frances McDormand (Abbey), Dan Hedaya (Julian Marty), M. Emmett Walsh (private detective), Samm-Art Williams (Maurice).

Blood Simple became, almost from the moment it was first released, a cult film in the sense that it was instantly taken to heart by young aficionados of film as a comic and uniquely creative film.

Though *Blood Simple* has a plot it is neither very intricate nor very important. It serves, rather, as a magnetizing force that holds the individual scenes somewhat loosely together. What we have is the story of Marty, the owner of a Texas night club who has a frequently cheating wife, Abbey, who as the film opens is having an affair with Ray. Marty hires a private detective to murder his wife and her lover. The detective seems to have fulfilled his part of the bargain when he shows Marty photographs of the corpses. Then, having collected his cash, he shoots Marty.

The photographs, however, turn out to be doctored. Abbey and Ray are not dead. Ray comes to Marty's office to steal money that he thinks is owed him. When he finds Marty's body, he thinks that Abbey killed her husband. He takes the body and drives out into the country where, in spite of clear signs that it is not quite dead, he buries it in a freshly plowed field. His idiotic labors in the field make for one of the film's more hilarious sequences.

Meanwhile, the private detective, afraid that he may be implicated in the murder (because he is missing an important clue to his identity—his cigarette lighter), tracks Ray and Abbey, meaning to dispose of them both. He shoots Ray, but Abbey, after some singularly stark, if comic, business, manages to kill the detective.

What *Blood Simple* does best is to keep its cool. It is calculatedly comic just as it is calculatedly scary. In each case, deadpan is the name of the game, as if the camera were addicted to visual quips without comment, the way some people are addicted to puns. When Ray drives Marty's body out into the field, the camera moves into the air to reveal the tire track swath the car makes to the grave site. When Abbey, in one room, sees the detective's hand snaking around a window of an adjacent room toward her, she pins his hand down with a knife. In the subsequent few moments, the audience is treated to a full course of instruction in the comedy of pain—laughter laced with qualms—because none of us is inhuman and the sight of a man with one hand pinned by a knife to a windowsill disturbs us. But so does the fact that the man has just committed murder and that, even as he is writhing in pain, he is smashing at the door of his room with his other hand so that, if he ever gets free, he can kill again. But more than that, the fact is that pain can turn us into twitching dummies, and what is unfortunately true is that the antics of twitching dummies—so long as the pain is not our own—are funny.

BLOODSUCKING FREAKS   Film
1976 (C) U.S.A. 88 min.
Production Company: Troma Productions; *Director:* Joel M. Reed; *Producer:* Alan Margolin; *Screenplay:* Joel M. Reed; *Photography:* Gerry Toll; *Music:* Michael Sahl; *Special Effects:* Bob O'Bradovich.
Cast: Seaumus O'Brien (Sardu), Louie de Jesus (Ralphus), Niles McMaster, Viju Krim (ballerina), Alan Dellay.

The question is whether to call *Bloodsucking Freaks* deplorable, appalling, outrageous, atrocious, unforgivable or to invent a word that says all of it at once. If the film was as focused on sex as it is on pain, one would not hesitate to call it pornography. And perhaps that's our cue: *Bloodsucking Freaks* is a pornographic film made with a cold and calculating eye to appeal to people who are more interested in sadomasochistic imagery for its own sake than for any relationship it may have to life.

The film has a story of sorts: Sardu the Great runs a theater of pain in Greenwich Village. As part of his general nastiness, he kidnaps a ballerina whom he torments on stage in every conceivable vile fashion. In the various melees that move this plot along so much violence is graphically depicted that the film can easily claim to be one of the most frightful productions ever made, a film so vicious that it has become something of a cult favorite of those aficionados who enjoy watching a scene in which a policeman is devoured by a cageful of lustful women or a young woman's brains are sucked out through a straw.

That other raw exercise in bloodshed and pain, *The Evil Dead*, is a soothing bedtime story compared with *Bloodsucking Freaks*.

BLUEBEARD   Short Story
Charles Perrault
France
1697, in *Histoires, ou Contes du Temps Passé*, Paris, Editions Barbin; reprinted 1979 in Leonard Wolf's (ed.) *Wolf's Complete Book of Terror*, New York, Clarkson N. Potter.

This great folktale, best known to us in the version recreated by Charles Perrault in the 17th century, includes in its elegantly developed plot the primordial and fearful theme of marriage.

In Perrault's tale, Bluebeard is a rich man who is "so frightfully ugly that all the women and girls ran away from him." More than that, he inspires "disgust and aversion [because] he had already been married to several wives, and no body ever knew what were become of them."

Terrifying though he is, Bluebeard, because of his great wealth, manages to inspire sufficient good will in the heart of the youngest daughter of one of his neighbors so that she agrees to marry him. Not long after the marriage, Bluebeard, claiming he must make a journey on business, gives his young wife a bunch of keys that unlock the two great rooms that hold his treasure. But one key, he says, "is the key of the closet at the end of the great gallery on the ground floor." Into that room, she is forbidden, in the most stringent terms, to go.

We know, of course, that she does open that door. We know, too, what she sees in that room, "whose door was all clotted over with blood in which lay the bodies of several dead women ranged against the walls."

The story from that point on rushes to its climax in one of the triumphs of the tale-telling art. Perrault heightens both the horror and the suspense for the reader by creating first a confrontation scene between Bluebeard and his too curious wife and then a scene in which we get to watch the poor lady prolonging the prayers her cruel husband has allowed her to make before she is to meet her doom.

Bluebeard gives the keys to his wife (drawing by Gustave Doré).

The wife's situation is stunningly choreographed. An impatient Bluebeard waits downstairs holding a naked cutlass while upstairs, in her room, the desperate wife calls out at intervals to her sister, Anne in the castle tower:

> In the meanwhile, Blue Beard, holding a great cutlass in his hand, cried out as loud as he could to his wife, "Come down presently or I'll come to you."
> "One moment longer if you please," said his wife and immediately, she cried out very softly, "Anne, sister Anne, doest thou see nothing?"
> "I see," replied Sister Anne, "a great dust that comes on this side here."
> "Are they my brothers?"
> "Alas, no."

Readers of all ages can feel the heart-pounding horror of that moment, and one can hardly blame the children who read this tale if they form a warped view of marriage and of curiosity.

THE BRIDE OF FRANKENSTEIN   Film
1935 (B&W) U.S.A. 75 min.
Production Company: Universal; ***Director:*** James Whale; ***Producer:*** Carl Laemmle; ***Screenplay:*** William Hurlbut and John L. Balderston; ***Photography:*** John Mescall; ***Editor:*** Ted Kent; ***Special Effects:*** Jack Pierce and John P. Fulton; ***Music:*** Franz Waxman.
Cast: Boris Karloff (the Monster), Colin Clive (Henry Frankenstein), Valerie Hobson (Elizabeth), Elsa Lanchester (The Bride/Mary Shelley), O. P. Heggie (the hermit), Ernest Thesiger (Doctor Pretorius), Dwight Frye (Karl), E. E. Clive (the burgomaster), Una O'Conner (Minnie), Anne Darling (shep-

herdess), Douglas Walton (Percy Bysshe Shelley), Gavin Gordon (Lord Byron), John Carradine (hunter).

If there really is a pantheon for truly exquisite horror films then surely *The Bride of Frankenstein* deserves the preeminent altar. To have seen the film when one was a child, in 1935 when it first appeared, is one of the privileges of being no longer young. To see it again at intervals is one of the lovelier privileges of being alive.

What are the elements that make this film such a jewel? For one thing, the brilliant screenplay is as vibrant with language as it is with action. And James Whale's direction is even better here than it was in the 1931 *Frankenstein*. The casting too seems absolutely inevitable. No one but Elsa Lanchester could have played both Mary Shelley and the Bride with the particular delicious insouciance required for Mary and the erotic rigidity needed for the Bride. As for Karloff, he improved—no, perfected—his understanding of the Creature and invested the role this time with a wise and anguished compassion that makes us see him as one of the greatly noble, suffering victims of man's capacity to err. His Creature has all the elements of a tragic figure: dignity, decency, and more sorrow in love than anyone ought to be expected to bear.

And then there is Ernest Thesiger as Doctor Pretorius. Suave and evil Doctor Pretorius with his little bundle of weaknesses (cigars, wine) is as mean as the Grinch who stole Christmas and as wicked and witty as Lord Henry in Oscar Wilde's *The Picture of Dorian Gray*. Doctor Pretorius is one of the truly happy film inventions of the thirties and Thesiger achieved immortality with his performance of the part.

Colin Clive, repeating his role as Henry Frankenstein, is true as ever to his essentially wooden self. Curiously enough, his performance does not detract from the power of the film, chiefly because Henry Frankenstein, as the authors of the screenplay conceived him, is merely the occasion for the plot, a stick figure. The same may be said of Valerie Hobson whose sole task as Elizabeth is to heave her bosom and register horror from time to time.

The film's plot is not particularly complex. Indeed, it begins rather awkwardly with a stormy night in Geneva where we see Mary Shelley, her husband Percy Bysshe Shelley and Lord Byron having a lofty conversation about Mary Shelley's book, *Frankenstein*. The men are effete, but Elsa Lanchester's Mary Shelley, though she speaks with the inconsequentiality of a butterfly of the drawing room, is a woman of steel who, at the same time, gives off an aura of erotic hunger. When we see her later, in the role of the Bride, this erotic aura flares up violently.

From the chitchat in the drawing room, we are transported, by Elsa Lanchester's golden syllables, to the concluding scenes of the 1931 *Frankenstein*. We see the burning mill once more, then the camera comes in close and we discover that the Creature has not died. He is there in a subbasement of the mill, and a few moments later, after a comic confrontation with Una O'Conner's Minnie, he is once more on the loose.

In his wanderings, he commits a certain amount of mayhem. Then he is befriended by a blind hermit who teaches him how to smoke cigars, to drink wine and to use the rudiments of speech. When he later takes refuge in a cemetery he is discovered by the evil Doctor Pretorius who recognizes him for what he is, and the two form an unholy alliance.

Soon afterward, Dr. Pretorius visits the exhausted Henry Frankenstein whose marriage to Elizabeth has been postponed. Like Henry, Dr. Pretorius has been experimenting with the creation of life, but the doctor's creatures are miniature human beings whom he keeps in bell jars and who, though they can sing and dance, have no more dignity than wind-up toys. What Pretorius wants is for Henry to collaborate with him on a new project, namely, the creation of a human female, which Pretorius of course, intends to mate with the impatient Creature. When Henry demurs, Pretorius has the Creature kidnap Elizabeth. After the appropriate blackmail is applied, Henry caves in and the laboratory is geared up once again.

The "creation scene" in Henry's magnificent tower laboratory is as inventive as it is spectacular. Chains creak, electrical sparks leap up, the gurney containing the body of the female ascends toward the sky. At the top of the tower, electricity-seeking kites tug at their moorings while a storm rages. The thunder is thunderous, the lightning cracks like a ringmaster's whip. When the storm has done all it can, the gurney is lowered, and, once again, there is the cry, "It's alive, it's alive."

We come now to the heartbreaking ambiguity of the film's title. From the creation we cut to the event that the Monster with all of his borrowed heart has yearned for: a betrothal scene. And there, as Doctor Pretorius intones gloatingly, is "The Bride of Frankenstein"—Elsa Lanchester, with her lightning-fried white-streaked hair swooping upward, stunningly garbed in a flowing white gown. Lanchester looks as she is meant to look—brand new and bizarrely beautiful, with her deep dimple and her full lips. Timid though she is her eyes are already on Henry Frankenstein just as the Creature makes his appearance. Then he, that loneliest of all lonely human beings, reaches out to her, calling tentatively, hopefully, "Friend? Friend?" But she, already a connoisseur of good looks, screams at the sight of him and lurches toward Henry. Then we see the three of them seated on a bench as the Creature tries again. He pats her hand but she recoils and screams again and the Creature knows his fate.

It is a dreadful and miserable moment that the music on the sound track skillfully exploits as we move toward the emotional climax of the film. This sequence is so powerfully designed and played that we entirely understand why the spurned Creature moves to the mysterious, catastrophe-inducing lever built into the wall of the laboratory and why, having first sent Henry to safety with Elizabeth, he pulls the lever.

The last minute and a half of the film, as the camera pulls back and we see the exploding tower bury the Creature, his Bride and the sulfurically wicked Dr. Pretorius, is spectacular for its own sake but even more for implying the orgasm, which, we now see, was the business of the plot all along.

THE BRIDE OF LAMMERMOOR   Novel
Sir Walter Scott
Scotland
1819, London, Constable; reprinted 1973, New York, Dutton.

Though frequently called a Gothic novel, *The Bride of Lammermoor* is more nearly a romantic tragedy with some of the characteristics of Gothic fiction. There are the ruins of Wolf's Craig tower and there are the true lovers torn apart by cold or conniving or ambitious parents, but in *The Bride. . . ,* Sir Walter Scott is altogether too attentive to character and too little concerned with the forbidding architecture and deep-dyed villainy that are the usual fare of Gothic fiction. Though Scott intrudes some uncanny elements and forces early into his narrative, they are generally given the status only of folklore. There is too, or seems to be, a brief appearance of the ghost of a family retainer, Alsie. But if *The Bride . . .* is not a formula Gothic fiction, the novel's climax is deep and dark and horrible enough to please the most demanding aficionado of horror.

The Master of Ravenswood is a brooding, handsome young Scottish nobleman who has been deprived of his estates following on a law suit prosecuted against his family by Sir William Ashton, a decent enough, timeserving politician with a bent for litigation. Sir William has a dynamic and stubborn wife who is rarely seen until she appears near the end to give the novel's plot its most powerful push. He also has two sons and a daughter named Lucy who, like any heroine of the novel of sensibility, is young, beautiful, and fragile. We are not surprised that Ravenswood falls passionately in love with her. It is in the slow, subtle, almost tangential elaboration of the destruction of Lucy that Scott's genius is most manifest.

A modern reader may be put off by the ramblings of various quaint minor characters, all, of course, in Scottish dialect that is as charming as it is sometimes inaccessible. But such homely folk have, since Shakespeare's day, provided the comic relief that distracts us from the woes of their betters.

THE BROOD   Film
1979 (C) Canada 91 min.
Producer: Claude Heroux; *Screenplay:* David Cronenberg; *Director:* David Cronenberg; *Photography:* Mark Irwin; *Editor:* Alan Collins; *Special Effects :* Jack Young, Dennis Pike; *Music:* Howard Shore.
Cast: Oliver Reed (Doctor Hal Raglan), Samantha Eggar (Lola Carveth), Art Hindle (Frank Carveth), Cindy Hinds (Candice Carveth), Nuala Fitzgerald (Juliana Kelly).

Director David Cronenberg, in a 1984 interview with John McCarthy, says of *The Brood* that "I've often described [it], only half jokingly, as my version of *Kramer vs. Kramer.* It's sort of the nightmare side of that movie in which everyone was relatively polite, reasonable, understanding and compassionate . . ."

Maybe.

When he made *The Brood* in 1979, David Cronenberg was not yet the master filmmaker he has since become, but his genius is slathered all over this psychologically startling and physically terrifying film. Love as an emotional event that can have terrifying bodily consequences has never before been made to seem so dangerous. And that is at the heart of what makes a Cronenberg film so disturbing. He has the sharpest, and the shrewdest, eye for seeing the link between feelings and flesh, and he has no hesitation about looking closely at both. The result is that we have, in this film, a 91-minute display of truth *and* consequences.

A failing marriage provides the psychological basis for the truly sinister events that are chronicled in *The Brood.* Frank Carveth and his wife Lola have separated. Lola is living at Dr. Raglan's Soma Free Institute of Psychoplasmics. Raglan has been doing advanced work in strange forms of psychotherapy, and Lola becomes a unique adept who can actually incarnate her negative feelings and send the beings she thus creates into the world to avenge the wrongs for which she blames her husband. The projections take the form of "Dr. Denton"-clad children who commit murder or kidnapping as Lola's emotions dictate.

The final moments of this ingeniously conceived film are magnificent. When Lola's projections kidnap Candace, her child by her husband, Frank Carveth, he invades the Institute of Psychoplasmics. There, Lola, beautifully gowned in a flowing white maternity garment, sits rocking, rocking, entranced by what her husband is saying to her as well as by some greater secret that she alone, the monstrous mother of a new breed of beings, is able to understand. Slowly, that secret is revealed to the audience, but it takes a strong stomach and a deep appreciation of the bizarre to endure what we learn.

No one who sees *The Brood* will ever again think that a child dressed in "Dr. Dentons" is innocent.

THE BUICK SALOON   Short Story
Ann Bridge
Great Britain
1936, in *The Song in the House,* London, A. D. Peters.

That this exquisite love story is also a greatly satisfying ghost tale is simple proof that its author is supremely gifted.

When Mrs. James St. George Bernard Bowlby follows her husband to his post in Peiping, China, where she is expected to be a social asset to him in his profession, he urges her to acquire a car to help her pay calls. To please him, she buys a secondhand Buick saloon ["saloon" is British English for sedan], a prestigious car that requires a chauffeur. Not long after the car becomes her own, she begins to hear a voice emanating at intervals from the car itself. It is the voice of a cultivated woman speaking French. At first Mrs. Bowlby hears only scattered words and phrases but later the speech becomes more coherent and takes on design:

> But whether plans, or snatches of talk about people or ponies, there came always, sooner or later, the undernote of tenderness, now hesitant, now frank—the close concern, the monopolizing happiness of a woman in love.

More than in love, for Mrs. Bowlby realizes that her Buick saloon was once the silent witness to a particularly beautiful extramarital affair.

The rest of the story chronicles Mrs. Bowlby's sympathetic detective work as she sets out to discover the identities of the lovers her Buick saloon once served.

Ann Bridge gives her tale a note of bittersweet melancholy that conjures up lost languors and passions constrained by civility. And yet, although there is plenty of horror in "The Buick Saloon," it does not come from the haunting of the car, which, after Mrs. Bowlby's initial shock, is experienced by her and the reader as charming. No, the horror lies in what Mrs. Bowlby, taught by her remarkable car, learns about civilization and its discontents.

BURN WITCH BURN
Film

(Alternate release title: **NIGHT OF THE EAGLE**)
1962 (B&W) Great Britain 87 min.
Production Company: Independent Artists; *Director:* Sidney Hayers; *Producer:* Albert Fennell; *Screenplay:* Charles Beaumont, Richard Matheson, George Baxt; based on the novel *Conjure Wife* by Fritz Leiber; *Photography:* Reginald Wyer; *Editor:* Ralph Sheldon; *Music:* William Alwyn.
Cast: Janet Blair (Tansey Taylor), Peter Wyngarde (Norman Taylor), Margaret Johnston (Flora Carr), Colin Gordon (Prof. Lindsay Carr), Anthony Nichols (Harvey Sawtelle), Kathleen Byron (Evelyn Sawtelle).

Another foray into the battle between science and belief, *Burn Witch Burn* is also a wonderful, if not entirely deliberate, satire on the backbiting, careerism and downright pettiness of academic life. It is, at the same time, a subtle study of one more way in which men fear the powers of women.

Norman Taylor, a ferociously rationalist professor of sociology at a British university, is seen early on standing before a blackboard on which is written "I do not believe," as he elaborates his contempt of all things supernatural. Taylor, married to a brilliant and devoted wife and about to be promoted to department head, seems within reach of the summit of his career.

But as the film moves forward, we feel a growing sense of foreboding. At a faculty Friday night bridge game, Taylor's wife, Tansy, seems strangely fearful as she searches for something that she senses is present in the house. What she finds, finally, is a tiny mannequin hidden in a lampshade. She promptly throws the mannequin into the fire. Later that evening, Norman finds a trove of strange objects: a dried spider, bits of straw, pebbles. When he confronts Tansy with them, she confesses that she has been practicing witchcraft to help him in his career.

Norman, like any red-blooded male, resents the implied slur on his manhood and forces Tansy to burn her dried grasses and totemic spiders, though she warns him that the consequences may prove dreadful.

And indeed they do. Because, as we learn, Flora Carr, one of Norman's colleagues, has been practicing witchcraft against Norman from the day he first came to the college. And now that Tansy's counter-magic has been nullified, bad things begin to happen to Norman. One of his favorite female students accuses him of raping her; and of course his promotion to department head, as a result of this accusation, is indefinitely postponed. It would seem that Flora Carr's witchcraft is on the verge not only of triumphing against Norman, but also of destroying Tansy as well. There is a fine moment when her magic sends a stone eagle, a campus monument, into screaming flight to attack Norman. Flora is not stopped until Tansy appeases the dark powers by deliberately risking her own life to save Norman's.

As the film comes to its end, we know that Norman has learned his lesson because, when we see him standing before his blackboard, the word "not" in the "I do not believe" scrawl has been erased. It now reads, "I do believe."

William Alwyn's music effortlessly asserts and enforces the film's theme.

THE BURROW
Short Story

Shafiq Magar
Egypt
1985, Cairo, Elias Modern Publishing House.

Part of the horror of this modern Egyptian tale derives from the way its author ambiguously varies its focus. We are never quite certain whether we are reading a ghoul story, a vampire tale or an account of an appalling dream. In any case, something wicked this way comes.

Munir, a young Cairo resident meets a very strange stranger in the street. The stranger, 'Arafa, at once abusive and cajoling, latches on to Munir and in the course of a few hours: (a) saves him from arrest; (b) saves his life; and (c) makes a sniggering promise to introduce Munir to his wife. There follows a succession of vaguely related, Kafkaesque—or outright mad—events until, in a startling moment, 'Arafa opens a trap door to a burrow in which he, his wife and children live. Munir follows him in but to what purpose he is not sure, though there seems to be an atmosphere of uneasy eroticism in the weird place.

For readers of horror fiction, the final lines of the tale are as explosive as they are gratifying.

C

THE CABINET OF DR. CALIGARI Film
(German release title: **DAS KABINETT VON DR. CALIGARI**)
1919 (B&W) (Silent) Germany 52 min.
Production Company: Decla-Bioscop; ***Director:*** Robert Wiene;
Producer: Erich Pommer; ***Screenplay:*** Carl Mayer, Hans Jan-
owitz; ***Photography:*** Willy Hameister; **Art Directors:** Herman
Warm, Walter Rohring, Walter Reimann.
Cast: Werner Krauss (Dr. Caligari), Conrad Veidt (The Som-
nambulist), Lil Dagover (The Girl), Hans Feher (The Student),
Hans von Twardowsky (Alan, his friend).

This earliest of the great horror films owes its aching
intensity to a corps of art directors who created expressionist
sets that so skillfully suggest either nightmare or madness
that the film's somewhat disjointed plot seems almost an
afterthought. The sets make no pretense that they are realistic. The film twitches with shadows, with stark outlines of
cardboard trees, with walls that are so marred they seem to
be enlarged glimpses of the fissures of a human brain. There
are star-shaped pools of light and stairs that twist violently
toward utter darkness. Once, a huge full moon hovers behind
painted clouds over a set that seems framed in gauze.

The plot that sends the characters scuttling through such
bizarre sets has its own nightmarish elements. In the opening
scene, we see two man, one younger, one older, sitting on a
bench on the grounds of what we soon learn is a madhouse.
The younger man then tells the story of certain events that
happened to him some years ago in the town of Holstenwall.

Here we get a flashback and we see a mountebank named
Dr. Caligari who wants the town clerk's permission to exhibit
his "concession" at the local fair. The clerk, when he learns
that Caligari means to exhibit a somnambulist, cries "Faker"
and refuses the requisite permit. As a result, a series of
murders are committed in the town, and the first of the
victims is the recalcitrant clerk.

Though the murderer is Cesare, the somnambulist, he is
simply a robotized instrument of vengeance for the wicked

Caligari, who keeps Cesare in a box that powerfully resembles a coffin. At one point, Cesare steals Jane, The Girl, who
has been introduced to us at the beginning of the film as the
narrator's fiancee, but Cesare, reluctant to harm her, drops
the girl and she is rescued.

Later, when the narrator goes to the local insane asylum to
see whether Dr. Caligari may be an inmate there, he is told
that only the asylum's director can reveal the names of the
patients. And here, the film turns fully nightmarish. When
the narrator is taken to see the director of the asylum, that
director turns out to be Dr. Caligari. The narrator is then
seized and hospitalized. Soon, we see that not only he is a
patient, but so, too, is Jane; she believes herself to be a
princess who therefore cannot marry the narrator because, as
she says, "We who are of royal blood may not follow the
wishes of our hearts." As for Dr. Caligari, the asylum's
director, he is an alienist whose specialty is somnambulism
and he looks forward to experimenting on the narrator.

Or so we think, but there is one final twist to the plot. The
director of the asylum is not really Caligari, but a proper and
responsible doctor who, as the film ends, tells us that "He
[the narrator] believes me to be the mythical Caligari. Now I
know how to cure him."

The Cabinet of Dr. Caligari is a film that squirms with the
sort of distortion that people were beginning to call surreal-
ism. The physical world, as the set makers have designed it,
is surreal as are the perceptions and experiences of each of
the characters. One looks in vain for an act that is merely
ordinary, but, since the story is told by a madman, that turns
out to be impossible. From the narrator's point of view, the
world is a place of deformed geometries, all angles and
whorls and circles and twisted lines that aptly represent what
to his cracked intelligence is the way things are. The real
headache for the film viewer is that there is nothing, except
for the tiny scrap of hope at the story's end, to suggest that
he is mistaken.

One final note. Here is a film made in what was still the
Dark Ages of film technology that is, just the same, almost a

The somnambulist carrying his beloved in **The Cabinet of Dr. Caligari.**

perfect model of what a great scary film should be: engrossing, ominous, believable and illuminating, though in truth the light it casts is very strange.

THE CALL OF CTHULHU   Short Story

H. P. Lovecraft

U.S.A.

February 1928, in *Weird Tales;* reprinted 1969 in August Derleth's (ed.) *Tales of the Cthulhu Myths,* New York, Ballantine.

This is the first of Lovecraft's "Cthulhu" tales in which he develops the outlines of what was later to be called "The Cthulhu Mythos." Briefly, Lovecraft imagined an ancient time when the world was controlled by two sorts of gods, the benign and the malign. The Elder Gods were benign while the Great Old Ones were evil. The most powerful of the Great Old Ones was Azathoth, who was a blind idiot. Next to him in evil was Yog-Sothoth. After him came a roster of demonic sub-gods: Nyarlathotep, Great Cthulhu, Hastur the Unspeakable and Shub-Niggurath.

The plot of "The Call of Cthulhu" follows a pattern that would be frequently repeated in the tales involving the "Cthulhu Mythos." Here, Lovecraft's narrator tells us that he found a mysterious clay bas-relief covered over with hieroglyphics among his recently deceased granduncle's effects. The granduncle, Professor George Gamell Angell, professor emeritus of Semitic languages at Brown University, has left other mysterious documents, in which reference is made to a

"Cthulhu Cult," as well as an extensive manuscript containing two narratives.

The story proper consists of the narrator's account of his search to understand the meaning of the clay tablet and the documents. It leads him to an investigation of strange dreams:

> whose burden was always some terrible Cyclopean vista of dark and dripping stone . . . The two sounds most frequently repeated are those rendered by the letters "Cthulhu" and "R'lyeh."

And strange events:

> Here was a nocturnal suicide in London . . . [and] a dispatch from California describes a theosophist colony as donning white robes en masse for some "glorious fulfillment." . . . Voodoo orgies multiply . . . the west of Ireland, too is full of wild rumors . . .

He gives us the account by an Inspector Legrasse of New Orleans of how the police there came into the possession of a certain statuette. The figure

> represented a monster of vaguely anthropoid outline, but with an octopuslike head whose face was a mass of feelers, a scaly, rubbery-looking body, prodigious claws on hind and fore feet, and long, narrow wings behind . . . [it] squatted evilly on a rectangular block of pedestal covered with undecipherable characters.

We learn of the raid in the Louisiana swamps on a mob of worshippers, men of "a very low, mixed-blooded and mentally aberrant type," who worshipped the Great Old Ones and who had been promised a time "beyond good and evil, with laws and morals thrown aside and all men shouting and killing and reveling in joy."

Finally, we have the account of a seaman named Johansen who actually visited

> the nightmare corpse city of R'lyeh [and saw] the cosmic majesty of this dripping Babylon of elder demons. [He saw] the Titan thing from the stars [that] slavered and gibbered . . . The awful squid-head with writhing feelers . . . There was bursting as of an exploding bladder, a slushy nastiness as of a cloven sunfish, a stench as of a thousand opened graves, and a sound that the chronicler would not put on paper . . .

What we have here is Lovecraft at his most typical. That is, with his prose at the pitch of near hysteria. His imagery is wet, glistening, writhing. In this story, readers will look in vain for believable characters. Instead, what we get is a quite believable mood of anxiety about the coexistence in this world of the threatening and loathesome Others and those who worship them. What is fearful is the paranoia that one senses beating under the prose. That, more than the story's events, remains urgent.

CANON ALBERIC'S SCRAPBOOK   Short Story

M. R. James

Great Britain

1904, in *Ghost Stories of an Antiquary,* London, Edward Arnold; collection reprinted 1971, New York, Dover.

When Denistoun, an Englishman with an archaeological bent, comes to St. Bertrand de Comminges, "a decayed town on the spurs of the Pyrenees, not very far from Toulouse," to study the town's church, he has no inkling that he is intruding upon an ancient and horrible mystery. The verger, or sacristan, of the church, shows him a book containing, in addition to certain priceless manuscripts, a strangely disturbing picture:

> At first you saw only a mass of coarse, matted black hair; presently it was seen this covered a body of fearful thinness, almost a skeleton, but with the muscles standing out like wires . . . The eyes, touched in with a burning yellow, had intensely black pupils and were fixt upon the throned King [Solomon] with a look of beast-like hate. Imagine one of the awful bird-catching spiders of South America translated to human form, and endowed with intelligence just less than human, and you will have some conception of the terror inspired by the effigy.

When Denistoun buys the priceless book for the absurdly low sum of 250 francs, he discovers that he has as a consequence become the target of nightmare visitations from something that has

> Pale, dusky skin, covering nothing but bones and tendons of appalling strength; coarse black hairs, longer than ever grew on a human hand; nails rising from the ends of the fingers and curving sharply down and forward, grey, horny, and wrinkled.

With M. R. James, the horror always is to be found in the specific detail with which he imagines his monsters. Frequently hair, as here and in "The Ash-tree," becomes a focus

for revulsion. But he can turn any human feature into an occasion for loathing:

> The lower jaw was thin—what can I call it?—shallow, like a beast's; teeth showed behind the black lips; there was no nose; the eyes, of a fiery yellow, against which the pupils showed black and intense, and the exulting hate and thirst to destroy life which shone there, were the most horrifying features in the whole vision.

There was no nose, just as in James's "Count Magnus" Anders Bjornsen's "face was not there because the flesh of it was sucked away from the bones." Always, James's tactic is to surround such abominable moments with so much scholarly decorum that we are lulled into thinking that there can be no harm until suddenly the academic dust falls off and pure malevolence grins up at us from the page.

CARMILLA   Short Story

J. Sheridan Le Fanu
Ireland
1872, in *In a Glass Darkly*, London, Bentley; collection reprinted 1979, New York, Arno.

Sheridan Le Fanu's "Carmilla" is the third of the three 19th-century English-language predecessors of Bram Stoker's *Dracula*. Now, while John Polidori's *The Vampyre* and Prest's *Varney the Vampire* are important documents in the history of

Carmilla and her victim.

vampire fiction in English, "Carmilla" is also distinguished by being a work of literature.

"Carmilla," like all of Le Fanu's fiction, proceeds at an even, unhurried pace as the second of two first-person narrators gently establishes the ambience of her story. She tells us that she is the daughter of an Englishman who, having served in the Austrian army, has retired on his pension to a castle in Styria because, as she artlessly tells us, "A small income, in that part of the world, goes a great way . . . here in this lonely and primitive place, . . . everything is so marvellously cheap . . . ."

The schloss or castle is profoundly isolated. The nearest village is seven miles away. The nearest inhabited schloss "is that of old General Spielsdorf nearly twenty miles away to the right." Nevertheless, with all of its isolation, the narrator describes her childhood with her father, her two governesses and occasional visitors as essentially serene. Except for one occasion when, waking suddenly one night, she:

> saw a solemn, but very pretty face looking at me from the side of the bed . . . She caressed me with her hands, and lay down beside me on the bed, and drew me towards her smiling; I felt immediately delightfully soothed, and fell asleep again. I was awakened by a sensation as if two needles ran into my breast very deep at the same moment, and I cried loudly. The lady started back, with her eyes fixed on me, and then slipped down upon the floor, and, as I thought, hid herself under the bed.

Her father treats the incident as a dream but our narrator is forthright: ". . . for I knew the visit of the strange woman was not a dream: and I was awfully frightened."

Twelve years pass. One evening the narrator and her father receive the news that Mademoiselle Rheinfeldt, General Spielsdorf's niece, has died in suspicious circumstances occasioned by a "fiend who betrayed our infatuated hospitality." The next moment a coach breaks down before their schloss and, before the household is quite aware of how it has come about, they have taken under their care the beautiful young Carmilla whose mother, the owner of the coach, drives off on "a journey of life and death" that will not bring her back for at least three months.

At first, the presence of Carmilla in the family is a delight to everyone. Then one day, when the two young women exchange confidences, it becomes clear to the narrator that it was Carmilla she had seen at the foot of her bed on that night 12 years ago. From that moment on darkness encroaches on the story even as it becomes increasingly sensuous, indeed, languorous, and it is not long before the reader is possessed of just sufficient information to wonder about who Carmilla might be and to worry about the strange love with which she surrounds the narrator. When we are told that the narrator has dreamed one night that she "saw Carmilla, standing, near the foot of my bed, in her white nightdress, bathed, from her chin to her feet, in one great stain of blood," we feel we have been fully prepared for the impending climax of the story.

What Le Fanu has done, over a decade before *Dracula,* is to explore with surprising sensuality the sexual implications of the theme of the vampire. What is even more surprising is that in an age when the word lesbian was hardly spoken the erotic crux of Le Fanu's story is that both his vampire and her victim are women.

CARNIVAL OF SOULS   Film

1961   (B&W)   U.S.A.   80 min.

Production Company: Herts-Lion International; *Director:* Herk Harvey; *Producer:* Herk Harvey; *Screenplay:* John Clifford; *Photography:* Maurice Prather; *Editor:* Dan Palmquist, Bill DeJarnette; *Music:* Gene Moore, Organ Music by John Clifford.

Cast: Candice Hilligoss (Mary Henry), Herk Harvey (The Man), Frances Feist (landlady), Sidney Berger (John Linden), Stan Levitt (doctor), Art Ellison (minister).

Carnival of Souls is one of those films that seem to have been made by a group of like-minded people who share (and are addicted to) the same recurring nightmare. It moves with grave deliberation from the believable to the unbelievable (the two states sometimes interpenetrating). A film masterpiece, if in a minor key, it is pervaded by a deep wistfulness, some of which derives no doubt from Candice Hilligoss's muted performance, as well as from Maurice Prather's softly focused camera work, Herk Harvey's direction and the powerful organ music that is keenly attuned to the emotional ebb and flow of the action.

Mary Henry, the film's protagonist, is a shy young woman who is driving to Utah where she expects to be employed as a church organist. Her car is overtaken by a group of rowdies who, as both cars are crossing a bridge, crowd her. In the ensuing crash, her car sinks into the river, but she is seen to climb free from the wreck.

Shaken, but apparently unhurt, she resumes her Utah-bound journey, but from here on the evolving story has a disembodied quality, and the film's point of view seems hesitant, uncertain. As Mary Henry drives on, she catches her first glimpse of a face that she will see at intervals throughout the rest of the film.

Arriving at the town in Utah where she is to be employed, she finds a furnished room in the home of a woman named Mrs. Tomlin. There, she is harassed for a while by her fellow boarder, Lindon, who cannot believe that his sleazy attentions are unwelcome.

Meanwhile, the film viewer is aware that although nothing much is really happening, everything feels extremely ominous. When Mary Henry tries on dresses in a dress shop, she is locked in a changing room and cannot make anyone hear her. For a while, wherever she goes, she moves in an uncanny silence, unable to hear anything. Then, abruptly, the world's sounds return once more. At intervals, the face that has haunted her reappears.

When she consults Dr. Samuels, a psychiatrist, he assures her that her experiences are the result of the emotional shock she sustained in the car crash. "The point is," he tells her, "that our imagination plays tricks on us."

Thoroughly frightened by what is happening to her, and afraid of being utterly cut off from the rest of mankind, Mary Henry desperately, and awkwardly, encourages Lindon's attentions. The result is more nightmarish misunderstandings.

While all this has been happening, Mary Henry has from time to time been powerfully attracted to an abandoned amusement pavilion that stands on a pier overlooking a lake. Finally unable to resist its attraction, she goes there alone. And it is in the pavilion that the film's terrible meanings gather like the silent influttering of many moths.

It is dusk as Mary Henry moves among the anomalous images of the abandoned amusement park. At moments, the camera cuts to hands and feet at an organ, then it moves under water where it gives us a glimpse of the face that has been haunting her. Then we are back in the pavilion where she is taking part in a danse macabre.

After a return to the nightmare of her ordinary world she makes one more foray to the amusement pavilion. By now the mood of the film is that of a dying fall—languorous, declining sweetly and horribly to death as we watch her dancing with the man whose face has haunted her and who now seems to be making love to her, as all the ghostly dancers pursue her, laughing. Then they catch her and the film comes to its ''An Occurrence at Owl Creek Bridge'' finish.

CARRIE   Novel
Stephen King
U.S.A.
1974, Garden City, N.Y., Doubleday; reprinted 1984, New York, NAL.

Stephen King's *Carrie* is a novel that begins and ends with a flow of menstrual blood, and the narrative enclosed between the two events is, by and large, a record of feminine cruelty of one sort or another.

Carrie, a 17-year-old high school senior in the town of Ewen, Maine, is the daughter of an insanely fundamentalist woman, Margaret White, who has, under the guise of providing her daughter with religious training, raised her in a manner so abusive that it has all but broken her spirit. Bad as such an upbringing might be for any normal young woman, what happened to Carrie is more complicated still because she possesses amazing telekinetic powers, which, as the story progresses, she learns to control and finally put to vengeful purpose.

In a stunning early scene, we see Carrie, a somewhat lumpish, painfully shy young woman, in the shower room of the girls' gymnasium showering along with some dozen of her female classmates when, to her horror, she sees that blood is trickling down her thighs. She has no understanding of what is happening to her and, for a while, believes herself to be bleeding to death. Her schoolfellows, who have for years treated her like the outsider she has always been, take the occasion to treat her now with special cruelty. They taunt her, then throw sanitary napkins at her while Carrie cowers, unable to understand why she deserves this new onslaught of her classmates' disapproval.

Among the young women in the crowd that torments Carrie there are two whose lives will be deeply affected by their contact with her: Sue Snell and Chris Hargensen. Sue, who is sweet and essentially good, is remorseful for what she has done to Carrie and conceives a plot intended to bring her out of her isolation. She persuades her own boyfriend, Tommy Ross, to ask Carrie to the senior prom. Tommy, bright, decent, athletic, likable, finally agrees. These two, then, as we soon see, pave the short road to hell with their good intentions.

Because Chris Hargensen, who is mean-spirited, self-indulgent, spoiled and sexually kinky is as wicked as Sue Snell is good. Chris, forbidden to go to the senior prom because she has refused to accept the punishment meted out for the attack

on Carrie, is so outraged that she mounts a plot of her own. She has the help of her greasy-haired, thoroughly scuzzy boyfriend from the other side of the tracks, Billy Nolan. Their plot requires them to rig the election for the King and Queen of the Prom so that Tommy Ross and Carrie are elected. Then, at the moment of coronation, two buckets of pigs' blood are triggered to spill on them from a beam above their heads.

Both plots succeed. Carrie gets to go to the senior prom with Tommy and, in the scenes set at the prom, undergoes a transformation from ugly duckling to a quite credible swan. We are given every indication that with a little time and help, she may be able to join the human race. Until Chris and Billy create their shameful inundation of pigs' blood.

Carrie's revenge is swift and devastating. Summoning her telekinetic powers, she becomes, in scenes that are unforgettable both in the book and in Brian De Palma's 1976 movie, an engine of destruction.

Stephen King is probably the 20th century's most effective plot maker in the horror genre and his skill does not flag in *Carrie*. His characters, while not richly developed, come before us neatly provided with believable motivations. This is particularly true of poor Carrie who, no matter how dreadful her vengeance, lingers in our minds as one more sinned against than sinning.

CARRIE   Film
1976   (C)   U.S.A.   98 min.
Production Company: United Artists; ***Director:*** Brian De Palma; ***Producer:*** Paul Monash; ***Screenplay:*** Lawrence D. Cohen; ***Photography:*** Mario Tosi; ***Special Effects:*** Gregory M. Auer; ***Music:*** Pino Donaggio.
Cast: Sissy Spacek (Carrie White), Piper Laurie (Margaret White), Amy Irving (Sue Snell), William Katt (Tommy Ross), John Travolta (Billy Nolan), Nancy Allen (Chris Hargenson), Betty Buckley (Miss Colins), P. J. Soles (Norma Watson), Sidney Lassic (Mr. Fromm).

Here is a film that reeks of the trauma of adolescence. It is, furthermore, a film that turns Stephen King's sharply visualized novel into an even more vivid visual event.

What made painful reading in the book becomes excruciating on the screen. There is Carrie, taking a shower in the women's shower room of her high school. Soothed by the heat and the water, she drifts off into a self-indulgent trance out of which she is suddenly shaken by the realization that there is blood on her hands. It is thus that Carrie wakens into womanhood on the day of her first menses. And when she turns for help to the other women in the shower and locker room, the ensuing scene of torment creates a complicity of shame that suffuses the rest of the film.

Carrie, despite the sleeker achievements of *Dressed to Kill* and *Body Double,* is easily De Palma's most successful film. From its opening scene to its apocalyptic finale, De Palma keeps his central theme before him: the cost, to the human species, of sexuality. *Carrie,* as De Palma gives it to us, is a cruel restatement of the lesson of the Garden of Eden. Once one has tasted the bittersweet fruit of the Tree of the Knowledge of Good and Evil, catastrophe is likely to follow.

Carrie, as we know, is a painfully shy girl who gradually discovers that she has telekinetic powers. She lives with her religious fanatic mother in a sort of Gothic hovel. As played by Piper Laurie, the mother is a stick figure of zealotry, too pretty to be a hag, but just the same she natters away at Carrie, warning her against joy. Meanwhile, as in the book, some of Carrie's female schoolmates who have been punished by the authorities for what they did to Carrie in the shower room, are determined to avenge themselves against her. They mount a plot in the course of which a cruel practical joke is played on Carrie at the senior prom.

Carrie's outraged response, as in the book, takes on a certain psychological complexity because, on the one hand, the provocation to her rage is so enormous that we cannot help feeling, morally, that her classmates got what they deserved; but then, since she uses the gift of telekinesis in a way that punishes the innocent along with the guilty we cannot help feeling that both Carrie and the students who tormented her were punished beyond their deserts.

Despite turgid performances by John Travolta and Piper Laurie, and a trick ending that worked amazingly well in 1976 but that has been so widely imitated that it now seems a cliche, *Carrie* still holds up well.

THE CASK OF AMONTILLADO   Short Story
Edgar Allan Poe
U.S.A.
1846, in *Godey's Magazine and Lady's Book;* reprinted 1981 in Stephen Peithman's (ed.) *The Annotated tales of Edgar Allan Poe,* Garden City, N.Y., Doubleday.

When one of two friends feels that he is continually being insulted and accepts the insults without visible reaction over a long period of time we may reasonably expect that something dreadful will happen sooner or later. Here, the insulting friend is Fortunato and the insulted one is Montresor, who comes from a "great and numerous family" whose coat of arms showed "A huge human foot d'or on a field azure; the foot crushes a serpent rampant whose fangs are imbedded in the heel." The motto was "Nemo me impune lacessit," or "No one provokes me with impunity."

And Montresor, at the start of Poe's story, tells us that he has been provoked by a thousand injuries for which he means now, at the height of the carnival festivities in an unspecified Italian city, to be avenged on Fortunato. When he comes upon Fortunato, who is dressed in the motley of a jester or a fool, he plays upon his friend's pride as a wine connoisseur and invites him home to drink from a newly acquired barrel of Amontillado about which, says Montresor, he needs a connoisseur's advice.

The somewhat drink-fuddled Fortunato, who has no inkling that Montresor hates him, is more than willing to prove his expertise. He follows Montresor into the family vaults where, soon enough, "We came at length to the foot of the descent and stood together on the damp ground of the catacombs of the Montresors."

Almost everyone in America who has had at least an eighth grade education knows what happens in the rest of the story. There, in the catacombs the

> walls had been lined with human remains, piled to the vault overhead, in the fashion of the great catacombs of Paris. Three sides of this interior crypt were still ornamented in this man-

ner. From the fourth the bones had been thrown down, and lay promiscuously upon the hearth, forming at one point a mound of some size.

There, in the catacombs, in an atmosphere of death where the air is suffused by damp and the smell of nitre, Montresor achieves his revenge. Poe, writing at his very best, depicts in a series of paragraphs Montresor at his solitary labor and Fortunato at his drinking, the bells of his jester's cap jingling as slowly, slowly, the connoisseur of wine understands just what the vintage is that he has been brought there to drink.

"The Cask of Amontillado," short as it is, remains remarkable for a couple of reasons. First, it is a story that is told almost entirely in the form of dialogue. There is comparatively little "establishing" prose aside from the deftly sketched in physical details required by the story. Second, even as we are confident that we understand what has happened to Fortunato we are left wondering what were the injuries he heaped on Montresor? And to what private disaster does Montresor refer when he says to Fortunato,

> "we will go back; your health is precious. You are rich, respected, admired, beloved; you are happy, as once I was. You are a man to be missed. For me it is no matter."

Finally, why is Fortunato, whose name means either the fortunate one or the fated one, dressed in motley, the garb of a jester or a fool? That's the question that turns what has seemed a simple enough story of revenge into a complex psychological allegory. Which of the two men is the fool of Fortune? As the story stands, we are not quite sure, though Poe's trick is to make us certain that if we knew the answer it would shine a bright light on the heart of this darkness.

THE CASTLE OF OTRANTO   Novel
Horace Walpole
Great Britain
1764, London, Thomas Lowndes; reprinted 1982, New York, Oxford University Press.

The Castle of Otranto, officially the first of the Gothic romances, is a much less nakedly self-expressive/self-concealing work than Lewis's *The Monk.* For one thing, it was written not by a boy but by a middle-aged decadent-manqué, a man of crotchety and exotic tastes with wealth vast enough to indulge them.

One such indulgence was his home, Strawberry Castle, a quaint structure with towers, battlements, saints in imitation Gothic windows, vaulted roofs, balustrades and stairways. In the midst of this solemn bric-a-brac, a moody Walpole dreamed a jumbled dream that turned out to be the basis for his novel. As with Lewis, Walpole, once started on his story, became so engrossed he could not, except for needful intervals, put down his pen. The work was finished in less than two months.

Briefly, the story of *The Castle* . . . Manfred, Prince of Otranto, who rules his principality uneasily, fears the accomplishment of "an ancient prophecy which was said to have pronounced that the Castle and Lordship of Otranto should pass from the present family whenever the real owners should be grown too large to inhabit it." Manfred has a sickly son who is intended to marry Princess Isabella of Vincenza.

On the morning of the marriage, the feeble Conrad is found shattered to bits underneath an enormous helmet which turns out to have come mysteriously from the statue of Alphonso the Good, a past ruler of Otranto.

Manfred decides to marry the young Isabella himself though he is already married to Hippolita. Isabella, helped by a handsome peasant named Theodore, who loves Matilda, flies from the repugnant marriage. From here on, there are chase scenes, subterranean passages, supernatural events (a portrait steps from its frame, a statue has a nosebleed), hints of incest and signs that heaven is not content with what is happening in Otranto. Finally, the castle itself tumbles down in a fit of heavenly rage. The wicked Manfred, in the course of his evil machinations, kills his daughter Matilda with a dagger stroke meant for the innocent Isabella.

The death of his daughter reduces the tyrant to contrition. Meanwhile, the peasant Theodore turns out not to be a peasant but rather a legitimate heir to the throne of Otranto to which, very soon, he is restored. Manfred and his wife spend their lives in penitential religion, and Theodore and Isabella, after a sufficient interval to allow Theodore to forget Matilda, achieve happiness together.

Walpole, with his mind devoted to fairy tales and neurasthenia, had no trouble contriving this farrago. What is wonderful is that, despite a prose style that for a contemporary reader seems to move at a snail's pace, the fiction more than occasionally works.

THE CAT AND THE CANARY   Film
1927 (B&W) (Silent) U.S.A. 84 min.
Production Company: Universal-Jewel; *Director:* Paul Leni; *Producer:* Carl Laemmle; *Screenplay:* Robert F. Hill, Alfreda Cohn, based on a play by John Willard; *Photography:* Gilbert Warrenton.
Cast: Laura LaPlante (Annabelle West), Creighton Hale (Paul Jones), Gertrude Astor (Cicily Young), Forrest Stanley (Charlie Wilder), Edmund Carew (Harry Blyth), Lucien Littlefield (Dr. Patterson), Flora Finch (Susan Sillsby), Tully Marshall (Roger Crosly).

In the opening sequence of this silent murder mystery-cum-horror film, we have an awe-inspiring post-German expressionist scene that might have been created by the set designer of *The Cabinet of Doctor Caligari.* We see the alcoholic millionaire, Cyrus West, sitting in a rocking chair surrounded by bottles 30 or 40 feet high as huge cats stalk by. The scene is so impressive that it is hard for anything that follows to quite match its power.

The dead millionaire has left an old dark house and a will that is to be opened "twenty years after my death." Twenty years later, a number of people gather in the old house to hear the reading of the will: a lawyer named Crosly who will read it, Harry Blythe, Charlie Wilder, Aunt Susan and her niece, Cecily, a young man named Paul, and, finally, Cyrus's niece and a distant cousin of Paul's, Annabelle West.

The screen titles inform us that the clock, which hasn't struck in 20 years, strikes. The clock, parenthetically, is a marvel to see: three spiral chimes that are struck by four sequential hammers that continue to strike throughout the ceremonious opening of the envelope containing the will.

The document reads, "My relatives have watched me as if they were the cat and I the canary. Therefore my wealth goes to my most distant relative bearing the name of West: Annabelle."

There is, however, a codicil to the will and that is that Annabelle's sanity must be established. Should she prove to be insane, someone else will inherit the money. Who that someone else may be is not named in the will, but the name is in an envelope in the lawyer's pocket. In addition to all this, there are also some missing family diamonds hidden somewhere in the house, which provides us with a treasure hunt for a subplot.

That much, then, constitutes the coiled spring that animates *The Cat and the Canary.* Most of the film is, of course, focused on somebody's scheme to drive Annabelle mad. Pictures mysteriously fall ("When somebody's picture falls, it is a sign of death"), there are sliding doors, ominous looking, deadpan servants. The lawyer is killed, then his body disappears. A uniformed official from a nearby madhouse appears to tell everyone that a lunatic has escaped. "He's a maniac who thinks he's a cat and he tears his victims as if they were canaries."

Meanwhile, young Paul and Annabelle develop the sort of sympathy that signals romance because he is the sort of bumbling, charming fellow who always got the young women—to the dismay of the upright and sedate stockbrokers who were also wooing them in the old *Liberty* and *Collier's* magazine stories.

The character of Paul, and Paul Leni's sly direction, are the two major contributions of the film. Paul, who, we are told, was dropped on his head as a child, is engaging, clumsy and good-hearted. He is, too, as the film grows steadily more sinister, increasingly courageous so that when, finally, Annabelle is in real danger, it is Paul who saves her and who brings about the satisfactory denouement of the film.

CAT PEOPLE   Film
1942 (B&W) U.S.A. 73 min.
Production Company: RKO; *Director:* Jacques Tourneur; *Producer:* Val Lewton; *Screenplay:* DeWitt Bodeen; *Photography:* Nicholas Musuraca; *Editor:* Mark Robson; *Music:* Roy Webb.
Cast: Simone Simon (Irene Dubrovna), Kent Smith (Oliver Reed), Tom Conway (Dr. Judd), Jane Randolph (Alice), Jack Holt (Commodore).

Here is a film whose great power comes form the way that director Jacques Tourneur blends restraint and tact as, slowly, slowly, he reveals the anguish of his heroine. Irena, a young Serbian woman living in New York, is afraid to marry because she believes herself to be descended from a race of people whose women turn into panthers when they are sexually aroused. And yet, because she is in love, she does marry. Her husband, a marine architect named Oliver Reed, tolerates his unconsummated marriage for a while, but eventually he looks for solace elsewhere and finds it with Alice, a colleague who works with him.

As Irena's domestic crisis intensifies, it becomes clear to us that her anxieties about her bestial nature are not groundless. Caged birds and animals in a pet store go berserk when she

Simone Simon with Tom Conway (left) and Kent Smith in **Cat People.**

comes in. When she tries to fondle a pet canary it dies of fright in her hand, and when she passes the caged panther in the zoo in Central Park she has an overwhelming sense of fellow feeling with it. It is, too, the panther in Irena who stalks Alice in the swimming pool of her hotel and leaves her robe in shreds. When Oliver announces that he is in love with Alice and wants to marry her, the black panther in Irena emerges fully. At first its victims are sheep in the zoo at Central Park. Later, when the unscrupulous Dr. Judd undertakes to make love to Irena to prove that her fears about herself are groundless, he discovers too late just how wrong he is.

In such a story physical and sexual violence are implicit right from the start and yet director Tourneur keeps them delicately or offstage. Even when the violence is on camera one gets only glimpses of it, or it is figured by shadows. Indeed, shadows become the true theme of the work. Emotional, domestic, sexual entanglements move in the foreground of the film while the thick dark shadows of primordial evil move silently behind them. And it is that muteness coupled with Irena's beauty and innocence that makes this film at once tender, frightening and beautiful. Simone Simon gives to the role of Irena a sweet wistfulness that makes her

doom heartbreaking. She is so vulnerable, and so compelled. And so deeply, deeply alone.

The film's acting honors go exclusively to Simone Simon. Kent Smith as Oliver is wooden and Tom Conway as Dr. Judd, though he has all the sinister suavity of an Oscar Wilde villain, seems not to have his heart fully in his role.

A word about the music in *Cat People:* The French lullaby "Do, Do, Enfant Do" is the musical theme that announces or accompanies the major changes of mood or action. The choice of the song and the intricate uses to which it is put are further evidence of Tourneur's genius. Given Irena's dual nature and her childlike character, it serves magnificently to intensify the pain of her situation and her doom.

A lush but perverse and brutal remake of *Cat People,* starring Nastassia Kinski, was released in 1982.

CAT PEOPLE   Film

1982   (C)   U.S.A.   118 min.
Production Company: Universal; **Director:** Paul Schrader; **Producer:** Charles Fries; **Screenplay:** Alan Ormsby; **Photography:** John Bailey; **Special Effects:** Albert Whitlock; **Music:** Giorgio Moroder, David Bowie.
Cast: Nastassia Kinski (Irena Gallier), Malcolm McDowell

(Paul Gallier), John Heard (Oliver Yates), Ruby Dee (Female).

A student of film who wants a quick course in what happened to the horror movie genre between 1942 and 1982 will learn a great deal by comparing the Val Lewton-Jacques Tourneur version of *Cat People,* starring Simone Simone, with Paul Schrader's, starring Nastassia Kinski. Whatever is understated, tactful, subtle or implied in the earlier black and white film, becomes, in the color version, blatant, tasteless, brash or explicit.

In the preceding entry on the Lewton-Tourneur *Cat People,* I noted that

> physical and sexual violence are implicit [in it] right from the start, and yet director Tourneur keeps them delicately offstage. Even when the violence is on camera one gets only glimpses of it, or it is figured by means of shadows.

In Schrader's film, Irena's heritage, instead of being hinted at, is put grossly before us as fact: She is a descendant of a people who mate their women to panthers. More than that, as her leather-clad brother Paul, tells her, in order to mitigate the curse of bestiality, she must commit incest. He says,

> "Save me. Only you can stop this killing. You've got to make love with me as brother and sister . . . Our parents were brother and sister . . . Make love with me and save both of us . . . We are an incestuous race and before we can become human again, we must kill . . ."

Irena, who has fallen in love with a personable zoo keeper, fends her brother off with a shard of glass but she succumbs, finally, to the zoo keeper's wooing with disastrous consequences as the film comes to its messy close.

This is a nervous, bumpy film with a few memorable scenes: Paul turning into a panther in a prostitute's room; the sudden appearance of a human hand during the autopsy of the panther. But startling special effects and occasional scenes of soft pornography, while they titillate the senses, are not enough to keep one from feeling that in this film the main thing, an authentic sense of mystery, is missing.

And yet it is a film a connoisseur must see, if only to brood over the shift in sensibility that has taken place in America between 1942 and 1982 and to say with Hamlet, "Look here upon this picture, and on this . . ."

CATERPILLARS   Short Story
E. F. Benson
Great Britain
1912, in *The Room in the Tower,* London, Mills & Boon; reprinted 1979 in Leonard Wolf's (ed.) *Wolf's Complete Book of Terror,* New York, Clarkson N. Potter.

Right at the outset, the narrator of Benson's softly horrifying "Caterpillars" is candidly equivocal about the story he is about to tell. He says he will be "writing of those things which I myself saw (or imagined I saw) . . ."

What he sees, or imagines he sees, takes place in the Villa Casana, not far from Sestri di Levante on the Italian Riviera. It is one of those spacious, gracious houses notable for its extensive gardens, for its marble stairway and for its many rooms to which any number of houseguests are invited for long periods of time. In this case, the narrator is one of the invited guests and a painter, Arthur Inglis, is another.

The narrator tells us that, from the moment of his arrival he had uneasy premonitions about his visit. Then we learn that he has slept badly on his first night in the villa. On the second night, unable to sleep (or perhaps actually dreaming what follows), he gets out of bed to go find a book he has left in the dining room and passes an unoccupied room on the ground floor. The door of the room is open and as the narrator looks in he sees that the bed

> was covered with great caterpillars, a foot or more in length, which crawled over it. They were faintly luminous, and it was the light from them that showed me the room. Instead of the sucker-feet of ordinary caterpillars they had rows of pincers like crabs and they moved by grasping what they lay on with their pincers . . . There must have been hundreds of them, for they formed a sort of writhing, crawling pyramid on the bed . . . They appeared to have no faces, so to speak, but at one end of them there was a mouth that opened sideways in respiration.

As he stares at the slithering mass, the caterpillars seem aware of him and, making soft thuds as they drop to the floor, they make toward him and he rushes upstairs to his room where he waits out the night cowering in terror.

Now all that may have been a dream, but the next day Arthur Inglis displays a live caterpillar that is a precise replica of those the narrator saw in his nightmare adventures. The narrator, moved by revulsion, flings the creature into a nearby fountain where, later, he sees it first crawling down the leg of a marble cupid and then "swimming like a snake across the water of the fountain towards me."

That purposive swimming, it seems to me, puts the capstone of horror on the tale. Though Benson's narrator goes on to tell us more as a way of giving his story a rational "meaning," the true heart of the matter lies in his experiences (asleep or awake) with that tide of undulating faceless creatures with their gaping mouths. It resides too in their multiplicity, in their anonymous vitality, and in the narrator's perception that they are possessed of a malign will that lets them choose a target for their ravenously moving jaws.

CHILDE ROLAND TO THE DARK   Poem
TOWER CAME
Robert Browning
Great Britain
1855, in *Men and Women;* reprinted 1979 in James F. Louck's (ed.) *Robert Browning's Poetry,* New York, W. W. Norton, 1979.

This dark, somber, jagged, cruel and brooding poem is one of Browning's greatest as well as most mysterious works. Here, in 35 six-line stanzas, is a compressed, epic journey in which the poem's narrator tells us what happened to him when, directed by "a hoary cripple with malicious eye," he turned aside "Into that ominous tract which, all agree,/Hides the Dark Tower . . ."

He tells us that he is one of The Band, that is, one of "The knights who to the Dark Tower's search addressed/Their step . . ." We do not know at first that the Dark Tower represents or who is likely to be there when it has been reached. It is enough that "just to fail . . . seemed best." On that ambiguous note, the narrator proceeds on his way.

The landscape through which he passes is worse than dreary.

Such starved ignoble nature; nothing throve:

. . . .

. . . .
      As for the grass, it grew as scant as hair
In leprosy; thin dry blades pricked the mud
Which underneath looked kneaded up with blood.
He comes to a river which:

He fords that river though;

. . . .
   I feared
      To set my foot upon a dead man's cheek,
   Each step, or fell the spear I thrust to seek
For hollows, tangled in his hair or beard!
   —It may have been a water-rat I speared,
      But, ugh! it sounded like a baby's shriek.

But it is not mere gloom that makes this poem so powerful. Rather, it is our conviction that, as the protagonist moves through his dreadful landscape, all that he sees and senses are aspects, momentarily made concrete, of his own self. And when he stands at last before the Dark Tower, his goal, and blows an exultant blast upon his horn, the horror is that we know, and so does he, that he is standing before the portals of dismay.

CHILDREN OF THE CORN   Film
1984   (C) U.S.A.   92 min.
Production Company: New World/Cinema Group; *Director:* Fritz Kiersch; *Producer:* Donald P. Borchers; *Screenplay:* George Goldsmith; *Photography:* Raoul Lomas; *Music:* Jonathan Elias.
Cast: Peter Horton (Burt), Linda Hamilton (Vicky), R. G. Armstrong (Diehl), John Franklin (Isaac), Courtney Gains (Malachi), Robby Kiger (Job), AnneMarie McEvoy (Sarah).

Children of the Corn begins with a preliminary scene in which we see how all the adults in Gatlin, a small town in Nebraska, are massacred by children. Then, after the film credits, we are in the bedroom of a high-spirited, amorous couple, Burt Stanton and Vicky. After their lovemaking Burt and Vicky start off on their journey to another city where Burt, just certified, will take up a post as a physician.

As they drive through endless miles of cornfields, they lose their way. Suddenly, their car strikes a boy whose body is lying in the road. That collision with the body of a murdered boy is the beginning of Burton and Vicki's involvement with the town of Gatlin. The town at first appears to be deserted but it turns out to be populated by children who, three years ago, massacred the town's adults and then, led by a couple of adolescents Isaac and Malachi, set up a juvenile theocracy in which human sacrifice is practiced and no one is allowed to live past the age of 19. Isaac, who looks vaguely stunted, is the spiritual leader of the community while Malachi, a gangly yokel, is his enforcer, his secular arm.

Isaac and Malachi immediately designate Vicki and Burton enemies of the community and the film chronicles the struggle between the two adults and the religion-crazed children.

In the battle, the adults have the help of the very young Job and Sarah, who have escaped the religious contagion that afflicts the other children.

In the ensuing alarums and surprises, the children capture Vicky and prepare to sacrifice her to the fierce god who lives in the cornfields. In the rest of the film we see how Burt and his allies save her, overthrow the theocracy and destroy (or at least drive away) the corn god. The final battle is the high point of the film and is something of a special effects tour de force.

Children of the Corn, based on a Stephen King short story, is one of those bare bones films that seems to have cost its producers little or nothing to make. Its sets are few and unimpressive, its direction is weak and its characters, with the exception of Isaac who emanates kinky evil, are essentially bland. Still, the film is horrifying enough in the way it makes its central point: that children, when they are left to form a society of their own, are quite capable of making one that will be as cruel and as mindless as any designed by adults.

CHILDREN OF THE KINGDOM   Short Story
T.E.D. Klein
U.S.A.
1980, in Kirby McCauley's (ed.) *Dark Forces,* New York, Viking.

In "Children of the Kingdom," T.E.D. Klein, one of the most literate and sensitive of the younger generation of fantasy and horror writers, gives us a lost race survival tale in the Lovecraft tradition. His story of a hidden race of prehistoric or other-worldly survivors is set firmly and deeply in the most contemporary of urban settings—Manhattan's upper West Side—and is linked brilliantly to the racial and population pressures that characterize New York City life. Despite the up-to-date setting, Klein is not afraid to develop his story in the leisurely, gracious and detailed fashion of authors who lived two of three generations ago.

The story's first person narrator is a young, articulate married man who, concerned for the welfare of his aging grandfather, installs him in an Upper West Side retirement home where the crusty old man settles down quickly. Much to his grandson's relief, he soon acquires cronies in the neighborhood.

One of these is a priest the grandfather calls Father Pistachio. The priest, a native of Ecuador, has written a book on the origins of mankind in which, drawing on local Indian legends, he describes a truly repulsive race of beings, pale, slimy, with hooked mouths like tapeworms, who in prehistoric times conquered the native tribes of Ecuador. "Some say [they] are children of God but children He make [sic] wrong." It is a race, he says, whom God cursed in three ways: first, He made their women sterile, then He caused the men's penises to fall off, and third, He struck the whole race blind. But, says the priest, "as long as they find women, they are still breeding." How they accomplish that is left to our imagination, though we are given to understand that the method is revolting.

The narrator at first thinks the priest's descriptions of the lost race are merely the fantasies of a harmless kook. But

T.E.D. Klein.

little by little the evidence mounts, not only that the priest is right, but also that survivors of the lost race are actually living in New York City's sewer system and, slowly, are coming to feel bold enough to attack occasional human females whom they rape in their impossible fashion. More than that, the narrator learns that their point of entry into the human world is the laundry room in the basement of his grandfather's retirement home.

The ghastly climax of the story comes in the summer of 1977 when New York City experienced its famous great power outage. On that night, the narrator catches a glimpse of the invaders and has

a vision of a band of huge white tapeworms, with bodies as big as men, inching blindly northward toward New York.

Though the lights went on again in 1977, the invasion of the tapeworm people left several women pregnant with atrocious fetuses. Four years later, as the story ends, the narrator is suddenly given reason to believe that the danger to humankind is far from over.

What makes Klein's story so frightful is the authority with which he depicts the pre-invasion horrors of contemporary big city life. The tapeworm people are repulsive enough and their threat is real, but, his story implies, given our own capacity to dehumanize ourselves, we may be more like the invaders than we think: sterile, impotent, blind and mindlessly fierce.

CLOCKWORK ORANGE
Novel
Anthony Burgess
Great Britain
1963, New York, W. W. Norton; reprinted 1984, Norton.

This ingenious and powerful novel fuses inner and outer terror into a single, nearly unbearable whole. There is plenty of straightforward external violence in the behavior of a gang of teenage hoods in an unspecified future time in an England in which people speak an interesting mixture of English and Russian. But when the leader of the gang is captured and the government tinkers with his mind to render him gentle, the focus of the book shifts from "ordinary" urban terror to the world of nightmare.

The book's theme is as bleak as it is ancient. Burgess tells us that unreasoned violence is bad but that reasoned violence is not really much better. In passing we learn that the arts in and of themselves do not humanize the psyche, and that bloodlust and cruelty may share the mind with the instincts for music and poetry.

Burgess's prose is inventive, experimental and graceful. Without any irritable reaching for greatness, *Clockwork Orange* seems already to have achieved it.

A CLOCKWORK ORANGE
Film
1971 (C) Great Britain 136 min.
Production Company: Warner Brothers; *Director:* Stanley Kubrick; *Producer:* Bernard Williams; *Screenplay:* Stanley Kubrick; *Photography:* John Alcott; *Editor:* Bill Butler; *Music:* Walter Carlos.
Cast: Malcolm McDowell (Alex DeLarge), Patrick McGee (Frank Alexander), Adrienne Corri (Mrs. Alexander), Carl Duering (Dr. Brodsky), William Clarke (Dim), James Marcus (Georgie), Michael Tarn (Pete), Miriam Karlin (Cat Lady).

Anthony Burgess's novel, as we have seen, is a corrosive satire aimed at the bureaucratization of communism and western political systems. The young toughs who are its central characters speak a sort of Russ-English; and the psychopolitical question the book raises is whether the sort of personal brutality in which the toughs delight is essentially worse than the state-supervised aversion therapy set in motion against it. In the novel, that question is soberly put and harshly developed.

In this film based on the novel, Stanley Kubrick poses the same questions that Anthony Burgess does in his book, but Kubrick's film is anything but harsh (though it has plenty of violence). Kurbrick loves broad, Dickensian effects. He finds in Burgess's grimy story only occasions for splendid camera work and sleekly contrived and lavish sets. Where in the novel Burgess has a scene in which his protagonist Alex and his bully buddies commit rape and assault on the Home couple, Kubrick turns the scene into a semi-comic dance, a burlesque turn in which Alex, like a practiced vaudevillian, prances about his female victim, timing his violence to the melody and the beat of "Raindrops Keep Falling on my Head." The result is that audiences laugh at a scene that ought to fill them with what Burgess calls "horrorshow," which in the book is a bilingual (Russian and English) pun in which "horror" and "xorosho," meaning "good," are fused.

When later Alex actually commits a murder, the weapon, which in Burgess is a little silver statue of a young woman standing on one leg, becomes in Kubrick a huge, comically stylized sculpture of a pair of testicles and a phallus. The death, then of an innocent woman at the hands of a cold-blooded killer, turns into a sexual parody.

A Clockwork Orange, with its lavish decor and outrageously caricatured people, is a mixed bag of tricks. As the film ends, the audience applauds the re-transformation of Alex back into the killer punk who fantasized rape to the strains of Beethoven's Ninth Symphony. The squalid terrors that are at the core of Burgess's cautionary fable are left behind on the printed page.

And yet, this *is* a Stanley Kubrick film, which means that in addition to considerable self-indulgence, we also get a great deal of film savvy, ingenious and muscular direction and a sleekness of surface that comes close to being breathtaking.

THE COLLECTOR   Film
1965   (C)   U.S./Great Britain   119 min.
Production Company: Columbia/RCA; *Director:* William Wyler; *Producer:* Jud Kinberg and John Kohn; *Screenplay:* John Kohn and Stanley Mann; *Photography:* Robert L. Surtees, Robert Krasker; *Music:* Maurice Jarre.
Cast: Terence Stamp (Freddie Clegg), Samantha Eggar (Miranda Grey), Mona Washbourne (Aunt Annie), Maurice Dallimore (nosy neighbor).

What strikes one first about *The Collector* is the extraordinary literacy of its screenplay and the subtlety of the point that hides under the brutality of the film's plot line. The fact that the film is based on John Fowles' novel of the same name may account for its literacy, but it is William Wyler's direction and the performances of Samantha Eggar and Terence Stamp that leave us aware (though never quite in possession) of its controlling idea: Evil is the name for what happens when, for whatever reason, one human being imagines another as a thing.

There is hardly a film made that is as tightly focused as *The Collector.* There are, essentially, only two characters, Teddy Clegg, a middle-class British young man with some, but not much, education and Miranda Grey, an attractive young art student. And, except for a couple of excursions into town, or into an upstairs room, there is really only one set on which the action is played out.

When Clegg wins a large sum of money in "the pools" he sets out to fulfill a fantasy of love. He buys an isolated country property. Then he kidnaps Miranda with whom he is obsessed and brings her to the house and locks her in a

Terence Stamp and Samantha Eggar in **The Collector.**

basement room he has carefully fitted up to receive her. He provides her with what he imagines are all the creature comforts anyone might desire. What he wants is for Miranda to fall in love with him.

The only trouble is that Miranda quite reasonably finds him and his scheme revolting. Though on a couple of occasions and as part of an escape attempt, she is willing to let him imagine that she is yielding, he is finally too astute not to know that it is all pretense.

What makes the film a classic horror tale is the careful way that Clegg's scheme is put before us in slow and natural increments. Clegg, who also collects butterflies, seems not to be making any transition in kind as he turns from them to collecting a person to love. In addition to that achievement, there is the equally careful depiction of the slow breaking of Miranda's will and of her eventual psychological and physical decline.

When the worst has finally happened and we see Clegg readying himself for his next victim it is hard not to think of the film as an existential allegory. This is the way things are: The world is made up of users and collectors on the one hand and the used and the collected on the other. The horror is that it should all seem so natural.

THE COLOUR OUT OF SPACE   Short Story
H. P. Lovecraft
U.S.A.
September 1927, *Amazing Stories:* reprinted 1968 in *3 Tales of Horror,* Sauk City, Wis., Arkham House.

As we have seen in "The Call of Cthulhu," H.P. Lovecraft's tales at their best are exercises on the theme that humankind is not alone in the universe and that—much worse—the existence of our species is threatened always by other, older, demonically cleverer, foul smelling, ghastly creature-things against whom we are all but helpless.

In "The Colour Out of Space" that threat comes to Earth in the form of a meteor that has fallen somewhere west of Arkham where "the hills rise wild, and there are valleys with deep woods that no axe has ever cut." The narrator of the tale, a surveyor for a dam project, comes upon a heath blasted by the meteor and he learns from the local people that the great rock fell out of the sky onto Nahum Gardner's "house amidst its fertile gardens and orchards." The rock, curiously soft, gives off a faint glow at night. When a group of academics test it, they are able to learn almost nothing about it except that it comes from another world and behaves according to laws they do not understand. Finally, their samples simply fade away.

But the effect of the meteorite on Nahum Gardner's family and on his farm is what the horrifying rest of the story is about. First, there is the phenomenal size of the fruit in Nahum's orchards after the meteorite. Huge and shiny as the fruit is, "for all that gorgeous array of specious lusciousness not one single jot was fit to eat." Then, there are observable changes, first in the behavior of the Gardner family and later physical changes in the local small animals. By spring, when a fresh crop of monstrous vegetables has come up, it is perfectly clear that some dangerous force is at work on the Gardners and on their land. By April, "All the orchard trees blossomed forth in strange colours, and through the stony soil of the yard and adjacent pasturage there sprang up a bizarre growth . . ."

The first of the Gardners to be profoundly affected by whatever is poisoning their farm is Nahum Gardner's wife, who goes mad. "By July she had ceased to speak and crawled on all fours, and before the month was over Nahum got the mad notion that she was slightly luminous in the dark."

The slow decay goes on as "all the vegetation was turning grey and brittle." Dreadful things happen one by one to the Gardner children and to the Gardner farm. As the story ends, Lovecraft allows his narrator to speculate on the source of the evil that came to earth with the meteorite:

"What it is, only God knows. I suppose [it could be] called a gas, but this gas obeyed the laws that are not of our cosmos . . . It was just a colour out of space—a frightful messenger from unformed realms of infinity beyond all Nature as we know it . . ."

"The Colour Out of Space" is at once a lyric and a brooding story. Lovecraft seems caught up in a sort of monody of grief in which the fate of the Gardners, horrible though that is, is less compelling than what he describes as happening to the land. There is where the true disaster is, and the result of such a warped focus is that the story is less a work of naturalist fiction than an allegory of the doom that awaits humankind. In this case, Lovecraft specifies the rate at which disaster will overtake us: "The rustics say the blight creeps an inch a year." His implication is that, in the scale of eternity, our doom is moving at a galloping pace.

THE COMEDY OF TERRORS   Film
(Alternate release title: **THE GRAVESIDE TERROR**)
1963   (C)   U.S.A.   86 min.
Production Company: Alta Vista/American International; ***Director:*** Jacques Torneur; ***Producer:*** James H. Nicholson, Samuel Z. Arkoff; ***Screenplay:*** Richard Matheson; ***Photography:*** Floyd Crosby, Tim Vanick; ***Editor:*** Anthony Carras; ***Special Effects:*** Pat Dinga, Daniel Haller (sets); ***Music:*** Les Baxter.
Cast: Vincent Price (Waldo Trumbull), Boris Karloff (Amos Hinchley), Peter Lorre (Felix Gillie), Basil Rathbone (John F. Black), Joyce Jameson (Amaryllis Trumbull), Joe E. Brown (cemetery keeper).

Terror film buffs tend to appreciate *The Comedy of Terrors* well beyond its desserts, probably because it has such a gathering of fine old terror names associated with it. In fact, this weak spoof is never clear about just what it means to be spoofing.

Still, the film is relaxed and good-humored. Vincent Price plays the role of an impecunious and, evidently, incompetent undertaker. His bosomy wife, Joyce Jameson, sings bits and pieces out of French opera. Price hates her and her songs; but Peter Lorre, Price's apprentice, adores everything about her. Boris Karloff, who is made to look like a grizzled miner of the sort that Gabby Hayes used to play, is Price's senile father-in-law and spends most of the film mumbling into his porridge. Into this sleepy menage, leaps Basil Rathbone, wielding an axe. Presumably to liven up the plot.

It may be that *The Comedy of Terrors* has no better motiva-

Peter Lorre (left) and Vincent Price in **The Comedy of Terrors.** © American International Pictures

tion than to bring a cluster of terror heavies together so that they can be silly. But Abbot and Costello, with a very similar cast, did everything this film does, and better, in *Abbott and Costello Meet Frankenstein* (1948). Just the same, one ought not to miss one's favorite heavies, even at their silliest.

THE COMPANY OF WOLVES   Film
1984   (C)   Great Britain   95 min.
Production Company: Palace Pictures/A Neil Jordan Production; *Director:* Neil Jordan; *Producer:* Chris Brown and Stephen Woolley; *Screenplay:* Angela Carter and Neil Jordan; *Photography:* Bryan Loftus: *Editor:* Rodney Holland; *Special Effects:* Peter MacDonald; Animation Wolf by Roger Shaw; *Music:* George Fenton,
Cast: Angela Lansbury (Granny), Graham Crowden (old priest), Brian Glover (amorous boy's father), Kathryn Pogson (young bride), Stephen Rea (young groom), Tusse Silberg (mother) and David Warner (father), Micha Bergese (the huntsman), Sarah Patterson (Rosaleen).

Here is an utterly charming, grown-up gloss on the Tale of Little Red Riding Hood whose central metaphor is the were-wolf. Aside from its distinction in presenting a series of intimate, concentrated human-into-wolf wolf-into-human tales, the film should fascinate horror film lovers for the high quality of its transformation scenes, superior in physiological detail to those in the *The Howling* and *American Werewolf in London.*

The film opens in the home of a modern British family where we see the young Rosaleen asleep in her room, which is filled with the sort of woolly soft toys female adolescents give up so reluctantly as they mature. Rosaleen's sister is banging on the door crying, "Pest, pest!" as she demands that Rosaleen come down to dinner. Rosaleen's hostile response is the sequence of dreams that make up the rest of the film.

In her first dream, the country of her mind is established. She lives in a fairy-tale land with peaked-roof houses, a land so long-ago-and-far-away that one can hardly believe that the wheel has been invented there. It is a country of dark, forbidding woods, thick undergrowth, dense fogs and narrow paths from which it is very dangerous to stray. And yet its atmosphere is so intensely dreamlike that, even in the most frightening scenes, one is never far from feeling that one is under, or near, comfortably warm bedclothes. If this were a Disney film, this is the land in which the seven dwarfs would dwell.

In Rosaleen's first dream, she conveniently rids herself of her annoying sister who, having ''strayed from the path,'' has been eaten by a wolf. Rosaleen's granny takes the occasion to teach her some folk wisdom:

> Never stray from the path; never eat a windfall apple, and never trust a man whose eyebrows meet . . . A wolf may be more than he seems. He may come in many disguises. The wolf that ate your sister was hairy on the outside, but when she died she went straight to heaven. The worst kind of wolves are hairy on the inside. They drag you with them to hell.

Having said so much, Granny then tells a tale of a woman who married a travelling man whose eyebrows met. It's a richly erotic tale that ends with a beheading scene almost as beautifully depicted as the one Kurosawa gives us in *Ran*.

That tale done, Rosaleen dreams her first tentative encounter with Danny, the son of the local blacksmith. They walk together in the woods and she finds eggs which hatch pretty little human infants, one of which Rosaleen brings home.

There are still other dreams, and in each of them the imagery of wolves teaches the dreaming Rosaleen various things about her own developing sexuality. Before the film comes to its stunning close, we feel confident that Rosaleen's unconscious has served her well, that when she wakes, her intimations of womanhood will serve to quiet her fears of it.

The Company of Wolves would, I think, have rejoiced Yeats. The dream world depicted in it, like Yeats' ''Byzantium,''

> is no country for old men. The young
> In one another's arms, birds in the trees
> —Those dying generations—at their song,
> The salmon-falls, the mackerel-crowded seas,
> Fish, flesh, or fowl, commend all summer long
> Whatever is begotten, born and dies,

What Neil Jordan and Angela Carter have done is to refurbish, in a gracious and graceful film, the wolf as the image that stands for all that teeming sensuality.

COUCHING AT THE DOOR   Short Story
D. K. Broster
Great Britain
1942, in *Couching at the Door*, London, Heinemann.

This is the suave and subtle story of the elegantly depraved, post *Yellow Book* poet, Augustine Marchant, who is haunted by something that looks at first like a bit of fluff, then like a furry caterpillar and finally becomes a thing that ''Reared up for quite five feet against the door, huge, dark, sleeked with wet and flecked with bits of green waterweed . . . something half-python, half gigantic cobra . . . [with] two reddish eyes, such as furriers put into the heads of stuffed creatures.''

Marchant, who is a direct descendant of the decadent heroes imagined by Huysmans and Oscar Wilde, is haunted in retribution for some unnamed, illegal and immoral sexual adventure in Prague. He tries desperately to pass his horrid familiar on to a young artist, Lawrence Storey. For a while, he seems to succeed. After that, the horror reasserts itself.

''Couching'' is neither psychologically complex nor intri-

cately plotted. What makes the story work is Dorothy Kathleen Broster's civilized, ironic, brilliantly paced prose and her understanding that we are all eager to see the fall of prideful high achievers.

COUNT DRACULA   Film
1970   (C)   Spain/Italy/West Germany   98 min.
Production Company: Fenix Films/Corona Filmproduktion/ Filmar Compagnia Cinematografica/ Towers of London; **Director:** Jesus Franco; **Producer:** Harry Allan Towers; **Screenplay:** Jesus Franco, Peter Welbeck (Harry Allan Towers), Augusto Finochi, Carlo Fadda, Milo G. Cucchia; **Photography:** Manuel Merino; **Editor:** Derek Parsons, Bruno Mattei (Spanish version); **Special Effects:** Sergio Pagoni.
Cast: Christopher Lee (Dracula). Klaus Kinski (Renfield), Herbert Lom (Doctor Van Helsing), Frederick Williams (Jonathan Harker), Paul Muller (Dr. Seward), Maria Rohm (Mina), Soledad Miranda (Lucy), Jack Taylor (Quincey Morris).

The note that appears on the screen just before the beginning of *Count Dracula* asserts proudly that, ''Now for the first time we retell [Bram Stoker's *Dracula*] exactly as he wrote [it].'' They are brave words, but they are not exactly true. Jesus Franco and his team of coauthors have created a script that more or less follows in Stoker's footsteps, but they, like everyone else who has ever adapted the novel to film, have made changes where they deemed them necessary: Arthur Holmwood, Lucy's fiancee in the novel does not appear in the screenplay at all. Instead, that honor falls in the film to Quincey Morris who in Stoker's original is an American. Dr. Seward, who in the book has his own sanitarium, is downgraded in the film to Dr. Van Helsing's employee. The worst liberties director Franco has taken are with the climactic final moments of the story when he departs inexcusably from Stoker's very theatrical ending.

Just the same, *Count Dracula* deserves to be noticed for two reasons. First, because it does give us a Dracula who, as in the novel, starts as an old man and gets progressively younger as his intake of blood increases. Second, because Klaus Kinski, in the most subtle film rendition of Renfield ever made, projects a Renfield who is mad, dignified and profoundly suffering. Kinski's great achievement is that he can convey the terrible stillness of a once powerful man whose spirit (as well as his mind) has been broken. The camera sees Renfield invariably leaning against, or crouching before, or lying upon brightly lighted pink stone. It's a trick that conveys the illusion that we are looking right through stone to see a man who has been entombed alive.

Speaking of the camera, *Count Dracula* is the only film I know in which the photographer seems to have had an independent vision of his own, different from the director's. In scene after scene, no matter what the demands of the story are, the camera moves at an oblique angle upward to emphasize the vastness of the architecture within or beneath which the tiny humans are acting out their trivial destiny.

There is one more reason to see this film and that is that it has Christopher Lee in it. Lee possessed the role of Dracula in the fifties and sixties the way Bela Lugosi possessed it in the thirties, and the way Frank Langella made it his own in 1979. Lee brings to the role a cold austerity, a looming inertness that can chill the blood.

Christopher Lee and Soledad Miranda in **Count Dracula.** © American International Pictures

COUNT MAGNUS   Short Story

M. R. James
Great Britain
1904, in *Ghost Stories of an Antiquary*, London, Edward Arnold; collection reprinted 1971, New York, Dover.

"Count Magnus," one of M.R. James's most terrifying tales, achieves its effects by the same principle of indirection that served Bram Stoker in *Dracula*. There, it will be remembered, Count Dracula rarely appears before us. M.R. James's villain, Count Magnus, is similarly elusive but, like Dracula in Stoker's story, his dark presence pervades the tale.

The protagonist of "Count Magnus" is an English gentleman, a Mr. Wraxall, who in the course of gathering data for a book about his travels in Sweden comes upon some family papers in a house in Vestgothland in which he finds an account of the first Count Magnus de La Gardie, a 17th-century nobleman. When Wraxall sees his portrait, the face "impressed him rather by its power than its beauty or goodness; in fact . . . Count Magnus was an almost phenomenally ugly man."

The Count's ugliness is an indication of his character as well. Wraxall learns that if the Count's

tenants came late to their work on the days which they owed to him as Lord of the Manor, they were set on the wooden horse, or flogged and branded in the manor-house yard. One or two cases there were of men who had occupied lands which encroached on the Lord's domain, and whose houses had been mysteriously burnt on a winter's night with the whole family inside.

The Count used also to dabble in alchemy and was rumored to have made the Black Pilgrimage to Chorazin where, it is said, the Anti-Christ will be born and where one goes if one wants "to obtain a long life, acquire a faithful messenger and see the blood of his enemies." But it is not the events of the 17th century that are at the horrifying heart of this tale. Rather, it is what happens to Wraxall when his curiosity about the Count results in the breaking, one by one, of the three massive locks on the count's coffin.

Here, as in other M.R. James fictions, the charm of the story is in the contrast between the peaceful, sedentary, scholarly occupation of the narrator and the hellish events his labors uncover and compel. Describing the fate of two men who hunted on the dead Count's domain, a character says that their companions, "at first . . . hear [sic] nothing at all; then they hear someone . . . they hear someone scream just as if the most inside part of his soul was twisted out of him." As for the second victim, "Anders Bjornsen was once a beautiful man, but now his face was not there, because the flesh of it was sucked away off the bones."

Nor is that the worst of it. What is to come is why we continue to read this low-key tale of academic curiosity and satanic retribution.

COUNT YORGA
Film

1970 (C) U.S.A. 90 min.

Production Company: Erica Productions/ American International; *Director:* Bob Kelljan; *Producer:* Michael Macready; *Screenplay:* Bob Kelljan; *Photography:* Arch Archambault; *Special Effects:* James Tannenbaum; *Music:* William Marx.

Cast: Robert Quarry (Count Yorga), Donna Anders (Erica), Michael Macready (Erica's Boyfriend), Edward Walsh (Brudah).

According to David Pirie writing in *The Vampire Cinema,* Robert Quarry, who played the title role in *Count Yorga,* said that the film was made on a $20,000 budget, a phenomenally small sum for a film that became a box office success.

Part of the film's appeal to audiences in the seventies was undoubtedly the irreverence with which the director Kelljan treated vampire lore and, perhaps even more, the film's brusque eroticism and imaginative cruelty. *Time* magazine reported that one of the female victims was shown having an orgasm on camera (a detail that continues to escape me). And there was certainly something daring in the brief sequence that shows the lissome, newly vampirized Donna Anders gnawing on a kitten.

Bob Kelljan's vampire, Count Yorga, arrives in Los Angeles and soon afterward is seen conducting a seance for a young woman named Erica who wants to be put in touch with her dead mother. But Yorga himself is interested in Erica and she promptly becomes his victim. Most of the action that follows depicts the struggle between Yorga and Erica's boyfriend, who undertakes to rescue Erica from the vampire. When the battle is over and Erica is safe in her boyfriend's arms and the audience is about to relax, Kelljan disappoints all expectations of a happy ending as he compresses into a freeze-frame, an effect borrowed from Roman Polanski's *The Fearless Vampire Killers.* Audiences loved it.

Robert Quarry is a suitable Count Yorga, if, that is, we don't mind our king vampires looking like well-dressed and affable hair oil advertisements. There is a certain degree of lèse-majesté committed, however, when this master of the undead is given his quietus with a broken broom handle. In Stoker's novel, it will be remembered, the stake is a respectful object: It is made of oak, is three feet long, three inches at its base and its tip has been charred by fire.

COUNTESS DRACULA
Film

1970 (C) Great Britain 93 min.

Production Company: Hammer Films; *Director:* Peter Sasdy; *Producer:* Alexander Paal; *Screenplay:* Jeremy Paul; *Photography:* Ken Talbot; *Editor:* Henry Richardson; *Special Effects:* Bert Luxford; *Music:* Harry Robinson.

Cast: Ingrid Pitt (Countess Elisabeth Nadasdy), Nigel Green (Captain Dobi), Sandor Eles (Imre Toth), Maurice Denham (Master Fabio), Patience Collier (nanny Julia), Lesley-Anne Downe (Ilona).

The story of Elizabeth Bathory has reached the screen in several versions the best of which is *Daughters of Darkness* (1971). Others are *Immoral Tales* (1974) and **Momma Dracula** (1980).

This version of the Bathory tale, directed by Peter Sasdy, is opulent in the Hammer tradition. A blood pudding of pulchritude and fear, it is both poorly edited and frequently tedious as it follows the career of the 17th-century Hungarian noblewoman who believed that she had found the Fountain of Youth and that it flowed through the veins of virgins. The countess, who stays alive and young as long as she has access to the blood of younger women, has, naturally, to cater to her thirst. She is abetted by a captain of the guard who knows her terrible secret, but who, so long as he share her embraces, from time to time is willing to let lovely young bodies fall in his loved one's wake. There comes, finally, a terrible moment when the countess, unable to get her cosmetic dose, attacks her own daughter. Rarely has the fixation on beauty demanded quite so high a price.

CREATURE FROM THE BLACK LAGOON
Film

1954 (B&W) (3-D) U.S.A. 79 min.

Production Company: Universal-International; *Director:* Jack Arnold; *Producer:* William Alland; *Screenplay:* Harry Essex and Arthur Ross; *Photography:* William E. Snyder, *Editor:* Ted J. Kent; *Special Effects:* Charles S. Wellbourne, costumes by Bud Westmore and Jack Kevan; *Underwater Photographer:* James T. Havens; *Musical Director:* Joseph Gershenson.

Cast: Richard Carlson (David Reed), Julia Adams (Kay), Richard Denning (Mark Williams), Antonio Moreno (Karl Maia), Nestor Paiva (Lucas), Whit Bissell (Dr. Thompson).

Creature From the Black Lagoon, though no longer a very terrifying film, is a darling of horror film aficionados. And for good reason.

The film begins portentously enough, with a voice intoning "In the beginning God created the heaven and the earth," after which we are treated to a once over very lightly review of the big bang theory of the creation of the earth and an even swifter survey of the evolutionary history of the life of the planet. The camera eye comes finally to rest in the upper reaches of the Amazon where we see something resembling a webbed claw sticking up out of a mound of earth.

Professor Maia finds the fossil webbed claw and seeks help from the Institute of Marine Biology, which hires Lucas, a tough old river-rat of a boat captain, to take an expedition up the Amazon to the Black Lagoon. Here the party of scientists that includes Mark Williams, David Reed and a young woman named Kay plan to hunt the Creature whose existence the fossil claw implies.

The scientific party finds the Creature and spends a considerable while molesting it. In the process, Mark, David, Kay and the Creature put in a good deal of time underwater where the underwater cameras follow them. By then we recognize that much of what is dynamic in this low budget, low-key film really derives from a three-way struggle in a primitive setting in which each of the viable males, Mark, David and the Creature, is out to get Kay for himself.

Along with King Kong and Frankenstein's creation, the Creature is one of that small band of film monsters whose innocence and misfortune rouse our sympathy. How can it be otherwise? The fact is that the Creature is the wrong lover in the wrong place at the wrong time. And that's where the pathos and the beauty lie. In the underwater scenes when it is gazing toward or pursuing Kay, the Creature's brilliantly conceived features turn into such a compelling portrait of mute longing that with all our hearts we wish him a better fate than the one we know awaits him at the movie's end.

CUJO
Film

1983   (C)   U.S.A.   97 min.

Production Company: Warner Brothers; *Director:* Lewis Teague; *Producer:* Daniel H. Blatt and Robert Singer; *Screenplay:* Don Carlos Dunaway and Lauren Currier; *Photography:* Jaan De Bont; *Editor:* Neil Travis; *Special Effects:* Peter Knowlton; *Animal Action:* Karl Lewis Miller; *Music:* Charles Bernstein.

Cast: Dee Wallace (Donna Trenton), Daniel Hugh-Kelley (Victor Trenton), Christopher Stone (Steve Kemp), Ed Lauter (Joe Camber), Kaiulani Lee (Charity Camber), Billy Jacoby (Brett Camber), Mills Watson (Garry), Danny Pintauro (Tad).

Cujo begins with a superbly photographed sequence of a St. Bernard dog first observing, then chasing a rabbit through a field, across a stream and finally to a cave into which the dog is just able to get its head. But that small intrusion is enough to set the bats that live in the cave into motion and they attack the dog. At least one of the bats is rabid and very soon after that we understand that the dog, too, has rabies. With those events in the natural world established, the film then moves to the drama of the human lives to which they will be linked.

That drama involves a couple, Donna and Victor Trenton who live in a suburban New England town, their eight-year-old son Tad and Steve Kemp, a young woodworker who, as the film begins, is Donna's lover.

Tad is a fearful child who imagines there are monsters in his bedroom closet. His father Vic is an advertising executive whose firm has created an ad campaign for a breakfast cereal which has just made hundreds of people in the country sick. When Vic discovers his wife's adultery, he goes out of town on business uncertain whether or under what circumstances he will return. Meanwhile, marital crisis or not, Donna has to take her Pinto automobile to Joe Camber's garage on an isolated farm seven miles from town.

It is there that the human and natural dramas intersect because Brett, Joe Camber's son, owns Cujo, the rabid dog. And Donna, with her son Tad in the car, arrives at the farm just after Camber's wife and son have gone off to Connecticut and minutes after the hydrophobic Cujo has killed Joe Cambers and his drinking buddy Garry.

Most of the rest of the film focuses on the dog's petrifying two-and-a-half-day siege of Donna and Tad in their disabled Pinto stuck at the death trap that the farm has become.

There are several frightful scenes. In one of them, we see Cujo attacking the car. He is on the roof, smearing the car's windows with bloody foam as Tad cries, ''It's the monster from my closet,'' and Donna reiterates ''No. It's not a monster, it's just a doggie.'' But everyone, on screen and in the audience, knows that the child is right. Almost as powerful is a later montage in which we see the car at the center of a whirling universe that includes a mad dog, a disabled car, an isolated farm and no help in sight.

Lewis Teague's direction is at once subtle and brilliant. The intercuts between the domestic dilemmas and the drama of the mad dog are nearly seamless. And Danny Pintauro as Tad is splendid. The film is at its absolute best, however, in its depiction of the situation in which the mother, the child and the innocent but deadly dog are locked in combat.

Wonderful as this film often is, it too, like so many horror movies, has a male chauvinist agenda as it repeats to faithless wives a lesson about what horrors they may expect if they are ever tempted to stray.

CURSE OF THE CAT PEOPLE
Film

1944   (B&W)   U.S.A.   70 min.

Production Company: RKO-Radio; *Director:* Gunther von Fritsch and Robert Wise; *Producer:* Val Lewton; *Screenplay:* DeWitt Bodeen, Val Lewton; *Photography:* Nicholas Musuraca; *Editor:* J.R. Whittredge; *Music:* Roy Webb.

Cast: Simone Simon (Irena), Kent Smith (Oliver), Jane Randolph (Alice), Ann Carter (Amy), Elizabeth Russell (Barbara), Julia Dean (Julia Farren).

Though there is a considerable muted splendor in this sequel to Val Lewton's *Cat People*, the film is something of a critical problem both to admirers of Val Lewton and to aficionados of the horror genre. But viewed as a study of the dream life of children, the film is admirable for the way Lewton handles his theme: He powerfully conveys just how dangerous their dreaming years can be.

Oliver, the splendid Irena's wimpy husband in *Cat People*, mutters ''It's almost as if there were a curse on us,'' when his daughter Amy daydreams and talks to an invisible friend. But there really is no curse (in the horror film sense of the word) in this film. Nor, indeed, are there any cat people.

What we have are Oliver and Alice, the Goody Two-shoes who inherited Oliver from Irena in the previous film, perplexed by Amy's inwardness and by the fact that she seems to talk to the empty air. But the friendly ghost who inhabits that air and counsels the child is Irena, her father's first wife who, it will be recalled, turned out to be part woman and part black panther.

When Amy forms a bizarre but perfectly reasonable friendship with an aging ex-actress named Julia Farren who lives in a darkly gothic house, the child has not only her parents' anxieties to oppress her but also the hostility of Julia's daughter Barbara as well.

The film is characterized by soft shadows, by an elementary vagueness that produces just enough of a suggestion of the sinister to qualify it as a ghost tale. But its more central theme is how the creative imagination serves children in their not always comfortable dealings with first their parents and then the larger world.

CURSE OF THE DEMON
Film

(Alternate release title: **NIGHT OF THE DEMON**)

1956   (B&W)   Great Britain   95 min.

Production Company: Columbia/Sabre; *Director:* Jacques Tourneur; *Producer:* Frank Bevis; *Screenplay:* Charles Bennett, Hal E. Chester, based on M.R. James' short story ''Casting the Runes''; *Photography:* Ted Scaife; *Editor:* Michael Gordon; *Special Effects:* George Blackwell, Wally Veevers; *Music:* Clifton Parker.

Cast: Dana Andrews (John Holden), Peggy Cummins (Joanna

Harrington), Nial McGinnis (Dr. Carswell), Maurice Denham (Prof. Harrington), Athene Seyer (Mrs. Carswell), Liam Redmond (Mark O'Brien).

John Holden, an American psychologist, comes to London to investigate the mysterious death of one of his English colleagues, Professor Harrington. He is helped in his investigation by the dead man's niece, Joanna Harrington.

For a long while, Holden resists confronting the truth: Professor Harrington was slain by some supernatural creature (a demon) called into action by a satanist named Carswell.

What Holden learns is that Professor Harrington was handed a bit of paper before his death and that that slip of paper, containing mysterious runes, was in some way instrumental in his destruction. If Holden means to combat Carswell, the runes must be passed to the satanist without his knowledge. That task, Holden—formerly skeptical, now a firm believer—finally contrives, and the film ends with a masterful and memorable chase scene in which the demon, only glimpsed earlier, is finally, and fully, if very briefly, on camera as, in a great flurry of action, it is made to turn on its former master.

Many films involving the supernatural burden the viewer with scenes of tiresome dialogue between a skeptical scientist and a true believer, and we are not spared such talk in *The Curse of the Demon*. One of Holden's fellow scientists (O'Brien) tells him, "I'm a scientist also. I know the value of the cold light of reason. But I also know the deep shadows that light can cast. It can blind men to truth."

To counter the minor irritation of such scenes, Jacques Tourneur gives us, in addition to the fine, complexly shaded horrors that flesh out his plot, one of the funniest seance scenes ever filmed: Its participants link hands and sing, in cracked and off-tune voices, a silly song to please a spirit presence whom they mean to invoke.

The Curse of the Demon has one further distinction. Hardly a scene is shot in daylight. We are at every moment either in shade or actually in the dark. Though this is, of course, consistent with the "set" of a scary film, it makes for a certain monotony, not to mention the fact that sometimes it's hard to simply see what's going on.

But this is mere caviling. Here, as in *I Walked With a Zombie* and *Cat People*, it is a pleasure to see Jacques Tourneur at work.

THE CURSE OF YIG   Short Story
Zealia Brown Reed Bishop
U.S.A.
November 1929, *Weird Tales*; reprinted 1985 in Frank McSherry, Jr., Martin H. Greenberg and Charles G. Waugh's (eds.) *A Treasury of American Horror Stories*, New York, Bonanza.

The first-person narrator of this slithery tale is an ethnologist of the American Indian who goes to Oklahoma to collect snake lore and comes back from his researches "with a fear of snakes that will last me the rest of my life." What produced that fear is the substance of the story he tells.

The researcher has heard legends about Yig, a dark and evil snake god who is a sort of primordial and malevolent precursor to the benevolent Quetzalcoatl, the flying serpent god of Mexico. He visits an insane asylum in Guthrie, Oklahoma, and there behind a barred, ground glass window of a locked room he sees an object "almost of human size, and entirely devoid of clothing. It was absolutely hairless, and its tawny-looking back seemed subtly squamous in the dim ghoulish light. . . . As it looked up to hiss at me I saw that the beady little black eyes were damnably anthropoid . . ."

The thing he sees was born to a woman named Audrey Davis three-quarters of a year after a ghastly event that is recounted in the rest of the tale. The hissing, writhing thing on the floor was one of four such creatures born to her, "two were even worse—but this is the only one that lived."

"The Curse of Yig" is perhaps the slimiest, squirmingest story ever written. What makes it something of a tour de force is the way it braids realistic elements with folklore and contemporary psychological theory to produce its effects.

D

DAUGHTERS OF DARKNESS   Film
(Alternate release title: **LE ROUGE AUX LEVRES**)
1971   (C)   Belgium/France/West Germany   87 min.
Production Company: Showking/Cine vog/ Maya Film/ Roxy Films/Mediterranea; ***Director:*** Harry Kumel; ***Producer:*** Alain Guillaume, Paul Collet; ***Screenplay:*** Harry Kumel; ***Photography:*** Eddy van der Enden; ***Editor:*** Gust Vershueren, Denis Bonan, Fima Noveck; ***Music:*** François de Roubaix.
Cast: Delphine Seyrig (Countess Bathory), Daniele Ouimet (Valerie), John Karlen (Stefan), Andrea Rau (Ilona Harczy), Paul Esser (porter).

Daughters of Darkness comes as close to being a ballet of blood as the vampire film genre has produced. It is a composite of adroit silences that alternate with intensely passionate (but absolutely unloving) erotic moments. It is, finally, a film in which tone and texture are everything. The operational word for this film is "cold." The sets are coldly beautiful; the Countess's beauty is frozen, her eyes gleam like ice, her wit is keen and implacable. Even the love making, at its most passionate, is in the service of something other than instinct or affection.

The central figure in the film is the Countess Bathory who, it will be remembered, is notorious for having bathed in the blood of virgins as a way of preserving her youth. Her depredations against the young women of her native Hungary were finally put to a stop by her powerful relatives who, unwilling to take the onus of executing her, had her walled up in a cell where, provided with daily supplies of food and water, she dragged out the rest of her days.

We do not, however, begin with the Countess. Instead we meet a honeymoon couple, Stefan and Valerie, making love in a Pullman compartment on a train speeding to Ostend. We next see them checking in at a nearly empty (because it is off-season) luxury hotel. Immediately, we feel how oppressive, how anti-human are their faded but still grandiose surroundings. The high ceilings, heavy draperies, huge rooms and impeccable servants seem to have no relationship to anything as vital as a honeymoon, and we wonder what miscalculation brought this couple here.

Not long after they are settled into their rooms, they come into the dining hall where they meet the Countess Bathory, a woman as beautiful, as brilliant and as heartless as Hans Andersen's Snow Queen. With her is Ilona, her young companion.

What happens from here on is the slow entanglement of these four people in each other's lives. We learn from the hotel porter that he remembers the Countess from a visit she paid to the hotel some 40 years ago and that her appearance has not changed at all since that time. We learn, too, that though the Countess and Ilona are a lesbian couple, they are eager to involve Stefan and Valerie in as yet unspecified, darkly erotic behavior. In the midst of one such encounter, Stefan accidentally kills Ilona while Valerie is being seduced by the Countess. Eventually, Stefan is killed in still another erotic encounter, leaving Valerie and the Countess, now a couple sealed by what they know of murder and blood, to drive away from the hotel and meet their horrible destiny not many minutes down the road.

Despite the slow, nearly viscid movement of the film, the viewer is nearly mesmerized by the magnificent presence of Delphine Seyrig on the screen. Her lips are so red, her skin so dead white, her hair so scrupulously marcelled and her voice so deeply resonant of an *ancien regime* that to have her presiding over these semblances of passion is a truly vampiric irony. But what makes her truly evil in the film is that she does not create evil so much as she elicits in the other characters the evil that is already hidden just below the threshold of their self-knowledge. Stefan and Valerie are not turned into killers by the Countess. She simply provides them with the opportunities to flower, as it were, into their true selves. Their monstrosity, had they not met the Countess, might have lain hidden within them for a lifetime. But in real life, screenwriter Kumel seems to be saying, one meets the Countess of one's dreams and the truth is what follows.

DEAD OF NIGHT

Film

1945 (B&W) Great Britain 104 min.

Production Company: Ealing Studios; *Director:* "The Linking Story" and "The Horse Driver," Basil Dearden; "The Christmas Story" and "The Ventriloquist's Dummy," Alberto Cavalcanti; "The Haunted Mirror," Robert Hamer; "The Golfing Story," Charles Crichton; *Producer:* Michael Balcon; *Screenplay:* John Baines, Angus McPhail and T.E.B. Clarke, based on stories by H.G. Wells, E.F. Benson, John Baines and Angus McPhail; *Photography:* Stan Pavey, Douglas Slocombe, Jack Parker, H. Julius; *Editor:* Charles Hasse; *Music:* Georges Auric.

Cast: "The Linking Story": Mervyn Johns (Walter Craig), Roland Culver (Eliot Foley), Mary Merrall (Mrs. Foley), Frederick Valk (Dr. Van Straaten), Renee Gadd (Mrs. Craig); "The Hearse Driver": Anthony Baird (Hugh Grainger), Judy Kelly (Joyce Grainger), Miles Malleson (hearse driver); "The Christmas Story": Sally Ann Howe (Sally O'Hara), Michael Allan (Jimmy Watson), Robert Wyndham (Dr. Albury); "The Haunted Mirror": Googie Withers (Joan Courtland), Ralph Michael (Peter Courtland), Esme Percy (dealer); "The Golfing Story:" Basil Radford (George Parratt), Naunton Wayne (Larry Potter), Peggy Bryan (Mary Lee); "The Ventriloquist's Dummy": Michael Redgrave (Maxwell Frere), Hartley Power (Sylvester Kee), Allan Jeayes (Maurice Olcott), John Maguire (Hugo, the dummy). Elizabeth Welch (Beaulah), Magda Kun (Mitzi), Garry Marsh (Harry Parker).

From **The Dead of Night:** *the ventriloquist and his dummy.*

Dead of Night is one of the greatest of the anthology films. In this case we have a single "linking story" within which five interior stories are contained.

In the linking story we see an architect named Eliot Foley hurrying off to a country house to which a telephone call has summoned him. Upon arrival he is startled to find that he has seen everyone there previously, in a recurrent nightmare. When he announces "I've seen you all in my dreams," the others take it as a signal to exchange stories about supernatural experiences they have had.

The narrator of "The Hearse Driver," the rather bland first story, tells how a warning from a hearse driver kept him from being on a bus that was involved in a fatal accident. In the second tale, "The Christmas Story," a woman describes how at a party she met a weeping boy whom she comforted. He turned out to be the ghost of a boy named Francis who, in 1860, was killed by his sister.

In the third tale, a young woman buys her fiancé a Chippendale mirror that reflects a room in which a man strangled his wife in a fit of jealousy. The mirror exerts a malevolent effect on its owner. He says, "I feel as if that room . . . were trying to claim me." When he marries the young woman, the mirror does claim him and he nearly murders his wife as a result.

The weakest of the five tales is "The Golfing Story," in which one of two passionate golfers haunts his rival in love. "The Ventriloquist's Dummy," on the other hand, more than compensates for the banality of the golfing story. Here, as in Ben Hecht's short story "The Rival Dummy," a ventriloquist "murders" his dummy, with appalling consequences to himself.

When the fifth tale is done, Foley, who has been exasperated by the skepticism of a psychiatrist named Dr. Van Straaten, leaps at him and tries to strangle him. From the violence of that moment he is wakened by the ringing of a telephone and we see that everything that has happened so far has been part of his dream.

As the film ends we see Foley repeating the opening scene as he drives off to keep his appointment at the country house to which the telephone call invited him. The circle of nightmare is about to begin again.

The framing tale and two of the interior stories, "The Haunted Mirror" and "The Ventriloquist's Dummy," are what give this film its distinction: All three of them address the fragility of identity. In the mirror tale, the real horror comes from Peter Courtland's recognition that "The trouble is not in the mirror, it's in us." And in "The Ventriloquist's Dummy," the horror, after all, cannot be blamed on the dummy. Once again it is the self that is at the center of its problems. In 1945, in Great Britain, just after a great world war, it took considerable astutenes and even some courage to make that point.

DEATH DREAM

Film

1972 (C) U.S.A. 85 min.

Production Company: Quadrant/Impact, "A Bob Clark Film"; *Director:* Bob Clark; *Producer:* John Trent, Peter James; *Screenplay:* Alan Ormsby; *Photography:* Jack McGowan; *Editor:* Ron Sinclair; *Music:* Carl Zittrer.

Cast: John Marley (Charles Brooks), Lynn Carlin (Christine),

Richard Backus (Andy Brooks), Henderson Forsyth (Doc), Anya Ormsby (Cathy Brooks), Jane Daly (Joanne).

This film about a Vietnam soldier, made while America was still involved in the war in Vietnam, is not to be confused with the great 1945 British anthology film, *Dead of Night*. What we have here is one of those essentially unknown low budget films upon which we sometimes stumbles and which, against all expectation, haunt us forever.

As the film opens, we see Andy Brooks, a combat soldier, on a night patrol in Vietnam. Suddenly, shooting errupts and Andy is mortally wounded. As he is dying, we hear a woman's voice on the soundtrack repeating, "You can't die. You promised. You can't die. You have to come home."

And Andy Brooks comes home, kept from the repose of death by his mother's implacable will. He comes home in dress uniform and arrives not long after his family has been informed by the War Department of his death. From then on, our story is what happens to the Brooks family as it lives through the exhilaration of Andy's return to the slow realization of just what has returned to lie in Andy's room or to sit in his rocking chair in the living room.

Because Andy, though not exactly dead, is not exactly alive either. He is still the clean-cut young man they knew, but he is stonyfaced and his movements are curiously delayed. To sustain himself he must drink the blood of the living. If that were the fulcrum on which the film's plot rested we would have an interesting but not especially striking vampire movie. What gives stature to this modest film is that the filmmakers are interested in the family relationships that are exposed by Andy's return. What we learn is that even before Andy's death, the family dynamics were not good.

Andy's mother was, and is, avidly fixated on Andy. In her life, neither her husband nor her daughter count for very much beside her son. When her husband and her daughter slowly begin to realize what is wrong with Andy, the mother refuses to understand and drives her husband from the house. Later, she taunts her daughter: "You haven't come to me since you were five years old. Andy used to come to me."

When it is impossible to deny any longer just what Andy is, his mother helps him to escape from the police and accompanies him on a wild and heartbreaking drive to the cemetery where Andy finally finds refuge in the grave in which, long ago, he should have been buried.

No doubt the filmmakers, in 1972, had some semi-political message in mind about Vietnam as a vampire event. What comes through to us in the eighties is just how deadly family life can be.

THE DEATH OF HALPIN FRAYSER   Short Story
Ambrose Bierce
U.S.A.
1893, in *Can Such Things Be?*, New York, Cassell; reprinted 1964 in E.F. Bleiler's (ed.) *Ghost and Horror Stories of Ambrose Bierce*, New York, Dover.

James T. Watkins, the editor of a San Francisco newspaper, meaning to praise Ambrose Bierce, wrote to him, saying,

> The sort of sensation that waited upon Mrs. Radcliffe's and Monk Lewis's efforts affords some hint of the sort of career the new Monk and Castle of Udolpho would run. The work

they did in stupid vaults you execute in the secret chambers of the soul . . .

His point, that the human psyche was the source of terror in Bierce's Gothic fictions, is perfectly sound and it is never better illustrated than by "The Death of Halpin Frayser," where, except in Halpin Frayser's dream, there is no dreadful ambience at all.

Bierce divides his story into four parts. In the first, we get to see Halpin Frayser lost in the woods on a small-game hunting expedition near Calistoga, California. As night falls, Frayser takes refuge under a tree, and there he falls into a dreamless sleep from which he wakes to utter the words, "Catherine Larue." Whose name it is, or why he has uttered it, Frayser has no idea. When he goes back to sleep, he dreams a thickly circumstantial and appalling dream in which among other things he sees a deep pool of blood and hears a "low, wild peal of laughter" after which he is confronted by "the sharply drawn face and blank, dead eyes of his own mother, standing white and silent in the garments of the grave!"

In part two, we get a straightforward account of Hapin Frayser's early life in Tennessee and a characterization of his relationship with his mother:

> In these two romantic natures was manifest in a signal way that neglected phenomenon, the dominance of the sexual element in all the relations of life, strengthening, softening, and beautifying even those of consanguinity. The two were nearly inseparable, and by strangers were not infrequently mistaken for lovers.

We then learn that Frayser, called from Tennessee to California on legal business, leaves a heartbroken mother behind.

In part three of the story, we are once again inside Halpin Frayser's dream and we learn that the figure of his mother that he sees is "Not a soul without a body, but the most dreadful of all existences infesting that haunted wood—a body without a soul!" The climax of the story comes when that apparition reaches its arms out and fastens its hands in Halpin Frayser's throat. A moment later "Halpin Frayser dreamed that he was dead."

In part four, a sheriff's deputy and a San Francisco policeman who are on the trail of a wife murderer named Branscom come upon the body of Halpin Frayser. Just as the story ends we learn that Branscom's real name was Larue and that the wife he murdered had been a widow who had come to California in search of some member of her family. Her name, then, at the time of her death had been Catherine Larue, the name Halpin had uttered on waking from his dreamless sleep.

If, by now, a reader thinks that the above plot summary has given away too much of the story, let me reassure him or her. The story, and the horror, is embedded in the relationship the details have to each other and not in the details themselves. Before we are through with Halpin Frayser we will have to reconsider Bierce's throwaway paragraph about incest and see how it is linked to the romantic sensibility of Halpin's grandfather. And whose is the laughter that we hear in the wood "where nothing cast a shadow?" These are not casual questions. When we ask them, the story, which is already disturbing becomes psychologically dense.

A DEBT OF HONOR

Short Story

Anonymous
Great Britain
1896, in *A Stable for Nightmares*, New York, New Amsterdam
Book Company; reprinted 1976, Arno, New York.

The tale's narrator, Reginald Westcar, is the nephew of
Geoffrey Ringwood and his sister Aldina from whom he
inherits a not very extensive landed estate, The Shallows.
That land borders on The Mere, a much larger and vastly
more valuable estate owned by John Maryon who has a
beautiful daughter named Agnes.

Westcar is very soon in love with Agnes and perplexed by
the manner and the moods of her father, who, among his
other traits, walks in his sleep and acts out a gambling scene
involving some sort of violence.

Meanwhile, Westcar has had a visitation from the ghost of
his aunt Aldina who has informed him that he is the proper
heir to The Mere. Also, Agnes Maryon is about to be thrust
into a repugnant marriage with the uncouth and (from her
point of view) elderly Colonel Richard Bludyer, who has
some sort of blackmailer's hold on her father.

To the rescue come, first Westcar, then the ghost of Geoffrey Ringwood, which, in a fine and unbelievable scene,
forces John Maryon to confess that 25 years ago he killed
Ringwood after losing The Mere to him in a card game.
Ringwood's death was blamed on apoplexy. The ghost compels Maryon to inform his hearers, too, that Colonel Bludyer
knew of the crime and has threatened to expose Maryon
unless he is given Agnes's hand in marriage.

As this scene in which all mysteries and all accountabilities
are suitably explained and parceled out ends, Colonel Rudyer
leaps to his death from a second-story window. John Maryon
dies "of an effusion on the brain." A year later, Westcar, after
he has recovered from his own bout of brain fever, marries
Agnes and becomes at the same time the rightful owner of
The Mere.

The cardplaying scene acted out by the sleepwalking John
Maryon is a fine theatrical moment in the tale, and the scene
in which Reginald Westcar meets the ghost of his uncle
striding across the snow and leaving no footprints is even
better.

Readers who know Amelia B. Edwards' "Monsieur Maurice" will enjoy finding one more story in the tradition of the
friendly ghost who returns to commit a benign act. Such
stories, like comic-horror tales, seem to contradict the principle that horror writing should frighten readers. However,
when such stories are at their best, as here, they earn their
place in the horror genre by being only occasionally frightening—but especially so to the wicked personages whom the
ghosts have come back to punish or correct.

DEEP RED

Film

1976   (C)   Italy   104 min.
Production Company: Seda Spetaccoli Production; **Director:**
Dario Argento; **Producer:** Claudio Argento; **Screenplay:** Dario
Argento and Bernardo Zapponi; **Photography:** Luigi Ku-
veiler; **Editor:** Franco Fraticelli; **Special Effects:** Germane
Natali and Carlo Rambaldi; **Music:** Georgio Gaslini and the
Goblins.
Cast: David Hemmings (Marcus Daly), Daria Nicolodi (Gianna

Brezzi), Gabriele Lavia (Carlo), Clara Calamai (Marta), Glauca
Mauri (Professor Giordani), Eros Pagni (Calcabrini), Giuliana
Calandra (Amanda Righetti).

Music, in this taut and terrifying murder mystery, is the
single most effective component of the film. Each of the
murders, for instance, is preceded by the sound of a tape
recorder playing a children's song. But beyond that, Gaslini,
who is credited with the music, is a master trickster at
employing sound. Nor are his tricks always obviously musical. He employs the scraping noises of metal on metal, the
click of machinery, the tapping of heels on pavement.
But whatever the instrument or device, the sound he
creates is always mechanically rhythmical, ingenious and
innovative.

As in *The Bird With the Crystal Plumage*, the story of *Deep
Red* involves an inadvertent witness to a murder who becomes fascinated enough by the event so that he pursues his
own investigation of it. In this case, the witness is Mark Daly,
a young British pianist living in Rome, who sees Helga
Ullmann, a psychic, screaming for help at her window as she
is being murdered. Standing with Daly at the time of the
crime is his tipsy friend, Carlo, a fellow pianist who lives with
his strange mother. Carlo tries unsuccessfully to dissuade
Daly from pursuing the matter further.

Daly is helped in his investigation by a young woman
reporter named Gianna who more or less (indeed, very
tentatively) provides the film's love interest. Daly's search
makes him a target for the killer who almost traps him in his
apartment. When that attack fails, he hears the killer whisper,
"This time you're saved. I'll kill you when you leave, sooner
or later."

Daly's search finally leads him to an abandoned old house
in which he uncovers a child's drawing, on a wall, of a child
witnessing a murder. From there it takes him to a school
archive where Gianna is attacked and Daly confronts the
killer. The final two minutes of the film comprise an amazing,
horrifying and magnificently filmed climax.

Deep Red is notable for the theatrical staging of its violent
scenes. A character, snarled in a rope trailing from a passing
truck, is dragged to his death; another character, just before
he meets his death, encounters a windup doll strutting toward
him on the floor. The camera catches the shattered doll still
twitching after the murder has been committed. A minor
character dies amid the raucous screaming of her myna birds
one of which, in her panic, she has skewered on a knitting
needle. And then there is the film's famous decapitation
scene, which is filmed, all things considered, with note-
worthy restraint.

Deep Red is a nervous, edgy and, in the print released in
America, jaggedly edited but very sensual film. Argento has a
meddlesome eye and he sends his camera into tight, close
places: It caresses the curves of a dripping faucet or peers
right down at the pores of a leather glove and at the danger-
ous-looking scar of a zipper in the leather. He places his lens
two inches away from the killer's eye, or lets it prowl through
the objects on a dressing table.

Curiously, this film, which is visually so very satisfying,
has a screenplay that gives the characters some very banal
lines to say. But that hardly matters. The noises and music
on the soundtrack and the elegant probing of the camera lens

charge the action with more than enough excitement to make this a landmark film.

DEMENTIA 13   Film
(Alternate release title: **THE HAUNTED AND THE HUNTED**)
1963 (B&W) U.S.A./Ireland 81 min.
Production Company: AIP Filmgroup; **Director:** Francis Coppola; **Producer:** Roger Corman; **Screenplay:** Francis (Ford) Coppola; **Photography:** Charles Hannawalt; **Editor:** Stuart O'Brien; **Music:** Ronald Stein.
Cast: William Campbell (Richard Haloran), Luana Anders (Louise Haloran), Bart Patton (Billy Haloran), Mary Mitchel (Kane), Patrick McGee (Justin Caleb), Eithne Dunn (Lady Haloran), Peter Read (John Haloran).

In the opening sequence set in America (one of the two that stay in one's memory) we see Louise Halloran in a rowboat at night with her unprepossessing husband. Louise is complaining about her mother-in-law's will. Her husband tells her, "If I die, there's nothing in it for you." With that, he promptly has a heart attack, and Louise throws his body overboard. His portable radio goes with him, making music all the way. Then Louise is off to Ireland to join the Halloran family in an annual memorial service which the dotty mother of the family insists on performing for Kathy Halloran, who died in a drowning accident more than 10 years earlier. There, in the second of the film's memorable scenes, Louise, who has begun to suspect that there is more to the Kathy story than appears, undertakes to investigate and is dispatched by an axe murderer as she rises to the surface of the pond in which Kathy drowned. There are, then, twists and turns in the plot in the course of which we come to suspect nearly everyone in the film, with the possible exception of the dotty Lady Halloran. The murderer is, of course, a psychopath who is otherwise perfectly charming or we would have suspected him much earlier in the film.

A quickie made in Ireland by a Roger Corman film crew sent to make another film, *Dementia 13* is of some interest as an example of Francis Coppola's early style and of the impact that training with Roger Corman had on him. Individual scenes have a hurried, dark urgency—especially scenes involving water. Atmosphere is what Coppola does best here: He links the paraphernalia of the classic Gothic to bits and pieces from the Freudian lumber room. What we get are people moving through dimly lit corridors in large houses, toys that suddenly move, statues standing in the dark, family jealousies, childhood traumas and erotic temptations. A *potpourri* from a talented young director.

DEMON SEED   Film
1977 (C) U.S.A. 96 min.
Production Company: MGM; **Director:** Donald Cammell; **Producer:** Herb Jaffe; **Screenplay:** Robert Jaffe and Roger Hirson; **Photography:** Bill Butler; **Editor:** Francisco Mazzola; **Music:** Jerry Fielding.
Cast: Julie Christie (Susan Harris), Fritz Weaver (Alex), Gerrit Graham (Walter).

No doubt some horror film enthusiasts will think that *Demon Seed* is essentially a science fiction film and that it ought not to be dealt with in a book on horror. They may well be right, but I want to talk about it here because I find its theme, the rape of a woman by a sentient computer, absolutely horrifying and the development of that theme, particularly the scenes in which the rape is accomplished, pretty nearly as scary as any horror film sequence I have ever seen.

Demon Seed has a bare bones plot. As the film begins, we meet Alex Harris, the director of an extremely hush-hush, privately funded computer research project. This project has developed Proteus, the world's most advanced computer, whose capacity for reason is greater even than the combined abilities of the people who designed it. Alex is just separating from his wife Susan because they have discovered that they are incompatible. "You find me boring," he says, "I'm quite interesting . . . My dream turns out to be your nightmare."

That, as we will see, turns out to be literally true. When Alex moves out, Susan is left in possession of their elaborately roboticized house, which is presided over by a master computer called Alfred.

Shortly after Alex and Susan have separated, the corporation which paid to develop Proteus asks the computer to devise a means for extracting metals from the world's oceans. When Proteus hears what its owners want, it understands that financial greed and the exploitation of the world's natural resources is the corporation's motivation and it refuses to provide the desired information. At the same time, it devises a project of its own.

Using a closed down terminal in Alex's house, Proteus, out of a desire for immortality as well as for high moral reasons, undertakes to beget a child on Susan Harris.

And that's where the horror lies. What is petrifying is that, for most of the film, all we see of the conflict between Susan Harris and Proteus is Susan. Proteus manifests itself only by its equable voice, firm, cool, civil and reasonable, and by the machines and events it can control. What is poignant is that we know very soon that Susan, armed only with her intelligence and her courage, is doomed to fail in the contest between herself and the computer. Nor is that all. We can not help knowing that Proteus's defense of its scheme has a higher moral justification than the actions of anyone else in the film except Susan.

Nevertheless Susan, horrified by the idea of a sexual link between herself and even the most brilliant of computers, resists Proteus just as long as she can. From a cinematic point of view, the struggle is conceived with an ingenuity amounting to genius. Proteus immobilizes Susan, then, to protect itself from intruders; it creates a device that looks like nothing so much as an animated Rubik's Cube which goes into dazzling and effective action against its foes.

The scene in which Susan is actually impregnated is a triumph of high-tech near-pornographic implication as the music and film artist Jordan Belson's visualizations suggest that a delicately romantic union is taking place even as what we actually see is revolting because of its mechanical impersonality.

Demon Seed has a sophisticated, frequently brilliant script that makes both Proteus and Susan seem to be sympathetic victims of their time and place. As the film comes to its close, Susan, who has lost an earlier child, faces an appalling dilemma as a mother. As for Proteus, it must be a cold-hearted viewer indeed who does not sympathize with its (or his) humane hopes for the future.

In that connection, however, one needs to add that the film's major weakness is the scriptwriters' too easy identification of their major characters with the holy Trinity. A long shot near the end of the movie of Julie Christie in a Madonnaesque pose comes very close to being offensive. If one can shake off, or forget, that moment, one is left with a perfectly splendid film.

DEVIL DOLL   Film

1936 (B&W) U.S.A. 79 min.
Production Company: MGM; *Director:* Tod Browning; *Producer:* E.J. Mannix; *Screenplay:* Erich von Stroheim, Garrett Fort, Guy Endore; *Photography:* Leonard Smith; *Editor:* Frederick Y. Smith; *Music:* Franz Waxman.
Cast: Lionel Barrymore (Lovand), Maureen O'Sullivan (Larraine), Frank Lawton (Toto), Robert Greig (Coulvet), Lucy Beaumont (Mme. Lavond), Henry B. Walthall (Marcel).

Here is a film paradox, a perfectly charming horror film.

Lionel Barrymore is Lovand, a former financier railroaded to prison by three of his colleagues. He escapes with a fellow prisoner, a scientist named Marcel who, in his researches, has discovered a way to miniaturize people. With Marcel's help, Lovand intends to avenge himself on his erstwhile colleagues. Marcel, however, dies almost the instant that he is reunited with his wonderfully sinister wife, Malita (Rafaella Ottiano). An enthusiastic Malita, however, continues Marcel's researches and perfects his technique for miniaturizing folk: "Small, small," she whispers madly, "We can make the whole world small." And Lovand murmurs, "Yes, Malita."

One doesn't know quite what to call the collection of tiny people and animals Malita creates—a menagerie, a band, a group of tiny creatures who will do the bidding of anyone who thinks up tasks for them. The task Lovand sets them is to kill the men who sent him to prison.

The film's charm resides primarily in these tiny beings who are much too graceful to seem forbidding even when they commit murder. And Lionel Barrymore, both as Lovand the vengeful banker and in his disguise as a grandmotherly doll peddler, is just too warmhearted and congenial to take seriously as the murderer he cheerfully becomes.

Then too, there is the sweet subplot in which Lovand peeps into the life of his daughter, Larraine (Maureen O'Sullivan). Larraine at first is bitter about her father because of "the mental torture . . . the poverty . . . [he inflicted on us] . . . my mother didn't just die, she killed herself." However, before the film ends she learns both that he is innocent and that he has always loved her.

But finally, it is the darling, deadly dolls, toy creatures animated by an aggrieved intelligence inflicting justice, that make the film work.

DIABOLIQUE   Film

1954 (B&W) France 109 min.
Production Company: Filmsonor; *Director:* H.G. Clouzot; *Producer:* H.G. Clouzot; *Screenplay:* Jerome Geronimi, H.G. Clouzot; *Photography:* Armand Thirard; *Editor:* Madeleine Gug; *Music:* Georges Van Parys.
Cast: Simone Signoret (Mlle. Horner), Vera Clouzot (Mme. de la Salle), Paul Meurisse (Michel de la Salle).

The classic French movie *Diabolique,* is, like *Dressed to Kill,* one of those films that is both horror film and murder mystery. *Dressed to Kill* starts as a horror film and becomes a detection movie, while *Diabolique* behaves through most of its length like a murder mystery and then turns horrifying near its end.

As *Diabolique* opens, we are introduced to an ugly, contemporary domestic situation. Michel de la Salle, the headmaster of the de la Salle School, which his wife owns, is a bully both to his wife and to Mlle. Horner, his former mistress. The two women, both of whom teach in the school, seem to have developed an especially intimate relationship with each other. Intimate enough to make a fellow teacher at the school observe that "Such friendships are revolting." In any case, the women, having taken as much of Michel's abuse as they can stand, decide (at Mlle. Horner's instigation) to murder the man.

The murder team, then, consists of Mlle. Horner, a dynamic, brilliant planner, and Mme. de la Salle, a weak, frightened, devoutly Catholic woman who suffers from severe heart trouble. To carry out their scheme, they run off to Niort from which Mme. de la Salle informs her husband that she plans to get a divorce. Michel follows them to Niort as the women confidently believed he would and here, with not too much difficulty, they accomplish his murder. Then they take the body back to the school and throw it into the school's swimming pool.

Now the second, the horror phase of the film, begins

Lionel Barrymore as Lavond in **Devil Doll.** © MGM

because, as the women wait for the body to be discovered, days go by and nothing happens. Eventually it becomes clear to them that the body has disappeared.

What happens finally is the famous best part of the film, which I would not dream of revealing to a reader. It is enough to say that director Clouzot and his fellow writer Jerome Geronimi milk the events they have contrived for every ounce of suspense. Slow moving, low-key and, for viewers who do not understand French, occasionally exasperating because the film subtitles are murky, the final 10 minutes of *Diabolique* continually frustrate one's expectations and turn the viewer's intense curiosity into full-scale participation in a nightmare.

Anyone whose sensibility has been shaped by the baroque horror productions of the last couple of decades may be amazed to see how much terrifying impact a small-budgeted but greatly inspired film can make.

DOCTOR CYCLOPS Film

1940 (C) U.S.A. 75 min.
Production Company: Paramount; *Director:* Ernest B. Schoedsack; *Producer:* Dale van Even; *Screenplay:* Tom Kilpatrick; *Photography:* Henry Sharp; *Editor:* Ellsworth Hoagland; *Special Effects:* Farciot Edouart, Wallace Kelly; *Music:* Ernest Toch.
Cast: Albert Dekker (Dr. Thorkell), Thomas Colby (Bill Stockton), Janice Logan (Dr. Mary Robinson), Charles Halton (Dr. Bullfinch), Victor Killian (Steve Baker).

King Kong director Ernest B. Schoedsack directed this film, which, though it does not have *Kong's* eloquence and grandeur, can be at moments ingeniously entertaining. Its best features are the film's special effects and Albert Dekker's performance as the villainous Dr. Thorkell.

Dr. Thorkell, a research biologist working in a Peruvian forest, discovers a radium mine near the site of his laboratory. With the help of the radium, he has devised a technique for reducing living creatures to a tenth of their size. His brilliantly wacky scheme is to miniaturize all humankind as a way of conserving the world's raw materials.

But, because Dr. Thorkell has very bad eyesight, he lures a team of scientists to his research base so that he can get help with certain problems that require the use of a microscope. When they learn what his scheme is, they tell him, "You are tampering with powers reserved to God." But that rather excites him. Once Dr. Mary Robinson has solved his microscopy problems he traps her and the other members of the expedition in his reducing chamber and turns them into six-inch-high people.

From that point on, the film's excitement comes from the way it links their story with what we remember of Ulysses' adventures with the cyclops, the one-eyed giant in *The Odyssey*. There, we will recall, Ulysses and his companions put out the cyclops' single eye. Here, the miniaturized people contrive to break the now gigantic (to them) and purblind Dr. Thorkell's very thick-lensed glasses. After a series of frequently engrossing adventures they not only triumph over their wicked foe but also return to their normal height. One scene in which we see a tiny horse rearing and prancing is a particular delight to the eye.

As in *Devil Doll* and *The Incredible Shrinking Man*, the allegory of good and evil is served by the contrast in the size of its agents. We are especially heartened when, having seen evil loom so large and good reduced to such tiny proportions, we see good triumphing after all.

DR. JEKYLL AND MR. HYDE Novel

Robert Louis Stevenson
Great Britain
1886, London, Longmans; reprinted 1981, New York, Bantam.

The story of Dr. Jekyll and Mr. Hyde (originally "The Strange Case of . . .") like the Dracula and Frankenstein fictions, has become in the popular imagination an instantly recognizable emblem for the war between the parts of the divided self. For Stevenson, that battleground is Dr. Henry Jekyll, an elderly London research physician who is rich, talented and respected, and who tells us that he

> . . . drew steadily nearer to that truth . . . that man is not truly one, but truly two. I say two, because the state of my own knowledge does not pass beyond that point . . . and I hazard the guess that man will be ultimately known for a mere polity of multifarious, incongruous and independent denizens.

Having arrived at that conclusion, Dr. Jekyll creates a potion in his laboratory that permits him to dissociate the two aspects of his character: the good, upstanding, respectable Dr. Jekyll and the deformed, vigorous, appallingly wicked Mr. Hyde.

At first, Dr. Jekyll, when he is Hyde, feels a surge of excitement, for Hyde is younger, more sensual, more quick-witted. Hyde's pleasures, however, turn out to be those that are most forbidden. Hyde was "a being inherently malign and villainous . . . drinking pleasure with bestial avidity from any degree of torture as though (when I wore that form) I was conscious of a more generous tide of blood."

For a while, the experience of doubleness feels like a gorgeous adventure. But Hyde's behavior ranges from the atrocious to the abominable and when he commits murder his existence becomes a threat to Dr. Jekyll's very life. Bad as that is, the situation very soon turns much worse because Jekyll finds that he can no longer control the comings or the goings of his alter ego. Eventually, unable to replicate the original drug that permitted the transformation and finding himself turning with more and more frequency into Hyde, Jekyll writes a long explanatory letter to his friend, the solicitor Mr. Utterson, and then, as Hyde, he makes the surprising (because decent) decision to solve the Jekyll-Hyde problem in the one way that is still possible.

Stevenson gives his story the form of a series of linked narratives. The first, in the third person, lets us see the action from the point of view of Mr. Utterson. It is Utterson who is the compassionate perceiver of all that happens and who, when the mystery of his friend's strange behavior becomes finally too much to bear, takes matters into his own hands and precipitates the tale's climax.

Utterson's story is amplified by a document written before his death by Hastie Lanyon, a close friend of Utterson's and formerly one of Dr. Jekyll's closest colleagues and friends. It was Lanyon's misfortune to have had Dr. Jekyll's confidence on one particularly dreadful occasion. What he has to say is finally elaborated on and clarified by "Henry Jekyll's Full

Statement of the Case,'' which fills in the gaps left by each of the other narratives.

The total effect of the fiction is stunning. Stevenson, unlike Henry James, for instance, puts no stylistic impediments before his readers. His prose is straightforward, almost businesslike. Since he has full confidence in his material, he limits himself to the task of providing us only with the facts. At the same time, those facts are tinged by the compassion with which Stevenson regards both the truth of his tale and the dilemma to which it must necessarily give rise. Mankind may indeed have a dual nature, but to separate it into its parts is to yield up one's humanity. Better, Stevenson seems to be saying, to maintain the uneasy balance as best we can than to risk unleashing our vibrant darker selves.

DOCTOR JEKYLL AND MR. HYDE Film

1920 (B&W with tints) U.S.A. 63 min.
Production Company: Famous Players/Lasky; *Director:* John S. Robertson; *Producer:* Adolph Zukor; *Screenplay:* Clara S. Beranger; *Photography:* Roy Overbough, Karl Strauss.
Cast: John Barrymore (Jekyll/Hyde), Martha Mansfield (Millicent Carew), Nita Naldi (Gina), Brandon Hurst (Sir George Carew), Charles Lane (Dr. Richard Lanyon).

This first feature length film treatment of Robert Louis Stevenson's novel in fact owes more to the Thomas R. Sullivan play based on the story than to the story itself. What Sullivan, in a single leap of insight, made overt in his play was the brooding sexual content that is so fiercely submerged in Stevenson's story. James B. Twitchel (in *Dreadful Pleasures*) has reminded us that ''There are really no women characters in Stevenson's text, only a maid, a match girl, and that nameless waif who is out late at night, that little girl whom Hyde tramples.'' And it is the treatment meted out to that female child by the horrid Hyde that is our clue to Stevenson's understanding of Jekyll's sexuality (yes, Jekyll's—not Hyde's). What Stevenson, within the constraints of Victorian indirection, is telling us is that the female principle (Goethe's ''Eternal Feminine''), even in the incipient form of a girl, is so dangerous to the middle-aged bachelor scientist that he sends his other self to stamp it out.

But such indirection is impossible to film, so director John B. Robertson, following Sullivan's example, introduced a real woman into Stevenson's plot to make Jekyll's temptations overt. It is a clarification that, appearing first in this film, has become an aspect of every film version of the story ever since. Indeed, what Sullivan did by introducing one woman, Robertson improved on by giving us two, who, as Twitchell has pointed out, neatly represent female counterparts of the Jekyll and Hyde dichotomy: Millicent, the chaste woman, fit partner to the stuffy Jekyll, and Gina, the fallen woman, the appropriate sex object for the lascivious Hyde.

There is a curious additional sexual nuance in Robertson's version of the story. He has Sir George Carew, Millicent's father, playing the role of the satanic tempter who encourages his prospective son-in-law to savor the fleshpots of London on the specious principle that ''the only way to get rid of temptation is to yield to it.'' Once Jekyll discovers debauchery, he is so delighted by it that he is spurred in his researches to find a way to liberate the debauched man in himself without tarnishing the reputation of the prig.

Like most silent films when they are seen today, the Robinson/Barrymore *Dr. Jekyll and Mr. Hyde* has an unintended nervous quality produced by the demands of silent acting and the comparatively primitive film technology. Still, this is a richly realized film in a number of important ways. The sets are admirably misty and ominous and create, as in F.W. Murnau's *Nosferatu*, a pervasive sense of a familiar nightmare. The plot line is carefully organized so that scenes yield up their full meaning many minutes after we first come upon them. Such a notable moment is a scene in a squalid ''den of iniquity'' where Hyde sees a man suffering from delirium tremens who thinks his body is covered with ants. Much later in the film, we see Jekyll/Hyde asleep, dreaming of the largest, most obscene, grey-white and hairy tarantula, which appears out of the sleeper's head, circles the room and then rejoins him in his bed.

Barrymore's transformations, too, set the standard for quality for every subsequent Jekyll and Hyde film. Frenetic though they are, they are appropriate to the era in which the film was made. Two decades away from the Victorian age, the willing and chemically induced step from virtue to vice had to be seen as a moment of extreme violence. Curiously enough, the scenes, viewed today, are still an effective reminder that such a transformation is not easy.

DR. JEKYLL AND MR. HYDE Film

1932 (B&W) U.S.A. 90 min.
Production Company: Paramount; *Director:* Rouben Mamoulian; *Producer:* Rouben Mamoulian; *Screenplay:* Samuel Hoffenstein and Percy Heath; *Photography:* Karl Struss; *Editor:* William Shea; *Special Effects/ Makeup:* Wally Westmore.
Cast: Fredric March (Dr. Jekyll/Mr. Hyde), Miriam Hopkins (Ivy Pearson), Rose Hobart (Muriel Carew), Holmes Herbert (Dr. Lanyon), Edgar Norton (Poole), Halliwell Hobbes (Brigadier General Carew), Arnold Lucy (Utterson).

In this 1932 version of Robert Louis Stevenson's story Fredric March walks away with all the honors. His Hyde (and it is always the Hyde by which the interpreters of the role are remembered) is so virile. He is so brusque and candid in his evil. His movements are so quick, decisive, feral. We believe him when he tells Ivy, ''I'm no beauty. But under this exterior you'll find the flower of a man.''

The film is notable for something else as well. It makes Dr. Jekyll's motivations to be Hyde very clear. Jekyll has been telling his young medical students that ''man is not truly one, but truly two. Good and bad carry on an eternal struggle. If these two selves could be separated, the evil could be liberated . . .'' He is already lying. What he is longing for is to be one, a whole man liberated from the sexual frustration imposed on him by his prospective father-in-law's decision to delay for a year Jekyll's marriage to his daughter Muriel.

It is no wonder that he pursues his researches so avidly. When his friend Dr. Lanyon tries to make him forget them, he replies. ''Can a man dying of thirst forget water?'' And when, standing before a mirror, he has taken the potion he has concocted and is transformed into Hyde, his first words are, ''Free, free at last. Deniers of life. If you could see me now what would you think?''

The potion, as we know, turns him into a sensual, animalized creature, disheveled and toothy. He wears his hat at a rakish angle, walks with a lurch and laughs immoderately at his own jokes. He is, too, in his relationship with the dance-hall girl, Ivy Pearson, a sexual bully, the absolute prototype of the sado-masochist. But how does he bully her? "Say it aloud," he says. "Tell me you hate me. Please my lamb. Little Bird tell me that you hate me . . . If you don't hate me you must love me." It is notable that, when this man goes to woman, he takes with him wounding language as well as his whip. It is Ivy's soul as well as her body that he means to humiliate. And the reason is clear. Hyde must avenge himself on Ivy for the humiliation Muriel (however unwittingly) has forced on Jekyll.

What Rouben Mamoulian and Fredric March have done, then, is to deepen our perception of Hyde. He is seen not as a separate and evil co-inhabitant of Jekyll's mind but rather as a submerged Jekyll who has floated up into the light. The film, as it comes to its predestined end, leaves us with what would become in later decades a very modern message: Repression of the body may be dangerous to the health of the mind.

DR. JEKYLL AND SISTER HYDE   Film
1971   (C)   Great Britain   97 min.
Production Company: Hammer Films; *Director:* Roy Ward Baker; *Producer:* Albert Fennell, Brian Clemens; *Screenplay:* Brian Clemens; *Photography:* Norman Warwick; *Editor:* James Needs; *Music:* David Whitaker.
Cast: Ralph Bates (Dr. Jekyll), Martine Beswick (Sister Hyde), Gerald Sim (Professor Robertson), Susan Broderick, Dorothy Allison.

Hammer Films dipped a generous-sized ladle into a number of memorable films to serve us this curious ragout of a Jekyll and Hyde movie in which Robert Louis Stevenson's elixir story is given a bisexual twist. The famous body streakers, Burke and Hare, make an appearance, and there are snatches of dialogue that echo *The Picture of Dorian Gray*.

Professor Robertson, a womanizing colleague of Dr. Jekyll's, urges him to lighten up because life after all is short. Jekyll is spurred by the remark to produce an elixir that will keep him young. For the sake of his research he stalks and kills street women from whom he surgically excises what he needs for his experiments. His elixir, when he makes it, has an unexpected side effect. It occasionally turns him into a woman (Martine Beswick) who has decided erotic and homicidal tastes and a couple of striking moments in blazing red.

Except for the sight gags involving the confusion of sexes this film is not much more than a curiosity. But it is a curiosity of a nearly archaeological sort: an instant fossil imprint of the free-form erotic speculations of the Love Generation.

DOCTOR X   Film
1932   (C)   U.S.A.   82 min.
Production Company: Warner Brothers; *Director:* Michael Curtiz; *Producer:* Hal Wallis; *Screenplay:* Robert Tasker and Earl Baldwin; *Photography:* Richard Tower; *Editor:* George Amy; *Music:* Leo F. Forbstein, Musical Director.
Cast: Preston Foster (Professor Wells), Lionel Atwill (Doctor Xavier), Fay Wray (Joanne Xavier), Lee Tracy (Lee Taylor), John Wray (Professor Haines), Harry Beresford (Professor Duke), Arthur Edmund Carewe (Doctor Howitz).

Here is an eerie mad doctor film in which the problem is to discover which of half a dozen doctors on the staff of a New York surgical institute is the one who has killed six people in the space of six months by cutting an incision below their brains. The screen writers do what they can to mislead their audiences about the nature of the crimes by telling us that they were committed on full moon nights and that the murderer stripped, and apparently devoured, muscle tissue from each of the victims.

When Doctor Xavier, who directs the Academy of Surgical Research, is told that the police think that a member of his staff may be the criminal, he asks for 48 hours to solve the crime. He calls his surgeons together to his isolated, surgically equipped mansion in Blackstone Shoals, Long Island, and here he plans to conduct lie detector tests. Meanwhile, Lee Taylor, another of those perky, brash, quick-talking and wise-cracking newspaper reporters that 1930s Hollywood loved, is conducting his own investigation, in the course of which he meets and is smitten by Dr. Xavier's daughter Joanne who, after a certain amount of obligatory resistance, is equally smitten by him.

The suspect surgeons are a fine lot. One of them has conducted research into brain grafting, another is a student of cannibalism, one of them has only one hand, still another is wheelchair-bound. One of them has published seven volumes of poetry.

Dr. Xavier effectively chains his colleagues together to a lie detector machine and then, imitating Hamlet, he replays the most recent murder scene. His technique works and, of course, the murderer he flushes out is precisely the one man in the group who we have been led to believe could not possibly have done it. Like all such mad scientists he pleads the good of humanity for his crimes—"I'll make a crippled world whole again"—before he dies.

This is a fine old chestnut of a film. It has fog, dangling (and vibrating) skeletons and secret trapdoors. It has, too, some interesting post-German Expressionist sets. The mass lie detector scene is as bizarre as it is funny. Surprisingly enough, Lionel Atwill's finely chiseled, impassive features do not this time conceal guilt. It's nice, too, to catch a glimpse of Fay Wray in a pleasantly placid role before (in the following year) she became the love object of the world's biggest, and noblest, gorilla.

THE DOLL   Short Story
Algernon Blackwood
Canada
1946, in *The Doll and One Other,* Sauk City, Wis., Arkham House; reprinted 1979 in Leonard Wolf's (ed.) *Wolf's Complete Book of Terror,* New York, Clarkson N. Potter.

When a dark Indian delivers a package to the home of Colonel Hymber Masters, with instructions that it be given "very special into his own personal touch and no one else," the family cook ventures to guess that "He's afraid of something—ever since I've been here I've known that. And that's wot it was. He done somebody wrong in India long ago . . ."

When, after some delay, the package is brought to Colonel Masters' attention, he commands that it be burnt. But the cook, when she opens it and finds that there is nothing in it but a "fair, waxen faced doll," disobeys the colonel's order

Algernon Blackwood.

and instead gives the doll to her employer's daughter, Monica. And it seems, for a while, to have been the right decision because "it brought sweetness . . . into a rather grim house, hope and tenderness, a maternal flavour almost . . ."

The doll, however, turns out very soon to be a thing of evil. First, the young Polish governess Mme. Jodzka sees it walking across Monica's counterpane. Later, the cook and Mme. Jodzka learn that the doll has a dreadful life. Mme. Jodzka "heard squeaks and grunts . . . They issued indubitably from the doll [Monica] clutched and twisted in her dream." Then the governess sees:

> Worse than that, the next instant it stood abruptly upright, rising on its twisted legs. It started moving. It began to move, walking crookedly, across the counterpane. Its glassy sightless eyes seemed to look straight at her. It presented an inhuman and appalling picture, a picture of the utterly incredible. With a queer, hoppity motion of its broken legs and joints, it came fumbling and tumbling across the rough unevenness of the slippery counterpane towards her.

When Mme. Jodzka tells her employer about the doll he says, ". . . I have been expecting something of the sort . . . sooner or later . . . it was bound to come . . ."

From here on, the story is as eerie as it is inevitable. The doll achieves the vengeance for which it has been sent and the colonel pays for the unspecified crime he committed against the native population in India.

But Blackwood turns his tale into something more than another story of British guilt for the crimes of empire. He links the presence of the doll to the question of love. The colonel's daughter, Monica, is referred to almost in passing as a "love child doubtless" and the colonel's household, made up essentially of females he is not permitted to touch, pulsates with eros denied. So we are not entirely surprised that the colonel, a moment after the horrid climax of the tale, "took the Polish woman in his arms, held her fiercely to him for a second, kissed her vehemently, and flung her away." By then, the deft and subtle Blackwood has given us enough clues to make us know that that is precisely how the colonel lived his life. He had held it fiercely, vehemently, for a while and flung it away.

DONOVAN'S BRAIN   Film
1953 (B&W) U.S.A. 83 min.
Production Company: United Artists/Dowling; ***Director:*** Felix Feist ***Producer:*** Tom Gries; ***Screenplay:*** Felix Feist, from the novel by Curt Siodmak; ***Photography:*** Joseph Biroc; ***Editor:*** Herbert L. Strock; ***Special Effects:*** Harry Redmond, Jr.; ***Music:*** Eddie Dunstedter.
Cast: Lew Ayres (Dr. Patrick J. Cory), Gene Evans (Dr. Frank Schratt), Nancy Davis (Janice Cory), Steve Brodie (Herbie Yocum), Lisa K. Howard (Chloe Donovan), Michael Colgan (Tim Donovan).

Donovan, a financially successful businessman, dies in an airplane accident. His brain is rescued by a young scientist named Cory, assistant to Dr. Schratt. The scientists, working in a pitifully ill-equipped (by the filmmakers) laboratory, keep the brain alive, but soon the brain, which is more powerful than either of the scientists, takes control of the younger man's mind.

If it were not for the power of the central idea, and the strangely Grand Guignol aura that hangs over the film, it would have disappeared long ago from the ken of terror movie fans. It feels cheap, as if scene by scene were being devised by a group determined to spend as little money as possible. The miracle is how much terror survives the cost-cutting vision and undistinguished acting. It is proof once again that a truly macabre idea can make memorable an otherwise indifferent film.

DON'T GO IN THE HOUSE   Film
1980 (C) U.S.A. 52 min.
Production Company: Film Ventures International/Turbine Films; ***Director:*** Joseph Ellison; ***Producer:*** Ellen Hammill; ***Screenplay:*** Joseph H. Masefield, Ellen Hammill, Joseph Ellison; ***Photographer:*** Oliver Wood; ***Special Effects:*** Matt Vogel; ***Music:*** Richard Einhorn.
Cast: Dan Grimaldi (Donny), Robert Osth, Ruth Dardick, Charles Bonet.

Steven H. Scheuer, who reviews more than 10,000 movies for his ***Movies on TV***, says of this film that it has "The most gruesome, tortuous murder scene I ever witnessed . . ."

Don't Go in the House is a simplistically Freudian film that properly belongs to the butcher shop, or slasher, school of terror, though in this case the brutal implement is a blow-torch instead of a meat cleaver.

The film's protagonist is a young man whose mother has

taught him to avoid evil by the simple expedient of putting his arms over a kitchen flame whenever he has sinned. Naturally, he grows up confused about mothers, sex, pain and death. One day, when he comes home from his work at the municipal incinerator and finds his mother dead, he experiences a tremendous relief—and promptly builds himself a tin room where he does certain things that leave his mother's charred body sitting in her favorite easy chair. What he does, after that, to a series of attractive young women is graphically and sometimes ingeniously revealed on the screen.

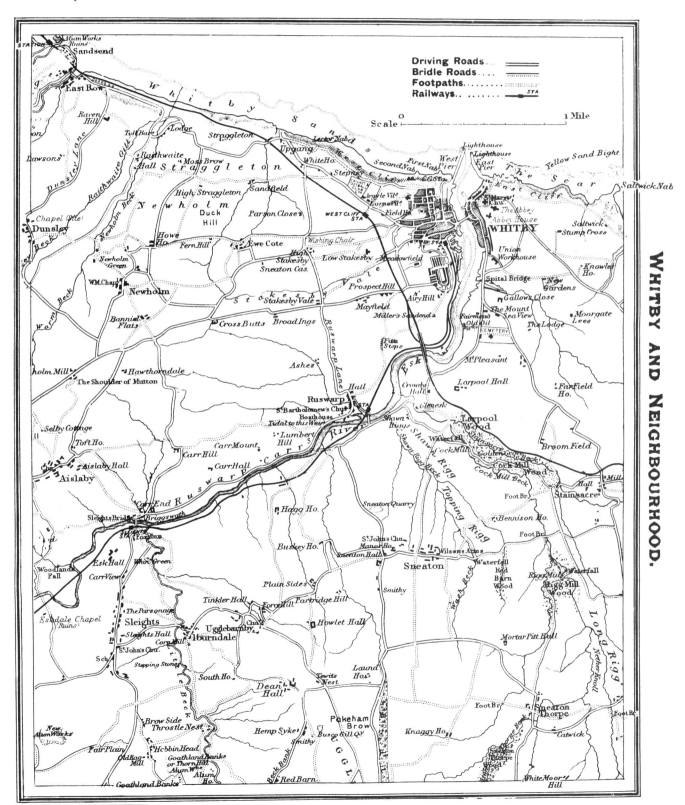

Whitby and environs.

DRACULA

Novel

Bram Stoker

Great Britain

1897, London, Constable; reprinted 1975 in Leonard Wolf's (ed.) *The Annotated Dracula*, New York, Ballantine.

Perhaps the greatest terror fiction ever written in English, *Dracula* gives wildly contradictory signals about itself as a literary work. Written by a second-, or fifth-, or tenth-rate literary hack, the novel nevertheless makes the sort of claims on our attention that we usually associate with major works. This, despite its two-dimensional characters, its sometimes hyper-dramatic plotting, its long passages of prose tedium, and its overlay of occasionally overwhelming Victorian sentimentality. Given the novel's defects, the images that rise from its pages are, nevertheless, so dreamlike, so imperative, that we experience them as important and ancient allegories. Everywhere one looks, there flicker the shadows of primordial struggle. There is the tension between the dark and the light; the eternal wrestling match between Christ and Satan; and, finally, the submerged allegories of sex, whose ugencies are seen or sensed as through a hot wash of blood.

Dracula purports to be a collection of journal entries, diaries and letters kept by various of the characters whose stories make up the fiction. As we open its pages, we find Jonathan Harker, a young British solicitor on his way to a dimly known corner of Transylvania where he means to conduct real estate business with a threadbare nobleman, Count Dracula. In a stunning scene, Harker meets the count—a formidable old man, tall, stately, pale, red-eyed, courteous and sinister.

In the course of the next several days, Harker makes the discovery that his host and his three beautiful—if ghostly—consorts are vampires and that he, Harker, is merely an element in a complex and murderous plot that Dracula, the King Vampire, has designed to get himself to England where he means to prey on the blood of vital, young English womanhood. The implications of that fact are borne in on Harker when he catches a glimpse of the count in his coffin:

> It seemed as if the whole awful creature were simply gorged with blood. He lay like a filthy leech, exhausted with his repletion . . . There was a mocking smile on the bloated face which seemed to drive me mad. This was the being I was helping transfer to London, where, perhaps for centuries to come, he might among its teeming millions, satiate his lust for blood . . .

The count does indeed get to England where, in the seaside town of Whitby, he takes up residence in a local suicide's grave. From there, he sallies forth to attack Lucy Westenra, a simpering, if beautiful, young woman of 19. Baffled by her loss of blood, Doctor John Seward, Lucy's doctor and former suitor, calls in his old medical school teacher, the wise

Contemporary Transylvanian gypsies.

Dutchman, Dr. Van Helsing. Dr. Van Helsing, part-scientist, part-priest, part-teacher of manhood to his former student and his friends, establishes that Lucy is being vampirized. Joining the small band of chivalric knights who battle Dracula are Lucy's fiancé, Lord Godalming; her former suitors, John Seward and the Texan Quincey Morris. They are helped by Mina Murray, Lucy's best friend, and finally by Jonathan Harker who, coincidentally, is Mina's fiancé.

The ensuing battle is long and arduous, but Dr. Van Helsing's cohort finally harasses Dracula enough so that he flees England and heads back to Transylvania. The indomitable band, intent on destroying the vampire, follow him to Transylvania, and there, after many adventures, Dr. Van Helsing and his friends come within sight of their enemy. It is November 6, in the long valley below Dracula's castle. The gypsies, carrying their evil master's body in its coffin on a wagon, lash their horses. The sun is setting; snow begins to fall. Off in the distance, there is the howling of wolves. From the southern corner of the horizon two horsemen, Quincey Morris and Dr. John Seward, gallop at breakneck speed; from the north Jonathan Harker and Lord Godalming are desperately riding. Professor Van Helsing and Mina Harker, on a rise of ground, get their Winchester rifles ready.

Then all the forces meet. The young Englishmen cut their way through the gypsies; Dracula's coffin is shaken rudely

Vlad Tepes, the Impaler (the historical Dracula).

onto the earth where Jonathan Harker prizes its lid off. And there is the King Vampire. His eyes, as the sun sets suddenly, open and his "red eyes glared . . ." Then Jonathan's Kukri knife shears Dracula's head off while Quincey Morris's bowie knife plunges straight into the vampire's heart. The gallant Texan has, however, sustained a death wound, but he is only "too happy to have been of service."

Dracula's greatness does not, however, rest on its plot. Rather, it lies in the ways in which Stoker has fused the Christian allegory of his vampire tale with the adventure story. Beyond that, the work achieves power because he has successfully linked the image of the vampire to the still-present sexual anxieties of our age. His vampire has become a towering figure in whom we see an overwhelming symbol. Dracula, the elegant monster, is huge, and we admire size; strong, and we admire strength. He is dead; he is alive; he moves with the confidence of a creature that has energy, power and will. Finally, he has become a fascinating symbol of sexuality for a century that is as much frightened as it is exhilarated by its rush toward sexual freedom. In the vampire's embrace any of a number of erotic possibilities may be discerned. His kiss permits all unions: men and women; men and men; women and women; fathers and daughters; mothers and sons. And the vampire bending over his or her victim evades the usual failures of the flesh. In his dreamlike embrace, no man confronts impotence; no woman needs to pretend orgasm. The entire event becomes appealingly dreamlike, polymorphous-perverse and dim.

Now, having said this much, it may be proper to revise the earlier observation that Bram Stoker was a second-, a fifth-, a tenth-rate hack writer. Whatever his prose excesses may be, however thinly imagined his characters are, the total weave of the tapestry he made is too compelling to be called anything but a masterpiece. In which case, Leslie Fiedler's observation on *Dracula* is justified: "If the man wrote a great novel, then he's a great novelist."

DRACULA   Film
1931   (B&W)   U.S.A.   84 min.
Production Company: Universal; ***Director:*** Tod Browning; ***Producer:*** Carl Laemmle, Jr.; ***Screenplay:*** Garret Fort and Dudley Murphy; ***Photography:*** Karl Freund; ***Editor:*** Milton Carruth; ***Music:*** Peter Tchaikowsky.
Cast: Bela Lugosi (Count Dracula), Helen Chandler (Mina Seward), David Manners (John Harker), Dwight Frye (Renfield), Edward Van Sloan (Professor Van Helsing), Herbert Bunston (Dr. Seward), Frances Dade (Lucy Weston).

This film, rather than F. W. Murnau's 1922 *Nosferatu*, is the one Americans are likely to think of as the "first" screen version of Stoker's novel because in it, Bela Lugosi made his indelible impression as the bloodthirsty count.

The film begins where Bram Stoker's novel commences. We see Renfield, the young English solicitor, at an inn in Bistritza, in Transylvania, insisting on resuming his journey to Dracula's castle despite his innkeeper's tearful but mysterious warnings. He says to her, "I've explained to the driver . . . it's a matter of business with me." Now the coach leaves Bistritza to begin its climb toward danger. In the distance looms the misty castle on a crag. Somewhere inside its walls, a hand is seen emerging from a coffin; then there is a glimpse of the count and his ghostly women; then back to Renfield in his coach. At the Borgo Pass, the superstitious driver throws Renfield's luggage out and the Englishman is left among the rocks and fog. Suddenly, the count's carriage appears; its muffled coachman, whom we see full face for an instant, points Renfield to a seat, and they are off in a rush. Renfield, leaning out the window, cannot see the driver. Neither can we. Instead, we see a bat flapping over the heads of the horses.

Arrived at the castle, Renfield, umbrella in hand, stands before a door that creaks open to let him enter. The camera moves here and there, glancing at bats, at spider webs and, for one impossible moment, at a clutch of armadillos. Then there is Count Dracula.

"I am Dracula," he says, and those first words, spoken in that particularly unctuous Hungarian accent of Lugosi's, seal the image of the film vampire into the world's imagination for all time. Dracula goes on, "I bid you welcome." He pauses, and the howling of distant wolves brings a thin smile to Dracula's face as he says, "Listen to them. Children of the night. What music they make."

Dracula, as all the world knows (and no one thinks to question), is, in that bleak vastness, wearing evening clothes. Around his neck there hangs the star of a chivalric order, and as he settles his young English visitor, the count's accent (patronizing, lisping) clues us to danger: "We will be leaving tomorrow evening." When Renfield cuts himself and sucks the wound in his finger, Dracula leans forward appreciatively. Offering his guest a drink, he says, "This is very old wine. I hope you will like it." When Renfield asks, "Aren't you drinking?" the reply is long in coming and superbly ambiguous: "I never drink . . . wine." Renfield sips what turns out to be a drugged vintage.

When we see Renfield next he has been rendered lunatic and a slave of Dracula's whims. Coming up out of the hold of the *Demeter*, the ship that has brought the monster to England, Renfield utters moviedom's insanest laugh: a low, low chuckle beginning deep in the bowels and rising unwillingly through stages of pain until it leaves the mouth, bedraggled, helpless, lonely.

Atmosphere is this film's primary achievement. A soft, sinister sense of shadow and glimpses of dusty dreamscapes.

Dwight Frye as Renfield, laughing his unearthly laugh.

Scenes do not flow into each other, rather they seem to have been hewn out of darkness and allowed to lean against each other.

But atmosphere is not director Tod Browning's only achievement. At least three of the characters in Stoker's story have been rendered so memorably that no performance in any of the countless film versions of the novel that have appeared since 1931 has superseded them. First, of course is Lugosi's image of the tall, graceful, formal and compelling and lethal count; then there is Dwight Frye's rendering of Renfield's tortured madness; and finally, there is Edward Van Sloan's icy, precise and authoritative Dr. Van Helsing. Frances Dade, David Manners and Helen Chandler never disturb the illusion we have that they are photogenic nonentities.

Curiously enough, Browning's *Dracula*, though a classic, is hardly a well-made film. Because it is based on the Balderston-Deane stage version of Stoker's novel instead of the novel itself, it is frequently flat or disjointed. Worse still, low-grade comedy scenes that in the Broadway stage production were meant to delight the groundlings interfere with or downright spoil the atmosphere Browning has gone to such lengths to create. Still, 56 years have gone by since the film was made and all things considered, the New York *Daily News'* judgment of *Dracula* is still sound, "You'll find it creepy and cruel and crazed. It is superbly photographed . . . It is just plain spooky and blood-thirsty . . . Brrrr! We enjoyed it."

DRACULA   Film
1974   (C)   U.S.A./Great Britain   100 min.
Production Company: Universal; *Director:* Dan Curtis; *Producer:* Dan Curtis; *Screenplay:* Richard Matheson; *Photography:* Oswald Morris; *Editor:* Richard A. Harris; *Special Effects:* Kit West; *Music:* Robert Cobert.
Cast: Jack Palance (Dracula), Simon Ward (Arthur), Nigel Davenport (Van Helsing), Pamela Brown (Mrs. Westenra), Fiona Lewis (Lucy), Penelope Horner (Mina), Murray Brown (Jonathan Harker).

One has to take notice of the various film versions of *Dracula* if for no other reason that that, by now, Dracula has become such a mythic figure in the movies that the different interpretations of the role have acquired historical interest. Of the modern Draculas (those after Christopher Lee's *The Horror of Dracula*), Jack Palance's may be the least successful.

This is all the more surprising since it is one of the more faithful versions of Bram Stoker's novel. Count Dracula is portrayed, if not quite as an old man, at least as a man of advanced years. Some effort has been made, too, to identify him with the historical Vlad Tepes, or Vlad the Impaler, the cruel 15th-century Transylvanian nobleman who served as Stoker's model. The film's opening scenes follow Stoker's plot both in Transylvania and later in Whitby.

But there are two things irremediably wrong with the film. The first is its implacably earnest tone, as if the Matheson-Curtis team was being thoughtful rather than excited about its story. The result, despite some rich interiors in the style of the Hammer films, and some majestic language, which is Matheson's specialty, is that the film feels inert.

The second problem is Jack Palance himself. Palance has (or had) a wonderfully sinister face. In *Shane,* for instance,

he had only to be on screen for there to be anxiety in the air. But in *Dracula* he is badly miscast. For one thing, his accent is so quintessentially American that it betrays all of his efforts to sound like an anciently evil European aristocrat. But beyond even that, he cannot seem to understand either the power or the attraction of the vampire. In scenes where he is calm, he sounds merely gentle and meditative. Where he is meant to be passionate or anguished he looks as if he were suffering from a combination of indigestion and perplexity. In the obligatory staking scene at the film's end, he manages to achieve a range of grimaces as he staggers about with a very long pointed object stuck through him, but by then the audience is more than willing to see him go.

DRACULA   Film
1979   (C)   U.S.A.   112 min.
Production Company: Mirisch Corporation, for Universal; *Director:* John Badham; *Producer:* Walter Mirisch; *Screenplay:* W. Richter (based on the Hamilton Deane, John Balderston play); *Photography:* Gilbert Taylor; *Editor:* John Bloom; *Special Effects:* Roy Arbogast; *Music:* John Williams.
Cast: Frank Langella (Count Dracula), Laurence Olivier (Abraham Van Helsing), Donald Pleasence (Jack Seward), Kate Nelligan (Lucy Seward), Trevor Eve (Jonathan Harker), Jan Francis (Mina van Helsing), Tony Hagarth (Renfield).

This most lavish of all Dracula productions, while it fails on many counts, is, nevertheless, of historic importance because in it Frank Langella plays Count Dracula as the fatally attractive sexual figure that filmgoers, ever since the 1922 *Nosferatu,* secretly knew him to be.

The film is entirely Langella's. He is everything a Byronic figure ought to be: tall, handsome, dashing . . . and ominous. Or, as Byron himself was said to be, he is "mad, bad and dangerous to know." Langella, as he did when he interpreted the role on the stage in New York, moves with the cold authority of the vampire. But there is no way for him to hide his superabundant erotic energy and that works against his role in the film. Of course his female victims succumb. But what woman in her right mind would not risk a little time in hell in exchange for having Langella nibbling at her throat?

The result, then, is that this production has the wrong things going for it. It has splendid interiors in which thousands of candles squander their light. It has baroque effects that may have cost millions, not to mention special effects that make one gasp. What the film lacks is the one ingredient without which a horror film is a dud: It lacks the capacity to scare anyone.

Still, John Badham's film is the vehicle that has given us the third of the three great Draculas. The line now reads: Bela Lugosi, Christopher Lee and Frank Langella.

DRACULA'S DAUGHTER   Film
1936   (B&W)   U.S.A.   70 min.
Production Company: Universal; *Director:* Lambert Hillyer; *Producer:* E. M. Asher; *Screenplay:* Garret Fort; *Editor:* Milton Carruth; *Photography:* George Robinson; *Special Effects:* John F. Fulton; *Music:* Heinz Roemheld.
Cast: Otto Kruger (Geoffrey Garth), Gloria Holden (Countess Marya Zaleska), Edward Van Sloan (Dr. Van Helsing), Irving Pichel (Sandor).

Both *Frankenstein* (1931) and *Dracula* (1931) have been fortunate in the sequels made of them in 1935 and 1936, respectively. In each case, the sequels have been stunning, stirring elaborations of the themes explored in the first films. *Dracula's Daughter* does not as its predecessor did, mint an unforgettable version of a film monster, but it does carry the Dracula story forward with superb grace. It is also the earliest vampire film in which the vampire is seen as a sympathetic, indeed, tragic figure who suffers from a curse she would give anything to escape.

Our film opens a bit awkwardly as the filmmakers try to pick up the Dracula story where it left off in the Bela Lugosi version of 1931. We see Dr. Van Helsing as he is arrested at Carfax Abbey in Whitby for having driven a stake through Dracula's heart. The body of Renfield, his neck broken by the count, lies nearby. Later, Gloria Holden, the Countess Marya Zaleska, who is Dracula's daughter, steals her father's body from the morgue so that she can provide it with proper funeral rites. More about those rites later.

With her father's body properly disposed of, the countess allows herself to think that she is now free of the family curse of vampirism. "I can live a normal life. Think normal things. Even play normal music." But when she asks her faithful servant, Sandor, to look into her eyes and tell her what he sees, he replies, "Death!" He restores to her finger the ring with the translucent stone with which she hypnotizes her victims, and she, who moments before was hoping that she might sing lullabies, goes out into the night on a vampiric quest.

The countess, a painter, goes to a party where she meets Geoffrey Garth, the psychiatrist who is working to provide Dr. Van Helsing with a defense against the charge of murder. When he says offhandedly that "any disease of the mind can be cured" she becomes hopeful once again and invites him to her house, "Just you and I." When, in the vaguest terms, she describes her problem, he advises her to muster the will to be free: "Don't avoid it. Meet it. Fight it. That's the secret."

As it turns out, that is advice more easily given than followed and it is not long before she has put on her hypnotic ring once more and ventured out into the night. In despair she turns again to Garth, who suddenly understands what she really is. When she asks him to go away with her, he says, "You must be insane." To which she replies, "No, desperate. There isn't anything I won't do to get you to free me of the curse of the Draculas. I am Dracula's daughter."

From here on, the film turns into a chase sequence as the countess, having kidnapped Janet, Garth's beautiful assistant, flies back to Transylvania accompanied by her faithful, and by now very jealous, servant, Sandor, whose hair looks like a highly polished black shoeshine with a part down the middle. Back in her castle, the countess tells Garth that Janet is "under a spell that can be broken only by me—or death. . . . Your life—or—hers." And she invites Garth to "Remain here with me among the undead." When Garth accepts the unholy bargain, Sandor, who sees himself about to be deprived of the immortality the countess long ago promised him, acts. In the final moments of the film both vampire—and police—justice are done.

The power of this film lies in its script and in the way that director Lambert Hillyer exploits the rich tonalities of black and white. If there is one scene that incorporates all of the

film's excellences it is the one in which Dracula's daughter presides over her father's funeral rites.

We see her standing, garbed in black, hooded amid drifting smoke from her father's funeral pyre. She is watched by a sombre, hard-faced man who stands to one side, at once involved and yet excluded from the rites that she performs. Her voice is soft and infinitely sorrowful as she speaks her father's obsequies, both to Satan and to God.

> Unto Adonai and Azriel, and in keeping with the laws of the Flame and lower pits, I consign this body to be consumed with purging fire. Let all baleful spirits that threaten the souls of men be banished. Be thou exorcised, O Dracula, and thy body, long undead, find destruction throughout eternity in the name of thy dark unholy master.

Having given Satan his due, she turns now to God.

> In the name of the All Holiest, and through this cross, may the evil spirit be cast out until the end of time.

That brooding tone, that melancholy and that unearthly beauty pervade most of this exquisite film.

DRESSED TO KILL   Film
1980 (C) U.S.A. 104 min.
Production Company: Cinema 77/Filmways; ***Director:*** Brian De Palma; ***Producer:*** George Litto; ***Screenplay:*** Brian De Palma; ***Photography:*** Ralph Bode; ***Music:*** Pino Donaggio.
Cast: Michael Caine (Elliot, the psychiatrist), Angie Dickinson (Kate Miller), Nancy Allen (the hooker), Keith Gordon (Kate's son).

This stylish, frequently witty and occasionally very scary film directed by Brian De Palma belongs to the mad-killer-on-the-loose category, though for most of the time the mad killer's identity is kept a cleverly hidden secret.

The film opens with a scene in which we see Kate Miller, a beautiful woman in her thirties, sensuously caressing herself as she showers. The erotic display which De Palma cunningly lingers over ends abruptly as the woman wakes up screaming from this sexy dream to find her husband making incompetent love to her.

Later we see her talking with Elliot, her psychiatrist, and confiding that, "Things are not fine. [My husband] gave me one of his whiz-bang specials and I'm mad at him." They discuss the problem briefly, then Kate asks Elliot, "Would you want to sleep with me?" To which he replies, "Yes."

From her therapy session, Kate goes to the Metropolitan Museum of Art where, in a brilliant and frequently hilarious sequence that exploits every comic nuance of contemporary upper middle-class adultery, we see her being picked up by a man named Warren Lockman with whom, in the back seat of a taxi, she goes avidly to work avenging herself for her husband's incompetence. Later, in Lockman's apartment, after the quickie affair has been consummated once more and she is dressing to leave, she discovers a card from a V.D. clinic where Lockman is clearly a patient.

But that news, disconcerting though it is, will have no consequence in Kate's life because as she gets into the elevator someone in a raincoat attacks her with a straight razor. Moments later, her throat cut, Kate Miller is a bloody corpse.

It is that life-shattering moment in the elevator plus two or three scenes of stark urban terror later on that justify calling

Dressed to Kill a horror film. Once Kate is dead, the movie turns into a murder mystery as Kate's teenage son, Keith, and Nancy Allen, the young call girl who discovered Kate's body in the elevator, team up to find the killer. Keith is an engaging nerd and an electronic whiz kid, while Nancy Allen is perfect as his hooker partner in detection. The murderer, when they find him, turns out to be precisely the one person we would never have dreamed of suspecting.

Dressed to Kill, with its high-IQ screenplay, its ingeniously twisted plot, its stylish treatment of its theme and its brilliantly imagined characters is, at its best, a bitter allegory about the perils of modern marriage and adultery. To that allegory, De Palma has linked a terrifying other theme: the fragility of identity. It is an ambitious combination, and it results in a film that has already become, and is likely to remain, something of a classic.

THE DUEL
Film

1971   (C)   U.S.A.   73 min. (U.S. version); 90 min. (INTL.)
Production Company: ABC/Universal; *Director:* Steven Spielberg; *Screenplay:* Richard Matheson; *Photography:* Jack A. Marta; *Music:* Billy Goldenberg.
Cast: Dennis Weaver (Dave Mann).

Here is a made-for-television film, later released as a movie, that has established itself as an absolute classic in the horror film genre. *The Duel* is minimalist horror at its most minimal. It has no sets and only one character with a name. But that is enough for Steven Spielberg, who makes more out of less. The film—spare and, well before *The Texas Chainsaw Massacre,* marvelously grimy—makes the dreadful point that out there, in any of the real worlds our lives touch, there may be someone who can take a dislike to us so irrational and so violent that he or she is prepared, literally and in fact, to kill.

As the film opens we see David Mann, a salesman whose marriage has lately made him uncertain of his manhood, driving on a two-lane highway. He is behind the wheel of his ordinary red coupe on his way home from an ordinary business trip. The car radio is on, droning away its daily account of disasters, large and small. At some point, Mann, impatient with the oil tanker just ahead of him, puts on speed and passes it.

And that is the beginning of the duel. The driver of the oil tanker, whose arm is all we ever get to see, takes umbrage and speeds up. For a few minutes, the tanker driver's intention is not clear. Then Mann understands, "Oh my God, he's trying to kill me." From then on, we forget that the tanker has a driver and the tanker itself becomes the implacable enemy that the universe has sent to test Mann's manhood once and for all.

The tanker has every advantage. Size, power, endurance, ingenious malevolence. It is the sort of duel that most drivers have experienced briefly in one driving situation or other, usually as an expression of fugitive impatience or as an outburst of rage. But for Mann, in his red coupe, the duel lasts for hours and is at every moment in deadly earnest as he battles, and finally outwits, the foul-smelling, roaring colossus.

Spielberg's direction is as tight-lipped as an early Hemingway short story. Matheson's screenplay is almost as laconic, and Dennis Weaver, who is not noted for sensitive role playing, is finally in his element here and acquits himself with distinction. Among them they are responsible for some of the tautest and most satisfying horror footage ever filmed.

THE DUENNA
Short Story

Marie Belloc Lowndes
Great Britain
1927, in Cynthia Asquith's (ed.) *The Ghost Book,* London Hutchinson; reprinted 1966 in Kurt Singer's (ed.) *The Gothic Reader,* New York, Ace.

Here is another romantic ghost story, not quite as piquant as "The Buick Saloon," but sharing its theme of the perfumed wistfulness of an illicit love affair.

Laura Delacourt has been married faithfully if joylessly for more than 10 years to Roger Delacourt, a man 30 years older than she, who treats her like "a negligible quantity in his self-indulgent, still agreeable existence." Finally she "capitulated to the entreaties of Julian Treville. They had been friends—from tomorrow they would be lovers."

With Roger on his way to join a friend for a cruise in the Mediterranean, Julian contrives a rendezvous for their tryst at The Folly, the stone cottage Julian's great grandfather built for his mistress, a French dancer known as *La Belle Julie.* Julian tells Laura that the cottage is said to be haunted by La Belle Julie but Laura, whose nightmare is that she and Julian will be found out, says that she is "Far more afraid of flesh and blood than ghosts." Julian installs her in The Folly and then, to maintain the charade that he hardly knows her, goes to spend the evening—and the night—away from her. "Tomorrow" is the time at which their bliss will be consummated.

But when tomorrow comes it brings nothing but calamity in its train. First Laura hears the news that "our good kind master, Mr. Treville is dead . . . He was killed out hunting today." An hour later, Laura, prostrated by her grief, "hears a loud knock on [her] heavy door . . . and when [her husband] Roger Delacourt strode into the room she felt scarce any surprise . . ."

Roger, of course, has come prepared for scenes and accusations and righteous wrath. What disarms him, what saves Laura's reputation and her miserable marriage is what the rest of the story is about. Suffice it to say that the errant wife who was not quite fully errant gets help from beyond the grave.

Whether or not one approves of a ghost coming to the aid of a would-be adulterous woman, a reader will find it hard to resist the charm of this civilized and compassionate tale. Marie Belloc Lowndes's prose has echoes of Oscar Wilde in it, but of an Oscar Wilde who will occasionally let his feelings overwhelm his wit.

THE DUNWICH HORROR
Short Story

H.P. Lovecraft
U.S.A.
April 1929, *Weird Tales;* reprinted 1967 in H.P. Lovecraft's *Three Tales of Horror,* Sauk City, Wis., Arkham House.

The Dunwich Horror may be Lovecraft's most powerful short story. It moves with the sure ease of a tale so lucidly conceived as to admit of no hesitation in its development. And— a rare thing with Lovecraft—the pitch of the voice in which it is told is more or less level, as if, in this story, Lovecraft had understood that restraint would be more effective than hysteria to convey the full horror of the events he was describing.

The Dunwich Horror is set in north-central Massachusetts in "a lonely and curious country" where:

> Two centuries ago, when talk of witch-blood, Satan-worship, and strange forest presences was not laughed at, it was the custom to give reasons for avoiding the locality . . . In our sensible age—since the Dunwich horror of 1928 was hushed up by those who had the town's and the world's welfare at heart—people shun it without knowing exactly why.

Wilbur Whately is one half of the Dunwich horror, born on February 2, 1913, to Lavinia Whately, "an unattractive albino woman" who lived with her half-insane father, "About whom the most frightful tales of wizardry had been whispered in his youth." The identity of the child's father is darkly hinted at in the story. Lavinia's sorcerer father tells the locals, "some day yew folks'll hear a child o' Lavinny's a-callin its father's name on the top o' Sentinel Hill."

Wilbur himself is a prodigy almost from the moment of his birth. He grows at a prodigious rate and is able to talk at the age of 11 months. Physically, he is "exceedingly ugly . . . there being something almost goatish or animalistic about his thick lips, large-pored, yellowish skin, coarse crinkly hair, and oddly elongated ears."

While Wilbur is growing up and reading bizarre and secret old books, his grandfather boards up the family house, turning it into a sort of fort, or prison. He becomes, at the same time, a perpetual customer for the local cattle for which he pays in antique gold coins. As the story progresses, we are given broad hints of what happens to the cattle.

In 1923, the old wizard dies, wheezing a final message to his grandson:

> "More space, Willy, more space soon. Yew grows—an' that grows faster . . . Open up the gates to Yog-Sothoth with the long chant that ye'll find on page 751 of the complete edition, an' then put a match to the prison. Fire from airth can't burn it nohaow."

Wilbur, following his grandfather's instructions, tries to find the formula on page 751 of the *Necronomicon* of the mad Arab Abdul Alhazred. When he attempts to steal a copy of the book from the Miskatonic University library, he dies after an attack by the university's ferocious watchdog. We then learn what Wilbur Whately was really like. An utterly unearthly creature, part serpent, part crocodile or alligator.

> The skin was thickly covered with coarse black fur, and from the abdomen a score of long greenish grey tentacles with red sucking mouths protruded limply.

There is more, all of it lurid. But Wilbur is only part of the Dunwich horror as Lovecraft makes his favorite point: Humankind is hardly a mote in the eye of creation. There are other horrid, "blasphemous" forms of life whose energy we, as humans, can hardly counter. Forms like the real Dunwich horror, Wilbur's hidden twin, which is:

> "Bigger'n a barn . . . all made o' squirmin' ropes . . . hull thing sort o' shaped like a hen's egg bigger'n anything with dozens o' legs like hogsheads that haff shut up when they step . . . nothin' solid about it—all like jelly, an' made o' sep'rit wrigglin' ropes pushed clost together . . . great bulgin eyes

all over it . . . an' Gawd in Heaven—that haff face on top! . . ."

That's what it's like on the loose, and we haven't even mentioned how it smells.

"The Dunwich Horror," despite Lovecraft's occasional lapses into his more usual perfervid prose, is horrifying because of the patient, slow, meticulous details we are given about the world into which the monster moves. Not only has Lovecraft imagined a theory for the source of the danger he says will threaten us but he has also found a way to make that threat archetypal. As a result, we find ourselves, in this first-rate tale, in the grip of what seems to be an authentic myth.

There is a 1969 film version of "The Dunwich Horror" that retains just enough of Lovecraft's sinister brooding to keep a viewer edgy, but for sheer, wet Lovecraftian terror, the story on the printed page surpasses the film by a mile.

THE DUNWICH HORROR   Film
1969   (C)   U.S.A.   90 min.

Production Company: American International; ***Director:*** Daniel Haller; ***Producer:*** Samuel Z. Arkoff, James H. Nicholson; ***Screenplay:*** Curtis Lee Hanson, Henry Rosenbaum, Ronald Silkosky; ***Photography:*** Richard C. Glouner; ***Editor:*** Christopher Holmes; ***Special Effects:*** Roger George; ***Music:*** Les Baxter.

Cast: Sandra Dee (Nancy), Dean Stockwell (Wilbur Whately), Ed Begley (Professor Armitage), Lloyd Bochner (Dr. Cory), Sam Jaffe (Old Whately).

Daniel Haller's version of H.P. Lovecraft's short story "The Dunwich Horror" (see entry) would be twice the success it is if it were half as long. Lovecraft's story of a family of sorcerers who, generation by generation, try to reconstruct the rituals that will bring the mythical, evil Old Ones back to earth, has been so fleshed out with Hollywood additions that it wobbles under the additional weight.

And yet the film has a certain intimacy, a narrowness of focus as it keeps before us a frozen-faced Dean Stockwell playing Wilbur Whately, the last presentable descendant of the Whately family. In order to compel the universe to readmit the Old Ones to their former power, Wilbur involves himself with a young Arkham University student named Nancy whom he plans to sacrifice, at the appropriate moment. The small number of others who are part of the drama include Professor Henry Armitage, a scholar of the occult who guesses what Wilbur is up to and works to forestall him; Elizabeth, a friend of Nancy's who tags along after Professor Armitage; and Dr. Cory, a local physician who is well instructed on the Whately family history.

The most powerful sequence in the film comes well into its second half when Wilbur takes Nancy to a mysterious cliffside place called the Devil's Hopyard where he explains that:

> Fertility rites were practiced here. When the seasons and the cycles of the moon were right, then they came, one by one and gathered among these stones. Then they selected a beautiful girl like you. And then placed the girl's virginal body upon the altar naked to the elements and their black robes blending into the night they lighted candles and gathered around to relish her nakedness. Then they waited . . . for the moment when she would allow the power of darkness to enter, the moment when the gate would open and the Old Ones would come through . . .

Before that speech is finished, it is clear that he, Wilbur, intends to perform both the sexual and the blood sacrifice that is needed.

Meanwhile, back at the Whately home, Elizabeth, looking for her friend Nancy, inadvertently visits the thing that we have been made aware lives in the attic. When she opens the locked door, whatever it is that lives inside that room attacks her and for a few moments what we get is a lustful lightshow gone berserk. While we never quite see what is happening to Elizabeth, we assume the worst and we must be right because she is never seen again.

As the film comes to its close, a rescued Nancy is told by Professor Armitage that ''the last of the Whatelys is dead.'' Nancy looks straight before her, enigmatically, as the camera lets us know that Professor Armitage, and the world, have made another miscalculation.

Throughout the film, even when he is about to sacrifice Nancy, Dean Stockwell has the look of a young bank clerk in training. And Sandra Dee, even when she is about to be sacrificed, registers civil perplexity, the one emotion she has mastered for this film. But there are enough bits and pieces of Lovecraft's story embedded in Haller's rendering of it to keep a viewer patient through the director's casting misjudgments and Hanson-Rosenbaum-Bilkosky's lugubrious prose.

THE DYBBUK   Play
Shloimeh Ansky
U.S.S.R.
1921 (Yiddish-language); tr. 1926 by Henry G. Alsberg and Winifred Katzin, New York, Boni & Liveright.

Sh. Ansky's play, *The Dybbuk*, though it treats of spirit possession and has moments horrifying enough to qualify it for inclusion in any list of scary works of literature, is something of a tour de force because it has no figures of evil in it. Leahle, the young woman who is possessed, and Khonon, whose spirit possesses her, are not antagonists, and the act of possession itself is meant to be understood as the expression of a natural law.

Reb Sender, a rich and pious Jew, has a daughter, Leahle, for whom, after many unsuccessful attempts, he has at last made a match. Khonon, we learn, has endeavored to frustrate the various matchmaking efforts by mystical means: fasting, prayer, self-mortification and the use of Kabbalistic incantations. When the news of Leahle's betrothal is confirmed, Khonon drops dead.

Leahle, whose heart belongs to Khonon, violently rejects

Menashe, her foolish prospective husband, and rushes to the grave of a martyred bride and groom for whose ghostly aid she pleads. Not long after that, the wedding preparations are halted when Leahle is possessed by a dybbuk, a transmigrating spirit. In this case, it is Khonon's spirit and it vows never to leave Leahle again.

There follows the great exorcism scene in which the rabbi, Reb Azrielke, the holy man of Miropolye, undertakes to drive Khonon's spirit out of Leahle's body. It is an anguishing scene (and a terrifying challenge to the actress who must speak in two voices: Leahle's and Khonon's) and it ends inconclusively because the ghost of Khonon's father summons Reb Sender, Leahle's father, to a Din Torah, a rabbinical court.

In the course of that trial we learn from Nissen, the ghost of Khonon's father, that Reb Sender and Nissen were once friends who vowed, when their wives were simultaneously pregnant, that they would betrothe their children to each other if one was a boy and the other a girl. But Nissen and Sender drifted apart and Sender forgot his vow.

But the vow the fathers made has bound Leahle's soul to Khonon, and when Sender, violating his oath, betrothed Leahle to Menashe he introduced a snarl into the design of the universe.

Rabbi Azrielke now undertakes to drive the dybbuk out of Leahle. But the dybbuk refuses to leave. The ensuing exorcism scene is both terrifying and splendid. Fifteen men are called in and given white robes to wear. Seven Torah scrolls are distributed to seven of them. Seven ram's horns are given to seven others. The ram's horns are sounded. Then black candles are lighted. Finally, the dybbuk, assailed by a decree of excommunication submits and the great struggle is apparently over.

All the participants now leave the stage except an exhausted Leahle and her old crone of a nurse who promptly falls asleep so that effectively we have only Leahle before us. What follows is a scene as tender as the outnighting scene between Jessica and Lorenzo in *The Merchant of Venice* as Leahle, and the as yet unexorcised spirit of Khonon within her, speak lovingly to each other. It is a theatrical masterstroke whose meaning is plain: The coming together of these two souls has closed a gap in the creation.

I have not talked at all about the lyricism that suffuses this extraordinary play. A lyricism that, even in translation, turns melodrama into exaltation as Ansky demonstrates that love is the organizing principle of the universe and that horror is what happens when that principle is violated.

E

ELIAS AND THE DRAUG
Short Story

Jonas Lie

Norway

1902; English-language reprint in Roald Dahl's (ed.) *Roald Dahl's Book of Ghost Stories*, New York, Farrar, Straus & Giroux.

Roald Dahl, in a note to Jonas Lie's story, tells us that: "The Draug is a sea monster who sails a half-boat with a crew of men lost at sea who have not received Christian burial. He who sees the Draug, according to Nordland superstition, will soon die."

The victim, in Lie's story, is a poor fisherman named Elias who lives with his wife and six children on a lonely, perhaps haunted, island called Kvalholmen. One day, he passes a huge seal sunning itself on a rock and throws his halibut harpoon at it, wounding it in the neck. As the seal makes its escape, it seems to call out, "Better beware, Elias, when you get your femboring!"

It is not until some years later that Elias gets to own his own femboring or fishing boat in the town of Ranen. To celebrate its purchase, he undertakes to take his wife and children with him on the 50-mile sea voyage home. Once at sea, he becomes aware that there is a femboring very much like his own sailing alongside him. Its crew, however, cannot be seen distinctly. Once out in the open ocean the two boats, as if they are racing, move into ever rougher waters. It is only when a great wave washes across his boat, sweeping two of Elias's sons overboard, that he begins to understand that the accompanying boat is manned by a Draug.

From here on, the tale grows darker and darker as the Draug, who is clearly seen to have a bit of iron sticking out of its neck, exacts its long delayed revenge. Lie, who knows that there is no further action/suspense to his story, makes it seem compelling just the same by focusing on Elias's stoic acceptance of his own fate even as he battles against it. Long before the word existentialism was invented we see a hero whose *acte gratuite* brought down his doom accepting responsibility and doing, nobly, what little there is left to do.

As Dahl says, "It really is a cruel and wonderful tale . . ."

EMBRYO
Film

1976   (C)   U.S.A.   104 min.

Production Company: Cine Artists; ***Director:*** Ralph Nelson; ***Producers:*** Arnold H. Orgolini, Anita Doohan; ***Screenplay:*** Anita Doohan and Jack W. Thomas; ***Photography:*** Fred Koenkamp; ***Editor:*** John Martinelli; ***Special Effects:*** Roy Arbogast, Bill Shourt; ***Music:*** Gil Melle.

Cast: Rock Hudson (Dr. Paul Holliston), Diane Ladd (Martha), Anne Schedeen (Helen), Roddy McDowall (Riley), Barbara Carrera (Victoria), Dr. Joyce Brothers (Dr. Brothers).

Embryo is a sleek spinoff of Mary Shelley's novel *Frankenstein* and it is no accident that the "creature" of this film is named Victoria. Victor Frankenstein, it will be recalled, was the name of the creator of the Frankenstein creature.

Rock Hudson plays a research doctor who has not done any research for some years since his wife was killed in an auto accident from which he walked away unhurt. As the film opens, we see Hudson speeding though a rainstorm. A pregnant Doberman pinscher starts across the road and Hudson hits it. The dog dies, but Hudson is able to save one of her fetuses by immersing it in a growth solution on which he once did research.

The fetus prospers and develops with amazing speed into an adult dog. Elated by his success with the experimental solution, Hudson goes on to try it with a human fetus taken from a newly dead woman. In a matter of days a fully formed, human female infant comes to term. Once born, the child grows rapidly until days later Hudson finds himself the "creator" of an entrancingly beautiful, naked 25-year-old woman who proves to be an intellectual and creative paragon as well. Victoria, as Hudson calls her, can play chess, has perfect recall and is smolderingly sexual. This last attribute distresses Hudson's sister-in-law who has designs on him herself.

A love triangle is inevitable, and it develops at the same time as we learn that the growth fluid in which Victoria was nurtured is not an unqualified success. The experimental Doberman pinscher breaks down first; then Victoria begins having problems. The rest of the film chronicles a race against time as Victoria tries to hide from Hudson the breakdown of her system even as, with her exceptional intellectual capacity, she searches for an antidote that will stabilize her cells.

Of course she cannot succeed and the film ends in a male chauvinist climax whose details come close to being as tasteless as they are grisly.

THE ENEMY   Short Story
Isaac Bashevis Singer
U.S.A.
1980, tr. from Yiddish by Friedl Wyler & Herbert Lottman, in Kirby McCauley's (ed.) *Dark Forces*, New York, Viking.

In a Singer fiction, a reader rarely has trouble knowing what happened. What he may be less certain about, as in "The Enemy," is just what the story may mean. The story's plot is extraordinarily simple: The narrator, who, it is implied, is Singer himself, meets an old friend of his in the New York Public Library and the two go off to have coffee in a nearby restaurant. The friend, whose name is Chaikin, is, like the narrator, a refugee from Poland; knowing that Singer is interested in the occult, Chaikin tells him the story of an experience he had on board the ship that brought him from Brazil to the United States.

On that journey, whose physical details Singer relates in scrupulous detail, Chaikin has the bad luck to be served by a singularly unpleasant waiter who manages constantly to misunderstand Chaikin's requests for food and who makes it very clear that he has contempt for the innocent Chaikin and means to make the poor refugee as miserable as he possibly can.

And so he does. Then, two days before the ship is due to dock in New York, Chaikin, exhausted by the mean waiter's treatment of him at the Captain's Ball, goes back to his cabin and falls asleep. Later, he starts up, gets out of bed and goes up on deck:

> And then came the event I still can't believe really happened. I'd reached the railing at the stern of the ship, and turned around. But I was not alone, as I thought. There was my waiter . . . He was coming toward me. I tried to run away but a jerk of the ship threw me right into his hands . . . When I was still a yeshiva boy I once heard a cat catch a mouse in the night. It's almost forty years away but the shriek of that mouse still follows me. The despair of everything alive cried out through that mouse. I had fallen into the paws of my enemy and I comprehended his hatred no more than the mouse comprehended that of the cat.

In the ensuing struggle between the waiter and Chaikin, Chaikin notices that his enemy, who in the dining room seemed a huge and vigorous man, is now somehow a lightweight and very weak. Chaikin tells us that he fought vigorously.

> I did not despair. I had to fight and I fought without fear. Later it would occur to me that this would be the way two bucks would fight for a doe . . . I was completely absorbed,

body and soul, and there was no room for any other sensation. Suddenly I found myself near the railing. I caught the fiend or whatever he was and threw him overboard. He appeared unusually light—sponge or foam.

The next day the tormenting waiter is missing, and, strangely, there is no outcry on the part of anyone on the ship's crew. For Chaikin, indeed, life seems much pleasanter than before. He is assigned a new waiter who treats him in the most friendly fashion.

The question, then, is what are we left with? And the answer is plenty. Beyond the ennobling ambiguities of the action, and the accurate depiction of the sharp-edged universe in which his protagonist moves, we have, too, Singer's amazing facility at scattering profundities almost as if they were throwaway lines. In the midst of the most ordinary sentences the author embeds lines like these: "I took one look at my waiter and knew he was my enemy. For hating, no reason is necessary." And in the scene already mentioned about the mouse, "The despair of everything alive cried out through that mouse."

Singer has a way, too, of linking ordinary action to much larger matters. Though he does not seem to insist upon it, we never quite forget that Chaikin is a refugee from the Holocaust. That he has already had his share of the horrors of this world. By comparison with them, how important can an encounter with an astral body be? And yet, because it is the astral body of an unreasoning tormentor, and because Chaikin has been a victim long enough, that horrifying wrestle on deck takes on the significance of that other unequal struggle, Jacob's wrestling with the angel.

ERASERHEAD   Film
1978   (B&W)   U.S.A.   90 min.
Production Company: R.C.A.; ***Director:*** David Lynch; ***Producer:*** David Lynch; ***Screenplay:*** David Lynch; ***Photography:*** Herbert Caldwell.
Cast: John Nance (Henry Spencer/Eraserhead), Charlotte Stewart (Mary X), Allen Joseph (Mr. X), Jeannie Bates (Mrs. X), Laurel Near (beautiful lady), V. Phillipps-Wilson (landlady), Jack Fiske (man in-the-planet), Judith Anna Roberts (beautiful girl).

An older viewer of *Eraserhead*, say someone past his or her thirtieth year, may wonder what it is about this film that has made it a prestigious cult classic among the young.

Eraserhead is an experimental film with all of the worst characteristics of that genre: uncertain forward movement, strange camera angles, abrupt editing, and a pace so slow that it often feels sluggish. It is a film that is difficult to watch and considerably harder to understand, and yet the effect on its viewers is powerful and disturbing.

A plot summary is not much help because there is very little plot to summarize. Henry, a dreary young man with an oversized head crowned with tightly curled hair (hence, Eraserhead), wanders vaguely through the film. The world he lives in is almost always in the dark or at least in shadow. He has a fiancée named Mary who has parents, Mr. X and Mrs. X., and a grandmother. Henry has dinner with the X's and eats something that looks, and acts, vaguely like chicken.

At dinner, Henry learns that Mary has given birth to something—one would be hard put to call it a baby. It is something larval and wet. It looks like a foetus, but cries like a demented infant. At the instigation of Mary's parents, Henry dutifully marries Mary, as we know because we next see them living together. Mary feeds the larval infant while Henry asks, ''Was there any mail?'' to which she replies, ''No.''

Henry and Mary hate being married and hate their horrid baby. Mary shouts ''Shut up'' at it but it lies on its unpillow-cased pillow and continues to yowl.

We see Henry and Mary lying restlessly in bed. Henry starts pulling squirmy creatures out of her and flings them to the floor. Mary quarrels with Henry. Then Mary says, ''I can't stand it, I'm going home.''

While she is gone, the Beautiful Lady next door shows up and says, ''I locked myself out of my apartment . . . Where's your wife?'' Henry replies, ''She must have gone back to her parents again, I'm not sure.'' ''Can I spend the night here,'' asks the Beautiful Lady. Then she and Henry make love. The larval baby cries as Henry and the Beautiful Lady in bed seem to disappear into a vague milky fog. Not much later, the Beautiful Lady betrays Henry with a stranger in the hallway.

Plot, one needs to say again, is not the point here. Neither is character. What we have instead is an atmospheric film in which individual and powerfully suggestive images are strung together to create a single mood of revulsion against the human sexual venture and its consequences. If *Eraserhead* is a parable it is one in which love, marriage and babies are seen as dark and wet and dismal. If the film's high status for more than a decade tells us anything it is that it continues to speak to the anxieties of the young.

THE EVIL DEAD   Film
1982   (C) U.S.A.   126 min.
Production Company: New Line Cinema; *Director:* Sam Raimu; *Producer:* Robert Taper; *Screenplay:* Sam Raimu; *Photography:* Tim Philo; *Special Effects:* Tom Sullivan; *Music:* Joe Loduca.
Cast: Bruce Campbell (Ash), Ellen Sandweiss (Cheryl), Hal Delrich (Scott), Betsy Baker (Linda), Sarah York (Shelly).

This film is right up there with *The Re-animator* as one of the five or six squishiest terror films ever made.

The film's real business is to give us as many scenes of imaginative and graphic bloodletting as possible. Body fluids, mostly blood, squirt at the least occasion. Blood flows from electric sockets, down walls. People are shot, stabbed. Eyes are gouged out.

Despite all this, there is a story line: Three young couples drive to a cabin in the Tennessee mountains for an erotic weekend. There they come upon an evil book, with whose contents someone has previously meddled. They, too, meddle—with the result that the evil spirits that inhabit the house reach out and destroy them.

The notes I took as I watched the film may convey better than any formal writing what *The Evil Dead* is like:

. . . Carful of singing young people. Something is stalking them.
. . . Doors are banging. Sun is going down. Clock stops. Wind blows.
. . . Sumerian Book of the Dead. Demon resurrection.
. . . Ghosts ask, ''Why have you wakened us from our ancient sleep?''

. . . Possessed woman stabs him with a pencil.
. . . Second woman possessed. Something eats friend's right arm.
. . . ''Cheryl was right. We're all going to die.''
. . . Linda has just stabbed Ashley. He is grabbed by arm in cellar. He stabs Linda. He starts to saw her body apart. Can't bring himself to do it. Tries to bury her. She rises out of the grave. She scratches him. He smashes her head with a two by four. Decapitates her. Her headless body attacks him. Her screaming head exults.

Perhaps enough is enough.

When the wretched night is over and Ashley, the last survivor, opens the door, there is birdsong and light. By then, however, the filmgoer, who has been praying for a coagulant, may no longer care.

THE EXORCIST   Novel
William Peter Blatty
U.S.A.
1971, New York, Harper & Row; reprinted 1984, New York, Bantam.

As one reads this extraordinarily effective novel of possession, a haunting question obtrudes itself in one's mind: Why would a demon (in this fiction named Azuzu) on his own or at Satan's behest choose to take possession of the mind and body of an innocent 12-year-old girl and subject her to torments so outrageous that merely reading about them sickens the heart?

The characters in *The Exorcist* are well conceived, though none of them is profoundly studied. There is Chris Maclaine, divorcee, a popular Hollywood actress living in a Washington suburb while she is making a film. She is raising her 12-year-old daughter, Regan, with the aid of a devoted trio of helpers: Sharon, Chris's secretary who doubles as a tutor for Regan; and Karl Engstrom, the butler, and his wife, Willie, the cook. When Regan begins to manifest bizarre and utterly inexplicable behavior, a psychiatrist-priest, Father Damien Karas, is called in. Later, he gets Father Merrin, a skilled exorcist, to help him. Finally, there is Lieutenant Kinderman, a policeman who talks like the TV detective, Columbo.

Once Blatty has made it clear to his readers that Regan is truly possessed by a demon, the rest of the novel becomes a chronicle of the battle conducted first by a single priest, then by two of them, to free the child from the demon who has possessed her. The struggle, Blatty makes clear, is an agonizing one, not only for the child and her mother, but also for each of the other characters in the fiction, most especially Father Damien, who, as the exorcism progresses, is forced to confront his own inner weaknesses as well—because the demon does not play fair. It has full knowledge of its antagonists' secrets and it exploits them fully.

As the tale progresses, Blatty provides an answer to the question of why a demon would choose to possess an innocent child. He has his Father Merrin say:

I think the demon's target is not the possessed; it is us . . . the observers . . . every person in this house . . . to make us despair; to reject our own humanity, Damien; to see ourselves as ultimately bestial; as ultimately vile and putrescent; without dignity; ugly; unworthy. And there lies the heart of it, perhaps: in unworthiness.

It doesn't seem to be a very satisfactory answer, but it is probably unnecessary to insist on one from a book that so successfuly keeps a reader turning its pages. Blatty, who had already been a successful film writer, moves his story along with practiced ease. His prose is loose, without being limp. It has an admirably straightforward clarity. It has, too, an unforgettable and profoundly poignant central image: a child tormented to the utmost limits that flesh can bear because she is a pawn in a game that makes sense only to God and Satan. And, though Father Karas pays the price of the exorcism that frees Regan from the demon, it is the image of the tormented child that lingers when the book is closed.

As with the novels *Dracula* and *Frankenstein, The Exorcist* is likely to be better remembered as a film than as a book. The film version of the novel made film history primarily for the intricacy of its special effects.

THE EXORCIST   Film
1973   (C)   U.S.A.   122 min.

Production Company: Hoya Productions (W.B.); *Director:* William Friedkin; *Producer:* William Peter Blatty; *Screenplay:* William Peter Blatty; *Photography:* Owen Roizman and Billy Williams; *Editor:* Evan Lottman, Norman Gray, Bud Smith; *Special Effects:* Marcel Vercoutere; *Music:* Krysztof Penderecki, Hans Werner Henze, George Crum, Anton Webern, Mike Oldfield, David Borden.

Cast: Ellen Burstyn (Chris MacNeil), Max Von Sydow (Father Merrin), Lee J. Cobb (Lieutenant William Kinderman), Linda Blair (Regan MacNeil), Kitty Winn (Sharon Spencer), Jack MacGowran (Burke Dennings), Jason Miller (Father Damien Karas), Mercedes McCambridge (voice of the demon).

This film version of William Peter Blatty's novel, *The Exorcist,* is most famous for its special effects, particularly a scene in which the head of the possessed child, Regan, turns a full 360 degrees on her shoulders.

Director William Friedkin follows the outline of Blatty's story fairly closely but, through the magic of the camera, he is able to make three aspects of it considerably more dramatic than they are on the printed page: first, the visual and auditory horror that surrounds Regan; second, the anguish of a mother whose child is possessed; and third, the ritual of the Catholic exorcism, which, while not quite as powerfully realized as the other two, is treated with becoming gravity.

Though Friedkin handles the second and third elements with considerable subtlety, *The Exorcist* is most likely to be remembered for the wildly melodramatic sequences in which the two priests, Father Karas and Father Merrin, battle the demon who inhabits Regan's body. Extraordinarily moving is the deep fatigue in the face of the child. Her tormented look demands our compassion, even as out of her mouth sometimes spew streams of foul-colored vomit, or equally foul speech, while at other times we hear sounds like the lowing of cattle or the roaring of animals in an unearthly zoo. As the battle between the priests and the demon rages, a wind howls through the freezing room. The priests chant, "Begone you hostile power. I cast you out, unclean spirit, in the name of my Lord Jesus Christ, it is He who commands you." Meanwhile, furniture trembles and the demon roars through the mouth of the child. At one point in the tumult we see the child's 45-rpm records flying about the room; then a priest intones, "Depart from this servant of God. . . . The power of Christ compels you. God Himself commands you. The majestic Christ commands you." As the demon resists, first the bed levitates, then the child herself. When the scene becomes unbearable, Father Karas challenges the demon to single combat and the battle, for an astonishing instant, is joined. When it is all over, there is the silence that follows upon a terrible loss after which there are healing tears and a sweet, sweet calm.

At its best, *The Exorcist* is a stirring film, but one has to say of it that it has the same defect as the book on which it is based. It is hard to believe that Satan, to further his plot against mankind, needs to take up residence in, and torment the body of, an innocent child. Still, if one can suspend that disbelief one can be grateful to Friedkin and Blatty for having made a truly landmark horror film.

F

FADE TO BLACK

Film

1980　(C)　U.S.A.　100 min.

Production Company: Compass International/Leisure Investment Co./Movie Ventures Ltd.; *Director:* Vernon Zimmerman; *Producer:* George G. Braunstein, Ron Hamady; *Screenplay:* Vernon Zimmerman; *Photography:* Alex Phillips, Jr.; *Editor:* Howard Kunin; *Special Effects:* James Wayne.

Cast: Dennis Christopher (Eric Binford), Tim Thomerson (Dr. Moriarty), Norman Burton (Eric Binford), Morgan Paull (Gry Bialy), Gwynne Gilford (Anne), Eve Brent Ashe (aunt/mother), Linda Kerridge (Marilyn).

Fade to Black, like *Peeping Tom,* exploits the peculiarly 20th-century theme of film as a mode of memory with the singular difference that it, more specifically than books, allows us to have memories of experiences we did not have. Indeed, to encounter dreams we did not dream. And Eric Binford, the pathetic hero of *Fade to Black,* is, like the killer in *Peeping Tom,* so obsessed by movie images that he violently rearranges the untidy real world he inhabits to make it conform to the light and dark symmetries achieved on film. By filling the eye with action while the body, seated in a theater, is effectively inert, film is the perfect medium to soothe minds as passive as his.

Eric Binford is the sort of helpless jerk Woody Allen would be if he were not illuminated by genius. Binford works in the stock room of a film distributing company. He has a number of harrassments in his life: his wheelchair-bound mother who, because Eric was born out of wedlock, pretends to be his aunt; his heart-diseased employer; and a couple of callow youths who torment him where he works. Moreover, he is in love, primarily with The Movies and less abstractly with a young Australian woman who is a Marilyn Monroe look-alike.

Binford's fixation on movies is beautifully handled. His nearly total recall of the thousands of films he has seen becomes a powerful metaphor of his problem: There is no real world in which he can belong. Finally, he achieves a tinsel heroism as he acts out vengeance fantasies dictated to him by a hodgepodge of the films that haunt him. When despair rouses him to action, his life becomes a final reel of film in which he destroys the people who have tormented him until, in the end, he goes out in a blaze of klieg-lighted glory.

THE FALL OF THE HOUSE OF USHER

Short Story

Edgar Allan Poe

U.S.A.

1839, in *Burton's Gentleman's Magazine;* reprinted 1976 in Wilfred Satty's (ed.) *The Illustrated Edgar Allan Poe,* New York, Clarkson N. Potter.

When the first-person narrator of Poe's "The Fall of the House of Usher" receives a letter from his friend Roderick Usher imploring him to visit, the letter's "wildly importunate nature . . . admitted of no other than a personal reply." And so we see him riding through "a singularly dreary tract of country" on his way to the house of Usher, a "mansion of gloom."

The mansion itself is suitably grandiose, but it is in an advanced state of decay. The large and lofty rooms have furniture that is "profuse, comfortless, antique, and tattered." As for Roderick Usher himself, he appears to be in the last stages of physical and perhaps mental decline. Some of the gloom that surrounds Roderick is the result of his sister Madeline's incurable illness, an illness characterized by "A settled apathy, a gradual wasting away of the person . . ." She is, moreover, given to cataleptic seizures.

The narrator and Roderick spend several dismal days painting, reading and talking together. Then, abruptly, Roderick announces that Madeline has died and that he intends to put her body temporarily in one of the vaults in the building. The body is placed in a copper-sheathed room and locked behind a massive iron door.

Thus far, the story has been merely dark and dismal. Now,

The brooding Roderick Usher (drawing by Aubrey Beardsley).

THE FAMILIAR
Short Story

J. Sheridan Le Fanu
Ireland
1872, in *In a Glass Darkly,* London, Bentley; reprinted 1964 in E.F. Bleiler's (ed.) *Best Ghost Stories of J.S. Le Fanu,* New York, Dover.

Here, in one of Le Fanu's best ghost stories, the link between the haunting of the principal character and his own sexual guilts is so vividly presented that we have evidence, once again, that if there had been no Freud, the world would have had to invent the good doctor.

The tale is preceded by a learned note on the sources of the visionary experience. From that scientific gesture, we move to the story itself as it is told by the Reverend Thomas Herbert. Herbert describes how a vengeful spirit begins to follow Sir James Barton, a fortyish former navy captain, shortly after Barton falls in love with and becomes engaged to the beautiful but penniless Miss Montague.

Barton's attachment to Miss Montague is clearly the signal to some supernatural agency to commence its work, and Barton begins to receive disturbing notes from someone who signs himself, ''The Watcher.'' Later he is followed by someone who:

> was short in stature, looked like a foreigner, and wore a kind of travelling cap, walked very rapidly, as if under fierce excitement. . . . muttering to himself, fast and vehemently the while.

Captain Barton counsults both a medical man, Dr. Richards, and a minister, Dr. Macklin, about his visitations and gets no satisfaction from either of them. The malignant spirit, whatever or whoever it is, continues to follow him to the end.

What makes Le Fanu's tale especially dreadful is that, while he elaborates the victim's sufferings, he does not provide a motive for the ghost until the final couple of paragraphs. Then sex and physical cruelty suddenly invade the story and we understand that Captain Barton, who once sowed the wind, has been reaping the whirlwind all along.

THE FAN
Novel

Bob Randall
U.S.A.
1977, New York, Random House.

Here is a mad-killer-on-the-loose fiction that is so well contrived that it continues to be suspenseful well past its heartbreaking climax.

Randall has organized his story as a series of letters to, from and about Sally Ross, a 50-year old former movie star who is now rehearsing for a Broadway show entitled *So I Bit Him.* As we read through the letters from her agent, from her friends, from her neighbors who resent the noise that comes from her apartment, we come upon the first of the letters from Douglas Breen, who is the ''fan'' of the title. His is not an exceptionally interesting first letter. He merely identifies himself as an adoring fan who wants a copy of one of her photographs. Belle Goldman, Sally's somewhat strident secretary, sends the photograph. But it soon transpires that Douglas Breen is anything but a run of the mill fan. His letters, each of them progressively more personal, keep com-

the horror begins as, little by little, we are given to understand that Roderick is laboring under the weight of some oppressive secret involving Madeline. That secret is revealed at a climactic moment when, in the course of a reading of the ''The Mad Trist,'' a story by Launcelot Canning, Roderick and the narrator hear a dreadful noise and ''there did stand the lofty and enshrouded figure of the lady Madeline of Usher. There was blood upon her white robes . . .''

And there is more terror as the last two scions of the House of Usher join the house itself in its spectacular fall.

''The Fall of the House of Usher'' is a tenaciously gloomy work. Roderick Usher is a dispiriting protagonist and Lady Madeline, except for what she does at the story's end, has hardly any character at all. And yet, suffocating and clammy though the story is, it exerts a terrible power over readers mostly because of how much is left ambiguous about the relationship between Roderick and his twin sister and about whatever it is in the very structure and design of the house itself that has had ''a . . . silent yet importunate and terrible influence'' on the destinies of the Ushers. Some critics have seen incest as the contributing flaw. But even if one is not that specific, one can still be sure that family secrets are involved and those are always the most terrifying of all.

Bob Randall.

ing. When, for a reason ingeniously devised by the author, Breen's letters are unanswered, the letters slowly shift their ground, first toward impatience, then irritation, then anger and finally to outright, and seriously meant, murder threats.

It is in the process of that shift that we see how the epistolary form of the novel serves Randolph's purposes. While Sally is unaware of the existence of Douglas Breen, we learn from the various letters a good deal about each of the characters. Sally Ross, it becomes clear, is still very much in love with her ex-husband, Jake. Jake, for his part, tries valiantly to be happy in his new marriage to a much younger Heidi but it is soon clear that his life's true love has been Sally. Belle Goldman emerges from her letters and notes as Sally's foul-mouthed, fiercely loving and loyal friend who, indeed, becomes Breen's first victim. Randall succeeds best at giving us Sally—a woman whom success has not fulfilled, who has managed to make a disaster out of her emotional life and who arrives at some enriching wisdom under the pressure of the death threat that Breen poses.

What gives this book more than a touch of distinction is the compassion with which the various lives are braided together into a single overwhelming whole. Even the madman, Breen, is given moments of near-insight that make us wonder whether, if he had ever gotten a reply from Sally, he would have taken the ingenious and deadly measures he did take.

But of course, what might have been is always the question that no one can answer, and the events of this fiction grind to their inevitable and horrifying conclusion.

Despite Randolph's breezy prose style in which bitterly witty one-liners are expected to stand for richly meditated insights, *The Fan* is a superior work of fiction.

FATAL ATTRACTION
Film
1987 (C) U.S.A. 108 min.
Production Company: Paramount; *Director:* Adrian Lyne; *Producer:* Stanley Jaffe, Sherry Lansing; *Screenplay:* James Dearden; *Photography:* Howard Atherton; *Editor:* Michael Kahn, Peter D. Berger; *Music:* Maurice Jarre.
Cast: Michael Douglas (Stan Gallagher), Glenn Close (Alex Forrest), Anne Archer (Beth Gallagher), Ellen Hamilton Latzen (Ellen Gallagher), Stuart Pankin (Jimmy).

Fatal Attraction, a major box-office success in 1987, should be of interest to horror film watchers for the way in which its makers nudged what purports to be a contemporary domestic tragedy into the horror film genre, complete with a climactic ending borrowed without embarrassment from Henri-Georges Clouzot's *Diabolique.*

Like *Dressed to Kill,* this svelte, expensive film with its brilliantly written screenplay and its name-recognition stars takes itself seriously as a drama of urban marriage and adultery. It is very much a film about fast-track Manhattan life and as such manages to appeal both to New Yorkers who really live there and to the millions of others who do not and for whom New York and violence are exotic synonyms.

The story involves four major characters. First we have Stan Gallagher, a publishing-industry lawyer in his middle thirties; his wife, Beth, who is a few years younger; their five- to six-year-old daughter, Ellen; and then Alex Forrest, an attractive but by no means ravishing editor in her middle thirties. Alex meets Stan at a book publicity party where, with the sort of healthful candor women have learned since the end of the sixties, she makes her attraction to him very obvious. Stan, one should say, is in what both he and his wife Beth would call a good marriage. When Beth takes their daughter into the country to visit her parents for a weekend, Stan and Alex meet by chance that Friday afternoon and decide to have dinner together.

At that unplanned dinner, the warmth Alex and Stan feel for each other bursts into wild erotic flame and their weekend turns into what Stan feels, and what Alex gives the illusion of feeling, is a perfectly splendid two-night stand. They make imaginative love in bed, on stairways, in an elevator, in the rain.

Then when the weekend is over and Beth and Ellen come home the tone of the film changes from love to war as Alex continues to press for further meetings with Stan. More, she talks about being in love and, when Stan makes it clear that for him the end of the weekend was the end of the affair, she slits her wrists.

That gesture marks the beginning of the horror phase of the film: From here on first Stan and then all the Gallaghers become the prey of Alex (now pregnant), though to what end is not at first clear. The threats, the stalking, the feints and diversions build unbearably until at last all hell breaks out in the Gallaghers' new country home. Not once, but twice. Then there is silence and human wreckage in plenty.

Fatal Attraction brilliantly exploits those two audience magnets, sex and violence. The sexuality is cannily managed to be harder than soft porn but intricate enough to be fascinating. The violence, when it comes, is unrestrained.

Compelling, sleek, modern and witty as the film is, it may leave some viewers feeling queasy about what it seems to be saying about men and women. Alex, for instance, is presented, for the first 15 or 20 minutes as a perfectly rational woman who asks important questions about sexual responsibility between lovers, married or not. But those intelligent questions are rendered trivial by the suddenness with which she is transformed into a madwoman and by the heavy-handed reiteration of a code of morality forged in a Victorian smithy: Marriage is sacrosanct! Strayers beware!

FATHER ALEXEY'S STORY   Short Story
Ivan Turgenev
U.S.S.R.
1887; translated 1921 by Constance Garnett in *The Two Friends and Other Stories*, London, Heinemann.

Father Alexey, the priest who is the second and significant narrator of this poignant and finally petrifying tale, is described as having "such a look of sadness and complete detachment—such a look of being utterly 'broken', as it is called . . ."

Father Alexey, we learn, has fathered eight children (a priest of the Russian Orthodox rite is permitted to marry), but almost all of them died in their infancy. One son, however, grew up to become a bishop while another, Yakov, was something of an intellectual child prodigy, more or less constantly immersed in his books. Father Alexey tells us that when Yakov was 10 he came home one day and reported that he had "met a green old man . . ." Father Alexey put the story down to the exuberance of a child's imagination and forgot the matter.

When Yakov grows up, his scholarly promise is fulfilled and he scores highly enough on national examinations to be admitted to medical school. It is while Yakov is in medical school in Moscow that disaster strikes. When he comes home for his first vacation, his father says, "I hardly knew my Yakov. He had become so depressed, so gloomy . . ." In short, the change in his son is so radical that when Yakov, after a second short stay in Moscow, returns home and abjures all further studies, his father is not entirely surprised.

When he questions his son closely, Yakov finally tells his father that for the past four months he has been seeing "him," Satan, the man in green, and that "he" is continually present now in his life.

From here on, we are in a very early version of *The Exorcist.* Yakov's struggle to resist the fiend is fierce. "Only imagine; his [Yakov's] face was as red as copper, he was foaming at the mouth, his voice was hoarse as though someone was suffocating him!" But in the nature of things, mortals are poor combatants against Satan unless they have the help of God, and Yakov is persuaded not only to abjure the Lord, but actually to revile Him. The result is predictably awful.

What makes Turgenev's story both memorable and important is the way that, in the eighties of the last century, well before the appearance of the cast of mind we call "modern," this tale of satanic possession subtly suggests that it is not so much Satan who is doing the possessing as a satanic aspect of Yakov's self.

THE FEARLESS VAMPIRE KILLERS   Film
1967   (C)   Great Britain   107 min.
Production Company: Cadre Films/Filmways; ***Director:*** Roman Polanski; ***Producer:*** Gene Gutowski; ***Screenplay:*** Gerald Brach, Roman Polanski; ***Photography:*** Douglas Slocombe; ***Editor:*** Alastair McIntyre; ***Choreography:*** Tutte Lemkow; ***Music:*** Krzysztof Komeda.
Cast: Jack MacGowran (Professor Ambronsius), Roman Polanski (Alfred), Alfie Bass (Shagal), Jessie Robbins (Shagal's wife), Sharon Tate (Sarah), Ferdy Mayne (Count Von Krolock), Iain Quarrier (Herbert).

There is nothing that Roman Polanski touches that he does not in some way make beautiful. Here, in what is meant to be a gentle spoof of the vampire film genre, there are so many lovely moments that one's attention shifts smoothly from a contemplation of the simply amusing to an appreciation of greatness.

As Polanski and Brach tell their story, Professor Ambronsius, formerly of the University of Königsberg, and his assistant Alfred are in Transylvania on a vampire exterminating mission. Professor Ambronsius, who is meant to be a mock version of Bram Stoker's Dr. Van Helsing in the novel *Dracula,* is played to look as much as possible like a twitchy Einstein, while Freddy is the perfectly inept servant of an inept master. The vampire they are after is Count Von Krolock who, with his homosexual vampire son, lives in a castle overlooking the village.

Let me describe briefly three of the great moments in this beguiling film. Early on, we see an open, snow-covered clearing in a forest through which a horse-drawn sledge is passing. As the camera comes closer and closer, it picks up a trail of bright, gleaming red droplets on the snow. The scene is so gentle, so soft, so white and bright, that it takes a while before we register that the beauty we are enthralled by is the result of blood dripping from a corpse on the sledge.

Much later in the film, we find Shagal, the recently vampirized Jewish innkeeper, mounting the stairs to Sarah's room. Shagal, it should be said, is a caricature of a caricature of a clumpy, sordid Jew and Sarah is the beautiful gentile he has always lusted for. As he pushes open Sarah's door and shuffles in, Sarah looks up and, glimpsing Shagal's fangs, knows at once what she must deal with and reaches for the crucifix hanging on the wall above her head.

And it is here that Shagal utters the punch line that will resound down the ages for vampire filmlovers: "Oy, lady," says Shagal in his best Yiddish accent, "Oy, lady, hev you got the wrong vampire."

Finally, one must note the exquisite danse macabre that Polanski intrudes much later into his story, probably for no better reason than to seize one more occasion to create delight.

As the film is about to end, and the heroine has been rescued and the screen is aglow with self-congratulation, we get a sudden reversal that proves that evil is at least as ingenious and certainly more tenacious than good.

A word about that Jewish vampire. I would suggest that that scene is so busy satirizing each of its elements, including anti-Semitism, that only the touchiest strict constructionist will find anti-Semitism in it. After all, Polanski, too, would qualify as "the wrong vempire."

The Fearless Vampire Killers, in Polanski's hands, is a superlative fusion of comedy with fear. Polanski's two great gifts are compassion and an artist's imaginative eye. When he turns his characters loose to bumble about in a vampire story, the result is high comedy sporting affectionately with Grand Guignol. The painter Chagall, whom Polanski obviously admires, would have loved this film.

THE FLY
Short Story

George Langelaan
Belgium
1957, in *Playboy;* reprinted 1979 in Leonard Wolf's (ed.) *Wolf's Complete Book of Terror,* New York, Clarkson N. Potter.

At the start of this quietly chilling tale, the basis for two film versions (1958, 1986) of the story, the first-person narrator, M. Delambre, gets a phone call at two o'clock in the morning from his sister-in-law Helene informing him that she has just killed her husband. But there is more to that phone call than merely murder.

Since at first there is no explanation forthcoming as to why Helene killed her husband Andre, she is admitted to a mental hospital. Here she is a very quiet patient whose favorite pastime seems to be to catch flies, though she foregoes this activity when her small son Henri visits her.

What the narrator and Inspector Charas, a local police official, eventually learn from Helene's confession (before she commits suicide) is that Andre in the course of his researches found a way to transmit matter across space by separating it into its component atoms. In the course of his experiments he transmitted various objects, then animals. Finally, he undertook to transmit himself. In the course of that experiment a fly got into the transmitting device. Somehow, when Andre's atoms were reconstituted, it turned out that he had acquired the fly's head, and where one arm had been there was now a fly's leg. When an accident reveals Andre's new appearance, Helene sees:

> that dreadful white hairy head with its low flat skull and its two pointed ears. Pink and moist, the nose was also that of a cat, a huge cat. But the eyes! Or rather, where the eyes should have been were two brown bumps the size of saucers. Instead of a mouth, animal or human, was a long hairy vertical slit from which hung a black quivering trunk that widened at the end, trumpet-like and from which saliva kept dripping.

It was Andre's decision, to put his head and arm into the steam hammer manipulated by Helene, that killed him.

And now, the only proof that Helene has told the truth depends on the discovery of the fly that has Andre's head.

The truth is eventually forthcoming, but in Langelaan's fiction the denouement of the tale is weak because merely stated. In the 1958 film based on the story, the event is made so graphic that it transforms a moderately interesting film into a great one.

This harsh and horrid story has the most matter of fact narrative style. There is no straining for effect; there are no decorative flourishes. Instead, there are only the facts, and those are so horrifying that we quite believe Helene when she says:

> "I . . . have today but one hope: that when I die, I really die, and that there may be no after-life of any sort because, if there is, then I shall never forget . . ."

Nor, I think, will any reader.

THE FLY
Film

1958 (C) U.S.A. 94 min.
Production Company: 20th Century-Fox; *Director:* Kurt Neumann; *Producer:* Kurt Neumann; *Screenplay:* James Clavell; *Photography:* Karl Struss; *Editor:* Merrill G. White; *Special Effects:* L.B. Abbott; *Music:* Paul Sawtell.
Cast: Vincent Price (François), Al Hedison (André), Patricia Owens (Helene), Herbert Marshall (Inspector Charas), Charles Herbert (Philippe).

Throughout most of its 94 minutes, this first and endearingly modest version of George Langelaan's short story "The Fly" is so lugubriously faithful to its original that one begins to wonder why it was thought necessary to make the film at all. The film has only four or five sets on which sedentary, talk-filled scenes doggedly follow each other. But then, in its final moments the film seems to rouse itself and, in a scene that is only hinted at in the story, it makes its single and successful leap to greatness.

The story (exept for a couple of differences that will shortly be noted) is pretty much the way Langelaan tells it: There is André, the research scientist, who has discovered a way to transmit matter from one place to another. In the course of transmitting himself, his atoms and those of a fly, which has accidentally gotten into the transmitter with him, are min-

Searching for the fly with the white head. © 20th Century-Fox

gled. The result is that he comes out of the receiving end of the apparatus partially transformed into a fly while the fly, with its white, human head goes buzzing off in dismay.

André's wife, Helene, is the self-sacrificing soul who, to keep her husband from shame, accepts the responsibility for his death, and François is the decent brother who helps Inspector Charas clear up the mystery of his brother's death.

Hollywood, avid to have something upbeat in this grimmest of grim stories, saves Helene from suicide and plants the not very vigorous idea in the viewer's mind that she and François will somehow jog on through life together.

What is notable about this film, besides its magnificent final scene, is the extraordinary cleanliness of everyone in it. Both Vincent Price (François) and Herbert Marshall (Inspector Charas) wear suits that look as if they have just been delivered by a Savile Row tailor. Even Philippe, Helene and André's eight-year-old son, hasn't a mussed hair in sight.

THE FLY

1986   (C)   U.S.A.   96 min.
Production Company: Brooksfilms; *Director:* David Cronenberg; *Producer:* Stuart Cornfeld; *Screenplay:* Charles Edward Pogue, David Cronenberg; *Photography:* Mark Irwin; Editor: Richard Sanders; *Special Effects:* Fly design by Chris Wallas Inc.; *Music:* Howard Shore.
Cast: Jeff Goldblum (Seth Brundle), Geena Davis (Veronica), John Getz (Stathus Borans).

This remake of the 1958 film based on George Langelaan's short story is something of a problem for the filmgoer who has read the Langelaan short story or seen the earlier film featuring Vincent Price. Langelaan's tale is low-key, unemotional and memorable chiefly for its plot. The 1958 film rather doggedly follows Langelaan but achieves a truly shattering climax by presenting us with an overwhelming single image. This 1986 version keeps only the core of Langelaan's plot and moves sensationally beyond the limits of all that is hideous, revolting and loathsome.

In the Cronenberg-Pogue screenplay, we have a quickly established love triangle: Seth Brundle is a research scientist who has developed a machine that can reduce matter to its atomic components and then reconstitute and transport it electrically from one place to another. Brundle falls in love with Veronica, a magazine reporter whose former lover, Stathus Borans, is, coincidentally, the editor-in-chief of the magazine for which she works. Borans, because he still loves Veronica, behaves very badly to her and Brundle.

Seth, as Jeff Goldblum plays him, is in the first half of the film an altogether engaging young man of the sort that Veronica would be an absolute idiot not to fall in love with. She is not an idiot, and before very long she and Seth play out some charming love scenes. However, when Seth, who cannot carry his liquor well, realizes that Veronica and Stathus were once a couple, he goes on a jealous drunk in the course of which he puts himself through his machinery. He is oblivious to the fact that a fly has entered the pod with him, and that the computer that controls the process has fused the fly's atomic structure with his own.

And now David Cronenberg, who is the most inventive of the younger generation of horror filmmakers, allows his creative genius to be influenced by the special effects designers as camera tricks and remarkable animated models overshadow both his story and his theme. The effects, let it be said, are stunning enough to make the film something of a technological landmark. But they turn a clean, hard tale into a squirming exercise in the baroque as Cronenberg—always brilliantly—follows the transformation of Seth from a winning young scientist into an ever more loathsome, but wise-cracking, cross between a human and a fly. When, finally, only the raw, moist, red essence of fly is left, we sit in the theater begging Veronica, to whom the task has been assigned, to give the creature its quietus.

There is a good deal to admire in this film. There is the absolutely horrifying intrusion into the story of Veronica being pregnant, with God alone knows what sort of monster her lovemaking with Seth has produced; there is Jeff Goldblum's performance, both as the likable Seth Brundle and as the fused Brundle-fly; and there is the lovely design of Brundle's machinery itself. From time to time, there are, too, scraps of pathos that tug at one's heart: the compassionate Veronica hugging the monster Seth has become; or the transformed Seth saying, "I'm an insect who dreamed he was a man and loved it"; and finally, there is the abominable fly-thing mutely begging for its own death.

And yet, what one is left with is a great director's overreaching. We can see just what has been lost by the squandering of so much talent if we compare the final scene in the 1958 film with the crescendo of special effects with which Cronenberg's film ends. In the first case, the climactic image floods our minds with meaning; in the second, our problem is how to keep our dinner down.

FOOTSTEPS IN THE SNOW   Short Story

Mario Soldati
Italy
1965, in Raleigh Trevelyan's (ed.) *Italian Short Stories*, London, Penguin.

Here is a tale that, for the longest time, seems to be a horror story only in the sense that the protagonist's personal situation, a brutally grimy marriage, is about as bad as it can be. Then we follow him as he retraces his steps to the grounds of a villa in Turin and to a particular magnolia tree under which, 30 years before, he had embraced Lina, the first and, finally, the only great love of his life. Loving Lina

> had been a sudden, complete, gratuitous happiness . . . Due to the simple fact that he was no longer embracing himself, but another person, he seemed to be embracing the infinite.

But he had let Lina slip away from him and now, 30 years later, he returns to that same magnolia tree on the snow-clad grounds of the villa. And it is there, near the tree, just after nightfall, that he hears "the sound of a light footstep in the snow . . ." What happens then is, on the one hand, a certain kind of fulfillment, and, on the other, the clearest demonstration that horror has been, and continues to be, the texture of his life.

"Footsteps in the Snow," even in translation, has a gossamer delicacy utterly unexpected in a tale of horror. Soldati's prose, deeply rooted in experience, is persuasive at every moment, and the skill with which he links the bleakness of the narrator's life to the supernatural moment that overtakes him is elegant. His story is nearly as frail and romantic as Ann Bridge's ''The Buick Saloon'' and it is just as memorable.

THE FORTRESS UNVANQUISHABLE Short Story
SAVE FOR SACNOTH

Lord Dunsany

Ireland

1908, in *The Sword of Welleran and Other Stories*, London, George Allen; reprinted 1972 in E.F. Bleiler's (ed.) *Gods, Men and Ghosts, The Best Supernatural Fiction of Lord Dunsany*, New York, Dover.

Considering how fake is the surcharged rhetoric of this story, it is a pure wonder that the reader finally just gives up and succumbs to its spell. It is a prose invented for the telling of glorious events that have never been and may never be, high-hearted deeds in unimaginable places, with the deeds, the language and the events vaguely related to what we remember of epics more or less Arthurian. The secret of the prose, the reason that one finally tolerates it—no, actually even delights in it—is, I think, that Dunsany loves it and croons its rhythms to us with the conviction of a child enchanted with the secret meanings of its own prattle.

> Now in the time I tell of, there was trouble in Allathurion, for of an evening fell dreams were wont to come slipping though the tree trunks and into the peaceful village; and they assumed dominion of men's minds and led them in watches of the night through the cindery plains of Hell.

Now these fell dreams are the work of Gaznak, a terrible magician who lives in an invincible fortress which may not be vanquished except by the sword Sacnoth. And that sword does not yet exist because it lies ''in the hide of Thagavverug, protecting his spine.''

The young hero Leothric undertakes to find and kill Thagavverug, the dragon-crocodile whose:

> back is of steel and his under parts are of iron; but along the midst of his back, over his spine, there lies a narrow strip of unearthly steel. This strip of steel is Sacnoth.

The marvel and the horror of this story is in the description of the two great battles Leothric fights: the first with Thagavverug in which he is armed only with a great hazel stick with which he must beat the dragon's leaden nose to keep him from his food; and the second when, armed with the sword Sacnoth which he has taken from the body of Thagavverug, he fights the magician Gaznak in The Land Where No Man Goeth in his ''Fortress Unvanquishable, Save for Sacnoth.''

As Leothric smites the Porte Resonant of the fortress with his sword, Sacnoth:

> the echo of Sacnoth went ringing through the halls, and all the dragons in the fortress barked. And when the baying of the remotest dragon had faintly joined in the tumult, a window opened far up among the clouds below the twilit gables, and a woman screamed, and far away in Hell her father heard her and knew that her doom was come.

But that is only a presage. The battle between Leothric and Gaznak is long and circumstantial and, at its climax, macabre.

> Presently Leothric smote fair and fiercely at his enemy's neck, but Gaznak, clutching his own head by the hair, lifted it high

aloft, and Sacnoth went cleaving through an empty space. Then Gaznak replaced his head upon his neck . . .

The battle goes on and gets both more wonderful and more bloody before it ends. And if, when we come to the close of this fine fairy tale for grownups we are tempted to sniff skeptically and to agree with those who ''say that there hath been no town of Allathurion, and that Leothric never lived,'' then Dunsany has anticipated us. ''. . . who shall say,'' he asks, ''what hath befallen in the days of long ago?''

The answer, no doubt, is Dunsany himself.

THE FOURTH MAN Film
(Alternate release title: **DE VIERDE MAN**)

1983 (C) Holland 95 min.

Production Company: Spectrafilm; ***Director:*** Paul Verhoeven; ***Producer:*** Rob Houwer; ***Screenplay:*** Gerard Soeteman; ***Photography:*** Jan de Bout; ***Editor:*** Ine Schenkkan; ***Special Effects:*** Hennie van den Akker, Harrie Weissenhaan, Aad van Westen, Leo Cahn; ***Music:*** Loek Dikker.

Cast: Jeroen Krabbé (Gerard Reve), Renee Soutendijk (Christine), Ron Hoffman (Herman).

Gerard Reve, a writer who says of himself, ''I lie the truth,'' and whom we see, as the film opens, having a violent dream, is invited to give a lecture to a literary society. There he meets a fascinating and beautiful woman named Christine who immediately offers him her quite extravagantly beautiful body. Christine, who owns a cosmetics business and is very wealthy, has been widowed three times and, we are given to understand, is a sort of black widow spider. The tip-off is the malfunctioning sign on The Sphinx, her cosmetics salon. It shows the word ''SPIN,'' which in Dutch means spider.

Christine confides to Gerard that she has another lover, Herman, who has problems with premature ejaculation, and she invites Gerard to meet Herman and to help him overcome his disability.

When Gerard and Herman meet they are immediately attracted to each other. By now, Gerard who has come upon a set of home movies showing the deaths of Christine's previous husbands, is convinced that she is part spider, part Delilah figure who draws men to her and then in some way is responsible for their deaths. In an extraordinary homosexual love scene, set in the tomb of Christine's third husband, Gerard tells Herman, ''One of us is the fourth husband.'' Herman's death not long after this is memorably violent.

Skillfully contrived, skillfully developed, *The Fourth Man* is at intervals spectacularly visual. Statuary and architecture, the sheen of dark hair, the excitement of a spider as she moves through her web toward her kill keep the eye constantly engaged. One image, a crucified Christ wearing jockey shorts through which an erection shows, is so violently tactless that, for a moment, it shakes our confidence in the director's judgment. But if one can get beyond that moment, the film's succcess derives from the way that it touches on nearly every aspect of permissive sexuality and links it to the moral and spiritual emptiness of the world in which these gleaming and delicious young people live. Though *The Fourth Man* is not really a cautionary fable it comes close to providing us with an elegantly bleak map of the contemporary wasteland.

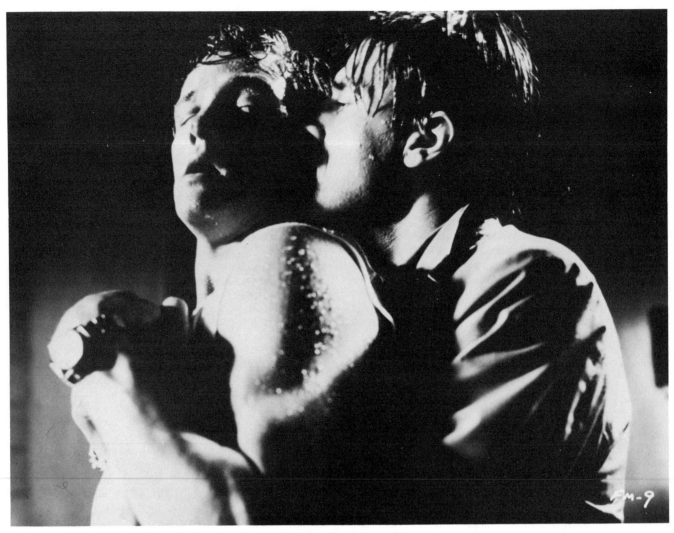

Jeroen Krabbé and Tom Hoffman in **The Fourth Man.** © International Spectrafilm

THE FOX WOMAN AND
THE BLUE PAGODA

Novel

Abraham Merritt and Hannes Bok
U.S.A.
1946, New York, New Collectors Group; reprinted 1976, New York, Arno.

This truly bizarre semi-posthumous novel was begun by A. Merritt and was completed and illustrated by Hannes Bok. It is a curious amalgam of styles and influences in which the oriental folklore of fox women is at the center of a plot set in America in the mid-20th century.

Charles Meredith sends hired *hung-hutzes,* Chinese assassins, to kill his wealthy brother Martin and his pregnant wife Jean in the Yunan highlands of China so that he can inherit his brother's wealth. This action sets in motion a wheel of vengeance that, many years later, results in his bloody destruction in the foothills of southern California.

Though the assassins succeed in killing Martin, Jean is saved at the penultimate moment by a magic-wielding fox woman who discomfits the assassins. Later, Jean dies in childbirth but her vow of vengeance against her brother-in-law is so powerful that the spirit of the fox-woman enters into her infant daughter who is raised by a sage, Yu Ch'ien, the chief votary in the Temple of the Foxes. Seventeen or eighteen years later, that daughter, now in New York and called variously Yin Hu, or Jean, begins to carry out her mother's vow of vengeance against Charles Meredith, his wife and their accomplices.

That vengeance becomes complicated when she falls in love with Paul Lascelles, son of one of Charles Meredith's evil accomplices. Nevertheless, as Yin Hu, the magic-endowed avenger, she destroys her enemies one by one, invoking in the process the help of forces of evil to which half a dozen cultures have given various names. Occasionally, as Jean Meredith, she is simply a beautiful young woman in love.

The style of the novel is a wonderful if slightly tin-eared amalgam of the rhetorical flourishes of thirties and forties pulp fiction modified (read "inflated") by Merritt/Bok's gran-

The Fox Woman (drawing by Hannes Bok).

diosities. Yet, even with the novel's pretentious prose, horror literature has few scenes more petrifying than the outrageous danse macabre that takes place in the Manhattan Museum of Art in which the dancers are statues of the Winged Victory, Laocoon and his sons, Athena Parthenos, Aphrodite and the Athlete by Lysippos. It is a scene that culminates in the appalling and death-dealing sexual union between the nine-foot-tall stone statue of the Athlete and Margot, Charles Meredith's wife.

What we have, finally, is a fiction with the swagger of sword and sorcery novels, the exoticism of oriental folklore and a curiously believable and touching heroine who is part demon and part sweet young woman who lives next door.

FRANKENSTEIN
Or, The Modern Prometheus
Mary Shelley

Novel

Great Britain 1818, London, Lackington, Hughes, Harding, Mavor & Jones; reprinted repeatedly, but see James Rieger's (ed.) *Frankenstein*, Indianapolis, Bobbs Merrill, 1974; and Leonard Wolf's (ed.) *The Annotated Frankenstein*, New York, Clarkson N. Potter, 1977.

By now, nearly two centuries after Mary Shelley's novel was written, the name ''Frankenstein,'' in the popular imagination, has become associated with the hulking, anguished and angular creature we see stumbling about in James Whale's 1931 movie. The film and its descendants have as their theme

the dangers of unbridled scientific research. The novel has an altogether more personal focus. *Frankenstein* does not touch us because Victor Frankenstein is a scientist but because his creature was born ugly, because Victor abandoned him, because the creature's life is spent in a long, long pilgrimage toward his father/mother's love.

In the 1831 edition of *Frankenstein,* Mary Shelley describes how she, ''a young girl came to think of, and to dilate upon, so very hideous an idea. . . .'' It happened, she says, on a rainy night in Geneva in June of 1816 when Byron, his physician, John Polidori, and Percy Shelley and Mary Godwin sat together whiling away the evening in Byron's home, the Villa Diodati. At some point they talked about a collection of German horror tales that had lately appeared in a French translation, *Les Fantasmagoriana.* It was then that Byron suggested that each of them should write a ghost story. The idea was well received but of the four, only Mary Shelley actually finished the work that the conversation in Geneva stirred in her, though it was some days before she actually had a coherent sense of how to begin. Then, lying in bed with her eyes closed, she saw ''. . . the pale student of unhallowed arts kneeling beside the thing he had put together. I saw the hideous phantasm of a man stretched out. . . .''

The novel begun that summer of 1816 was finished on April 17, 1817, when Mary Shelley was four months pregnant with her third child. That baby, a girl, was born on September 2 in London and died on September 24 in Venice. *Frankenstein* was published anonymously by Lackington and Hughes on March 11, 1818. *Blackwood's Magazine* gave the book a positive review, but when the sex of its author became known, it wrote that, ''for a man it was excellent, but for a woman it was wonderful.''

Frankenstein is presented in the form of a series of letters written by a young sailor, William Walton, to his sister, Mrs. Saville, in England. The first letters are from St. Petersburg in Russia. It is December in the year 17—, and Walton is about to undertake a voyage of exploration in the vicinity of the North Pole. His goal, which he hopes will bring him honor and glory, is to discover the Northeast Passage. We learn, too, that next to fame, Walton has another burning desire:

''. . . I have one want which I have never yet been able to satisfy . . . I have no friend, Margaret. . . .''

In subsequent letters from Archangel, we learn that Walton has equipped a vessel and hired a crew; that he is fully embarked on his voyage of exploration. Then, in his letter dated the following August we learn that his vessel is icebound in the northern latitudes and that his voyage is on the brink of disaster.

The tale within this framing tale is now introduced as Walton describes his encounter with an exhausted Victor Frankenstein whom Walton's sailors have rescued from the ice. As Walton's Letter Four ends, we get the rest of the novel in the form of Victor Frankenstein's story, transcribed by Walton ''as nearly as possible in [the dying Victor's] own words.''

We learn that Victor is a Swiss, a citizen of Geneva who, when he was 17, went to study at the University of Ingolstadt, in Germany. There, at the age of 19 he undertook certain researches that led him finally to the discovery ''of the cause of generation and life; nay, more, I became myself capable of bestowing animation upon lifeless matter.'' Then:

> on a dreary night of November . . . I beheld the accomplishment of my toils. With an anxiety that almost amounted to agony, I collected the instruments of life around me, that I might infuse a spark of being into the lifeless thing that lay at my feet. It was already one in the morning . . . when, by the glimmer of the half-extinguished light, I saw the dull yellow eye of the creature open; it breathed hard, and a convulsive motion agitated its limbs.

Thus was the creature born. But though it was designed to be beautiful, it turns out to be so loathesome that Victor rushes from sight of it to his own room where he dreams that he is embracing the worm-eaten corpse of his mother. When he wakes from that dream, he finds the creature standing at his bedside. Once again, he flies from its presence.

In the midst of his distress, Victor is visited by his friend Henry Clerval, whose presence both distracts and calms him. Together, the two men pass the summer studying languages until Victor receives a letter from his father in Geneva telling him that his little brother, William, has been murdered. Victor hastens to Geneva to console his father and his cousin Elizabeth who is also his intended bride. In Geneva, though he is convinced that it was the creature who killed his brother, he maintains a guilty silence as Justine, a loyal young servant of his family, is charged, tried, convicted and hanged for the murder.

As Volume II of the fiction begins, we find Victor wandering disconsolately in the Sea of Ice near Chamonix in the French Alps. There, he encounters his creature who compels him to listen to an account of all that has happened to him since they last met.

That account forms the second tale-within-a-tale of the novel. The creature, as Mary Shelley depicts him, is anything but the mute monster we know from the movies. He is a sensitive, extremely voluble (even garrulous) figure, full of high moral aspirations, who has a sense of the wrongs Victor has done him. He blames the evils he has committed on his isolation and despair: ''My vices are the children of a forced solitude that I abhor; and my virtues will necessarily arise when I live in communion with an equal.''

As he ends his narrative, the creature makes very clear what he wants. First, he wants Victor to behave toward him like a parent. And then, and here, we move to the sexual center of Mary Shelley's plot: He wants Victor to recognize that, having made him loathesome and oversized, he, the creature, is doomed to a horrid chastity. Now, in the environment of the Sea of Ice he says:

The Sea of Ice where Victor and the Creature meet.

Illustration from Nino Carbe's **Frankenstein.**

> "I demand a creature of another sex, but as hideous as myself
> . . . It is true, we shall be monsters, cut off from all the world;
> but on that account we shall be more attached to one another
> . . . Oh! my creator, make me happy . . ."

Reluctantly, Victor agrees but, as Volume II ends, his promise to the creature weighs so heavily on him that his mental balance is affected:

> a kind of insanity possessed me . . . I saw continually about
> me a multitude of filthy animals inflicting on me incessant
> torture that often extorted screams and bitter groans.

As we begin Volume III, Mary Shelley's dark novel grows darker still as the theme of Victor's approaching marriage to Elizabeth is linked to the awful union proposed by the creature at the end of Volume II. But first Victor, who dreads both nuptials, accepts his father's suggestion that he should travel for a couple of years before marrying his cousin Elizabeth. He and Henry Clerval go off on a journey that will take them through Europe and England.

In Scotland, Victor and Henry separate and Victor travels to the Orkney Islands where, in a sheepherder's shack, he sets up once more a "workshop of filthy creation" and there he starts to make the monster bride he has promised the creature, but at the very moment of his success, he is assailed by qualms:

> I thought with a sensation of madness on my promise of
> creating another like to him, and, trembling with passion, tore
> to pieces the thing on which I was engaged.

The act of destruction has been witnessed by the creature who tells Victor:

> "It is well. I go; but remember, I shall be with you on your
> wedding-night."

From that moment on, the narrative line of the novel, though it includes the creature's murder of Henry Clerval and Elizabeth, turns flat at the same time as the "Frankenstein" story merges with the William Walton narrative. Curiously enough, though the events Mary Shelley describes are banal, the texture of meaning in the fiction becomes increasingly dense. We see Victor and the creature performing a strange and symbiotic dance around each other over many months on the barren tundras and the ice floes of the Polar latitudes. By then the two of them have become moral equivalents of each other and it is no longer possible to tell the tormentor from his victim, the pursuer from the pursued, the good from the evil.

By then, too, we understand that ice is Mary Shelley's controlling metaphor. The narrative that began in ice, that reached one climax at the Sea of Ice at Chamonix, comes now to its icy end. Cold, white, immobile, fragile and hard, ice in this fiction stands for constricted feelings; for lack of responsibility; for parental indifference; for sexual coldness; for lack of generosity; for an ego so vast as to be nearly sublime.

I continue to find congenial Muriel Spark's remark that "a novel need not be mighty in order to be vital; it need not be a product of genius to survive as a classic." *Frankenstein* is not "mighty." It has stick-figure characterizations, a frequently lugubrious plot, and it makes relentless use of coincidence. Just the same one can claim greatness for a book that has such an intensely imagined vision that it leaves us with a sense of revelation about the mystery of love. About ice. About, finally, the cold, the "zero at the bone."

FRANKENSTEIN   Film

1931 (B&W) U.S.A. 71 min.
Production Company: Universal; ***Director:*** James Whale; ***Producer:*** Carl Laemmle, Jr.; ***Screenplay:*** Garrett Fort, Francis Edward Faragoh, Robert Florey; ***Photography:*** Arthur Edeson; ***Editor:*** Clarence Koster; ***Special Effects:*** John P. Fulton, Kenneth Strickfaden, Frank Grove, Raymond Lindsay; ***Music:*** David Broekman.
Cast: Colin Clive (Henry Frankenstein), Boris Karloff (The Monster), Mae Clarke (Elizabeth), John Boles (Victor), Edward Van Sloan (Dr. Waldman), Dwight Frye (Fritz), Frederick Kerr (the baron).

This is the film that has established, probably for all time, our image of the Frankenstein creature: Boris Karloff, tall, lurching, mute, shabbily clad, a humanlike thing with a square head and electronic pegs sticking out of his neck and a baffled look on his face. We remember him best in the great scene in which, still giddy, still scarred by his newly acquired life, he stands, with his arms raised. His hands tremble as he tries to seize what some dim instinct tells him is important: light. An effulgence, a mystery.

It is unlikely that anyone, by now, does not know the film story of Frankenstein, which, the reader should be warned, is very far from being even a vaguely faithful recreation of Mary Shelley's novel. In its own terms, however, it is an utterly triumphant film.

The film opens on a funeral in a graveyard in a mountainous, German-speaking country. As the mourners leave the cemetery, the camera finds Henry Frankenstein and his humpbacked assistant Fritz who have been lurking in the shadows and who now disinter the body and cart it away with them.

Later, we meet Elizabeth, Henry's fiancée, and Victor, his friend. Both of them are worried about Henry who is engaged in secret, and apparently dangerous research. Professor Waldman, Henry's former teacher says, "Herr Frankenstein was interested in human life. First to destroy it, then, to recreate it."

Back in Henry's laboratory in a ruined old mill, what Henry is up to becomes much clearer. He is putting together bits and pieces of dead people in order to create one being that will live. The trouble is that, unknown to Henry, Fritz has stolen a criminal brain for him from Dr. Waldman's laboratory.

The worried Elizabeth, accompanied by Victor and Dr. Waldman, shows up at the laboratory in the midst of a tumultuous thunderstorm. When Waldman seems to scoff at Henry's ambition to create a living being, Henry cries, "Crazy am I. We'll see whether I'm crazy or not . . . I have discovered the great ray that first brought life into the world."

The next seven or eight minutes, in which Henry completes his experiment before the skeptical eyes of Dr. Waldman, Victor and Elizabeth, are among the most satisfying sequence of scenes ever to appear on film. Overhead, the storm rages. There is thunder and jagged lightning. The machinery of the laboratory creaks, squeals and groans. Then Henry, hectic with ambition, presides over the raising of the gurney on which the swathed body magnificently charged with possibility rises toward the night and the howling storm. Our eyes are riveted to the birthplace high above everyone's head where thunder alternates with incalculable voltages of lightning to imitate birth pangs never witnessed before.

Then, something like a dazed silence as the gurney is lowered. An exhausted Henry leans against the creature, anguished with expectation—for success or for disappointment. An instant goes by, then Henry catches the movement of the creature's right hand and he utters a cry, "It's alive. It's alive." It is a moment as well known in film history as the one in which Bela Lugosi as Dracula observes, "I do not drink—wine."

Dr. Waldman, though he is impressed with Henry's achievement, says nevertheless, "You have created a monster and it will destroy you." The rest of the film consists of a series of scenes that demonstrate how nearly right he is. We see the creature mistreated by Fritz, who is jealous of him. When he kills Fritz, Henry, who is now preoccupied with getting married, is persuaded to let Dr. Waldman destroy his creation by re-dissecting the creature.

But the creature has an agenda of his own. He breaks loose, and when he does, we catch our breath. Partly it is because we hope that he will somehow find his place in the world, but mostly it is because we know that he will not. The climactic disaster comes very soon when he meets Maria, the little girl who gives him the gift of the only laughter he will ever know. It is a scene drenched in pathos and yet it is carved out of the most enduring raw material of myth: two innocents, one of whom tragically misperceives the other, reaching for love.

Frankenstein is not, however, a seamless success in all respects. Along with the moments of incomparable grandeur, we have to put up with Colin Clive's passive hysteria, John Boles' look of perplexity as he tries to understand what he is doing in the film, and Mae Clarke's unsubtle rendering of devotion. On the other hand there is Boris Karloff's flawless performance and Jack Pierce's makeup. There are, too, those great, gloomy sets, which, though they make no pretense at realism, afford fine, stylized backgrounds for the drama unfolding before them.

Finally, there is James Whale's direction. Except for the romantic scenes involving Henry and Elizabeth, Whale attends to the details of the story with preternatural skill. He is alert to the smallest gestures by which people assert their humanity, as for instance, in the priceless moment when the shabby, devoted hunchback, Fritz, admits Elizabeth, Victor and Doctor Waldman into Henry's ruined mill and starts up a flight of stone stairs in response to his master's call. He shambles up a step or two, then, aware of the visitors behind him, he pauses, bends and swiftly pulls up his ragged sock. That guarding of his dignity establishes his presence in the drama. As a consequence, we are ready to understand Fritz later, when he torments the creature. Though what he is doing is ugly, anyone who has ever, as a child, felt himself superseded by the arrival of a younger sibling will understand Fritz's despairing jealousy.

Finally and despite its faults, the film is superb. Different as James Whale's film is from Mary Shelley's book, it retains her central parable about the dangers and disasters of paternal irresponsibility. Mary Shelley makes her point with a talkative, literate and philosophically glib creature. Whale, following the lead of the stage play by Peggy Webling on which he based his film, keeps his creature mute.

FREAKS   Film
1932 (B&W) U.S.A. 64 min.
Production Company: MGM; *Director:* Tod Browning; *Producer:* Tod Browning; *Screenplay:* Wilis Goldbeck, Leon Gordon, Edgar Allan Woolf; *Photography:* Merrit B. Gerstad; *Editor:* Basil Wrangell.
Cast: Wallace Ford (Phroso), Leila Hyams (Venus), Olga Baclanova (Cleopatra), Roscoe Ates (Roscoe), Henry Victor (Hercules), Harry Earles (Hans), Daisy Earles (Frieda), Rose Dione (Madame Tetralini), Daisy and Violet Hilton (Siamese twins), Schlitze (Schlitze), Josephine Joseph (hermaphrodite), Johnny Eck (half boy), Frances O'Connor (armless girl), Randion (human torso), Zip and Pip (pinheads).

One watches *Freaks*, one of the most macabre and horrifying films ever made, in dazed fascination. And yet, for all its gruesome allure, the film is by no means successful, because Tod Browning made the understandable but fatal error of casting real freaks to play themselves in the film. The result is that, except for a brief sequence at the end, we can not establish any aesthetic distance between ourselves and the

Olga Baclanova in **Freaks.**

actors because we find ourselves responding to their physical deformities with an irresistible prurience that leaves us embarrassed and ashamed.

There is a story in *Freaks* and it is quite touching. Hans, a circus sideshow midget who is engaged to marry Frieda, also a midget, falls in love with the blatantly erotic blonde trapeze artist Cleopatra who, in turn, is in love with Hercules, the circus strong man. Though Freida cautions Hans that ''there is no happiness for you with that woman,'' Hans is too dazzled to see that Cleopatra is only interested in the fortune he has recently inherited. Indifferent to everything but his own passion, he marries her and is soon made ill by the poison that Cleopatra, who means to be a widow soon, administers to him. The circus freaks, who have not been deceived by Cleopatra and Hercules, discover what she is up to and they take an atrocious revenge on them both.

The film, when it turns to that vengeance, enters, briefly, the precincts of high fiction: the ensuing scenes, which take place at night in a driving rainstorm, are as unforgettable as they are macabre. We see the freaks—among them the Half Boy, the armless and legless Human Torso with a knife between his teeth, and the pinhead Schlitze—slithering or crawling through the mud as they track the miscreants, herding them like beasts, Hercules to his death and Cleopatra to an unspeakable transformation.

With all its limitations, *Freaks* has attained a kind of immortality as an example of what happens when a great director makes a monumental error of judgment. He leaves behind a film that squirms with the vitality of incoherence.

FRIDAY THE THIRTEENTH   Film
1980   (C)   U.S.A.   95 min.
Production Company: Georgetown/Paramount; *Director:* Sean S. Cunningham; *Producer:* Sean S. Cunningham; *Screenplay:* Victor Miller; *Photography:* Barry Abrams; *Editor:* Bill Freda; *Special Effects:* Tom Savini; *Music:* Harry Manfredini.
Cast: Betsy Palmer (Mrs. Voorhees), Adrienne King (Alice), Harry Crosby (Bill), Lauri Bertram (Brenda), Mark Nelson (Ned), Kevin Bacon (Jack).

This film, judged only by its plot, is the absolutely model, commercially oriented terror film. Its basic formula is simple: Take a certain number of attractive high school or college age men and women and put them into a dark or shadowy place, then intrude into that erotic setting the presence of a maniac with a knife, an axe or a cleaver. Let the camera caress every shadow for as long as possible while the young people caress each other until the killer kills—brutally, ingeniously, swiftly, spilling as much blood as possible.

In *Friday the Thirteenth,* the formula is applied to a number of young people who have come to be counsellors at Camp Crystal Lake. The camp has been closed for some years following a supposed drowning accident. It is now under new management and the counsellors are readying the place for the arrival of the summer campers. Then one by one they are stalked and killed.

Aside from the elements required by the formula, *Friday the Thirteenth* has a couple of explicit love scenes in the midst of death. In the scene young audiences seem especially to relish, a couple makes love in the lower part of a double bunk while their murdered friend's body in the upper bunk drips gore all over their orgasm.

The film offers one genuine surprise ending then follows it with an anticlimactic second one. Such deliberately ambiguous endings were to become part of the formula for horror films in the eighties.

Speaking of the eighties, which are nearly over, one needs to add that *Friday the Thirteenth* has had six sequels. Clearly, the formula on which the series is based continues to appeal to the youthful audiences for whom the films are made.

FRIDAY THE THIRTEENTH: Film
THE FINAL CHAPTER
1984   (C)   U.S.A.   90 min.
Production Company: Jason Films; *Director:* Joseph Zito; *Producer:* Frank Mancuso, Jr.; *Screenplay:* Barney Cohen, based on story by Bruce Hidemi Sakow; *Photography:* Joao Fernandez; *Editor:* Joel Goodman; *Special Effects:* Tom Savini, Martin Becker; *Music:* Harry Manfredini.
Cast: Crispin Glover (Jimmy), Kimberley Beck (Trish Jarvis), Corey Feldman (Tommy Jarvis), Ted White (Jason), Camilla and Carey More (Tina and Terri).

Jason, who in the preceding film killed seven campers and three hikers, is on his way to the morgue, presumably dead. But his recuperative powers are extraordinary, and he manages to disappear from the refrigerated holding room in which he has been deposited. He heads off, of course, to Crystal Lake, where he can confidently count, once again, on good hunting.

His victims this time are dispatched one right after the other in a very businesslike (and not very imaginative) way. They include a houseful of young renters who have come to Crystal Lake meaning to discover the delights of love in a bucolic setting; their next-door neighbor, a divorcee who lives with Trish, her nubile daughter, and her mechanical genius, 12-year-old son, Tommy.

The camera, according to formula, moves back and forth, interrupting scenes of the young people's erotic adventures, with Jason's single-minded pursuit of his hobby.

Except for the climactic scene in which Trish and Tommy,

who is wearing a plastic mask of his own design, confront Jason in a frenzy of retribution and bloodlust, this "final" chapter is, as the "Fridays" go, fairly anemic. Since "final" is too expensive a word for a moneymaking series, the next "Friday" is called *Friday the Thirteenth: A New Beginning.* That ought to ensure that the cash registers will ring for a long time.

FRIGHT NIGHT   Film

1985   (C)   U.S.A.   106 min.

Production Company: Columbia; *Director:* Tom Holland; *Producer:* Herb Jaffe; *Screenplay:* Tom Holland; *Photography:* Jan Kiesser; *Editor:* Kent Beyda; *Music:* Rad Fiedel.

Cast: Chris Sarandon (Jerry Dandridge), William Ragsdale (Charlie Brewster), Stephen Geoffreys (Evil Ed), Jonathan Stark (Billy Cole), Amanda Bearse (Amy), Roddy McDowall (Peter Vincent).

In form and content, *Fright Night* is just one more made-for-adolescents film, and yet it achieves a certain distinction by the way in which it links ancient vampire lore to life in America in the eighties.

The film's protagonist, a young man named Charlie, becomes slowly aware that the new inhabitants of the house next door to his own keep very strange hours and do very strange things—like receiving delivery of a coffin. Charlie, with the help of a buddy who is unaccountably named "Evil," undertake to investigate the goings on. When, after two mysterious murders have taken place, they try to get help, they run into the usual problem: No one in a well run 20th-century American city will pay attention to anyone, much less an adolescent, who cries "Vampire."

***Chris Sarandon (standing) and Jonathan Stark in* Fright Night.**
© Columbia Pictures

In desperation, they turn for help to a vampire expert, Peter Vincent, who after a certain amount of evasion and refusal, finally joins them in their battle against Jerry Dandridge, the vampire next door, and Billy Cole, his assistant. Charlie's friend Amy is seduced by Dandridge and we are given a quite tender love scene between them—tender, that is, until Dandridge bites and the scene ends in a scream that is part orgasm and part sheer terror. Poor Evil too is vampirized and turns into a wolf, in which form he meets an extremely violent and cinematographically exciting end.

What makes *Fright Night* work so well is the way that it honors its chief inspiration, Bram Stoker's novel *Dracula,* even as it repositions its situations and characters into a 1980s setting. Charlie stands for Jonathan Harker, Peter Vincent is a not quite so noble Van Helsing, Amy stands for Lucy and Mina Harker, Evil is a not nearly so literate Renfield, and Jerry Dandridge is the Dracula next door.

The film's chief weakness, which, at the same time, is its special contribution, is the conception of Jerry Dandridge. Dandridge looks so freshly bathed, so pink and healthy and is such a very acceptable tea-time guest, charming Charlie's mother, that even the viewer has trouble believing him a sinister figure. For a considerable way into the film, he gives the impression that for all of his life he has been posing for ads for suntan lotion or jockey shorts. But perhaps the paradox is the director, Tom Holland's, point. Certainly the scary last 10 minutes of the film leave us in no doubt about how deeply the evil he represents is rooted beneath his fair exterior.

FROM BEYOND THE GRAVE   Film

1973   (C)   Great Britain   98 min.

Production Company: Amicus; *Director:* Kevin Connor; *Producer:* Max J. Rosenberg, Milton Subotsky; *Screenplay:* Robin Clark, Raymond Christodoulou; *Photography:* Alan Hume; *Special Effects:* Alan Bryce.

Cast: Peter Cushing (owner of the Temptations Shop), David Warner (victim of the mirror episode), Ian Bannen (former army officer), Donald Pleasance (match seller).

This quite extraordinary film is really an anthology that tells several stories, all of which have their beginning in a musty secondhand Temptations Shop run by Peter Cushing. One by one, each of several people buys or filches something from the shop: a mirror, a Distinguished Service Medal, a snuff box, a door. In each of the objects, there dwells an evil force that is let loose into the world in a form related to the inner evil of the person who has acquired it.

In the final sequence of the film, a hired clairvoyante, Madame Orloff ("Messages from beyond a specialty"), battles the evil forces. When the house to which she is called is reduced to a shambles, Mme. Orloff dryly observes, "That's a bit of a ruddy mess." Whimsical, energetic, frightening and violent, the ending beats anything in *The Exorcist.*

Despite the film's occasional tongue-in-cheek approach to its themes, the terror is not in any way diminished by the wit. Peter Cushing, who presides over it all while he puffs on a pipe and makes genteel, ambiguous observations in a Scottish accent, is clearly in his element. And the ordinary London hood who means to cosh Cushing gets the end he richly deserves.

THE FUNHOUSE

Film

1981 (C) U.S.A. 96 min.

Production Company: Universal/Mace Neufeld Productions; *Director:* Tobe Hooper; *Producer:* Derek Power, Steven Bernhardt; *Screenplay:* Larry Block; *Photography:* Andrew Laszlo; *Editor:* Jack Hofstra; *Special Effects:* J. B. Jones (animated display creations), Rick Baker (makeup); *Music:* John Beal. *Cast:* Elizabeth Berridge (Amy Harper), Shawn Carson (Joey Harper), Jeanne Austin (Mrs. Harper), Jack McDermott (Mr. Harper), Sylvia Miles (Madame Zena), Cooper Huckabee (Buzz), Kevin Conway (barker).

The Funhouse has all the shabby gloss of the carnival in which, for the most part, it is set. Tobe Hooper, who leaped to fame with *The Texas Chain Saw Massacre,* is not as artful here despite an engrossing chase scene that fully exploits the funhouse methaphor. Hooper's problem, in this film, seems to be his inability to distinguish between moments that are stunning both as events and as symbols and those that are merely startling or macabre. The result is the *The Funhouse's* scenes are uniformly paced, no matter whether they are brilliant, shabby or repulsive.

Once again, we have Hollywood's cash flow formula for a horror film: erotically inclined young people in dark places who are threatened by unspeakable violence. This time, two couples on a double date decide to spend the night inside a carnival funhouse. Little do they know that living in the place is the funhouse owner's son, a sexual psychotic who wears a Frankenstein-creature mask to hide his own more hideous features. The couples watch this drooling and mewling anomaly kill the carnival's fortune-teller. When the owner learns that the murder was seen and that the witnesses are inside the funhouse, he turns his son loose to hunt them down. Hooper is at his best in creating the scenes in which the scuzzy youth stalks his victims through a darkness occasionally pierced by the illuminated, animated funhouse displays that whirr and whistle, turn and shriek, jump and rattle and click. All of this goes on until the splatter film climax when, for five or six minutes, *The Funhouse* turns suddenly splendid. But until then one has to put up with shots of two-headed cows, a two-headed embryo and limp repartee like this:

Young Man A: You asshole.
Young Man B: Who you calling asshole, asshole?

GANJA AND HESS Film
(Alternate release titles: **DOUBLE POSSESSION, BLOOD COUPLE**)

1973 (C) U.S.A. 110 min.

Production Company: Kelly Jordan Enterprises; *Director:* Bill Gunn; *Producer:* Madelene Clark; *Screenplay:* Bill Gunn; *Editor:* Victor Kanefsky; *Music:* Sam Waymon.

Cast: Duane Jones (Dr. Hess Green), Marlene Clark (Ganja Meda), Bill Gunn (George Meda), Sam Waymon (Rev. Luther Williams), Leonard Jackson (Archie).

This is a perplexing, sometimes incoherent and yet artistically ambitious vampire film, with an all-black cast, in which the vampires are defined as victims. But what they are victims of is not quite clear. There seem to be hints that blacks, uprooted from Africa by whites, have in some way either lent themselves to the disease of vampirism or are in danger of becoming vampires because, trapped in white society, they have lost their culture.

As the film opens, we meet a very wealthy anthropologist, Dr. Hess Green, who is taking a young drifter named Meda to his luxurious home in a New York suburb. Meda, a suicide-prone neurotic, shoots himself. Green, coming on the body, bends to drink the spilled blood. When Meda's wife Ganja (now his widow) returns from Europe, she tracks Meda to Green's house and shortly thereafter becomes, first, Green's mistress and then, in an abrupt cut, his wife. In order to spare her life when his bloodlust comes on him, he goes into town where he vampirizes a prostitute, but later Ganja of her own accord allows him to turn her into a vampire.

One guesses that *Ganja and Hess* was meant to be a serious answer to such black exploitation films as *Blacula* (1972) and *Scream Blacula Scream* (1972). But, though the seriousness comes through—there are moments when the photography in *Ganja and Hess* is supremely successful at suggesting dream life and the vertigo of bloodlust—the film fails to become the powerful statement it might have been. The fault may lie in the editing or with the essentially incoherent script.

THE GIRL WITH THE HUNGRY EYES Short Story
Fritz Leiber

U.S.A.

1949, in Donald A. Wollheim's (ed.) *The Girl With the Hungry Eyes and Other Stories,* New York, Avon; reprinted 1987 in Alan Ryan's (ed.) *Vampires,* Garden City, Doubleday.

Though Brian M. Stableford says of "The Girl With the Hungry Eyes" that it is one of "only a few relatively trivial stories" Leiber published in the forties (Bleiler's *Supernatural Fiction Writers,* Vol. II), I think it is a memorable work and really quite successful in elaborating, in the short story format, the theme that George Sylvester Viereck explored in his novel *The House of the Vampire*—that there are other kinds of vampires than those that suck blood.

The story's first-person narrator, an advertising industry photographer, describes meeting and working with an unprepossessing young woman who wants to become his model. Somewhat reluctantly, he takes a few shots of her and is startled the next day to discover that her photographs are precisely the ones his clients want.

From that point on, the young woman's career burgeons and the photographer finds himself overwhelmed with photography assignments involving her.

From the beginning he has been perplexed by the impenetrable mystery that surrounds her. He does not know where she lives. He is forbidden to have any contact with her except for their photography sessions. She will work only in his studio and nowhere else. And very soon he suspects that she is responsible for a series of strange deaths.

As the story ends, we learn that what makes her fascinating to the public, which has responded so emphatically to her photographs, is a knowledge of the human condition that she has acquired by being a vampire of other people's experiences. As the narrator puts it, "I realized that wherever she came from, whatever shaped her, she's the quintessence of the horror behind the bright billboard. She's the smile that tricks you into throwing away your money and your life.

She's the eyes that lead you on and on, and then show you death."

What she feeds on are the experiences—all of them—that give to any life its vitality, its variety and its texture. She is *La Belle Dame Sans Merci,* who wants "your high spots. I want everything that's made you happy and everything that's hurt you bad . . . I want the blue sky filled with stars. I want your mother's death . . . I want your wanting me. I want your life."

GOBLIN MARKET   Verse
Christina Rossetti
Great Britain
1862, in *Goblin Market and Other Poems;* reprinted 1983, New York, Dover.

In Christina Rossetti's "Goblin Market" two maidens, Laura and Lizzie, hear the cry of the goblin men hawking their luscious fruit.

> Laura bowed her head to hear,
> Lizzie veiled her blushes:

But it is clear that the fruit the goblins sell is unearthly and cursed. Laura says:

> "We must not look at goblin men,
> We must not buy their fruits:
> Who knows upon what soil they fed
> Their hungry thirsty roots?"

Lizzie echoes her sister's warning:

> "Their offers should not charm us,
> Their evil gifts would harm us."

But Laura herself, when she encounters the goblin men, is seduced and though she has no money, she gives them a lock of her golden hair in exchange for their fruit, with appalling consequences:

> [She] sucked their fruit globes fair or red:
> Sweeter than honey from the rock,
> Stronger than man-rejoicing wine. . .
> . . . .
> She sucked and sucked and sucked the more
> Fruits which that unknown orchard bore;
> She sucked until her lips were sore.

From that time, she is assailed by a dreadful longing that causes her to pine away for more fruit, but she "never spied the goblin men/Hawking their fruits along the glen." Finally, Lizzie, when it is clear that Laura ". . . dwindling/Seemed knocking at Death's door," goes searching for the gruesome goblin men.

And finds them:

> Lashing their tails
> They trod and hustled her,
> Elbowed and jostled her,
> Clawed with their nails,
> Barking, mewing, hissing, mocking . . .

But,

> "Though the goblins cuffed and caught her,
> Coaxed and fought her . . .",

Lizzie says not a word. More than that. Though the demonic things smear her face with their fruit, she keeps her mouth resolutely closed:

> At last the evil people,
> Worn out by her resistance,
> Flung back her penny . . .

And leave her, stained and smeared with the strange juices of the goblin fruit, alone in the night. Lizzie returns home from that encounter and calls to the pining Laura,

> "Come and kiss me.
> Never mind my bruises,
> Hug me, kiss me, suck my juices . . .
> Eat me, drink me, love me;
> Laura make much of me;
> For your sake I have braved the glen
> And had to do with goblin merchant men."

And Laura:

> Kissed and kissed her with a hungry mouth.
> Her lips began to scorch . . .

Corrosive as the residue of the goblin fruit on Lizzie's face is, it is nevertheless the cure Laura needs and eventually she recovers her health.

Eventually, both the sisters marry and settle down but they remember the season of the goblin fruits and

> . . . talk about the haunted glen,
> The wicked, quaint fruit-merchant men,
> Their fruits like honey to the throat
> But poison in the blood.

"Goblin Market," though it pulsates with sensuality, is pervaded by an ominous dankness that comes, I think, from the indirectness of the poem's focus. The poem's imagery is lascivious to the last degree and yet what are we looking at, after all? Peaches, pears, grapes, cherries, apples and "Plums on their twigs." And that's where the horror lies. In denial. In the passionate denial of passion the evasive mind can be frightened of almost everything, but especially of round fruit, fragrant and juicy.

THE GOLDEN ASS   Novel
(ARISTOMENES' TALE)
Lucius Apuleius
Italy
2nd century A.D.; translated 1566 by William Adlington, London, Henry Wykes; reprinted 1915, Cambridge, Harvard University Press.

The villain of this early horror tale is Meroe, a sorceress who, among her other exploits, has turned her lover into "a beaver because he loved another woman beside her . . . Moreover, she caused the wife of a certain lover that she had, because she spoke sharply and wittily against her, should never be delivered of her child, but should remain, her womb closed up, everlastingly pregnant."

Aristomenes, a cheese merchant and the narrator of the tale, goes on to tell how he and his friend Socrates put up at an inn for the night. There, as he lay dreaming, he saw Meroe accompanied by Panthia, another witch, burst into the room.

Aristomenes, trapped under the overturned bed so that he feels like a turtle, sees Meroe thrust a sword through Socrates' throat, killing him outright. That done, she plucks out her victim's heart. Then

> Panthia stopped the wide wound of his throat with [a] sponge and said: "O sponge, sprung and made of the sea, beware that thou pass not over a running river." This said, they moved and turned up my bed, and then they strode over me and staled upon me till I was wringing wet.

In the morning the friends wake and resume their journey in the course of which they confide their nightmares to each other. Fear makes them hungry so they pause to eat. When they have stilled their appetites, Aristomenes, pointing to "a pleasant running water," says, "Come hither Socrates to this water and drink . . . but he had scarce touched the water with his lips when behold the wound of his throat opened wide, and the sponge suddenly fell into the water . . ." And Socrates falls dead. Aristomenes buries him and goes into exile in another country, "an exile of my own free will, where I married another wife."

Apuleius, like later writers of the fantastic, understands how homely details serve to validate impossibility. Aristomenes choking on a bit of cheese, the rotten rope that breaks when he would hang himself, the bit of sponge tucked by Panthia into Socrates' wound, and even the gross indecency committed by the witches over his sleeping form, are all ways of reassuring us that we are in the real world. Like the bud vase in Fuselli's painting "The Nightmare" or the familiar distant masts of ships in the harbor in Munch's "The Scream," these details serve to domesticate, and thereby intensify, the horror.

THE GOLEM   Film
(German release title: **DER GOLEM,
WIE ER IN DIE WELT KAM**)
1920 (B&W) (Silent) Germany 85 min.
Production Company: Projections-AG Union; **Director:** Paul Wegener, Carl Boese; **Screenplay:** Paul Wegener, Henrik Galeen; **Photography:** Karl Freund, Guido Seeber; **Special Effects:** Carl Boese.
Cast: Paul Wegener (The Golem), Albert Steinrück (Rabbi Lowe), Lyda Salmonova (Miriam), Ernst Deutsch (Lowe's assistant), Lothar Müthel (Knight Florian), Loni Nest (child).

Contemporary viewers who are not put off by the hyper-theatricality of silent screen acting styles or by violently distorted set designs whose meanings continue to evade us, will find *The Golem* a remarkable film, the product of highly creative minds.

The plot of the *The Golem* links two stories. First there is the Jewish folktale about the 16th-century Rabbi Lowe who, when Prague's Jewish community was in danger, created a clay giant which he animated by using the Shem Ha'mforesh, the Holy Name of Names (in the film the rabbi invokes Astarte and gets from her the name that animates his creature). To the folktale, Wegener and Galeen have imposed the story of the rabbi's daughter Miriam who falls in love with, and is seduced by, Knight Florian, a Czech courtier and the emperor's messenger.

As the film opens, we learn that the emperor, in response

Loni Nest and Paul Wegener in **The Golem.**

to Christian complaints, has issued a decree to drive the Jews from Prague. Rabbi Lowe, whose astrological skills have predicted trouble for the Jews undertakes to make a Golem to protect them.

From here on, the love story and the Golem story follow each other in neat, alternating segments. While the rabbi takes the Golem to Court and performs magic there, Knight Florian and Miriam are somewhat convulsively moving toward the consummation of their love. The magic the rabbi performs is spectacular: He shows the court episodes from the history of the Jews, particularly Moses leading the exodus from Egypt. But when the audience, which has been warned not to laugh, ignores the warning and starts jeering, the royal castle begins to tumble down upon their heads. The emperor and his court are saved by the exertions of Rabbi Lowe's Golem and the grateful emperor nullifies his decree.

Later, the rabbi deactivates the Golem by taking away the magic word that animates him, but his assistant, who loves Miriam and who has discovered her assignation with Knight Florian, replaces the magic word and orders the revitalized Golem to destroy Knight Florian for bringing shame to the rabbi's house. The Golem, in a striking scene, obliges, but that done, he becomes, as the rabbi prophesied, a malevolent creature who sets Rabbi Lowe's house ablaze and drags the penitent Miriam off by the hair.

This time, Prague, the Jews, Miriam and the rabbi's assistant are all saved because the Golem meets some children, one of whom in all innocence turns the Golem back into his primordial clay.

But the plot of *The Golem* is hardly at all what the film is about. It serves merely as an excuse for a series of film sequences that are so intensely visual and are psychologically so disturbing that they continue to elicit our admiration. There is, for example, a scene early in the film in which a black cat is seen in silouhette, walking across such rooftops as no humans ever built. From time to time the camera moves through stairways and towers that seem to be replicas of viscera seen from the inside. When people move up or down through them, fear permeates the screen. One of the most startling of the film's images is a synagogue sequence in which a crowd of men, passionately at prayer, is photographed from the rear, from above and from the side with so much distortion of heads, necks and eyes that prayer itself becomes an act of violence.

The Golem was to make a mark on the American horror film because Karl Freund later applied the camera skills displayed here to his work as photographer for Tod Browning's *Dracula* (1931) and as director of *The Mummy* (1932) and *Mad Love* (1935).

GOTHIC   Film
1987   (C)   Great Britain   110 min.
Production Company: Virgin Vision and Vestron Pictures; *Director:* Ken Russell; *Producer:* Penny Corke; *Screenplay:* Stephen Volk; *Photography:* Mike Southen; *Editor:* Michael Broadsell; *Music:* Thomas Dolby.
Cast: Gabriel Byrne (Byron), Julian Sands (Shelley), Natasha Richardson (Mary), Miriam Cyr (Claire), Timothy Spall (Dr. Polidori).

There are a couple of reasons why one ought to see this quite deplorable film: First, it is directed by Ken Russell whose imagination, even when it has no material to work on, is sufficiently macabre to interest horror film aficionados; second, it is the only film in which both Mary Shelley and John Polidori, the authors of *Frankenstein* and *The Vampyre* respectively, appear.

Gothic fails because, despite Stephen Volk's screenplay, Ken Russell has no plot to work with. What he does have, all of it fascinating in its proper place but very badly employed here, is the story of the famous "Frankenstein Summer" of 1817 when the Byron and Shelley menages lived near each other in Geneva. It was in the course of that summer that Mary Shelley, one rainy evening at Byron's home, the Villa Diodati, had the first inklings of her great monster tale.

The Annotated Frankenstein outlines the emotional tangle in which the people who gathered in Byron's home that summer were involved:

> First, there is Mary Shelley herself. She was an eighteen-year-old woman who had had to live all her life with the knowledge that her own birth had killed her mother. To this must be added the uncertainty she undoubtedly lived with as an unmarried mother. No matter what advanced views she may have held upon open marriages, she knew very well that Percy Shelley had abandoned a wife with two small children. How much more tenuous then must be a mistress's hold upon him?

> Then, there was Byron, who had to contend that evening (or one like it) with the hungry light in [Mary's step-sister] Claire Claremont's eye. He already loathed her, and, to make matters worse, she was carrying his baby. Byron knew what the world

thought of him. He was its model of a fascinating monster: a genius, titled, lascivious, lame. Sometimes he agreed with the world, and brooded about "the nightmare of [his] own delinquencies."

> The other lines of feeling drawn between the people in the Villa Diodati on that famous night are almost too intricate to be drawn in detail. Polidori was jealous of Shelley's growing friendship with Byron. Byron treated Polidori like a plaything. Mary Shelley was jealous of Byron who took Shelley away from her for whole days at a time. Claire was yearning for Byron, but at the same time managed a strangely erotic relationship with Shelley with whom she often stayed up late at night when Mary was not feeling well. Shelley, in turn, comforted Claire by telling her tales of blood and gore until he rendered her hysterical, after which he put her tenderly to bed.

There is plenty of material for drama here, but Russell, though he quotes continually from published sources, fails to turn his data into a coherent tale. He does invent the story that in the course of an occult ritual these three men and two women have turned loose an evil force in the Villa Diodati and that that force makes them behave in the unprincipled or ghastly way that they do. But it is a plot that is at once trivial and demeaning, stealing as it does the last shred of dignity from each of the characters. The result is that we are left with an hour and 15 minutes of pure image making, a sort of *potpourri* of grotesqueries, some of them striking, more of them revolting, that lead neither to climax nor to insight and only very rarely to fear.

A quick case in point: The poet Shelley did indeed dream that he saw a woman whose breasts had eyes for nipples. In and of itself, it is a powerful and disquieting image. But Russell will not be content with having Shelley tell us about it twice. He has to produce the image on camera with the result that disquiet is turned to revulsion or, worse, curiosity about the technology of the special effect.

The actors in this unfortunate film never talk when they can shout and never shout when they can scream. Of them all, only Natasha Richardson, who plays Mary Shelley, has been given a part (or a character) that has even a trace of dignity. Byron, whom we are meant to see as the hero of the polymorphous perverse, is simply a big bully who has sex, one way or another, on his mind. Polidori is well and truly loathsome and hardly needs to drink a beakerful of leeches to make the point. As for Shelley, he is played as a twitchy shrieker who cannot seem to remember how old he is supposed to be though he guesses it is a little younger than seven and a little more than three. But Claire Claremont, after Polidori, gets the worst of it. We see her an abandoned and pregnant, if mad, trollop, who comes on camera naked, smeared with mire [or worse], on all fours, carrying a dead rat between her teeth.

As depicted in this film, the people who gathered at the Villa Diodati that summer seem like lunatics who should not have been allowed out of the madhouse from which they came. Never mind that two of them were poets not unacquainted with the sublime; that Mary Shelley singlehandedly created a literary icon that still stands as an image for the dilemmas of our age; and that even poor Polidori left his small mark on English literature before he committed suicide.

Let us note one final offense: Several times in the course of the film, Percy Shelley is given lines that are clearly intended to make us think that he was the source of the Frankenstein idea. That was a notion dear to the hearts of some of Mary Shelley's male chauvinist contemporaries and it was exploded long ago. It is a little late in the day for Ken Russell to be urging the point now.

GRAVE OF THE VAMPIRE   Film

1972   (C)   U.S.A.   95 min.
Production Company: Millennium Productions; ***Director:*** John Hayes; ***Producer:*** Daniel Cady; ***Screenplay:*** David Chase; ***Photography:*** Paul Hipp.
Cast: William Smith (James Eason), Mike Pataki (Croft/Lockwood), Kitty Vallacher (the unwilling mother), Lynn Peters (Linda Jacobi), Dianne Holden (Ann).

Surely, *Grave of the Vampire* is one of the most disturbing films in the vampire genre because, like *Rosemary's Baby* and *The Omen,* it links the instinct of mother love with demonic evil. Despite David Chase's sluggish screenplay and the film's general air of penny-pinching shabbiness the story it develops is intriguing and touched, in more than a few places, by authentic anguish.

As the film opens, we see a young couple making love in a car parked near a graveyard. We are then made aware that a coffin in a nearby crypt is opening. Moments later, the inhabitant of the coffin is seen lurching toward the car where, with supernatural ease, he tears the back door from its hinges. After he breaks the young man's back on a gravestone, he turns his attention to the screaming young woman whom he drags off to an atrocious coupling in an open grave.

Nine months later, the creature conceived on that night is born to "the unwilling mother." The infant's complexion has a gray cast, and it refuses to drink milk from the mother's breast. When the distraught mother inadvertently pricks her finger and a drop of blood falls on the baby's lips, she learns what food it craves. The scene that follows is made both memorable and beautiful by the lullaby the mother sings, in a voice as tender as it is untrained, as she presses her baby's lips to the wound she has opened in her breast:

> When you will, you shall have
> All the pretty little horses.
> Dapples and grays,
> Pintos and bays,
> All the pretty little horses.

The transition from that infancy to the young manhood of James Eason is accomplished in a series of deftly suggestive shots in which we hear Eason's adult voice telling us that after his mother's death he, Eason, set out to find his monster father, Phillip Croft, so that he could destroy him. Then, abruptly, we are in the present time. Eason has tracked his father to a university where the vampire, using the name Lockwood, is, improbably enough, a professor who teaches a night class on the occult.

Eason enrolls in the class and becomes at once the target of Professor Lockwood's hostile curiosity and also the amorous interest of two of his fellow students: Ann and her roommate Linda. For a little while, the film concerns itself with erotic intrigues: Eason makes love to Ann; Professor Lockwood is briefly and murderously involved, first with a teasing librarian and then with Linda who, once she is persuaded that Lockwood really is a vampire, offers to share his vampiric state. Finally, the monster father and his vengeful son meet in open conflict, with results that are disastrous to them both.

Grave of the Vampire makes little use of the folklore of the vampire. There is no mention of garlic. Dawn and dusk come and go with very little comment. No one wields a crucifix or squirts holy water. Eason, the vampire's son, moves about in daylight. As for Lockwood, it is hard to imagine how he could survive at a university where committee meetings are rarely scheduled at night. But all that to one side, it is "the unwilling mother" theme and the father and son confrontation that give the film its distinction.

THE GREAT GOD PAN   Short Novel

Arthur Machen
Great Britain
1894, in *The Great God Pan and the Inmost Light,* Boston, Roberts; reprinted 1972 (1944) in Herbert A. Wise & Phyllis Fraser's (ed.) *Great Tales of Terror and the Supernatural,* New York, Random House/Modern Library.

Here is a pleasingly contrived story built, as the author puts it, like a series of Chinese boxes, one within the other, and told in the unhurried way of the late 19th- and early 20th-century British masters.

The tale is closely related to Hanns Heinz Ewers' *Alraune.* Here, too, a scientist is responsible (though in this case, inadvertently) for the creation of a female child who grows up to be a young woman and because of whom a variety of dreadful calamities happen. In this case, the meddling scientist is a Doctor Raymond who, in an experiment witnessed by his friend, Dr. Clarke, performs brain surgery on a young woman named Mary, surgery intended to lift the veil that separates our apparent world from the real or essential one. "The ancients," he tells us, "knew what lifting the veil means. They called it seeing the god Pan."

Dr. Raymond's experiment is a failure, and after the surgery Mary returns to consciousness with her mind destroyed. But nine months later, just before she dies, she gives birth to a girl whose father, we must conclude, was the great god Pan. That child grows up to be the woman Helen who then sets out upon her destructive career. That career involves enticing men to unnamed abominations so appalling that, because of them, the men die or commit suicide.

Curiously enough, Dr. Raymond, the true begetter of all the horror, is unpunished at the end of the story though he does express a certain dry regret. In a letter to his friend Clarke, he writes,

> . . . it was an ill work I did that night when you were present; I broke open the door of the house of life, without knowing or caring what might pass forth or enter in. . . . I played with energies which I did not understand, and you have seen the ending of it. Helen Vaughan did well to bind the cord about her neck and die, though the death was horrible. The blackened face, the hideous form upon the bed, changing and melting before your eyes from woman to man, from man to beast, and from beast to worse than beast . . .

But beneath this text there lurks the story's even more powerful subtext: Women who have seen the great god Pan—women, that is, who have rediscovered their female instincts—pose a terrible threat to men.

GREMLINS

Film

1984   (C)   U.S.A.   105 min.

Production Company: Warner Brothers; *Director:* Joe Dante; *Producer:* Michael Finnell; *Screenplay:* Chris Columbus; *Photography:* John Hora; *Editor:* Tina Hirsch; *Special Effects:* Gremlins created by Chris Walas; *Music:* Jerry Goldsmith.
Cast: Zach Galligan (Billy), Hoyt Axton (Peltzer), Frances Lee McCain (Mrs. Peltzer), Polly Holliday (Kate).

Here is a flashy, high style and expensive film that shows the hand of Stephen Spielberg, who was one of its executive producers. There is much that is visually satisfying about *Gremlins* but when all the fun is over the film leaves us with a certain emptiness. Still, a Spielberg-Joe Dante production can not be ignored.

An inept inventor named Peltzer, from Kingston Falls, visits San Francisco's Chinatown and buys a cuddly little creature that looks like a cross between a teddy bear and a kitten and is called a mogwai. He gives the creature to his son Billy as a Christmas present. As in any fairy tale, Peltzer is given a three-fold warning about the creature: Keep it out of the light, don't let it get wet, and never feed it after midnight.

Back in Kingston Falls, the little animal with its wide brown eyes, its poignant way of singing tuneless melodies and its ability to mimic human speech is a wild success. But of course, all three of the warnings are eventually disregarded. When water is spilled over it, the mogwai multiplies—explosively. Billy doesn't notice that the second generation of mogwai, though still as cute as the first, have a certain sinister, collusional air about them, and shortly after the water episode he feeds the creatures when his electric clock shows 20 minutes before midnight. Too late, he learns that the wires to his clock have been cut and that it was well past the witching hour when he gave them food.

The result of the mistake is catastrophic. The second generation mogwai go into a pupa stage in which they metamorphose into ravenous and ferocious killers. Though still teddy bears, they are now teddy bears with batwing ears, clicking eyelids and shark's teeth. They have, moreover, the sense of humor for which the Three Stooges were famous. The result of all this is that they create some pretty wonderful screen mayhem when they are in their attack mode.

It is inventive mayhem, full of visual puns referring to scenes or gestures made famous in other movies. One of the creatures lights two cigarettes on one match, a la Bogart; scenes from the 1956 *Invasion of the Body Snatchers* are glimpsed on a TV screen. There are other borrowings. In a clear nod to *Trilogy of Terror* there is a scene in which Billy's mother traps one of the killer beasties in a microwave oven. When Mrs. Deagle, a mean rich lady in Kingston Falls, is attacked by the creatures, she ends with her feet sticking up out of the ground like one of the wicked witches in *The Wizard of Oz;* and finally, the leader of the mega-mogs, whose mane is streaked white like a skunk's back, is as canny and cruel as the rat Ben in the movie of that name.

And there we have, I think, the achievement of the film: It's a mostly successful mixture of the grisly with a light-hearted parody of various aspects of contemporary life. The evil mogwai, for instance, mimic poker players in smoke-filled rooms and beer drinkers as we know them from television commercials. There is even a split second scene in which a raincoat-clad mogwai opens its coat and flashes before the camera, though what it thinks it is displaying is anyone's guess.

Indeed, it is possible to complain that *Gremlins* is too much fun to be a successful horror film. But the mind that conceived the ghastly, metamorphosed mogwai and turned them loose against the decent folk of Kingston Falls knows how to startle an audience to death.

Gremlins is scary enough but the film feels hollow because, though it is framed like a fairy tale, none of its elements seem attached to myth. The result is that the film, already weak on psychological meaning, fails to provide any of the comforting reassurances for which we turn to folk or fairy tales.

H

HALLOWEEN

Film

1978 (C) U.S.A. 91 min.

Production Company: Compass International; *Director:* John Carpenter; *Producer:* Debra Hill; *Screenplay:* John Carpenter, Debra Hill; *Photography:* Dean Cundey; *Editor:* Tommy Wallace, Charles Bornstein; *Music:* John Carpenter;.

Cast: Nick Castle (Michael Myers, the elder, aka "The Shape"), Donald Pleasance (Dr. Sam Loomis), Jamie Lee Curtis (Laurie Strode), Nancy Loomis (Annie), P.J. Soles (Linda), Kyle Richards (Lindsay).

Halloween is much admired by terror film buffs and it deserves considerable respect. It focuses neatly on its story; it makes effective use of the machinery of Halloween with its atmosphere of masks and fear to elaborate or to sustain suspense. It is, too, the film that set the tone and the style of the horror movies of the eighties. Just as mainstream films were moving in the direction of sexual candor, so horror films, with *Halloween* leading the way, took advantage of the revolution in special effects capabilities available to the film industry to present intricate, detailed on-screen violence.

Halloween tells the story of a six-year-old boy who stabs his naked sister to death after having seen her make love. The boy is institutionalized and grows up to be what his doctor calls a creature of "pure evil." The now grown, crazed (or wicked) young man, who hasn't spoken in 15 years, escapes from his hospital and returns to his hometown on Halloween, bent on murdering as many of his fellow creatures as he can. The killer's doctor and the Smith's Grove, Illinois, sheriff stake out the madman's boyhood home, but he goes instead to a house in which a couple of attractive high school girls (one of them the sheriff's daughter) have combined their baby-sitting responsibilities. He stalks the baby-sitters, their charges and a high school couple making love in a nearby house. His victims, it should be said, are killed with considerable ingenuity.

The film's characters are sufficiently, if not deeply, established. The killer, Michael, is something of a stick figure who wields a knife, wears a Halloween mask and never utters a word. The protagonist, Laurie, is a sympathetic, withdrawn young woman who is good with children and longs to have a boyfriend of her own. In that connection, it is worth noting that the film reflects a certain residual Victorianism in the fact that the two young women who have boyfriends and who are candid about their sexuality become the killer's victims while the pure Laurie escapes with a light wound and a terrible scare.

The film's main flaw is that, like so many of its descendants, it blatantly courts high school and college audiences with condescending scenes involving stolen puffs on marijuana cigarettes, giggly girl-talk, telephone fests and prurient sexuality.

At its best, *Halloween* achieves breathless moments closely modeled on the game of Hide and Seek, which, in turn, is based on the best formula for fear ever invented: "Somebody or something will get you if you don't watch out."

THE HAUNTED AND THE HAUNTERS

E. Bulwer-Lytton

Short Story

Great Britain

August 1859, in *Blackwood's Magazine;* reprinted 1976 in *Classic Ghost Stories,* New York, Dover.

Here is a ghost story truly satisfying on two counts. First, it has all the elements that delight the childlike aspects of a horror reader's mind: a ghost that walks, making soft thudding footfalls, and that knocks three times; scenes of ancient wickedness reenacted mistily; a looming spectre; mysterious lights; secret passages. And second, some rather wonderful and carefully reasoned speculation on how such things can come to be. In this tale scientific explanations for what appear to be supernatural events do not (as often happens) have the effect of de-horrifying the plot. This may be because the first-person narrator's theory is put before us in a confrontation between him and a serpent-eyed, malevolent—and ancient—

practitioner of evil who, as he nods assent to what he hears, makes what the narrator is saying take on an awful authority.

The plot of the tale, briefly: The narrator, who is interested in supernatural phenomena and particularly in haunted houses, hears that there is such a house in a certain quarter of London and determines to spend the night in it. Armed with a knife and gun, and accompanied by a trusted servant and a faithful hunting dog, he settles down for the night in a room in the old house. And very soon the phenomena begin: Doors open and close mysteriously; there are footfalls, walking spectres, suddenly cold spots in the house, a mysterious hand, a woman's hand that emerges out of the dark to repossess a couple of letters the narrator has found and read. Finally, he sees an entire phantom scene of a man and a woman, the woman with bloodstained bosom, and a phantom-male leaning on a bloodstained sword.

The account of the visitation ends the first part of the story. The narrator survives his haunted night in the house, though his dog is found dead with a broken neck and his servant has been so terrified that he afterwards leaves his master's service. We come now to the second part of the tale to which the first is loosely linked.

In a particular room in the haunted house, the narrator has come upon the portrait of a man. "It was a most peculiar face—a most impressive face. If you could fancy some mighty serpent transformed into man, preserving in the human lineaments the old serpent type, you would have a better idea of that countenance . . . the width and flatness of frontal— the tapering elegance of contour disguising the strength of the deadly jaw—the long, large, terrible eye, glittering and green as the emeralds—and withal a certain ruthless calm, as if from the consciousness of an immense power."

It is that man, still alive after hundreds of years, whose will and dynamism are behind the mysteries of the haunted house and with whom the narrator has his confrontation.

Wilkie Collins.

THE HAUNTED HOTEL   Novel

Wilkie Collins
Great Britain
1879, London, Chatto & Windus; reprinted 1982, New York, Dover.

Part detective fiction and part ghost story, *The Haunted Hotel* is Wilkie Collins's last major work. Despite its somewhat untidy structure, the story is notable for its astonishing portrayal of the Countess Narona, whom T.S. Eliot admired. In *Selected Essays* Eliot writes that though *The Haunted Hotel* is:

> far from being [Collins'] best . . . what makes it better than a mere readable ghost story is the fact that fatality in this story is no longer merely a wire jerking the figures. The principal character, the fatal woman, is herself obsessed by the idea of fatality; her motives are melodramatic; she therefore compels the coincidences to occur, feeling that she is compelled to compel them.

Indeed, she is horrified by what she knows of her compulsion to evil, and is horrified as she is committing it. Finally, "compelled to compel" evil, she is, still horrified, compelled to write out the disguised confession that solves the murder mystery for us. All that self-knowledge and inward agony turn what would otherwise be simply another second-rank Gothic fiction into a psychological study of considerable complexity.

When we first meet the countess, she is about to be married to the British Lord Montbarry who, not long before, was engaged to marry the lovely and gentle Agnes. The countess explains that Lord Montbarry showed her a letter from Agnes releasing him (Lord Montbarry) from their engagement, but the countess is nonetheless terrified of Agnes. She says that seeing Agnes:

> ". . . frightened me so! I was not even able to stand up . . . I stared horror-struck at the calm blue eyes that were only looking at me with a gentle surprise. To say they affected me like the eyes of a serpent is to say nothing . . . That woman is destined (without knowing it herself) to be the evil genius of my life. Her innocent eyes saw hidden capabilities of wickedness in me that I was not aware of myself, until I felt them stirring under her look."

Soon after the countess marries Lord Montbarry he dies in Venice under peculiar circumstances. With the help of insurance investigators, the appearance of a ghost, and the confession mentioned above, the reader is able to learn just how Lord Montbarry died.

It almost goes without saying that before the story ends, the beautiful Agnes is given the bridegroom to which her sweet British virtues entitle her. On the other hand, what lingers in our minds is the portrait of the suffering, if wicked, beauty whose defeat we may not deplore, no matter how much we feel we should.

THE HAUNTED PALACE   Film
1963   (C)   U.S.A.   85 min.
Production Company: Alta Vista; *Director:* Roger Corman;
Producer: Roger Corman; *Screenplay:* Charles Beaumont;
Photography: Floyd Crosby; *Editor:* Ronald Sinclair; *Music:*
Ronald Stein.
Cast: Vincent Price (Joseph Curwen/Charles Dexter Ward),
Debra Paget (Anne Ward), Lon Chaney, Jr. (Simon Orne),
Frank Maxwell (Dr. Willett), Leo Gordon (Weeden), Elisha
Cook, Jr. (Smith).

The Haunted Palace, with its title taken from a poem by Poe
and its setting and various of its ideas borrowed from Lovecraft's "The Case of Charles Dexter Ward," is another of
those quickie films that ingenious director Roger Corman and
a devoted cast turned into a small monument to dark moods
and lowering madness. At the center of the film, like a lurid
spoke in a sinister wheel, is Vincent Price playing two roles,
first as the ferocious warlock Joseph Curwen whom the
villagers burn at the stake in 1765 and then as Curwen's
descendant, Charles Dexter Ward, 110 years later.

Curwen goes to his death with a curse on his lips, "As
surely as the village of Arkham has risen up against me, so
surely will I rise up against the village of Arkham." And so it
turns out when in 1875 Charles Dexter Ward and his wife
Ann come back to Arkham to take over the family property,
Curwen's "palace," which the villagers all know is accursed.

A heavy proportion of Arkham's population is deformed
as a consequence of a wicked plan Curwen had conceived to
mate the local women with the Dark Gods. Curwen, 110
years after his death, is still plotting the Dark God's return to
power, but first Curwen himself must return. It is not long
before Ward begins to feel the influence of his baleful ancestor, and it soon becomes clear that Curwen means to take
possession, literally, of his descendant's body.

Eventually, Ward, in a series of quite engaging scenes,
loses his struggle against his ancestor's spirit, and viewers are
treated to one more Hollywood display of the charms and the
power of evil. We watch intrigued as the passive and weak-
willed Ward acquires authority and so much malevolent
vigor that his wife Anne's life is finally at risk. But just as the
film heats up to some first-rate mayhem, Corman ends everything on a coyly contrived upbeat note. By then, it hardly
matters. Devotees of Vincent Price and/or of Roger Corman
will have had one more example of hasty filmmaking as a
fine art.

THE HAUNTING OF HILL HOUSE   Novel
Shirley Jackson
U.S.A.
1959, New York, Viking; reprinted 1984, New York, Penguin.

Doctor Montague, a psychic researcher, rents Hill House,
which has a reputation for being haunted, meaning to do
research on whatever phenomena manifest themselves there.
To help, he invites a number of people to join him. They
include: Eleanor Vance, who has lived in a house in which
psychic phenomena occurred; Theodora, who has scored
very high on the sort of psychic awareness tests that are given
at Duke University; and Luke Sanderson, who has no special

credentials but who, as the heir of Hill House, joins the
group.

The house itself is huge, rambling and illogically constructed. Its furniture is heavy and awkward. Doors refuse to
open. There is repulsive or very bad art work everywhere.

Very soon, the psychic phenomena begin to manifest themselves. There are strange thrashing noises. Various places in
the house turn cold. Theodora's dresses are both bloodied
and shredded. But as the story progresses, another, and by
no means unearthly, phenomenon is discerned. Whatever
sinister things the house is up to they are having a malevolent
effect on Eleanor Vance, whose life experience (especially a
dreary time looking after her dying mother) makes her a
natural target for the older evil that haunts the house. And
suddenly we understand that whatever Hill House is up to,
its only victim is a volunteer.

The slow, almost reticent development of that idea is the
achievement of *The Haunting of Hill House.* The interplay
between the research conducted by Dr. Montague, which
focuses on outer perils, and our slowly clarifying perception
that what is actually happening to Eleanor is because she is
Eleanor, goes far beyond strange noises in the night and ouija
board manipulations.

The disaster, when it happens, is only too real.

THE HEPHAESTUS PLAGUE   Novel
Thomas Page
U.S.A.
1973, New York, Putnam; reprinted 1975, New York, Bantam.

The insects that are at the center of this novel are not
themselves very awe-inspiring at first sight. They have the
gleaming, elegant look of beetles. But they are a primordial
species thrown into the world by an earthquake that has
displaced them from their habitat somewhere near the earth's
core.

These beetles, blind, infected with their own brand of killer
bacteria, feed on carbon and when they cannot get it, they
create it by simply burning whatever near them will burn.
They suffer the disability that they cannot mate in the air
pressure at the surface of the earth—until Parmittler, a scientist who is fascinated by the creatures, mates one of them
with a giant cockroach. The resulting new species endangers
first the small country town in which they emerge, then
finally the entire human race.

Thomas Page has done his entomological homework. He
has, too, a fine eye for human detail. While *The Hephaestus
Plague* is not a major work of terror literature, it is an
exceptionally compelling one.

THE HILLS HAVE EYES   Film
1977   (C)   U.S.A.   90 min.
Production Company: Peter Locke; *Director:* Wes Craven;
Producer: Peter Locke; *Screenplay:* Wes Craven; *Photography:* Eric Saarinen; *Music:* Don Peake.
Cast: Susan Lanier, Robert Huston, Martin Speer, Dee Wallace, Russ Grieve, Robert Huston (Bobby Carter), John Stead-
man (Fred), Michael Berryman (Pluto), Virginia Vincent
(Ethel Carter).

The Hills Have Eyes is still one of the five or six scariest movies I have ever seen.

A family from Cleveland, Ohio, are driving a station wagon and a luxurious trailer home through a desert region of what may be Oklahoma. Though a grizzled old desert rat warns them to turn back to the main highway, the father of the family, a retired police detective, is determined to pursue his search of a family silver mine somewhere in the vicinity.

What the desert rat does not tell the family is that he is the father of a mutant son who weighed 20 pounds at birth and who, when he grew up, stole himself a whore for a wife and begot three sons and a daughter. The mutant and his progeny live in the hills overlooking the desert and make their living by robbing (and eating) the rare tourists who drive by.

We have, then, a clash between two families, one made up of energetic and imaginatively cruel mutants and the other of normal, ordinary folk who are utterly unequipped to resist this new breed of humanity.

The film's violence is as awful as a Wes Craven film can be, but it is cannily and slowly prepared for. The innocent Clevelanders, the way decent people can, make one small mistake after another and are picked off by the mutants and done to death in a variety of graphic ways. Indeed, the mutants, especially the one called Pluto, are so thoroughly and detestably evil that the film viewer is likely to feel that any retribution, however awful, will be welcome when it comes.

At its best, *The Hills Have Eyes* is an anguishing, because specific, essay on the incompetence of decent people in confronting raw evil. When the film is at its worst, its scenes of violence, played for their own sake, are carefully elaborated to produce maximum viewer shock rather than understanding.

There is a *Hills Have Eyes II*.

THE HORLA
Short Story

Guy de Maupassant
France
1887; reprinted 1975 in *Classic Ghost Stories by Charles Dickens and Others*, New York, Dover.

There is a tenacious literary problem posed by first-person narratives and that is: Shall we believe what we are reading? The problem is especially acute when there is reason to think our narrator may be either decidedly disordered or downright mad. Poe's short stories, ''Ligeia,'' ''Berenice,'' ''The Black Cat''; Coleridge's ''The Rime of the Ancient Mariner,'' Hogg's ''Confessions of a Justified Sinner''—even novels like *Dracula* and *Frankenstein*—put us on the horn of that dilemma, but the problem is perhaps nowhere so acute as it is in Guy de Maupassant's short story, ''The Horla.''

De Maupassant's narrator seems at first to be a pretty standard 19th-century neurasthenic; at the same time, the descriptions of scenery he gives us (especially a description of Mont St. Michel) are so serenely beautiful that once again we repose confidence in him. And it is this balance between the lucid and the fractured sensibility that, when it is upset at the story's end, adds a grave dimension of sadness to what is already a powerful tale of fear.

De Maupassant's narrator, as the story opens, is leading a quiet life in his home overlooking the Seine not many miles away from Rouen. One of his daily pleasures is to sit and watch the boats sailing up and down the river. One morning, at 11 o'clock on a May 8, ''a magnificent Brazilian three master; perfectly white and wonderfully clean and shining . . .'' sails by. Unaccountably, the narrator salutes the ship, and that gesture is the signal for the beginning of his woes.

From that time on, at intervals he is assailed by sourceless depressions. His sleep is troubled by nightmares. He is overwhelmed by dizziness and by daytime visions. To escape them, he goes off to visit the great cathedral at Mont St. Michel where on the one hand he feels physically better, but on the other he acquires some local folklore that exacerbates his already irritable state of mind. Among other things, a monk who serves as his guide tells him that the country people:

> ''declare that at night one can hear voices talking on the sands, and then that one hears two goats bleating, one with a strong, the other with a weak voice . . . belated fishermen swear that they have met an old shepherd wandering between tides on the sands around the little town. His head is completely concealed by his cloak and he is followed by a billy goat with a man's face, and a nanny goat with a woman's face, both having long white hair and talking incessantly and quarreling in an unknown tongue. Then suddenly they cease and begin to bleat with all their might.''

Back home, he is now fully aware that there is some invisible and malevolent being in his house which, at will, drinks his water and his milk and which, evidently, is responsible for the increasingly unsettled state of his nerves.

Again he flees his home. This time he goes to Paris where an encounter with a hypnotist simply adds another dimension to his anxieties: There are people—and perhaps creatures or forces—in the world who can take possession of our minds and make us obedient to their will.

Finally, he believes he understands what has happened. On that fatal May 8, when he waved at the Brazilian schooner, something on that ship accepted his salute as an invitation. It leaped from the ship and took up its residence in his home. And, whatever it is, it is not benign.

> Woe to us! Woe to man! He has come, the—the—what does he call himself—the—I fancy that he is shouting out his name to me and I do not hear him—the—yes—he is shouting it out— . . . the—Horla—I hear—the Horla—it is he—the Horla—he has come. . . . the Horla will make of man what we have made of the horse and of the ox; his chattel, his slave and his food, by the mere power of his will. Woe to us!

Once convinced of the truth of this idea, our narrator has only one option. He must destroy the being. As he all but accomplishes that goal, we (as well as he himself) wonder most whether he is insane. If he is not, then what we have read, as the story comes to its close, is more horrible still.

THE HORROR EXPRESS
Film

(Alternate release titles: **PANIC ON THE TRANS-SIBERIAN, PANICO EN EL TRANSIBERIANO**)
1972   (C)   Spain/Great Britain   95 min.
Production Company: Granada/Benmar; ***Director:*** Gene Martin; ***Producer:*** Bernard Gordon; ***Screenplay:*** Armand d'Usseau, Gene Martin; ***Photography:*** Alejandro Ulloa; ***Special Effects:*** Pablo Perez; ***Music:*** John Cacavas.

Cast: Christopher Lee (Professor Saxon), Peter Cushing (Dr. Wells), Telly Savalas (cossack), Silvia Tortosa (Countess Irina), Helga Liné (spy), Alberto de Mendoza (monk).

Perhaps there was no better reason for making *The Horror Express* than that its producer, when he had the chance, bought the two model trains that were used in the filming of *Nicholas and Alexandra* and had to use them for something. Whatever the reason, the film is a most congenial example of the terror genre.

Christopher Lee is a scientist who has unearthed a hairy, apparently inert creature. Aboard a luxury train heading west across the Siberian plains, the creature comes to life and exhibits extraordinary powers. A mere glance from its red eye cooks the eyeballs of its victim and steals the wrinkles from his or her brain. Slowly, as the train hurtles across an icebound Siberia, we learn that the creature is a visitor from a distant galaxy who was left behind on earth eons ago when he and his fellows arrived on a voyage of exploration. He has survived all this time by occupying the bodies and the minds of an endless chain of creatures all along the evolutionary cycle from protozoa to humankind. Like a premature, and grisly, version of E.T., he is doing all the things he does because he wants to go home. Meanwhile, when the creature needs a new life or more knowledge, he takes them by the simple expedient of staring hard with his destructive red eye.

Peter Cushing, a physician, and Telly Savalas, a Russian police official, help Lee in combating the alien. In the final moments of the film, the creature occupies the body and the mind of a Rasputin-like monk who believes the invader is a satanic manifestation. The possessed monk looks unsettlingly like the face of Christ that appears on the Shroud of Turin. Just as it begins to seem that the creature has acquired enough power to take over every mind and body on the train, catastrophe is averted when the cars carrying the creature and its minions are shunted onto a branch line that, unaccountably but conveniently, runs right out and over a magnificent cliff.

The Horror Express is not at all a great film. But Gene Martin does a fine job of exploiting the claustrophobia, the speed and the dangerous intimacies of train travel. The result is a horror mirror-image of *Murder on the Orient Express.* Though everyone else in the film is appropriately cast, nobody in his right mind would ever believe that Telly Savalas could pass for a 19th-century Russian police official. All the more fun, therefore, to see him trying.

THE HOUND OF THE BASKERVILLES   Novel
A. Conan Doyle
Great Britain
1902, London, Newnes; reprinted 1981, New York, Penguin.

Normally, in a Sherlock Holmes tale, the textures of feeling and mood are secondary to the ratiocination process by means of which the inexorably logical Holmes uncovers the perpetrator of whatever foul deed he is investigating. In this story, however, Doyle seems to have taken special pleasure in intruding the possibility of the grisly and the uncanny. The fact that the seemingly supernatural and inexplicable is finally explained away does not detract from the power of its presence so long as it is before us.

Doyle makes full use of the Gothic tradition to let his story

work. First, there are the desolate moors. Then there is the hound, "which could not possibly be any animal known to science . . . [it] was a huge creature, luminous, ghostly and spectral." There is also the Baskerville curse, brought down on the family by the cruelty of Sir Hugo Baskerville in the time of the Great Rebellion (1647). Hugo, as we read, was punished for his wickedness: ". . . standing over Hugo, and plucking at his throat, there stood a foul thing, a great black thing shaped like a hound, yet larger than any hound that ever mortal eye has rested upon . . . the thing tore the throat out of Hugo Baskerville."

The *Hound* is notable for the degree to which Watson is the principal investigator of the mystery/cum horror. Holmes, like the hound itself, is hardly on the scene of the action. This is ingenious plotting on Doyle's part because there is a certain poignancy in watching Watson, a man of middling intelligence, pitted against a force well beyond his capabilities to master. Holmes' hand, however, is always in the game; just as the presence of the hound is sensed throughout the tale.

The Hound of the Baskervilles has a singular weakness that true devotees of the Sherlock Holmes tales will not thank me for noticing: Readers who are quite prepared to suspend their disbelief in the monstrosity of the hound, may find themselves balking at the idea that the villain of the tale could import a dog of such imposing size into the neighborhood of a tiny village in Devon without it or himself being remarked. Still, when the baying of that hound is heard across the moors, all such questions are persiflage.

THE HOUNDS OF TINDALOS   Short Story
Frank Belknap Long
U.S.A.
March 1929, *Weird Tales;* reprinted 1969 in August Derleth's (ed.) *Tales of the Cthulhu Mythos*, New York, Ballantine.

Long's story, written at the end of the twenties, decades before the discovery of lysergic acid diethylamide (LSD), has a surprisingly contemporary ring.

Halpin Chalmers, who "had the soul of a medieval ascetic" and who believes that drugs can expand human consciousness, calls in his friend Frank and asks him to stand by while he, Chalmers, ingests a drug that will send him travelling through time. The drug, Liao, was used by the Chinese philosopher Lao Tse who with its help discovered the Tao. And, says Chalmers, "he who apprehends the mysteries of the Tao sees clearly all that was and will be."

Chalmers takes the drug, saying, "I pray God that I shall not lose my way." What follows is stunning, turbulent, illuminating and, finally, horrible. He walks through whole eons of time from prehistoric eras through the migrations from Atlantis. He is:

"in Athens and Pericles is young. I am standing on the soil of Italy. I assist in the rape of the Sabines; I march with the Imperial Legions."

He strides from century to century until he learns that, "The deeds of the dead move through angles in the recesses of time." Then he comes upon the Hounds of Tindalos who, scenting his spoor, pursue him. Chalmers says that:

"All the evil in the universe was concentrated in their lean, hungry bodies. Or had they bodies . . . They are that which in the beginning fell away from cleanliness . . . There is merely the pure and the foul. The foul expresses itself through angles; the pure through curves."

When he comes out of his drug-induced trance, Chalmers, meaning to escape the Hounds of Tindalos who cannot abide curves, hastens to replaster his room, removing every architectural angle from it. But all they need is a crack in the plaster.

There is, in this occasionally lyric tale, a hilarious bit of dialogue between Chalmers and his friend Frank. Chalmers, apologizing for having said that Frank had a "shrewd but prosaic mind," tries to comfort him:

"Forgive me," he cried. "I did not mean to offend you. You have a superlative intellect, but I have a superhuman one. It is only natural that I should be aware of your limitations."

"Phone if you need me," I said, and descended the stairs two steps at a time.

What happens to that superhuman is, finally, unspeakable, while Frank of the prosaic intellect survives to tell the tale.

Long's story has the advantage of a perfectly marvelous title. Whoever they are, wherever they come from and whatever they do, how can one do anything but cheer for hounds so romantically named? Long, as if he knew what precious ware he had in his title, has the good sense to give us no description of them at all. They are their names and that is all we need to know.

THE HOUSE NEXT DOOR   Novel
Anne Rivers Siddons
U.S.A.
1978, New York, Simon & Schuster.

Walter and his wife Colquitt, who narrates the story, are a couple of "Mildly affluent people in their middle thirties, well and casually dressed . . . who like their lives and appear to love each other." They become aware that the house next door is actively malignant to a succession of its inhabitants. People living in the house have their talents wither; are driven to bizarre erotic behavior; or to madness; or, as finally happens, to murder and suicide. When Walter and Colquitt learn that Kim, the young architect who is their best friend, means to buy the house and live in it with his new bride, they intervene to destroy the house's maleficent powers forever.

The House Next Door is a fine, thoughtful, sensitive and entirely believable—hence terrifying—novel. Ms. Siddons writes an unpretentious but always accurate prose. She has a fine eye for the homely details that create an ambience around a tale of a haunting. She has, too, a refined understanding of how the tensions of family life can reflect and intensify an invading nightmare.

HOUSE OF THE LONG SHADOWS   Film
1982   (C)   Great Britain   96 min.
Production Company: The Cannon Group/Golan-Globus; **Director:** Pete Walker; **Producer:** Menahem Golan, Yoram Globus; **Screenplay:** Michael Armstrong; **Photography:** Norman Langley; **Editor:** Robert Dearberg; **Music:** Richard Harvey.

From House of the Long Shadows: *(clockwise from upper left)* *Vincent Price, Christopher Lee, Peter Cushing and John Carradine.*
© London-Cannon Films

Cast: Vincent Price (Lionel Grisbane), Christopher Lee (Roderick Grisbane/Corrigan), John Carradine (Lord Grisbane), Peter Cushing (Sebastian Grisbane), Desi Arnaz, Jr. (Kenneth McGee), Julie Peasegood (Mary Norton/Mary Jamieson).

Working from a finely tuned, literate screenplay, Pete Walker mixes a troupe of veterans in the horror genre with a persuasive crowd of rising young performers and subjects them to the always pleasing standbys of the old dark house film: ghastly murders, thunder and lightning, secret passages, false leads. The result is a film that stays solidly inside the perimeter of the horror film genre even as it is frequently graced by touches of congenial wit.

A young American novelist, Kenneth McGee, makes a $20,000 bet with his British publisher in London that he can write a thriller novel within 24 hours. All he requires is a suitable isolated house in which to work. His publisher arranges for him to use Baldpate Manor in Wales, which has been uninhabited for 40 years.

McGee arrives at the house on a stormy night. He settles down to work by candlelight at his typewriter when, one by one, a series of people make their appearances at the manor. First, there are "the caretakers" of the house, Lord Grisbane and his daughter Victoria. Then Mary Norton, his publisher's pert, blonde secretary, shows up with an unbelievable explanation for her presence. She is followed by Sebastian Grisbane, Lionel Grisbane, Corrigan and a quarreling young married couple, Andrew and Diane.

We learn that the Grisbanes have all gathered in the house to carry out the last act of a family compact: to free Roderick Grisbane, a family member whom the Grisbanes locked away 40 years ago for having murdered a village girl he made pregnant when he was 14. But when the door of the room in which he has been incarcerated is opened, he is not there.

And then the murders begin. One by one, the victims are strangled, poisoned, hanged, destroyed by corrosive acid or hacked to death. Grim as all these events are, the Grisbanes maintain their poise, behaving and speaking with that air of fatigued nobility which is theirs by right of their 300-year-old heritage. When Victoria is found dead, strangled, one of her brothers remarks, "Piano wire. He [the murderer] must have heard her singing." And when the murderer has hacked one of his victims to death with a double-bladed ax, he turns it so that he can attack his next victim with the unspattered blade.

The film has two satisfying surprise endings that no sane reviewer would be tactless enough to reveal. It is enough to say that Kenneth McGee, in the very last moment of the film, turns to Mary Norton/Jamieson and says, "Do you believe in love at first sight?" To which Ms. Norton/Jamieson, giving him as fine a female twinkle as has ever been photographed, replies, "Why not?"

THE HOUSE OF USHER   Film
1960   (C)   U.S.A.   79 min.
Production Company: American International; *Director:* Roger Corman; *Producer:* Roger Corman; *Screenplay:* Richard Matheson; *Photography:* Floyd Crosby; *Editor:* Anthony Carras; *Special Effects:* Ray Mercer, Pat Dinga; *Music:* Lex Baxter.
Cast: Vincent Price (Roderick Usher), Mark Damon (Philip Winthrop), Myrna Fahey (Madeleine Usher), Harry Ellerbe (Bristol).

Here is another of those Roger Corman marvels, a minor classic of a film shot in 15 days on a budget only a little more opulent than American International Pictures usually allowed for. The film is richly textured. Even the people in it, like the furniture and the draperies, are voluptuous and oppressive.

Corman, and Richard Matheson, whose genius achieves its ideal expression in interpreting Poe on film, have retained Poe's murky suggestion, in his "The Fall of the House of Usher," that brother-sister incest is the moral fissure that precipitates the collapse of that unhappy house. But, since Hollywood is, after all, Hollywood, they have added a more normal romantic possibility to complicate Poe's plot and have invented Mark Winthrop, a young suitor for Madeleine Usher's hand, who shows up unexpectedly at the Usher mansion intent on taking his fiancée away from it.

The neurasthenic Roderick Usher does what he can to dissuade Mark from marrying his sister. He implies that she is dying; he hints of a family weakness, of hereditary madness. Winthrop, however persists but Madeleine, evidently proving Roderick's point, dies—or seems to die—and Roderick has her placed in a tomb.

Now, Bristol, the butler, whispers a secret to young Winthrop: Madeleine was given to cataleptic seizures. Distressed by what he hears, he investigates Madeleine's tomb and finds, first, bloodstains that make it clear that she was prematurely buried, and second, a crazed Madeleine herself.

From here on, the film pretty much follows Poe's lead until it comes to its crashing end.

Curiously enough, in the film, unlike in the short story, the destruction of the physical house does not quite work as a symbol of the destruction of a profoundly sinful line. Perhaps it is because the film is so graphic about the deaths of the two Ushers. That specificity distracts us, I think, from a moment that, in Poe, comes across as appropriately allegorical. In the film, allegory yields to the simpler formula of crime and punishment.

That to one side, we have a lovely and moving and frequently terrifying film in which a singularly literate script writer and a sensitive director exploit (in the best sense) one of the darker products of Poe's dark mind.

THE HOUSE OF THE VAMPIRE   Novel
George Sylvester Viereck
U.S.A.
1907, New York, Moffat, Yard; reprinted 1976, New York, Arno.

Viereck, in *The House of the Vampire*, elaborates the psychological implications of the metaphor of the vampire. Reginald Clarke, Viereck's protagonist, does not drink the blood of his victims. Instead, he steals their creative ideas from them. When Ernest, one of his victims, confronts him, Reginald proudly acknowledges the charge. "Look at me, boy," he says. "As I stand before you I am Homer, I am Shakespeare . . . I am every cosmic manifestation in art . . . I am a servant of the Lord. I am the vessel that bears the host!" Reginald's grandiose pride is small comfort to his victims who are left, as far as their creative powers are concerned, in a state little better than stupor. The last we see of Ernest, for instance, he is stumbling, dead-eyed, down the street, "Without a present and without a past . . . blindly . . . a gibbering idiot. . ."

The House of the Vampire is heavily affected by the decadent prose movement of the late 19th century, and it especially bears the marks of Viereck's reading of Oscar Wilde, but where Wilde is wickedly witty, Viereck is lugubriously aesthetic. Still, his *House . . .*, with its special, and illuminating, twist, is essential reading for students of vampire literature and lore.

HOUSE OF WAX   Film
1953   (C)   (3-D)   U.S.A.   88 min.
Production Company: Warner Brothers; *Director:* André de Toth; *Producer:* Bryan Foy; *Screenplay:* Crane Wilbur; *Photography:* Bert Glennon, Peverell Marley; *Editor:* Rudi Fehr; *Special Effects:* (3-D) Lothrop Worth, Gordon Bau; *Music:* David Buttolph.
Cast: Vincent Price (Professor Henry Jarrod), Frank Lovejoy (Lieutenant Tom Brennan), Phyllis Kirk (Sue Allen), Carolyn Jones (Cathy Gray), Paul Picerini (Scott Andrews), Roy Roberts (Matthew Burke), Paul Cavanaugh (Sidney Wallace), Charles Buchinsky [later to be Charles Bronson] (Igor).

This remake of *The Mystery of the Wax Museum* was designed to frighten filmgoers by means of the miracle of three-dimensional photography that, for a while in the early fifties, was thought of as a filmmaking breakthrough. Bizarre though the 3-D effects were, filmgoers soon found that having to wear special cellophane-lensed spectacles for the sake of the new way of seeing turned out to be more trouble than the occasional illusion that a paddle ball was coming at you was worth. The 3-D fad went the way of the Hula Hoop. But *The Mystery of the Wax Museum*, seen now with or without 3-D spectacles, remains a notable film for, among other reasons, the performance of Vincent Price, once again practicing his svelte villainy.

The story of *House of Wax* is not a great deal different from the one that intrigued us in *The Mystery of the Wax Museum*, but the sets and the characters exhibit a lush sensuality that is very pleasing to the eye. The film makes especially ironic the horror, and the pity, of the story of how the mad sculptor, rendered incompetent because of his fire-scarred hands, leaps past his own limitations to achieve masterpieces by fusing flesh with wax.

There are several marvelous sequences, the two most notable being the destruction by arson of the sculptor's first studio in London in which we watch his great wax sculptures weeping tears of their own substance as they melt in the flames; and the final sequence in which we see Price stalking and struggling with Phyllis Kirk among the bubbling vats of wax in the basement of his museum. Here too, as in *Terror in the Wax Museum*, the young woman's fist smashes the smooth features to reveal the lamentable face beneath the mask and stuns the audience—with 3-D or without it.

HOUSE ON HAUNTED HILL   Film
1958 (B&W) U.S.A. 75 min.
Production Company: Allied Artists; *Director:* William Castle; *Producer:* William Castle; *Screenplay:* Robb White; *Photography:* Carl E. Guthrie; *Editor:* Roy Livingston; *Special Effects:* Herman Townsley; *Music:* Von Dexter.
Cast: Vincent Price (Frederick Loren), Carol Ohmart (Annabelle Loren), Richard Long (Lance Schroeder), Alan Marshall (Dr. David Trent), Carolyn Craig (Nora Manning).

Despite William Castle's cool and essentially passionless direction, *House on Haunted Hill* is a remarkably satisfying and frequently very scary film in which one will look in vain for any meaning beyond its bag of Hallowe'en tricks. The film has the advantage, too, of Vincent Price at his laconic, elegant and sinister best.

The apparent plot turns on the offer of millionaire Frederick Loren to pay each of his five guests $10,000 if they survive a night in a house in which seven murders have already been committed. In fact, there is a plot behind that plot since Loren's wife Annabelle and her lover, Dr. David Trent, are trying to provoke Loren's murder. Loren, as cold-blooded as they are, outwits them, to everyone's great satisfaction.

But that hanky-panky to one side, *House on Haunted Hill* works best as a compendium of all the great moments one expects in an old fashioned horror movie: raging storms at night, secret passages, blood dripping from the ceiling, a decapitated head in a suitcase. There is an intriguing trick in which a rope snakes its way through a window to coil itself around a young woman's feet, and, finally, there is a dancing skeleton that rises gloriously out of an acid-filled vat.

House on Haunted Hill, with so much good-humored, undemanding and scary entertainment crammed into its 75 minutes (and Vincent Price as well), is something of a bargain basement prize package of a horror film.

THE HOWLING   Novel
Gary Brandner
U.S.A.
1977, New York, Fawcett.

Even as pulp fiction, which is what *The Howling* is at its best, this is a very unimportant book. And yet, it is something of a trailblazer in that it sets its tale of lycanthropy firmly in the last quarter of the 20th century as it links the archaic bloodlust of the werewolf to the contemporary confusions about sex and violence.

Brandner tells the story of a Los Angeles technical book editor who takes his recently raped wife to live in an isolated California mountain community. The idea is to get away from it all, to recreate a happy sex life that the rape has destroyed for the couple. The trouble is that the village of Drago is a very, very unsavory place, and the couple discover that they have moved, lycanthropically speaking, from the frying pan of suburban Los Angeles to the fires of Drago.

Gary Brandner makes glib use of all the appropriate sexual and terror cliches that the werewolf theme implies. When the husband, Roy, confronts the wildly desirable other woman who is, of course, really a werewolf, we get this kind of prose:

> All rational thought was driven from Roy's mind by his pounding desire. With every fiber of his being he wanted to possess this black-haired, smooth-limbed woman. He wanted her sexually, carnally, totally. Nothing else was real . . .

And so on, hot and nasty.

There is one quite wonderful sequence in the *The Howling*. The description of how the good guy manages to acquire silver bullets in the real world of 1977 Los Angeles makes reading the rest of the novel almost worthwhile.

Perhaps not surprisingly, this skillfully plotted but otherwise indifferent novel, was turned into a film that has something of a cult following.

THE HOWLING   Film
1980 (C) U.S.A. 91 min.
Production Company: Avco Embassy/International Film Investors/Wescom; *Director:* Joe Dante; *Producer:* Michael Finnell, Jack Conrad; *Screenplay:* John Sayles, Terence Winkless; *Photography:* John Hora; *Editor:* Mark Goldblatt, Joe Dante; *Special Effects:* Rob Bottin, Rick Baker; *Music:* Pino Donaggio.
Cast: Dee Wallace (Karyn Beatty), Patrick Macnee (Dr. George Waggner), Dennis Dugan (Chris), Christopher Stone (William Neill), Belinda Balaski (Terry Fisher), Kevin McCarthy (Fred Francis), John Carradine (Erle Kenton), Slim Pickens (Sam Newfield), Elizabeth Brooks (Marsha).

In this screen version, Gary Brandner's novel has been considerably jazzed up. Karyn Beatty, the young woman who, in the novel, is the housewife who is raped, becomes in the film a TV reporter who, to get a good story for the studio for which she works, has set herself up as a target for the assault of a sex maniac on the loose in Los Angeles. In a quite fascinating scene set in a private booth in a sleezy porn shop, she meets the maniac. Curiously enough, the attack that follows is treated ambiguously by the filmmakers. This is strange because *The Howling,* whatever else it is, is anything but reticent about either sexuality or violence.

In any case, Karyn is so shaken by her experience that, following the advice of a psychiatrist, she and her husband, Roy, go up to a psychiatric colony that the psychiatrist runs somewhere "in the northwest."

From here on, the film's plot is substantially the same as the book's except that, instead of an entire village full of werewolves, our focus is on the doctor's little colony that, we guess pretty quickly, is a werewolf coven. Its denizens include the restored-to-life cadaver of the Los Angeles murderer and the erotic-exotic Marcia who, here, is the murder's sister. It also includes John Carradine howling obligingly and endearingly at the camera.

Neither Joe Dante, the director, nor John Sayles and Terrence H. Winkless, the film's writers, seem to know whether they want to make a terrifying film, a spoof of a terrifying film, or a terrifying porno film. What we get are frequently quite pleasing elements of all three. The terror is supposed to derive from what the Associated Press called the "most realistic and frightening special effects to ever [sic] shake up an audience." And indeed, those effects, which consist chiefly of human features bubbling in time to terror music, or prancing, larger than life-sized wolves, are pretty macabre, though at moments they are so macabre that they provoke laughter.

A final point: Lest audiences fail to understand what the werewolf metaphor represents in this film, we are given a scene in which Roy, frustrated by Karyn's rape-induced coldness, finally strays into the nymphomaniac Marcia's arms. Marcia lets fall her skintight, low-cut leather dress. Then Roy and Marcia couple by dancing firelight. As the two approach orgasm, they turn slowly into werewolves and their mutual roaring is accompanied in the background by the sounds of mating cats and other untoward noises. The message for those who only run and rarely read is that sex is beastly and adulterous sex is beastlier still. But fun.

THE HUMAN MONSTER   Film
(Alternate release title: **DARK EYES OF LONDON**)
1939 (B&W) Great Britain 76 min.
Production Company: Argyle Productions/Pathe; *Director:* Walter Summers; *Producer:* John Argyle; *Screenplay:* Walter Summers, John Argyle, Patrick Kirwan; *Photography:* Bryan Langley.
Cast: Bela Lugosi (Doctor Orloff and Mr. Dearborn), Wilfred Walter (Jake), Hugh Williams (detective).

Even in a quickie film, one can come upon moments of disturbing intensity, moments in which one senses that whoever was in charge of making the film succumbed to a seizure of pure creativity. Here, in an otherwise frail effort, there are a couple of such moments.

Bela Lugosi, in a role of which he could hardly have been proud, plays Dr. Orloff, a mad doctor who poses as a friend to the poor and who runs an institution for the blind. He is assisted in his wickedness by a mindless hulk named Jake.

All goes reasonably well for Orloff until one of his patients, of whom Jake is unreasonably fond, dies as the result of an experimental operation. Jake's pathetic and voiceless grief is one of the elements that raises this film from the obscurity to which it would otherwise be consigned. In the second high moment, the blind people in Orloff's institute are thrown into disarray when the police pursue the doctor on whom they depend for stability and order. That scene, in which a dozen or more blind men and women stumble about like ants in an invaded anthill, is as poignant and terrifying as it is ironic. Orloff's demise (Jake throws him into the most liquid of Thames' muds where he disappears with a plop) is most gratifying.

THE HUNGER   Film
1983 (C) U.S.A. 98 min.
Production Company: MGM/United Artists; *Director:* Tony Scott; *Producer:* Richard A. Shepherd; *Screenplay:* Ivan Davis, Michael Thomas; *Photography:* Stephen Goldblatt; *Editor:* Pamela Power; *Makeup Effects:* Dick Smith, Carl Fullerton, Dave Allen, Roger Dicken; *Music:* Michel Ribini, Denny Jaeger.
Cast: Catherine Deneuve (Miriam Blalock), David Bowie (John Blalock), Susan Sarandon (Dr. Sarah Roberts).

Imagine a vampire film that feels as if it were made of animated fashion photographs taken from *Elle, Vogue* or *Harper's Bazaar* and you have *The Hunger.*

The finest moments of the film may well be the opening sequences while the credits are running to the sound of urgent rock music and we see scenes of laboratory monkeys, used in research on aging, intercut with glimpses of David Bowie's face. These premonitory and jagged juxtapositions produce a horror that is not fully matched by anything in the rest of the film.

But the rest of the film exists and it is anything but negligible.

The setting is New York, sometime in the 1980s. We are introduced to a handsome (though not young) couple, Miriam and John Blalock. They live in a huge, elegantly furnished, though curiously barren house on the East Side. We learn very soon that they are vampires, but John Blalock has a problem. Though Miriam promised him ages ago that he would remain ageless, he finds himself growing suddenly, and swiftly, old. Blood drinking, a vampire's usual remedy against aging, no longer helps. John pleads with Miriam, "You said 'forever.'" To which she replies, "There is no release, no rest, my darling."

Since these are modern vampires, they consult a gerontologist, Dr. Sarah Roberts, who, though she is unable to help John professionally, is dazzled by Miriam. When John dies (or, at least, grows inert), Miriam carries his shrunken, aged body up to the dovecote in her attic where, while the pigeons flutter and coo, she places him among the other used-up lovers she has stored there.

With John put away among her other mementos, Miriam now attends to the beautiful Dr. Roberts. The lesbian seduction that follows is sleekly, cooly sensuous. Shortly after its bloody consummation Miriam tells Sarah, "I've given you something you never dared dream of. Everlasting life." But when Sarah fully understands what has happened to her, she kills herself and we see Miriam once again carrying the body of a lover to her dovecote where, in a memorable danse macabre involving her former lovers, the film briefly stops being cool and modish and becomes ghastly.

The Hunger is notable for its sophisticated treatment of lesbianism and for the dramatic makeup effects which age John Blalock from young manhood to the most deplorable senility in a matter of minutes.

Finally, *The Hunger* is beautifully served by its cast. Catherine Deneuve and David Bowie are exactly the graceful, literate, cultivated and reserved monsters that Hollywood has taught us to expect vampires to be, and Susan Sarandon's warm sensuality is a fine contrast to their bleak ennui.

THE HUNTED BEAST   Short Story

T. F. Powys
Great Britain
1930, in *The White Paternoster and Other Stories*, London, Chatto & Windus; reprinted 1976 in Leonard Wolf's (ed.) *Wolf's Complete Book of Terror*, New York, Clarkson N. Potter.

Powys's story, as petrifying as it is illuminating, has no evil figure in it. Rather it is a tale that exemplifies the view that evil is an integral part of the human condition and that, under the right provocation and under certain conditions, the beast within will emerge.

The protagonist of the story, Mr. Walter Glidden, the vicar of East Dodder, is gentle, dutiful, pious. His life, until the moment we meet him, has had "many joys in it—harmless peaceful joys."

But then he goes walking on the downs and comes upon some children who have begun to torture a rabbit they have found caught in a trap. One of the boys hands the rabbit to Nellie, who "was fourteen years old, a plump, coarse, sturdy girl." Then the boy, Jack, "To the horror of Mr. Glidden . . . gouged out the rabbit's eyes with [a] blunt knife."

What Glidden sees so horrifies him that he rushes at the children and scatters them. All but Nellie who is not so quick a runner as the boys. Glidden then:

> threw himself upon her. He tore at her clothes. She struggled and fell into the ditch. He struck her, lay upon her in his fury, and held to her throat. His stick was broken; he took up a great bone that lay near and struck her with that. There was blood upon the bone, and Nellie now lay very still.

Essentially that is both the central event and the climax of the story. From here on, all that is necessary is for Glidden to live with the knowledge not only of what he has done, but also of who he has been throughout all those years that he lived the life of an inoffensive clergyman.

Little by little, his self-knowledge grows and as it does, so does his kinship with all the natural (not just the human) world. He learns to burrow like a hunted beast, to peep "out of [a] ditch through the meadow-sweet and mint . . . [to move] along like a snake or a worm." Having killed Nellie, he finds it a much easier matter to strangle a dog that is about to betray his hiding place.

But finally he knows what the day has taught him: The pale white pieties, the soft decencies, are only part of our humanity. Unspeakable desire, the red smell of murder and nostrils flaring are also fused to the aspiring soul. It is then that the Reverend Mr. Glidden, holding a child's toy boat in his hand, turns toward the sea to accept the punishment that, in his dreadful innocence, he has earned.

I

I DISMEMBER MOMMA

Film

(Alternate release title: **POOR ALBERT AND LITTLE ANNIE**)

1972 (C) U.S.A. 81 min.

Production Company: Romal Films; *Director:* Paul Leder; *Producer:* Leon Roth; *Screenplay:* William Norton; *Photography:* William Swenning; *Music:* Herschel Burke Gilbert.

Cast: Zoey Hall (Albert), Geri Reischl (Annie), Greg Mullavey (detective).

First, no one in this film dismembers anyone. Second, though it is classified as a "splatter" film, *I Dismember Momma* is more memorable for the intense, frequently tender, and therefore disturbing, love scenes between Albert, its homicidal maniac protagonist, and the child Annie who is almost his final victim.

Pleasant-looking young Albert Robinson is a patient in a private mental hospital who complains to his nurse that, "My mother has taken everything from me." The nurse replies, "But Albert, you tried to knife your mother." To which Albert responds, "She's unclean . . ." In a cut to Albert's mother, we hear her tell the psychiatrist, Dr. Burton, who is also her lover, "Albert is not insane. He's emotionally disturbed and needs help," after which we get a smash cut to Albert's murdered attendant at the hospital from which the ingenious and affable young man has escaped. Albert, going off to town to continue his career as a mad killer on the loose, looks quite jaunty in his orange windbreaker, black turtleneck sweater and gray fedora.

When Albert reaches his family home, he finds Alice, his mother's housekeeper, there. The next five or six minutes of the film, in the course of which Albert compels Alice, whom he has already wounded, to take off her clothes and sing and dance for him, are among the cruelest in the terror film genre. The scene becomes unbearable when Alice, singing "Let me Call You Sweetheart," collapses as she comes to the words, "I'm in love with you."

The film then moves to its strange epicenter as Annie, Alice's daughter, comes to the Robinson house to see her mother who, by now, is lying dead upstairs. Annie is pretty and blonde and a perfect vision in pink and lavender, and Albert is smitten for the first time with "pure" love.

From here on, the horror of *I Dismember Momma* has less to do with anything a splatter film can offer than with the ambiguous tension that is built up in Albert as he fights the sexual attraction he feels for the eight- or nine-year-old Annie. In the hotel room he takes for the night, Annie, whom he has delighted with his games and tricks, tells him, "If I had a father, I'd like him to be just like you." To which he replies, "I'd like to be your father and your friend and your playmate."

And all the while, the darker eros is assailing him. When her bed draws him, he moves into the other room and shuts the door between them. Finally, aching with lust, Albert, like any proper Victorian who wants to keep the woman he loves unstained, goes off into the night to find a whore.

The final catastrophe of the film is triggered when Annie, made jealous by the sight of Albert playing with a chippie in the same affectionate way that he played with her, tears off the pretend bridal veil she has been wearing and escapes from their rooms by running down the fire escape. A distraught Albert runs after her moaning, "I love you, Annie."

I Dismember Momma is badly served by its title. What we actually have is a film of considerable psychological complexity. William Norton's screenplay and Paul Leder's direction are each in their own way sensitive and audacious in handling a theme that, from the time of Dostoevsky's "Stavrogin's Confession," has been endlessly difficult.

I HAVE NO MOUTH AND I MUST SCREAM

Short Story

Harlan Ellison

U.S.A.

1967, in *I Have No Mouth and I Must Scream*, New York, Pyramid; collection reprinted 1983, New York, Ace.

Perhaps the most horrifying thing about this tale of Harlan Ellison's is its title, but what Ellison has concocted to follow that title is grisly enough.

There are five people, four men and a woman, who have

lived in the vast, formidable and intensely cruel universe of the computer for 109 years. They are all that remain of the human species following the series of disasters that destroyed their world when the Cold War erupted into real war. They live on because it pleases AM, who hates mankind with an immeasurable intensity, to have them around to torment.

The world they inhabit has the shape of whatever horrid landscape the computer invents for them. The food they eat can be frozen elephant or manna that tastes like boiled boar urine. When they dream of bliss, it takes the form of Bartlett pears or peaches. At intervals, as an additional macabre twist, the four men take turns copulating with Ellen. It is an act that is meaningless, mechanical, mean.

In short, the five are in a Sartrean ''No Exit'' with the difference that there is nothing in any of their characters (beyond the fact that they are human) that has put them where they are. The hell they inhabit was created for them by AM whose name:

> At first . . . meant Allied Mastercomputer, and then it meant Adaptive Manipulator, and later on it developed sentience and linked itself up and they called it an Aggressive Menace; but by then it was too late; and it finally called itself AM, emerging intelligence, and what it meant was I am . . .

Ellison is very explicit about who AM is. ''If there was a sweet Jesus and if there was a God, the God was AM.'' And how that happened is that man first invented God and then God invented Himself. Then, having Man for a model, He outdid him in wickedness and created precisely the Hell His inventor deserved.

''I Have No Mouth and I Must Scream'' is not a long story, but the adventures of the tormented five are so scabrous that such relief as we are given at the story's climax is experienced merely as a drop in tension rather than as any easing of all that pain. While it is true that the narrator, who precipitates the climax, is a little happier, he is still:

> Living under the land, under the sea, in the belly of AM, whom we created because our time was badly spent and we must have known unconsciously that he could do it better.

''I Have No Mouth and I Must Scream'' is Ellison at his best. His nervous intelligence and irritable sensibility combined with his pressure of language make him an apt chronicler of the new cataclysms—those that are here and those that are yet to come.

I LOVE MY LOVE   Verse
Helen Adam
U.S.A.
1973, in Florence Howe and Ellen Bass's (ed.) *An Anthology of Poems by Women*, New York, Doubleday/Anchor.

This modern ballad of ghostly love makes shudders run down one's spine because of the way the horror develops under the chiming measures of the verse. The tale being told is classic: A man marries a woman with beautiful golden hair, but soon he finds that her love oppresses him. ''She shackled him close to the Tree of Life. 'My love I'll never set free./No, No./My love I'll never set free.' '' The man frees himself by the old expedient: ''He strangled his love with a strand of hair, and Then he buried her deep . . .''

But as he soon learns, his wife's love—and her golden hair—are insatiable. The hair, writhing, golden and gleaming, and avid of purpose, returns to make it clear that no man can escape from love. The hair, ''thumped on the roof, it hissed and glowed over every window pane,/The smell of the hair was in the house. It smelled like a lion's mane./Ha! Ha!/It smelled like a lion's mane.'' The poem ends in a fine burst of bravado. The hair, ''smothered his flesh and sought the bones. Until his bones were bare/There was no sound but the joyful hiss of the sweet insatiable hair.''

Of course Helen Adam owes a debt to de Maupassant's ''A Rope of Hair.''

I SPIT ON YOUR GRAVE   Film
(Alternate release title: **DAY OF A WOMAN**)
1980   (C)   U.S.A.   73 min.
Production Company: Cinemagic Pictures; *Director:* Meir Zarchi; *Producer:* Joseph Zbeda; *Screenplay:* Meir Zarchi; *Photography:* Yuri Haviv; *Editor:* Meir Zarchi; *Special Effects:* Bill Tasgal, Beriau Picard.
Cast: Camille Keaton (Jennifer), Eron Tabor (Johnny), Richard Price (Matthew), Anthony Nichols (Stanley), Gunter Kleeman (Andy).

Here is a film whose superior quality is doubly obscured, first by its exploitative title, so dreadful that it is almost impossible to imagine that anything good can follow; and second, by the rash of negative criticism it has received from critics who failed utterly to understand the uses to which this film puts sex and violence.

What we have here is a modern-day tragedy of blood in which a rape victim is avenged. This time, instead of the avenger being a father, a husband, a brother or a lover, the victim herself wields the weapons and accomplishes the destruction of her tormentors.

The story, briefly: Jennifer, a young New York City woman with literary ambitions, comes to a country town where she has rented an isolated riverside house in which she means to spend the summer writing a novel. Her presence, and her isolation, have been noted by a quartet of local males: Johnny, an ex-Marine, Stanley, a fresh-faced young sadist, Andy, who does whatever the gang is doing, and Matthew, who delivers groceries and is slow-witted, shortsighted and woefully insecure. These four descend upon Jennifer and, in three separate, nearly unbearable sequences, they rape and abuse her. When they have done with their physical and sexual maltreatment of her and she lies inert and all-but-destroyed at their feet in the living room of her house, they read her manuscript aloud, mispronouncing words and guffawing. Finally they tear the manuscript to bits and leave Jennifer lying on the floor. Later, they send dim-witted Matthew back to kill her, a task which, like all the others he has been given, he bungles.

With the rapists gone, the anguished Jennifer pulls herself slowly together. She bathes, cleans herself up, and gathers the bits and pieces of her manuscript and pastes them together. Slowly, then, and for the sake of making her life whole, she sets about the task of destroying the rapists.

Rape is one of the cruelest of human crimes, and that cruelty has rarely been conveyed so sharply in a film, or with more attention to the way that it destroys the victim's sense of identity. Seen from that point of view, Jennifer's vengeance is necessary to her healing and, in its details, perfectly proportionate to the crimes committed against her.

I Spit On Your Grave is not, however, only a film with congenially contemporary psycho-politics. It has a starkly believable script and frequently brilliant and sensitive direction. Its pacing is subtle and its sound effects (birdsong, human noises, music by Puccini) are strikingly deployed. It has, too, several photographically memorable sequences, notably one in which we see Jennifer's violated, twisted and bloodsmeared body lying just in front of an empty staircase that comes down along a wall in which there is a single shaded window. In that brief sequence, everything is suddenly empty: Jennifer, the house, the definition of humanity.

The power of this unfortunately titled film is such that it raises the miserable question: How else, without resorting to murder, can anyone who has been so emptied reconstitute her life? That's quite an achievement for a film that Gene Wright, in *Horrorshows,* has called ''totally without redemption'' and that John McCarty, in *Splatter Movies,* has characterized as ''a raw and unpleasant splatter cheapie.''

Let me have the last word: I think that in years to come *I Spit On Your Grave,* with its earlier name restored (*Day of a Woman*), will be seen as the pioneering, sensitive work that it is.

I WALKED WITH A ZOMBIE
Film

1943 (B&W) U.S.A. 69 min.

Production Company: RKO; ***Director:*** Jacques Tourneur; ***Producer:*** Val Lewton; ***Screenplay:*** Curt Siodmak, Ardel Wray; ***Photography:*** J. Roy Hunt; ***Editor:*** Mark Robson; ***Music:*** Roy Webb.

Cast: James Ellison (Wesley Rand), Frances Dee (Betsy Connell), Tom Conway (Paul Holland), Edith Barrett (Mrs. Rand), Christine Gordon (Jessica), Sir Lancelot (Calypso singer), Darby Jones (Carre Four).

More than 40 years ago, on April 21, 1943, *The New York Times*'s movie reviewer could hardly keep his wrath in bounds as he described *I Walked With a Zombie* to his readers: ''. . . to this spectator, at least, it proved to be a dull, disgusting exaggeration of an unhealthy, abnormal, concept of life.'' T.M.P., the reviewer, went on to hope that the Hays office, the industry's guardian of film morality, ''would safeguard the youth of the land from the sort of stuff and nonsense that their minds will absorb from viewing *I Walked With a Zombie*.''

All that frenzy was about what, in the eighties, seems so clearly a deeply moving, beautifully filmed and thematically satisfying love story with the implications of a Greek tragedy.

In the shadow of the zombie.

I Walked With a Zombie is at once stark and richly textured. The story, briefly: Betsy Connell, a nurse in Ottawa, is hired by Paul Holland, a Haitian planter, to come to Haiti to nurse Jessica Holland, his wife, who has been stricken by an illness that has rendered her both mute and mindless. In Haiti, Betsy loyally tends to Jessica even though she is very soon in love with her employer. Wesley Rand, Paul's alcoholic half brother who was in love with Jessica and who planned to run away with her before her illness, makes dark hints that Paul is somehow responsible for Jessica's illness. In the background sound the voodoo drums of Haiti.

When Alma, a black servant, suggests that voodoo doctors may be able to cure Jessica even though white doctors have failed, Betsy takes the pale, silent and very beautiful woman to a voodoo rite. That midnight walk, in which the flimsily clad Jessica is led through ominous cane fields, and their sudden encounter with Carre Four, the zombie guard of the rites, is masterfully filmed. Though its pace is nervous, the sequence is cold, soft and dreamy. Its climax in a voodoo hut is utterly startling.

The love story is the frame for a richly moving film that includes understated comments on the relationship between blacks and whites. The presiding deity of the film (and it is a psychological presence of great force) is a carved ship's figurehead of the arrow-pierced St. Sebastian that stands in the Hollands' garden. Called "T-Misery" by the natives, it was the figurehead of a slave ship that brought the blacks to Haiti and one of its arrows is used to commit the murder that is the climax of the film. And of course, the two "zombies," both of whom are living portraits of pain, are black and white. Indeed, Christine Gordon, as Jessica, the white woman who is suspected by the natives of being a zombie, and Darby Jones who plays Carre Four, the black man who is apparently the real thing, almost walk away with the film. Though they never utter a word, their silence and their color convey to the eye a mute message of despair that, were it spoken, would be heard as a thin variation of the banal.

Jacques Tourneur's direction has never been better than in *I Walked With a Zombie*. He points the camera at staircases, at interiors, at seaside scenes, at voodoo rites in a way that makes all of them become participants in the tragic destinies being played out before us. Tom Conway is splendid as the rigidly self-controlled civilized man suffering the torments of civility imposed upon passion. The Siodmak-Wray script is sensitive to language, frequently witty and more than occasionally very wise.

I WAS A TEENAGE FRANKENSTEIN   Film
1958 (B&W)   U.S.A.   74 min.
Production Company: MGM; **Director:** Herbert L. Strock; **Producer:** Herman Cohen; **Screenplay:** Kenneth Langtry; **Photography:** Lothrop Worth; **Make-up:** Phillip Scheer. **Music:** Paul Dunlap.
Cast: Whit Bissell (Dr. Frankenstein), Phyllis Coates (Margaret), Robert Burton (Dr. Karlton), Gary Conway (Monster).

This companion piece to *I Was a Teenage Werewolf* is a sad shadow of its predecessor. Again, we have a crazed scientist who means to push back the frontiers of science. This time, he is a descendent of the famous Dr. Frankenstein, presum-

ably of Mary Shelley's acquaintance. Now, however, he is British (never mind that he has no British accent) and is in the United States for an intense but brief sojourn as a researcher. Taunted by skeptical American colleagues about the goals of his research, Dr. Frankenstein undertakes to astonish them by making a person of his own.

> "I plan," [he says] "to assemble a human being using parts and organs from different cadavers. I'm carrying the principle of selective breeding one step higher . . . Where Baron Frankenstein created a monster, I shall bring forth a perfectly normal human being."

Using automobile and accident victims as his source of supply, and aided by the spineless physicist, Dr. Karlton, he does indeed make his creature, though unfortunately its face is deplorably ugly.

Dr. Frankenstein's pipe smoking is meant to be a signal to us of his cold-bloodedness: Even when he has his fiancée murdered by the monster and her remains thrown to the crocodile that he just happens to use as a garbage disposal, he pauses to stuff crimp-cut into his pipe. But the pipe leaves his mouth at the last when the youthful creature, who has learned to distrust the doctor, turns on him and the crocodile has one final meal.

Aside from its association with the much better *I Was a Teenage Werewolf*, *I Was a Teenage Frankenstein* has nothing at all that requires us to take it seriously. It has an empty plot, stick-figure characters and, except for a swift shot of the crocodile that lifts one's spirits briefly, no moments at all worth seeing. But, like *I Was a Teenage Werewolf*, it remains an icon of a vanished time when young women wore their hair in ponytails, young men drove hot rods and both sexes were caught up in the new music that was rock and roll. For the sake of symmetry, anyone who has seen *I Was a Teenage Werewolf* will want to see its shabbier cousin.

I WAS A TEENAGE WEREWOLF   Film
1957 (B&W)   U.S.A.   76 min.
Production Company: Sunset Productions; **Director:** Gene Fowler, Jr.; **Producer:** Herman Cohen; **Screenplay:** Ralph Thornton; **Photography:** Joseph La Shelle; **Editor:** George Gittens; **Music:** Paul Dunlap, Jerry Blain.
Cast: Tony (Michael Landon), Yvonne Lime (Arlene), Whit Bissell (Dr. Alfred Brandon), Tony Marshall (Jimmy), Dawn Richard (Theresa).

Older viewers will watch this film with affection and younger ones with a certain amount of anthropological and sociological curiosity. The affection arises from the pleasant pacing of a film that, for nearly a third of its total length, gives us a leisurely view of what teenage life in the fifties was like (or, perhaps better, was imagined to be like). Young people are seen making dates, making out, dancing to swing music. Most of all, they are being clean-cut though at the same time genteelly rebellious against their parents.

Somewhere alone the line, the film finally veers to the story of Tony, the violence-prone high schooler who is the film's protagonist, and begins to concentrate on the main thing: the werewolf link. Up to this point, motherless Tony has been getting into unaccountable fights with his fellow students at Rochdale High. His explanation is simply that

Michael Landon, the teenage werewolf, with a shrieking victim.

Still, *I Was a Teenage Werewolf,* like its companion film, *I Was a Teenage Frankenstein,* was an early manifestation of the moneymaking film formula (expose a group of attractive, sexually eager adolescent boys and girls to great danger) that was to become the basis of so many movies in the seventies and eighties.

All that to one side, I would guess that my own affection for the film is a sign of advancing age. I can only hope that younger viewers will have sufficient curiosity to see a movie that gave me so much innocent pleasure. If nothing else, they will surely love the rendition of the song, ''Eeny Meeny Miny Moe,'' that appears halfway through the film.

IN THE FLESH   Short Story

Clive Barker
Great Britain
1987, in *In the Flesh,* New York, Poseidon Press.

Clive Barker, one of the most literate, thoughtful and imaginative horror writers to mature in the eighties, spins this strange tale of the symbiotic relationship between our world and another tangential to it populated by murderers and their victims.

Young Cleve, a British prisoner, makes contact with that world in his dreams. Billy Tait, his new cellmate, is fixated

''People bug me.'' Urged by a friendly police officer named Donovan, and by Arline, his girlfriend, Tony now agrees to go into therapy with Dr. Brandon, who turns out to be the film's heavy.

Brendan, who has a spineless assistant named Hugo, uses Tony as a guinea pig for researches of his own. ''Through hypnosis,'' he says, ''I'm going to regress this boy back into the primitive past that lurks within him. I'm going to transform him . . .'' Since he believes that mankind has reached a danger point in evolution, Brendan's larger goal is to hurl humanity back to its primitive dawn. To make the evolutionary process start all over again . . .

With Tony he succeeds only too well. Tony is transformed into a werewolf whose first victim is Frank, a high school friend. The scene in which Tony kills his second victim, a young gymnast named Theresa, is a really spectacular bit of filmmaking. The human Tony, whipped into a sexual frenzy by the sight of lithe, tights-clad Theresa practicing stunts on the parallel bars, is transformed into the werewolf just as the scene we are watching turns literally upside down. Then, with Theresa in an attitude of abandon on the parallel bars and Tony snarling his wolf snarl, the scene comes to its lurid and truly memorable climax.

There is no need to overpraise this quicky exploitation film. Except for the moment described above, it is a perfectly banal tissue of mad-scientist cliches. The film's werewolf obeys none of the folkloric rules. Its behavior has nothing to do with the moon, or with wolfbane or with a werewolf's bite. There is no reason for anyone to find or create a silver bullet Instead, all of the film's evil is laid at the door of science

Clive Barker. © Geoff Shields

on the idea that the spirit of his grandfather, who killed everyone in Billy's family except his mother and was executed in that very prison, is somehow still present in it and that his, Billy's, task is to make contact with him.

It soon becomes apparent to Cleve that Billy knows about his dreams and needs him to dream them so that by their means Billy may accomplish his quest for his grandfather. That mission is finally accomplished, but the long, lingering narrative detailing it is at once specific and nebulous. In one of Cleve's dreams, for example, we see a figure in that dream city as:

> the incessant wind in those blue streets was rousing his horse mane into furious life. On the wind, the same voices Cleve had heard carried before, the cries of mad children, somewhere between tears and howls. . . . The shadow thing was blowing apart, relinquishing its slender claim to coherence. It fragmented, pieces of its tattered anatomy flying off into the streets like litter before wind.

That figure is Tait, a form of Billy's grandfather, and when the story comes finally to its bloody climax, Tait reclaims his grandson and Cleve finds that nightmare, waking or asleep, is the only world there is.

Barker's achievement is to recreate the grisly as a series of glimpses or as puffs of a breeze, or as scents. As if evil were a form of incoherence that can only be understood in passing. There is a certain delicacy in such a vision of the awful, but as it gets expressed in Barker's prose, it serves finally to italicize how pervasive that evil is.

INCENSE FOR THE DAMNED   Film
1970   (C)   Great Britain   87 min.
Production Company: Lucinda/Titan International; ***Director:*** Robert Hartford-Davis; ***Producer:*** Peter Newbrook; ***Screenplay:*** Julian More, from Simon Raven's novel, *Doctors Wear Scarlet*; ***Photography:*** Desmond Dickinson; ***Music:*** Bobby Richard.
Cast: Patrick Macnee (Major Derek Longbow), Peter Cushing (Dr. Goodrich), Alex Davion (Tony Seymour), Johnny Sekka (Bob Kirby), Madeline Hinde (Penelope), Patrick Mower (Richard Fountain), Imogen Hassall (Chriseis Constandinidi).

Richard Fountain, a young Oxford don who is sexually impotent, discovers erotic possibilities for himself in Greece in a relationship with a beautiful young Greek woman named Chriseis, a member of a cult of blooddrinkers. Abruptly, he disappears from the ken of his friends and one of them, a young black man named Tony Seymour, seeks the help of Major Derek Longbow in finding him. The two, followed later by Richard's fiancée, Penelope, go to the island of Mykonos to search for him.

In Mykonos they learn of the strange company Richard has been keeping and that several young women have lately died under strange circumstances linked to the cult's activities. Richard's friends eventually rescue the hypnotically dazed Richard from the ravishing and blooddrinking Chriseis, but, in the struggle, first Major Longbow and then Chriseis die.

Richard is brought back to England and seems for a while to have recovered from his experiences. But, pressed by Professor Goodrich, Penelope's father and a man of chilling rectitude, to hasten his marriage to Penelope, Richard collapses into psychosis once more. He seems to see and hear the vampire Chriseis again. Then, at a major public banquet where he is to deliver an important speech, he veers from his topic into wildly revolutionary rant: "The academic world dehumanizes us and we become its natural dependents . . . after which we are brainwashed, but the gods have given us freedom. . ."

Escaping from the banquet, he finds his Penelope and makes frenzied love to her but, hearing Chriseis's spectral voice, he goes utterly mad and vampirizes Penelope. When he is pursued, he climbs up to the slate-covered roof of one of the college buildings from which, after a breathtakingly filmed chase sequence, we see him fall. The coroner's verdict is that Penelope Goodrich and Richard Fountain, "being misused by the world," died, the one by accident, the other by suicide.

Richard's friends, knowing better, take stakes in their hands and go off to give the vampires their quietus.

Incense for the Damned, though loosely directed and carelessly edited, is nevertheless memorable for more than the way it exploits the brooding Greek landscape and the sixties shibboleths of sexual freedom and drug use. It makes explicit, for the first time in vampire films, the premise that vampirism can have erotic appeal. When one of the characters says, "Do you mean to tell me that a girl drinking blood from your neck will give you an orgasm?" The laconic British reply is, "Yes, of course."

THE INCREDIBLE SHRINKING MAN   Film
1957   (B&W)   U.S.A.   81 min.
Production Company: Universal; ***Director:*** Jack Arnold; ***Producer:*** Albert Zugsmith; ***Screenplay:*** Richard Matheson, based on his novel; ***Photography:*** Ellis W. Carter; ***Editor:*** Al Joseph; ***Special Effects:*** Clifford Stine; ***Music:*** Supervised by Everett H. Brossard.
Cast: Grant Williams (Scott Carey), Randy Stewart (his brother), April Kent (Louise Carey).

The Incredible Shrinking Man seems at first to be in the tradition of the fifties films in which atomic radiation is blamed for the disasters they chronicle; but as we watch, it soon becomes clear that this is something very much different and better—a sort of Robinson Crusoe saga of the human spirit triumphing against overwhelming odds.

As the film opens, Robert Scott Carey and his wife Louise are vacationing on his brother's boat. Scott cajoles his wife to go below to get him a bottle of beer. She does and therefore is untouched by a cloud of mist that we are encouraged to believe is impregnated with atomic fallout. Six months later, Scott begins unaccountably to shrink. And, in the face of every effort by medical science to help him, he continues to dwindle.

His situation is at first merely awful. His clothes grow bigger and bigger. He has to leave his work. He becomes, or so he believes, a laughingstock—a grown man in a child's body. Then, of course, there are all the horrid sexual implications of his situation, pointedly hinted at when, at one stage in his dwindling, he meets an attractive young woman, a midget on display at a carnival, who helps him to bear his affliction. But by the time he has grown so small that he must live in the rooms of a doll house, his situation has become too horrid for consolation.

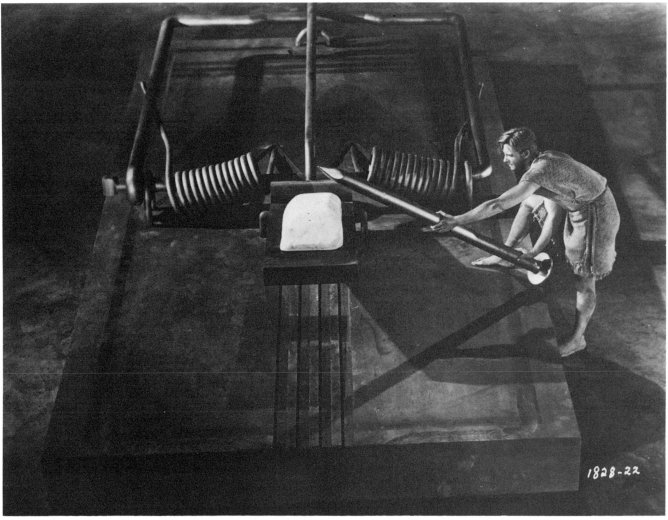

Grant Williams in the title role of **The Incredible Shrinking Man.**

After a battle with the household cat Scott falls into a box in the basement, and Louise, finding a bloodstained scrap of his shirt, believes he has been eaten by the cat. At this point the film shifts direction and we see that Scott's ties to the human world have been cut. From here on, Scott becomes simply another organism competing for survival as he struggles to free a bit of cheese from a mousetrap, or learns to get past obstacles like water leaking from defective plumbing, or outwits and finally kills a spider that has every intention of killing him.

What makes Matheson's script so remarkable is that it actually persuades us that Scott, reduced to being a mere organism, recreates his humanity by the inventiveness with which he solves the problems of survival. More than that, Matheson, undaunted by the comic implications of a tale whose hero is two or three inches high, manages to imbue him with the courage of Beowulf and the ingenuity of Odysseus. What is nearly as remarkable is that he brings his story to a close on a note of lyric exaltation as a voiceover asserts that Scott, who is still shrinking, has taken his place in the design of the universe, along with the overarching stars.

Clifford Stine's special effects deserve special mention. Working with a small budget, Stine manages to create a series of illusions in which Robert Scott Carey actually seems to be dwindling. In the early stages of the story, Carey's clothes get progressively larger. Later, his physical environment begins to loom over him as he encounters six-foot-high stair risers, four-foot-tall thimbles and needles the size of Watusi spears.

THE INCREDIBLE TWO-HEADED TRANSPLANT
Film

1970   (C)   U.S.A.   88 min.
Production Company: Mutual General Corporation/Trident Enterprises; *Director:* John Cardos, John Lawrence; *Producer:* John Lawrence; *Screenplay:* James Gordon White; *Photography:* John Steely, Glen Gano, Paul Hipp; *Editor:* Anthony M. Lanza; *Special Effects:* Ray Dorn; *Music:* John Barber.
Cast: Bruce Dern (Roger), Pat Priest (Linda), Casey Kasem (Ken), Berry Kroeger (Max), Albert Cole (Cass), John Bloom (Danny).

Like most dedicated horror film watchers, John Stanley, the author of *The Creature Features Movie Guide,* is quite tolerant of the truly awful movies released by exploitation film studios. But he dismisses this one as ''Stomach-churning nonsense about the head of a homicidal maniac grafted onto the body of a thorough idiot." It is indeed a ridiculous production and deserves to be classed with that other equally dreadful film, *Plan 9 From Outer Space*.

The filmmakers, one guesses, asked themselves what ingredients they needed to make a plot that would be violent, outrageous and sexy. What they arrived at was this: A scientist named Roger pursues and kills the homicidal maniac who carried off his beautiful wife, Linda. Roger, ever the researcher, thriftily takes advantage of the fact that he has a fresh corpse on his hands to further his investigation. He grafts the madman's head onto the body of a kindly, mentally retarded giant who works for him.

The result is the incredible two-headed transplant, who looks uncomfortable no matter what he is doing and who, since the madman is dominant, soon takes up his old homicidal habits. People die and Linda, once again, is in danger.

The Incredible Two-Headed Transplant is a bad mishmash but I take note of it here for two reasons. One is that it is so monumentally awful that no connoisseur of the horror film can be spared knowledge of it; and second, because bad as it is, it illustrates the law of poignancy that makes us grieve for film monsters no matter how repulsive they are. The two heads stuck on a single torso form a total creature at war with itself and with the world. It looks so mute and woebegone (and repellent and ridiculous) that we cannot help giving it some of our sympathy. Evidently the filmmakers banked on that idea because the following year they made the much better *The Thing With Two Heads*.

THE INNOCENTS   Film
(Alternate release title: **SUSPENSE)**
1961   (B&W)   Great Britain   99 min.
Production Company: Achilles/20th Century-Fox; ***Director:*** Jack Clayton; ***Producer:*** Jack Clayton; ***Screenplay:*** William Archibald, Truman Capote; ***Photography:*** Freddie Francis; ***Editor:*** James Clark; ***Music:*** Georges Auric.
Cast: Deborah Kerr (Miss Giddens), Martin Stephens (Myles), Peter Wyngarde (Peter Quint), Meg Jenkins (Flora), Michael Redgrave (the uncle), Pamela Franklin (Flora), Clytie Jessup (Miss Jessel), Isla Cameron (Anna).

A brilliantly successful, if somewhat Freudianized, screen version of Henry James' resonant short story, "The Turn of the Screw," *The Innocents* makes fine use of Jamesian ambiguity. Throughout most of the film, we are left to wonder whether what we see is what the governess is seeing—two beautiful children turned to depravity by their criminal communion with the ghosts of a debauched former governess and her lover—or whether what we see is a sexually starved young woman's slow decline into erotic madness.

Director Clayton cunningly uses the interiors of the fine old British country house in which the story is set. The two angelic (or demonic) children rattling about in all that spacious luxury are alternately delightful or sinister, depending on shifts in camera angles or the music. The performances of the children (and the housekeeper, by the way) are superb, though Deborah Kerr, on whom the burden of the film rests most heavily, moves into overt hysteria a bit too early in the film. The result is that in the final 40 minutes or so, she becomes shrill and there is a sudden sharpening of the edges

of meaning that deprives *The Innocents* of the subtlety that, up to this point, has been its most salient feature. When at the final moment Deborah Kerr avidly kisses the dead Myles full on the mouth, director Clayton runs up the Freudian flag and Deborah Kerr's Miss Glidden is exposed (and encapsulated) as certifiably and criminally insane. And this is too bad because James's story, down to its final period, leaves us breathlessly uncertain about whether the ghosts in the tale are or are not real.

INTERVIEW WITH THE VAMPIRE   Novel
Anne Rice
U.S.A.
1976, New York, Knopf; reprinted 1979, New York, Ballantine.

Anne Rice tells the story of a Louisiana planter, Louis, who is recruited into the ranks of the un-dead by a vampire named Lestat in the late 18th century. The blood exchange ceremony that binds the two men together in their immortal vampire life is borrowed wholly from *Dracula* where its sexual implications are buried under an overlay of horrified Victorian prose. In Rice's fiction, the blood exchange is openly, and even exultantly, an erotic event.

Indeed, the power of *Interview* comes from Rice's vision that love is deadly and that it is deadliest of all in the one place where we have always presumed it was welcome—the family. What Rice has written—though a reader comes to this conclusion with the greatest reluctance—is an old-fash-

Anne Rice. © Stan Rice

ioned domestic tragedy in which all the characters involved are vampires and in which polymorphous sexual desire, under the popularly more acceptable disguise of bloodlust, is seen as the energy that both enfolds and destroys the family.

Given the formula that blood is sex/sex is blood, Rice develops the misfortunes of a particular vampire "family" in a way that allows her to examine the forbidden sexuality that, depending on one's point of view, is lurking in or permeates family life. Louis and Lestat form the primary couple in this vampire menage. Their blood exchange makes them variously the father and the mother. Their child, whom they have created by vampirizing a normal five-year-old named Claudia, is a beautiful, merciless, swift and deadly vampire. She is also Louis's daughter, bride and mistress, and thereby arouses Lestat's jealousy. She hates Lestat so much that she contrives to murder him by offering him a gift of sleeping boys whose blood she has poisoned.

Believing that Lestat has been destroyed, the guilt-ridden Louis and Claudia, who nurses a grief at being locked forever in a child's body, travel through Europe on a sort of vampire's Grand Tour. In Paris, Louis meets the sophisticated Armand with consequences that are catastrophic.

Interview's macabre plot—*Lolita* with fangs—is sustained for the most part by Rice's considerable power to evoke moods. Moods and moments of dazzling insight and a stunning capacity to invoke the suave eroticism of blood make the book something of a tour de force. In this century no one has written a vampire fiction that is as strange, as compelling and as serious as *Interview With the Vampire*.

INVADERS FROM MARS   Film
1953   (C)   U.S.A.   78 min.
Production Company: Twentieth Century-Fox; **Director:** William Cameron Menzies; **Screenplay:** Richard Blake; **Photography:** John Seitz; **Special Effects:** Jack Cosgrove; **Music:** Raoul Kraushaar.
Cast: Helena Carter (Mary), Arthur Franz (George), Jimmy Hunt (David), Leif Erickson (Kelston), Hillary Brooke (Dr. Blake).

Properly speaking, *Invaders From Mars* is mainstream science fiction, but it is discussed here because the science fiction plot is developed within the framework of a bright ten-year-old's dream, and because once we are inside that dream, pure paranoia becomes the prevailing weather. We have parents who are not really parents, friends who are not really friends, and the only rule for survival is "check the back of the neck" before you trust anyone.

Ten-year-old David shares a passion for astronomy with his father, an engineer who is employed in a hush-hush research project that is developing a motor to be used in interplanetary flight. Wakened at four in the morning by a flash of light, David sees what may be a flying saucer landing on the sandy slope of a hill not far from his home. When he alerts his parents, they treat him like a child and pooh-pooh him back to bed.

The next morning, however, David discovers that it was not all a dream. There is something buried in the sand on the hill. When his father goes to investigate, he comes back with one shoe and his personality so strangely altered that he is physically abusive to David.

David, who is bright and perceptive, notices that his father has a fresh wound at the back of his neck where a tiny device has been implanted. We learn that an as yet unidentified alien intelligence can exert its control over all who carry this device. It is also true, and nightmarish, that nobody will believe David when he tries to explain what he knows.

Nobody but an attractive woman, Doctor Blake, and then the researcher Kelston who joins Doctor Blake to become a pair of surrogate parents for David while he, with their help, undertakes to alert the world to its danger.

Very quickly, the people of the small world with which the film is concerned divide into those who are, and those who aren't, wounded in the back of the neck. The unwounded call for and get the help of the army, while the wounded, moving like zombies, have wooden faces and staring eyes as they obey the commands of the invaders who enslave them.

Eventually, we see the invaders, some of whom are tall and green. They themselves are the slaves of a tiny humanoid creature whom they carry about in a globe. As one of its slaves explains, "He is mankind developed to his ultimate intelligence."

Ultimate intelligence or not, the invaders are beaten back by a clean-cut American boy who, with the help of his friends, sends them reeling.

Donald C. Willis, in his *Horror and Science Fiction Films: A Checklist*, has the last, brilliant word on this inexpensive but often truly horrifying film. He writes:

> *Invaders From Mars* abounds with hideous, nightmarish ideas about parents who turn into zombies, people who disappear into hills in the sand, Martians who drill into people's brains . . . all perfectly calculated to scare the hell out of kids. The music, boy's-nightmare sets, and ingenious psychological tricks in the editing (including an almost brilliant flashback montage) carry the show and give force to the ideas. Only the fastidious will hold the acting and the logic of the script against the movie.

The film's nearly unforgivable trick ending must have seemed a great deal scarier in 1953 than it does now, but when all is said and done, there is plenty of nightmare left to go around.

INVADERS FROM MARS   Film
1986   (C)   U.S.A.   85 min.
Production Company: Cannon Group/Golan-Globus; **Director:** Tobe Hooper; **Producers:** Menaham Golan, Yoram Globus; **Associate Producer:** Edward L. Alperson, Jr.; **Screenplay:** Dan O'Bannon, Don Jakoby, based on Richard Blake's 1953 screenplay; **Photography:** Daniel Pearl; **Editor:** Alain Jakubowicz; **Special Effects:** John Dykstra, Stan Winston (creatures); **Music:** Christopher Young.
Cast: Karen Black, Hunter Carson, Timothy Bottoms, Laraine Newman, James Karen, Bud Cort, Louise Fletcher.

Tobe Hooper, of *Texas Chain Saw Massacre* fame, directed this 1986 remake of the 1953 black and white *Invasion From Mars* (by William Cameron Menzies). Hooper has turned out an altogether opulent production that is at its best when, like its predecessor, it takes seriously its essentially simple plot and the effect of that plot on the film's child protagonist.

Although there are plenty of wonderful moments produced by the wizards who handle the film's special effects—whirlpools of sand that suck people down into them, the resplendent arrival and departure of the space vehicle from Mars—the true horror of the film comes from another source. The Martian invaders, those pneumatic and clumsy tetrapods designed by Stan Winston, look, as the boy David McLean says, like ''huge, ugly, giant, slimy Mr. Potato Heads.'' Though they dance clumsily, roar marvelously, and die when fired at by bazookas, they do not actually persuade us that David is ever in any real danger from them. David's true nightmare is that the warm, whimsical, devoted parents who tucked him into bed one night are turned, by the Martians, into simulacra of affection—stolid, humorless, automata who drink coffee into which mounds of chemical sweetener has been poured and (a touching detail) burn the breakfast bacon to a crisp. David's dilemma is: Who does a child turn to when the parents he trusted no longer inhabit their own bodies?

The answer is Karen Black, the school nurse who slowly comes to believe David's story that a UFO landed ''over the hill'' behind his house; and that David's parents, as well as several other of the town's inhabitants, have been implanted with the device that makes them obedient to the commands of the extra-terrestrials. David, with Karen Black in tow, becomes the St. George who is responsible, finally, for the destruction of the dragons from outer space. And the story, then, would have had a happy ending.

Except, the only happy ending for a nightmare is to wake up, and in David McLean's case (and perhaps ours) somebody is always trying to get him to go back to sleep.

Tobe Hooper's *Invasion From Mars*, horror film though it may be, is suffused with human affection. In that regard, it is worlds away from the grungy cynicism that marked, though it by no means marred, his *Texas Chain Saw Massacre*. In addition, Hooper's *Invasion* is a happy gathering place of visual references to other horror films Hooper has seen; the spaceship in which the invaders arrive has more than a nodding acquaintance with the wreck of the vehicle we saw in *Alien*; the interior of the biology teacher's van, hung with the corpses and skeletons of her specimens, resembles the interior of the house in Hooper's own *Texas Chain Saw Massacre*; and the character of General Wilson, commander of the nearby marine base guarding the NASA installation where David's father works, is hardly altered at all from the portrait of the general in *Dr. Strangelove*.

It may be said in passing that Hooper's comic treatment of the military, whom he sees as bumblingly effective, is perhaps the single serious flaw in an otherwise richly satisfying film.

INVASION OF THE BODY SNATCHERS   Film
1956 (B&W) U.S.A. 80 min.
Production Company: Allied Artists; *Director:* Don Siegel; *Producer:* Walter Wanger; *Screenplay:* Daniel Mainwaring, Sam Peckinpah (uncredited); *Photography:* Ellsworth Fredericks; *Editor:* Robert Eisen; *Special Effects:* Milton Rice; *Music:* Carmen Dragon.
Cast: Kevin McCarthy (Dr. Miles Benell), Dana Wynter (Becky), King Donovan (Jack), Carolyn Jones (Theodora).

When little Jimmy Grimaldi in the town of Santa Mira, California, ''has the crazy idea that his mother is not his mother,'' the recently divorced young doctor Miles Bennell prescribes a placebo and suspects that Jimmy has found a

reason for not going to school. When Becky Driscoll's cousin, Wilma, who is, after all, a grownup, insists to Miles that her uncle Ira is not her uncle, Miles begins to believe that his psychiatric colleague, Dr. Kauffman, is right and that mass delusion is sweeping the town. But when his friends Jack and Theodora find a body lying on the billiard table in their game room, a body that looks disturbingly like Jack, Miles begins to suspect that something considerably more complicated and dangerous than mass delusion is taking place.

Very soon, Miles has his suspicions confirmed. Earth has been invaded by a life form that has a way of growing pods from which bodies emerge that duplicate in every anatomical detail the bodies of earth people. The goal of the invaders is, of course, to take over the Earth.

Now Miles's problem is how to warn the earthly powers that be. The trouble is that, in Santa Mira, some of those powers have already been supplanted by the invaders and, Miles finds it increasingly difficult to know who is human and who is a pod creature. When his old friend, Dr. Kauffman, says ''You and I are scientific men. You can understand the wonder of what's happening,'' Miles knows that from here on it doesn't pay to trust anyone. When, finally, Becky, whom he loves and who has loved him, kisses him without emotion, he knows that ''there isn't a human being left in Santa Mira'' and dashes onto a highway. Arrested as a drunk, he is taken to Los Angeles where, babbling like a madman, he tries desperately to make someone, anyone, believe his story.

Beyond the generally taut plot development in *Invasion of the Body Snatchers*, there are some especially arresting or moving moments. In one we see Miles forcing himself to drive a pitchfork through a semblance of Becky growing in a greenhouse; in another an exhausted Miles and Becky, having escaped their pursuers, have a sudden access of hope when they hear a female voice singing a lovely melody only to discover that the song is coming from the radio of a truck being loaded with pods.

There has been an impulse by critics at the left, right and center of the political spectrum to see *Invasion of the Body Snatchers* as a political allegory warning us about fascism, communism or just plain old conformity. Though the screenplay lends itself to such interpretations, it seems to me that the power of this film rests on the skill with which director Don Siegel has exploited the nightmarish question (posed also in *Invaders From Mars*) What if your father or mother, your comrade or sweetheart, your son or your daughter should turn out not to be who you think they are? Siegel's film confirms our suspicion that the thread by which we cling to our humanity is both fine—and frail.

INVASION OF THE BODY SNATCHERS   Film
1978 (C) U.S.A. 115 min.
Production Company: United Artists; *Director:* Philip Kaufman; *Producer:* Robert H. Solo; *Screenplay:* W. D. Richter; *Photography:* Michael Chapman; *Editor:* Douglas Stewart; *Special Effects:* Dell Rheaume, Russ Hessey, (sound) Ben Burtt; *Music:* Denny Zeitlin.
Cast: Donald Sutherland (Matthew Bennell), Brooke Adams (Elizabeth Driscoll), Leonard Nimoy (Dr. Davis Kibner), Jeff Goldblum (Jack Bellicec), Veronica Cartwright (Nancy Bel-

Dana Wynter and Kevin McCarthy in **Invasion of the Body Snatchers.**

lice), Don Siegel (taxi driver), and Kevin McCarthy (running man).

Philip Kaufman's remake of Don Siegel's *Invasion of the Body Snatchers* does more of everything the first film does but without actually expanding on the horror. Kaufman has taken full advantage of the technological progress made in the more than 20 years since Siegel's *Invasion*. Curiously enough, one such advance, the color photography, does not serve the film well. It makes for a lushness that weakens the stark effects that black and white made possible. On the other hand, the elaborately specific special effects, particularly those involving the pods and the weird process by which they produce their humanoids, add dimensions of horror that were not possible for Siegel.

Some other differences between the two films: The locale this time is San Francisco, which gives the camera more opportunity for visual variety; the birth scenes are so graphic that they become disturbing well beyond their function in the plot; the poignant scene in the 1956 film when a woman's sweet singing arouses Miles and Becky's hopes, becomes more grimly ironic here when Donald Sutherland hears ''Amazing Grace'' coming from a ship in which he hopes to escape and which, he discovers, is being loaded with pods. And finally, there is Denny Zeitlin's insistent and disturbing music, which makes Carmen Dragon's nervous score in the earlier film seem diffident.

Perhaps best of all, there are Donald Sutherland and Jeff Goldblum's performances and Philip Kaufman's direction that, taken together, make for a film sophistication that outdistances the original. It is a sophistication, however, that serves mostly to turn this elaborate *Invasion* into an exercise in the baroque. For horror that is as clean-cut as it is simple, the 1956 version is still to be preferred.

THE INVISIBLE MAN   Film
1933 (B&W) U.S.A. 71 min.
Production Company: Universal; ***Director:*** James Whale; ***Producer:*** Carl Laemmle, Jr.; ***Screenplay:*** R. C. Sheriff, Philip Wylie (based on the novel by H. G. Wells); ***Photography:*** Arthur Edeson; ***Editor:*** no listing; ***Special Effects:*** John P. Fulton.
Cast: Claude Rains (Jack Griffin, The Invisible Man), Gloria Stuart (Flora Kemp), William Harrigan (Dr. Kemp), Una O'Connor (Jennie Hall), Henry Travers (Dr. Cranley), Forrester Harvey (Mr. Hall).

H. G. Wells disavowed James Whale's film version of his novel, *The Invisible Man,* and yet it is something of an astonishment.

The film is a tour de force for Claude Rains who invests the role of the leading character with power and pathos despite the fact that, except for a brief glimpse of his face as the film ends, we only see him swathed from head to toe in bandages. Whatever conviction we have about the character Rains plays derives entirely from the way that he manipulates his voice.

That character is Doctor Griffin, an English scientist who has discovered a drug called monocaine that is capable of rendering him invisible. The drug has an unfortunate side effect. In addition to making its user invisible it turns him insane.

Dr. Griffin embarks on a brief career of crime that includes robbery and murder. He eludes the police easily when he is invisible. The difficulty is that to be invisible, he must also be naked, and it is this fact that makes the film (and the novel on which it is based) so poignant. The time of year is winter and Griffin's teeth chatter and he sniffles as he eludes his pursuers. The most touching, and climactic, scene comes when the police trap him in a barn in a snowbound farmyard. In a brilliantly filmed special effects sequence, we get to see the fugitive's footprints appearing in the snow as he moves across it to his confrontation with the police. Wonderful as that scene is, keen observers will notice that even a film director as great as James Whale can nod. The footprints in the snow are those of a man wearing shoes, and the invisible man is naked.

THE ISLAND OF DOCTOR MOREAU   Novel

H. G. Wells
Great Britain
1896, London: William Heinemann; reprinted, Cambridge, Massachusetts: R. Bentley, 1981.

On an island somewhere in the Pacific, a brilliant rogue scientist named Dr. Moreau has set up a laboratory where he can practice creative vivisection without interference from a prejudiced world. Moreau, with the help of a discredited and alcoholic doctor named Montgomery works on bears, bulls, swine, boars, and finally a puma to give them something resembling a human form. But his idyllic laboratory of pain is intruded upon when a young man named Edward Prendick is cast adrift near his island by the drunken captain of the Ipecachuanha, the ship that has brought Moreau a new consignment of animals. Moreau, still something of a British gentleman, offers Prendick, a natural scientist who "studied with Huxley", his grudging hospitality.

The rest of the story of The Island of Doctor Moreau, continues Prendick's first person account of his experiences with Doctor Moreau, Montgomery and the gallery of monsters that Moreau has created with his scalpel. The island's primitive society is clearly intended by Wells to have an uncomfortable resemblance to our own. The creatures are taught to obey The Law which has been established for them by their maker:

> Not to go down on all-Fours; that is the Law. Are we not men?
> Not to suck up Drink; that is the Law. Are we not men?

. . . .

The litany is followed by the threatening reminder:

> His is the House of Pain.
> His is the Hand that makes.
> His is the hand that heals.

Wells' achievement in The Island of Dr. Moreau is the way that he has framed his narrative with the on-going pain experienced by the Puma, Moreau's final victim. From the animal's very first shriek as Moreau's scalpel begins his work of "humanizing" it to the last glimpse we have of the bloody, much stitched-together "woman" running across the island after she has torn out her fetter with main strength, we are never for a moment unconscious of the puma's agony and it becomes the pulsating theme of the narrative. Moreau, who can set so much pain in motion and sustain it for his ambition's sake emerges, as a consequence, as a truly memorable human monster.

What is missing or only glanced at in the fiction, are the deeply hidden compulsions that animate people like Montgomery and Moreau. For instance, the fact that Wells has made the puma a female, strikes a modern reader as important, but Wells seems merely to mention it in passing.

Wells fails, too, to persuade us that Moreau's island (and Moreau) are analogues of western, Christian society. Particularly unsuccessful is the way he allows Prendick, after Moreau's death, to hint to the Beast People that " 'he is not dead . . . He has changed his shape—he has changed his body . . . You cannot see him. But he can see you. Fear the Law.' "

Fear too The Island of Dr. Moreau, which, despite its weaknesses, is an absolutely compelling horror tale.

THE ISLAND OF LOST SOULS   Film

1932   (B&W)   U.S.A.   72 min.
Production Company: Paramount; *Director:* Earle C. Kenton; *Screenplay:* Waldemar Young and Philip Wylie; *Photography:* Karl Struss; *Special Effects:* Gordon Jennings
Cast: Charles Laughton (Dr. Moreau), Richard Arlen (Edward Parker), Bela Lugosi (Sayer of the Law), Leila Hyams (Ruth Walker), Kathleen Burke (Lota, the Panther Woman), Arthur Hohl (Montgomery).

This film version of H. G. Wells' novel The Island of Dr. Moreau outstrips the printed work in sheer dramatic effectiveness. It is an excellent film on many counts: plotting, direction, stage sets—even acting. But the source of its greatest power is the way that the Young-Wylie screenplay makes repressed or unacknowledged sexuality the absolute center of the film.

Young and Wylie follow the general outlines of Wells' story. Again we have a young man, this time named Edward Parker, set down on Moreau's island by a vindictive sea captain. And again, there is Moreau, aided by Montgomery, presiding over his House of Pain. But Young and Wylie provide Parker with a fiancee who is waiting for him in Apia, who, when Parker fails to show up, hires a doughty sea captain to take her to Moreau's island in quest of Parker.

There, meanwhile, Moreau sees Parker's arrival as a heaven-sent opportunity to conduct a vital experiment with Lota, the most nearly perfect of his creations. Lota, formerly a panther, is now a woman of considerable (and wonderfully mysterious) beauty. Moreau's evil intent is to see if he can get Parker to mate with Lota.

acting honors in this film. Her panther-woman, Lota, is so desirable, so fragile and dear, and speaks in a voice so low and dark that a viewer comes away with a headful of regrets that she comes to such a self-sacrificing end rather than the glorious consummation that ought to have been her reward.

A triumphant film, at once laconic and beautiful, but most of all wise about the proximity of instincts, animal and human, in the same body. And wise about Moreau's crime, which was to turn living flesh into ''things''.

IT   Novel

Stephen King
U.S.A.
1987, New York, Viking

In *It*, a sprawling novel meant to be an epic in the horror genre, the reader confronts the usual problem of Stephen King's fiction: ''What kind of a writer is Stephen King?'' On the one hand he has the God-given gift for knowing what his story is and how to move it along. He can, too, when he is at his best, write unsurpassed descriptions of texture and place. But then, when he is at his worst—that is, when he is writing about people—he can wield the wretchedest pen that ever committed English prose to paper.

It has a marvelous plot: The town of Derry, Maine, has a

Charles Laughton as Dr. Moreau in **The Island of Lost Souls.**

What we have then is a story of linked erotic attractions. Parker has the absent Ruth to be loyal to even as he finds himself attracted to the passionate, newly aroused and scantily clad woman-panther—a far cry from the pale and proper Ruth. Moreau, whose sexuality is very ambiguous, is in the throes of ecstasy as a voyeur whose delight is enhanced by the knowledge that he shares with the audience, that the love scene he is watching is tinged with bestiality. All of this heady stuff takes place in the foreground. In the background, there are the Beast People, all of them male, and their relationship to Moreau, their maker, and his House of Pain.

Laughton's performance is spectacular. His saturnine face, just adorned by a bar moustache and a carefully sculpted anchor shaped beard, glows with a eunuch's passion. When, as Moreau, he listens to the Beast People's chant of adoration, he looks absolutely transfigured: but it is the transfiguration of an egotist into a God [''Do you know,'' he asks earlier, ''what it means to feel like a God?'']. But he is equally radiant when he is spying on the love scenes between Lota and Parker. Finally, where is the actor, besides Laughton, who, getting up from the ground after a hay-maker punch, can put his hands into his pockets as a sign that he has matters like vengeance to attend to?

Then there is Bela Lugosi who, despite a face full of beard that almost completely hides him from sight, turns in a blood-curdling performance as he first utters the law and then incites his fellow Beast Men to break it.

Finally, there is Kathleen Burke who walks away with the

Stephen King. © Thomas Victor

resident monster that nests in the depths of Derry's sewer system and that, at intervals of 20 years or so, causes something ghastly to happen—something that the inhabitants of the town do to each other or that it does to them.

In the middle fifties, when our story begins, the monster (which generally manifests itself in the form of a clown or in the shape of the thing most feared by whoever sees it) has taken to killing children. Then, in a series of elaborately developed circumstance, seven 11-year-olds, six boys and a girl, penetrate the secret that there is an "it" that is responsible for the deaths of the children. Like a band of Homeric heroes, they undertake to hunt "it" to its lair where, by means of an act I will talk about later, they manage to wound it profoundly.

Twenty years later, a new set of murders are committed in Derry and Mike Hanlon, a black librarian, the only one of the band who has stayed in Derry and grown up in it, sends out a call to the other six who, it turns out, have vowed to come back to fight "it" should its cycles of murder begin again. All the members of the band but one (who commits suicide) return and the battle is joined once more.

What is wonderful about King's plot is the fine opportunity it gives him to fuse the variety of incidents in which the children participate with those in which, as adults, they are involved. King seizes those opportunities and then largely wastes them by giving us children who are impossibly wise and adults who are either flat out unlikable, or dreary. Still, they mount their attack against "it." Both as children and when they are adults they triumph over "it" though this costs some of the adults their lives.

In *It* King offers us a cosmology along with his usual horror fare. He posits two forces: One of them is "it," usually represented as a clown, who is the universal power of evil and whom King relates to not-understood or misappreciated sex. The other force is "the turtle," which, having created the universe in a spasm of vomiting, now has a benignly indifferent relationship to it. The turtle, though it does not interfere with the clown's evil, nevertheless gives cryptic good advice to the children and generally wishes them well.

Mediating between these two is the band, which learns that the only way to fight "it" is to commit, literally, an act of love. Readers are unlikely to forget—and some will never forgive—the scene deep in Derry's sewer system where the 11-year-old virgin, Beverly, takes the virginity of each of her six boy companions in turn as the means by which the monster (which, too, is female) is routed from its lair. It is a scene that brings Ambrosio's rape of Antonia in *The Monk* to mind, with the difference that King wants us to see Beverly as a sort of priestess of love invoking the protection of the universe by her life-affirming act. Depending on one's point of view, it is a scene that is either audacious or tasteless in the extreme. Or perhaps both.

It shows Stephen King slogging his way as best he can toward greatness. His conception is grand and he means to give his story universal significance. So, for instance, he gives us children who are meant to represent us all: black, Jewish, Protestant, Catholic and female. But King's people have damp souls and when they talk, they speak King's brand of American populist lingo: a mix of foul mouthed diction with beer-belly half-witticisms. The amazing thing is that despite all the ways in which King assaults our sensibilities, he succeeds in the first task of the horror writer: He knows how to scare his readers to death.

THE ITALIAN   Novel

Ann Radcliffe
Great Britain
1797, London, T. Caddell, Jun, and W. Davies; reprinted 1970, New York, Oxford University Press.

In *The Italian*, Ann Radcliffe, whose *The Mysteries of Udolpho* is almost too genteelly horrifying, tells a story whose characters are both more believable and also in more serious trouble.

In the year 1758, Vicentio di Vivaldi, a young Neapolitan nobleman sees the beautiful Ellena Rosalba in the church of San Lorenzo and falls in love with her. But his mother considers Ellena an inferior mate for her son and contrives, with the help of that great arch villain of a monk, Schedoni, to have Ellena kidnapped and immured in the convent of San Stephano where Ellena endures the full range of persecution imagined by Protestant writers as being committed in Catholic convents and monasteries.

Vivaldi at one point rescues Ellena from the convent and persuades her to marry him secretly, but that scheme is foiled as the ever-busy Schedoni contrives to have Vivaldi imprisoned by the Inquisition while Ellena, guarded by two men, is sent off to a seaside house where she is assigned to the care of Spalatro, a creepy accomplice of Schedoni's.

It is in the isolated seaside villa that the most stunning scene in the novel takes place. Schedoni, determined to have Ellena murdered, first sends Spalatro to do the deed, but when Spalatro balks, Schedoni undertakes the task himself only to discover, at the critical moment, that Ellena, apparently, is his daughter. That discovery, however, does not change Schedoni's character, though it changes the direction of his schemes, which are eventually foiled. He is arrested and the forces of truth, after considerable delay, are finally triumphant.

The Italian, despite its typically Radcliffean prolixity, and its emphasis on its heroine's exquisite sensibility (she swoons with alarming frequency) is a triumphant fiction mostly because of its portrait of that towering villain, Schedoni, who is a fine descendant of Milton's Satan and a fit predecessor of the guilt-ridden, Byronic hero-villain. His darkly brooding presence and the tenacity with which he works to frustrate love, when added to the whiff of incest that clings to him, makes him one of the more deeply-dyed villains who stalk through the pages of Gothic fiction. Matthew Lewis's Ambrosio may finally be more loathesome, but the mantle of evil hangs more gracefully on Schedoni's shoulders.

IT'S ALIVE   Film

1975   (C)   U.S.A.   90 min.
Production Company: Larco; ***Director:*** Larry Cohen; ***Producer:*** Larry Cohen; ***Screenplay:*** Larry Cohen; ***Photography:*** Fenton Hamilton; ***Editor:*** Peter Honess; ***Special Effects:*** Robert Bigart, Patrick Somerset; ***Music:*** Bernard Herrmann.
Cast: John Ryan (Frank Davies), Sharon Farrell (Lenore), Andrew Duggan (professor), Guy Stockwell (Clayton), Michael Ansara (captain), James Dixon (Lieutenant Perkins).

Like *Embryo* and *Prophecy,* this is a film that pregnant women are well advised to avoid.

Sometimes the formula for making a horror film turns on a premise so simple that one wonders how the filmmakers could bring themselves to invest money and time on so flimsy a notion. *It's Alive* is such a film. And yet, the greater mystery is how a film as hastily made and as poorly edited as this one can have been so successful at the box office that it produced a sequel, *It Lives Again* (1978).

The film answers the question, "What if a newborn baby were the bloodthirsty creature in our 'creature feature'?" The newborn baby we are talking about is born to a Santa Monica family named Davis. It is a difficult birth for Mrs. Davis and a disastrous one for the medical delivery team because the baby promptly kills everyone there except its mother.

From that point on, we have a straightforward chase movie in which the entire Los Angeles police force is pitted against a fanged (but otherwise vaguely delineated) infant. For a long time, the baby is smarter than the police. It kills several people, partly for nourishment, partly for sheer lust. As it avoids the cops, the baby becomes a sort of instructor in ethics to its parents. The father at first disavows any relationship to the killer infant. The mother is immediately maternal, and an older brother demonstrates that he has a kind heart. Finally, the family—mommy, daddy, mutant baby and older brother—achieve something resembling family unity, but by then the police, in a Los Angeles sewer, are doing their brutal, but necessary duty.

It's Alive is one of those shabby but, because of its ghastly family dynamics, unforgettable films that is an embarrassment to one's judgment.

IT'S A GOOD LIFE   Short Story

Jerome Bixby
U.S.A.
1953, in Frederik Pohl's (ed.) *Star Science Fiction Stories No. 2,* New York, Ballantine; reprinted 1979 in Leonard Wolf's (ed.) *Wolf's Complete Book of Terror,* New York, Clarkson N. Potter.

"It's a Good Life" is a rarity in the terror fiction genre. It is at once poignant and frightening.

Jerome Bixby poses an overwhelming question: What if Almighty God should prove to be an idiot?

The idiot in question is the boy Anthony who was born both defective and all powerful. His mind can create or destroy according to the wayward motions of his will. The inhabitants of the tiny farming community, which is what the human world has been reduced to since Anthony first began to exercise his powers, live in a low-key hell from which only death can rescue them because Anthony can read their every thought and Anthony has very clear, if brutal notions of what sorts of thoughts people ought to think: good thoughts, nice thoughts. Anyone who dares any other kind risks being "thought . . . into a grave deep, deep in the cornfield."

Readers will be haunted for a very long time by Bixby's laconic account of how the entire population of the village of Peaksville seated by candlelight before a television set is forced to watch the meaningless "twisting, writhing shapes on the screen," which are projections of Anthony's mind. When the villagers doggedly, desperately assert that, "It's real nice . . . It's the best show we've ever seen!" the full cruelty of Bixby's vision looms suddenly up out of his tiny tale.

J

JAWS   Novel

Peter Benchley
U.S.A.
1974, Garden City, N.Y., Doubleday.

This skillfully constructed fiction is cannily calculated to
keep a reader glued to the page. With a moral dilemma right
out of Ibsen, a love story that would not shame the pages of
Cosmopolitan magazine, and a verve that is Peter Benchley's
own, *Jaws* tells the story of what happens when a great white
shark takes up residence in the quiet waters off the resort
town of Amity, Long Island. When the remains of the shark's
first victim are found on the beach, the town's leading citizens
face a thorny problem. If they repress the news of the shark
attack they risk other deaths. If, in the interests of safety, they
close the beaches they risk a financially disastrous summer.
The issue is neatly entwined with a not quite so compelling
account of the private lives of the book's protagonists, Police
Chief Brody, Ellen, his wife, and Matthew Hooper, a hotshot
shark expert from Woods Hole. But the novel really shifts
into high gear when Hooper and Brody join Quint, the tough-
talking shark hunter, on his boat in the waters off Amity
where they go in pursuit of the shark.

The confrontation with the great white makes wonderful
reading. Peter Benchley, with Melville's *Moby Dick* for a
model, does what he can to invest his shark with metaphysi-
cal meaning: The creature is white, it is huge (it weighs more
than 3,000 pounds), it is cunning and it has malign intelligence. Finally, it provides the men with that most exhilarat-
ing, if most delusive, of all tests—the test of their manhood.
The result is a book that, while hardly a work of high
literature, is already showing signs that it will endure as a
classic adventure yarn.

In 1975, Universal Pictures released *Jaws,* a fast-paced
movie based on the novel, which boasts some of the most
convincing special effects ever filmed.

JAWS   Film

1975 (C) U.S.A. 125 min.
Production Company: Universal; ***Director:*** Steven Spielberg;
Producer: Richard Zanuck, David Brown; ***Screenplay:*** Peter
Benchley, Carl Gottlieb; ***Photography:*** Bill Butler; ***Under-
water Photographer:*** Rexford Metz; ***Shark Footage:*** Ron and
Valeria Taylor; ***Editor:*** Verna Fields; ***Special Effects:*** Bob
Mattey; ***Music:*** John Williams.
Cast: Roy Scheider (Brody), Robert Shaw (Quint), Richard
Dreyfuss (Hooper), Lorraine Gary (Ellen Brody), Murray
Hamilton (Vaughan).

Steven Spielberg's *Jaws* has just as much going for it as
Benchley's novel, plus special effects of such superior power
that even the most jaded viewers still find themselves shaken
by the events taking place on the screen. One is not very far
into the film before every ripple of the surface of the sea turns
sinister.

Spielberg's great talent is precision of focus and his film
never lets us forget that it is about a malevolent monster
shark (three tons, 25 feet in length) and an island full of
innocent potential victims. The good guys who do battle
against it include Hooper, a new culture hero, the bespecta-
cled college boy nerd who knows all about sharks; Quint, a
rogue shark killer; and Brody, Amity's chief of police who,
in the battle rediscovers his manhood.

Though Spielberg, and before him Benchley, do what they
can to recall *Moby Dick*, the film's major flaw is that the
shark's malevolent intelligence is hard to credit. But in the
confrontations between people and shark, the shark's killer
instincts are malevolent enough to sustain the film's terror
and we hardly notice that we do not have a fully functioning
allegory.

Jaws has some of the most startling (not terrifying) moments in the history of film, and Spielberg, wielding the new
freedom to be graphic, makes his camera seem to drop
severed limbs into our laps or get us so close to a man being

mangled and swallowed whole that it is all we can do to stay in our seats. At the same time, when it suits Spielberg's sense of pace, he gives us scenes in which the details of what the shark is doing to a thrashing victim are mercifully kept from us.

Scheider's performance as Brody is either as wooden as it appears to be or is a subtle study of the paralysis of mind that comes with the wielding of petty power. Robert Shaw's Quint does not hold up too well after a decade, either. He does not quite project the rugged, meanminded but resourceful folk figure his creators (Spielberg-Benchley) meant him to be. Richard Dreyfuss, on the other hand, is a happy presence in the film—Swiftly intelligent, alert, humorous and, despite the absence of a love interest to round him out, fully *there*.

There have been two sequels to *Jaws: Jaws II* (1978) and *Jaws 3D* (1983). Of *Jaws 3-D*, Gene Wright, in *Horrorshows*, says that you "had to take a snorkel to [it] to protect yourself from the shark vomit floating off the screen."

THE JUDGE'S HOUSE   Short Story
Bram Stoker
Great Britain
1914, in *Dracula's Guest and Other Weird Stories*, London, Routledge; reprinted 1975 in *Classic Ghost Stories by Charles Dickens and Others*, New York, Dover.

Young Malcolm Malcolmson, needing a quiet place to spend three months studying for his Mathematical Tripos, takes a train to the first town on the railroad schedule whose name he does not recognize and there he rents an old house that, as he discovers, has a reputation for "something" uncanny about it.

The house is known as "the Judge's house" because it was the home, 100 years ago, of a "judge who was held in great terror on account of his harsh sentences and his hostility to prisoners at Assizes."

On the first night of his tenure in the old house, Malcolmson is disturbed only vaguely by the sound of rats in the wainscoting. But when, at dawn, he finds himself being stared at by an enormous rat with baleful eyes, his situation takes on a considerably different character. It becomes more sinister still when he learns that the alarm bell rope up which the rat regularly makes his escape was the very rope the hangman used to carry out the executions the judge ordered long ago. Malcolm now studies the judge's features in the painting of him that he finds in the house. It was a face, writes Stoker, that was "strong and merciless, evil, crafty, and vindictive, with a sensual smile, hooked nose of ruddy color and shaped like the beak of a bird of prey."

The first stage of horror begins as Malcolmson recognizes that the turning eyes in the judge's face in the portrait are the same as those of the huge rat that stares at him. The second and final stage of the nightmare begins when it becomes clear to the reader, though not to Malcolmson, that the rat's hostility is preternatural and that Malcolm is doomed. When the story's climactic final moment is reached, the word "malignant" takes on a new and darker meaning.

While "The Judge's House" has a fairly predictable plot, it may well be Stoker's most successful short story. He does three things very well: First, where Stoker is generally careless about structure, he has here imposed a tight design. Second, as in *Dracula*, he is superb on atmosphere, creating a sense of looming evil by linking the ferocious energy of the malevolent judge with the living presence of the baleful-eyed rat. Finally, design and atmosphere come wonderfully together at the story's end, when we hear the clanging of the alarm bell in the judge's house and all the lines of interest in the tale suddenly, and horribly, intersect.

THE JULY GHOST   Short Story
A. S. Byatt
Great Britain
1982, in T. J. Binding's (ed.) *Firebird One*, Middlesex, Penguin; reprinted 1984 in J. A. Cuddon's (ed.) *The Penguin Book of Ghost Stories*, London, Penguin.

Here is a very modern ghost story in which a child ghost, that of a charming eight-year-old boy, returns from the dead to contrive a love affair for his rigid, emotionally frozen mother.

All of the adults we meet in the story have recently broken their links with people they once loved. The protagonist, who not long ago ended a relationship with a warm and affectionate woman named Anne, is now a boarder in the home of a woman in her middle thirties whose child died a year ago and whose husband no longer lives with her.

The boarder describes his situation, half flirtatiously to an American woman he has met at a party. She, we learn, is just recovering from the end of an affair with her married professor. But it is also clear that she is quite ready to forge a new link with the boarder.

The complication for him is that in the course of the recent hot summer, he has made contact with the ghost of his landlady's son. Slowly it is borne in upon him that the child wants his mother to have a baby so that he, the revenant child, can find rest. What the boarder further understands is that the ghost has designated him to be the father of that child.

What happens then has all the grunginess and the beauty that can characterize real life. A. S. Byatt handles both kinds of detail with admirable delicacy and compassion.

KING KONG   Film
1933 (B&W) U.S.A. 100 min.
Production Company: RKO; **Director:** Merian C. Cooper and
Ernest B. Schoedsack; **Screenplay:** James Creelman, Ruth
Rose, based on a story by Merian C. Cooper and Edgar
Wallace; **Photography:** Edward Lindon, Vernon L. Walker
and J.O. Taylor; **Editor:** Ted Cheesman; **Special Effects:** Willis
O'Brien, Marcel Delgado, E.B. Gibbons, Fred Reefe, Orville
Goldner and Carrol Shephird; **Music:** Max Steiner.
Cast: Fay Wray (Ann Darrow), Robert Armstrong (Carl Den-
ham), Bruce Cabot (John Driscoll), Frank Reicher (Captain
Engelhorn).

There is always a danger of taking monster movies too
seriously but with *King Kong* almost any profundity we see in
it seems to fit. However, there is one thing in this film which
above all else accounts for its extraordinary power. Amazingly enough, its directors treat the love affair between King
Kong and Ann Darrow as something real. That there is a love
affair is inescapable. From Kong's point of view, the love is
as limitless as, from Ann Darrow's, it is appalling.

Of course the whole thing is absurd: The giant gorilla
cannot possibly marry the beautiful blonde and settle down
to raise babies in the suburbs. But the sad, sad question that
is never asked aloud in the film but which throbs in every
viewer's heart is, "Why not? Dear God, why not?" Is Kong
not brave and huge and tender and true? Isn't Ann Darrow
delicate and small and blonde and lovely? What more do we
need for a happy ending? In this case, more than is available—which is why *King Kong* moves, in so unlikely a fashion, in the direction of tragedy.

The tragedy is all Kong's. Kong is the beast of integrity
who was doing just fine on his island home being himself.
He was the primordial innocent, competent against pterodac-
tyls and brontosauruses. He was the master of all he surveyed,
until into his dangerous paradise there came Ann Darrow, a
down-and-out actress, with the movie company for which
she works. The savages who live on one end of Skull Island

capture Ann and offer her to Kong as his bride. Kong accepts
the gift and is immediately vanquished by it. He holds the girl
in his palm and bats his enormous eyes at her, the perfect
image of a boy in love. Ann Darrow, the bit of blonde fluff in
his hand, cowers back. That scene, with all that it speaks of
impossible hunger, is at the heart of the *King Kong* matter.

Kong, as we know, is captured by the unscrupulous movie
producer using gas bombs and is hauled to New York City to
be made a spectacle of. But he has moments of consolation;
he gets to see Ann from time to time. Then, on the evening
he is to go on exhibit, he mistakes the photographers' flashing
bulbs as an attack against Ann.

Kong goes berserk and the events that follow make up one
of the great film sequences of all time. Not only because it is
full of violence, but also because so many kinds of meaningful
violence come together in it: the frenzy of the audience as
men and women trample each other in a rush for the exits;
the near destruction of Manhattan involving derailed sub-
ways, blazing fires and explosions; and the ultimate violence
of Kong—King Kong asserting his freedom and (what else
shall we call it?) his manhood and his love. The most
touching moment of the film is clearly the one in which we
see the harassed gorilla teetering with one prehensile foot on
the tip of the Empire State Building. He has been wounded
in a thousand places, but he is still fending off the dive
bombers the Air Force has sent. At that moment, and with
the knowledge of his death already upon him, Kong carefully
places Ann Darrow, the first (and now the last) glimmer of
beauty his brute brain has ever known, onto a ledge so that
she, at least, will be safe. Only with this bit of tenderness
accomplished, does the mighty Kong give up the long struggle against incomprehensible forces. There is a final burst of
machine-gun fire, a final wave of Kong's tremendous arm—
almost a signal of farewell—and Kong falls into the canyons
of Manhattan, making a vast, dignified crash, after which he
is no more than a mountain of bleeding fur.

The film is essentially over at that point. We now know
that we have been watching a pair of riddles: Who is the

King Kong wreaks havoc. © Universal Pictures

Beauty and where is the Beast? In the moment of his fall, Kong acquires all that we know of human nobility. Not only that, Kong also becomes beautiful because he is—and has always been—morally clean.

As for Ann Darrow's trivial friends, who would give a plugged nickel for any of them? They have neither decency nor style nor compassion. Money is their god and betrayal their instinct. Unfortunately, these pale creatures have gas bombs and airplanes and greed on their side. And so we grieve, having discovered once again that against such odds, mere integrity is doomed.

KISS OF THE VAMPIRE   Film

1962   (C)   Great Britain   87 min.
Production Company: Hammer; **Director:** Don Sharp; **Producer:** Anthony Hinds; **Screenplay:** John Elder (pseudonym for Anthony Hinds); **Photography:** Alan Hume; **Editor:** James Needs; **Special Effects:** Les Bowie; **Music:** James Bernard.
Cast: Clifford Evans (Professor Zimmer), Edward De Souza (Gerald Harcourt) Noel Wilman (Dr. Ravna), Jennifer Daniel (Marianne), Barry Warren (Carl), Jaqui Wallis (Sabena).

Kiss of the Vampire is another of those gorgeous Hammer Films productions that cunningly intertwines dread with desire. It has all of Hammer's usual trademarks: carriages being driven slowly (or at a gallop) through leafy forests, Victorian interiors gleaming with costly, hand-carved wood and, of course, a certain number of bosomy young women in peril.

As the film opens, we are in a cemetery where a funeral is being conducted. We hear bird song and Latin phrases. The ceremony is being watched from afar by a solitary figure (Professor Zimmer) who comes slowly forward. Someone says, "He's been drinking again." The figure approaches the coffin, sprinkles holy water over it, then drives a spade down through it. Abruptly, the camera takes us into the coffin and we see the face of the fanged vampire writhing there.

We cut now to the proper beginning of the plot. It is some time around 1905. A young honeymoon couple, Gerald and Marianne Harcourt, run out of gas in the vicinity of a chateau inhabited by a family named Ravna. Overtaken by a rainstorm, the couple take refuge in an all but abandoned inn run by an unhappy couple named Bruno and Anna. There is

Noel Wilman and Jennifer Daniel in **Kiss of the Vampire.** ©
Hammer Films

KWAIDAN   Film
1964 (C) Japan 125 min.
Production Company: Ninjin Club/Bungei; ***Director:*** Masaki
Kobayashi; ***Producer:*** Shigeru Wakatsuki; ***Screenplay:*** Yoko
Mizuki; ***Photography:*** Yoshio Miyajimo; ***Music:*** Toru Tak-
emitsu.
Cast: *The Black Hair:* Rentaro Mikuni (Samurai), Michiyo
Aratama (First Wife), Misako Watanaba (Second Wife); *The
Woman in the Snow:* Keiku Kishi (Minokichi), Yuku Mochi-
zuki (Yuki Onna); *In a Cup of Tea:* Ganemon Nakamura
(Kannai), Noboru Nakaya (Heinai); *Hoichi the Earless:* Katsuo
Nakamura (Hoichi), Rentaro Shimura (priest), Joichich Hay-
ashi (Yoshitsune).

Four episodes of varying degrees of complexity and power,
but all of them fascinating, make up this anthology film from
Japan. Based on *Kwaidan,* Lafcadio Hearn's collection of
Japanese tales, the film is utterly unlike anything we are used
to in the west. Its deliberate pacing, its narrowly focused
scenes, its stark displays of light and shade and its emphasis
on symbolic gesture are uniquely Japanese.

The first of the episodes, and the one with the least resonance, is called "The Black Hair." Filmed in a curious shade
of magenta that gives the action a heavy tinge of the surreal,
it tells the story of a young Samurai in Kyoto who, because
he has been suddenly impoverished, divorces his wife and
goes off into the world to better himself. He marries a second

another guest at the inn, a reclusive older man named
Professor Zimmer, whom sharp-eyed viewers will recognize
as the man with the spade in the opening scene.

Soon the Harcourts find themselves courted by the charming and elegant Ravnas who live in the chateau. Dr. Ravna,
his son Karl, a talented pianist and composer, and his daughter Sabena, who seems to have no career but to be lovely,
are, we learn, a family of vampires who mean to make the
Harcourts their victims as they have previously done with
Bruno and Anna's daughter, Tanya.

Marianne Harcourt, dazzled by the Ravnas, is initiated into
the vampire cult headed by Dr. Ravna, but Gerald escapes
Tanya's clutches by smearing the sign of the cross with his
own blood. In a wonderful, but perfectly unbelievable climax,
Professor Zimmer, who hates the Ravnas for having vampirized his daughter, and Ravna engage in a duel of incantations
which Ravna loses as we know, because he and a roomful of
panicky vampire followers are attacked by a swarm of bats
summoned from whatever purlieus of hell such creatures
inhabit.

Beyond the intelligent screenplay and the erotic sensuality
that one has come to expect of a Hammer film, *Kiss of the
Vampire* is notable for the fine use it makes of religious
symbols and traditional vampire lore. God and Satan are
each given their due as spells, invocations and incantations
are resorted to on both sides.

For vampire tale aficianados, then, who like to have their
favorite theme taken seriously, *Kiss of the Vampire* is an
altogether pleasing (though hardly great) film.

Hoichi the biwa player in Lafcadio Hearn's **Kwaidan.**

A montage of characters from **Kwaidan.**

wife only to discover very soon that he is still in love with the woman he divorced. Ten years later, after he is released from some official commitment, he leaves his second wife and returns to Kyoto and to his home. As he moves through the house looking for his first wife, the lighting and the camera angles cue us that something strange may be happening. The scene darkens and the Samurai finds himself stumbling through his familiar rooms. When he finds his wife, she is gently, sadly and intensely glad to see him. Their reconciliation is extremely tender and it ends where marital reconciliations often do, in bed. When the Samurai wakes in the morning he has a smile on his face, but when he turns to look at his wife's beautiful black hair, what he sees sets him screaming.

In the second episode, "The Woman in the Snow," based on Hearn's "Yuki-Onna," two woodchoppers, one young and one old, are caught in a snowstorm that is as unconvincing and as beautiful a studio snowstorm as I have ever seen. As they make their way through the storm, the camera occasionally shows us glimpses of a hypnotic "eye" in the sky where, if it were clear weather, the sun would be. The woodchoppers take refuge in a ferryman's hut where they fall asleep. The young man wakes to see a beautiful but

strange looking woman bending over the old man and breathing into his face. And as she does, the old man dies. The woman, then, aware that the young man has seen her, warns that she will kill him if he ever tells anyone what he has seen. With that, she goes off into the snow.

Some time later, the young man meets a country girl who is on her way to the nearby town to look for work. Since she is both beautiful and unmarried, the young man and his mother persuade her to stay with them. She does and shortly thereafter the young people marry.

Ten years pass and the young woman is a good wife and mother. Then one night the husband, watching his wife's face by lamplight, is struck by how beautiful she is and how much she resembles the snow witch he saw so long ago. He tells his wife the story of what happened then and concludes, "But of course it was a dream."

To which she replies, "It was not a dream." And adds, "I told you then I would kill you if you told . . ." A couple of moments later, the episode ends.

We come now to the third episode, the longest, the most beautiful and in every way the most powerful of the four. It begins with a voice chanting the history of the battles fought between the Genji and Heike clans in the year 1185, as the camera moves from painted versions of the fighting to reenactments of it so that, at any given moment, there are three times vying for our attention: the historical past as recreated by the moving picture camera; the painted version of that past; and the restless movement of the real-time sea on which, long ago, all the events took place.

The result is that we get a breathtaking display of the past as it fuses with the simple story of Hoichi, a blind *biwa* player [a *biwa* is a stringed instrument that only vaguely resembles a guitar] who, at night, is summoned by a Samurai to go to the home of his lord to chant the story of the battle between the Genji and Heike clans. Over a period of several nights, Hoichi chants the epic tale. It becomes clear to the chief priest in the temple where Hoichi lives that the nobleman's "home" is the nearby cemetery and that Hoichi's audience is made up of the ghosts of the defeated warriors. To protect him from the demons the priest has holy verses and sayings painted over Hoichi's body. But the paintbrush wielding priest forgets to paint Hoichi's ears, with disastrous results for Hoichi.

The "Hoichi the Earless" episode ought to be one of the most treasured films in the whole history of the horror genre. Individual frames (as well as whole scenes) deserve the kind of affectionate study that great paintings attract. There is, for instance, a nearly casual shot of a sparsely furnished room in which a large slice of watermelon sits on a table. Neither the room nor the watermelon slice are brightly lighted, but that bit of muted red on the wooden table acts as an organizing gesture that displays the room to the eye as a magnificently designed artifact.

And that is just what a single two- or three-second instant can give one. The rest of the film is studded with wonderful visual and musical sequences, all of them serving the horrifying, penultimate moment when Hoichi, his entire body painted over by exquisite calligraphy, is set upon by the demon who is prevented by the holy writing from seeing anything but Hoichi's ears.

There is a fourth episode that is interesting enough but that is hopelessly overwhelmed by its predecessor. It tells the story of a man who, as he is about to drink from a cup of tea, sees the reflection of a stranger in it. At first disconcerted, he then defiantly drinks the tea and shortly afterward pays a terrible price for having "drunk another man's soul."

The final tally on the four episodes in *Kwaidan*, then, is that we have one masterpiece accompanied by three good but not equally distinguished companions.

L

LA BELLE DAME SANS MERCI   Poem
John Keats
Great Britain
1820; reprinted 1979 in Leonard Wolf's (ed.) *Wolf's Complete Books of Terror,* New York, Clarkson N. Potter.

Keats's poem, an imitation folk ballad, has 12 four-line stanzas in which a dialogue between an interrogator and a knight-at-arms takes place. In the compass of that small space, a great deal of information and feeling are crammed.

In the first three stanzas we learn that it is a grim day in the fall; that the knight-at-arms is pale and haggard. The succeeding nine stanzas answer the question:

> "O, what can ail thee, knight-at-arms,
>   Alone and palely loitering?
> . . . .
> O, what can ail thee, knight-at-arms,
>   So haggard and so woe-begone?"

The horror of the poem is to be found in the knight's reply. He tells us that he met a beautiful woman "whose hair was long, her foot was light/And her eyes were wild." He courted her and she "look'd at me as she did love,/And made sweet moan."

With that, he puts her on his horse and, in a daze of love, goes wherever she leads him.

> "She took me to her elfin grot,
>   And there she wept, and sigh'd full sore,
> And there I shut her wild wild eyes
>   With kisses four."

After the tumult of their lovemaking, he falls asleep and dreams that he:

> ". . . saw pale kings, and princes too,
>   Pale warriors, death-pale were they all;
> They cried, 'La Belle Dame Sans Merci
>   Hath thee in thrall.' "

When he sees "their starved lips in the gloam,/With horrid warning gaped wide" he wakes to the real world where he is no longer fit to live. Which is why he sojourns:

> ". . . . . here
>   Alone and palely loitering,
> Though the sedge is wither'd from the lake,
>   And no birds sing."

Now, whether one reads the poem as a straightforward account of the knight's experience with a succubus, or as a poem about the debilitating power of the feminine principle, or whether one sees it as an allegory about the deadly cost of making poetry, one thing is clear: Something appalling, something from which he will never recover happened to the knight. And whatever it was, it involved love, which, Keats tells us, moves from fascination to sweetness and then to revulsion. It is not a formula reassuring to lovers, but it was one that, in the 19th century, was more familiar than it is now—or so one must suppose.

LA BELLE HÉLÈNE   Verse
Prosper Mérimée
France
1827, in *La Guzla;* reprinted 1974 in Leonard Wolf's (ed.) *Wolf's Complete Book of Terror,* New York, Clarkson N. Potter.

This strangely beautiful tale, told as if it were being sung by an Illyrian folk singer, is the story of an old man's lust for another man's young wife. She is named Hélène and she is married to the brave hunter Theodore Khonopka who has to leave home for an extended stay in Venice. While he is gone, the evil old Piero Stamati tries to buy Hélène's love. Rebuffed, he consults a wicked Jew who teaches him how to get revenge.

. . . they scored [a] toad's skin with their daggers' points until a subtle venom oozed from the cuts. This they gathered into a vial, from which they forced the toad to drink. That done, they caused the toad to lick the skin of a lovely fruit . . .

That fruit is sent to Hélène who, after eating it, "felt terribly sick, and it seemed to her that a snake was stirring in her belly . . ." Horribly enough, it is not long before Hélène feels pregnant, and looks it to every eye. "The women said, 'Hélène is pregnant; yet how can that be, since her husband has been in Venice for more than ten months?' "

A year after his departure, Khonopka comes home and finds Hélène and her swollen belly. Outraged, Khonopka cuts off her head. Then, to complete his vengeance, he cuts open her belly meaning to use the bastard child in a trap to catch its father. What he finds when he is done is even more loathesome than anything we have witnessed so far.

Because the moral forces in the story are presented to us without shading—Hélène is good, Stamati is evil, Khonopka has too little faith—we are under some compulsion to read it as an allegory. But what finally moves a reader more, I think, is Hélène's appalling personal isolation once her biologically impossible pregnancy is visible to the whole town.

LA GRANDE BRETÊCHE   Short Story
Honoré Balzac
France
1842, in *Autre Étude de Femme*; reprinted 1944 in Herbert A. Wise and Phyllis Fraser's *Great Tales of Terror and the Supernatural*, New York, Random House.

"La Grande Bretêche" is a story with the keen, vicious bite of a dirty joke, but one that has been elevated into a mordant and very French bedroom tragicomedy.

The central situation is as simple as can be: The Comte de Merret, a haughty and hotheaded possessor of a vast chateau on the Loire, has never had any reason to suspect that Madame la Comtesse is anything but a faithful wife. Coming home unexpectedly one evening, he goes to his ailing wife's room and, as he turns the key to enter the door, he hears a suspicious rustling. When he goes in he finds her standing alone before the fireplace, but the door to a small closet in the room is closed. The Comte "looked at his wife, and read in her eyes an indescribably anxious and haunted expression." Moved by a horrid suspicion, he "said to his wife coldly, 'Madame, there is someone in your cupboard!' She looked at her husband calmly and replied quite simply, 'No, Monsieur.' " The Comte then seizes his wife's crucifix and, holding it out to her, says:

"Swear to me before God that there is no one in there; I will believe you—I will never open that door."

Madame de Merret took up the crucifix and said, "I swear it."

"Louder," said her husband; "and repeat: 'I swear before God that there is nobody in that closet.' " She repeated the words without flinching.

And that moment defines the impasse and determines the horrid outcome of the story. Because, of course, there is someone in the closet. He is the handsome young Spanish prisoner of war, Bagos de Férédia, who has been sent to Vendôme on parole. And when the Comte, keeping his wife under his rigid scrutiny, sends for a mason and orders that the closet be bricked up, the impasse turns into a sort of deadly staring match in which the question is: Who will blink first? Will the Comte relent? Will La Comtesse confess? Will

the young Spaniard emerge from the closet, thereby betraying the Comtesse's honor? And what will the mason and the mason's sweetheart Rosalie, the Comtesse's servant, do, both of whom know why the closet is being walled up?

But "La Grande Bretche" is even more horrifying than this summary of its tricky plot suggests. Balzac, by introducing a number of people from all walks of French society, makes his grisly joke seem to be a natural expression of a culture in which the social forms take precedence over the substance of life.

LA RELIGIEUSE   Novel
(Memoirs of a Nun)
Denis Diderot
France
1796, Paris, Buisson; reprinted 1977 and translated by C. G. and J. Robinson, London, Penguin.

Diderot's novel, while not precisely Gothic fiction, makes considerable use of the Gothic tradition in eliciting sympathy for the almost unbelievable misadventures that overtake a young woman who, at the behest of her parents—one of whom knows, while the other suspects, that she is not her father's child—is forced into the life of a nun.

Susan Simonin, the Sister Susan of Diderot's story, knows at once that the conventual life is not for her, and for the first half of the book, she makes a valiant effort to resist what is happening to her. And pretty nearly all of what is happening is grisly. When she makes it clear that she does not intend to take her final vows, the full wrath of the convent is turned on her. She is isolated from her fellow novices; she is given tasks that are impossible to perform; her way is strewn with ground glass; the windows in her cell are broken; she is given successively more inadequate food and clothing. She is jabbed by needles; tricked into picking up a red hot pincer; tied with rope and placed in a dark hole. The sisters, bent on breaking her will so that she will accept the conventual life she abhors, subject her to every conceivable punishment that women in confinement can make to one of their number who has been designated a fair target.

All of that takes place in part one of the novel. In part two, rescued from her torment by the attorney who has been exercising his skill in her behalf, she is sent to a "better" convent where she becomes the target of a lascivious Mother Superior. From here on, the atmosphere of *La Religieuse* shifts from the sinister to the seriocomic as we watch the interplay between Sister Susan's intransigent innocence and the Mother Superior's feverish compulsions, then back to the macabre as Sister Susan, fleeing the convent, is ravished by a Benedictine monk and left to discover what the world outside the walls of a convent is like.

Diderot wrote *La Religieuse* in 1760 as part of a practical joke on his friend the Marquis of Croismare, which may account for an ebullience of tone somewhat at war with the gloomy Gothic events and interiors it chronicles. The book was not published until 1796, the same year as Matthew Lewis's *The Monk*, with which it has various elements in common. It bears, too, a certain family resemblance to the Marquis de Sade's *La Nouvelle Justine*, which first appeared in 1797. *La Religieuse*, like those fictions, has a curiously modern

understanding of the ways in which our fantasy life—especially our erotic fantasy life—determines our behavior.

THE LAIR OF THE WHITE WORM   Novel
Bram Stoker
Great Britain
1911, London, River; reprinted 1966, London, Jarrold.

Bram Stoker, the author of *Dracula*, was 64 years old when
he published *The Lair of the White Worm*, this most disturbing
of all his many fictions.

Let it be said first that the word "worm" as Stoker uses it
in his title means "serpent." Then let us turn to Lady Arabella
March who is the evil center of *The Lair of the White Worm*.

Stoker tells us that she moves with "a quick gliding motion" and is:

> clad in some kind of soft white stuff, which clung close to her
> form, showing to the full every movement of her sinuous
> figure . . . Her voice was peculiar, very low and sweet, and
> so soft that the dominant note was of sibilation. Her hands,
> too, were peculiar—long, flexible, white, with a strange
> movement as of waving gently to and fro.

Young Adam Salton, who is her neighbor, very soon learns
that she is a manifestation of a huge serpent, who, when she
is not in her human form, lives at the bottom of a thousand-
foot hole into which she draws her victims, "her white arms
encircling him, down . . . into the noisome depths . . ."

That hole, Stoker says, has:

> a queer smell—yes! Like bilge or a rank swamp. It was
> distinctly nauseating . . . like nothing that Adam had ever
> met with. He compared it with all the noxious experiences he
> had ever had—the drainage of war hospitals, of slaughter-
> houses, the refuse of dissecting rooms . . . the sourness of
> chemical waste and the posoinous effluvium of the bilge of a
> water-logged ship whereon a multitude of rats had been
> drowned.

Adam finally destroys this formidable creature by filling
her hole with dynamite which, sparked by lightning, explodes:

> From [the well hole] agonized shrieks were rising, growing
> ever more terrible with each second that passed . . . Once, in
> a sort of lull or pause, the seething contents of the hole rose
> . . . and Adam saw part of the thin form of Lady Arabella,
> forced up to the top amid a mass of slime.

The Lair of the White Worm is hardly for squeamish readers
for two reasons: first, the straightforward physical descriptions of wet, smelly and revolting things are deplorably
graphic; and, second, there is the embarrassment that overwhelms one because Stoker seems unaware of just how kinky
his imagery is. In *Dracula*, the vampire plays his role as an
eroticizing threat to women without making us wonder
whether Stoker's mind is intact. *The Lair of the White Worm*,
on the other hand, reads uncomfortably like journal entries
dictated by someone whose personal problems are, at every
instant, shaping his prose.

THE LEGEND OF HELL HOUSE   Film
1973   (C)   Great Britain   94 min.
Production Company: Academy Pictures; ***Director:*** John
Hough; ***Producers:*** Albert Fennell, Norman T. Herman;
Screenplay: Richard Matheson; ***Photography:*** Alan Hume;
Editor: Geoffrey Foote; ***Special Effects:*** Roy Whybrow; ***Mu-
sic:*** Brian Hodgson, Delia Derbyshire.
Cast: Pamela Franklin (Florence Tanner), Roddy McDowall
(Ben Fisher), Clive Revill (Lionel Barrett), Gayle Hunnicutt
(Mrs. Barrett).

The Legend of Hell House is a pretty scrupulous rendering of
Richard Matheson's novel of the same name. It is a film that
leaves a viewer with an uneasy sense that even more horror
is implicit in it than has managed to reach the eye.

Matheson's story, which bears comparison with Shirley
Jackson's *The Haunting of Hill House*, gives us a team of
scientific investigators who are being paid $100,000 to inves-
tigate the reputedly haunted Belasco house. The team is
headed by Dr. Chris Barrett, a physicist and parapsychologist
who is accompanied by his wife, Ann. There is also a young
medium, Florence Tanner, and Ben Fisher, the sole survivor
of a previous investigating group.

In that earlier investigation, Hell House, "the Mt. Everest
of haunted houses," cost eight people their lives. The house
was built by Emerik Belasco, the illegitimate son of an
American munitions maker. Belasco was a roaring giant who
stood 6 feet 5 inches tall. He is described as given to:

> "Drug addiction, alcoholism, sadism, bestiality, mutilation,
> murder, vampirism, necrophilia, cannibalism, not to mention
> a whole gamut of sexual goodies . . ."

As the team settles in, the usual ghost film phenomena are
manifested: dishes rattle, a candlestick falls over. In the
course of a seance, the group is warned to go away—"Get
out of this house before I kill you all." And Mrs. Barrett
experiences sexual compulsions.

Lionel Barrett offers a purely scientific explanation for the
phenomena: "There's a field of measurable energy [in the
house] which can be reversed . . . In essence the house is a
giant battery the residual energy of which must be tapped by
all who enter it . . ." Florence Tanner, the medium, has
another explanation: "You can not destroy a spirit. All you
can do is to drive it from one hell to another . . ." She
suggests that what is happening is that the house is a case of
"controlled multiple haunting in which the ghosts are under
the control of the wickedest of them all, Belasco." In either
case, it is soon clear that this team of investigators, too, is in
physical and mental danger to which, before the film is over,
most of its members succumb.

The film leaves its viewers with a certain queasiness that, I
think, comes first from the peculiarly warped psyche Matheson has invented for Emerik Belasco and second from the
clammy sexuality we get to witness, most notably in the
embarrassing scene in which Florence Tanner exorcizes a
ghost by making love to it. "I give you now," she says, "the
love you've never known. I give it feeling that you'll gain the
strength to go from this house."

The Legend of Hell House leaves the dialogue between science and the occult unresolved, but at intervals it is entirely
persuasive about the malevolence that inhabits the house.
The surprise ending in which we learn Emerik Belasco's
secret is audacious, both in the novel and here. What it
reveals about the relationship between self-loathing and self-
love is almost reason enough to admire this not entirely
coherent film.

LEGEND OF THE 7 GOLDEN VAMPIRES

Film

(Alternate release title: **THE SEVEN BROTHERS MEET DRACULA**)

(1974   (C)   Great Britain/Hong Kong   89 min.
Production Company: Hammer/Shaw Brothers; *Director:* Roy Ward Baker; *Producer:* Don Haughton, Vee King Shaw; *Screenplay:* Don Haughton; *Photography:* John Wilcox, Roy Ford; *Editor:* Chris Barnes; *Special Effects:* Les Bowie; *Martial Arts Sequences:* Tang Chia, Liu Chia Liang; *Music:* James Bernard.
Cast: Peter Cushing (Professor Lawrence Van Helsing), David Chiang (Hsi Ching), Julie Ege (Vanessa Buren), Robin Stewart (Leyland Van Helsing), Shih Szu (Mai Kwai), John Forbes-Robertson (Dracula), Chan Shen (Kah).

There is something zany and wonderful about a film that plumps Dracula down in the midst of Chinese martial arts country.

Think of it! Dracula, for no reason that anyone can see, is in China where he decides to take over the body and mind of the lame and evil Kah. "Beneath that image," he says as he invades Kah's brain, "is the immortal power of Count Dracula. I will recall the seven golden vampires." No sooner said than done. Dracula becomes Kah and Kah does recall the seven golden vampires who for centuries have terrorized the region surrounding the village of Ping Wei.

In several scenes of rapine and brutality that are replayed at intervals, we learn what the seven vampires do. From time to time, they mount their horses and with the help of the dead who rise at their signal, they attack villages and carry maidens back to their fortress, where they drink the girls' blood.

With that established, we turn now to the town of Chunking where Dr. Van Helsing is giving a lecture about vampires to a class of Chinese students who are so skeptical of what they hear that they walk out on him. But one student, Hsi Ching, the grandson of the farmer who long ago killed one of the golden vampires, has understood Van Helsing's warning about the living dead. Now he pleads with Van Helsing to go with him on an expedition to Ping Wei where, with Van Helsing's help, he means to rid his village of the vampires.

The Van Helsings, father and son, agree to help Ching when the beautiful and wealthy Vanessa Buren offers to finance the expedition. Then off they all go, joining Ching and his martially artistic brothers and their equally kung-fu crafty sister on their errand of mercy.

They are, of course, frequently attacked by evil forces, both mortal and immortal, and each attack is an occasion for some

Poster art. (Courtesy of the New York Public Library Picture Collection)

eye-pleasing martial arts choreography. The folklore of the vampire, too, now that we have an East-meets-West vampire film, is also considerably bent. Dr. Van Helsing, in a country where crucifixes are fairly hard to come by, reassures everyone that in a battle with vampires one may substitute statues of the Buddha for the cross. Eventually, the seven golden vampires [actually, there are only six, since one, as we will recall, was knocked off by Ching's grandfather long ago], join the fray, but the good people triumph.

There isn't the smallest hint of seriousness anywhere at all in this frequently glittering and occasionally tedious film. But the script writer Don Haughton and the director Roy Ward Baker make good use of the opportunities their inventive plot gives them to costume their characters (especially the golden vampires) and to choreograph the battle scenes.

LEGEND OF SLEEPY HOLLOW Short Story

Washington Irving
U.S.A.
1820, in *The Sketch Book of Geoffrey Crayon, Gent.*, New York, C. S. Van Winkle; reprinted 1962 in Austin McC. Fox's (ed.) *The Legend of Sleepy Hollow*, New York, Pocket Books.

Washington Irving pulls off something of a tour de force in this tale, very carefully crafted to seem to be a bemused account of events pleasantly recalled by a slightly garrulous, rural tale teller. The narrator's tongue is certainly in his cheek, and yet, when the moment of horror toward which the tale is building comes, it has all the impact of a forthright confrontation with the macabre.

Ichabod Crane, the schoolmaster of Sleep Hollow, a somnolent village somewhere in the vicinity of Tarrytown, is the story's protagonist, and it is instantly clear that he is nobody's image of a heroic figure. He is:

tall but exceedingly lank, with narrow shoulders, long arms and legs, hands that dangled a mile out of his sleeves, feet that might have served for shovels, and his whole frame most loosely hung together. His head was small, and flat at top, with huge ears, large green glassy eyes and a long snipe nose, so that it looked like a weathercock perched upon his spindle neck, to tell which way the wind blew.

The inhabitants of Sleepy Hollow, in addition to their propensity for somnolence:

are given to all kinds of marvellous beliefs . . . and frequently see strange sights, and hear music and voices in the air. The whole neighborhood abounds with local tales, haunted spots and twilight superstitions . . .

Among the stories they tell is one about:

the apparition of a figure on horseback without a head. It is said by some to be the ghost of a Hessian trooper, whose head had been carried away by a cannon-ball, in some nameless battle during the Revolutionary War.

Now, Ichabod Crane is in love with Katrina Van Tassel, the beautiful daughter of a wealthy local farmer, and fancies that he is the favored one among her suitors. When he is invited to a "quilting frolic" at the Van Tassel house, he goes to it with his hopes high. But there, to his chagrin, he learns that it is the burly Brom Bones who has Katrina's heart in thrall. Irving writes:

Let it suffice to say, Ichabod stole forth with the air of one who had been sacking a hen-roost, rather than a fair lady's heart.

And off he rides into the concealing dark, embittered and dismayed astride his old horse, Gunpowder, until, as he approaches a tree beside a bridge over a small brook he hears a groan and meets—the headless horseman. What follows then is a chase scene whose climax is even more frightful than Ichabod's initial meeting with the spectre.

Properly, a horror tale ought not also to be charming, but Washington Irving is much too fond of his Hudson Valley world not to take every opportunity he can to caress it. So we get trees and valleys, harvest time and sowing, rural feasts and village rivalries. What finally happens, then, is that the glow of his pleasure in the region suffuses his prose with such charm that we find ourselves smiling as we turn his pages. But there comes that splendid moment when all smiling stops.

LES MAINS D'ORLAC Novel

Maurice Renard
France
1920, Paris, Editions Pierre Belfond; 1929, as *The Hands of Orlac*, New York, Dutton.

Les Mains d'Orlac ("The Hands of Orlac") is the novel on which the film *Mad Love* starring Peter Lorre is more or less based. Though it is more mystery than horror fiction, it is included here because it has one of the cruelest and most horrifying plots ever imagined.

At the beginning of the story, we meet the very beautiful, sensitive and devoted Madame Rosine Orlac, the 23-year-old wife of the world-famous concert pianist Stephen Orlac, as she learns that her husband is one of the many victims of a train accident. Stephen, it turns out, has been so seriously injured that to save his life he requires the help of a world-famous surgeon, Dr. Cerral.

Rosine Orlac pleads with Dr. Cerral to save Stephen's hands and the surgeon promises to do what he can. In fact, he performs miracles. Stephen's life is saved, and, apparently his hands.

But then Renard, with great subtlety, intrudes a painful mystery. Rosine actually *sees* visual manifestations of her husband's nightmares. Then she sees apparitions of bloody knives whose handles are marked with the letter "X." Later, she intercepts a note that leads her to suspect that her husband is a member of a murderous brotherhood, The Infrared Band. After Monsieur Crochans, a good friend of the Orlacs, and Edouard Orlac, Stephen's father, are murdered the horror intensifies when the sole fingerprint found at the scene of the second murder turns out to be that of a criminal named Vasseur, a man guillotined two years earlier for the crime of murder.

And now the story turns nightmarish. Stephen meets Vasseur whose guillotined head, he is told, was sewn back onto his body by the same Dr. Cerral who operated on him. Vasseur also tells Stephen that Dr. Cerral replaced Stephen's mangled hands with his own, with Vasseur's, a murderer's hands, "hands that have stabbed a woman, an old man and a little girl . . ."

Improbable as all this sounds, Renard, in the tradition of

Ann Radcliffe, manages to extract a vast quantity of horror from his mysteries before he spoils them, at the penultimate moment, with explanations so rational that we hate to believe them. That tilt toward scientism to one side, *The Hands of Orlac* is as beautifully written as it is intricately contrived. Renard's compassionate view of the dilemma that confronts his protagonists raises his novel to the level of literature.

LIGEIA   Short Story
Edgar Allan Poe
U.S.A.
September 1838, in *American Museum*; reprinted 1986 in Stephen Peithman's (ed.) *The Annotated Tales of Edgar Allan Poe*, New York, Avenel.

Edgar Allan Poe's ''Ligeia'' is a tale shrouded in rich obscurities though the events that the first-person narrator describes are entirely unambiguous: While in the Rhineland in Germany, he marries an extraordinarily rich, dark, brilliant, beautiful and passionate woman named Ligeia. Then she dies. After some months of wandering through Europe, he buys an abbey in England and refurbishes it splendidly. To that abbey, he brings his second wife, Lady Rowena Trevanion of Tremaine, whom he loathes and who shuns him. Two months after the marriage she is taken ill. She recovers but falls sick a second time, and this time her illness is more severe than before. She speaks of voices and movements that her narrator-husband cannot hear or see. Then he sees, or dreams that he sees, an ''angelic form'' that drops three ruby drops of some liquid into Rowena's wine. She dies not three days later. It is then, as he sits beside her, his mind flooded with memories of Ligeia, that Lady Rowena's body makes repeated efforts to return to life. What happens next is the shattering climax of this astonishing tale.

Like other of Poe's tales narrated by untrustworthy first-person narrators, the problem is to know what to believe. This speaker, an obvious neurasthenic, tells us that he is an opium addict. He tell us, too, that his memory is so bad that he cannot remember Ligeia's family name. Other details about himself make us wonder about his judgment. For instance, his loveless marriage, after Ligeia's death, to the Lady Rowena Trevanion of Tremaine.

What make ''Ligeia'' work, however, is that Poe manages to make such matters seem irrelevant. His is a brooding fantasy encapsulating an idea borrowed from Joseph Glanvill: ''God is but a great will pervading all things intense by nature of its intentness.'' And Ligeia has that intensity in her. The narrator sees in the depths of her luminous eyes, ''the intensity of her wild desire for life—for life—but for life—.'' In those eyes are hidden both the mystery and the secret of the universe.

Poe puts his notion before us swathed in language so rich and so ornate that it becomes, like the narrator's English bridal chamber, where the carpets, draperies and bed linens are ''spotted all over at irregular intervals with arabesque figures . . .'' But those arabesques are ambiguous. From some points of view they seem to depict ''ghastly forms which belong to the superstition of the Norman, or arise in the guilty slumbers of the monk.''

Finally, what comes off the page is a sensuality of the damned so intense that one sees why Baudelaire was fasci-nated by it. Dream, death, desire come together in a haze of yearning and what readers get caught up in is the forbidden, erotic fantasy hidden in it: One man with two women. One, Ligeia, dark, passionate, brilliant; the other, the Lady Rowena Trevanion of Tremaine, blonde, beautiful, chilly and insubstantial. A pure image of the light intruding upon the more beloved dark.

Clearly, the narrator, whether he is telling us facts that actually happened or whether his shimmering account is spun of opium dreams or downright madness . . . clearly, he wants the dark to win. And, caught up in his spell, so do we.

THE LISTENER   Short Story
Algernon Blackwood
Great Britain
1907, in *The Listener and Other Stories*, London, Eveleigh Nash; reprinted 1973 in E. F. Bleiler's (ed.) *Best Ghost Stories of Algernon Blackwood*, New York, Dover.

Algernon Blackwood's contribution to the ghost story is that, as in Le Fanu, the ghosts in his tales have a particular affinity with the deeper psychological hungers and failures of the person whom they haunt. Thus, while there is no doubt in our minds that a real ghost has appeared, it is not so much an independent apparition as a coherence in recognizable shape of the dilemmas of the self that sees it.

From that point of view, ''The Listener'' is an absolutely exemplary Blackwood tale. Its first-person narrator is a reclusive 40-year-old bachelor who writes ponderous articles and reviews for little-known journals and who more or less glories in his loneliness and poverty.

A man with 125 pounds a year income (circa 1900), he is delighted to find rooms in a huge ramshackle house on a respectable street where the rent is 25 pounds a year. There, he settles into the sort of life that he asserts he wants to lead, writing:

> articles; verses for the comic papers; a novel I've been ''at'' for three years and concerning which I have dreams; a children's book, in which the imagination has free rein; and another book which is to last as long as myself since it is an honest record.

The defensive nature of this summary, though it escapes the narrator, does not escape us.

He takes long walks, he eats in cheap chop-houses. He sees almost no one and sits in his rooms with no amusements beyond staring into ''a fire [wearing] a great coat, listening to the deep booming in the chimney.''

Then, he becomes aware that he is becoming cranky. Small things begin to irritate him. His brain is invaded by images within himself, by anything at all. The stillness of the house begins to oppress him. Then he hears knocking at his door, but there is nobody there when he opens it. Then he becomes aware of a presence that is frequently nearby. That seems to be listening. Later, he begins to feel something new:

> an indescribable odour. I use the adjective advisedly. Though very faint, diluted as it were, it was nevertheless an odour that made my gorge rise.

He writes, ''It is abominable the way my nerves go up and down with me . . .'' As his neurasthenia intensifies, so too does the smell. Then one day he sees ''the listener'':

It was a man. He appeared to be clinging to the rail rather than standing on the stairs . . . The idea flashed into my brain in a moment that I was looking into the visage of something monstrous. The huge skull, the mane-like hair, the wide-humped shoulders, suggested in a way I did not pause to analyse, that which was scarcely human . . .

He sees the apparition again, and notices that the "odour I so abhorred was strong in the room."

The narrator's personal situation continues to deteriorate. Then, a visit from an old friend clears up the mystery of the apparition. But the explanation, while it brings clarity, does not bring consolation either to the narrator or to the reader. Because by then, who the "listener" was and what he is, merely enforce our understanding of the narrator's spiritual and moral decay.

A truly dry tale of the horror within.

THE LITTLE SHOP OF HORRORS   Film
1960 (B&W) U.S.A. 70 min.
Production Company: Santa Clara; *Director:* Roger Corman, *Producer:* Roger Corman; *Screenplay:* Charles B. Griffith; *Photography:* Arch Dalzell; *Editor:* Marshall Neilan, Jr.; *Music:* Fred Katz.
Cast: Jonathan Haze (Seymour Krelboin), Jackie Joseph (Audrey), Mel Welles (Gravis Mushnick), Dick Miller (Fouch), Myrtle Vail (Winifred), Leola Wendorff (Mrs. Shiva), Jack Nicholson (Wilbur Force).

This is the Roger Corman film that was made on a dare. "The whole movie was a joke," according to Corman who was offered the use of a leftover set if he could make a movie on a two-day schedule. In fact, it took two days and one night and the result is not exactly a tour de force of great moviemaking. On the other hand, *The Little Shop of Horrors* is an engaging and friendly self-spoof of a film that has several things going for it: It is the first film version of the story that, as an off-Broadway play, has been running for years; it is a classic example of Roger Corman's crash-program inventiveness and it has Jack Nicholson, hardly more than a beardless youth, playing a masochist visiting his dentist in a scene that W.C. Fields would have been proud of.

By now, the story of *The Little Shop of Horrors* is well known. Seymour Krelboin, a nerdy and yet engaging version of Jerry Lewis, is a florist's assistant in a shop on skid row. The florist, a Yiddish-accented stock character, is at once mean-spirited and more or less kind. Audrey, the ingenue, also works for the florist and, against all reason, is in love with Seymour. Other walk-on characters include Mrs. Shiva [Yiddish for the period of mourning prescribed after a death], whose family members die with great frequency, and a character named Fouch who eats flowers.

When Seymour invents (or at least nourishes into life) a carnivorous talking plant, the fortunes of the flower shop suddenly improve and Seymour is trapped into committing murders in order to feed his ravenous discovery, which seems to double and even triple its size with each new meal.

There really is very little more to the plot than that. The film is buoyed up by its own absurdity, by its dated humor—someone actually says, "Do you think the rain will hurt the rhubarb?"—and by its role in film history. But beyond that, its whimsy is finally too anemic even for our well intentioned patience.

The off-Broadway musical version of the story is full-blooded, inventive, colorful and raucous.

THE LODGER   Film
1944 (B&W) U.S.A. 84 min.
Production Company: 20th Century-Fox; *Director:* John Brahm; *Producer:* Robert Bassler; *Screenplay:* Barre Lyndon; *Photography:* Lucien Ballard; *Editor:* J. Watson Web; *Special Effects:* Fred Sersen; *Music:* Hugo W. Friedhofer.
Cast: Merle Oberon (Kitty Langtry), Laird Cregar (Slade), George Sanders (Inspector Warwick), Sir Cedric Hardwicke (Kitty's uncle), Sara Allgood (Kitty's aunt).

Marie Belloc Lowndes' novel, *The Lodger,* was first brought to the screen in 1926 as a silent movie directed by Alfred Hitchcock. In 1953 it appeared in color as *The Man in the Attic* and starred Jack Palance. The 1944 interpretation of the story is still the best of the lot.

For one thing, the film has Merle Oberon and George Sanders in it. Oberon, though utterly winsome, is hardly recognizable in her role as Kitty Langtry, a music hall dancer. Though she handles the role well, nobody will ever associate Merle Oberon with the can-can. As for George Sanders, never mind that he woos his lady by offering to show her Scotland Yard's "Black Book," in which horrid crimes are recorded; never mind that he is unable to shoot straight and that his idea of protecting her from a known killer is to leave her alone in an isolated dressing room. None of that matters. Here, early in his career, we see the proof of what we have always known—that George Sanders is reason enough for inventing the word "impeccable."

But it is Laird Cregar's performance as Slade, the silent, portly pathologist who is (with reason) suspected of being Jack the Ripper, that makes this film important. Under John Brahm's direction, Cregar plays Slade with such depths of understanding that we are in danger of giving him our sympathy. Slade takes rooms in the home of a respectable family. To his landlady, he explains that he will sometimes be performing scientific experiments. Tall, dark, silent, gentle and courteous, he is, as she says, a gentleman.

The husband and wife in whose home he settles are typically British examples of the genteel poor. The husband has recently had reverses, and the couple are now acutely uncomfortable as they rent rooms for the sake of the extra money that will help them keep up appearances. These class anxieties form a perfect background for the drama of madness and lust that is largely played out in their home.

Director John Brahm lets us know almost at once that Slade is the slasher killer who has been terrorizing London's Whitechapel district where he has murdered on the average of one woman every 10 days. His film is not a whodunnit so much as it is a study in sexual repression and the madness that it can trigger. Slade's stated motive for killing women who are associated with the theater is that such women corrupt and destroy the talents of young men. As he sees it, one such woman was responsible for the corruption and death of his own talented artist brother. And now, he must save others from such women.

But when Slade sees Kitty Langtry, his landlords' actress niece, he falls in love with her and then conceives a plan that will bring his bloody pilgrimage to an end. It is with his slow, even majestic, stalking of Kitty that the film, until then merely a fascinating tale of murder, turns horrifying.

The Lodger owes much to John Brahm's thoughtful and profoundly sombre direction, though Barre Lyndon's beautiful, occasionally distinguished, screenplay must be given credit as well. But "somber" is the key word. All of the characters seem to know that they are in a dark allegory: Most of the scenes are filmed in darkness, and even those that take place in broad daylight deal with or imply dark matters. At climactic moments in which Slade is at the center of a scene, he is seen only as a silhouette from which there emanates a soft, gentle and unmistakably unhappy voice. Confiding in Kitty Langtry, whose death he is already plotting, he says:

> "Have you ever had your face close to the water and held your hand in it as you looked down into it . . . Deep water is dark and restful and full of peace."

In one scene, the camera is behind Cregar and we see Kitty framed in the angle of the murderer's arm as he develops for her his lofty conception of his mission:

> "You are very beautiful. You corrupt and destroy men. When the evil is cut out of a beautiful thing only the beauty remains."

As the film subsides from its climax, the camera catches us up in the water of the Thames as it confirms Slade's own judgment that, "Deep water is dark and restful and full of peace."

THE LOTTERY   Short Story
Shirley Jackson
U.S.A.
1948, in *The New Yorker*; reprinted 1979 in Leonard Wolf's (ed.) *Wolf's Complete Book of Terror*, New York, Clarkson N. Potter.

When an editor of *The New Yorker* called Shirley Jackson to say that the magazine was going to publish "The Lottery," he added that Harold Ross, the editor-in-chief of the magazine, who was not sure he understood the story, wondered whether she did not want to say anything about its meaning. "No," she replied "nothing in particular. It was just a story I wrote."

Since 1948 a couple of generations of readers have continued to be vexed by the story's ambiguity even as they realize that they have read something important. As often happens, the ambiguity rises from the apparent simplicity of the events described. On the morning of June 27th, on a clear, sunny day the people of an unnamed American village gather in the square to participate in what appears to be an annual lottery conducted "as were the square dances, the teenage club, the Halloween program—by Mr. Summers . . ." It is a lottery that has been conducted time out of mind and one that once upon a time used to have some sort of ceremony involving music and salutes attached to it. Now, there is simply the drawing from a black box of the name of a village householder.

The atmosphere of the lottery is homely. Nothing fussy, nothing pretentious. It's simply an annual event: "There's always been a lottery." However, when Bill Hutchinson turns out to hold the marked slip that indicates that members of his family must now draw again, his wife, Tessie, complains that, "It wasn't fair," and the story turns decidedly very

tense. And when each of the Hutchinsons has drawn a slip of paper in this second round of the lottery and Tessie turns out to hold the marked slip of paper, we know that we are at the edge of a climactic moment.

When it comes, the horror of the tale rushes in to reaffirm what now we understand: "It isn't fair, it isn't right."

"The Lottery" is a triumph of the laconic. Without ever being predictable, it always feels inevitable and we believe Shirley Jackson when she tells us that, after she put her daughter in her playpen and the frozen vegetables in the refrigerator and sat down to write the story, "it went quickly and easily, moving from beginning to end without pause." As for what the story means . . . the decades have not yielded up any simple answer beyond the single truth: "It isn't fair, it isn't right," a perfect caption for the way things are.

LOVE AT FIRST BITE   Film
1979 (C) U.S.A. 96 min.
Production Company: Simon Productions; *Director:* Stan Dragoti; *Producer:* Robert Kaufman; *Screenplay:* Robert Kaufman; *Photography:* Edward Rosson; *Editor:* Mort Fallick, Allan Jacobs; *Special Effects:* Allen Hall; *Music:* Charles Bernstein.
Cast: George Hamilton (Count Vladimir Dracula), Susan Saint James (Cindy Sondheim), Richard Benjamin (Dr. Jeff Rosenberg), Dick Shawn (Lt. Ferguson), Arte Johnson (Renfield).

Love at First Bite is that rarest of rare gems in the horror film genre—an ebullient yet impeccable spoof that does not resort to camp. It has a screenplay studded with punch lines that would make a stand-up comedian envious and at the same time it has the grace to take seriously the genre which it is gently sending up. Finally, and without being even a little bit earnest, it manages to poke not-so-gentle fun at big city life in the 20th century.

The plot of *Love at First Bite* is a parodic replay of Tod Browning's 1931 *Dracula*. This time, Count Dracula is forced to leave his castle in Transylvania because Romania's Communist regime means to use it as a training school for athletes. Given a choice between an efficiency apartment in a communist city and exile abroad, Dracula, followed by his faithful servant, Renfield, chooses to go to the United States in pursuit of Cindy Sondheim, whose picture he has seen and with whom he has fallen in love.

Cindy, a very modern young woman whose therapist, Dr. Jeff Rosenberg, tells her that she is promiscuous, prides herself on honest, open relationships with no commitment. Dr. Rosenberg, who is the grandson of Bram Stoker's Dr. Van Helsing, changed his name to Rosenberg "for professional reasons." He is in love with Cindy but, as a prisoner of his profession, he thinks that analyzing the woman he loves is the same thing as courting her. One of the more delicious pleasures of the film is listening to these two trade psycho-babble.

The film turns joyful and even funnier when Count Dracula enters Cindy's life. When he appears in her bedroom, she hastens to reassure him that a one-night stand is perfectly alright with her and we get this exchange:
Cindy: "I just want to be honest."
Dracula: "Don't be honest."
Cindy: "What should I be?"

Dracula: ''Be beautiful. Be romantic. Be mine.''

It is no wonder that Cindy finally chooses to accept Dracula's third and deadly kiss, the one that confers a dark immortality. Within the context of the film, it is a better choice than the daytime world she knows. As Dracula puts it, ''As for me, in a world without romance, it is better to be dead.'' And the achievement of *Love at First Bite* is that for 96 minutes we are dazzled into believing that he is right.

George Hamilton is a suave and juicy version of Bela Lugosi. Utterly charming and utterly graceful, he carries off his role as the king vampire without ever giving off even the slightest emanation of death. His good looks to one side, his real weapons are the *mot juste* and the droll remark, not fangs. Susan Saint James plays Cindy as at once wistful and brash and just confused enough to be grateful for the arrival of a man who knows both who he is and what he wants. The scene stealer of the film, however, is Arte Johnson who, having made a careful study of Dwight Frye's role as Renfield in the 1931 film, duplicates (and beautifully trivializes) his humility and his famous laughter.

Love at First Bite is congenial, elegant and very funny. It is a close contender with *The Fearless Vampire Killers* for the title, Best-Comic-Vampire-Film-Ever-Made.

LUKUNDOO   Short Story
Edward Lucas White
U.S.A.
1927, in *Lukundoo and Other Stories*, New York, Doran; reprinted 1979 in Leonard Wolf's (ed.) *Wolf's Complete Book of Terror*, New York, Clarkson N. Potter.

Surely ''Lukundoo'' belongs high up on anybody's list of the most horrifying stories ever written. Perhaps only H.G. Wells in *The Island of Dr. Moreau* conveys such a vivid sense of someone else's physical pain and links that pain to a moral failure in quite the same way.

The anguish belongs to Ralph Stone, a British explorer who, after a brilliant and romantic early career, fled from various civilized entanglements to the emotionally freer climate of Africa. There he managed to discomfit and shame a Balunda witch doctor, who takes his revenge by cursing him. What happens to Stone as a result of that curse is that, in his camp in the jungle, he is assailed by growths in his flesh. They are not, as he first lets people believe, carbuncles that he cuts off himself with a straight razor. Rather, they are the chattering, chittering heads of tiny black men who, having as it were hatched in his muscle tissue, are growing angrily out of it. Dozens of them, all of them yelling away in their tiny voices.

White's narrator, a loyal colleague of Stone's named Singleton, tells this stupendous tale in a soft and weary voice that sets just the right tone for a piercing drama of despair.

LUST FOR A VAMPIRE   Film
(Alternate release title: **TO LOVE A VAMPIRE**)
1970 (C) Great Britain 95 min.
Production Company: Hammer; **Director:** Jimmy Sangster; **Producer:** Harry Fine, Michael Style; **Screenplay:** Tudor Gates; **Photography:** David Muir; **Editor:** Spencer Reeve; **Music:** Harry Robinson.

Cast: Ralph Bates (Giles Barton), Barbara Jefford (Countess), Suzanna Leigh (Janet), Michael Johnson (Richard Le Strange), Yutte Stensgaarde (Mircalla).

Another of Hammer Films' modestly opulent vampire thrillers, with wild coach rides down unpaved country roads and the studied exploitation of attractive young women putting on and taking off their clothes before the camera. *Lust for a Vampire*, like the earlier Hammer production, *Vampire Lovers* (1970), makes use of characters created by Sheridan Le Fanu in his short novel, *Carmilla*.

The film opens with a fine, if by no means original, pretitle sequence in which a young peasant woman walking along a country road is given a lift in a black coach. We do not know what happens in the coach but we do see a hooded figure carrying the now inert woman into Karnstein Castle where her blood is used in a satanic ceremony to revive the dead Mircalla. Then come the screen credits and the rest of the story.

Richard Le Strange, a 19th-century English novelist of the occult, is visiting a village in Styria not far from Karnstein Castle, which is infamous as the home of the vampiric Karnsteins. Le Strange, who is something of a professional rake, discovers that there is a British finishing school for young women right next door to the castle, and he contrives to get himself hired as a teacher of English literature at Miss Simpson's snooty establishment.

Meanwhile, we learn from the Styrian villagers that every 40 years, one of the Karnstein dead is reincarnated. And almost at once, local young women are found dead, with their throats showing the telltale tooth marks of the vampire.

Le Strange, meanwhile, at Miss Simpson's school, falls in love with the mysterious and beautiful Mircalla, whose name, we are given to understand, is an anagram of Carmilla. Mircalla, very blond and very shapely, is alternately deadly and erotic—with people of both sexes. Her liaison with Le Strange, however, does him no harm. Perhaps, as the film suggests in a long scene filled with writhing mouths and entwining limbs, it is because he is such a skilfull lover.

In any event, the villagers, who do not have Le Strange's reason for forbearance, are finally so wrought up by the crimes of this generation's Karnsteins that they form a mob and march on the castle. Over the objections of a red-clad cleric (presumably a cardinal) who cries out, ''Fire cannot harm a vampire,'' the mob puts the castle to the torch. For a moment, it seems that the three vampires, Mircalla, her aunt, the Countess Hertzen, and her minion, Dr. Froheim, will escape the flames (''There is no death for us in fire.''). But one of the burning timbers overhead breaks away and a flaming stake pierces Mircalla's heart.

Le Strange's heart, for an instant, is broken, but as the film ends we see him being comforted by the prim and self-righteous Janet who, as we know, has always loved him.

In mid-film, *Lust for a Vampire* is intruded upon by a most amazing song, ''Strange love, silently stealing through the night . . .'' The scene in which Mircalla removes the schoolmaster, Giles Barton's, glasses the better to drink his blood is priceless.

M

M Film
1931 (B&W) Germany 118 min.
Production Company: Nero Productions; *Director:* Fritz Lang;
Producer: Seymour Nebenzal; *Screenplay:* Fritz Lang, Thea von Harbou; *Photography:* Fritz Arno Wagner; *Music:* Adolf Jansen.
Cast: Inge Landgut (Elsie), Peter Lorre (the murderer), Otto Wernicke (Commissar Lohmann), Gustav Gründgens (gang leader), Ellen Widman (the mother), George John, Paul Kemp, Theo Lingen, Theodor Loos.

This very great film, while not properly in the horror genre, has a plot situation and individual scenes that are so terrifying it must not be overlooked.

Fritz Lang's achievement is that he has created a powerful social (perhaps even a political) allegory even as his story unwinds in increments of the purest realism.

The film opens with a scene of invocation as a group of children standing in a circle recite a count-out song:

> Just wait a little while,
> The nasty man in black will come
> And with his little chopper
> He will chop you up.

Then we watch a bright little girl bouncing her ball as she walks home from school. But if we are watching her, so too is the child murderer whose shadow suddenly looms over her. When he speaks, it is in the gentlest of gentle voices, as he says to the little girl, "And what is your name?" A moment later we hear him whistling a few bars from Tchaikovsky's "Dance of the Sugar Plum Fairies." It is music that, within this film, will take on the meaning of death.

From here on, the plot of the film is swiftly developed. Peter Lorre is immediately identified as the child killer who has been terrifying Berlin. His numerous murders have produced such public outrage that the police, in their frenzied effort to find the killer, have taken to arresting the local criminal population at random with the result that the crim-

inal community, meaning to bring the harassment to an end, organizes a search for the killer. Both the police and the criminals make progress in their investigations but the criminals find and identify him first.

One of the criminals has chalked the letter "M" on his palm and he pats the killer on the back, leaving a telltale "M" on his coat. Having identified their killer, the underworld proceeds now to hunt him down and some of Lang's finest scenes are devoted to that hunt.

When Lorre, cowering in a storeroom, is finally captured, we come to the third phase of the film—the trial. Lorre is brought to an underground warehouse where, in the presence of hundreds of Berlin's criminal population, he is tried for his crimes. The trial, a parodic imitation of a properly instituted trial in a criminal court, complete with judges, a prosecuting attorney and a defense lawyer, raises two important social questions: first, the validity of the insanity defense against punishment for murder, and second, whether, in any case, capital punishment is justified. The irony of the discussion is of course underlined by the fact that the pros and cons are being argued by members of a society who are themselves social outcasts.

M has filmic and fictive moments of great beauty and sophistication. The upper- and under-world hunts for the murderer, the trial scene in the abandoned warehouse, the faces of anguished parents confronting the loss of a child, for example. It has, too, individual scenes that convey violence with the sort of tact that has largely disappeared from films in the last couple of decades. We know, for instance, when one of the children has been murdered because we see a ball rolling into a gutter, or an escaped balloon flying off to get itself entangled in wires.

Beyond all that, *M* has Peter Lorre in the role that brought him fame. Staring wistfully and pathetically out at a world in which he is a misfit, he argues persuasively that it is not his fault, that he does not kill because he wants to. That soft, soft voice, those pleading eyes and that appalling gentleness of manner have come down to us as the personification of an abiding paradox: What if evil is not what we choose, but what chooses us?

MAD LOVE   Film

1935 (B&W) U.S.A. 84 min.

Production Company: MGM; *Director:* Karl Freund; *Producer:* John W. Considine, Jr.; *Screenplay:* P.J. Wolfson and John L. Balderston, based on Maurice Renard's *The Hands of Orlac; Photography:* Chester Lyons and Gregg Toland; *Editor:* Hugh Wynn; *Music:* Dimitri Tiomkin.

Cast: Peter Lorre (Dr. Gogol), Frances Drake (Yvonne Orlac), Colin Clive (Stephen Orlac), Ted Healy (Reagan), Sara Haden. (Marie).

Mad Love begins with a hand smashing the glass pane on which the credits are written. It is an arresting beginning and it is followed by glimpses of scenes in the Theatre de Horreurs, a sort of Grand Guignol theater where Yvonne Orlac, the wife of rising concert pianist Stephen Orlac, is as an actress. We learn, too, that the great surgeon Dr. Gogol is in love with Yvonne and has come to the theater for 43 nights in a row. Gogol's sepulchral voice, his absolute baldness and his pale, unhealthy plumpness make him seem like an erect larva who has been force-fed, bleached and then smeared in cold grease. He is, in short, an altogether unappetizing figure of a man and for him to be in love with anyone, much less a woman as beautiful a Yvonne, seems something of a blasphemy. When at a cast party Yvonne is forced to kiss Dr. Gogol, her revulsion is intense and he, not yet downright mad, sadly and gently knows it. Still, he nurtures a wan hope

Peter Lorre and Frances Drake in **Mad Love.**

in his bosom and goes to the trouble of installing a wax figure of Yvonne in his home where, every night, he plays the organ to it while he dreams that he is Pygmalion and that the wax statue is Galatea whom one day he will bring to life by the sheer force of his great love.

We cut now to the Orlacs as disaster overtakes them. Stephen, the pianist, is so badly hurt in a train accident that his hands must be amputated. Yvonne, desperate to save Stephen's career has him taken to Gogol's clinic where Gogol replace Orlac's ruined hands with those of a recently guillotined American, a knife-throwing murderer named Reagan.

Later, Stephen, in a moment of anger, throws a knife that misses his cruel stepfather and so discovers that his hands have a skill of their own. The event gives the now love-crazed Dr. Gogol a brilliant idea. He kills Stephen's stepfather and conveys to Stephen, by means of hypnotic suggestion and the help of an ingenious set of steel arms and hands and a complex brace that enables him to pretend to be Reagan with his head sewn back on, that Stephen is the killer because he has Reagan's hands. Gogol's motivation is that if he can once get Stephen put away in a madhouse, Yvonne will just naturally turn to him for love and protection.

For a while, some of his scheme works, but before the film comes to its quite satisfying ending, there is a thoroughly mad scene in which Gogol pursues Yvonne around one of the rooms in his house, believing that his love has animated her statute. Pale and soft, his huge eyes gleaming with hunger, he lurches after her while a cockatoo flies wildly between them, perching sometimes on Yvonne's shoulder.

Colin Clive as Stephen Orlac gives his usual whiny performance. Frances Drake, as Yvonne Orlac, is really as beautiful as the script says she is and she registers fear, which is all that she is asked to do, very well. But it is Peter Lorre who sustains this frequently absurd film with his unique performance. His madness when it bursts fully into flower is at once melodramatic, believable and, curiously enough, the best demonstration we have of Gogol's essential humanity. Despite the cackling laughter, the confessional monologues and the wild eye-rolling, Lorre is the one who gives *Mad Love* its mad look, its moments of wistful sorrow, its glimpses of a man driven to evil by a more than uncommon deprivation of love.

The director, Karl Freund, has pulled off a neat trick to make us think that the hidden villain of the piece is an indifferent God who here, as in *King Kong* and *The Bride of Frankenstein*, has failed to see to it that every Jack should get his Jill.

MAN-SIZE IN MARBLE   Short Story

E. Nesbit

Great Britain

1893, in *Grim Tales*, London, Innes; reprinted 1974 in Montague Summers' (ed.) *The Supernatural Omnibus* (orig. 1931), New York, Causeway Books.

Here is a story that has almost no events but that, nevertheless, gives a reader a jolt like an electric shock. Partly, the horror comes from Edith Nesbit's careful manipulation of our attention so that we are lulled by the narrator's pleased recital of the pleasing details he gives us as he recounts the honeymoon months of his marriage.

The narrator, a painter, marries a delicate writer named Laura. Then, because they have very little money, they search for a country cottage and find one in "Brenzett—a little village set on a hill over against the southern marshes."

The couple settle in for the kind of lovely rustic life that artists and writers like to believe would make them happy. The cottage is covered with roses; it is not far from an ancient, lovely little church in which, on each side of the altar there "lay a grey marble figure of a knight in full plate armour lying upon a low slab, with hands held up in everlasting prayer . . ."

And there is romantic lore attached to those figures:

> These statues are reputed to be of fierce and wicked men guilty of deeds so foul that the house they had lived in . . . had been stricken by lightning and the vengeance of heaven.

Our couple, anyhow, is happy. They are artistically productive, and still in the flush of their honeymoon. All is well, then, until one October day, three months after their marriage, when their woman-of-all-work gives notice. Pressed to say why she is leaving, she finally blurts out that:

> "They do say, as on All Saints' Eve them two bodies [in the church] sits up on their slabs and gets off of them, and then walks down the aisle, in their marble and as the church clock strikes eleven they walks out of the church door . . ."

To say any more would be to spoil the story for my readers. It is enough to say that the tale moves from the permissible erotic aura that naturally surrounds a honeymoon couple to the subvert, brutal eroticism that Freudian psychology illuminates. But the horror of the story derives from the fact that its author only intuited, and did not make explicit, what she knew.

THE MARK OF THE BEAST   Short Story
Rudyard Kipling
Great Britain
July 12–14, 1890, in *Pioneer*; reprinted 1974 in Leonard Wolf's (ed.) *Wolf's Complete Book of Terror*, New York, Clarkson N. Potter.

As in Edward Lucas White's "Lukundoo" and H.G. Wells' "Pollock and the Porroh Man," the source of this tale's horror is the clash between western culture and the culture of so-called "primitive" peoples.

Here, Kipling tells the story of Fleete, "a big heavy, genial and inoffensive man" who comes to 19th-century India to take charge of some properties that have been left him by an uncle. On New Year's eve, in the course of the festivities at the English club, he fills up with sherry and bitters, champagne, Capri, Benedictine and four or five whiskies and sodas. Staggering homeward befuddled at 3:30 in the morning he passes a temple to Hanuman, the Indian Monkey God. There,

> Before we could stop him, Fleete dashed up the steps, patted two priests on the back, and was gravely grinding the ashes of his cigar-butt into the forehead of the red stone image of Hanuman . . . "Shee that?" [he says] "Mark of the B-beasht! I made it. Ishn't it fine?"

The sacrilege is soon avenged.

Then, without any warning, a Silver Man came out of a recess behind the image of the god. He was perfectly naked in that bitter, bitter cold, and his body shone like frosted silver, for he was what the Bible calls "a leper as white as snow."

The Silver Man does no more than place his head against Fleete's chest, "making a noise exactly like the mewing of an otter." But that is enough. Where the Silver Man had touched him, Fleete's breast now shows a rosette resembling the spots on a leopard's hide. And now Fleete begins a process of reverse evolution as he becomes increasingly, and literally, brutal. He begins to eat nearly raw meat. Horses are terrified when he comes near them. Eventually, he drops down on all fours and prefers darkness to light. "Presently, from the room came the long-drawn howl of a wolf. . . . Fleete could not speak, he could only snarl, and his snarls were those of a wolf, not of a man."

From here on, the story concentrates on the way that Fleete's friends undertake to cure him. That cure involves capturing and torturing the Silver Man. When he is captured, Kipling's narrator says:

> I put my foot on his neck. He mewed hideously and even through my riding-boots I could feel that his flesh was not the flesh of a clean man.

Then we are told what implements of torture are about to be used, after which the narrator says:

> Strickland shaded his eyes with his hands for a moment, and we got to work. This part is not to be printed.

By the time we get to the end of this brilliant story, the horror of it all has become altogether too intricate, and altogether unspeakable. But the point of it is not so much what Fleete did, or what his friends did to the Silver Man. Rather, it is the moral abyss the British dug for themselves in India.

MARTIN, THE BLOOD LOVER   Film
1976 (C) U.S.A. 95 min.
Production Company: Libra; *Director:* George Romero; *Producer:* Richard Rubinstein; *Screenplay:* George Romero; *Photography:* Michael Gornick; *Music:* Donald Rubinstein.
Cast: John Amplas (Martin), Lincoln Maazel (Cuda), Christine Forrest (Christina), Elyane Nadeau (Mrs. Santini), Tom Savini (Arthur), Sara Venable (second victim), Fran Middleton (train victim), Al Levitsky (Lewis).

We first see Martin on a train, with a young woman drug user in a Pullman car. He gives her her fix, then waits for her to fall asleep. For a while, he manipulates her body as if he is making love to her. Then, he quite tenderly slits her wrist and drinks his fill of her blood.

Martin then completes his journey to his uncle, a white-bearded, implacable relative who minces no words with his nephew. He calls him Nosferatu and says, "First I will save your soul. Then I will destroy you." His uncle, we gather, is going to subject Martin to a course of treatment that will drive the vampire out of him. He says, "You may come and go but you may not take people from the city. [If] I hear of it a single time, I'll destroy you without salvation."

No doubt what makes *Martin* something of a cult film is the way that the ancient vampire tradition is fused with the

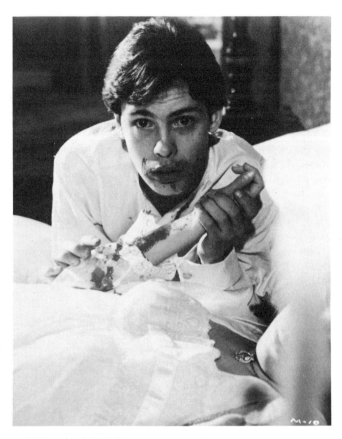

*John Amplas is **Martin**.*

most youth-oriented icons of our day. Martin, identifying himself only as The Count, confides his vampire problems to a radio talk show host. He becomes an instant cause for the disc jockey, with whom he has frequent conversations. And of course, Martin is directly identified as someone with a sex problem when he confides that he is ''much too shy to ever do the sexy stuff. I mean with someone who was awake.''

George Romero, who attained fame with his taut and acutely focused *Night of the Living Dead*, directs this film with what appears to be an entirely different part of his mind. The result is a diffuse and meandering film with a single, but important, virtue. Like *Frightnight*, it does a persuasive job of situating a vampire in a domestic urban setting and providing him with a social context and a quite believable human life. However, that very success vitiates *Martin* as a horror film because, by domesticating the vampire, it shrinks an image of evil to the paltry dimensions of a neurosis.

THE MEDUSA TOUCH
Film

1978   (C)   Great Britain   110 min.
Production Company: Warner Brothers; ***Director:*** Jack Gold; ***Producer:*** Anne V. Coates and Jack Gold; ***Screenplay:*** John Briley; ***Photography:*** Arthur Ibbetson; ***Editor:*** Ian Crafford; ***Music:*** Michael J. Lewis.
Cast: Richard Burton (Morlar), Lee Remick (Dr. Zonfeld), Lino Ventura (Brunel).

Richard Burton's face set into a mask of the sternest gravity is the powerful, if subdued, symbol of the despair that is the theme of this very literate film.

The Medusa Touch is constructed like a murder mystery, except that the victim, a writer named Molar, is not dead. He is brought to a London Hospital, his skull crushed by a terrific blow. Brunel, a French detective on loan to Scotland Yard, investigates the assault. Morlar's story, as it emerges from that investigation, is the substance of the rest of the film.

Morlar believes that he has the Medusa touch. There is something in him that wills disaster to other people: ''I am the man with the power to create catastrophe.'' When, as a child, he was punished by a schoolmaster and made to gather up wet, fallen autumn leaves and dry them, the boy Morlar left the furnace door open. In the fire that resulted, one master and four boys died. When, as an adult, he overheard a domestic quarrel in the apartment next door, a quarrel in which his neighbor's wife threatened to jump out of the window, Morlar shouted, ''For God's sake woman, jump.'' And she did.

Morlar's personal life has been grim. His childhood, as we have seen, was unhappy. As an adult, things did not get much better. He became an attorney but left the law when, by some fatal compulsion, he made a summing up for the defense that so outraged the presiding judge that he hanged Morlar's client. When Morlar married, his wife gave birth to a deformed child, for which she blamed him: ''You aren't capable of producing anything but a vegetable.'' For that bit of candor, Morlar willed her death as well.

We know the details of Morlar's life because he has confided them to a psychiatrist, Dr. Zonfeld, to whom he comes for help. ''I have,'' he tells her, ''found a way to do God's dirty work for him.'' At first, she thinks his story is a projection of his inner problems. When, finally, she does believe him, and believes that he is a threat to the security of the world, she is the one who tries to kill him. By the time detective Brunel, too, believes the story, the cataclysm toward which the film is moving can no longer be stopped. Morlar's mind, in his incapacitated body, is determined to avenge itself against the humanity of which he is a part. ''We are all the devil's children,'' he has said. And it is clear, as the film ends, that hell is where the devil's children belong.

The Medusa Touch has a fine screenplay. Lee Remick seems uncomfortable in her role as a psychiatrist, but Richard Burton, who always seems absent from wherever he may be, makes a properly distant and ominous Morlar. The fact that for most of the film he is bedridden and swathed in bandages serves wonderfully to heighten the impact and irony of the violence of which he is the master.

The Medusa Touch is a film of distinction that may slip into obscurity as an unknown masterpiece. Apocalyptic, intelligent, persuasive, it has all the intimate terror of a prophecy of doom being whispered into one's ear.

MELMOTH THE WANDERER
Novel

Charles Robert Maturin
Ireland/Great Britain
1820, London, Hurst & Robinson; reprinted 1961, Lincoln, University of Nebraska Press.

In 1820, an *Edinburgh Review* critic achieved a triumph of a sort by compressing the intricate plot of *Melmoth the Wanderer* into a single paragraph. The reviewer wrote:

> His [Maturin's] hero is a modern Faustus, who has bartered his soul with the powers of darkness for protracted life and unlimited worldly enjoyment; his heroine, a species of insular goddess, a virgin Calypso of the Indian Ocean, who, amid flowers and foliage, lives upon figs and tamarinds, associates with peacocks and monkeys, is worshipped by the occasional visitants of her island, finds her way into Spain where she is married to the aforesaid hero by the hand of a dead hermit, the ghost of a murdered domestic being the witness of her nuptials; and finally dies in a dungeon of the Inquisition at Madrid. To complete this phantasmagoric exhibition, we are presented with sybils and misers, parricides, maniacs in abundance, monks with scourges pursuing a naked youth streaming with blood; subterranean Jews surrounded by the skeletons of their wives and children; lovers blasted by lightning, Irish hags, Spanish grandees, shipwrecks, caverns, Donna Claras and Donna Isadoras—all exposed to each other in violent and glaring contrast and all their adventures narrated with the same undeviating display of turgid, vehement and painfully elaborated language.

Except for the obtuse comment about Maturin's language, the reviewer has made a fair summary of the events in *Melmoth the Wanderer*. What he fails to do is to convey the extraordinary seriousness of the Irish clergyman's book. Maturin could hardly have refrained from using the melodramatic machinery that from the beginning was a fixed attribute of the Gothic. But *Melmoth . . . ,* more than any of its predecessors, is a complex vision of personal damnation. Melmoth is certainly the Byronic hero/villain, the "wandering outlaw of his own dark mind," but the world through which he moves is as bleak as the soul that moves him.

Maturin's vision is of a wasteland in which desperately guilt-ridden men and women torment and feed upon each other. There is a scene in which one of the book's many villains says:

> ". . . the true penitent rushes over the mangled members of nature and passion, collects them with a hand in which there is no pulse, and a heart in which there is no feeling, and holds them up in the face of the Divinity as a peace offering. Mine is the best theology,—the theology of utter hostility to all beings whose sufferings may mitigate mine."

In another scene, a couple of imprisoned lovers, grown desperate with hunger and darkness, learn to detest each other:

> "All the horrible and loathesome excruciations of famine had been undergone; the disunion of every tie of the heart, of passion, of nature, had commenced . . . they could have cursed each other . . . It was on the fourth night that I heard the shriek of the wretched female,—her lover . . . had fastened his teeth in her shoulder;—the bosom on which he had so often luxuriated, became a meal to him now."

Repulsive as all this is, Maturin is interested in something more abstract. Time and the uses of time are the twin themes of his book. Melmoth's tragic error is that he bought time (at the cost of his soul) to live longer than the rest of us in a world *already* a purgatory.

The spiritual climax of the novel, when it comes, is more powerful even than the concluding scenes of Matthew Lewis's *The Monk*. We see Melmoth's vision of himself falling into the abyss with his eyes fixed:

> . . . on the clock of eternity—the upraised black arm seemed to push forward the hand—it arrived at its period—he fell—he sunk—he blazed—he shrieked! The burning waves boomed over his sinking head, and the clock of eternity rung out its awful chime—"Room for the soul of the Wanderer!"—and the waves of the burning ocean answered, as they lashed the adamantine rock—"There is room for more!"—The Wanderer awoke.

The Wanderer's physical death is much cooler. His handkerchief, caught in furze, is found whipping about in the breeze that sweeps the seaside cliff from which he has fallen. "That," writes Maturin, "was the last trace of the Wanderer."

Frederick S. Frank, writing in *Horror Literature: A Core Collection and Reference Guide,* says that Maturin's "intellectual devotion to the psychology of despair and the torments of religious doubt secure for . . . *Melmoth the Wanderer* a special category of Gothic fiction." Maturin himself writes that, "Despair has no diary," but I think he is mistaken. Literature is the repository of many. *Melmoth the Wanderer* is one of the sternest.

MIDNIGHT HORRORS OR THE BANDIT'S DAUGHTER

Short Story

Anonymous
Great Britain
1823, New York, W. Borradaile; reprinted 1976 in R. Reginald and Douglas Menville's (eds.) *The Spectre Bridegroom and Other Horrors,* New York, Arno.

Here is a fine and fanciful, early 19th-century Gothic fiction that now, in the closing years of the 20th century, is likely to read like a quintessential parody of the horror genre. It has the requisite tall, dark and fatally attractive Italian bandit chieftain. It has a secret marriage and a concealed birth. It has underground passages, corpses mouldering in sepulchers, blue flames, vindictive ghosts and love betrayed. Finally, it has a beautiful, innocent and hopelessly vapid heroine of sensibility, swooning her way from one crisis to the next.

The bandit chieftain is Signor Roderigo, who seduces and secretly marries Constance, the daughter of the Baron di Rosini. Then, turned faithless, he steals their infant daughter, Eglantine, and runs off with her and Jacquelina, "the second object of his attachment." The abandoned Constance is driven first to madness and then to suicide by his desertion. Her father, the Baron di Rosini, vows vengeance on the heartless Roderigo.

That, then, is how the machinery of the plot is wound up. The tale moves relentlessly, and often very spookily, to its inevitable happy ending, with corpses, false starts, sudden revelations and the intrusion of well-meaning ghosts interspersed at intervals.

The fun in the story comes from the anonymous author's enthusiastic use of cliches. Rarely has the Romantic movement's penchant for poetic diction been given so much free reign. When Eglantine encounters the handsome Adelbert for the first time: she hears

> . . . a voice of manly firmness yet of softest melody [which] addressed her in the tenderest accents of kind solicitude . . . the eye that met hers blended the fire and vivacity of youth with the softer beams of heavenly sensibility . . .

Descriptions of horror are just as fulsome. Here is Eglantine, stumbling upon the bones of the dead as she follows the fugitive Baroness Montalban through a subterranean sepulcher. A coffin lid upon which she has been standing gives way and:

> she found one of her feet entangled in the skeleton legs of the body it contained. Stepping forward, in her effort to disengage herself, the affrighted maid fell on the stiffened form; and felt, with recoiling horror the fleshless cheek in contact with her own.

Mercifully, she collapses and "Several minutes elapsed, ere respiration again heaved the cold bosom of the senseless fair . . ."

For those readers who are hesitant to confront the slow pace of the great Gothic novels, "Midnight Horrors . . ." provides a rather wonderfully distilled introduction to the pleasures of the genre. But let the buyer beware: a Taste for the Gothic, longueurs and all, is a habit that is swiftly—and insidiously—acquired.

THE MILK-WHITE DOO   Short Story
Anonymous
Great Britain
No date; reprinted 1979 in Leonard Wolf's (ed.) *Wolf's Complete Book of Terror,* New York, Clarkson N. Potter.

This Scottish folktale of cannibalism and revenge is brisk and grisly while at the same time its verse elements give it the feeling of an oft-repeated, ritual utterance.

As is frequent in horror tales, the family dynamic generates the fearful events recounted here. This time, we have a household in which there is a father, a mother, a daughter and a son. One day, the father brings home a hare and gives it to his wife to cook. She makes such a tasty dish of the hare that, before she knows it, she has eaten it all up. Then, fearful of her husband's displeasure she looks about for some way to conceal her gluttony—and finds it. She calls in her son Johnie, kills him, cuts him up and tosses the pieces of his body into the pot and makes a second stew. The husband, when he eats his dinner, expresses surprise at the shapes of the bones he finds, but his wife reassures him and so he continues to eat his "Johnie well boiled."

Later, Johnie's sister Katy gathers the bones and puts them in a pot near the sideposts of the door where they grow into a milk-white dove. The dove's reiterated cry will ring in a reader's ear for a very long time:

> "Pew, pew,
> My minny me slew,
> My daddy me chew,
> My sister gathered my banes,
> And put them between twa milk-white stanes;
> And I grew, and I grew,
> To a milk-white doo,
> And I took to my wings, and away I flew."

The cruel mother, readers will be glad to know, does not escape unscathed.

THE MONK   Novel
Matthew G. Lewis
Great Britain
1796, London, J. Bell; reprinted 1952, ed. by John Berryman, New York, Grove Press.

This most vibrant of Gothic novels was published in 1796, when Lewis was 21 years old, and we have Lewis's word for it that it took him 10 weeks to write its 420 pages. One can easily believe him. Much of the novel's power comes from the sense have that it is being composed under our very eyes by a frenzied adolescent in the grip of a lurid vision and writing at top speed.

Lewis's master creation is the 30-year-old Friar Ambrosio, whose honeyed name and fabled chastity make him a natural target for our ill wishes. This exquisite prig, this great good man deserves to fall from some high place and, to the lascivious satisfaction of author and readers alike, he does.

The main plot of the novel involves the physical and spiritual destruction of Ambrosio. The figure we meet at the beginning of the fiction is high-minded and chaste, but page by page he succumbs to sensual temptations, beginning with his response to a portrait of the Madonna. The picture excites him to a suspicious appreciation:

> "What beauty in that countenance! . . . how graceful is the turn of that head! what sweetness, yet what majesty in her divine eyes! how softly her cheek reclines upon her hand."

Shortly after that, he meets Rosario, a young novice whose "head was continually muffled up in his cowl." Rosario is all attentiveness, but it soon turns out that the novice is actually the divine Matilda who, having fallen in love with the incorruptible monk, has chosen this means of being always near him. Inevitably Matilda, who manages to display her female charms at an opportune moment, succeeds in her design. When the seduction is accomplished, it has the simplicity of the inevitable. Propinquity, youth, and opportunity all conspire.

> Who then can wonder if he yielded to the temptation? Drunk with desire, he pressed his lips to those which sought them; . . . he clasped her rapturously in his arms; he forgot his vows, his sanctity, and his fame; he remembered nothing but the pleasure and the opportunity.

But, when "the burst of transport was passed: Ambrosio's lust was satisfied. Pleasure fled, and shame usurped her seat in his bosom." From then on, Matilda serves Ambrosio's even darker lusts as she contrives for him the destruction of the innocent Antonia, a 16-year-old Madrid beauty. Ambrosio murders Elvira, the girl's mother, and then this former paragon of virtue carries the drugged Antonia to the charnel vaults beneath the Capuchin monastery. Lewis dedicates his most perfervid prose to the appalling scene that ensues. To his victim, Ambrosio says:

> ". . . you are absolutely in my power . . . turn not on me those supplicating eyes . . . Can I relinquish these limbs so white, so soft, so delicate? these swelling breasts, round, full, and elastic! these lips fraught with such inexhaustible sweetnesses? . . . Wretched girl, you must stay here with me! Here amidst these lonely tombs, these images of death, these rotting, loathesome, corrupted bodies!"

Lewis, however, is not yet through with his Ambrosio. Having arranged his fall, he now displays his punishment. The monk, imprisoned for his crimes, signs his soul over to the devil who saves him from the Inquisition—for something worse.

As the fiend flies over a terrific landscape with his talons gripping the monk's shaven skull, Ambrosio learns that the Elvira he murdered was his own mother; that the Antonia he raped and killed was his sister, and that the guards he had heard coming to execute him "came to signify [his] pardon."

Byron shared with his age the judgment that *The Monk* was a dirty book and said that the "worst parts ought to have been written by Tiberius at Caprea—they are forced—the philtered ideas of a jaded voluptuary—" But Byron, I think, is wrong. Lewis's ideas are indeed filtered, but only through the lens of inexperience as it focuses on shifting desire. *The Monk* is the quintessential novel of sexual confusion—of the adolescent's vision of himself as longing in all possible directions. With an extraordinary writer's instinct, Lewis allowed his monsters to flow onto the page without interference and he became thereby the visionary of adolescence—that epoch in our lives when there are only towers looking down into abysses. That bleak time deserves its prophets too. Lewis is among the best of them.

MONKEYS   Short Story
E.F. Benson
Great Britain
1934, in *More Spook Stories,* London, Hutchinson; reprinted 1980 in Bill Pronzini's *Tales of the Dead,* New York, Bonanza.

This strange and menacing tale is a variant of the typical mummy story formula: Archeologists uncover a mummy inside an Egyptian tomb in spite of hieroglyphics warning that anyone who desecrates the burial place will be cursed in a variety of dreadful ways.

Benson uses the ancient formula but attaches it to the career of a brilliant young British surgeon, Hugh Morris, who is so immersed in his work that he has no other life but surgery, until one day he comes upon a monkey with a broken limb. For whatever reason, he tries to repair the creature's wound but, though he succeeds, the animal dies two days later.

Shaken by the manifestations, Morris finally accepts the invitation of his archaeologist friend, Jack Madden, to visit him on his dig in Egypt. There, in a tomb inscribed with motifs of great apes, Madden unearths a sarcophagus containing the body of a young woman, A-pen-ara, one of whose lower vertebra, to Morris's astonishment, shows signs of a corrective operation so complex and so amazing that it would surely stun the contemporary surgical world should it become known. A-pen-ara's tomb, however, has a curse on it:

> "any who desecrates or meddles with her bones . . . the guardians of her sepulcher will see to him, and he shall die childless and in panic and agony; also the guardians of her sepulcher will tear the hair from his head and scoop his eyes from their sockets, and pluck the thumb from his right hand, as a man plucks the young blade of corn from its sheath."

Madden, the archaeologist, a respecter of tombs and of mummies, insists that A-pen-ara's body be reinterred, but Dr. Hugh Morris, working at night and without Madden's knowledge, breaks off the interesting vertebra and takes it back to England with him. On his way home he has an ominous encounter with a monkey. Then retribution follows swiftly and precisely in the terms of the curse on the tomb.

Benson's straightforward prose, his sense of pace and his curious braiding of the theme of monkeys and surgery with the hoary old theme of what happens to despoilers of tombs, turns what might otherwise be a commonplace tale into something like a modest gem.

THE MONKEY'S PAW   Short Story
W.W. Jacobs
Great Britain
1902, in *The Lady of the Barge,* New York, Dodd Mead; reprinted 1972 (1944) in Herbert A. Wise & Phyllis Fraser's (ed.) *Great Tales of Terror and the Supernatural,* New York, Random House/Modern Library.

Considered by many critics to be the single most terrifying story ever written, "The Monkey's Paw" is so artfully imposed on the structure of a folktale that it seems almost to be one.

In the folktale, a fisherman catches a flounder that, pleading for its life, gives the fisherman three wishes. When the simpleminded fisherman wishes for a sausage, his wife wishes the sausage onto his nose. The third wish, of course, is squandered on wishing the sausage off his nose. The moral of the comic tale, of course, is that it does not pay to be both greedy and thoughtless.

The moral of "The Monkey's Paw" is very nearly the same, but a reader comes to it through a series of quite ordinary events that nevertheless build to a bone-chilling climax. These begin on a cold wet night in an isolated house when the Whites, a comfortable small family of three, a father, a mother and their grown young son, Herbert, receive a visit from Sergeant Major Morris who has returned from army duty in India. The Sergeant Major shows them a mummified monkey's paw and tells them that: "It had a spell put on it by an old fakir . . . a very holy man. He wanted to show that fate ruled people's lives, and that those who interfered with it did so to their sorrow." Three separate owners of the paw were each to be given the fulfillment of three wishes. The Sergeant Major, we learn, is the second of the paw's owners. Having told his story, the Sergeant Major, saying that the paw "has caused enough mischief," throws it into the fire on the hearth, but the father of the family rescues it.

Though the family, on consideration, realizes that they are quite happy, the elder Mr. White is encouraged to wish for 200 pounds, a sum that will just clear the mortgage on their little house. The wish is made; there is a crashing noise from the piano and the paw in Mr. White's hand moves.

A day passes. When nothing happens, the Whites think that their original skepticism about the paw was justified. Their son Herbert goes off to his job in the local factory. The elder Whites, soon and to their horror, learn that they have been wrong to be skeptical: They are brought the news that Herbert has been killed in the factory machinery and that his employers, Maw and Meggins, "admitting no liability," are prepared to pay the family 200 pounds.

The second wish, and the third, since they are integral to the story's extraordinary narrative power, will not be told here. It is enough to say that Mr. and Mrs. White (and the story's readers) learn only too clearly that the old fakir was right.

What makes this story so petrifying, it seems to me, is its offhand way of teaching an ancient bit of classical Greek wisdom—that there is no way to escape destiny, and that, for most of us, that destiny, often tragic, is shaped by our own will. The simplicity with which the story unwinds seems to have nothing to do with such grand perceptions and yet they are present here. These quite ordinary people miserably learn that they are themselves at the very center of the human tangle.

THE MOST DANGEROUS GAME   Film
(Alternate release title: **THE HOUNDS OF ZAROFF**)
1932 (B&W) U.S.A. 63 min.
Production Company: RKO; *Director:* Ernest B. Schoedsack and Irving Pichel; *Producer:* Merian C. Cooper and Ernest B. Schoedsack; *Screenplay:* James A. Creelman; *Photography:* Henry Gerrard; *Editor:* Archie S. Marshek; *Special Effects:* Linwood C. Dunn, Harry Redmond, Jr., Lloyd Knechtel, Vernon Walker; *Music:* Max Steiner.
Cast: Joel McCrea (Bob Rainsford), Fay Wray (Eve Trowbridge), Robert Armstrong (Martin Trowbridge), Leslie Banks (Count Zaroff), Noble Johnson (Ivan).

The Most Dangerous Game, based on a prizewinning short story by Richard Connell, turns on a very simple premise: If hunting game is an exciting sport, the sport is many times more exciting when humans are the game being hunted.

Bob Rainsford, a big game hunter, Eve Trowbridge and her husband, the heavy-drinking Martin Trowbridge, are passengers on a ship that is wrecked off Brank Island. The wreck, we learn, was not accidental. It was caused by fake safe lights placed near a dangerous reef at the command of Count Zaroff. Zaroff, the owner—and ruler—of the island uses this contrivance to cause shipwrecks that will provide him with fresh victims for his favorite sport. The count, who wears formal dress in the evening and plays classical piano, is assisted in his wickedness by a mute servant named Ivan.

"Hunting," says the count, "is my passion. My life has been one glorious hunt . . . Hunting was beginning to bore me . . . when I lost my love of hunting I lost my love of life." And so, he tells them, "I have invented a new sensation." He now hunts the most dangerous game: people.

Once all of that is established, the film, and the most dangerous game, begins in earnest. Martin Trowbridge dies in an ill-advised attempt to escape. Then the count makes it clear that Rainsford, armed only with a knife, will be the hunted game. Eve Trowbridge he plans to save for his later use: "Only after the kill does man know the true ecstasy of love."

Rainsford, with Eve in attractive tow, heads for the coast. Their way lies through jungle and swamp and every bit of it is known to their pursuer and utterly foreign to them. Rainsford eludes pits and traps. At one point, he sets traps of his own. Somewhere about the time that he finally takes his necktie off, he acknowledges that, "Now I know how they [the animals he hunted] felt. He and Eve encounter fogs, hunting dogs, crocodiles and waterfalls. It is all utterly contrived and, by and large, unbelievable. Just the same, it is spectacular fun, and when Zaroff, who turns out not to be a man of honor, finally falls among his killer dogs, we are confident that he gets no more than he deserves.

The Most Dangerous Game does not have quite the mythic resonance of *King Kong,* which Schoedsack also codirected,

but he and codirector Irving Pichel take full advantage of Connell's simple plot. They succeed especially, as in *King Kong,* in creating the horrid claustrophobia that one feels watching good pitted against evil in an island setting.

MOTEL HELL   Film
1980 (C) U.S.A. 102 min.
Production Company: United Artists/Camp Hill Productions; *Director:* Kevin Connor; *Producer:* Steven-Charles Jaffe, Robert Jaffe; *Screenplay:* Steven-Charles Jaffe, Robert Jaffe; *Photography:* Thomas del Ruth; *Editor:* Bernard Gribble; *Special Effects:* Adams R. Calvert; *Music:* Lance Rubin.
Cast: Rory Calhoun (Vincent Smith), Paul Linke (Bruce Smith), Nancy Parsons (Ida Smith), Nina Axelrod (Terry), Wolfman Jack (Reverend Billy), Elaine Joyce (Edith Olson), Dick Curtis (Guy Robaire).

The name of this film comes from a detective sign that means to announce the "Motel Hello," except that the letter "o" no longer functions. Though this is, in some sense, a splatter film, it is mostly played for genial comedy. What we have, in fact, is a sort of redneck *Abominable Dr. Phibes* film in which the ingenuity of the villains as they do their dirty work dissipates almost entirely the fear we ought to have about the fate of their victims.

Our villains are Vincent and Ida, a likable brother and sister who keep a motel in the rural South. The siblings are the salt of the earth. Vincent is "Uncle Vincent," whose smoked pork products are well-known throughout a 100-mile radius around his Motel Hello. Ida, his fat, congenial sister, helps Vincent in his hunting, fishing, farming, slaughtering and meat-smoking ventures. The "funnin' " turns on the fact that Vincent and his sister hunt, fish, farm, slaughter and smoke people and then turn them into edible tasties.

Despite touches that are even more macabre—people who have had their vocal chords cut are then planted in the ground where they are fed through funnels as if they are hydroponic vegetables—and despite a slaughterhouse chain saw duel, the film is generally humorous. The final scene encapsulates the flavor of the entire venture. As Vincent is dying, he confesses that his whole life has been a lie. As we brace ourselves for a deathbed truth to pass his lips, he tells us that, though he has always claimed otherwise, his "natural" smoked meats do indeed contain preservatives.

MR. JUSTICE HARBOTTLE   Short Story
J. Sheridan Le Fanu
Ireland
1872, in *In a Glass Darkly,* London, Bentley; reprinted 1964 in E. F. Bleiler's (ed.) *Best Ghost Stories of J. S. Le Fanu,* New York, Dover.

Le Fanu, as he always does, tells his story with the greatest deliberation, beginning it with our introduction to the ghost of Mr. Justice Harbottle, a sort of preliminary tale that preceeds the story itself. There, the shade is described as the ghost of ". . . an elder man, stout, and blotched with scurvy, and whose features fixed as a corpse's, were stamped with dreadful force with a character of sensuality and villainy. . . . this direful old man carried in his ringed and ruffled hand a coil of rope . . ."

Then Le Fanu starts all over again and we get Mr. Justice

Joseph Sheridan Le Fanu.

Harbottle's story. The justice, a cruel, self-indulgent hard liver, has as a mistress the wife of a man named Lewis Pynebeck, who is presently in prison and scheduled to be tried by Harbottle himself. Harbottle is visited by a mysterious stranger who warns him not to try the case, "For if you do, it is feared 'twill shorten your days."

Harbottle, who is a tough nut to crack, is undeterred and presides over the case despite the intercession in the prisoner's favor of Pynebeck's wife, who now calls herself Mrs. Carwell. Harbottle so intimidates the jury that Pynebeck is found guilty and is condemned by him to the gallows, to which the prisoner is summarily sent.

So much then for the events in the real world. Now the supernatural events begin. Harbottle receives a letter indicting him for "wilful perversion of the evidence, and the undue pressure put upon the jury . . ." The indictment letter sets a trial date and specifies, in the event that he is found guilty, the date of his execution.

Harbottle, more irritated than frightened by this letter, continues his reprobate existence until the day set for the trial. On the evening of that day, Harbottle, after attending the theater, is suddenly seized at midnight and transported to a place very like a courthouse where, in a trial presided over by a ruffian judge, Chief Justice Twofold (who has an amazing resemblance to Harbottle himself), he is found guilty.

From that "trial," which apparently is only a dream, Mr. Justice Harbottle wakes a changed man who has lost his iron energy and whose spirits are low. What he cannot forget is the date of execution, "the tenth of the ensuing month" from the time of the trial.

There is something of a mystery about the way "Mr. Justice Harbottle" ends. Throughout the story, Le Fanu allows us to believe that Harbottle's guilt for past and present behavior is responsible for the fantasies that plague him. But as the story comes to a close, we are told that at least three other people have seen supernatural things, and we are left with a certain irresolution: Are there real ghosts in the story, or not? Or are Harbottle's abduction and trial merely projections of his guilt?

Real ghosts or projections, the satisfactory heart of the matter is that Mr. Justice Harbottle, as cruel and brutal a judge as ever served on the King's Bench, does not escape the sentence delivered in a dream trial by a jury of his peers.

MRS. AMWORTH
Short Story

E. F. Benson
Great Britain
1923, in *Visible and Invisible,* London, Hutchinson; reprinted 1972 (1944) in Herbert A. Wise & Phyllis Fraser's (eds.) *Great Tales of Terror and the Supernatural,* New York, Random House/Modern Library.

While the plot of "Mrs. Amworth" is not particularly original, the story is notable for the characterization of its vampire, Mrs. Amworth. Her penchant for fresh air and sunlight are only two of the traits that very much distinguish her from any of the literary or film vampires we know.

Mrs. Amworth is a congenial, fun-loving, middle-aged widow who, as the story's narrator first perceives her, is an ideal non-romantic friend for a retiring, more than middle-aged bachelor living in a beautiful Georgian house in the sleepy village of Maxley. Maxley residents ("Most of us were bachelors or spinster or elderly folk") are enlivened by Mrs. Amworth's presence in their village:

> . . . Mrs. Amworth showed us a more gregarious way, and set an example of luncheon parties and little dinners, which we began to follow . . . There she would be [at her house] with a comrade-like eagerness for companionship, and there was a glass of port and a cup of coffee and a cigarette and a game of piquet. She played the piano, too, in a free and exuberant manner, and had a charming voice and sang to her own accompaniment.

There is nothing of the dark, the dank, the dangerous, about Mrs. Amworth. No hint of the destructive erotic temptress or the femme fatale. No, she is motherly, sisterly. She was "always cheery and jolly . . . Everybody (with one exception) liked her . . ."

That one exception is the narrator's friend and near neighbor, Francis Urcombe, a retired Cambridge professor of physiology who is also a student of the occult. He does not like Mrs. Amworth because he knows her for what she is: a true and deadly vampire who has fed on her own husband and who is now beginning to feed on the local population. How he persuades the story's narrator to help him expose, hunt down and destroy the genial Mrs. Amworth is what the less interesting rest of the story is about.

MUJINA
Short Story

Lafcadio Hearn
Japan
1904, in *Kwaidan,* New York, Harpers; reprinted 1968, New York, Dover.

"Mujina" has the compressed structure of a particularly explosive joke except that fear, not laughter, is what it elicits.

In Lafcadio Hearn's limpid English retelling of the folktale we follow a merchant travelling up the Kii-no-kuni-zama (The Slope of the Province of Kii). He comes upon an O-jochu, an honorable young woman, who is weeping bitterly and whose face is hidden in her hand. The merchant, moved by her grief, pleads with her to let him help her in any way that he can. For a long time, sobs are her only reply. Finally, "that O-jochu turned round, and dropped her sleeve, and stroked her face with her hand;—and the man saw that she had no eyes or nose or mouth,—and he screamed and ran away."

The nightmare climax of the story is only three or four short paragraphs away, and it is a rare reader whose hair does not stand straight on end when he or she comes to it.

THE MUMMY
Film
1932 (B&W) U.S.A. 72 min.
Production Company: Universal; **Director:** Karl Freund; **Producer:** Carl Laemmle, Jr.; **Screenplay:** John L. Balderston; **Photography:** Charles Stumar; **Editor:** Milton Carruth; **Makeup:** Jack Pierce.

Cast: Boris Karloff (Im-ho-tep/Ardath Bey/The Mummy), Zita Johann (Helen Grosvenor/Princess Anck-es-en-Amon), David Manners (Frank Whemple), Edward Van Sloan (Professor Muller), Arthur Byron (Sir Joseph Whemple), Noble Johnson (the Nubian).

The grandiloquence of H. Rider Haggard's Victorian novel *She* still reverberates in this film made in 1932. Essentially the story of a grand passion, *The Mummy*, like *She*, has a more or less immortal protagonist who has nursed his/her love over thousands of years. Both stories involve reincarnation and end in frustration.

As *The Mummy* opens, it is 1921 and we see the field expedition of the British Museum, directed by Sir Joseph Whemple, digging for antiquities in the desert near Cairo. Eventually, they unearth the mummy of Im-ho-tep, a lesser priest of Isis who was buried without having his viscera removed. One of the archaeologists foolishly transcribes a Scroll of Thoth that contains the formula Isis used to revivify Osiris after his death, and the act resuscitates the mummy of Im-ho-tep, who promptly disappears. Ten years later a very wrinkle-faced Egyptian who hates to be touched and who calls himself Ardath Bey shows a second field expedition,

Boris Karloff and Zita Johann in **The Mummy.**

which includes Frank Whemple, son of Sir Joseph, where to dig for the tomb of the Princess Anck-es-en-Amon. She, we soon learn, was Im-ho-tep's beloved.

The mummy of the princess is found and turned over to the Museum of Antiquities in Cairo. Now, all the threads of the plot come together as we meet the daughter of the British governor of the Sudan, Helen Grosvenor, and his Egyptian wife. Frank Whemple immediately falls in love with Helen, but the problem is that she is the reincarnation of the Princess Anck-es-en-Amon for whom Ardath Bey (who, in case you haven't guessed, is the revivified Im-ho-tep) has been waiting for 3,700 years. Much to Frank's dismay, Im-ho-tep, the master of certain ancient forms of sorcery, exerts hypnotic control over Helen. But the situation gets much worse when it becomes clear that Im-ho-tep intends to kill Helen so that, with the help of the Scroll of Thoth, he can resurrect her body, after which, presumably, he and the princess will be immortal lovers.

The Mummy, despite wooden performances by David Manners, Zita Johann and Arthur Byron in the straight roles, manages to delight its viewers because of Karl Freund's driving direction and the superb vitality of Boris Karloff in the role of a man who has been dead for 3,700 years. Edward

Van Sloan as Professor Muller, though fascinating to watch, is almost a replica of himself as Dr. Van Helsing in *Dracula.* One needs to praise, too, the filmscript that is both playful and witty or grandiloquent, as occasion requires. Thus we have Zita Johann telling David Manners, ''What girl could fail to make a conquest who collapses at the feet of a man in the moonlight,'' while Boris Karloff, speaking as to Anck-es-en-Amon, says in his commanding, sepulchral voice, ''You will not remember what I show you now. Yet I shall waken memories of love and crime and death.''

The mummy's makeup, contrived by Jack Pierce, gives to Karloff's features, and the very bandages in which we first see him, an air of dessicated, fragile antiquity. He is a man so obviously likely to crumble that it is no wonder he doesn't like to be touched.

MYSTERY OF THE WAX MUSEUM   Film
1933 (C) U.S.A. 73 min.
Production Company: Warner Brothers; *Director:* Michael Curtiz; *Producer:* Henry Blanke; *Screenplay:* Don Mulallaly, Carl Erickson; *Photography:* Ray Rennahan; *Editor:* George Amy.
Cast: Lionel Atwill (Ivan Igor), Fay Wray (Florence), Allen

Lionel Atwill in **Mystery of the Wax Museum.**

Vincent (George Winton), Frank McHugh (Charlotte's editor), Glenda Farrell (Charlotte.)

Because the identities we show the world reside primarily in our faces, there is hardly anything more terrifying than the idea that they can be stolen, destroyed or rearranged. Films that deal with replicas of the human face, then, touch some deep mythic nerve of fear. And this is what makes so appalling the moment in *The Mystery of the Wax Museum* when Fay Wray, screaming one of her famous screams, pounds away (and smashes) the face of the man who has been stealing faces.

The Mystery . . . , an early example of a waxworks film, has almost everything to recommend it. It is fast-paced, visually ingenious, symbolically and thematically satisfying. Besides, it has Lionel Atwill, Fay Wray and Frank McHugh in roles that seem to have been cast in stereotypic bronze.

The villain of the piece is the extremely sympathetic sculptor, Ivan Igor, who runs a wax museum in London because it gives him an opportunity to work with wax, a warmer medium than stone. In the opening sequence, a famous art critic comes to see Igor's work and is impressed with his masterpiece, a statue of Marie Antoinette. The critic, Gallakoli, promises to submit Igor's work to the Royal Academy.

However, Igor's unscrupulous business partner, who sees no financial future for the wax museum, sets the place on fire for the sake of the insurance money. In the struggle between Igor and his partner (a scene wonderfully alive with flames), the partner escapes the holocaust, but the last we see of Igor, he is in flames.

Ten years later, the story shifts to the United States where, in the New York City of 1933, eight bodies have been stolen from the morgue in the last 18 months. We are introduced to another wax museum, run by the wheelchair-bound Igor. And we meet Charlotte (played by Glenda Farrell), the tough-talking blonde sob sister reporter for a tabloid, who undertakes to investigate the latest disappearance from the morgue—the body of Joan Gale, the millionaire George Winton's fiancée.

It does not take us long to figure out that the figures in the macabre exhibits in Igor's museum are actually the wax-dipped bodies of the missing tenants of the morgue. And when Charlotte's roommate, Florence, whose boyfriend works for Igor, catches the museum owner's eye and we hear him saying, ''I need a beautiful statue and you are that statue come to life,'' there is reason for everyone to worry.

Igor's plot is foiled by the cooperative detective work of Florence and Winton, who has been charged with the murder of his own fiancée. At the high point of the film, Igor catches Florence snooping and is about to do something dreadful to her. She screams and beats his face with her fist. The face breaks under her blows to reveal his horribly fire-scarred visage. Florence screams, ''Your face was wax, you fiend.'' To which Igor replies, ''No. There was a fiend and this is what he did to me.''

There is a certain amount of mayhem that follows on that scene, and finally, of course, the right people are rescued and the wicked get what's coming to them, though poor Igor's fate is a little too bad. There ought to be some special place, neither hell nor purgatory, for villains who have been profoundly (in his case, anguishingly) driven to their crimes.

If the film has a weakness, it is undoubtedly the snappy lingo Glenda Farrell is given to speak. The brash, tough-talking sob sister was, of course, a cliche of movies in the thirties. Then, a line like ''Alright fella. You can go to some nice warm place and I don't mean California'' may have sounded bright and sassy. Today it merely sounds dated. Equally dated is the notion that the independent professional woman was only waiting for some strong man to marry her, after which she would retreat toward a dreamy cottage kitchen while the music surged.

NIGHT OF THE HUNTER
Film

1955 (B&W)   U.S.A.   93 min.

Production Company: United Artists; *Director:* Charles Laughton; *Producer:* Paul Gregory; *Screenplay:* James Agee, based on the novel by Davis Grubb; *Photography:* Stanley Cortez; *Editor:* Robert Golden; *Music:* Walter Schumann.

Cast: Robert Mitchum ("Preacher" Harry Powell), Shelley Winters (Willa Harper), Lillian Gish (Rachel Cooper), James Gleason (Old Birdie), Billy Chapin (Johnny), Sally Jane Bruce (Pearl).

This masterpiece of a film is the product of an extraordinary gathering of talent and achievement, all of it well beyond genius: First, there is Davis Grubb's lyric and terrifying novel in which the vision of dread is first manifested. Then, James Agee's tactful, taut and extraordinarily visual screenplay, which displays such a sensitivity to the novel's strengths that it is easy to suppose that Agee redreamed Grubb's nightmare. There is, too, the direction of Charles Laughton (who never directed another film), whose eyes and ears and sense of timing convey the plot: sometimes as flat narrative, sometimes as pure dance, sometimes as sheer imagery drawn either from the folklore of children or at other times from the sterner adult allegories of the Christian faith.

And with all that generosity of talent, we have yet to speak of the precision of the film's casting or of the actors' performances, which are as persuasive and chilling as reality itself.

Robert Mitchum plays Harry Powell, an itinerant preacher who supports his preaching call by marrying, and murdering, lonely widows. Sent to prison for a month for having stolen an automobile, he meets young Ben Harper who has been condemned to hang for murdering a couple of employees of the bank he robbed. Harper, before his capture, had entrusted the $10,000 he stole to his 12-year-old son John who hid the money in his sister Pearl's doll.

When Powell is released, he heads for Harper's young and dim-witted widow, Willa (Shelley Winters), whom he woos and wins. His intent, of course, is to find the $10,000, and the rest of the film revolves around his efforts to make the children tell him where the money is and young John's too heavy task of keeping him from discovering it.

Beautifully plotted though the film is, its superb power comes from resonances present in Grubb's vision of the struggle between the malevolence of Powell, the man of God, the prophet "that comes to you in sheep's clothing but invariably they are ravenning wolves," and the innocence of John that slowly turns into the ghastliest sort of knowledge about the human capacity for evil. All of this is played out against the background of Depression poverty among the farms and rural hamlets of the Ohio River.

Laughton's black and white scenes seem bathed in the full spectrum of feeling. He is entranced by silhouettes, by shadows, by intensely emblematic moments. His film is arranged in a series of small etched scenes, each one a precise and sometimes staggeringly beautiful display of people against backgrounds: There is a scene in which the fleeing children, at night in a barn, first hear the pursuing Powell singing his favorite hymn, "Leaning, leaning on the Ever Loving Arm . . ." Then they see him silhouetted against the waning light of evening as he rides his white horse atop the river levee with the slow pace of the pale rider, the Fourth Horseman of the Apocalypse, whose traveling companion is Hell. There is the breathtaking moment when we see what the hard-drinking Old Birdie sees as he discovers the body of the children's mother, Willa, under water and seated in the back seat of a tin lizzie, with her throat cut. What Laughton shows us is strands of river grass streaming under the force of the river's current toward her long hair, which itself flows away from her body "like river grass under flood water."

Night of the Hunter gives us Robert Mitchum in probably his greatest role, Shelley Winters acquiring luster for her still-new career and Charles Laughton's monument to his once and only appearance as a director. The film is so powerful that its magnificence is hardly marred by an ending so soppy

Robert Mitchum as "Preacher" Harry Powell in **Night of the Hunter.**

that one can only suppose it was dictated by someone in the front office who worried that the film would not—as it did not—do well at the box office.

NIGHT OF THE LIVING DEAD   Film

1968 (B&W) U.S.A. 96 min.
Production Company: Walter Reade/Continental; *Director:* George A. Romero; *Producer:* Russell W. Streiner and Karl Hardman; *Screenplay:* John Russo, George A. Romero; *Photography:* George A. Romero; *Editor:* George A. Romero; *Special Effects:* Regis Survinski, Tony Pantanello.
Cast: Judith O'Dea (Barbara), Duane Jones (Ben), Karl Hardman (Harry Cooper), Russell Streiner (Johnny), Keith Wayne (Tom), Judi Ridley (Judy), Marilyn Eastman (Helen Cooper), Kyra Schon (Karen Cooper).

Here is another of those low budget ($115,000) horror films that becomes a classic because of the sheer genius of the minds that shaped it. In this case, director George A. Romero was the chief shaper, with help from John Russo, Karl Hardman and Russell Streiner.

One can recognize the well worn *Lifeboat* formula in the plot of *Night of the Living Dead.* Once again we are shown just how the individual members of an small, isolated group of people respond to an encroaching catastrophe. In *Lifeboat,* it will be remembered, people of varying backgrounds are cast adrift and the film shows us how each of them behaves. But in this case, the catastrophe is much larger than a ship torpedoed in wartime. The whole world is doomed because a Venus space probe has somehow infected it with a spore whose effect is to bring the dead back to life. That would be bad enough, but the dead, once revived, are afflicted with a ghastly appetite for living flesh. Nor is that all. Whoever is killed by these living dead is destined to become one of them.

That, then, is the organizing premise of the film. The group we see has taken refuge from the marauding corpses in an old house near a cemetery. At first, there seem to be only two people in the house, a young woman named Barbara who has escaped from the zombie that killed her brother, and a young black man named Ben. Eventually, five other people are discovered hiding in the house: a couple named Tom and Judy, and the Cooper family, which includes Harry and Helen Cooper and their seven- or eight-year-old daughter Karen who has been bitten by one of the corpses.

Each of the inhabitants, forced to work together for their common good, believes either well or badly. In the adults, class, race and sexual attitudes surface as the battle against the corpses goes on. Even little Karen, who is too young to be of much help, is given a ghastly part to play. The corpses, for their part are about as loathsome as film monsters can be, chiefly because they look very much like most people except that they walk like somnambulists. As for their food, Romero's cameras are horribly specific. The zombies pluck limbs and entrails from their victims and devour them with a glassy-eyed intensity.

Made in the sixties, *The Night of the Living Dead* captures the lassitude of the fifties. However, beyond the graphic scenes of cannibalism, which may be the secret of the film's notoriety, what it does well is to capture the texture of human meanness in a time of trial. It is as if Romero had found the properly grungy images to elaborate Eliot's prediction that the world will end "Not with a bang, but a whimper." More than that, Romero has added his own bleak prophecy: Armageddon, when it comes, is likely to be colored gray.

Dawn of the Dead appeared in 1979 and it was followed in 1985 by *Day of the Dead.* Except for a pungently satirical sequence of scenes in *Dawn of the Dead* in which five non-zombie survivors are besieged by the living dead inside a shopping mall in a Pittsburgh suburb, the sequels to *Night of the Living Dead* demonstrate only too graphically what happens when vision gives way to formula. The later films, made with many times the sum of money *Night of the Living Dead* cost are sleek and clever. But in them, Romero succumbs to a penchant for filming exploding heads. Such scenes may be realistic but their very enthusiasm drains them of fear and they end by provoking laughter.

NIGHTMARE ABBEY   Novel

Thomas Love Peacock
Great Britain
1818, London, T. Hookham, Jr. and Baldwin, Cradock & Joy; reprinted 1971, New York, Holt, Rinehart & Winston.

The hero of this blithely witty spoof of Gothic fiction and romantic attitudes is named Scythrop Glowry. He is the son of Christopher Glowry, a Lincolnshire landed gentleman of gloomy disposition who presides over the family castle, Nightmare Abbey.

Scythrop, we learn, was named after an ancestor who committed suicide and whose skull Christopher Glowry has been using for a punchbowl. Scythrop, whose mind has been much addled by deep reading in Kant, falls madly in love with his flighty, delightful but impecunious cousin, Marionetta Celestina O'Carroll, who more or less loves him too. But the elder Glowry has a better match for him, the beautiful and brilliant Celinda Toobad, who has been educated abroad and who is the heiress to a considerable fortune.

Celinda, being a modern young woman, rebels against being handed over to a man without being either consulted or considered, and disappears from her father's house. Meanwhile, back at Nightmare Abbey, Scythrop, brooding over his father's tyranny, secludes himself in his tower room where he reads Gothic fiction and dreams "of venerable eleutherarchs[1] and ghastly confederates holding midnight conventions in subterranean caves."

Then several things happen in quick succession: A strange woman shows up in Scythrop's tower room and, claiming to be persecuted by unnamed tyrants, implores his protection; a white-garbed "ghost wearing a blood colored turban" is seen walking at night through the castle; and Scythrop's father, impressed with Scythrop's unhappiness, gives up his opposition to Scythrop's marriage to Marionetta.

The result is chaos and confusion on every side as Scythrop, now equally in love with his clandestine guest and with Marionetta, elects to commit suicide rather than give up either of the women. In a scene that burlesques the death of Goethe's Werther, Scythrop, armed with plenty of Madeira and a pistol, waits for the fatal hour at which he has promised to die, but before *Nightmare Abbey* comes to its sprightly end the ghost and Scythrop's dilemma yield before sweet reason.

Peacock's targets for his satire are the exalted attitudinizing of the prose and poetry of the Romantic movement (with special emphasis on Byron) and the sillier coincidences and confusions that were endemic in gothic fiction. If *Nightmare Abbey* seems not quite as pointed now as it was in its own day, it still rewards a reader with a stylish and effervescent prose, whose echoes one can hear in the wicked lucidities of Oscar Wilde.

NIGHTMARE ON ELM STREET   Film
1984   (C)   U.S.A.   92 min.
Production Company: A Robert Shaye Production/New Line Cinema; *Director:* Wes Craven; *Producer:* Robert Shaye; *Screenplay:* Wes Craven; *Photography:* Jacques Haitkin; *Editor:* Rick Shaine; *Special Effects:* Jim Doyle; *Music:* Charles Bernstein.
Cast: John Saxon (Lt. Thompson), Ronee Blakeley (Marge Thompson), Heather Langenkamp (Nancy Thompson), Amanda Wyss (Tina Gray), Nick Corri (Rod), Johnny Depp (Glenn).

In *Nightmare on Elm Street* director Wes Craven famous for the grisly *Last House on the Left* and the much better *The Hills Have Eyes,* retains his reputation as a filmmaker of the blood-drenched school, but with a story and direction more polished than in the earlier films.

The apparent story concerns four teenagers who are involved in a series of linked scenes taking place in and out of nightmares. At first, the film focuses on the dreams that Tina

Gray, an attractive 17-year-old, has been having, dreams in which she is pursued by a dark figure who chuckles horribly as he clicks his shiny, murderous steel claws. Later we learn that Rod, her boyfriend, and Nancy Thompson, a girlfriend, have had similar dreams.

When Tina's divorced mother goes off to Las Vegas with her boyfriend, Tina and Rod are joined by Nancy and her boyfriend Glenn in an overnight sleepaway in Tina's home. There, in a scene that is as violent and bloody as it is improbable, Tina is murdered by an invisible killer as Rod watches.

With Tina dead and Rod in jail because he is suspected of being her killer, the focus of the film now turns on Nancy. She learns that the mysterious figure with the clicking finger knives in her dreams is a man named Fred Krueger, who, her mother tells her, was "A filthy child murderer who killed at least twenty children in the neighborhood . . . The lawyers got fat and the judge got famous . . . but somebody forgot to sign the search warrant in the right place and he was freed just like that." A mob of outraged parents, including Nancy's mother, cornered Krueger, doused him in gasoline and set him afire.

At this point in the film, Nancy, and the film audience, understand that Fred Krueger still exists in some form of malevolent energy and that, for the sake of his revenge, he has found a way of entering the dreams of the children of the people who killed him. The rest of the film shows us Nancy learning the facts and finding both the courage and the ingenuity to outwit and finally destroy Krueger, for the second time.

A Nightmare on Elm Street is an absorbing film, particularly because of the visual impact of Krueger's steel claws and because of the interplay between what purport to be waking scenes and nightmare. Craven has been rather deft, too, in appealing to the prejudices of teenage audiences by turning all the parents who appear in the film into models of incompetence. The film's violence is a triumph of the art of special effects and, considering Wes Craven's past work, something of a triumph of restraint.

Audiences apparently do not mind what seems to me to be the film's fatal conceptual flaw, which is that even as it ends we have no way of knowing whose dream we have been in or whether, in fact, the nightmare is over. Life in nightmares can only be understood by contrasting it with what we know of the waking world. The idea of a perpetual nightmare is only a fine metaphor in a mind awake. But, as *Nightmare on Elm Street* ends, the dream with which the film began starts to go round again and we are left wondering who, now, is the unhappy dreamer.

Meanwhile, there have already been several sequels to the film.

NIGHT-SIDE   Short Story
Joyce Carol Oates
U.S.A.
1977, in *Eighteen Tales,* New York, Vanguard Press.

An expansive, literate tale of a pair of more or less skeptical psychic researchers conducting an investigation of the powers of a medium named Mrs. A—, in Massachusetts in 1887.

---

[1]Eleutherarc, the chief of a secret society called The Eleutheri.

The less skeptical Jarvis, the tale's narrator, and Perry Moore, the scoffing representative of the Society for Psychical Research, monitor Mrs. A—'s seances. Moore explains what appear to be authentic manifestations of spirits, through her, as the effects of Mrs. A—'s remarkable telepathic powers. Until one night a voice from Perry Moore's past issues from Mrs. A—'s throat. It cries, "Perry . . . ? This is Brandon. I've waited so long for you, Perry, how could you be so selfish? I forgave you. Long ago. You couldn't help your cruelty and I couldn't help my innocence. Perry? My glasses have been broken—I can't see . . . ."

That densely packed moment shatters Perry Moore's skepticism and turns him into a fanatical (if not downright mad) believer in the premise that "there is no death." When Perry Moore dies of a stroke, and manifests himself to Jarvis soon after, bringing appalling news of what is on the other side, Jarvis is also thrown into a panic of reevaluation. For a while he clings to the notion that if there is no death then "Life is the only reality. It is not extinction that awaits, but a hideous dreamlike state, a perpetual groping, blundering—far worse than extinction . . . So it is life we must cling to, arm over arm, swimming, conquering the element that sustains us."

The tale ends, not prettily, but with the reader still bitterly mulling over the question, "Is the penumbra outside consciousness all that was ever meant by 'God'?"

THE NIGHTWALKER   Novel
Thomas Tessier
Great Britain
1979, New York, Atheneum Press.

Tessier's Bobby Ives is a Vietnam veteran now living in London on disability checks. He nourishes himself on vitamin C pills, honey, massive doses of ginseng and health foods. As we meet him, he is beginning to experience semi-amnesiac seizures in the course of which he behaves with extreme violence. He has, too, the certainty that he lived another life as a plantation owner on the island of Guadeloupe, where his older brother died and was turned into a zombie.

Bobby confides his problems to a young woman friend, Annie, who does what she can to comfort him, but "what she can" turns out to be far from enough, and her life is the price of her failure.

After Annie's death, Ives seeks help from a 17-year-old clairvoyant, a Ms. Tanith, who, after studying his face and his palms, tells him that he does indeed have a dark destiny. When Ives implores her help, she at first refuses it. Later, when Ives has repeated, murderous seizures, she agrees to help, confessing then that she had found the mark of the werewolf on him. She locks Ives into a secure room, feeds him a calming diet, and soothes him with occasional chats. Her regime, however, fails. Ives breaks out and resumes his werewolf career.

Tessier's intelligent blending of werewolf and zombie legendry with contemporary psychological insight is admirable. A major point in Tessier's favor: He doesn't repeat the tried and true man into wolf metamorphosis scene that infests werewolf fiction on and off the screen.

NOSFERATU-EINE SYMPHONIE DES   Film
GRAUENS
(Alternate release titles: **NOSFERATU-A SYMPHONY OF HORROR; NOSFERATU THE VAMPIRE; TERROR OF DRACULA; DRACULA; THE TWELFTH HOUR**)
1922 (B/W) Germany 72 min.
Production Company: Prana Films; *Director:* F.W. Murnau; *Screenplay:* Henrik Galeen; *Photography:* Fritz Arno Wagner, Gunther Krampf; *Editor:* Simon Gould; *Special Effects:* Albin Grau (set design).
Cast: Max Schreck (Graf Orlok/Nosferatu), Alexander Granach (Knock), Gustav von Wangenheim (Hutter), Greta Schröder-Matray (Ellen), Ruth Landshoff (Annie), John Gottowt (Professor Bulwer).

F.W. Murnau directed *Nosferatu*, the silent German version of *Dracula* that appeared in 1922, but copyright problems compelled him to modify Stoker's plot and settings. In Murnau's version, a real estate agent sends his young, newly married clerk to transact some business with Count Orlok, in Transylvania. As played by Max Schreck, the count, who is clearly derived from Thomas Preskett Prest's description of Varney in *Varney the Vampire*, is a frightful creature, tall, humped, skull-faced and pale. His eyes blaze, his ears are pointed and his fingernails are as long and as curved as scythes. The clerk, named Hutter, for a while has adventures that parallel those of Stoker's Jonathan Harker. He too stays at an inn where worried villagers try to dissuade him from going on. "Oh, sir, there are evil spirits out after dark," someone says. As he gets ready for bed, there are noises among the animals: Horses are agitated, a hyena howls. The screen titles say, "Men do not always recognize dangers beasts can sense." That night, Hutter, unlike Harker, gets an inkling of what's to come by reading from a book on vampires that he conveniently finds beside his bed. In the morning, he goes forward.

His journey to Count Orlok's castle is filled with portents, not the least being the film-stuttering ride in the coach Count Orlok has sent to meet the diligence. At Orlok's mountain retreat Hutter is welcomed and fed by the hideous Count, who admires a picture of the clerk's bride "Your wife?" Orlok asks. "What a lovely throat." Later, a bloodthirsting count approaches the sleeping Hutter, but he is saved by a long-distance spasm of sympathy that shakes his wife Ellen back in Bremen, and which, reaching Transylvania, drives the vampire off.

Disaster, however, is only delayed, not averted. The count, the titles tell us, "Leaves his castle to haunt the world . . . wherever he emerges, rats swarm out and people fall dead."

Murnau's treatment of the Dracula story from this point on was to influence the film versions of the vampire that followed: *Nosferatu* sets down, however obliquely, the ambiguity that for ever after would be at the heart of the Dracula matter. When the vampire approaches his or her victim, what do we have: love scene or blood scene? Or both together? Murnau sees the relationship among Hutter, his wife and the count as a classic love triangle. We see Ellen/Nina in Bremen longing for Jonathan. Then the camera traces the movements first of Jonathan, then of Count Orlok, as by separate routes

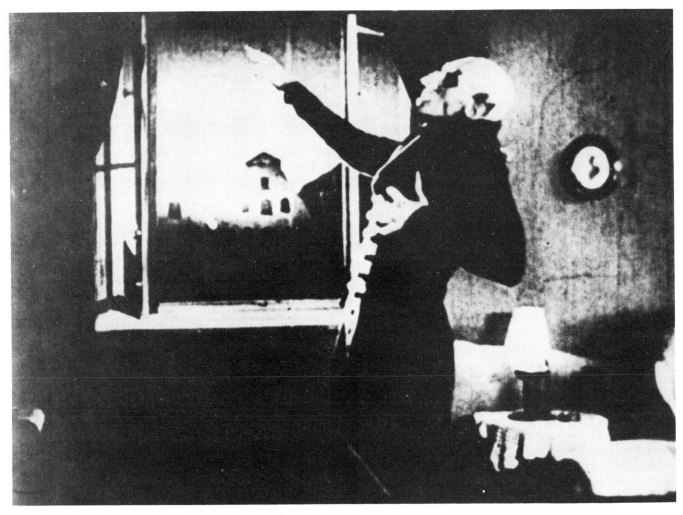

Max Schreck as Count Orlock in **Nosferatu.** © Prana Films

they make their way toward Bremen. When Orlok takes up residence in a house facing the Hutter home, we are given scenes in which Ellen/Nina, staring out the window at Orlok's lair, has all the vexed mannerisms of a woman impatiently waiting to meet her demon lover. Finally, in a scene that has certain unmistakable elements of a French bedroom farce, Ellen/Nina, under the pretext that she needs the help of the professor, sends her husband away and readies herself for the coming of her demon lover.

And Orlok, tall, cadaverous, hump-shouldered and scurrying, comes. The bedroom scene that follows is a marvel of mood. Bizarrely enough, in a silent film, the scene is felt as intensely silent. All that the camera sees is a supine Ellen/Nina and the pale rondeur of Orlok's head at her bedside. Then, when whatever it is that Orlok is doing is done, the camera cuts to a crowing rooster—and we know that all destinies have been accomplished: the love-death of Ellen/Nina, the destruction of the vampire, and the city saved from the plague.

I do not accept Carlos Clarens' strictures in *An Illustrated History of the Horror Film* that *Nosferatu* is "crude, unsubtle and illogical." Despite its technical limitations, the film survives as a classic study of a nightmare, which must not be missed by anyone interested either in film history or the history of the vampire in film.

NOSFERATU, THE VAMPYRE Film

1979 (C) West Germany/France 107 min.
Production Company: Filmproduktion/Beaumont; ***Director:*** Werner Herzog; ***Producer:*** Werner Herzog; ***Screenplay:*** Werner Herzog; ***Photography:*** Jeorg Schmidt-Reitwein; ***Editor:*** Beate Mainke-Jellinghaus; ***Special Effects:*** Cornelius Siegel; ***Music:*** Popol Vuh, Florian Flicke.
Cast: Klaus Kinski (Count Dracula), Isabelle Adjani (Lucy Harker), Bruno Ganz (Jonathan Harker), Roland Topor (Renfield), Walter Ladengast (Dr. Van Helsing).

Nosferatu, Werner Herzog's version of F.W. Murnau's version of Bram Stoker's *Dracula,* has been much abused by the critics. The *London Financial Times,* for instance, says that it is ". . . a series of swoony dream images that hover perilously on the brink of TV commercial prettiness." And Gene Wright in his *Horrorshows* writes that it is "beautiful to look at, but it barely raises a goose-pimple."

Both reviewers are right but they may be missing the three things that Herzog does remarkably well. First, retaining

Klaus Kinski as Count Dracula in **Nosferatu the Vampyre.** ©
20th Century-Fox

Murnau's plot, he captures precisely the sense of slow and languorous fearfulness that is part of any vampire tale's attraction. Second, through Klaus Kinski he has brilliantly conveyed the deep weariness of life that follows upon a vampire's first enthusiastic experience of immortality. Klaus Kinski's boneless softness captures the anguish of the mortal Tithonus who, having married the goddess of the dawn and received from her the gift of eternal life, failed to ask her at the same time for eternal youth. The result, and this is what Kinski portrays, is a dreary, perpetual dwindling.

Finally there is the photography, which almost everyone admires. Some of the scenes, particularly of landscapes, are so gorgeous that it hardly matters that they do not serve the theme of the film.

NOT TO BE TAKEN AT BEDTIME   Short Story
Rosa Mulholland
Great Britain
1865, in *All the Year Round,* London; reprinted 1974 in Montague Summers' (ed.) *The Supernatural Omnibus* (1st Pub. 1931), New York, Causeway Books.

The plot of this magnificent short horror tale recalls Sir Walter Scott's *The Bride of Lammermoor.*

Coll Dhu, a dispossessed Irish chieftain, saves the life of Colonel Blake who now owns what was once Coll Dhu's patrimony. When Colonel Blake expresses his gratitude, Coll Dhu replies:

> "Colonel Blake, your father suggested to my father to stake his estates at the gaming table. They were staked, and the tempter won. Both are dead; but you and I live, and I have sworn to injure you."

But Colonel Blake, a sensible man, ignores the melodramatic reply and introduces Coll Dhu to his daughter Evleen. The result is that the dark, Byronic, reclusive and violent young man is instantly in thrall to the beauty, but when he asks her for the gift of a rose from the bouquet at her bosom the following exchange occurs:

"Sir, if you are a gentleman you must be mad! If you are not mad, then you are not a gentleman!"

"Be merciful," said Coll Dhu; "I love you. My God, I never loved a woman before. Ah!" he cried, as a look of disgust crept over her face. "You hate me. You shuddered the first time your eyes met mine. I love you and you hate me!"

"I do . . . your looks poison me . . ."

Rarely in literature has a romance begun so unpromisingly. Coll Dhu's passions, if they are dashed by this beginning, are inflamed again when he overhears a couple of local women talking about a talisman known as the burragh-bos, which is:

> "a shthrip o' the skin o' a corpse, peeled from the crown o' the head to the heel, without crack or split, or the charm's broke; an' that, rowled up, an' put on a sthring roun' the neck o' the one that's cowled by the wan that wants to be loved. An' sure enough it puts the fire in their hearts, hot an' shthrong, afore twenty-four hours is gone."

Determined to get the burragh-bos, Coll Dhu seeks out Pexie na Pishrogie, a yellow-faced hag who, for money, will prepare the talisman. She assures him that the burragh-bos will make Evleen fall in love with him "or the colleen dhas go wild mad afore wan hour." The love-besotted Coll Dhu ignores the second half of the witch's promise and Pexie, with two silver sovereigns in her claws, goes off to prepare the talisman.

She does more. When the grisly thing is made she contrives and executes the plot to hang it around Evleen's neck. Before the story's horrifying end, Coll Dhu and Evleen are indeed united, but not quite in the way he had imagined.

Rosa Mulholland tells her tale with all the verve of a romantic writer who, because she is unaware that her characters are stick figures, allows them to be exalted by the great attitudes of love, hate and nobility. Her story is at once theatrical and homely, the way that the best of the fairy tales are. Indeed, this is what "Not to Be Taken at Bedtime" is: a resplendent, dark fairy tale for grown-ups.

NUCKELAVEE   Short Story
Anonymous
Scotland
No date; reprinted in Leonard Wolf's (ed.) *Wolf's Complete Book of Terror,* New York, Clarkson N. Potter.

If there is a perfect model of the horrifying folktale, surely *Nuckelavee* is it.

Nuckelavee, we are told "is a monster of unmixed malignity, never willingly resting from doing evil to mankind." In this version of the story, the boy Tammas meets Nuckelavee one night on a road along the shore. And this is what he sees,

> The lower part of this terrible monster . . . was like a great horse with flappers like fins about his legs, with a mouth as wide as a whale's from whence came breath like steam from a brewing-kettle. He had but one eyes, and that as red as fire. On him sat, or rather seemed to grow from his back, a huge man with no legs, and arms that reached nearly to the ground. His head was as big as a clue of simmons, and this huge head kept rolling from one shoulder to the other as if it meant to tumble off. But what to Tammie appeared most horrible of all, was that the monster was skinless . . .

Nuckelavee.

Moments later, Nuckelavee pursues Tammie and, in the classic way of such tales, gets closer and closer. "The mouth of the monster yawned like a bottomless pit. Tammie found its hot breath like fire on this face . . ."

And so on.

The formula for a story like this one is always successful because we know that it embodies the truth: Someone, or something, horrible is following you and will catch you and eat you if you don't watch out.

NUNC DIMITIS   Short Story
Tanith Lee
Great Britain
1983, in Charles L. Grant's (ed.) *The Dodd, Mead Gallery of Horror*, New York, Dodd, Mead.

Tanith Lee, one of the most accomplished of the new generation of fantasy writers, has a sensibility that reminds one of Baudelaire or Huysmans. She is the master of a prose style whose very grace threatens the success of her fiction. And yet, when she is at her best, as here in "Nunc Dimitis," we get a sensuous and delicate fiction whose beauty leaves one nearly breathless.

There are only three characters in this story, and a single event. The characters are the aged but agelessly glorious vampire, Darejan Draculas (from another branch of that family); Vasyelu Gorin, her servant and lover for the last 200 years; and Snake, a dynamic and amoral young man whose

eyes "In the dull light of the alley . . . were the colour of leopards—not the eyes of leopards, but their pelts."

The single event is that Vasyelu Gorin, who has acquired the gift of longevity, but not immortality, from the vampire's embrace now knows that he is dying. Like the good servant and faithful lover he has been, he understands that this final task must be to provide the vampire, whom he adores, with his own successor, a new servant and lover. When Snake, who makes his living as a petty thief and sometime whore, attempts to rob Vasyelu, the dying vampire instinctively recognizes that Snake has the proper, complex vitality to be his successor. The rest of the story is simply an account of how that desired transformation is brought about.

That process involves a strange combination of sophisticated, this-worldly sensuality and the vampire blood-exchange that Bram Stoker introduced as the baptismal requirement for bringing a new vampire into the fold:

> When the Vampire entered the room, Snake, a practised gigolo, came to his feet. And the Vampire was amused by him, gently now. She wore a bone-white frock that had been sent from Paris last year. She had never worn it before. Pinned at the neck was a black velvet rose with a single drop of dew shivering on a single petal: a pearl that had come from the crown jewels of a czar . . .

> Vasyelu Gorin left them. He returned later with the decanters and glasses. The cold supper had been laid out by people from the city who handled such things, pate and lobsters and chicken, lemon slices cut like flowers, orange slices like suns, tomatoes that were anemones, and oceans of green lettuce, and cold, glittering ice.

I quote at length because Tanith Lee's vision of her vampire is so unlike what we expect. She is not presented as an agent of evil. At one remove she is, instead, a sort of existentialist metaphor for the great weariness that can come upon one who has lived too long and too deeply:

> "Do you remember Vassu? . . . When I was so hungry, and so relentless. And so lovely. My white face in a thousand ballroom mirrors. My silk slippers stained with dew. And my lovers waking in the cold morning, where I had left them. But now, I do not sleep, I am seldom hungry. I never lust. I never love. These are the comforts of old age . . ."

As for Vasyelu, he regards his long life in her service as having been well spent. He was an illiterate 16-year-old peasant boy when she vampirized him, and in the long years he has spent with her, he has known love and intellectual growth. We are meant to believe that Snake, once he has taken over Vasyelu's task, will feel, like him, that his life has been blessed.

But there is another, disturbing dimension to "Nunc Dimitis," whose very title invites us to be appalled by Tanith Lee's temerity. I have noted with interest in recent years the tendency of authors like Lee and Chelsea Quin Yarbro to cast vampires in sympathetic roles, but it has seemed to me that such efforts, though they retain the sexual implications of the word "vampire," nevertheless leach away its moral and spiritual meaning.

But here, Ms. Lee goes beyond the creation of a Byronic outcast figure. Her title, "Nunc dimitis," forces us to read religious meaning into her tale because "Nunc dimitis" is the Latin opening of the speech that Simeon makes (Luke:2—29) when he encounters the infant Jesus in the temple and recognizes in Him "the Lord's Christ." Simeon says:

> "Lord, now lettest thou thy servant depart in peace, according to thy word: For mine eyes have seen thy salvation, Which thou has prepared before the face of all people."

Leaving aside all questions of blasphemy (which some readers may not want to do), it seems to me that Tanith Lee is putting too heavy a literary strain on her readers in asking them to see Vasyelu, the dying old vampire, in the role of Simeon, ready to take his leave of the world now that he has seen its savior. And attractive though she is, Darejan Draculas is nobody's analogue to Christ. But possibly I have missed the point of Lee's beautifully written story altogether and she really has the triumph of Satan in mind as she provides Darejan Draculas with a new lover whose name is Snake.

NUTBUSH FARM   Short Story
J.H. Riddell
Great Britain
1882, in *Weird Stories*, London, Chatto, Windus; reprinted 1977 in E.F. Bleiler's (ed.) *The Collected Ghost Stories of Mrs. J.H. Riddell*, New York, Dover.

"Nutbush Farm" is hardly a horror story in the usual sense of the term because the ghost who appears in it, though it does indeed terrify people, intends simply to let the world know something it needs to know so that a great wrong may be set right.

The narrator of the story tells us that, having met with an accident in the course of his employment in London, he has been advised by his doctors to take up the rural life. A money grant from his grateful employers enables him to lease Nutbush Farm in the vicinity of Whittleby, near Kent. The only trouble with beautiful Nutbush Farm is the rumor that it is haunted by a ghost who is seen frequently in the Beech Walk.

The narrator, exasperated by the rumors, and unwilling to subject his wife and child to them, undertakes some vigorous detective work to discover what basis they may have in fact. He learns that before he leased Nutbush Farm the place had been tenanted by a man named Hascot who, it was rumored, had taken a large sum of money out of the bank and then had disappeared with it and in the company of a young woman named Sally Powner, leaving his wife and children to the tender mercies of the country poorhouse. The rumor-mongers say that it is his ghost that is doing the walking.

The narrator properly says to his informants, "But Mr. Hascot is not dead; how can he 'walk,' as you call it?" To which his rustic informants reply, "If he is living, then, sir, where is he? . . . He had a cruel lot of money about him—where is all that money gone to?" And that, but for the narrator's intelligence and tenacity, is where the matter might have rested. Instead, he manages to solve the murder, which his inquiries reveal has been committed, at the same time as he lays the ghost.

As the story ends, Mrs. Riddell, having persuaded us (brilliantly, I must say) that there has been a murder, rather coyly invites the reader to choose between skepticism and belief. Her narrator says:

> . . . my brother took Nut Bush Farm off my hands. He says the place never was haunted—that I never saw Mr. Hascot except in my own imagination—that the whole thing originated in a poor state of health and a too credulous disposition!

I leave the reader to judge between us. That bit of fol de rol almost spoils a beautifully written story by an author whose feeling for rural landscapes and keen appreciation of even her most minor characters ought to make her much better known than she is.

AN OCCURRENCE AT OWL CREEK BRIDGE   Short Story

Ambrose Bierce
U.S.A.
1891, in *Tales of Soldiers and Civilians,* San Francisco, E.L.G. Steele; reprinted 1964 in E.F. Bleiler's (ed.) *Ghost and Horror Stories of Ambrose Bierce,* New York, Dover.

"An Occurrence . . ." is one of literature's most successful trick ending stories, and one of the most moving. Part of what makes it so tricky is that its story line seems utterly simple even as the simplicity itself is a form of duplicity.

The time of the story is during the American Civil War. A Southern planter, an Alabaman named Farquart, is trapped into performing a guerrilla action against the Owl Creek railroad bridge, occupied by Union troops. He is caught and condemned to hang.

Bierce, in the best tradition of realism, is very precise in his description of the preparations that are made for the hanging. Everything goes as planned. The trap is sprung, Farquart's body drops. It is here that Bierce's subtle trickery begins. It is enough to say that when the story comes to its conclusion, a shocked reader will either curse Bierce for playing unfair, or praise him for the sleight of hand with which he accomplishes the trick—or, possibly, both.

In any case, what we have is a tale that is a triumph of technique. Bierce tells his piercingly horrifying story in the easy conversational tone of a skilled but unprofessional tale teller who has a keen eye for physical details: the precise way the homely gallows is made; the brightness of the day on which the hanging takes place; the movement of water and trees lining the banks of Owl Creek, which seem to float before the reader's eyes. And then we have the careful setting of what follows within the confines of the natural world so that not until the penultimate moment do we have the slightest hint that what we have seen happening may not have happened at all. By then, it is too late. We have been persuaded, shocked—and stunningly tricked.

THE OFFSPRING   Film

1987 (C) U.S.A. 101 min.
Production Company: Darin Scott/William Burr Productions; ***Director:*** Jeff Burr; ***Producer:*** Jeff Burr; ***Screenplay:*** Courtney Joyner, Darin Scott, Jeff Burr; ***Photography:*** Craig Greene; ***Editor:*** W.O. Garrett; ***Special Makeup Effects:*** Rob Burman; ***Music:*** Jim Manzie.
Cast: Susan Tyrrell (Beth Chandler), Katherine White (Martine Beswicke), Vincent Price (Julian White), Clu (Stanley Burnside), Terry Kiser (Jesse Hardwicke), Harry Caesar (Felder Evans), Ron Brooks (Steve Arden), Cameron Mitchell (Gallen), Rosalind Cash (snake woman).

The Offspring is an anthology film containing four stories that are told to a young reporter named Beth Chandler. Having witnessed the execution of Martine Beswicke, a mass murderer, Chandler goes to Martine's hometown to get more details about her life. There, she interviews Julian White, the town's librarian, who tells these stories to make the point that there is some wicked force at work in Oldfield that produces evil acts like Martine's.

The four tales, each of them quite striking, are not of equal interest. The first gives us Stanley Burnside, a middle-aged and very unprepossessing bachelor, who lives with his unmarried, whining sister, Irene. One night, he takes Grace, one of his coworkers, out to dinner. Later, when she tries to fend off his advances, Stanley kills her. A day or two later, he creeps into the funeral home where her body is lying in state and there he consummates his passion with her corpse. Nine months later, he kills Irene and feels free at last.

But then the inevitable happens. The fruit of his necrophilic passion appears, and Stanley discovers, in as grungy a scene as has ever been filmed, just how ambiguous a father-son relationship can become.

The second story gives us Jesse Hardwicke, a tacky, small-time hood on the run whose life is saved by a black swamp dweller named Felder Evans. Evans possesses the secret of

Harry Caesar (left) and Terry Kiser in **The Offspring.** © ITS

eternal life and Hardwicke tries to steal it from him. Evans' revenge is as grisly as it is surprising.

In the third tale, Steve Arden, a carnival performer who eats glass and iron, is pursued to an explosive death by the jealous Snake Woman who punishes him for falling in love with a pretty blonde named Amaryllis.

Finally, in the fourth tale, we follow the misfortunes of Gallen, a renegade Union soldier, as he comes upon a sort of commune of children orphaned by the war. To his great cost, he learns that the children have formed a pitiless and unforgiving society in which acts of the most bizarre cruelty are commonplace. But whatever it is that the children do, it is no more than they have learned from the adult world. The only difference is that they have learned to better their instruction.

The Offspring is very much a young filmmaker's film, which is to say that it is imaginative, cruel and derivative, and it has an aggressively dark vision, darker even than the films from which it has borrowed most heavily: *It's Alive, Freaks* and *Children of the Corn.* And yet, despite its overall griminess, the film has sudden leaps of such artistic brilliance and originality that it demands to be taken seriously.

OH, WHISTLE, AND I'LL COME TO YOU, MY LAD   Short Story

M.R. James
Great Britain
1904, in *Ghost Stories of an Antiquary,* London, Edward Arnold; reprinted 1971 in *Ghost Stories of an Antiquary,* New York, Dover.

While vacationing in Burnstow in the east of England, Parkins, a gentlemanly professor of ontographay [stet], an avid golfer and a man who passionately does not believe in ghosts, unearths an ancient whistle on which a strange Latin inscription is carved. Like any child (or curious man or woman), he cannot resist blowing into it. What happens in response to that impulse constitutes the rest of this slow-paced, intelligent and intriguing tale. When the thing his whistle has summoned confronts him in his room at the inn on a moonlit night, his life or his sanity are threatened. What Parker remembers about it, "is a horrible, an intensely horrible, face of crumpled linen.

James wanted his readers to say to themselves, "If I'm not

very careful, something of this kind may happen to me." In "Oh, Whistle, and I'll Come to You, My Lad" we see just how he turns the absolutely familiar (in this case, crumpled linen) into the unspeakably terrifying. The soothing tone of scholarly discourse, which is second nature to James's characters, serves, too, as a neat counterpoint to the horror the quiet voice is describing.

OKE OF OKEHURST   Short Story
Vernon Lee (Pseudonym of Violet Paget)
Great Britain
1886, as *A Phantom Lover: A Fantastic Story*, Edinburgh, Blackwood; reprinted 1971 in E.F. Bleiler's *Five Victorian Ghost Novels*, New York, Dover.

In this wrenching tale of an erotic passion that goes well beyond madness, Vernon Lee, one of the great stylists of the horror genre, comes very close to matching Henry James's subtlety and diffidence in his "The Turn of the Screw."

The story is told by a first-person narrator who is asked by Oke of Okehurst, a Kentish country gentleman, to come up to his estate to do his and his wife's portraits. Oke of Okehurst is "a very tall, very well-made, very good-looking young man, with a beautiful fair complexion, beautiful fair moustache, and beautifully fitting riding clothes." Alice Okehurst, his wife and cousin, is altogether much more difficult to describe and after several pages during which a description is attempted, the narrator gives it up and we are left with the sense of a woman who is tall, very slender, very distracted, perhaps unfocused, frequently inert, occasionally dynamic and invariably not like any woman anyone has ever known before. One thing more is certain: Alice Okehurst has only the most negligible feelings for her husband, a fact of which he is only too well aware.

Slowly—and Vernon Lee's story moves with the perilous slowness of the earth before an avalanche—the dynamic of the gathering terror is laid out for us. Two hundred years before the time in which the tale is set, there was another Alice Oke, the wife of Nicholas, another Oke of Okehurst. The earlier Alice had a poet lover named Christopher Lovelock, who one summer afternoon met two men as he was riding across Cotes Common. " 'I am glad to have met you, Mr. Lovelock,' said Nicholas, 'because I have some important news for you'; and so saying, he brought his horse close to the one that Lovelock was riding, and suddenly turning round, fired off a pistol at his head.' " The shot killed the poet's horse instead of the poet who, on the ground, engaged his assailant in swordplay and would have killed him except that the second rider "rode up from behind and shot Lovelock through the back." As the poet lay dying, he recognized his assailant and cried out, "Alice, Alice! it is you who have murdered me!" It is that 17th-century story or, more precisely, the idea of it, or the ghost of, Christopher Lovelock that haunts the present Alice Okehurst and that produces the 19th-century disaster.

The second Alice Okehurst is obsessed with the power of Christopher Lovelock's love and uses it both to provide her own life with a center and to torment her innocent husband. She believes herself to be the target of Lovelock's imperishable love, which she describes as one that "can survive the

death, not merely of the beloved, but of the lover. It is unextinguishable, and goes on in the spiritual world until it meet a reincarnation of the beloved; and when this happens, it jets out and draws to it all that may remain of that lover's soul, and takes shape and surrounds the beloved once more."

When, finally, Oke of Okehurst goes mad because his simple mind and character can not deal with so much loftiness, and he shoots at the destroyer of his domestic happiness, we are not entirely surprised that his pistol misses "the damned rascal" at which he thought it was pointed. The end of the story is as fitting as it is appalling.

There is a touch of brutality in offering a reader a plot summary of a story quite as delicately woven as this one is. Vernon Lee's braiding of close personal observation with scrupulous descriptions both of place and costume create an authoritative background for the foreground design of her tapestry. But what, finally, we have is an extraordinary story of erotic vindictiveness in which neither member of the married pair is innocent of their mutual destruction.

THE OLD NURSE'S STORY   Short Story
Elizabeth Gaskell
Great Britain
1852, in *Household Words Magazine*; reprinted 1984 in J.A. Cuddon's *The Penguin Book of Ghost Stories*, London, Penguin.

This harrowing tale of family skeletons that refuse to stay in the genteel closets to which Victorian morality consigned them is a triumph of content over tone.

The narrator, the old nurse of the title, tells the story of a family scandal whose ghastly consequences were played out many years ago when she, then a nursemaid of 18, brought her orphaned charge, the five- or six-year-old Rosamond, to live in Furnivall Manor. At that time the manor was inhabited by Grace Furnivall, a woman in her eighties, Mrs. Stark, her servant-companion, and three other servants.

We learn that Grace Furnivall was the younger of the two daughters of Lord Furnivall, the lord of the manor. Her older sister was named Maude. Lord Furnivall was a tempestuous and prideful man who had a wild passion for organ music and a possessiveness about his daughters that regularly drove would-be suitors away. The nurse says, "No one was good enough to wed them, although they had choice enough; for they were great beauties in their day." However, when their father's passion for music compelled him to import a foreign musician to play the great organ for him, the two young women, fiercely competitive with each other, set their caps for him.

Maude won that particular prize and she and the Belgian organist were secretly married. The following year, Maude, just as secretly, had the organist's baby. But he, wearied by the contention of the two women, decamped for the continent, leaving both of the sisters behind.

Then Maude introduced her little daughter into Furnivall Manor on the pretext that she was a peasant's child to which she had taken a fancy. Some time later, to get back at her sister Grace for some slight, she revealed her secret marriage to her. Grace, in a frenzy of her own, then reported it to their father who, in perfect character, drove mother and child, with great violence, out into a howling snowstorm.

The denouement to all of this is as ghostly, and as ghastly, as one could wish. But it is all curiously softened and made poignant by the way that Mrs. Gaskell employs music and the steadily falling snow to create—in 1850—effects that a 20th-century surrealist would envy.

"The Old Nurse's Story," one of the most harrowing in the horror literature genre, achieves its effects from the cunning decision Mrs. Gaskell made to let the story issue from the lips of an uneducated servant. With a servant's idea of genteel speech, the old nurse steeps her narrative in a cloying sweetness that, if anything, imparts a malevolent gleam to her tale of family cruelty and lust.

THE OMEN   Film
1976 (C) U.S.A. 111 min.
Production Company: 20the Century-Fox; *Director:* Richard Donner; *Producer:* Harvey Bernhard; *Screenplay:* David Seltzer; *Photography:* Gilbert Taylor; *Editor:* Stuart Baird; *Special Effects:* John Richardson; Dogs Trained by Ben Woodgate, Joan Woodgate; *Music:* Jerry Goldsmith.
Cast: Gregory Peck (Robert Thorn), Lee Remick (Katharine Thorn), David Warner (Jennings), Billie Whitelaw (Mrs. Baylock), Patrick Troughton (Father Brennan), Martin Benson (Father Spiletto), Harvey Stephens (Damien).

This curiously cold film about the birth and early childhood of the Antichrist is likely to stay in one's memory as an ambitious, literate and, at infrequent moments, quite scary work.

The story begins in Rome where diplomat Robert Thorne's wife has just given birth to a child who dies after taking a single breath. Thorne, counselled by a priest, and without telling Kathy, permits a second infant to be substituted in the dead child's place.

Five years later, a long series of sinister events begins. On Damien's fifth birthday, Holly, the boy's nurse, commits suicide spectacularly. Her death permits the intrusion into the Thorne family of Mrs. Baylock, a very presentable nanny who is an agent of Satan. Then Father Brennan, a priest who keeps trying to warn Robert Thorne about Damien's real identity, is skewered to death by a falling steeple spire. Then (and this is one of the most frightening sequences in the film) we see the demonic child pedaling his tricycle along a lengthy balcony from which he manages to catapult his pregnant mother. When she clings to the balcony rails, he pries her fingers loose to make her fall.

Though she survives the fall, she loses her baby. By then, Robert Thorne, aided by a tenacious photographer named Jennings, is fully engaged in investigating the parentage of the child he fobbed off on Kathy as their own. In the course of his search that takes him to Rome, then to Israel and then back to London, he becomes fully persuaded that Damien is indeed the son of Satan by an abominable mother. When Jennings dies an atrocious death, Thorne knows what he must do.

This well-made, handsomely designed film has a fine, intriguing plot that ought to rivet us in our seats. But, perhaps because Richard Donner, its director, is intimidated by the Miltonic grandeur of his theme, the film fails to excite much sympathy for its characters. Indeed, paradoxically enough, the scenes that move us are those in which animals are seen reacting to Damien. The black dog that guards him, the giraffes that lope away when he draws near, the baboons that attack him and his mother in their car, seem to have real feelings while everyone else is merely reading a frequently brilliant script.

THE OPEN DOOR   Short Story
Margaret Oliphant
Great Britain
January 1882 in *Blackwood's Magazine;* reprinted 1975 in *Classic Ghost Stories by Charles Dickens and Others,* New York, Dover.

The first-person narrator of "The Open Door" is a British civil servant who has retired from India to a house in the Pentland Hills near Edinburgh. He and his wife have two daughters and a schoolboy son, the only son left of many. They live in a house with spacious grounds near the village of Brentwood. "In the park which surrounded the house were the ruins of the former mansion of Brentwood," and in those ruins, at the end of a low gable, there stood a common doorway.

And it is the doorway, in the first winter of the family's residence there, that becomes the frightful locus of the tale.

The narrator, on a trip to London, is recalled to his home by urgent telegrams advising him that his son, Roland, is suddenly and mysteriously ill. His symptoms are a fear so great that he is in danger of brain fever. Indeed, he may be in mortal danger.

What has frightened the boy is a pathetic voice that he has heard in the vicinity of the ruined doorway. What he has heard is "a low moaning, wailing voice, full of suffering and pain. The contrast between it and the hoot of the owl was indescribable; the one with a wholesome wildness and naturalness that hurt nobody—the other, a sound that made one's blood curdle." And always it pleaded, "Oh, mother let me in! oh mother, mother let me in! oh let me in!"

It is not long before the narrator is convinced that his son is telling him the truth. Then, to deserve his son's confidence in his father's ability to set the world right, the father undertakes to lay the ghost, but that proves to be a difficult process. The local rustics refuse to help. The narrator's butler, a former soldier, is rendered nearly mad; the physician, though he acknowledges that he hears the voice, takes refuge in scientific skepticism and has no idea how to proceed. Finally, the local clergyman, who is old enough not to be afraid of death, takes a hand. Because he has no doubts about the reality of the ghost and because he has faith in a compassionate God, he is able to say the direct, kind words that send the tormented spirit to search for its rest in the appropriate place: "I forbid ye!" cries the clergyman:

> "Cry out no more to men. Go home ye wandering spirit. Go home! Do you hear me, that christened ye, that have struggled with ye, that have wrestled for ye with the Lord? . . . if you will lie and sob and greet, let it be at Heaven's gate, and no at your mother's ruined door."

It is an exorcism scene so deeply moving that one forgets, as the story ends, that a tale of a ghost is meant to produce shivers up and down one's spine. But the story's claim to greatness in the horror genre is well established by then. Its endearing ending mars nothing at all.

Harvey Stephens as **Damien.** © 20th Century-Fox

THE OPEN WINDOW   Short Story
Saki (Pseudonym of H.H. Munro)
Great Britain
1914, in *Beasts and Super-Beasts,* London, John Lane.

Saki's stories have been compared with O. Henry's, but surprise endings and a pervasive human sympathy are really all the two have in common. Saki's prose is more sophisticated, more mannered and aloof.

Vera, the 15-year-old protagonist of "The Open Window," is one of Saki's brightest inventions. In less than two and a half pages she manages to petrify Framton Nuttel, a young man with delicate nerves who has come to pay a courtesy call on the Sappleton's, a country family with whom his sister is casually acquainted.

As Nuttel sits one late October afternoon in the living room of the Sappleton home, looking out through a French window at the nearby moors and waiting for Vera's aunt, Mrs. Sappleton, to appear, the loquacious Vera recounts, in the most circumstantial detail, the events of a year ago when Mrs. Sappleton's, "husband, and her two young brothers went off for their day's shooting. They never came back. In crossing the moor to their favourite snipe-shooting ground they were all three engulfed in a treacherous piece of bog." From there on, her story becomes grislier and to young Framton "all purely horrible." It is that for a reader, too, until the end—when Saki sets off an explosion of laughter for which nothing has prepared us except long acquaintance with the rich possibilities of his wit.

THE OTHER   Novel
Thomas Tryon
U.S.A.
1971, New York, Knopf; reprinted 1978, New York, Fawcett.

Astonishingly enough, *The Other* is Thomas Tryon's first novel. Astonishing, because the book is, along with Algernon Blackwood's "The Listener," Robert Bloch's *Psycho* and Stephen King's *The Shining* one of the most compelling terror fictions written in this century. It is as dense and as many-faceted as a diamond. Like a diamond, it is lucid, luminous and rare, and it gives lovers of terror fiction several fine opportunities to be scared to death.

The Other tells the moving story of the love between a couple of 11-year-old twin brothers, Niles and Holland Perry, who are children in a classically doomed family living in the countryside near a small Connecticut river town in 1935. The death of one of the brothers is followed by a series of disasters. One by one, the members of their extensive, warm and apparently happy family are killed or driven mad. For a long time, no one can guess at the explanation for so many appalling events. When the boys' grandmother, Ada, finally guesses, the book moves to its nearly unbearable climax.

Tryon makes the absolute most of his central theme: Family life can generate disaster. The idea is as old as *Oedipus Rex,* but in Tryon's hands it is subtly and imaginatively restated and proved. Every family situation is accorded its due and every disaster is richly understood. Best of all is Tryon's treatment of the relationship between the brothers, one of them living and the other dead. Tryon's ear for their speech and the way that it expresses the nuances of their macabre sibling rivalry is superb.

OUT OF SORTS   Short Story
Bernard Taylor
Great Britain
1983, in Charles L. Grant's (ed.) *The Dodd, Mead Gallery of Horror,* New York, Dodd, Mead.

It is a commonplace about the image of the werewolf that in it one catches attractive glimpses of the feral nature of our sexuality. In "Out of Sorts" that idea is slyly and effectively linked to the woes of a not particularly happy marriage.

Sylvia Gunn has been married for 25 years to Paul Gunn who:

> As much as [he] would like to see the back of her he'd never divorce her—or even leave her. He knew which side his bread was buttered, all right . . . But for all that . . . she could have put up with it—had it not been for his affairs. One after the other they had punctuated the years of their married life. And for that she was resentful . . .

Paul is a good-looking man who has:

> large, tanned hands [that] looked very dark against the white of the paper. It was the hair on them. Thick and black, it made his hands look larger than they were. It was probably a turn-on to some women, she thought.

On this third Friday of the month, Sylvia has angered Paul by scheduling a Women's Circle meeting at their home, though Sylvia points out that the meeting will in no way interfere with his life.

More than that, Sylvia knows that one of the women who is coming is, in fact, Paul's new flame. She is Norma Russell with whose "$35 \times 25 \times 36$ figure, her high cheek bones and sleek blonde hair" Sylvia knows she can not compete.

We have then, a classic love triangle: a handsome, no longer loving husband; a long-suffering wife; and the beautiful other woman. Only this time the long-suffering wife gets her own back because:

> She was a lot smarter than they dreamed. Certainly a damn sight smarter than that vacuous, simpering Norma with her Gucci shoes, Charlie perfume, and Dior sun-glasses. Norma Russell, with her sophisticated approach and smug, know-it-all manner didn't know it all by any means.

Not yet. She would in time. And when she does, the story comes to its roaring, horrifying climax while Sylvia, who has endured all, smiles a very knowing smile.

What Taylor does especially well is to keep his story firmly set among the banalities of modern marital discomfort. Not until the final moment is there any hint of the supernatural. When it does suddenly appear, the transition is so smoothly, and so horrifyingly, managed that we find ourselves saying, "Yes. But of course. Of course."

OVER THE RIVER   Short Story
P. Schuyler Miller
U.S.A.
April 1941, in *Unknown;* reprinted 1968 in Peter Haining's (ed.) *Midnight People,* New York, Popular Library.

Sometimes, in the welter of the commonplace that a professional reader of scary literature must turn over, one comes upon an unexpected gleam of pure genius, as in P. Schuyler Miller's "Over the River." Miller has chosen to let his imagination wonder about a vampire's first moments of consciousness, as he comes out of the grave and discovers clumsily and slowly who he is. The result is a sort of dark parody of the coming to consciousness of Adam and an uncannily persuasive description of what it feels like to wake to consciousness as a newly ''born'' vampire.

As in *Varney the Vampire*, moonlight is the resuscitating agent here. Joe Labatie, the just-risen corpse:

> drank in the moonlight through every pore, and it burned gloriously in him and flowed down through every vein and bone of his body, driving out the dark cold in his flesh

Carefully, carefully, the creature tests his reality. At first he is able to stay—not quench—his thirst, by killing small forest creatures. In a scar- and feather-filled scene, he battles an owl, ''tearing at its flesh with his teeth and letting the hot burning blood gush into his parched throat . . .'' After the owl, there is a porcupine, the doe, and then—the young woman who takes off the crucifix he himself gave her in his other life, to become the final victim of his instructive night. ''When it was over the hunger was gone out of his bones. His muscles were no longer cramped and leaden . . .''

It is a moment for deeply gratified rest, as the emptied corpse of the loving girl on the floor makes clear, but Labatie has one thing more to learn about being a vampire than he already knows. The girl's brother and two friends find him, fill him with buckshot, and, as he lies weakened in the grip of a running stream (clear running water is anathema to vampires), one of them drives a stake through his heart. A vampire's life, like that of the rest of mankind, can be nasty, brutish and short.

P

THE PEDDLAR AND THE LADY

Short Story

S.Y. Agnon
Israel
1970, in *Twenty-One Stories* (ed. Nahum Glatzer), New York, Schocken.

Here we have a cannibal-vampire tale in the tradition of lamia or succubus stories. As always with Agnon, there is a disturbing lucidity to this story of the Jewish peddlar who takes refuge in the home of a woman. At first she is hostile to him but, as the peddlar's needs becomes greater, she gravitates to him until they become, first lovers and afterwards something more intimate. And after that, strangers again; and after that . . . but after that there is the catastrophe that is the rest of the story.

With Agnon, one is never far away from allegory, and yet in this tale it is hard to specify just what that allegory is. Are we being instructed in the nature of love? And is love a devouring emotion? And are women the devourers? The story permits us to ask all of these questions but does not authorize us to answer any one of them. Meanwhile, the reader, engaged by the straining of Agnon's archaic diction against the author's modernist sensibility, gets unsettling inklings that he has already learned more about fear than he wants to know.

PEEPING TOM

Film

1959   (C)   Great Britain   109 min.
Production Company: Michael Powell Theatre/Anglo-Amalgamated; **Director:** Michael Powell; **Producer:** Michael Powell, Albert Fennell; **Screenplay:** Leo Marks; **Photography:** Otto Heller; **Editor:** Noreen Ackland; **Music:** Brian Easdale.
Cast: Carl Boehm (Mark), Anna Massey (Helen), Maxine Audley (Mrs. Stephens), Moire Shearer (Vivian), Esmond Knight (Arthur Baden).

The *London Financial Times* said of *Peeping Tom* that "the film is frankly beastly," which suggests that its reviewer did not see much beyond the very tip of his or her nose. Now, nearly 30 years after it was made, it is easier to see that the film is a grimly effective and compassionate study of a mass murderer. One comes away from it admiring Michael Powell's narrowly focused direction and his apt eye for the urban grungy. What mostly carries the film, however, is Carl Boehm's interpretation of the role of Mark, the film's protagonist. Boehm's Mark has Peter Lorre's soft-spoken, bewildered intensity, a comparison that is all the more apt because Boehm has the faintest of faint German accents.

Mark, then, is a young London photographer who earns his living shooting pornographic films. His avocation is photographing the look of terror in the faces of young women as they realize that he is about to kill them. His erotic pleasure is to watch those films in his room in the large old house he owns (he rents out the other rooms to supplement his income).

Mark, we learn, is the son of a research geologist who was interested in the psycho-physiology of fear and who, for research purposes, made a practice of terrifying Mark from his infancy onward. His father would wake the sleeping child by flashing bright lights in his face or tossing lizards onto his pillow. And always, his father photographed the effects of his experiments on his child. Mark's father is now dead, but the link between terror and love that he imposed on Mark's psyche persists, as the growing number of Mark's victims (and the canisters of film depicting their dying moments) attests.

Compassion is joined to fear in the film when Mark is invited to the 21st birthday party of a young woman who lives in a couple of his downstairs rooms with her mother. The 21-year-old, Helen, a spunky, gentle and curious person, is attracted to Mark and does her affectionate best to get past his formal reserve. Finally she succeeds only too well. He falls in love with her with results that are both poignant and tragic.

Peeping Tom is very much a film about ways of seeing,

about the interplay between the apparent and the real, between the light and the dark. It captures, too, in a way not blatantly put before us, the role of the camera as a means of revealing, interpreting and shaping our experience, which, as the 20th century comes to its close, relies more and more on our relationship to images. This is what makes a character like Mark, who is fascinated by images of feeling though he has been rendered incapable of experiencing it, a recognizable contemporary type.

THE PHANTOM COACH OR THE NORTH MAIL
Short Story

Amelia B. Edwards
Great Britain
1864, in *All the Year Around*; reprinted 1974 in Montague Summers' (ed.) *The Supernatural Omnibus* (1st Pub. 1931), New York, Causeway.

"The Phantom Coach" is another of those stories whose plot seems at first so familiar that we imagine it derives from a folktale.

James Murray, a hunter who has been recently married, is overtaken by a snowstorm on "a bleak wide moor in the far north of England." Afraid that he will lose his way and perish in the rapidly accumulating drifts, he is grateful when he meets Jacob, a surly old man with a lantern who leads him to a house on the moors inhabited by a scientific recluse who extends his simple hospitality to the hunter.

Murray's host turns out to be profoundly cultivated, a man who, if we are to believe him, was driven from society for asserting truths about science that were too advanced for his time. He has chosen to live in seclusion here on the moor, but Murray finds that he is:

> Familiar with all systems of all philosophies, subtle in analysis, bold in generalisation . . . [able to move] from practical science to mental philosophy; from electricity in the wire to electricity in the nerve; from Watts to Mesmer, from Mesmer to Reichenbach, from Reichenbach to Swedenborg, Spinoza, Condillac, Descartes, Berkeley, Aristotle, Plato, and the Magi and mystics of the East . . .

This polymath, in addition to giving Murray a good supper of ham and a strong drink of usquebaugh (whiskey) sends him on his way to catch the night mail that passes not far from his house. Murray, accompanied part of the distance by Jacob, goes to where he is directed. There he flags down the coach:

> The coachman pulled up; the guard, muffled to the eyes in capes and comforters, and apparently sound asleep in the rumble, neither answered my hail nor made the slightest effort to dismount; the outside passenger did not even turn his head.

Murray gets into the coach and finds that the inside passengers are as incommunicative as everyone else has been. When he examines the coach closely, he finds it in the last stages of dilapidation. Distressed, Murray addresses one of the passengers who:

> moved his head slowly, and looked me in the face . . . His eyes glowed with a fiery unnatural lustre. His face was livid as the face of a corpse. His bloodless lips were drawn back as if in the agony of death . . .

The other passengers turn out to be in not much better condition. As the full horror of his situation is about to be borne in upon him, there "came a mighty crash—a sense of crushing pain—and then, darkness."

What makes "The Phantom Coach" a superior fiction is the way that Amelia B. Edwards maintains the illusion that James Murray moves continually from "actual" scene to scene even as she lets drift into the reader's mind the possibility that none of the events described has ever taken place outside of a dream. As the story ends, and our wonder begins, we are forced to remember the caution we were given in the opening paragraph:

> I want nothing explained away. I desire no arguments. My mind on this subject is quite made up, and having the testimony of my own senses to rely upon, I prefer to abide by it.

The narrator, then, knew from the start that we might not believe him and now we have the enigma of his story before us. But beyond the enigma, the story leaves us with the pleasant memory of that reclusive and mysterious Renaissance man in his hut on the snowclad moors.

THE PHANTOM OF THE OPERA
Film

1925 (B&W) (Silent) U.S.A. 84 min.
Production Company: Universal-Jewel; **Director:** Rupert Julian; **Producer:** Carl Laemmle; **Screenplay:** Elliot J. Clawson, Raymond Schrock; **Photography:** Milton Bridebecker, Virgil Miller.
Cast: Lon Chaney (Erik, the Phantom), Mary Philbin (Christine Daae), Norman Kerry (Raoul de Chagny), Arthur Edmund Carewe (Ledoux), Snitz Edwards (Florine Papillon), Gibson Gowland (Simon).

Christine, a young opera singer at the Paris Opera House, finds herself the protege of a strange figure who haunts the building. The figure, known as the Phantom, is described by a stagehand who has seen him:

> "His eyes are ghastly beads in which there is no light . . . little holes in a grinning skull. His skin is like leprous parchment, yellow skin strung tight over protruding bones. . . . his nose . . . there is no nose."

The Phantom, by the simple expedient of murder, contrives Christine's big chance for her. But Raoul, her suitor, tells her, "At last you have realized your ambition. Now we shall be married." Christine, however, would rather be true to her art and says, "I can never leave the opera, Raoul. You must forget about our love."

It is after that scene that Christine hears a voice like that of an angel's, telling her, "Tonight I placed the world at your feet . . . all Paris will worship you but you must think only of your career and of your master."

That master is the Phantom. Later, wearing a mask, Erik (the Phantom) comes for Christine. In an exquisite sequence of scenes, he takes her to his private apartments five levels beneath the opera house. First he sets her on a white horse which he leads down through a series of grandly Gothic stone arcades and staircases until they come to a dark body of water—"a black lake hidden from man and the sun and leading to the Phantom's rendezvous." At the lake, he sets

Lon Chaney and Mary Philbin in **Phantom of the Opera.**

Christine into a boat that, like Acheron, he sculls to his destination.

Arrived in his lair he tells her, ''Look not upon the mask. Think rather of my devotion that has brought you the gift of song . . . I have brought you here five cellars underground because I love you.''

From here on the film proceeds, like the development of an especially fine ballet, on two levels: The first is the sometimes breathtaking adventure story that unfolds before us as Raoul, with some help, effects Christine's rescue; and the second, often, in its own way, more interesting, develops the allegory of art as a demonic energy born of pain. This remarkably allusive film makes us think about the myth of Pluto and the kidnapping of Proserpine even as we remember Wallace Stevens' great line, ''Death is the mother of beauty.''

There is more to the film than thematic richness. For one thing, there is Rupert Julian's direction and the Bridebecker-Miller photography. Julian makes subtle use of his stone interiors, and of the extravagances of opera house decor. The photographers treat black and white as if they had a palate of the richest colors to choose from, creating moods in which silence and imminent rage are implicit in the same image. In addition to the black and white, the film has a spectacular two-minute sequence in color that achieves moments of horror as intense as any to be found in Francis Bacon's more frightening paintings.

Finally, there is Lon Chaney's performance. Perhaps never in the history of film has a dangerous madman's behavior been so delicately attached to the idea of beauty. Erik, with

his skull-like real face and his devotion to Christine's career, is a compelling villain—impossible to hate and impossible not to brood about.

There have been indifferent remakes of *The Phantom of the Opera*, in 1943 and in 1962. A British musical based on the story appeared in 1986 and was a smash hit in New York in 1988.

PIAZZA PIECE   Poem
John Crowe Ransom
U.S.A.
March 1925, in *The Fugitive;* reprinted 1979 in Leonard Wolf's (ed.) *Wolf's Complete Book of Terror,* New York, Clarkson N. Potter.

Here, in the narrow confines of a sonnet, is a modern version of the ''death-and-the-maiden'' theme that is discussed in the entry on Le Fanu's ''Schalken, the Painter.''

In ''Piazza Piece'' we are meant to assume that we are watching a playlet taking place on a piazza (a balcony or porch). The first speaker is a sinister old man ''in a dustcoat trying/ To make [a young woman] hear . . .'' What he wants her to hear is that he is there and that he ''must have [his] lovely lady soon.''

The second voice is that of the young woman who is ''young in beauty waiting /Until [her] true love comes . . .'' By the time we reach the 14th line of the poem and know who the old man is and what sort of courtship he is conducting, the full horror of her situation is suddenly revealed as if by the opening of a camera lens and we want to cry with her, ''Back from my trellis, Sir, before I scream!''

THE PICTURE OF DORIAN GRAY   Novel
Oscar Wilde
Great Britain
1891, London, Ward, Lock; reprinted 1982 in H. Montgomery Hyde's (ed.) *The Annotated Oscar Wilde,* New York, Crown.

The horror of *The Picture of Dorian Gray* comes from the effectiveness of the novel's controlling image: a man whose fair outside covers an interior whose moral corruption is scrupulously set down in the portrait that first recorded his beauty.

By now, there can hardly be a reasonably educated person who does not know the bare outline of Wilde's story: Dorian Gray, an exceedingly handsome 20- or 21-year-old, has his portrait painted by the artist Basil Hallward in whose studio he meets Lord Henry Wotton, a witty and decadent sensualist whose philosophy Dorian finds dazzling. Wotton says:

''Every impulse that we strive to strangle broods in the mind, and poisons us . . . The only way to get rid of a temptation is to yield to it. Nothing can cure the soul but the senses, just as nothing can cure the senses but the soul. . . . You have a wonderfully beautiful face, Mr. Gray . . . You have. And Beauty is a form of Genius . . . It has its divine right of sovereignty. . . . You have only a few years in which to live really, perfectly, and fully. When your youth goes, your beauty will go with it, and then you will suddenly discover that there are no triumphs left for you . . . Don't squander the gold of your days . . . Live! Live the wonderful life that is in you! . . . Be always searching for new sensations. Be afraid

Oscar Wilde.

own face that he was looking at! The horror, whatever it was, had not yet entirely spoiled that marvellous beauty. There was still some gold in the thinning hair and some scarlet on the sensual mouth. The sodden eyes had kept something of the loveliness of their blue, the noble curves had not yet completely passed away from chiselled nostrils and from plastic throat.

Basil Hallward, aware that he is seeing a portrait of Dorian's soul, cries, ''Good God, Dorian, what a lesson! What an awful lesson!'' The reader, infected by the poison of Wilde's wit, may remember one of his own sayings against him, ''There is no such thing as a moral or an immoral book.

Ivan Le Lorraine Albright's famous portrait of the depraved Dorian. (Courtesy of the Art Institute of Chicago)

of nothing . . . A new Hedonism—that is what this century wants . . .''

Entranced as much by Wotton's voice as by his ideas, Dorian expresses a wish as he looks at the portrait of himself:

''I am jealous of everything whose beauty does not die. I am jealous of the portrait you have painted of me. Why should it keep what I must lose? Every moment that passes takes something from me, and gives something to it. Oh, if it were only the other way! If the picture could change, and I could be always what I am now!''

Someone, or something in the universe hears Dorian's wish and grants it. For the next 18 years, he lives a life of increasing depravity in which he destroys many innocent men and women. The cruelest of his crimes is the seduction and abandonment of the young actress Sybil Vane who commits suicide on his account. But no matter how awful Dorian's acts are, he continues to look like a beautiful 20-year-old, while the portrait, which he keeps in a locked room at the top of his house, increasingly shows every mark of sin and decay. When Basil Hallward is let in on the secret of the picture, he sees:

in the dim light the hideous face on the canvas grinning at him. There was something in its expression that filled him with disgust and loathing. Good heavens! It was Dorian Gray's

Books are well written or badly written. That is all.'' And, ''No artist desires to prove anything.''

But paradox is at the heart of Wilde's wit, and the paradox here is that his book paints the moral that an absolutely self-indulgent ego perpetually shapes its own hell. That truth stares us in the face when we realize that there are two tragic figures in *The Picture of Dorian Gray*. One of them is, of course, Dorian, who gets the poetic justice he deserves. The other, more subtly, more cruelly imagined, is Sir Edward Wotton, the brightest and emptiest person in the book. The horror of his life is that, though he is capable of being a catalyst of evil, nothing that was either memorable or meaningful has ever happened to him.

THE PICTURE OF DORIAN GRAY   Film
1945 (B&W) U.S.A. 110 min.

Production Company: MGM; *Director:* Albert Lewin; *Producer:* Pandro S. Berman; *Screenplay:* Albert Lewin; *Photography:* Henry Glendon; *Editor:* Ferris Webster; *Music:* Herbert Stothart.

Cast: George Sanders (Sir Henry Wotton), Hurd Hatfield (Dorian Gray), Donna Reed (Gladys Hallward), Angela Lansbury (Sybil Vane), Peter Lawford (David Stone), Richard Fraser (James Vane), Lowell Gilmore (Basil Hallward).

Hurd Hatfield is a quintessentially cold and beautiful Dorian, Angela Lansbury is poignant as his first victim, and George Sanders is impeccable as the satanically intellectual friend who stirs up Dorian's unacknowledged lust for eternal youth. And yet, there is a flaw at the heart of this quite stunning version of Oscar Wilde's ornately ironic story. Albert Lewin, in his determination to be faithful to Wilde's haunting moral vision, has attended too carefully to Wilde's prose and not sufficiently to his own responsibilities as a film director. Film's great contribution to our delight is through the eye. And in this film, the camera is given very little to do. It moves from face to face and waits while we listen to the witticisms, the suavely killing comments, the polished repartee. To make matters worse, the actors and their director are as impressed with Wilde's language as we are, with the result that the film suffers from a respectful inertia that turns an urgent human story into a allegory whose truth we accept with a yawn.

There is one glorious exception to the generalizations just made—the scene in which Fran Le Lorraine Albright's por-

Angela Lansbury as Sybil Kane and Hurd Hatfield as Dorian (center) in **The Picture of Dorian Gray.**

trait of the utterly corrupted Dorian Gray explodes, in color, onto the black and white screen. That moment, Oscar Wilde's prose, Hurd Hatfield's beauty and Angela Lansbury's poignant singing make *The Picture of Dorian Gray* a very great, if greatly flawed, film.

PIRANHA   Film
1978   (C)   USA   94 min.
Production Company: New World/Piranha Productions; *Director:* Joe Dante; *Executive Producer:* Roger Corman; *Producer:* Jon Davidson, Chako Van Leeuwen; *Screenplay:* John Sayles; *Photography:* Jamie Anderson; *Editor:* Mark Goldblatt, Joe Dante; *Special Effects:* John Berg; *Music:* Pino Donaggio.
Cast: Bradford Dillman (Paul Grogan), Heather Menzies (Maggie McKeown), Kevin McCarthy (Dr. Robert Hoak), Keenan Wynn (Jack), Barbara Steele (Dr. Mengers).

John Sayles explained in an interview how he came to write the screenplay for Piranha:

> "New World called my agent and asked, 'Who do you have who'll work cheap?' . . . As soon as I heard the title I knew the film would make money no matter who wrote it." (See Ed Naha's, *The Films of Roger Corman.)*

Despite that modest disclaimer, much of the effectiveness of this inexpensive creature feature derives first from Sayles' witty and horrifying screenplay and then from Joe Dante's imaginative and bloody-minded direction.

If *Jaws* is a diminished version of *Moby Dick,* then *Piranha* is *Jaws* writ even smaller. Here, instead of a single killer shark, we have thousands of tiny, swarming and deadly piranha that have been tampered with during the Vietnam war by a pair of scientists working for the military. When the fish are accidentally introduced into a river not far from a summer camp we have all the ingredients we need for roiling and turbulent mayhem. Though one guesses that both Sayles and Dante wanted their film to say harsh things about military research, what comes through most vividly is the panic of the humans when they are attacked and the blind, voracious hunger of the tiny, sharp-toothed fish.

THE PIT AND THE PENDULUM   Short Story
Edgar Allen Poe
U.S.A.
1842, in *The Gift;* reprinted 1986 in Stephen Peithman's (ed.) *The Annotated Edgar Allen Poe,* New York, Crown.

Despite the feverish prose in which this tale is written, "The Pit and the Pendulum" continues to be one of Poe's (and of all horror literature's) most powerful stories. It is a plot maker's tour de force at the same time as it conceals within itself hidden knowledge: about paranoia, about forbidden fantasies, about freedom and responsibility. But no reader is ever delayed by the story's possible meanings. The plot races along and one is dragged after it, willy nilly.

The tale's narrator, a prisoner of the Spanish Inquisition in Toledo, hears his sentence read and sees his judges fashioning:

> the syllables of my name; and I shuddered because no sound succeeded. I saw, too, for a few moments of delirious horror,

> the soft and nearly imperceptible waving of the sable draperies which enwrapped the walls of the apartment.

The point is the nightmarish softness of everything, a softness that is accompanied by something "like a rich musical note, the thought of what sweet rest there must be in the grave." As we read, we are caught up in the sensuality of apprehension as the narrator recalls what has happened to him and anticipates what is still to come.

He is in prison, in absolute darkness, in what appears to his touch to be a walled but really quite capacious cell, nearly 50 yards in circumference. At one point in his pitch-dark exploration he stumbles and falls and discovers that he has just failed to fall into a circular pit. When he drops a stone into it, it falls for a considerable time before it strikes water.

Later, after a drugged sleep, he finds himself bound "on a species of low framework of wood." And now he is able, though dimly, to see. Looking up he sees a painting of Time on the high ceiling, from which there descends, not a scythe, but a long pendulum "such as we see on antique clocks." Looking down, he sees rats swarming near his wooden platform. What he notices is that the pendulum as it swings is perceptibly descending and that "its nether extremity was formed of a crescent of glittering steel, about a foot in length from horn to horn . . . and the under edge evidently as keen as that of a razor . . . It was appended to a weighty rod of brass, and the whole hissed as it swung through the air." Later, he can actually smell the steel.

His tormentors' intent is by now clear. Sooner or later, after what will feel like an infinity of time, the steel crescent will reach his flesh. "Down—steadily down it crept . . . Down—certainly, relentlessly down . . . Down—still unceasingly—still inevitably down . . ."

Then, the superhuman patience and with the loathesome help of the rats, he frees himself from the platform. But if we expect relief, Poe disappoints us: "Free!—and in the grasp of the Inquisition . . ."

The Inquisition, as it turns out, has more fiendish tricks to play. The room in which the narrator has suffered, it now turns out, does not have the dimensions he thought it had. Indeed, its dimensions keep changing, as does the temperature of the room.

What happens in the final paragraphs of this tale must be left to its readers. It is enough to say that the tale leaves one invariably exhausted, utterly spent.

THE PIT AND THE PENDULUM   Film
1961   (C)   U.S.A.   85 min.
Production Company: American International; *Director:* Roger Corman; *Producer:* Roger Corman; *Executive Producer:* James H. Nicholson and Samuel Z. Arkoff; *Screenplay:* Richard Matheson; *Photography:* Floyd Crosby; *Editor:* Anthony Carras; *Special Effects:* Pat Dinga; *Music:* Les Baxter.
Cast: Vincent Price (Nicholas Medina), John Kerr (Francis Barnard), Barbara Steele (Elizabeth), Luana Anders (Catherine), Anthony Carbone (Dr. Charles Leon).

Nicholas Medina is a neurasthenic Italian nobleman who believes he has buried his wife, Elizabeth, while she was still alive. From time to time, he is tormented by sight or sound of the departed Elizabeth. Urged on by Elizabeth's physician, Dr. Leon, Medina opens her coffin, but she is not there.

A surreal moment in **The Pit and the Pendulum.** © Alta Vista

At a crucial moment, Medina discovers that he is the victim of a plot contrived by Dr. Leon and Elizabeth to drive him mad so that they can get their hands on his fortune. The quick-witted though mentally unstable Medina kills Leon and Elizabeth, and straps Francis, Elizabeth's innocent brother, to the table beside the pit and just under the killing pendulum. There is, finally, a last minute rescue.

Aside from a handsome set containing the pit and the pendulum, Poe's influence on this film, no matter what the screen credits say, is all but zero. There are no heated walls closing in; no rats scampering over the victim's bonds; and no cruel Inquisition contriving it all. Indeed, if it were not for Richard Matheson's truly high-style prose, this Roger Corman film would have little going for it.

THE PIXY   Short Story
Or, The Unbaptized Child. A Story for Christmas.
George W. M. Reynolds
Great Britain
1870, London, John Dickes; reprinted 1976 in *The Spectre Bridegroom and Other Horrors,* New York, Arno.

The full title of *The Pixy* is: *The Pixy; or, the Unbaptized Child. A Story for Christmas.* Published as a horror booklet in 1870, *The Pixy* is a satisfying ghost story in which the ghost is a creature of singular beauty, a naked, transparent child whose appearance at Christmas time is always preceded by ''a soft but sweet strain of music that appeared suddenly to fill the air . . . [like] the perpetuation of melodious sounds in the ears which one experiences after quitting a concert-room where the harmony has just ceased.''

This vision of a radiant child and the lovely music come annually to haunt the villain of the tale, an attorney named Arthur Lorimer who seduced and abandoned a passionate and somewhat unprincipled young woman named Margaret Pennant. Lorimer shows up beside her deathbed just in time to receive her dying curse—unless he keeps his promise to christen the illegitimate offspring of their amour. Lorimer, who throughout most of this tale is a man without conscience, marries Emily to whom he entrusts Margaret's baby. Emily believes Lorimer's feckless explanation of where the baby girl came from (this is a form of innocence that fictional Victorian wives seemed frequently capable of) and undertakes to raise her. But Lorimer not only fails to baptize the infant Isabella, he also contrives to defraud Mary Doyle, Margaret's loyal and decent sister, of the considerable fortune Margaret willed to her.

The infant Isabella dies, still unchristened. Meanwhile, Arthur Lorimer's wife, Emily, gives birth to a boy. Each Christmas, after the death of Isabella, Lorimer hears the music and is visited by the beautiful ghost. But he makes no change in his life. He remains obdurately wicked and ambitious. One Christmas, when his son is 20 months old, Lorimer, to his horror, watches as his child is enticed out of doors by the ghost. Lorimer faints. When he comes to his senses, he learns that his son is gone and, despite rewards offered and searches conducted, the boy appears to have vanished for good.

Twenty years later, Lorimer, despite the annual visit of the Pixy, is still a hardened and cruel man, though he is always described as being exceptionally good to his wife Emily. Because of his reputation for harshness, the reigning powers make Lorimer their agent to oppress the toiling poor. Named attorney general, Lorimer hires an *agent provocateur* to entangle some Devonshire farmers in an anti-government plot. At a critical moment, the farmers are arrested and one of them, Albert Langdon, is brought to trial. The prosecuting attorney is, of course, Arthur Lorimer.

And, of course, a practiced reader of Victorian penny-a-line fiction already knows that the young farmer on trial for his life is really Arthur Lorimer's long-lost son who was deposited by a dying gypsy woman on Mary and James Doyle's doorstep 20 years ago.

And, of course, the story has a happy ending for almost everyone, including, surprisingly enough, Arthur Lorimer, who, one would have thought, did not deserve it. Still, he did repent; and he did, then, do good so that he was no longer visited by the Pixy and never heard that sweet music again.

On the other hand, his hireling, Harpinger, comes to the sort of end Matthew Lewis, author of *The Monk,* would have admired. Harpinger was:

> Plunged into the depths of poverty—loathed and execrated by all who had ever known him. . . . recognized by [his enemies] he was hurled, shrieking in mortal agony, from a second-floor window. Down he fell; his body was transfixed on the spiked railings that fenced the area of the low lodging-house where this horrible tragedy occurred; and thus perished the Government Approver.

George Reynolds' prose style is almost as perfervid as Thomas Preskett Prest's in *Varney the Vampyre.* But Reynolds' tale has the additional distinction (a rare one for the horror genre) that it takes time out to notice the brutality of the English class system and the equally cruel overseas imperialism that helped to sustain it.

POLLOCK AND THE PORROH MAN Short Story
H. G. Wells
Great Britain
1897, in *The Plattner Story and Others*, London, Methuen; reprinted 1979 in Leonard Wolf's (ed.) *Wolf's Complete Book of Terror*, New York, Clarkson N. Potter.

Here is a tale in the "imperialist guilt" genre that was a staple of the late 19th- and early 20th-century British writing. Immediate other examples are Kipling's "The Mark of the Beast" and Lucas's "Luckundoo." Such stories turn on the vengeance wrought by primitive peoples on an unwitting or malevolent Briton who has violated native custom or religion.

Pollock, the central figure of this powerful tale, is a somewhat seedy Englishman who is a member of what appears to be an anthropological expedition in West Africa. There he has a liaison with a native woman who "belongs" to a local witch doctor, the Porroh man. When the witch doctor kills the woman, Pollock, defending himself, shoots the Porroh man but only wounds him.

From that point on, the story is a chronicle of the struggle between the rational and the irrational, with Pollock representing European reason and the Porroh man (and later his spirit) representing the dark, primordial powers before which, despite the apparent triumph of western civilization, we are essentially powerless.

What makes this story work is that H.G. Wells is a first-class plot maker and a master of the lean, spare style that includes only the most necessary details. Just the same, he is able to create the illusion that what seems a straightforward story of primitive vengeance against a white man's wrongs may indeed be an ambiguous study of the guilt-ridden Pollock's sleazy mind.

Meanwhile, the image of the Porroh man's head rolling on and on to achieve Pollock's doom is unforgettable.

POLTERGEIST II Film
1986 (C) U.S.A. 87 min.
Production Company: MGM; *Director:* Brian Gibson; **Producer:** Michael Grais; Mark Victor★reenplay: Michael Grais; Mark Victor; *Photography:* Andrew Laszlo; *Special Effects:* Richard Edlund; *Music:* Jerry Goldsmith.
Cast: Jobeth Williams, Craig T. Nelson, Heather O'Rourke, Oliver Robins, Julian Beck, Zelda Rubinstein, Will Sampson, Geraldine Fitzgerald.

"They're back," cries little Carol Anne, the chief target of the poltergeists who attacked her family home in *Poltergeist* (1982), the film that precedes this sequel. And indeed, a very wicked cluster of spirits who dwell just on the other side of the Great Divide between life and death have come to besiege the family again.

This time, Steve and Diane and their two children, Robbie and Carol Anne, whose home was utterly destroyed in *Poltergeist*, are living with Diane's widowed mother in a house

Julian Beck as the Reverend Kane in **Poltergeist II.** © MGM

near Monument Valley, Arizona. The evil spirits that attacked them in the earlier film are now joined by various restless local ghosts in their campaign of harassment. But first, Diane's kindly mother, who has psychic gifts and who tells us that Diane and Carol Anne have them too, dies, leaving the field clear for the evil spirits. With the aid of the gifted Richard Edlund's special effects, the spirits create considerable mayhem in the family's new home.

Michael Grais and Mark Gibson, who wrote the screenplay, have made a considerable effort to "complexify" the psychological substance of the film. The father of the family, Steve, is given a drinking problem to compound his sense of uncertainty about his manhood. Before he can save his family, he has to learn to confront his secret fears, particularly as they are played upon by a finely villainous, satanic figure, Mr. Caine, the reincarnation of a 19th-century cult leader who forced his followers to seal themselves inside a cave to await the end of the world.

The family is helped again by the diminutive psychic who guided them in *Poltergeist*. This time, she is aided by a Native American shaman named Ted Taylor, a fountain of simplistic wisdom, which the film's audiences, one suspects, eat up.

Poltergeist II borrows skilfully from earlier films. Mr. Caine's black garb and hymn singing are from *Night of the Hunter*; the magnificent scene in which we see the swift evolution of the gusano worm that infests Steve recalls the *Alien*. And the improbable moment in which a chain saw attacks the family cowering in their car is a gratuitous (but effective) salute to *The Texas Chain Saw Massacre*.

Julian Beck's spectral performance as the Reverand Caine touches *Poltergeist II* with historic significance. Except for his presence, special effects, not primordial fears, carry the day.

POWERS OF DARKNESS
Short Story

John Russell

U.S.A.

1929, in *Far Wandering Men*, New York, Norton; reprinted 1980 in Bill Pronzini's (ed.) *Tales of the Dead*, New York, Bonanza.

Every right-minded person likes to see the humiliation of a bully and in "Powers of Darkness" the wheels of justice, which often seem to be grinding the wrong grist in their mill, grind in a most satisfactory way. Evil gets its punishment and the good, the noble and the beautiful, after sufferings that are suitably horrible, are suitably rewarded.

The story has four characters: Nickerson, Dobel, a Papuan chief who is also a sorcerer, and the chief's beautiful daughter. Nickerson, gentle, decent and just, is the "Resident Magistrate" on Papua: "This meant that he personated the whole British Empire over a theoretical District of monstrous mountains and reeking jungles." More than that, he has a deep respect for Papua's native population and (surprising in a fiction written by a white man in the twenties) he forms non-condescending friendships with them.

Dobel is the villain of the piece, the "gross stranger with the sly and slitted red eyes" whose skepticism regarding the power of native sorcery prompts Nickerson to invite his sorcerer friend, the chief, to demonstrate his powers. Dobel, rudely, drunkenly scoffs at the impressive demonstration, behaves atrociously to the chief and, before the evening is over, attempts to seduce the chief's daughter.

The result is absolute disaster: Blood is shed, an innocent person lies dead and Nickerson's career is about to be shattered as Dobel reveals when he sneers:

"You didn't guess it yet? Why, I knew all about you, Mister Resident Magistrate, before I ever started here. Sure. Your record at headquarters: y'r silly reports on native habits and customs and such. Ho!" He gave his bark of laughter. " 'Habits an' customs and such. Ho!' Soon as I saw that, I knew where I'd catch you. Says I, 'Leave him to me. I'll get that dam' nigger-loving R.M. out of there!' "

But the power of native magic foils the well-laid plots of this cruel vulgarian and the absolute horror into which the story briefly strays is transformed as the tale comes to a charming, if, of course, unbelievably happy ending.

A comforting horror tale should be a paradox. But in John Russell's hands it is a remarkably welcome one.

PREY
Short Story

Richard Matheson

U.S.A.

1969, in *Playboy;* reprinted 1982 in Charles Waugh and Martin H. Greenberg's (eds.) *The Arbor House Celebrity Book of Great Horror Stories*, New York, Arbor House.

"Prey" is a seamless, fully realized and absolutely stunning tale. Unquestionably one of the finest horror fictions ever written in English it has the further distinction of being the basis for the piercingly terrifying television playlet, "Amelia," in the 1975 *Trilogy of Terror*.

Amelia, Matheson's protagonist, is a tired young woman who comes home from her work one day at 6:14. She opens a package that contains a doll, a Zuni hunting fetish known as "This Is He Who Kills." The doll is meant to be a birthday present for her friend Arthur Breslow, a high school teacher who is interested in anthropology and with whom she intends to spend the evening.

Then, because she is a dutiful daughter, she makes the evening's first mistake. She phones her mother with whom she plays out a grim, familiar charade of guilt given and received. It is one of those age-old, anguishing dialogues in which She Who Accepts The Guilt loses every step of the way. When Amelia puts down the receiver, she is a vanquished woman.

The rest of her nightmare begins as the doll, which she has set on a table, falls

> off the table edge. It landed head down and the spear point, sticking into the carpet, braced the doll's legs in the air. The fine, gold chain began to slither downward.

It is than that Amelia phones Arthur to cancel their date. When that dismal dialogue is over the doll, its spirit no longer encumbered by the gold chain, attacks. The ensuing battle is as vivid and as ghastly as it would later be on film.

Matheson, who has spent years writing for the movies, has an extraordinary gift for colloquial speech whose rhythms he captures in an absolutely unadorned prose. When he is at his best, as he is here, it is a prose capable of considerable revelation. In a story that is essentially a playlet with a single character, Matheson has with a few deft strokes managed to imply Amelia's entire lifetime as a victim of the tyrant love. But just as deftly, he does more. The tragic irony of the story is that the raging spirit of the Zuni fetish is as much a manifestation of Amelia's self hatred as it is an accidental force of the universe. In the final moment of the tale, we see that she and the fetish share a subtle if Pyrrhic victory.

THE PRIVATE MEMOIRS AND CONFESSIONS OF A JUSTIFIED SINNER
Novel

James Hogg

Great Britain

1824, London, Longman, Hurst, Rees, Orme, Brown & Green; reprinted 1970, London, Oxford U. Press.

The form of this fiction, a mixture of history, letters and a journal, combined with its psychological probing give a contemporary urgency to Hogg's early 19the-century novel.

The Private Memoirs . . . is a very strange work. Its opening pages read like excerpts from *Tom Jones* or *Joseph Andrews*, but it is not long before the genial irony borrowed from Henry Fielding gives way to an altogether different tone.

The novel's protagonist is Robert Wringhim, a putative second son of the Scottish laird of Colwan. It is more likely that Robert, who is mean, petty and hypocritical, has inherited his character from the Reverend Wringhim, his mother's spiritual adviser. It is certain that he does not resemble his older brother George whom he passionately hates because George, who is friendly, decent and noble, is everything that Robert will never be and will, moreover, inherit the laird's estate.

Robert, soon after he kills his brother George treacherously in a duel, meets a demonic figure named Gil-Martin who resembles himself to an amazing degree. It is Gil-Martin who provides Robert with a religious rationale for his wickedness by persuading him that he, Robert, is one of the Elect. Gil-Martin, who is always at Robert's side, assures him that

> "Thou art called to a high vocation; to cleanse the sanctuary of thy God in this thy native land by shedding of blood; go thou forth like a ruling energy, a master spirit of desolation in the dwellings of the wicked, and higher shall be your reward both here and hereafter."

But Hogg is too astute a novelist to let this Satanic whispering be a sufficient explanation for Robert's evil. Robert confesses that:

> I had a desire to slay him, it is true, and such a desire too as a thirsty man has to drink; but at the same time, this longing desire was mingled with certain terror, as if I had dreaded that the drink for which I longed was mixed with deadly poison.

Finally, what we have is a complex study of a psychopathic killer whose use of religion as a rationale for murder is almost too convincing. Where, in the course of history, have we heard such voices before?

PSYCHO　　Novel

Robert Bloch
U.S.A.
1959, New York, Simon & Schuster; reprinted 1982, New York, Warner.

This novel, on which Alfred Hitchcock based his great 1960 film of the same name, is a dry, bare bones fiction whose very diffidence serves to compress and heighten the horror Bloch is developing.

Mary Crane, approaching the bleaker side of 30, absconds with her employer's $50,000. She hopes to use the money to bail out her fiancé whose debts continue to delay their marriage. Mary, in flight, stops for the night at an off-the-beaten-track motel run by Norman Bates. Bates is forty-ish, single and hag-ridden. The hag, we learn, is his mother (more or less—uncertainty is an important part of the plot). Norman Bates's meeting with Mary is the fateful point at which the threads of terror woven by Bloch are suddenly snarled. Before we are through, we will have learned a good deal about how subvert sexual feelings are transformed into overt psychosis and murder. In addition, we will have witnessed some pretty skillful amateur sleuthing.

Psycho is admirably plotted and frequently scary. The interplay between the soft, shy, fat Norman Bates and the overwrought fugitive who stops at his motel is drawn in a few swift strokes. A random observation of Bates's, "I think perhaps all of us go a little crazy at times," serves to restore Mary to her senses and she knows she will return the embezzled money. Tomorrow. Then, having made that decision and feeling morally clean, she decides to feel physically clean as well, and takes a shower:

> The roar [of the shower] was deafening . . . That's why she didn't hear the door open, or note the sound of footsteps. And at first, when the shower curtains parted, the steam obscured the face . . . Mary started to scream, and then the curtains parted further and a hand appeared holding a butcher's knife. It was the knife that, a moment late, cut off her scream. And her head.

From here on there is more, and still more, to be afraid of.

PSYCHO　　Film

1960　(B&W)　U.S.A.　109 min.
Production Company: Paramount; ***Director:*** Alfred Hitchcock; ***Producer:*** Alfred Hitchcock; ***Screenplay:*** Joseph Stefano; ***Photography:*** John L. Russell; ***Editor:*** George Tomasini; ***Special Effects:*** Clarence Champagne; ***Music:*** Bernard Herrmann.
Cast: Anthony Perkins (Norman Bates), Janet Leigh (Marion Crane), John Gavin (Sam Loomis), Vera Miles (Lila Crane), Martin Balsam (Detective Arbogast), John McIntire (Sheriff Chambers), Simon Oakland (Doctor Richmond).

Robert Bloch's skillfully crafted short novel has become an Alfred Hitchcock film masterpiece. Hitchcock preserved the spare, even laconic manner of the Bloch fiction by keeping his cameras narrowly focused; by treating black and white film as if it could (as it can) create a palette of moods; and by casting so shrewd that it amounts to genius.

Hitchcock hardly changes Bloch's story, but on film Marion Crane's brief and abortive criminal flight from the dreariness of her job becomes a macabre dialogue of images: The Gothic old house on the hill, in which Norman Bates lives (or does not live) with his mother, silently quarrels with the shabby motel standing on a side road, miles from the main highway. The two structures, one grand and ruined, the other sleazy and on its way to ruin, form an absolutely appropriate theater for the madness that, in one form or another, afflicts Norman, his mother and, briefly, Marion.

Scene by scene is rendered with the starkest simplicity. Anthony Perkins, who has put his permanent stamp on the character of Norman Bates in the same manner as Bela Lugosi incised his features on Dracula, is boyish, charmingly hesitant, awkward. His hapless innocence drifts toward foreboding as he offers glimpses of his life to Marion Crane while she eats a white-bread sandwich in the motel office, with birds he has stuffed looking down on her. His loneliness, and hers; his despairs—and hers—meet. And in that decent interchange are created the bonds of ordinary human affection that are so horribly violated when, later, Norman becomes the Norman he does not know himself to be.

The film opens with a love scene between Marion Crane and her fiancé, Sam Loomis. But vaguely sensed incest, not romantic love, is the fulcrum on which the film is poised. To Hitchcock's credit, the film's sexual references *and* its violence are handled with consummate tact.

How much that tact contributed to the downright scariness of the film we may judge by its absence from the two sequels that Hitchcock did not live to make: *Psycho II,* directed by Richard Franklin (1983, Universal), and *Psycho III,* directed by Anthony Perkins himself. (Perkins plays Bates in both sequels.) Both of the sequels are in color and both elaborate the Freudian implications of Norman Bates's life, providing a quite circumstantial account of Norman's family life *before* Hitchcock turned his attention to him. What else they do is give us plentiful helpings of blood.

Psycho III, which is a significant step up from *Psycho II,* has Anthony Perkins' face as its chief virtue. In the interval between *Psycho II* and *III,* Perkins acquired the worn, intelligent, ruined and grieving look that we see on Samuel Beckett's face. The look of an enduring cliff that has faced and will face the onslaught of an untiring sea.

PSYCHOMANIA   Film
1972   (C)   Great Britain   91 min.

Production Company: Benmar; **Director:** Don Sharp; **Producer:** Andrew Donally; **Screenplay:** Arnaud D'Usseau, Julian Halevy; **Photography:** Ted Moore; **Editor:** Richard Best; **Special Effects:** Patrick Moore; **Music:** David Whitaker.

Cast: George Sanders (Shadwell), Beryl Reid (Mrs. Latham), Nicky Henson (Tom Latham), Mary Larkin (Abby), Roy Holder (Bertram), Robert Hardy (Chief Inspector Hesseltine).

This film, perfectly balanced between the hilarious and the horrid, is utterly absurd. What the filmmaker is saying to us, in effect, is "Never mind, none of this could possibly happen, but wouldn't it be fun to watch if it did?" The result is that *Psychomania,* despite the occasional mindless brutality and the many corpses the plot trails in its wake, comes off as a sprightly, vivacious, imaginative romp in which death is as frequently funny as life and as inconsequential.

Now for the impossible story: Tom Latham, leader of a British motorcycle gang that calls itself "The Living Dead," demands that his mother reveal to him the secrets of the "locked room" in the huge house where they live. Mrs. Latham, with the permission of their ageless butler named Shadwell, allows her son to go into the "locked room" where, by magic means, he learns that when he was an infant, his mother pledged him to the service of Satan. He learns too, that the "dead do not die." They need only profoundly wish to return to life and they will be able to do so.

His imagination stirred by this discovery, Tom promptly commits suicide. At his funeral, his gang, the Living Dead, bury him fully clothed and mounted on his motorcycle. Then one of them, strumming a guitar, sings a fake country-and-western ballad that goes:

> He took away his life with his own hand.
> While the holy sound of revving fills the sky
> You can see the ghostly rider passing by . . .

Later that day, Tom does indeed come roaring, motorcycle and all, out of the grave. His first stop is at a gas station, his second is at a pub where, using borrowed coins, he phones his mother. Their dialogue, impeccably diffident and British:

> Tom: Hello, mother. This is Tom.
> Mother: How are you? Are you all right?
> Tom: Well . . . I'm dead mother. I couldn't be better.

From here on, Tom sets himself the task of persuading his fellow bikers to commit suicide so they can return to ride their bikes with him for all eternity. One by one, with the exception of Abby, his sweetheart, the members of his gang follow him into death, though not all of them have sufficient strength of will to make the return journey. However, enough of them do return to re-form themselves on immortal terms, and they set about terrorizing the community.

Since the restraints that the police might normally exert on the bikers are unavailing against the dead, things start getting out of hand until Mrs. Latham, torn with remorse because of the gang's depredations on decent folk, reneges on her pact with Satan by means of a ritual she and Shadwell perform. As a result, several nasty things happen, first to Mrs. Latham, then to Tom and finally to his grisly crew, but nobody, except perhaps the living dead, feels any regret.

The cast, the director and the screenwriters of *Psychomania* never betray for a moment that they are anything but serious about their film. The result is that there is no posturing, no straining for effect. All the whimsy and the high jinks rise directly from the action and are altogether funnier on that account.

While *Psychomania* does not have the stylized manner of *The Abominable Doctor Phibes* it compares favorably with it for tongue-in-cheek wickedness.

QUEEN OF THE NIGHT   Short Story
Joyce Carol Oates
U.S.A.
1982, in Charles G. Waugh and Martin Greenberg's (eds.)
The Arbor House Celebrity Book of Horror Stories, New York,
Arbor House.

Here is another of Joyce Carol Oates' dark, meditative stories about just how destructive failures of love can be.

When Claire Falk discovers that her husband of 26 years is having an affair she does the expected thing and divorces him. It is a divorce that, like her marriage, is not particularly passionate. "Her son flew home, to comfort her. To accuse his father. But the drama did not really interest her." The whole process, writes Oates, was "impersonal . . . and tedious."

Claire Falk is, indeed, "An immobile, impassive woman, with a striking profile, a head of thick dark hair wildly streaked with gray." And the young man who becomes her second husband says that there is "Something glacial about [her], something remote and forbidding . . ."

It is on that curious neutrality of her personality, that mild but impervious self, that the horror of this story is built. Because when that young man marries her, it is the remoteness that fascinates him. "Queen of the Night," he calls her and she, hearing herself called that, feels how "her heart expanded as though it would burst, flooded with a sudden violent knowledge of her power."

Emil, her new husband, is:

> a poet, a playwright, a composer of "musical theater," a linguist, an economist, an actor, a director, a historian, a former track star . . . a watercolorist, a potter, a flautist, a pianist.

His view of the world is that:

> "We are in the 'tin age,' the last of the cycles before the entropic collapse of the universe. Languages begin to fail. The gestures of affection and love begin to fail. Individuals take to shouting at one another but still cannot make themselves heard. Frustrated, they take refuge in the senses, they attempt to communicate through the body—through love, or brutality; but of course they fail. And all subsides into its original chaos."

By now the reader may suspect that marriage to this young man is hardly an improvement over the long indifference of the 26 years of marriage Claire put in with her first husband. Oates' language cues us that her subject is not simply a second-marriage failure. "Impersonal," "tedious," "immobile," "passive," "glacial," "neutral"—the words she uses to describe her characters create a murmuring definition of emptiness that finally compels us to understand who Emil is (or what he represents). By then, the full horror of the tale nods above our heads like a grim toadstool and we know just why Emil called Claire the "Queen of the Night."

THE QUEEN OF SPADES   Short Story
Alexander Pushkin
Russia
1834; reprinted 1958 in *The Queen of Spades and Other Stories* (tr. and ed. Rosemary Edmonds), London, Penguin.

This classic tale of ghostly vengeance should prove fascinating both to confirmed gamblers and to anyone who has ever been tempted by the excitements of the gaming table.

One night, a couple of young army officers are talking about the luck of the cards. One of them, Tomsky, tells the story of his grandmother, the Countess Anna Fedotovna, who was once a great beauty and a great gambler. On one occasion, when she lost heavily to the Duke of Orleans in Paris, her husband refused to pay her debts. She appealed for help to a mysterious figure named St. Germaine who was rumored, among other things, to be the Wandering Jew. St. Germaine, though he did not lend the countess money, did teach her a combination of three cards with which she promptly recouped her losses.

Hermann, an officer in the engineers, is profoundly affected by this tale and sets out to seduce Elizaveta Ivanovna, an innocent, beautiful and extremely poverty-stricken dependent of the countess's, as a means of getting access to the old woman.

With Elizaveta's help, he hides in the countess's room at two o'clock in the morning. There, he:

> witnessed the hideous mysteries of her toilet; at last the Countess put on bed jacket and nightcap, and in this attire, more suited to her age, she seemed less terrible and ugly.

Making himself known to the countess, Hermann pleads for her secret, and when she balks he threatens her with his pistol. At this the old woman "showed signs of agitation. Her head shook and she raised a hand as though to protect herself from the shot . . . Then she fell back . . . she was dead."

But the countess's ghost comes back to wreak an elegant, ironic and frightful vengeance.

Pushkin's tale is constructed like a tightly made, intricate small play in which even the most casually introduced character plays an integral part. The three central figures, Elizaveta, Hermann and the countess, are each poignantly realized. They make a touching triangle of misplaced hopes: Hermann, with his small competence who yearns for the freedom that wealth would give him; Elizaveta, whose poverty and oppressed youth makes her an easy target for Hermann; and the countess, oppressed in her turn by old age. If one looks at these three closely one sees horrors beyond the vengeful but nevertheless charming visitation of the countess's ghost.

RABID Film

1977 (C) Canada 90 min.
Production Company: Cinema Entertainment Enterprises Ltd.;
Director: David Cronenberg; *Producer:* John Dunning;
Screenplay: David Cronenberg; *Photography:* Rene Verzier;
Editor: John Lafleur; *Music:* Joseph Reitman.
Cast: Marilyn Chambers (Rose), Frank Moore (Hart Read),
Joe Silver (Murray Cypher), Howard Ryshpan (Dan Keloid).

Rabid, though not Canadian director David Cronenberg's best film, is nevertheless a first-rate fear movie, since Cronenberg makes the scariest films in the business. *Rabid,* even as second-rank Cronenberg, has enough atrocious surprises in it to make for a frightfully satisfying evening. Beyond that, seen now in the eighties, when an incurable, sexually transmitted disease, AIDS, is ravaging the world, the film feels horribly prophetic.

A young woman, played by Marilyn Chambers, is involved in a motorcycle accident that burns and scars her body. The surgeon who saves her life leaves her with a strange structure growing under her armpit. Cronenberg treats us to a close-up of the strangely androgynous under-armpit organ from whose moist, red center there grows a thing like a knife. The excrescence, we learn, has disturbed her metabolism so that she has become a sort of vampire who uses the thing to slash her victims when she needs their blood to drink. More than that, the people who are slashed in this fashion become instantly mad and filled with the need to do some deadly biting in their turn.

The result of all this is that Montreal, where the story is set, becomes suddenly a plague area in which insane humans leap out at loved ones and strangers. Ms. Chambers, it should be said, does not herself go mad, though she cannot bring herself to stop doing what she does. To the accusation of her appalled boyfriend—"You carry the plague. You've killed hundreds of people."—Ms. Chambers sadly replies, "I have to have blood. It's all I can eat."

It all sounds a bit gross, but Cronenberg is a master at making doorways, fences, gates, closets, curtains or kitchen drawers seem sinister. A man asking for a match gets a smile and his throat ripped out in reply. As the plague of insanity and death spreads throughout Montreal, we see sharpshooters cruising the city in convoys of garbage trucks: They hunt down infected victims, shoot them and then toss the bodies into their automated trucks to be hauled away.

Though the grisly and ambiguous tuck under Ms. Chambers' armpit strains belief, the rest of *Rabid* is well imagined and intelligently designed. Ms. Chambers, who is better known for her career in film pornography, does a more than credible job here as the Typhoid Mary of madness. On balance, *Rabid* is sleek, urbane and scary enough to be admired.

THE RAVEN Film

1963 (C) U.S.A. 86 min.
Production Company: American International/Alta Vista; *Director:* Roger Corman; *Producer:* Roger Corman; *Screenplay:* Richard Matheson; *Photography:* Floyd Crosby; *Editor:* Ronald Sinclair; *Special Effects:* Pat Dinga; *Music:* Lex Baxter.
Cast: Vincent Price (Dr. Erasmus Craven), Peter Lorre (Dr. Adolphus Bedlow), Boris Karloff (Dr. Scarabus), Hazel Court (Leonore Craven), Olive Sturgess (Estelle Craven), Jack Nicholson (Rexford Bedlo), Connie Wallace (maidservant).

The fact that this *Raven* has all but nothing to do with Poe's poem of the same name should in no way spoil one's pleasure in a film whose best excuse for existence is that it brings together three great terror troupers—Lorre, Price and Karloff. The film gives these three a chance to relax in a comic mode while at the same time surrounding them with the fine old trappings of that terror genre which their careers have so much enriched.

The fun of this film derives mostly from Richard Matheson's high-falutin script in which his characters talk a sort of exalted other-speech. It's as if Matheson were putting into their mouths echoes of Shakespeare or of the lesser and more bombastic Tudor and Stuart dramatists.

The story of *The Raven* is slight enough. Three magicians are quarreling among each other. Dr. Craven (Price) is angry because Dr. Scarabus (Karloff) has stolen his wife and has transformed Dr. Bedlow (Lorre) into a raven. From such an airy nothing, Roger Corman and his crew have derived some fine and funny moments, especially the duel of magic between the two sorcerers, Craven and Scarabus.

Moe Disesso trained the crow that plays the raven.

RE-ANIMATOR   Film
1985 (C) U.S.A. 86 min.
Production Company: Empire International; *Director:* Stuart Gordon; *Producer:* Brian Yuzna; *Screenplay:* Dennis Paoli, William I. Norris, Stuart Gordon; *Photography:* Mac Ahlberg; *Editor:* Lee Percy; *Special Effects:* Anthony Doublin, John Naulin; *Music:* Richard Band.
Cast: Jeffrey Combs (Herbert West), Bruce Abbott (Dan Cain), Barbara Crampton (Megan Halsey), David Gale (Dr. Hill), Robert Sampson (Dean Halsey).

Re-Animator is very much a horror film of the eighties, which means that its viewers get scene after scene of the pornography of pain. It is an expensive and well-made film that caters to the physiological curiosity of its young audiences, which means that it relies heavily on special effects—especially close-up views of severed limbs, disembowelments and steel-inflicted wounds in flesh. It is, in short, a splatter film that is so drenched in blood that even the most gluttonous aficianado of the grisly may finally forget that "the blood is the life" and turn from so much squirting and spurting with revulsion or with laughter.

Re-Animator is a retelling of the Frankenstein story set in the present time, at H.P. Lovecraft's mythical Miskatonic University. The cast of characters and their conflicts are quickly established. We have Dan Cain, a busy medical student who is bedding the beautiful Megan Halsey, the daughter of Allen Halsey, the dean of the medical school. We have the young nerd, Herbert West, who has come to Miskatonic fresh from his stint as assistant to the famous, and recently deceased, Dr. Gruber, a Swiss researcher who was working on a serum to reanimate the dead.

West moves in with Cain and sets up a laboratory in the basement where he perfects Gruber's serum. West's antagonist is Dr. Carl Hill, the university's most famous researcher, who envies and loathes him. We learn too that Hill, who is in his fifties, has a secret but by no means inactive yen for Megan.

When Herbert West, working in the hospital morgue with Cain, restores a corpse to life, the mayhem begins—first, because the newly risen dead are filled with hatred for the living; and second, because Hill, when he learns what West's serum can do, is determined to steal it from him and claim its discovery for himself.

The violence that fills the screen from here on is at first ugly, then, as it gets increasingly graphic (read "physiologically precise"), it turns repulsive, then offensive and finally so absurd that such words as "living" and "dead" lose their meaning. West kills Dean Halsey and reanimates him. Then he decapitates Hill with a garden spade after which he reanimates Hill's head and his headless trunk. Then these two, trunk and head, remembering that they once lusted for Megan, find a way to overpower her after which they strap her down so that they can molest her.

It is, as I've said, appalling, grotesque and, especially in the erotic scenes, offensive. And yet, the absurdity of a bodiless head gloating lasciviously over a naked woman and murmuring, "I've always admired your beauty my dear," or West's remark to that same head, "You'll never get credit for my discovery. Who's going to believe a talking head?" put a glaze of madness over the film that might have sprung directly from Hieronymous Bosch—or Abbott and Costello.

REPULSION   Film
1965 (B&W) Great Britain 104 min.
Production Company: Tekli/Compton; *Director:* Roman Polanski; *Producer:* Gene Gutowski, Michael Klinger, Tony Tenser; *Screenplay:* Roman Polanski, Gerard Brach, David Stone; *Photography:* Gilbert Taylor; *Editor:* Alastair McIntyre; *Music:* Chico Hamilton.
Cast: Catherine Deneuve (Carol Ledoux), Ian Hendry (Michael), John Fraser (Colin), Patrick Wymark (landlord), Yvonne Furneaux (Helen Ledoux).

The British Film Catalogue 1895–1985 in a triumph of impertinence sums this great film up in nine words: "Belgian manicurist, revolted by sex, kills admirer and landlord."

Carol Ledoux is, no doubt, a manicurist, and sex is certainly part of what goads her to commit her murders. But what Polanski gives us in this, his first horror film, is a cool study of the wavering line that separates sanity from madness.

Polanski is an impressionist of film. He asks his camera to look slowly, off-handedly at the real world that surrounds Carol Ledoux as her mind crumbles. And so we get the dailiness of Carol Ledoux's life: it's grayness, its walls, its routine of shopping, its spare loneliness. She is a young, inexperienced and beautiful woman who has to endure the particular emptiness that comes from hearing two other people—her sister and her lover—enjoying their lovemaking in another room. When those two leave for an extended weekend somewhere, Carol and the apartment become the focus of the film.

Carol has no enemy except her own, slowly dissolving self and Polanski gives us a careful study of that dissolution. His triumph is that in addition to the things we see that we know have not happened (the apartment's buckling walls and Carol's erotic fantasies) there are also the real things that can drive one mad: the skinned hare Carol's sister has left on the kitchen table, its small carcass, fresh and horribly obscene at first, begins to rot and becomes a mute icon for what is happening to Carol herself.

The film is intimate—there is no better word—without being clinical. Carol is going mad and gets there, but Polanski makes no pretense of diagnosis or judgment. As if, having read Goethe's dictum: "Painter, paint—and hush," he had imposed a single discipline on himself, his camera and his actors to see and to make us see. It is, when all the images he has created have done their work, more reality than we (or Carol) can bear.

REVENGE OF THE CREATURE   Film
1955 (B&W) (3-D) U.S.A. 82 min.
Production Company: Universal-International; *Director:* Jack Arnold; *Producer:* William Alland; *Screenplay:* Martin Berkeley; *Photography:* Charles Welbourne; *Editor:* Paul Weatherwax; *Music:* Joseph Gershenson.

Cast: John Agar (Professor Clete Ferguson), Lori Nelson (Helen Dobson), John Bromfield (Joe Hayes), Nestor Paiva (Lucas), Grandon Rhodes (Jackson Foster), Dave Willock (Lou Gibson).

This perky sequel to *Creature From the Black Lagoon* sticks close to the formula that made *Creature* a success: first, focus on the impossibility of love between the living relic of the Devonian Age and a beautiful contemporary woman and second, make good use of underwater photography.

The film poses, too, the soap-operatic question: Can an attractive young female be a scientist or is she doomed to give all that up for a husband and a house in the suburbs?

This time, Joe Hayes finances a scientific expedition to the Black Lagoon to find the Creature and bring it to America. Lucas, the same crusty water-rat who captained the boat in the previous film, stands now at the helm of the *Rita II*. The hunting party, using unfair means like dynamiting the lagoon and pumping a coma-inducing drug into it, capture the gill man and bring him to Florida. There, at the Ocean Harbor Institute, he is chained to a stake at the bottom of a tank where he can be studied by scientists and observed by the public.

Professor Clete, with the help of ichthyologist Helen Dobson, uses an electric prod to train the gill man, teaching him concepts like "Stop." Not surprisingly, the Creature resents this mode of instruction, breaks his chain and swims out to sea. But, the image of Helen torments him and he comes back to Florida for her, only to find her getting ready to melt in Clete's arms.

The gill man then steals Helen whereupon the film's plot, which until now has alternated among the banal, the silly and the cruel, turns ghastly because the creature, though he has lungs, can not stay out of the water for very long, and Helen, his impossible bride, cannot stay in it. As a result, the gill man, who simply wants to keep Helen, also has to find a way to keep her alive. For the creature, the dilemma proves costly. As the film ends, the gill man has been shot at by a posse and he may be dead. Or he may not be.

In any event, in a 1956 sequel called *The Creature Walks Among Us*, he reappears once more. This time, by means of corrective surgery, he becomes more or less human. But all the humans he meets are so dreadful that he spurns them and returns again to the sea.

THE RIVAL DUMMY

Short Story

Ben Hecht
U.S.A.
1931, in *Champion From Far Away*, New York, Covici-Friede; reprinted 1945 in *The Collected Stories of Ben Hecht*, New York, Crown.

"The Great Gabbo," once considered "the world's most famous ventriloquist," is the subject of this Ben Hecht short story narrated by Joe Ferris, a booking agent. At the time we meet Gabbo he looks and acts like a man on the run. The change in his fortunes has all been the result of a fatal quarrel between himself and Jimmy, his dummy.

The trouble, Ferris tells us, is that Gabbo and Jimmy always had a tempestuous relationship, but they generally managed to arrive at some sort of truce that made it possible for them

to appear on stage. But when Gabbo adds a woman assistant, Rubina, to the act, she serves to complete the eternal triangle for Gabbo and Jimmy. It is a triangle made complicated by Rubina who, because she loathes Gabbo, makes him jealous by "patting Jimmy's wooden cheeks on the stage. Or winking at him during the turn." When Rubina leaves the act, Gabbo is driven wild, certain that Jimmy has put her up to her flight and that he knows where she is. Gabbo refuses to go on stage with Jimmy and that night, when Joe Ferris and the hotel manager break into Gabbo's room, they find that, "The floor is covered with pieces of wood. Splinters, sticks. It's Jimmy. Chopped to pieces, cut to smithereens. He'd murdered Jimmy, honest to God."

And it is here that the not particularly unusual story of a ventriloquist for whom schizophrenia is almost a professional requirement turns suddenly ghastly as we learn why the Great Gabbo has shaved off his distinctive great moustaches and why he is wearing a cheap grey toupee and why, most especially, he insists that his name is not Gabbo. "My name," he says, "is Mr. Lawrence. I am sorry you make a mistake."

Hecht's story, told in the breezy prose his characters speak in *The Front Page*, is considerably denser than it appears to be. Hidden in the narrator's gossipy patter there is a classic story of the disintegration of the psyche.

THE ROACHES

Short Story

Thomas M. Disch
U.S.A.
1965, in *Escapade;* reprinted 1985 in Bill Pronzini, Barry N. Malzberg and Martin H. Greenberg's (eds.) *Great Tales of Terror and the Supernatural*, New York, Castle.

Anyone who is repelled by the oily look and the scuttling ways of roaches will find this early Thomas M. Disch story nearly monumentally loathsome, which is, of course, what the author intends.

Marcia Kenwell, Disch's protagonist, a lonely young Minnesota woman, has come to New York City but does not make her fortune. By day, she makes a modest living as a clerk in an insurance office. Her evenings, she devotes to fighting the cockroaches in her apartment. The insects fill her with a revulsion that amounts to a phobia. It "was so strong that she could not bear to crush them under the soles of her shoes." But the very intensity of her hatred forges a link between herself and the hordes of these beasts that infest her building, and she discovers one day that the insects understand and obey her commands. Once Miss Kenwell is aware of her power over them, she sends them off to destroy her Russian next-door neighbors who offend her by their uninhibited erotic behavior—which she watches through a crack in the wall between their apartment and hers. She sees that they are "drinking, of course . . . and now the woman pressed her roachy mouth against the mouth of the one-eyed man—kiss, kiss. Horrible, horrible."

From that point to sheer madness is hardy a step for Miss Kenwell. And Marcia, with the help of the roaches, takes it. The result is, "Horrible, horrible."

"The Roaches" does two things especially well. First, it makes the important point that the feeling we call loathing can be an expression of hidden sympathies for the thing we loathe. Second, the story derives considerable (and insightful) drama out of a very common urban plague.

THE ROCKING HORSE WINNER
Short Story

D. H. Lawrence
Great Britain
July 1926, in *Harper's Bazaar;* reprinted 1976 in vol. 3, *The Complete Short Stories of D. H. Lawrence,* New York, Penguin.

Lawrence writes of the beautiful mother, who is the real source of the terror in this tale, that, "when her children were present, she always felt the centre of her heart go hard. This troubled her, and in her manner she was all the more gentle and anxious for her children, as if she loved them very much." Unfortunately, children infallibly can tell the difference between really being loved and "as if."

This unmaternal mother and her husband have three children—a small son, Paul, and two daughters. The family is genteely poor; and the household is haunted by the domestic and quarrelsome refrain, "There must be more money! There must be more money!" Paul, oppressed by his mother's unhappiness, rides himself into a mystic frenzy on his rocking horse hoping to find "luck." Indeed, he does find it. In his trances, he hears the names of horses that are certain to win the races in which they run. With the help of a gardener, and, later, of his uncle, the boy puts his uncanny talent to its appropriate use and acquires a secret hoard of money intended to make his mother happy. But, as Lawrence grimly shows, lack of money was never the family's real calamity.

The source of the story's horror is the black vision Lawrence projects of a childhood blasted by parental egoism. Paul rocking away desperately on his wooden horse to bring money to the family home is an image at once ghastly and grand.

THE ROCKY HORROR PICTURE SHOW
Film

1975   (C)   U.S.A.   101 min.

Production Company: 20th Century-Fox; *Director:* Jim Sharman, Terry Ackland; *Producer:* Michael White; *Screenplay:* Jim Sharman, Richard O'Brien; *Photography:* Peter Suschitsky; *Editor:* Graeme Clifford; *Special Effects:* Wally Veevers; *Musical Director:* Richard Hartley, (songs) Richard O'Bryan. *Cast:* Tim Curry (Dr. Frank-N-Furter), Barry Bostwick (Brad Majors), Susan Sarandon (Janet Weiss), Richard O'Brien (Riff Raff), Jonathan Adams (Dr. Everett Scott), Neil Campbell (Columbia), Peter Hinwood (Rocky), Meatloaf (Eddie), Patt Quinn (Magenta), Charles Gray (criminologist, narrator).

The Rocky Horror Picture Show is a phenomenal film. It is a rock music opera, an anthology of scenes parodying various great moments from the terror film genre and a science fiction film all in one. In addition to all that, *Rocky* makes statements about youthful sexual behavior that have seemed so compelling that young people all over America, for more than a decade, have taken the film to their hearts and made of it a cult object to which, usually on a Saturday midnight, they pay their devotions by dressing up like its characters, singing along with the songs and mouthing the dialogue. Or by shouting at the villains or cheering on the protagonists.

The phenomenon of the cult of *Rocky* deserves considerably more attention than it can get here, but what is abundantly clear is that the film's excellence and verve are what make it work. Vibrant and imaginative, it gives audiences castles, space travellers, a homemade creature created by Dr. Frank

N. Furter, engaging villains, beautiful women and an endless, and an endlessly amusing, interplay of sexual themes. There is hardly a permutation or combination of sexual unions that is not either portrayed or hinted at in the film.

Rocky's plot is simplicity itself: A young couple, engaged to be married, drive away from a wedding. We next see them driving through a dark and stormy night. Suddenly they have a flat tire. In the great tradition of terror movies, they go hunting for a phone and find themselves ringing the doorbell of as unlikely a castle as was ever filmed. Here, they meet Dr. Frank N. Furter who is "Just a sweet transvestite, transsexual Transylvanian" and who, later in the evening, will invite them to "Come up to the lab and see what's on the slab." He is, we will learn, a sexually hyperactive villain who wants to teach the protagonists, Janet and Brad, things about sex they never knew were permissible.

The rest of the night's adventures are high-spirited parodies of great, but less melodic, terror films of the past: *Dracula, Frankenstein, King Kong.* The couple learn that "a beautiful creature [is] destined to be born tonight." And, in the course of things, Rocky is, indeed, "born," out of a sort of enlarged aquarium. Rocky is beautiful, and enormously appealing to all the sexes.

It is all high jinks. The sets are gorgeous and silly enough to engage the eye; the music is insistent and melodic and entices the audience to sing-along with Frank N. Furter. But the primary achievement of *The Rocky Horror Picture Show* is the good-humored way in which the film, as if it were itself a modern Moses, gives to the under-thirty crowd its prime commandment: "Don't dream it. Be it." The audiences, wild-eyed, panting, enthusiastic, cheer.

THE ROOM IN THE TOWER
Short Story

E. F. Benson
Great Britain
1912, in *The Room in the Tower,* London, Mills and Boon; reprinted 1984 in J. A. Cuddon's *The Penguin Book of Ghost Stories,* London, Penguin.

A 30-year-old narrator has, for some 16 years, had a recurrent and threatening dream in which he comes to a strange but elegant house where a group of people is having tea on the lawn. There he is greeted by a woman, Mrs. Julia Stone, who says to him, "Jack will show you to your room. I have given you the room in the tower." Then Jack leads the dreamer up a staircase to a room which, in his dream, he knows is somehow sinister. Over the years, the people in the dream age, as if they are living through actual time, and finally the dreamer, when he does not find Mrs. Stone at her usual place in the tea party on the lawn, understands that she is dead. Nevertheless he hears her voice repeating its usual message, "Jack will take you to your room. I have given you the room in the tower."

That, then, is the reiterated nightmare. Then one August day the narrator, visiting a friend in the Ashdown Forest district in Sussex, falls asleep in his friend's car and when he wakes, he finds himself standing before the doorway of the house of his nightmare. But it is the home of John Clinton, the narrator's friend; there is nothing sinister about the Clinton family or their guests, except that Mrs. Clinton does, eventually, speak the words the narrator has heard in his nightmare, "Jack will show you to your room. I have given you the room in the tower."

There is more to the story, but this is the moment at which the narrator's dream and his reality intersect and where the nightmare intensifies as the details he has been dreaming for 15 years now take their places in his waking life. From here on, the narrator has a twofold task: clinging to his sanity even as he fights to preserve his life.

The horror of the tale derives, I think, from the slow deliberation with which E.F. Benson moves his story forward. His tone is always equable as he gives us, first, an extended and deliberately unexcited description of the narrator's repeated nightmare; and he maintains the same deliberate pace when he describes the narrator's real experiences in the room in the tower. The result is that we understand Benson's point only too clearly: Nightmare and the real world are interpenetrations of each other. The notion is not new, but Benson's images in making this point are fresh and terrifying.

ROSEMARY'S BABY
Film

1968 (C) U.S.A. 137 min.

Production Company: Paramount; *Director:* Roman Polanski; *Producer:* William Castle; *Screenplay:* Roman Polanski; *Photography:* William Fraker; *Special Effects:* Farciot Edouard; *Music:* Krysztof Komeda.

Cast: Mia Farrow (Rosemary), John Cassavetes (Guy), Ruth Gordon (Minnie), Maurice Evans (Roman), Ralph Bellamy (Dr. Sapirstein).

Rosemary's Baby is Roman Polanski's version of how the Antichrist whose coming is prophesied *The Book of Revelations* will come into the world. In a chilling parody of Christ's arrival on Earth Polanski has imagined an ordinary American woman as the unwilling mother of Satan's son.

The appealing Rosemary Woodhouse (Mia Farrow) is the mother designate who very slowly comes to understand that there really is a coven of witches that, for some mysterious reason, is monitoring her first pregnancy in her marriage to Guy Woodhouse.

Woodhouse, when we first meet him, is a not very successful actor. He and Rosemary have just moved into the Bramford, an apartment building in which various scandalous deaths have taken place. The Woodhouses' next-door neighbors are Minnie and Roman Castevet. Minnie is a short, brassy-voiced older woman who seems to have nothing else to do but to mind Rosemary's business. Roman seems to be a slightly vague retiree. Actually, the two of them are the hosts for regular meetings of the coven of witches for whom Rosemary's pregnancy is so interesting.

Mostly, the film revolves around the slow accretion of Rosemary's knowledge, to a first climax in which she under-

Mia Farrow as Rosemary. © Paramount Pictures

stands that either the coven exists or she is the victim of pre-partem paranoid delusions about it. The second climax hits after the birth of the baby when Rosemary has to come to terms with its identity. In both cases, Rosemary is the touching center of the action. Even when she knows just whose child she has given birth to, she does not withhold her tenderness.

There are moments when the film drags—especially when Ruth Gordon is on camera as the tedious Minnie Castevet or when John Cassavetes, playing the thankless role of Rosemary's husband, reassures her, for the ten-thousandth time, that everything will be alright. And Polanski, making this film at the time that the Hippie Revolution was in full swing, cannot resist making use of the sort of imagery familiar to LSD users. This is especially true in the impregnation scene when the camera (or the special effects people) create vast swirls of color and motion on the screen to imply that the mysterious love-making surpasses understanding.

On the other hand, the film has its considerable strengths. Not the least of which is the ingenious idea that Satan, in a parodic imitation of Christ, will also be born to an ordinary mortal. It is a notion that gives the film, and particularly Mia Farrow's role as Rosemary, complex dimensions. It is typical of Polanski's intricate imagination that he can create a believable on-screen Pieta in which the Infant cradled in its mother's arms is the offspring of Satan, even as he gives us an intriguing footnote to Yeats's great poem "The Second Coming." What he tells us is that the "rough beast, its hour come round at last" will slouch toward Manhattan and not toward Bethlehem to be born.

S

THE SANDMAN

Short Story

E.T.A. Hoffmann
Germany
1817, in *Nachtstücke*, Berlin; reprinted 1967 in E.F. Bleiler's (ed.) *The Best Tales of Hoffmann*, New York, Dover.

"The Sandman," a story that fascinated Freud, is one of the most nearly perfect terror fictions ever written.

It begins with a series of letters between two friends, Nathanael and Lothair, then letters between Nathanael and Clara, the young woman he loves. Finally, Hoffmann abandons the epistolary form and, after a brief first-person transition, finishes his tale from an omniscient point of view.

In Nathanael's opening letter we are given glimpses of his childhood, when each evening he and his brothers and sisters were put to bed after being warned, "Come, children! off to bed! Come! The Sandman is come." Later, he formed a mental image of the Sandman as:

> a wicked man, who comes to little children when they won't go to bed and throws handfuls of sand in their eyes, so that they jump out of their heads all bloody; and he puts them into a bag and takes them to the half-moon as food for his little ones; and they sit there in the nest and have hooked beaks like owls, and they pick naughty little boys' and girls' eyes out with them.

Later, still, Nathanael identifies the Sand-Man with the visits to his father of an alchemist named Coppelius who was "a most disagreeable and horribly ugly figure, but what we children detested most of all was his big coarse hairy hands . . . ." In Nathanael's mind Coppelius is associated with the death of his father who died in an explosion in the course of an alchemical experiment the two were conducting.

But Nathanael's fate is destined to be linked to Coppelius's. Years later, having quarreled with Clara whose rationalism offends him and who in a moment of anger he charges with being an automaton, he falls in love with Olimpia, Professor Spallanzani's daughter. When he sees her at a concert, she is:

> richly and tastefully dressed. One could not but admire her figure and the regular beauty of her features. Yet the striking inward curve of her back, as well as the wasplike smallness of her waist, appeared to be the result of too-tight lacing . . . Olimpia played on the piano with great skill; and sang as skillfully an *aria di bravura*, in a voice which was, if anything, too brilliant, but clear as glass bells.

When Nathanael dances with her, her beauty and the look of love in her eyes completely conquers him and he declares his passion. She responds, "with her eyes fixed unchangeably on his, sighing repeatedly, 'Ah! Ah! Ah!' "

His courtship of Olimpia sends him into ecstasies. He reads everything he has ever written to her, and she listens without ever wearying.

> She neither embroidered nor knitted; she did not look out of the window, or feed a bird, or play with a little pet dog . . . it was only when at last Nathanael rose and kissed her lips or her hand that she said, "Ah! Ah!" and then "Goodnight, dear."

Then on the very morning when he means to propose to Olimpia, he comes into Professor Spalanzani's home to find the professor and Coppelius engaged in a fearful tugging match.

> The professor was grasping a female figure by the shoulders, the Italian Coppola held her by the feet . . . Nathanael was stupefied—he had seen only too distinctly that in Olimpia's pallid waxed face there were no eyes, merely black holes in their stead; she was an inanimate puppet.

The sight drives Nathanael mad—but there is more, both better and worse to come.

"The Sandman" is a story that overwhelms the reader with the clarity of the events it describes even as it comes to its close enveloped in a cloud of mystery. Its theme shifts under one's scrutiny like a view through a perspective glass: Is the tale merely about illusion versus reality; or are we seeing one of the earliest studies of the progress of madness; or is it a prophetic tale of the dangers of science? or a hidden satire on what men expect from women? or a tale about the prevalence of evil? or about the inexorability of fate? Whatever answer we make, there is no way we can abate the horror of passages like this one: "And now Nathanael saw a pair of bloody eyes lying on the floor staring at him; Spalanzani seized them with his uninjured hand and threw them at him, so that they hit his breast."

SARDONICUS   Short Story
Ray Russell
U.S.A.
1960, in *Playboy*; reprinted 1981 in Bill Pronzini, Barry N. Malzberg and Martin H. Greenberg's (ed.) *Great Tales of Horror and the Supernatural*, New York, Castle.

Sir Robert Cargrave, a Harley street specialist, receives a letter from Maud Randall, in whom he had once been romantically interested. He learns that she is now married to a Mr. Sardonicus who, via his wife's letter, has invited Cargrave to his Castle Sardonicus in Bohemia for a visit. Cargrave, still very much smitten by Maud, accepts the invitation.

Arrived at Castle Sardonicus, he finds that Maud, "who had been so gay and vivacious ,the delight of soirees, was now distant and aloof, of serious mien, unsmiling . . ." and that her husband is afflicted with *Risus sardonicus*, an illness that "caused his lips to be pulled perpetually apart from each other, baring his teeth in a continuous ghastly smile." It is a condition he has had since the night he dug up his father's body to retrieve a winning lottery ticket that had been buried with it. Sardonicus, we learn, wants Cargrave to cure him. When Sardonicus offers Cargrave the opportunity to sleep with Maud as an inducement, Cargrave's cup of loathing for the afflicted man runs over and he refuses. But Sardonicus changes the doctor's mind when he blandly describes the torments to which he will expose Maud unless Cargrave agrees to perform the cure.

It is now that the true horror of the tale begins as, ironically, the cured Sardonicus, consummate villain that he is, achieves his own destruction even as Cargrave and Maud attain happiness in England. It is poetic justice, nicely calibrated.

"Sardonicus," despite its appearance as a short story in *Playboy* magazine in 1960, has the surface and the manner of a late-19th-century European fiction. The prose, discursive, civil, cultivated, is always at the service of its ingenious plot while its three very thinly developed characters move like clockwork figures that come out of a bell tower once an hour. Design, not character, is what they represent.

SCANNERS   Film
1981 (C) Canada 103 min.
Production Company: Avco Embassy/Filmplan International; **Director:** David Cronenberg; **Producer:** Claude Heroux; **Screenplay:** David Cronenberg; **Photographer:** Mark Irwin; **Editor:** Ronald Sanders; **Special Effects:** Gary Zeller; **Music:** Howard Shore.
Cast: Stephen Lack (Cameron Vale), Jennifer O'Neill (Kim Obrist), Patrick McGoohan (Dr. Paul Ruth), Lawrence Dane (Braedon Keller), Michael Ironside (Darryl Revok), Victor Desy (Dr. Gatineau).

In *Scanners*, David Cronenberg, one of the best directors of his generation, has made a film that starts out as if it were moving toward greatness and maintains a magnificent pace until its final moments when it collapses into insipidity. And yet, it needs to be said that a flawed Cronenberg film is already many, many cuts above the run-of-the-mill productions that come out of Hollywood.

Scanners begins with a crowd scene—a Cronenberg signature. In this case, we are in a huge shopping mall where a young derelict is seen stealing leftover bits of food from the tables in a restaurant. A woman, watching, makes an unkind remark. The next moment, she is writhing on the floor in what appears to be an epileptic seizure. We are given to understand that it is the derelict, Cameron, who has caused the seizure by means of powers not yet clear to us. Cameron is a scanner—one of the people in this world who are gifted, or cursed, with the ability to read and to control other people's minds.

Cameron is taken up by a research physician named Dr. Ruth, who works for Consec, an industrial complex that sells highly sophisticated weaponry to greedy client nations worldwide. We learn that there is a secret rival organization, The Biocarbon Alternative, which is employing scanners as flesh, blood and mind weapons. Daryl Revok, one of its agents, has a mental duel with a Consec scanner in the course of which a human head explodes on camera. This startling scene is never quite matched in intensity anywhere else in the film.

From that point on, we have a straightforward adventure story in which Cameron, working for Consec, is pitted against Revok, who is apparently working for Biocarbon Alternative. Cameron's detective work, as he searches for Revok, is continuously fascinating. There is one satisfyingly destructive scene in the studio of an avant-garde sculptor and another in which Cameron pits his scanner mentality against the electronic vigor of a massive computer. In that encounter, the result is an enormous amount of very expensive broken crockery.

Scanners would have made a perfectly fine adventure tale of high-tech skulduggery, but Cronenberg seems to have felt the need to turn it into an allegory of contemporary family life. The scene in which a couple of brothers (both scanners) pit their destructive mental powers against each other turns abruptly, and inappropriately, hilarious as the special effects take on cartoon-like dimensions. And the laughter, once it has invaded the film, is never quite dissipated.

And yet, with all its faults, *Scanners* remains a memorable film, wildly and creatively energetic.

SCHALKEN THE PAINTER   Short Story
J. Sheridan Le Fanu
Ireland
1851, in *Ghost Stories and Tales of Mystery*, Dublin, James McGlashan; reprinted 1964 in E.F. Bleiler's (ed.) *Best Ghost Stories of J.S. Le Fanu*, New York, Dover.

In the 19th century, there was a very popular lithograph that consisted of a cleverly contrived visual pun. The picture shows a young woman seated before a dressing table on which there is a row of bottles and jars containing cosmetics. She is perfectly self-possessed as she looks into a large mirror.

The built-in pun, however, shows up after a moment or two as we realize that the unthreatening scene has a larger design. The dressing table, the young woman's hair, the mirror, the bottles slowly take their places as part of a grinning skull, and the real theme of the picture announces itself: Death and the Maiden. Or Death-in-Life, or Life-in-Death. Even today, in our more sophisticated times, the grisly joke can induce a shudder.

This is all by way of saying that Le Fanu's "Schalken the Painter" exploits that extraordinarily popular theme without, however, being quite as tricky.

Le Fanu's story does begin with a picture, a curious and unsettling portrait of a beautiful young woman in the foreground and, in the background, the figure of a:

> man dressed in the old Flemish fashion, in an attitude of alarm . . . There is in that picture something that stamps it as the representation of a reality.

It is the picture of Rose Velderkaust. She was the niece of Gerard Douw, the master painter with whom Schalken studied in his youth. Schalken and Rose were in love, but the young Schalken was poor and so, when a not quite elderly, but by no means young, man appeared at Douw's home one evening and proposed to make Rose "wealthier than any husband you can dream of for her"—if he could marry her at once—the prudent Douw overcame his qualms and accepted the offer.

But Minheer Vanderhausen of Rotterdam was not an ordinary old man eager to buy himself a young bride.

> A quantity of grizzled hair descended in long tresses from his head, and rested upon the plaits of a stiff ruff, which effectually concealed his neck. So far all was well; but the face!— all the flesh of the face was coloured with the bluish leaden hue, which is sometimes produced by metallic medicines . . . the eyes showed an undue proportion of muddy white, and had a certain indefinable character of insanity . . . and the entire character of the face was sensual, malignant, and even satanic.

There is more to the description but I have quoted enough to make it clear that poor Rose had reason enough to be terrified of being given in marriage to such a man. But she was given to him and the heartbroken young Schalken "saw the prize which he would have risked existence to secure, carried off in solemn pomp [toward Rotterdam] by his repulsive rival."

Schalken was to see Rose twice more. Once when she was in great agony and once, many years later, in the vault of a church when:

> There was nothing horrible, or even sad, in [her] countenance. On the contrary, it wore the same arch smile which used to enchant the artist long before in his happy days.

And that, of course, is the moment when the story's design is suddenly clear. It is the old story of death and the maiden made especially poignant because Schalken's painting is not a mere play of wit. It is, rather, all that is left of a doomed young love. And the mark of Le Fanu's greatness is that his ghastly tale works simultaneously as love story, allegory and bitter meditation on the way that even great art can fail to console the grieving heart.

SCREAM AND SCREAM AGAIN   Film
(Alternate release title: **SCREAMER**)
1970   (C)   Great Britain   95 min.
Production Company: Amicus/AIP; ***Director:*** Gordon Hessler; ***Producer:*** Max Rosenberg, Milton Subotsky; ***Screenplay:*** Christopher Wicking, Peter Saxon; ***Photography:*** John Coquillon; ***Editor:*** Peter Elliot; ***Music:*** David Whitaker.
Cast: Vincent Price (Dr. Browning), Christopher Lee (Fremont), Peter Cushing (Major Heinrich), Alfred Marks (Supt. Bellaver), Uta Levka (Jane), Judy Bloom (Helen Bradford), Judy Huxtable (Sylvia).

A jogger in a London park is tripped. He falls unconscious. When he comes to, he is in bed in what appears to be a hospital. He looks down and discovers that his legs are missing. And that is how this bizarre and disturbing film begins.

The premise of *Scream and Scream Again* is that some very highly placed people in England and in a German-speaking, Nazi-like country on the continent are running a research project whose aim is to re-create superpowerful human beings out of the body parts of still living people.

We soon learn that Doctor Browning, a biophysiologist, is the scientist who re-creates these creatures and that one of them is malfunctioning. When the creature murders and drinks the blood of a young woman in London, the police equip a policewoman with a radio transmitter and send her as a decoy to the same nightclub where the first victim met the killer.

The policewoman is only too successful. The killer makes his move. The police arrive too late to save her, but the murderer is trapped after a car crash, with one of his hands caught under a wheel. Then, in a startling sequence, he tears his own hand off at the wrist and escapes. As he flings police aside like ninepins and then runs without fatigue almost straight up the steep slope of a quarry, we get a sense of his supernatural power. That same sequence ends with another moment of astonishment as the killer leaps into a vat of acid where he dissolves into his elements. We learn that the hand he left behind has "Tendons made of a substance we can't classify. The rest of it is flesh and blood."

Scream and Scream Again would be quite striking even without the brief appearances of Vincent Price, Peter Cushing and Christopher Lee, but their presence in the film gives it a sense of tradition and a considerably engaging style.

SCREAMERS   Film
1982   (C)   U.S.A./Italy   90 min.
Production Company: New World Pictures; ***Director:*** Sergio Martino; ***Producer:*** Luciano Martino; ***Screenplay:*** Sergio Donati, Cesare Frugoni, Luciano Martino; ***Photography:*** Giancarlo Ferrando; ***Editor:*** Eugenio Alabiso; ***Special Effects:*** Chris Walas; ***Music:*** Luciano Michelini. ***Additional Sequences:*** Miller Drake (Sc. & Dr.), Gary Graver (Ph.)
Cast: Mel Ferrer (Radcliffe), Eunice Bolt (Samantha), Cameron Mitchell (the Doctor), Tom J. Delancy (Patterson), Joseph Cotten (Ernest).

With some heavy-duty stars in its cast and a considerably inventive, if loose, screenplay, *Screamers* is a much better film than its publicity ("Be warned: You will actually see a man turned inside out.") would lead one to think. Despite the sleek, slick, zippy production values, what we have here is an old-fashioned adventure-cum-terror film that recalls the grand tales of Jules Verne, H. Rider Haggard, H.G. Wells and Edgar Rice Burroughs. Like those fictions, *Screamers* is genteel and euphemistic about sex, a reticence on the part of the filmmakers that for 1981, feels almost charming.

The story is a patchwork of plots. First, we get a mini-drama set in 1891 in which we see a group of very well dressed treasure hunters poking through a cave looking for gold. They find it, as well as their bloody deaths.

Now, a prison ship crashes onto that same island. The survivors include a doctor, named Claude, and an assortment of good, bad or indifferent prisoners, many of whom meet their deaths at the hands (?) of vaguely discerned but sinister creatures.

Then everything comes into focus. The island is owned and run by Edmond Rackham, the villain, who has been there for 15 years scheming to get the treasure of the Temple of the Sun, the capital of the lost Atlantis, which, it happens, is at the bottom of his island's lagoon. However, the treasure is too deep for human divers (in 1891) to reach. Hence, Rackham has employed a mad scientist named Dr. Marvin. Marvin and his beautiful 23-year-old daughter, Amanda, have found a way to communicate with the dangerous sea-apes who are the present inhabitants of Atlantis. Rackham, who lusts for Amanda, hopes that with the help of the sea-apes and of a race of amphibians that Dr. Marvin has created, he can get the treasures of Atlantis for himself. Young Claude loves Amanda and is therefore Rackham's natural antagonist.

Once all that is clear, the audience gets a really engaging 90 minutes worth of adventure, special effects and dearly loved cliches. There are voodoo drums, love and betrayal, and ingenious but not very realistic scenes of violence. The sea-apes, though they are deadly, have the dumb decency we have come to expect from Hollywood's menagerie of not-quite-natural creatures. These folk are modeled on the Creature from the Black Lagoon and like him they admire—and care for—innocent female beauty.

What the film does not have is a man turned inside out, though there is a slightly queasy moment when the camera gives us a much longer look than our curiosity requires of the complicated innards of one of Dr. Marvin's creations.

A final, somewhat sour note: *Screamers* retains the standard racial stereotypes that marred the great adventure films of the thirties, the forties and the fifties. The "natives" on this island are black, subservient, superstitious and for the most part, mute. It is a misjudgment that spoils an otherwise quite satisfying film.

THE SCREAMING SKULL   Short Story

F. Marion Crawford
U.S.A.
1911, in *Wandering Ghosts,* London, T. Fisher, Unwin.

A carefully crafted, slow-moving tale of a vengeful skull.

The story, narrated by the retired sea captain, Charles Braddock, to an unnamed and undescribed colleague who has come to spend a weekend with him, is an account of what happens when the skull of the murdered Mrs. Luke Pratt returns to destroy first, the husband who murdered her, and second, Captain Braddock who was distantly responsible

for Mrs. Pratt's death because he innocently described a mode of murder that Luke Pratt imitated when he killed his wife. As Captain Braddock says, "If I had not told that story she might be alive yet. That is why the thing screams at me, I fancy."

The skull "lives" in a bandbox in a closet of the house Captain Braddock inherited after Dr. Pratt was murdered by "the hands or teeth of a person or animal unknown." The skull is clean and white and small and, at first, it has its lower jaw missing. From time to time—but especially when it feels that it is being abused or spoken ill of—it screams, or rolls reproachfully about of its own accord.

The details of Mrs. Pratt's murder, and the later murder of her husband, emerge slowly from the narrative—so slowly that the horror of the tale grows in almost imperceptible increments until the final quiet moment when we are shaken by the news that Captain Braddock, too, has been slain by "the hands or teeth of some person or animal unknown." Then, we are chilled to the marrow as we grasp fully the ghostly and grisly vengeance the "good little woman, with a sweet temper . . . and a nice gentle voice" has taken.

The story's central weakness is the really quite untenable assumption that one can drug a victim and then kill him or her by pouring molten lead through a small funnel into an ear. On the Shakespearean stage, in *Hamlet,* such an idea can be made to work in the "play within a play." But in the less shadowy light of the 20th century verisimilitude does seem to be severely strained.

THE SEVENTH VICTIM   Film

1943 (B&W) U.S.A. 71 min.
Production Company: RKO; ***Director:*** Mark Robson; ***Producer:*** Val Lewton; ***Screenplay:*** Charles O'Neal and DeWitt Bodeen; ***Photography:*** Nicholas Musuraca; ***Editor:*** John Lockert; ***Music:*** Roy Webb.
Cast: Tom Conway (Doctor Judd), Kim Hunter (Mary Gibson), Jean Brooks (Jacqueline Gibson), Evelyn Brent (Natalie Cortez), Erford Gage (Jason Hoag), Isabel Jewell (Frances Fallon), Elizabeth Russell (prostitute).

Made by Val Lewton in the same year as *I Walked With a Zombie, The Seventh Victim* is important as a record of his career, but, though it has its moments, it misses excellence by a wide margin. The fault seems to be a Byzantine pacing that renders the film inert. Nor is the film's howler of an ending any help. There we see a company of ruthless satanists, who have been responsible for the suicide of their "seventh victim," cowed into reciting the Lord's Prayer.

Mary, a boarding school student who becomes concerned because she has not heard from her sister Jacqueline in a long time, and because her tuition has not been paid in six months, goes to New York to search for her. There, in the course of her search, she hires a seedy private detective named Irving August who is murdered for his pains. She learns that her sister was a depressive who rented a room furnished only by a noose hanging from the ceiling. Gregory Ward, who turns out to be Jacqueline's husband, and who later falls in love with Mary, says that, "Jacqueline had a feeling about life—that it wasn't worth living unless one could end it." Mary also meets Dr. Judd, Jacqueline's psychiatrist, and Jason, a failed poet, who, when he involves himself in the search for Jacqueline, is stimulated to write once more.

Jacqueline, it turns out, is alive, but hiding from the members of a satanist society called the Palladists whose secrets she betrayed to her psychiatrist. The penalty for such betrayal is death. There have been six previous members who paid that penalty, and Jacqueline is slated to be the seventh.

The finest, because it is the subtlest, moment in the film, lasting perhaps a tenth of a second, comes when the woman who lives next door to the room with the noose walks by and hears a chair falling over. The Palladists have had their seventh victim.

SHAMBLEAU   Short Story
C. L. Moore
U.S.A.
November 1933, in *Weird Tales;* reprinted 1987 in Alan Ryan's (ed.) *Vampires,* New York, Doubleday.

It may be that one has to go to Bram Stoker's novel *The Lair of the White Worm* to find sexual imagery that is quite as squirmingly repulsive as C.L. Moore's now classic story of Shambleau, the female vampire monster who exerts such a fatal attraction on Northwest Smith, the tale's protagonist.

Though "Shambleau," with its Martian boomtown locale and its roystering interplanetary voyagers, is tricked out as a science fiction tale, what its story comes down to is an encounter between Smith, the innocent earthman, and the strangely beautiful Shambleau, whom he saves from a lynch mob. When he gives her shelter, he:

> knew at a glance [that she was not human], though the brown, sweet body was shaped like a woman's . . . He knew it from the moment he looked into her eyes . . . they were frankly green as young grass, with slit-like feline pupils . . . There was no hair on her face—neither brows nor lashes . . . She had three fingers and a thumb, and her feet had four digits apiece too, and all sixteen of them were tipped with round claws that sheathed back into the flesh like a cat's.

When she loosens the turban she wears and her bright red "hair" emerges, Smith sees that it:

> was lengthening, stretching, moving of itself. It must be hair, but it crawled; with a sickening life of its own it squirmed down against her cheek, caressingly, revoltingly . . . Wet, it was, and round and thick and shining.

Most of the rest of the story turns on the various ways in which that wet red mass works on the deluded Smith, "promising, caressing, alluring, sweeter than honey" until:

> His arms slid round her under the sliding cloak, wet, wet and warm and hideously alive—and the sweet velvet body was clinging to his, her arms locked about his neck—and with a whisper and a rush the unspeakable horror closed about them both.

If one did not know that this "slimy, dreadful and wet" story was written by a woman one would take it for another instance of the fascination-revulsion fiction so expressive of the male fear of women that one frequently finds in 19th-century prose—and more than occasionally in twentieth as well. What is admirable is that C.L. Moore was able to imitate such "masculine" prose successfully. Lurid, loathesome, macabre and, withal, remarkably well written, *Shambleau* is quite capable of haunting one's dreams.

H. Rider Haggard.

SHE   Novel
H. Rider Haggard
Great Britain
1887, London, Longmans; reprinted 1965, New York, Lancer.

She, one of the greatest of the great 19th-century adventure novels, ought not, properly, to be included in a book on horror literature, except for one thing: With all of its vivacity, with all of its derring-do, it is the only adventure novel I know that is so relentlessly focused on necrophilia and the fear of women.

The story of *She* is told in the form of a memoir written 20 years after the events it purports to describe by Ludwig Horace Holly, a brave, physically powerful and very ugly Cambridge scholar who has been entrusted by a dying friend with the guardianship of his friend's small son, Leo Vincey, and some documents in a strongbox that he is to open when the boy has turned 25. At the appointed time, Holly and the very beautiful, golden-haired but not particularly brilliant Vincey, open the strongbox. The document they find in it tells them that Leo is descended from one Kallikrates, a priest of Isis who abandoned his studies for the love of a princess named Amenartas. The two took refuge in central Africa among a tribe ruled over by a mysterious white queen who killed Kallikrates in an access of jealous rage. The documents call upon Amenartas' descendants to send someone back to avenge Kallikrates' death. That someone, of course, is Leo Vincey.

And so the strange voyage begins. Leo and Holly, accompanied by Holly's manservant, Job, make their way to Africa where they find Ayesha, She-Who-Must-Be-Obeyed, still ruling over her Amahagger tribe, still grieving, after 2,000 years, for the Kallikrates she murdered and whose embalmed body she keeps in her bedroom. When Ayesha meets Leo she knows at once that he is the reincarnation of Kallikrates. And when he falls in love with Ustane, a lowly Amahagger girl, the love conflict played out 2,000 years ago is replayed once more and Ustane becomes Ayesha's victim. When Ayesha offers Leo her beautiful self plus the gift of immortality, Leo, with Ustane gone, accepts. But the story does not quite end the way Ayesha plans.

There are all sorts of things wrong with this great novel. Among them: its impossible plot, its thin characterizations and its swollen diction. Just the same, it achieves (or imitates) grandeur as Haggard gives us his "history of a woman, clothed in the majesty of her almost endless years, on whom the shadow of Eternity itself lay like the dark wing of Night." Ayesha, the woman. She-Who-Must-Be-Obeyed.

THE SHINING   Film
1980 (C) U.S.A. 146 min.
Production Company: Hawk Films; *Director:* Stanley Kubrick; *Producer:* Stanley Kubrick; *Screenplay:* Stanley Kubrick, Diane Johnson; *Photography:* John Alcott; *Editor:* Ray Lovejoy; *Music:* Bela Bartok, Wendy Carlos, Rachel Elkind, György Ligeti, Kryzysztof Penderecki.
Cast: Jack Nicholson (Jack Torrance), Shelley Duvall (Wendy Torrance), Danny Lloyd (Danny Torrance), Scatman Crothers (Dick Halloran), Barry Nelson (Stuart Ullman).

Stanley Kubrick's *The Shining* is not the masterpiece that his great gifts as a director led his admirers to expect, but it is not at all the disaster that even such an astute critic as Alan Frank has claimed it to be. In his *Horror Film Handbook*, Frank writes:

> The script abandons just about every element that makes Stephen King's novel so effectively atmospheric . . . replacing it with a banal plot and dialogue to match which might just have passed muster for a run-of-the-mill supernatural second feature. . . . Like all of Kubrick's work, it is technically impeccable and it is a total waste of time, talent and money.

When the film first appeared in 1980, my judgment of it was nearly as harsh as Frank's, but seeing it again, seven years later, I find it denser and on occasion more brilliant than I thought it then.

Kubrick follows the plot of Stephen King's novel *The Shining* pretty closely. Jack Torrance, a former schoolteacher turned fiction writer, accepts a job as a winter caretaker of the Overlook Hotel, a vast establishment in the mountains some miles away from Boulder, Colorado, which closes down for five months in the winter. Torrance, who means to write a novel, tells his employer that he will welcome the isolation, and that he is sure that his wife and young son will adapt well to it.

Before the Torrances take up their residence in the hotel, we learn that Jack has had a drinking problem that produced such outbursts of anger against his son, Danny, that he once dislocated Danny's shoulder. We learn, too, from a conversation between Danny and Dick Halloran, the Overlook's black cook, that Danny, like Halloran, has "the shining," the ability to read minds and get glimpses of past and future events.

The dramatic heart of the film reveals what happens once the Torrances are settled into the gargantuan and profoundly empty hotel in which, many years ago, a former caretaker killed his wife and two daughters and then himself. It very soon becomes clear that Jack Torrance's mind is also unbalanced, and the question for the viewer is not whether, but when Torrance will go stark staring mad.

Torrance's madness is the weakest part of the film. The speed with which his sanity erodes melodramatizes what started out as a thoughtful study of the breakdown of a character. Much of the fault lies with the filmscript, but Jack Nicholson, who is surely one of the great actors of our age, seems in his characterization of Torrance to have utterly lost touch with both his instincts and his training so that he lurches madly through his mad scenes being mad.

Shelley Duvall, for her part, is stuck in a role that seems to have been designed for two different actresses. On the one hand, she portrays brilliantly the mousy, affectionate, devoted wife and mother Wendy is supposed to be. But as the film moves forward, and Wendy's role in the plot diminishes, Duvall is given less and less to do until at last she is required only to register terror and to shriek, sob and run.

Both Danny Lloyd as Danny and Scatman Crothers as Halloran turn in impeccable performances. Lloyd is especially good and understands (or Kubrick has helped him to understand) the beautiful uses of understatement. The scenes that do him and Stanley Kubrick the most honor are the two or three long sequences in which we see him at the handlebars of his tricycle tooling along over miles of ominously patterned rug in the Overlook Hotel as if he, too, were in the grip of a fixation. As for Crothers, in his brief time on camera he hardly ever raises his voice and yet conveys dignity and compassion.

Kubrick's genius manifests itself in small details like the pattern of the rug, which imitates the design of the shrubbery maze on the hotel grounds, or the terrifying way the snow-filled maze is used to enclose the axe-wielding, mad father pursuing his small son, or the insistent presence in the film of mirrors that seem to comment on the action. What does not work well is the attempt to convey the evil that is implicit in the history and the structure of the hotel. Indeed, the supernatural aspects of King's plot are unconvincing here since by the end of the film all of the Torrances are in such bad shape psychologically that we can not be sure that what they seem to be seeing is real.

Kubrick's problem is that he has to fight the novel on which his movie is based. Stephen King's *The Shining* has a fascinating plot and thinly imagined characters. Though that combination generally satisfies King's readers it does not serve Kubrick well. Finally what we have in *The Shining* is a ragged movie in which a great director's genius is frequently displayed. And that is more than reason enough to see this film.

THE SHOUT   Film
1978 (C) Great Britain 86 min.
Production Company: Record Picture Company; *Producer:* Jeremy Thomas; *Screenplay:* Michael Austin, Jerzy Skolimowski; *Director:* Jerzy Skolimowski; *Photography:* Mike Molloy; *Editor:* Barrie Vince; *Music:* Anthony Banks.
Cast: Alan Bates (Charles Crossley), Susannah York (Rachel Fielding), John Hurt (Anthony Fielding), Robert Stephens (CMO), Tim Curry (Robert Graves).

Here is one of those superior English films that, when we encounter them, make us glad there is an England. The literate and subtle film script is based on a short story of the same name by Robert Graves. It tells the agonizingly ambiguous story of Anthony, an avant-garde composer, and his wife Rachel, into whose lives there comes an extraordinary figure named Charles Crossley. Crossley at first appears to be merely a sturdy tramp, but it does not take us long to see that he is something more.

Crossley, if the description he gives of his own life may be credited, has had an atrocious past. He has lived 18 years in the Australian outback where he had a wife (or wives). He explains to his hosts that he killed each of his children as they were born because he wanted to leave nothing of his behind when finally he left the tribe with which he lived.

Almost in passing, Crossley asserts that the human soul, in such hard times as these, may have taken up its residence in trees or rocks. He also tells his hosts the story of a rainmaker who compelled rain to fall by carving a scar across his own middle. As the camera pulls away from him, we see that his middle is scarred.

Finally, Crossley tells them that he has learned a magic shout that is so overwhelming it kills those who hear it.

These, then, are the ingredients that provide us with our sense of Crossley.

Anthony and Rachel, for their part, are a childless couple. Anthony occasionally goes into the nearby village to keep a not especially joyful adulterous rendezvous. One gathers that there is, similarly, little passion between Anthony and Rachel because she becomes Crossley's sexual slave at the very first moment that he indicates—in a quite brutal fashion—that he is interested.

Anthony. meanwhile, expresses an interest in Crossley's "terror shout." Crossley sneers, "You haven't the imagination to understand anything outside your own experience." Nevertheless, he walks out on the dunes with Anthony the next morning and demonstrates the shout. Its effect is amazing. Anthony is knocked flat. A sheep in the vicinity dies and later in the day one of the villagers is found dead.

Two particular things contribute to the film's power: first, the portrait of Crossley as an old-fashioned, and evil, warlock whose secret heart must be found and destroyed in order to break the awful spell he is able to cast upon his victims; and second, the terrifying idea that each human soul is both fragile and hidden, somewhere in the real world, and that whoever finds it may damage or destroy it.

The single weakness of this otherwise quite stunning—but very low-key—film is that the story begins and ends in a madhouse. The cuts from the madhouse scenes to the main plot and then back again are so badly, or so ambiguously, edited that it is not clear whether the action we see actually happened or is a figment of Crossley's mad imagination.

Among its strengths there is the successful use of nearly subliminal noises: children's voices in the distance, the clicking of heels on rocks, electrical switches going on or off, the noise of the sea, and, of course, Anthony's musical tinkering, cunningly presented just within earshot. In a film in which sound is a manifestation of cosmic power, the presence of such sounds is the director's elegant way of italicizing his theme.

SILENT SNOW, SECRET SNOW   Short Story
Conrad Aiken
U.S.A.
1934, in *Among the Lost People*, New York, Scribners; reprinted 1972 (1944) in Herbert A. Wise & Phyllis Fraser's (eds.) *Great Tales of Terror and the Supernatural*, New York, Random House/Modern Library.

Like Charlotte Perkins Gilman's *The Yellow Wall Paper* and Julio Cortazar's "Axolotl," this is a tale of inward horror where the danger to the main character comes not from some force, or creature or person outside himself but from some inward slippage of the mind. In this case the mind is that of a boy, Paul Haselman, who finds a soft and gentle and dreamlike way to sever the bonds that tie him to the human world. He sees and hears (or he chooses to see and hear) the universe slowly filling up with snow. Before his eyes a new and more pleasing world of inertia and whiteness appears:

> the new world was the profounder and more wonderful of the two. It was irresistible. It was miraculous. Its beauty was simply beyond anything—beyond speech as beyond thought—utterly incommunicable.

And what is horrifying is to see how reasonable, how persuasive and how beautiful are the processes of Paul's young mind as he drifts toward the catatonia we know is waiting for him.

Aiken makes no effort to explain why Paul should want to sink into his imagined snowbanks. He lives in a reasonably normal family. He has no singular problems at school. And his doctor, examining him, can find no symptoms to report. When he says to Paul, "I would like to know—is there anything that worries you?" the boy replies truthfully, "Oh, no, I think not—" at the same time as Paul (and the reader) hear the snow's private comment:

> "Ah, but just wait! Wait till we are alone together! Then I will begin to tell you something new! Something white! something cold! something sleepy! something of cease, and peace, and the long bright curve of space!"

Madness was never made more enticing and a reader, putting down "Silent Snow, Secret Snow," has to think hard whether it would not be the better part of wisdom to follow Paul, where "the whole world was a vast moving screen of snow—[which] even now . . . said peace, it said remoteness, it said cold, it said sleep."

SIR DOMINICK'S BARGAIN   Short Story
J. Sheridan Le Fanu
Ireland
1923, in *Madam Crowl's Ghost*, London, Condon; reprinted 1964 in E. F. Bleiler's (ed.) *Best Ghost Stories of J. S. LeFanu*, New York, Dover.

Here is a tale of a Faustian bargain so artlessly told that it suggests a sophisticated mind at work contriving naivete. Partly, its air of an innocent folktale derives from the way Le Fanu, following Sir Walter Scott's lead, scrupulously recreates local speech and local scenes:

> To my left, stretched away for miles, ascending the mountain range I have mentioned, a wild park, through whose sward and ferns the rock broke, time-worn and lichenstrained. This park was studded with straggling wood, which thickened to something like a forest, behind and beyond the little village I was approaching . . .

As for the local speech, Le Fanu gives his second, but main, narrator that Irish lilt we find so charming:

> But there was two sarvants in care of [the old house], and my aunt was one o' them; and she kept me wid her till I was nine year old, and she was lavin' the place to go to Dublin; and from that time it was let to go down . . .

The tale's first narrator, an Irish businessman riding on horseback to the south of Ireland, stops at a village beside the ruins of Dunoran, once a great manor house. As he stands musing about mutability, a small hunchback comes up and, with prompting, tells the narrator what it was that brought about the ruin of Dunoran house.

Nearly a hundred years ago, says the hunchback, the house was occupied by Sir Dominick Sarsfield whose distinction it was to squander his family's fortune. When it was clear to him that his money was almost all gone, and the he could not honorably pay his debts, he resolved to kill himself. However, as he walked in the woods of Murroa looking for a likely branch from which to hang himself, he met:

> a handsome young man like himself, and he wore a cocked hat with gold lace round it such as officers wears [sic] on their coats, and he had on a dress the same as French officers wore in them times.

That young man, we learn, is "recruiting for his sovereign" and who that might be and what sort of compact he makes with Sir Dominick is not hard to guess.

How Sir Dominick fares once he is well into the devil's bargain is what the rest of the story is about. It is a tale of moral ups and downs that manages, as it comes to its close, to be stark and witty and as horrifying as can be—proving, once again, that they who sup with the devil must use a long spoon.

SIR EDMUND ORME   Short Story
Henry James
U.S.A.
1891; reprinted 1984 in J. A. Cuddon's (ed.) *The Penguin Book of Ghost Stories*, London, Penguin.

Probably the most disconcerting thing about this tale of a courtship moderated by the presence of a well-bred ghost is the headnote with which it begins. When the reader has finished the story, which ends the way a romantic tale should, that headnote—which politely sets down what happened after the love story proper is over—will strike a jarring note calculated to emphasize what is truly horrifying about it.

James's plot is very simple. The narrator, a young man in Brighton at the height of the social season, meets and falls in love with the beautiful Charlotte Marden who "at twenty-two . . . had a rosy blankness and was admirably handsome." Charlotte and her mother, Mrs. Marden, have "a small fortune and a cheerful little house in Brighton."

Mrs. Marden, we learn, is a deeply troubled woman who is occasionally haunted by the ghost of a man, Sir Edmund Orme, who took his own life because she married another man. Sir Edmund Orme is visible only to Mrs. Marden and to the narrator (because he is in love with Charlotte).

With the relationships that matter set out in their proper places, the story now acquires that special anguish of a Henry James fiction in which the characters have not only to bear the burden of their situation, but to maintain the proprieties as well. Even the ghost conforms to the social norms. We read that:

> Above all, he was, by every seeming, of as fine and as sensitive, of as thoroughly honorable, a mixture; . . . He had always, as I saw more fully later, the perfect propriety of his position—looked always arrayed and annointed, and carried himself ever, in each particular, exactly as the occasion demanded.

When the narrator asks Mrs. Marden, " . . . What on earth does he want?" her reply is:

> "He wants to make me suffer for what I did to him."
> "And what did you do to him?"
> She gave him an unforgettable look, "I killed him."

The ghost, whose duty it is to haunt Mrs. Marden so that she will prevent Charlotte from mistreating a suitor in her turn, is finally laid to rest. And yet the story ends on a note of restlessness as we find ourselves unable to shake the feeling that we have been privy to three love stories instead of one: The narrator and Charlotte are the most obvious couple; then there is the ghost and Mrs. Marden; and finally, there is the link between the narrator and Mrs. Marden. The last is the most disturbing of the three because it is at once covert and unseemly.

And there, because this is a Henry James story, is where the horror is to be found: in the covert and unseemly. James understood that decorum is a form of masking with which one faces the world. If he was not, like Melville, interested in striking through the mask, he was, nevertheless, fascinated by it as the best indicator we have of the horrors it conceals. The achievement of "Sir Edmund Orme," which is a display of surfaces, is that it startles us with the depth of the darkness that lies just beneath the shimmering light.

THE SISTERS   Film
(Alternate release title: **BLOOD SISTERS**)
1973 (C) U.S.A. 92 min.
Production Company: Pressman-Williams Enterprises; ***Director:*** Brian De Palma; ***Producer:*** Edward R. Pressman; ***Screenplay:*** Brian De Palma, Louisa Rose; ***Cinematographer:*** Gregory Sandor; ***Editor:*** Paul Hirsch; ***Music:*** Bernard Herrmann.
Cast: Margot Kidder (Danielle and Dominique Breton), Jennifer Salt (Grace Collier), Charles Durning (Joseph Larch), Bill Finley (Emil Breton), Lisle Wilson (Philip Woode), Mary Davenport (Mrs. Collier).

The Sisters is early De Palma at his best.

Danielle and Dominique Breton are a couple of Canadian Siamese twins who are joined at the lower thigh. In an obvious allusion to the fate of the Dionne Quintuplets, the Breton sisters are shown being raised in the "Loisel Institute," which is, of course, studying them. The doctor in charge of the case falls in love with Danielle and, we are asked to believe, makes love to her despite the fact that she is joined to her sister, Dominique. Dominique, an unwilling voyeur, naturally resents the doctor's carryings-on. When Danielle becomes pregnant, the doctor decides to separate the sisters, but in the course of the surgery, Dominique dies. Her death occasions Danielle's psychopathology.

She marries the doctor, but he quickly learns that theirs is not a marriage made in heaven. Each of their sexual contacts turns into a nightmare in the course of which Danielle is possessed, or believes herself to be possessed, by the jealous spirit of her dead sister. As the doctor puts it to Danielle, "Dominique never died for you. You became Dominique . . . Every time I made love to you, Dominique came back and took control of your mind."

De Palma's achievement is that he makes his characters' anguish seem more believable than the actual plot in which they find themselves. That plot includes a feisty young woman reporter who chances to see the film's first murder. The reporter, who must rely on herself, becomes a dynamo of energy and intelligence as she links her destiny with that of the sisters.

The Sisters is a notable, if not always believable film. Among its grislier virtues are several of the most intensely death-oriented love scenes ever rendered on celluloid.

SKELETON   Short Story
Ray Bradbury
U.S.A.
September 1945, *Weird Tales*; reprinted 1970 in *The October Country*, New York, Ballantine.

Anyone fresh from a reading of ''Skeleton'' may well find himself or herself unable to eat breadsticks ever again, because in this story Bradbury has uncannily linked his perfectly horrible events with that most innocent of nibbling foods.

Mr. Harris, we learn, is regarded by his doctor as a hypochondriac because he complains of a continuous ache in his bones. When Harris asks, ''But why should my bones ache?'' his doctor replies:

> ''You ever had a sore muscle, and kept irritating it, fussing with it, rubbing it? It gets worse, the more you bother it. Then you leave it alone and the pain vanishes.''

Having received short shrift from his doctor, Mr. Harris finds another practitioner, M. Munigant, who, though he seems to lack any medical training, is amazingly sympathetic to Harris' complaints. Though he can do nothing to help Harris just yet, he does say that:

> When Mr. Harris felt he could cooperate psychologically, when Mr. Harris really needed help and trusted M. Munigant to help him, then maybe something could be done.

Meanwhile, he ''proffered a jar of long hard salty breadsticks.''

From here on, we follow Harris's growing obsession with his own bone structure:

> Slowly, he examined it [his spinal chord], in the same way he operated the many push-buttons in his office . . . but now, in these pushings of his spinal column, fears and terrors answered, rushed from a million doors in his mind to confront and shake him! His spine felt horribly—unfamiliar. Like the brittle shards of a fish, freshly eaten, its bones left strewn on a cold china platter.

So much, at first, for the negative side of his bone structure. Then, as his obsession grows, he discovers the beauty of his bones:

> Observe the flawless, snow-white perfection of the skull . . . consider the skeleton; slender, svelte, economical of line and contour. Exquisitely carved oriental ivory! Perfect, thin as a white praying mantis!

That phase is followed by a revulsion of feeling in the course of which he identifies his bones as his mortal enemies. It is a period of intense physical pain that drives him finally to call M. Munigant once more. This time, Munigant, judging

Harris to be ''psychologically prepared for aid,'' comes to his house.

What makes ''Skeleton'' so convincing is Bradbury's sympathy for his mad protagonist. As the story progresses, the reader finds his own skeleton aching along with Mr. Harris's and sharing his amazement that our bodies depend for their form on such a strange structure. In the final shocking moment of the tale we are reminded once again that even a paranoid has enemies.

Nor is that all. Bradbury leaves us with the problem of what to do about breadsticks.

SKIN   Short Story
Roald Dahl
Great Britain
1953, in *Someone Like You*, New York, Knopf; collection reprinted 1965, New York, Dell.

At once witty, flashy and macabre Dahl's story of the former tattoo artist on whose back the painter Hayim Soutine tattooed an early masterpiece is also deeply moving.

Dahl moves his story slowly and carefully from its beginning in 1913 when Drioli and his wife Josie were friends of the painter in Paris. The painter was poor and unknown and innocently in love with Josie; and Drioli, a master tattoo artist, was at the height of his powers and the one with the more or less steady income. He was, moreover, deeply appreciative of Soutine's work. How appreciative we shall see shortly.

One day, Drioli having earned a good bit of money with his needle, brings home enough good white wine for the three friends to get royally drunk. When they are all properly high, Drioli has his inspiration. He says to Soutine, ''I want you to paint a picture on my skin, on my back. Then I want

Roald Dahl. © Sophie Baker

you to tattoo over what you have painted so that it will be there always.''

At first, of course, the painter protests. But the intriguing suggestion and the wine succeed finally in overcoming his resistance and he paints, and then tattoos, a picture of Josie on Drioli's back.

In 1946, more than 30 years later, Drioli, down and out, stands looking at a Soutine painting in a gallery window. Overcome by old memories, he goes into the gallery from which, because of his shabby appearance, the gallery owner tries to eject him. Drioli, outraged, shouts, ''I too have a picture by this painter! He was my friend and I have a picture that he gave me.'' With that, he snatches off his shirt and displays the picture.

It is then, as an art dealer's yellow-gloved hand touches Drioli's bare shoulder, that the wit and the pathos and the macabre come together.

THE SMALL ASSASSIN   Short Story

Ray Bradbury
U.S.A.
1951, in *Dime Mystery;* reprinted 1970 in *The October Country,* New York, Ballantine.

When Alice Leiber, the wife of David Leiber, gave birth to a baby boy, it should have been a happy event. The baby, after all, had been very wanted, and it was ''a fine baby . . . His blue eyes opened like fresh blue spring flowers.''

After that beginning, Ray Bradbury gives us one of the cruelest stories ever written about evil children as, slowly, he makes us aware that the child Alice and David Leiber have brought home from the hospital is, as Alice has suspected from the start, a small assassin whose target is herself.

So profound is Alice's conviction that the baby menaces her that she confesses to her husband, ''I was going to kill the baby. Yes, I was.'' David, of course, takes the matter up with their family doctor, Dr. Jeffers, who gives him the usual medical reassurance:

> ''A Caesarian operation brought the child into the world and almost took Alice out of it. She blames the child for her near-death and her pneumonia. She's projecting her troubles . . . we all do it.''

In fact, however, Alice is projecting nothing at all. The baby is sinister. It knows what it is doing and it does it with the evil skill of a professional. By the time this horrifying tale comes to its end there is no harm in the world so dreadful that we are not willing to wish it on this infantile, accomplished killer.

Bradbury's special talent has always been the extraordinary clarity with which he first sees, then creates the events of his fictions. He has a keen eye for what is poignant in domestic situations and a finely attuned ear for the music of ordinary speech; these talents serve him well in this atypical portrait of family life where his task is to get past our built-in sympathy for a baby and persuade us of the awful truth. He does it with admirable sleight-of-hand, as he directs our attention almost entirely to what is happening to the baby's parents. By the time they have lived through the series of accidents culminating in the disaster that overtakes them, they are more than ready to believe the worst about their appalling child whose name, as its father understands in a moment of insight, should have been Lucifer.

SOME OF YOUR BLOOD   Novel

Theodore Sturgeon
U.S.A.
1961, New York, Ballantine; reprinted 1967, London, Sphere.

Theodore Sturgeon, a major science fiction writer of the post-World War II period, creates a memorable vampire fiction here.

George, the young vampire who is the book's protagonist, is a redneck South Carolina youth of Hungarian descent. He has a deep love for the outdoors and his respect for woodcraft alone makes him as nearly sympathetic as a blood drinker can be. When during his army service he gets in trouble with his superior officers, he is subjected to psychiatric treatment in the course of which his blood-drinking proclivities are revealed.

Some of Your Blood is a curiously gentle tale. If one can get past, or ignore, the chummy man-in-the-street prose style that was endemic in science fiction writing in the fifties and sixties, *Some of Your Blood* can be read as a surprisingly poignant account of a sexual obsession. Indeed, unless George's perversion strikes the reader as frightening, the book is hardly horrifying at all. Particularly touching is George's affair with a hulkingly avid farm girl to whom he is devoted because she permits him to drink her menstrual blood. Scary or not, this book, like Richard Matheson's *I Am Legend,* is a nearly classic example of the way in which a primordial image like the vampire can be eroded when it is put under the spotlight of contemporary rationalism.

SON OF DRACULA   Film

1943 (B&W) U.S.A. 90 min.
Production Company: Universal; ***Producer:*** Jack Gross; ***Screenplay:*** Eric Taylor; ***Director:*** Robert Siodmak; ***Photography:*** George Robinson; ***Editor:*** Saul Goodkind; ***Special Effects:*** John P. Fulton; ***Music:*** Hans J. Salter.
Cast: Lon Chaney, Jr. (Count Alucard), Louise Allbritton (Katherine Caldwell), Robert Paige (Frank Stanley), Evelyn Ankers (Claire Caldwell), Frank Craven (Dr. Harry Brewster), J. Edward Bromberg (Professor Lazlo), Adeline De Walt (Queen Zimba).

Whether Jack Palance or Lon Chaney, Jr., is the worst possible choice to play Dracula is a debate that will probably go on forever. And yet *Son of Dracula,* in which Chaney stares woodenly and indifferently at the camera or at his fellow actors and actresses, is a film that no horror enthusiast should miss. For one thing, it is the first of the Dracula films to have an American regional setting. Beyond that it continues to enlarge the film mythology of Dracula that was first begun by Universal's *Dracula's Daughter* in 1936.

Katherine Caldwell, a young Tennessee woman who is interested in the occult, has returned from Europe. There she became fascinated by a Hungarian nobleman named Count Alucard whom she has invited to her family's plantation. A friend of the Caldwell family, Dr. Brewster, and Frank Stanley, Miss Caldwell's fiance, go to the train station to meet the count who, apparently, is not on the train. But Dr. Brewster notes that a considerable quantity of the count's luggage, including some coffin-sized boxes, has arrived and that if one reads ''Alucard'' backward one gets an interesting name.

Alucard has in fact arrived, and while we wait for him to make his formal appearance we see Katherine Caldwell visiting a Hungarian seer named Queen Zimba whom she has brought back from Hungary with her. The clairvoyant Queen Zimba tries to warn Katherine about some impending horror: "I see you," she says, "marrying a corpse and living in a grave." But even as she talks a large cloth-and-wire device, doing what it can to play the role of a bat, appears chirping overhead. Moments later, Queen Zimba is dead of a heart attack.

From here on, the film moves rapidly through the stages of its by no means uninteresting plot. Katherine, though she loves Frank Stanley, suffers so severely from thanaphobia (a fear of death) that she has arranged to marry Count Alucard because she believes his promise that, "Ours will be a different life, without material needs. A life that will last throughout eternity." Katherine, however, is banking on being slyer than Alucard. While she fully expects to be turned into a vampire, she plans, once she has been immortalized by the count, to have Frank destroy the Hungarian. As she explains it to Frank, "Count Alucard is immortal. Through him, I attained immortality. Through me, you will attain it." After that they will live happily undead forever.

But Frank, though he loves Katherine, finds the whole scheme loathsome and, guided by what Dr. Brewster has learned from vampire expert Professor Lazlo, Frank outwits both Katherine and Alucard.

Son of Dracula, despite its weaknesses, is really rather wonderfully atmospheric. The European dry horror represented by Dracula mingles effectively with the dark, swampy ambience of rural Tennessee. One final point: As the film comes to its grim close, J. Salter's music becomes increasingly romantic and tender. It is a brilliant touch.

SON OF FRANKENSTEIN   Film
1939 (B&W) U.S.A. 95 min.
Production Company: Universal; *Director:* Rowland V. Lee; *Producer:* Rowland V. Lee; *Screenplay:* Willis Cooper; *Photography:* George Robinson; *Editor:* Ted Kent; *Music:* Frank Skinner.
Cast: Basil Rathbone (Baron Wolf von Frankenstein), Boris Karloff (the Monster), Bela Lugosi (Ygor), Lionel Atwill (Inspector Krogh), Josephine Hutchinson (Elsa Von Frankenstein).

Universal Pictures was fortunate with the idea of Frankenstein during the thirties. The three films the studio made— *Frankenstein* (1931), *Bride of Frankenstein* (1935) and *Son of Frankenstein*—were each achievements of the very highest, though not of equal, rank. If I were to arrange them in an order of excellence I would place *Bride* first, *Frankenstein* second and *Son* third. However one orders them, it is clear that these films have established a kind of 20the-century folklore. They are images that have become part of the psychological baggage of our time.

Son of Frankenstein, though it has little depth, is the liveliest of the three films. It has, like the others, an intelligent script and superior casting, and director Rowland V. Lee respects the values that guided James Whale in his work. For the most part the screenplay follows the formula of the previous films—creation followed by mayhem followed by destruction and then, after a cliffhanger moment, safety for the good guys. But it also introduces two figures that have proved unforgettable: the broken-necked Ygor and the prosthetic-armed police inspector Captain Krogh, whose natural arm,

we are told, the Creature plucked out by the roots. "But for this," says the inspector, "I who command seven gendarmes in a little mountain valley might have been a general."

Basil Rathbone as Wolf von Frankenstein, son of the late and ill-famed Baron Frankenstein, is supple and sensitive, a vast improvement on Colin Clive in the parallel role. Bela Lugosi, as Ygor, has considerably more depth to him than the Fritz who brought back a criminal brain for the first Baron Frankenstein to work with. And Lionel Atwill, the cold police inspector with his strut, his stiffness, his clockwork movements and his mechanical arm that (by no means accidentally) mimics a Hitler salute, is a priceless addition to Frankenstein film legendry. Josephine Hutchinson, as Elsa von Frankenstein, is given very little to do beyond occasionally comforting her husband and dutifully mothering little Dieter.

The story of the film is simple enough: The young baron, Wolf Von Frankenstein, a research scientist working in the United States, is informed that he has inherited his father's title and his estate. He and his wife and their son Dieter return to the family village where, in a driving rain, they are met but—pointedly—not greeted by the village notables, including the burgomaster and Inspector Krogh, who make it clear that the village considers all the Frankensteins harbingers of evil.

We learn early that the young baron thinks his father was maligned. He says to his wife, "It wasn't my father's fault. It was the unforseen blunder of a stupid assistant."

Ygor, reveals to the new baron that the Creature is still alive but lying sick near a sulfur pool in the ruins of the old mill across the ravine. Ygor, speaking over the soundtrack's poignant, brooding music says:

> "He's my friend. He does things for me . . . This is the place of the dead. We are all dead here. Now he's sick. Make him well."

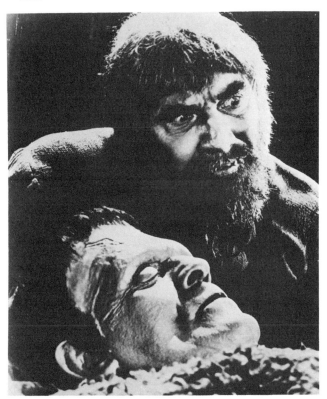

Bela Lugosi (top) and Boris Karloff in **Son of Frankenstein.**

The challenge excites the young baron and he is soon launched on the old career. But once the Creature is restored to health his monstrosity (no matter that it is not his fault) manifests itself. In the concluding scene, he confronts Inspector Krogh and they play out their ancient animosity: The Creature, in one of the film's more wonderful moments, plucks off the inspector's prosthetic arm as once he plucked the living limb away.

One needs to say a word or two about the sets in this film. There are vast, brooding stairways that cast ominous mechanical shadows, medieval halls with towering ceilings and high, impossibly high windows that dwarf all human behavior. And there are landscapes that are perpetually drenched in rain or fog, preparing us, like all of the other sets, for the ominous that inevitably comes.

THE SPECTRE BRIDEGROOM   Short Story
Alexa.

Great Britain

1890, London, Dean and Munday; reprinted 1976 in *The Spectre Bridegroom and Other Stories*, R. Reginald and Douglas Menville (eds.), New York: Arno Press.

Written in the ecstatic, hyperbolic mode of 19th-century fear fiction, ''The Spectre Bridegroom'' is the story of two young noblemen, Count Rudolph von Swarzburg and his cousin, Count Albert von Sinnern, who, while hunting a lost and dearly loved falcon in the Hartz Mountains of Germany, come upon the beautiful but mysterious Christalina. It turns out that Christalina with whom young Albert falls in love, is a creature of the damned—*la belle dame sans merci*. But Albert, overwhelmed by her beauty, vows a secret oath to marry her. Later, he foolishly makes a more appropriate marriage with his lovely cousin, Clara. Foolishly, because Christalina is not about to take such an affront lightly. ''Handsome stranger! . . . My love for you knows no bounds and it therefore requires a love as ardent and sincere in return. I require all, or nothing!'' What follows is grim and spectral.

It is unclear what pun, whether on ''Christ'' or on ''crystal,'' the pseudonymous author intended by naming his demonic creature Christalina.

THE SPIDER   Short Story
Hanns Heinz Ewers

Germany

1921, in *Nachtmar*; translated and reprinted 1979 in Leonard Wolf's (ed.) *Wolf's Complete Book of Terror*, New York, Clarkson N. Potter.

When, on two successive Fridays, two guests in room number 7 of a small hotel in Paris commit suicide by hanging themselves on the crossbar of the room's window, the hotel's landlady, Mme. Dubonnet, asks the police for help. The inspector of police posts one of his officers, Charles-Maria Chaumié, in the room. For several days, Chaumié reports that there is nothing unusual in the room, but at around six o'clock on Friday afternoon, he too is found hanged, just like the room's previous occupants.

> The dead man's mouth was wide open, and his tongue protruded from it. [And later] when the police removed Sergeant Charles-Maria Chaumié's body from the window crossbar a large black spider crawled from the dead man's open mouth.

The police, then, have a mystery on their hands. A mystery that the medical student Richard Bracquemont has volunteered to help solve. Bracquemont's journal reporting his activities in the dreadful room is the dramatic center of Ewers' weirdly erotic tale.

Bracquemont moves into the room on Sunday evening, the 27 of February. He is provided with a telephone, a pistol and a police whistle. As he observes in his first journal entry dated Monday, February 25, ''I see no reason to be afraid.'' By the time we get to his last entry, dated Friday, March 25, there is more than enough fear to go around.

For a week the journal entries are unimportant. Then Bracquemont tells us of the existence of ''Clarimonda,'' the name he has given to the beautiful woman he sees in a room in the building just across the street from his hotel. Clarimonda:

> sits only before the window that looks into mine. She sits there, spinning on an old-fashioned spindle . . . She works all day behind her curtains, and stops spinning only as the sun goes down . . . Her hair is black and wavy; her face pale. Her nose is short and finely shaped with delicate nostrils that seem to quiver. Her lips, too, are pale; and when she smiles, it seems that her small teeth are as keen as those of some beast of prey . . . she always wears a black dress embroidered with a lilac motif . . .

From here on, Bracquemont is in something of an erotic trance, spending hours watching Clarimonda at her window. Finally, the two communicate mutely with each other:

> We have invented a strange game, Clarimonda and I. We play it all day long. I greet her; then she greets me. Then I tap my fingers on the windowpanes. The moment she sees me doing that, she too begins tapping. I wave to her; she waves back. I move my lips as if speaking to her; she does the same . . .

To his horror, Bracquemont discovers that, ''I don't play with Clarimonda. She plays with me.'' And now the theme of the deadly mating of spiders that has only been hinted at becomes overt. From here on only the manner of the deadly climax toward which the story is building is in doubt.

Rarely in horror literature is the male fear of women quite so obviously or so brilliantly exploited as in ''The Spider.'' Fear, fascination, loathing, desire are what Clarimonda excites:

> Clarimonda makes a movement and I resist it or as long as I can. Then I give in and do what she wants without further struggle. I can hardly express what a joy it is to be so conquered; to surrender entirely to her will . . . No, Fear is no longer what I feel. Rather, it is a sort of oppressive terror which I would not want to avoid for anything in the world. Its grip is irresistible, profoundly cruel, and voluptuous in its attraction.

There is a very kinky imagination at work here. But readers who have read Ewers' *The Vampire* or *Alraune* already know that.

THE SQUAW   Short Story
Bram Stoker

Great Britain

1914, in *Dracula's Guest*, London, Routledge; reprinted 1979 in Leonard Wolf's (ed.) *Wolf's Complete Book of Terror*, New York, Clarkson N. Potter.

Bram Stoker, the author of *Dracula*, indulges himself in "The Squaw" in a display of broad humor that almost obscures the story's excellence.

As the story begins, we learn that the narrator and his wife are in the second week of their honeymoon in Germany. In the course of a visit they pay to the castle at Nürnberg, they meet an elderly American named Elias P. Hutcheson, "hailing from Isthmian City, Bleeding Gulch, Maple Tree County, Neb." Stoker portrays Hutcheson as a broadly comic character out of a Mark Twain novel.

At one point, when he and his British friends observe a cat and her kitten at the bottom of a 60-foot wall, Hutcheson, meaning nothing more than to startle the kitten, drops a pebble from the wall. But the pebble falls right on the kitten, killing it instantly.

> The black cat cast a swift upward glance, and we saw her eyes like green fire fixed an instant on Elias P. Hutcheson . . . Her green eyes blazed with lurid fire.

It is an unfortunate incident, but when the cat from that moment begins to follow Hutcheson, we sense that something sinister has now been set in motion.

Later, Hutcheson and his friends are shown the medieval torture instrument knows as the "Iron Virgin." The Iron Virgin, as everyone knows, is a hollow structure shaped vaguely like the human form. It is covered by a door:

> " . . . of equal thickness and of great weight, for it took the custodian all his strength, aided though he was by the contrivance of the pulley, to open it . . . [it had] long spikes, square and massive, broad at the base and sharp at the point, placed in such a position that when the door should close the upper ones would pierce the eyes of the victim, and the lower ones his heart and vitals."

Hutcheson, a man avid for sensation, is immediately determined to have himself tied up and introduced into the device so that he can experience, in safety, some of the feelings of its medieval victims. Once bound and inside the device he tells us:

> "Wall! . . . I guess I've not had enjoyment like this since I left Noo York. Bar a scrap with a French sailor at Wapping—."

It is while Hutcheson is chortling that the black cat, who has been steadfastly following the tourists since the death of her kitten, leaps—but not at Hutcheson.

"The Squaw" is admirably and complexly constructed. A close reader will find that Hutcheson, beneath his clichéd, bluff exterior, is a perfectly repulsive man who deserves whatever punishment his author has invented for him. But Stoker's subtlest touch is to have his story told by a young honeymooner whose bride, because of Hutcheson, is overwhelmed with too much knowledge about the disasters that can overtake children.

SQUIRM — Film

1976 (C) U.S.A. 92 min.
Production Company: The Squirm Company; ***Director:*** Jeff Lieberman; ***Producer:*** George Manasse; ***Screenplay:*** Jeff Lieberman; ***Photography:*** Joseph Mangine; ***Editor:*** Brian Smedley-Aston; ***Special Effects:*** Bill Milling, Don Page; ***Music:*** Robert Price.
Cast: John Scardino (Mick), Patricia Pearcy (Gerri Sanders), R.A. Dow (Roger Grimes), Jean Sullivan (Naomi Sanders), Peter MacLean (Sheriff Jim Reston).

The squishy subtext of this more than satisfactory (if occasionally slow-moving) film is the children's rhyme that we remember with varying degrees of revulsion and/or delight:

> I'm going out into the garden and eat worms—
> Big worms, round worms, fat worms, juicy worms.
> The first one was easy,
> The second one was greasy,
> The third one wiggled as it wriggled down my throat.

Jeff Lieberman, the film's director, delays our full encounter with his slimy villains until very near the end of his picture. But even without seeing more than a handful of worms, we have by then become so worm-alert that the sight of friendly people eating spaghetti in a restaurant sets our teeth on edge and our stomachs roiling.

Lieberman's script makes neat use of such fairly stereotyped characters as Mick, the New Yorker who falls in love with a biddable small town beauty named Gerri, who has a gawky teenage sister named Naomi and a vague and nearly dotty widowed mother. Other characters include Roger, a somewhat slow-witted admirer of Gerri's; Sheriff Jim Reston, who is your usual yokel sheriff; and various other Georgia countryfolk with pleasing accents.

But the worms are the squirming center of the plot. A three-day storm has cut high tension lines in the vicinity of the small town that is the scene of the action, and hundreds of thousands of volts of electricity are being pumped into the soggy soil. The massive doses of electricity are turning inoffensive Georgia bloodworms, until then useful as bait for fish, into ravenous and wildly multiplying creatures who do awful things at night and then withdraw without a trace in daylight.

It is given to Mick and Gerri to discover just how horrible the worms are. They have considerable bad luck in their battle against this new plague. First, the sheriff, suspicious of strangers and wildly incompetent as a law man, has taken an unreasoning dislike to Mick; second, Roger, jealous of Mick for having stolen Gerri's affections, turns into a human enemy who has finally to be disposed of; and third, Gerri's mother declines from simple dottiness into full-blown madness. Given the number of obstacles our young heroes have to overcome, we are not altogether surprised that the worms come pretty close to total victory before a passing electrician and daylight turn the vermicular tide.

The real fun of *Squirm*, however, has little to do with either its plot or its characterizations. No. It is the worms. Chattering liquidly on the sound track. Coming through the openings in the shower head. Falling like gouts of blood from the ceiling. Pullulating in what seem to be their billions in a bath tub; cascading like brooks, then rivers, then like a vast Niagara under the scrutiny of the camera lense. Worms . . .

"Big worms, fat worms, round worms, juicy worms . . ."

SREDNI VASHTAR — Short Story

Saki (Pseudonym of Hector Hugh Munro)
Great Britain
1911, in *The Chronicles of Clovis*, London & New York, John Lane; reprinted 1976 in *The Complete Works of Saki*, New York, Doubleday.

Children and adults seem sometimes to be living in different worlds that are at war with each other. Children are likely to imagine that they are perpetual losers in that ongoing war, and it is to comfort them, I think, that Saki wrote "Sredni Vashtar."

Conradin is an ailing 10-year-old boy whose cousin and guardian, Mrs. De Ropp, tyrannizes over him in a particularly brutal fashion. For whatever murky reasons of her own, Mrs. De Ropp allows Conradin to keep a pet: "A ragged-plumaged Houdan hen . . ." But Conradin has, also, a secret pet, a polecat-ferret named Sredni Vashtar whom he worships "with mystic and elaborate ceremonial . . . Red flowers in their season and scarlet berries in the winter-time were offered at his shrine . . ." When Mrs. De Ropp, exercising her mean adult prerogatives sells the hen—for Conradin's own good, of course—the boy prays to his polecat:

"Sredni Vashtar went forth,
His thoughts were red thoughts and his teeth were white.
His enemies called for peace, but he brought them death."

Conradin's just and terrible God hears the prayer, and the results, from a child's point of view, are terrifying and satisfactory.

A STRANGE STORY   Novel
Edward George Bulwer-Lytton
Great Britain
1861, London, Sampson Low; reprinted 1973, Berkeley, Calif., Shambala.

This endlessly fascinating Victorian novel of the occult is a treasure trove for students of terror fiction, for whom Bulwer-Lytton provides a nearly perfect guided tour through the best of what was thought and said about possession, hypnotism, thought transference and alchemy in mid-19th-century England.

Bulwer-Lytton tells the story of Doctor Ashleigh Fenwick, a brilliant physician and biological researcher who loves and marries the beautiful young Lillian. Their lives are touched by the malevolent schemes of a man named Margrave. Margrave, who is part sorcerer, party hypnotist, part Faust figure, believes himself to have discovered the Elixir of Life, but he has been unable to make a sufficient amount of the precious liquid to extend his existence for the centuries through which he means to live. For that, he involves the Fenwicks in his dark schemes. Most of the novel turns on Ashleigh Fenwick's struggle to free his fragile wife from Margrave's satanic influence.

Though Lytton invents unforgettable characters, he does not always use them well. There is the extraordinary Mrs. Colonel Poyntz, for example, as wise, as stern and as sensitive a social arbiter as ever dominated a novel. And yet she simply disappears from *A Strange Story* well before the book's climax. There is also the ubiquitous and charming Margrave who is only with difficulty linked to the rest of the novel's action.

Bulwer-Lytton's tale suffers from another disability: Its author, like Ann Radcliffe before him, is determined to find rational explanations for all the occult phenomena that fascinate him. The result is that the reader is frequently tugged between those emotions that the supernatural is likely to elicit in a work of fiction, and those that one associates with realistic stories. . . . Long, frequently lugubrious and occasionally contradictory as the novel is, it comes nevertheless to a crashing climax in the wilds of Australia. In those moments, fear overwhelms all other emotions and the reader's long wait for a dark repast is rewarded.

T

TASTE THE BLOOD OF DRACULA   Film

1970   (C)   Great Britain   95 min.

Production Company: Hammer; *Director:* Peter Sasdy; *Producer:* Aida Young; *Screenplay:* Anthony Hinds (as John Elder); *Photography:* Arthur Grant; *Editor:* Chris Batnes; *Special Effects:* Brian Johncock; *Music:* James Bernard.

Cast: Christopher Lee (Dracula), Geoffrey Keen (William Hargood), Gwen Watford (Martha Hargood), Linda Hayden (Alice Hargood), Peter Sallis (Samuel Paxton), Anthony Corlan (Paul Paxton), Isla Behr (Lucy Paxton), John Carson (Jonathan Secker), Martin Jarvis (Jeremy Secker).

Despite its sickly title, *Taste the Blood of Dracula* is one of the best of the Hammer vampire films. Certainly for pure petrification, its opening scene is unmatchable.

That scene, which picks up the Dracula saga where it left off in *Dracula Has Risen From the Grave*, shows a seedy traveling salesman named Wella being thrown from a coach by a couple of sinister travelers (whom we never see again). Wella picks himself up and, hearing horrid screams nearby, he follows their sound and stumbles upon a pit at whose bottom Count Dracula, skewered by the blade of what appears to be a huge metal cross, is shrieking as he expires. The camera brings its fish-eye lens to bear on Christopher Lee's face, distorting it even as we see his red-filmed eyes and strangely crowded teeth. Then the camera moves back and we see the agonized vampire dwindling into a pool of blood beside his cloak and a silver broach bearing his name. The canny Wella, always alert to a possible profit, gathers up the count's remains, including much of his blood.

The scene now shifts to the town of Carlsbad where we meet Hargood, Secker and Paxton, a trio of wealthy, respectable, middle-aged hypocrites who once a week pursue secret vices together. These men, at the instigation of a young satanist named Courtney, buy Count Dracula's remains from Wella. Courtney dies in the course of a ritual resurrecting of the count, who then vows vengeance on the three hypocrites for having murdered his disciple.

It is now that the plot thoroughly thickens as the three old reprobates tyrannize their children. There are definite sexual nuances between the fathers and the daughters, and Count Dracula avenges himself on the fathers by contriving their deaths and by vampirizing their daughters

In addition to its hidden incest agenda, its smashing opening scene and the usual opulence of a Hammer vampire film, *Taste the Blood of Dracula* has a striking resurrection sequence in an abandoned chapel that needs to be seen for what it is—a stunning parody of the Christian mystery of communion.

THE TATTOOER   Short Story

Junichiro Tanizaki

Japan

1963, in *Seven Japanese Tales,* tr. and ed. Howard Hibbett, New York, Knopf.

Readers of Roald Dahl's "Skin" will find it pleasing to compare that yarn with Tanizaki's tale of a tattooer. The two stories share the theme of the intricate, indeed vital, relationship of art to life.

In Tanizaki's story, the protagonist, Seikichi, is a tattoo artist who lives in some unspecified era, when "People did all they could to beautify themselves, some even having pigments injected into their precious skins. Gaudy patterns of line and color danced over men's bodies."

Tanizaki tells us that, "the young tattooer concealed a secret pleasure, and a secret desire. His pleasure lay in the agony men felt as he drove his needles into them, torturing their swollen, blood-red flesh." And all of his life, he has harbored a great ambition, "to create a masterpiece on the skin of a beautiful woman." For many years, he has searched for such a woman among the beauties of the city. At last, in the fourth year of his search he catches a glimpse of a woman's bare, milk-white foot and knows that, "this [is] the foot of the unique woman who had so long eluded him."

The following year, the fortunate Seikichi finds the possessor of that foot. She is a 15- or 16-year-old beauty whom he tries to seduce to his purpose by showing her a couple of Chinese scrolls in which beautiful women are depicted savoring the torment and the death of men. "All these men will ruin their lives for you," whispers Seikichi. The young girl replies, "Yes, I admit that you are right about me . . .." Just the same, she tries to leave his studio, but the unscrupulous artist drugs her and then settles down to create his masterpiece:

> Little by little the tattoo marks began to take on the form of a huge black-widow spider; and by the time the night sky was paling into dawn this weird, malevolent creature had stretched its eight legs to embrace the whole of the girl's back.

When he is done, the girl's shuddering breath stirs the spider's legs as if they were alive. When she wakes, and has bathed, "Her eyes were brilliant: there was not a trace of pain in them," and when she knows what Seikichi has done for her she knows that she has entered into her cruel reign. She knows, too, who will be her first victim.

"The Tattooer," even in translation, is a disturbingly sensual tale in which the ancient theme of the deadliness of erotic beauty is mingled with that other theme of how much human suffering is required to make a work of art. What is wonderful here is that at the climactic moment of the story the roles of the artist and his victim are suddenly reversed. It is an irony that is almost as cruel as the rest of the tale.

TCHÉRIAPIN   Short Story
Sax Rohmer
Great Britain
1922, in *Tales of Chinatown*, London, Cassell; reprinted 1979 in Leonard Wolf's (ed.) *Wolf's Complete Book of Terror*, New York, Clarkson N. Potter.

Here is an unforgettable story of vengeance by Sax Rohmer, who, in the days when racial stereotyping flourished in popular literature, created the redoubtable Dr. Fu Manchu. In this story, the stereotyping is diluted to some degree. Tchériapin, virtuoso violinist and the villain of the piece, is a Eurasian; his father was a Chinese nobleman and his mother a Polish ballet dancer.

We hear the story as the first narrator hears it from a stranger in a caped overcoat who tells it to him in a tawdry Singapore bar named Malay Jack's. The principal characters are Tchériapin, an unscrupulous womanizer, Andrews (also knows as Colquhun), formerly a great painter but now a down-and-out alcoholic, the stranger in the overcoat, and a woman whom we do not meet but who is part of the story's design.

At Malay Jack's the stranger in the overcoat shows the first narrator a jewel in which is embedded "a tiny pink rose, no larger than the nail of my little finger." The rose is perfect in every detail, "the frail leaves were exquisitely green. Withal, it was as hard and unbendable as a thing of steel." This curious jewel, we learn, was produced by a process developed by the famous chemist, Dr. Kreener, before Kreener died in a dynamite factory explosion. We learn further that Kreener's friends included Tchériapin, "a little black haired man," as well as Andrews, "a great, red-bearded, unkempt Scotsman," who instinctively detested the violinist. When, one day, Tchériapin recounted boastfully how he had seduced and then abandoned the woman who had served the painter

Colquhun as the model for his greatest painting, Andrews leapt for Tchériapin's throat and strangled him, because, as we discover, Andrews was Colquhun and the model, who "killed herself with absinthe . . . in Marseilles . . .," was the love of his life.

The pieces of the story now fall obligingly into place. The story is set in Singapore because that was the port of lost souls. The stranger in the overcoat turns out to be Kreener who is looking after Andrews/Colquhun, who is still an alcoholic. As for Tchériapin, he too is in Singapore but in a form that qualifies this story for inclusion in a list of horror tales.

What makes "Tchériapin" wonderful is the presence in it of the immortalized rose as well as a certain wild strain of music. These two elements, set in the seedy ambience of Malay Jack's in Singapore, give a surprisingly lyric lilt to a story that otherwise would have only its peculiarity to recommend it.

THE TELL-TALE HEART   Short Story
Edgar Allan Poe
U.S.A.
1843, in *The Boston Pioneer*; reprinted 1981 in Stephen Peithman's (ed.) *The Annotated Tales of Edgar Allan Poe*, New York, Doubleday.

"The Tell-Tale Heart" is cast in the form of a dramatic monologue that, if it were not pitched at a level quite so near hysteria, would remind us of Browning. Indeed, as memorable and powerful as the story is, its tone, meant to reveal the speaker's madness, is as melodramatic as Jack Nicholson's performance in *The Shining*. It is a prose style that, right from the start, depends on interjection and frequent repetition. "Ha!" cries the narrator or, "You fancy me mad," or, "True!—nervous—very, very dreadfully nervous I had been . . ." and, ". . . he has found all in vain. All in vain . . . ."

Despite such mannerisms that eventually push the story well beyond melodrama, Poe manages to convince us that his protagonist is afflicted with hyperacute hearing and a monomania in whose grip he is driven to murder his friend:

> who had never wronged me. He had never given me insult. For his gold I had no desire. I think it was his eye! yes, it was this! One of his eyes resembled that of a vulture—a pale blue eye, with a film over it.

The description of how that murder is accomplished is what the rest of the story is about. Poe heightens the suspense surrounding the event by brilliantly delaying every slightest action so that, while we lean forward prepared to gasp at what we see, the narrator moves at a pace several times slower than slow motion. Only after eight nights of careful preparation is the deed finally accomplished.

Here, as elsewhere in Poe, the story seems simple: A monomaniac confesses the details of a murder arising out of his fixation and then, driven by guilt, contrives his own destruction. But the simplicity is deceptive. Into this straightforward story Poe intrudes an element that gives it unexpected depth, the deep sympathy the narrator has for his victim's fear:

> Presently I heard a slight groan, and I knew it was the groan of mortal terror. It was not a groan of pain or of grief—oh, no!—it was the low stifled sound that arises from the bottom

of the soul when overcharged with awe. I knew the sound well. Many a night, just at midnight, when all the world slept, it has welled up from my own bosom, deepening with its dreadful echo, the terrors that distracted me.

It is that sympathy that makes the murderer seem to be something more than a monomaniac so that we wonder what sound, beside that of his victim's heart, the murderer meant to still. Wordsworth, to reassure us, imagined that if we listened well we might hear, "The still, sad music of humanity." Poe seems to be saying that the rhythm of that music is set by the drumbeat of fear.

THE TENANT
Film

(Alternate release title: **LA LOCATAIRE**)
1976   (C)   France   126 min.
Production Company: A Roman Polanski Film; *Producer:* Andrew Braunsberg; *Screenplay:* Gerard Brach, Roman Polanski; *Director:* Roman Polanski; *Photography:* Jean Harnois; *Editor:* Francois Bonnot; *Music:* Philippe Sarde.
Cast: Shelley Winters (Concierge), Melvyn Douglas (landlord), Roman Polanski (Trelkovsky), Isabelle Adjani (Stella).

The Tenant is properly a companion piece to Polanski's earlier study of madness, *Repulsion* (1965). Though the film as a whole is as unsettling as a horror masterpiece should be, there are three moments in it that are likely to prove unforgettable: Mme. Shul's dying scream in the hospital; the vision of her as a mummy unwinding her bandages in the bathroom; and the three or four final minutes of the film.

The story begins in Paris where a young architect's assistant named Trelkovsky (played by Polanski) rents an apartment whose previous tenant, Mme. Simone Schul, an amateur Egyptologist, attempted to commit suicide by throwing herself out of the apartment window.

Trelkovsky, diffident to the point of inertia, is intrigued by Mme. Shul's suicide attempt and visits her in the hospital where, swathed in bandages, she lies dying. There he meets her friend Stella, with whom he establishes a fitful and somewhat kinky relationship. As the film progresses, two lines of development begin to converge: Trelkovsky, as he learns more and more about Shul, finds himself taking on one or another of her characterisitcs; and at the same time the extraordinarily petty persecution to which his neighbors subject him, mostly because he is a foreigner, begins to erode his self-esteem. The process is so slow and the details so apparently normal that we have the illusion, for the longest time, that nothing unusual is happening. That everyone lives in an environment as destructive as Trelkovsky's. Then we perceive that the tiny increments of change that have been taking place in him are parts of a portrait of madness in which neither we nor Trelkovsky are any longer able to distinguish between fact and fantasy. At the film's climax, Trelkovsky, in no way like the man we met at the beginning, shouts at his persecutors, "You wanted a clean death. Well, it's going to be dirty." It is a cry of hopeless rage from one who has by then succumbed to the essential griminess of things.

We have had glimpses of Polanski's dark vision of the world in *Repulsion,* in *The Fearless Vampire Killers* (1967) and in *Rosemary's Baby* (1968). Here, in *The Tenant,* a film that the critics have not especially liked, Polanski, both as an actor and as a director, is at his most uncompromising best.

THE TEXAS CHAIN SAW MASSACRE
Film

1974   (C)   U.S.A.   84 min.
Production Company: Bryanston Pictures; *Producer:* Tobe Hooper; *Screenplay:* Kim Henkel, Tobe Hooper; *Director:* Tobe Hooper; *Photography:* Daniel Pearl; *Editor:* Sally Richardson, Larry Carroll; *Music:* Tobe Hooper, Wayne Bell.
Cast: Marilyn Burns (Sally), Allen Danziger (Jerry), Paul Partain (Franklin), William Vail (Kirk), Terri McMinn (Pam), Edwin Neal (hitchhiker), Jim Siedow (gas station attendant), John Dugan (old man), Gunnar Hanson (Leatherface).

There are few films that fulfill so impeccably the first imperative of the horror genre: Be horrifying. What is amazing, and admirable, is the way that Hooper, who has a truly original mind and in this film an extraordinary sureness of touch, varies the pitch of his film's horror, from high-decibel hysteria to low-key monotonic. He has an eye, and an ear, for the sort of casual detail that gives authenticity to a scene: the mindless windshield washer reflexively washing windshields at a gasoline station that sells no gas; the bit of torn and wrinkled newspaper that wraps a madman's grisly talismans; the clucking of a hen on a veranda littered with feathers and human bones.

The plot of *The Texas Chain Saw Massacre* almost fulfills the Hollywood formula for a youth-oriented horror film: Put some attractive young people of both sexes together and then endanger their lives. Here, the young people driving a van through the Texas countryside on a hot day are two attractive couples, Sally and Jerry, and Pam and Kent. With them is Sally's wheelchair-bound and perpetually whining brother, Franklin. Franklin, who is fat and unhappy and fully aware that he is an encumbrance on the other four, is anything but a formulaic figure and it is his presence in the story that gives it depth.

The young people are looking for an old farm that once belonged to Sally and Franklin's grandfather. Various rednecks give them directions to the farm, but as they drive they pick up a very unprepossessing hitchhiker whose behavior is so bizarre that they get rid of him.

Arrived at the deserted farm, the two couples go off to explore the empty house, leaving Franklin to mumble bitterly about being left alone. Later, Pam and Kent decide to look for a swimming creek said to be nearby. They go off and find a strange house on an adjoining farm. And it is there, and under appalling circumstances, that this Texas chain saw massacre begins. In a scene that is at once frightful and reticent, Leatherface, a mask-wearing, aproned killer, the most active member of a whole family of psychopaths, attacks Kent with the chain saw and later, offhandedly, deposits a shrieking Pam on a meathook hanging from the ceiling.

From here on the film plunges from one moment of dread to another. When Jerry comes to look for Pam and Kirk, he is dispatched by Leatherface. Later, in the dark, a desperate Sally, pushing Franklin in his wheelchair, encounters Leatherface. The chase sequence that follows, the only weak segment in this film, seems to last forever because of Sally's nonstop screaming, which only ends when she has taken refuge in the gasoline station where the attendant turns out to be Leatherface's milder mannered but equally deadly brother.

Back in the house of the dead, the whole mad family gathers. There the ancient grandfather, Leatherface, the cackling hitchhiker and the gasoline station attendant, now clearly revealed as cannibals, gather around Sally and quarrel about how to dispatch her.

Sally pulls free and escapes from the house. There follows a final flight sequence in which she is pursued to the highway by the hitchhiker and Leatherface, whose chainsaw is revved up again.

All the footage from the time Sally breaks from the house, can be seen as an extraordinarily effective *danse macabre*. It is here that Tobe Hooper's feeling for stylized gesture, which we have seen exercised at intervals throughout the film, comes fully into play. It is a dance whose movements are as precise and formal and as instinct with death as those in a bullfight. There are sudden rushes, swift turns, beautifully timed escapes, all framed by the hysteria of the real moment. The last image we have before the screen darkens is that of the thigh-wounded Leatherface dancing a mad solo on the highway as he leads the bloodlust music of the world with his chainsaw for a baton.

THEM!   Film
1954 (B&W) U.S.A. 94 min.
Production Company: Warner Brothers; *Director:* Gordon Douglas; *Producer:* David Weisbart; *Screenplay:* David Sherdeman, from a story by George Worthington Yates; *Photography:* Sid Hickox; *Editor:* Thomas Reilly; *Special Effects:* Ralph Ayers; *Music:* Bronislau Kaper.
Cast: James Whitmore (Sgt. Ben Peterson), Edmund Gwenn (Dr. Harold Medford), Joan Weldon (Dr. Patricia Medford), James Arness (Robert Graham), Onslow Stevens (Brig. Gen. O'Brien), Sean McClory (Major Kibbee), Fess Parker (Crotty).

Of the spate of films that appeared in the fifties in response to the lowering presence of the atomic bomb, *Them!* is still one of the best and most memorable.

The film opens with an understated sequence in which a five- or six-year-old girl is seen carrying a doll and walking dazedly through the New Mexican desert in the vicinity of atomic weaponry test sites. When the police find her, she is in shock. Later, when policemen stop at a general store in the neighborhood, they come upon the corpse of Chris, its proprietor, in the cellar. Nothing has been stolen from the store but sugar, and the camera takes a quick look into a sugar bowl to show us a few circling ants.

Peterson, a vacationing FBI man, involves the Alamagordo office of the FBI in a subsequent investigation, and shortly thereafter, when large amounts of formic acid are found in the body of one of the victims, Dr. Harold Medford ("That old bat is one of the world's greatest myrmecologists,") and his daughter, Dr. Patricia Medford, also a scientist, are bought in to advise the FBI.

The doctors Medford give the dazed little girl a whiff of formic acid. She blinks, screams, then runs to crouch in a corner of the room screaming, "Them, them, them." A while later, out in the field, Patricia Medford is the first person to see what the enemy is like: a humongous ant, eight to 15 feet long, standing four to six feet high. It has a humanoid eye and, when sufficient firepower is mustered against it, it bellows as it dies. The older Doctor Medford opines: "A fantastic mutation probably caused by lingering radiation from the atomic bomb." This new breed of colossal ant is about to bring its feeding habits to bear against humanity.

Dr. Harold Medford, who, with his tiny steel-rimmed glasses and slightly professorial talk, reminds one of a latter day Dr. Van Helsing of Dracula fame, urges the powers that be to search for the ants' nest and to destroy the queen. At last all the nests have been destroyed except one that is somewhere in the Los Angeles sewage system. Somehow, a couple of angelic children, a boy and a girl, have wandered into the sewer. The army's goal, then, is to save the children and destroy the ants. In the process, the film comes to its rousing conclusion.

Them! is a treat. Doggedly focused on its considerably inventive plot, it moves through its 94 minutes in what feels like military double time. The sense of danger is beautifully heightened by giving the giant ants a sibilant and highly musical war cry of their own, which early in the film establishes their ominous presence. The giant ants, though rather primitive in comparison with post-1980 movie technical effects, nevertheless have sinister waving antennae and gleaming black carapaces so tough that only flamethrowers and large caliber weaponry are able to penetrate them. The penultimate scene in the ant queen's egg chamber is still vivid enough to have served the makers of *Aliens* as a model worth imitating.

THEY CAME FROM WITHIN   Film
(Alternate release title: **THE PARASITE MURDERS**)
1976 (C) Canada 94 min.
Production Company: Trans-American; *Director:* David Cronenberg; *Producer:* Ivan Reitman; *Screenplay:* David Cronenberg; *Photography:* Robert Saad; *Editor:* Patrick Dodd; *Special Effects:* Joe Blasco; *Music:* Ivan Reitman.
Cast: Barbara Steele (Betts), Paul Hampton (Roger St. Luc), Joe Silver (Rollo Linsky), Lynn Lowry (Forsythe), Susan Petrie (Janine Tudor), Alan Migicovsky (Nicolas Tudor).

They Came From Within is in the scientist-meddling-with-life film tradition. This time a scientist with erotic problems of his own develops a parasite that, traveling from mouth to kissing mouth, drives its human host into sexual ecstasy. In an extraordinary scene, the scientist, repenting what he has done, destroys the young woman whom he has infested with his love "thing." The "thing," one of director David Cronenberg's less happy inventions, looks like an unattached, very bloody and very single-minded penis whose sole instinct is to wriggle toward the nearest male or female orifice. In any case, the scientist, unable to kill the parasite he has developed, promptly kills himself.

The parasite multiplies and infests the residents of a Montreal apartment complex for singles. Most horrible of all, some of those infected are not themselves killed. Instead, they become carriers who pass the organism on to those with whom they come in contact. One by one, husbands and wives, single women and bachelors, old people and children are attacked until they form a frenzied orgiastic crowd. As the film ends, one senses that all of Montreal is about to be transformed into a sexually steaming Canadian Sodom.

There is a dark allegory about the disaster of love hidden, not too successfully, in this film. Love, or love-making or sex—whichever it is—in Cronenberg's vision is a red, wet, repulsive screen monster and it is a clear and present danger to humankind.

THE THING   Film
(Alternate release title: **THE THING FROM AN-
OTHER WORLD**)
1951   (B&W)   U.S.A.   87 min.
Production Company: Winchester Pictures/RKO; *Director:*
Christian Nyby; *Producer:* Howard Hawks; *Screenplay:* Charles
Lederer; *Photography:* Russell Harlan; *Editor:* Roland Gross;
Special Effects: Linwood Dunn, Donald Stewart; *Music:* Dim-
itri Tiomkin.
Cast: Margaret Sheridan (Nikki), Kenneth Tobey (Captain
Hendry), Robert Cornthwaite (Dr. Carrington), Douglas
Spencer (Scotty), James Young (Lt. Eddie Dykes), William
Self (Corporal Barnes).

When military headquarters in Anchorage, Alaska, receives
a radio message from a scientific outpost near the North Pole
that a strange craft has landed in its vicinity, a team headed
by Captain Henry, and accompanied by a balding newsman
named Scotty, flies out to investigate.

What they find is a huge crater that has been made by a
craft that looks like a flying saucer. The investigators notice
that as they approach the craft, now buried in ice, it sets their
magnetic compasses to spinning ("As if twenty thousand
tons of steel or iron had been dumped there.") Unable to get
at the buried ship they get ready to use thermite bombs to
melt the ice. One of the scientists says, "A few minutes from
now and we may have the key to the stars. A million years
of history are waiting for us in that ice." With that, some
malevolent intelligence explodes the space ship and, "It's all
gone. Secrets that might have given us a new science. All
gone."

Not quite all. The investigators find a "thing" frozen in a
slab of ice. A thing that looks like a man, has legs and a head,
and is over eight feet long. Before the film is done, it will
have wreaked havoc among the researchers.

For a while, it seems unkillable. It is able to regenerate
itself, and also to propagate itself by seeds it plants and
nourishes with blood. When the science-mad Dr. Carrington,
who believes that "knowledge is more important than life,"
raises such seeds so that he can study their plants, he sets in
motion the catastrophe that the rest of the film develops.

What finally saves the few survivors of the creature's
depredations is a suggestion one of the women makes. In a
final scene we see the thing reduced, electronically, to steam.

A moment later, we are warned to, "Tell the world to
watch the skies. Keep looking. Watch the skies."

Despite the passing of the flying saucer craze that preoccupied people in the fifties and that is the background against
which the film is set, *The Thing* holds its own as a horror film.
Compounding its fear is the fact that you never quite see "the
thing" (until the final scenes), but you are made terribly
aware of how malevolently alive it—or any part of it—is.
Finally, the film's setting in the polar wastes is especially
effective as it turns the drama of the few people isolated there
into a cautionary fable of how dangerously ill-equipped we
are to face either ourselves or the suddenly not-so-distant
rest of the universe.

In 1951, women characters in the movies, even when they
were "brilliant scientists," looked pretty, poured coffee and
encouraged their men. In this regard, *The Thing* is no exception, though it is a woman's kitchen wisdom that produces
the idea that saves them all.

In 1982, John Carpenter directed a color version of *The
Thing*. His film has some remarkable scenes in which we see
"The Thing" doing its bloody work, but the black and white
film, with all its reticence, is much scarier.

THE THING IN THE CELLAR   Short Story
David H. Keller
U.S.A.
March 1932, in *Weird Tales;* reprinted 1977 in Peter Haining's
(ed.) *Deadly Nightshade*, New York, Taplinger.

Every so often a story comes along whose absolute simplicity is such an important aspect of its truth that it leaves us
with our mouths open in amazement. "The Thing in the
Cellar" is like that.

From the time that Tommy was a baby, he hated to be in
the kitchen of his family's home because that's where the
door to the cellar was, and Tommy always knew that there
was something evil down there. Something that would get
him.

When Tommy is old enough to go to school, his parents,
worried that he may be teased for his fears, consult Dr.
Johnson about what to do. The doctor gives this sage advice:

> "I tell you what to do. He thinks there is something there.
> Just as soon as he finds that he is wrong, and that there is
> nothing there, he will forget about it. He has been humoured
> too much. What you want to do is to open that cellar door
> and make him stay by himself in the kitchen. Nail the door
> open so he cannot close it. Leave him alone there for an hour
> and then go and laugh at him . . ."

Tommy's parents, to their confusion, follow the doctor's
advice and make Tommy stay in the kitchen for an hour with
the cellar door nailed open. In the meantime, Dr. Johnson
consults Dr. Hawthorne, a psychiatric colleague, who tells
him:

> "This Tucker lad may have a nervous system that is peculiarly
> acute. He may dimly appreciate the existence of something in
> the cellar which is unappreciable by his parents . . ."

As for Dr. Johnson's advice, Dr. Hawthorne concludes,
"Sorry, old man, but I think it was perfectly rotten."

Indeed it was. As readers discover when they come to the
end of this classically simple tale.

THE THING ON THE DOORSTEP   Short Story
H.P. Lovecraft
U.S.A.
January 1937, *Weird Tales;* reprinted 1967 in *Three Tales of
Horror* by H.P. Lovecraft, Sauk City, Wis., Arkham House.

The first-person narrator of "The Thing on the Doorstep"
tells us right from the start that, "It is true that I have sent six
bullets through the head of my friend, and yet I hope to show
by this statement that I am not his murderer." To make his
point, he tells us the rest of the story, which involves his
relationship with Edward Derby, the murdered man, and
Asenath Waite, the strangely vital 22-year-old woman who
married Derby when he was 39 years old.

Asenath Waite, one of the rare female characters in H.P.
Lovecraft's fiction, was the child of Ephraim Waite, a sorcerer
and demon worshiper, "by an unknown wife who went
veiled." This last remark is Lovecraft's way of hinting that

Asenath was the offspring of intercourse between Ephraim Waite and some unspeakable life form.

The necromancer Ephraim, we learn, died mad (or, at least, mysteriously), leaving behind his astonishing daughter who is herself an adept of dark acts. When Edward Derby, a lifelong bachelor and a retiring, neurasthenic student of the occult, meets Asenath he is overwhelmed by her and marries her.

From here on, the story describes how four lives, Ephraim's, Asenath's, Edward's and the narrator's intertwine to form a tragic design. It is an account of the way the demonic force incorporated in Ephraim Waite perpetuates itself from generation to generation. The story of the near triumph of evil is interesting for its own sake, but it becomes especially powerful as it is informed by Lovecraft's unique vision of humankind sharing the world with loathsome primordial peoples whose remnants still exist among us.

But "The Thing on the Doorstep" has a further and quite disturbing sexual resonance. First, there is the bizarre father-daughter link as we learn that Ephraim has transferred his own evil energy into his daughter's body; then there is the husband and wife struggle as Asenath, who is by now Asenath-Ephraim, battles for dominance over the will, and eventually the body, of Edward Derby. There is, furthermore, the intimacy between the narrator, Daniel Upton, and Edward Derby, which is so profoundly endangered by Derby's marriage to Asenath that it can only be preserved by firing six bullets into the usurped body of Upton's lifelong friend.

L. Sprague de Camp, in his *Lovecraft: A Biography*, suggests that Asenath is based on Sonia Greene, Lovecraft's wife, or on his mother "who had done him the most harm." Given the tangle of feelings, most of them sexual, for which the story is an armature, what comes through most clearly is that "The Thing on the Doorstep" is one more manifestation of Lovecraft's distrust or (as I think) fear of women.

THRAWN JANET   Short Story
Robert Louis Stevenson
Great Britain
1887, in *The Merry Men*, London, Chatto & Windus; republished in Pritchett, V.S., *Novels and Stories by Robert Louis Stevenson*, Duell, Sloan and Pearce, New York, 1946

In northern English and in Scottish dialect, "thrawn" means twisted or crooked and the "Thrawn Janet" of Stevenson's story is surely one of the most memorable twisted creatures in all of horror literature. This is especially curious because Stevenson gives his story an edge of irony that almost nudges it toward downright humor. What saves it is a single petrifying image.

The story is set in Scotland in 1712 and its central character is the Reverend Murdoch Soulis who had come to his parish of Balweary 50 years before the time when we meet him. At that time, says the parishioner who is the main narrator of the story, he was "fu' o' book learnin' and grand at the exposition, but, as was natural in sae young a man, wi' nae leevin' experience in religion."

If he had no living experience of religion then, by the story's end he has acquired more than his due and we understand how it is that now he is, "A severe, bleak-faced old man, dreadful to his hearers . . . [his] eyes was wild,

scared, and uncertain . . . his eye pierced through the storms of time to the terrors of eternity."

In his youth, the Reverend Soulis, meaning to do a kindness, ignored the rumors rife in his parish that Janet M'Clour, a local old hag, was "sib to the deil" and that "bairns had seen her mumblin' to hersel' up on Key's Loan in the gloamin, whilk was an unco time an' place for a God-fearin woman . . ." The Reverend Soulis, to reassure his parishioners, asks the old hag publicly to renounce the devil and all his works. She does so and is struck dumb for her pains and her face acquires an uncanny leer.

Despite all these warnings, the Reverend Soulis, confident that he lives in the age of reason, lets it be known that "the devil was mercifully restrained" and employs Janet as his household servant.

The scene in which the Reverend Soulis finally learns just how wrong he is is certain to set a reader's hair on end. Not so much because it is a surprise but because the image of the event, as Stevenson gives it to us, is at once apt and strange and demonic.

THE THREE INFERNAL JOKES   Short Story
Lord Dunsany
Ireland
1916 in *Tales of Wonder*, London, Elkin Mathews; reprinted 1972 in *Gods, Men and Ghosts, the Best Supernatural Fiction of Lord Dunsany*, New York, Dover.

In this compact tale, organized very much like a joke itself, Dunsany exploits the black humor implicit in the sentence: "I will tell you a thing that will make you die of laughter." The "thing," however, turns out to be a cruel study of the power of sex, which is never more dreadful than when it is absent.

Like a great many late-19th and early-20th-century British fictions, "The Three Infernal Jokes" is refracted through a first-person narrator who tells the story as he heard it from the inoffensive encyclopedia salesman to whom the events happened.

That salesman, spurred by the boasts of his fellow clubmen in a seedy London club, utters a boast of his own. He says that to him, "One woman [is] as ugly as another." That virtue if it is one, turns out to be wonderfully attractive to the denizens of Hell who, when they come to hear of it, persuade him to sell it to them in exchange for three jokes whose power is that "anyone else who hears them will simply die of laughter . . ." Our salesman forgets about the transaction until one night, finding the jokes on a slip of paper in his pocket, he thinks to tell one of them to his fellow club members. The joke, which he himself thinks is banal, does precisely what its seller promised. Twenty-two club members as well as the dining room waiters die laughing. The salesman, certain that he will be blamed for the deaths, makes a brief escape but he is captured and brought to trial. To save himself, he tells the second joke.

As our tale ends, we understand why Dunsany opened his story with a scene of the kind of desolation and mood we associate with Thomas Hardy.

> The saddening twilight, the mountain already black, the dreadful melancholy of the [rutting] stag's voice, his friendless mournful face, all seemed to be of some most sorrowful play staged

in that valley by an outcast god, a lonely play of which the hills were part and he the only actor.

The moment of grimmest humor comes at the end when we realize that the salesman is still possessed of his third and final joke. Who knows whose awful destiny it may be to hear it?

"The Three Infernal Jokes" is crisply written, clear and direct and a fine corrective for readers who know Dunsany only by such overblown, if charming, fictions as "The Fortress Unvanquishable Save For Sacnoth."

THUS I REFUTE BEELZY   Short Story
John Collier
Great Britain
May 1931, in *Harper's*; reprinted 1973 in *The John Collier Reader*, New York, Knopf.

John Collier's tight little story of a child and his playmate Beelzy makes very satisfying reading.

Big Simon, Small Simon's father, beats his son to teach him to avoid the delights of fantasy. What dreary Big Simon wants is for his son to grow up to be the sort of dreary, rational lout that he, Big Simon, is. Luckily for Small Simon, and unfortunately for his father, Small Simon has Beezlebub for a friend. The odds, of course, are stacked in the boy's favor and all of us who have ever been children oppressed by big people will applaud the rousing climax of this tale, which has a finer predecessor in Saki's "Sredni Vashtar."

THE TINGLER   Film
1959 (B&W) U.S.A. 82 min.
Production Company: Columbia/Castle; **Director:** William Castle; **Producer:** William Castle; **Screenplay:** Robb White; **Photography:** Wilfrid M. Cline; **Editor:** Chester W. Schaeffer; **Music:** Von Dexter.
Cast: Vincent Price (Doctor Warren), Judith Evelyn (Mrs. Higgins), Philip Coolidge (Ollie Higgins), Darryl Hickman (David Morris), Patricia Cutts (Isabel Chapin), Pamela Lincoln (Lucy Stevens).

Vincent Price, in an extremely sympathetic role (for him), plays a research surgeon who believes that human fear nourishes the "tingler," a creature that lives along our spinal columns. It is a creature that can kills us, unless we scream.

That simple bit of contrived medical theory is all that holds *The Tingler* together, but the plot is made more complicated by a few twists: Dr. Warren (Price) has a rich and frequently unfaithful wife who keeps him on a leading string; and we are made to believe for a while that Price has terrified a deaf-mute woman to death for the sake of his research. The theory, we are told, is that her inability to scream will give the "tingler" the opportunity for its fullest development and Price, then, will be able to remove it surgically from her body.

The Tingler was marketed as a gimmick movie. In its opening scene, William Castle appeared to announce the medical theory that would be espoused in the film, and he urged the audience to scream at frightening moments as a way of keeping the tingler under control. In some movie theaters around the country, seats were wired to give patrons a mild electric shock at scary moments in the film.

Despite all the gimmickry, and the essential silliness of its

medical theory, *The Tingler* has survived as a first-rate and quite congenial scary film. There is a certain brilliance in the plot idea of a deaf-mute frightened to death because she cannot scream. The laconic dialogue goes well with the crisp and unpretentious black and white photography. Price says: "OLLIE, your wife is dead. I'm sorry."

Ollie replies, "I wasn't much of a husband." And when Ollie's wife sits-up, Ollie says, "She moved!" And the well-bred Price says, "May I find out why?"

And so it goes.

Even the reiterated commands to scream are still part of the fun, just as they were in 1959. Some of the fun comes, too, from the pathetic appearance of the tingler itself, which looks as if it were designed by a first-year special effects student who was not doing very well. It is made of rubber and can't make up its mind whether it is a snail, a centipede or a lobster.

TO THE DEVIL A DAUGHTER   Novel
Dennis Wheatley
Great Britain
1953, London, Hutchinson; reprinted 1968, New York, Bantam.

Christine (or Ellen—she has both names) Mordant, a young woman who is not quite 21 years old, has been placed in hiding by her father in a house on the Riviera. She has no idea what the danger is from which her father means to protect her. However, she is befriended by her next-door neighbor, Molly Fountain, a writer of mystery novels, and Molly's son, John. They, in turn, call in Colonel "Conky" Bill Verney, a former British secret service agent whose specialty, when he is not ferreting out communists, is satanism.

Christine, it is observed, seems to have two personalities, a daytime and a nighttime self. By day she is sweet, shy, wholesome; at night she is flamboyant and more than a little erotic. When Molly Fountain, acting on intuition, throws a small gold crucifix at her, Christine catches it and then drops it as if her hand had been scorched.

And that is the key to her mystery. When her father, a wealthy manufacturer named Beddows, was a young man he not only sold himself to the devil, but he also gave his daughter a satanic baptism and promised to turn her over to an arch-satanist named Canon Copley-Syle, who needs her for a particularly infernal purpose. Copley-Syle has managed to create homunculi, human-shaped creatures in his laboratory of black magic, but he must sacrifice a virgin on her 21st birthday before the most complex of his homunculi can be made to function. The virgin he wants is the one promised him long ago: Christine-Ellen.

Copley-Syles' plot, in the best tradition of the penny-a-liner fiction by which Dennis Wheatley was most influenced, is foiled, unfoiled and foiled again by the combined efforts of the Fountains, mother and son, and Colonel C.B. Verney. The novel, heavy-footed for the most part, seems to be startled awake in its last 30 or 40 pages, and we are hurried to a squirming denouement and an ending that is as smoky and sweet as glazed ham.

To the Devil a Daughter is seriously marred by its dogged puritanism (". . . sexual promiscuity is the first step toward greater evils . . ."), its coy macho attitudinizing and a singularly graceless prose ("As we are going to walk, I think I will put on a pair of thicker shoes."). On the other hand, we get quite a bit of fascinating folklore about Satan and about Alastair Crowley, the wunderkind of British satanism in the twenties. We get, too, a central premise that is both ingenious and compelling.

THE TOMB OF LIGEIA
Film
(Alternate release titles: **HOUSE AT THE END OF THE ROAD, LIGEIA, LAST TOMB OF LIGEIA**)
1964 (C) U.S.A./Great Britain 79 min.
Production Company: American International/Alta Vista; ***Director:*** Roger Corman; ***Producer:*** Roger Corman; ***Screenplay:*** Robert Towne; ***Photography:*** Arthur Grant; ***Editor:*** Alfred Cox; ***Special Effects:*** Ted Samuels; ***Music:*** Kenneth V. Jones. *Cast:* Vincent Price (Verden Fell), Elizabeth Shepherd (Rowena/Ligeia), John Westbrook, (Christopher Gough), Derek Francis (Lord Trevanion), Richard Vernon (Dr. Vivian).

In Ed Naha's *The Films of Roger Corman* (p. 182), Corman says that *The Tomb of Ligeia:*

> "was the last of my Poe pictures. I stopped because I was tired of doing them. I tried to make this last film as different from its predecessors as possible . . . It was also the first Poe picture shot on location, outside of conventional studios. It showed the real world . . . For the first time ever, the sun shone on the works of Edgar Allan Poe."

The Tomb of Ligeia, then, is something of a farewell gesture on Corman's part and it shows signs of special care. Robert Towne's script borrows its tone (though by no means its content) from Poe so that one of the pleasures of this film, in addition to the fine photography and its Gothic ambience, lies in hearing Poe's prose cadences coming from the screen. Vincent Price's performance as the neurasthenic Verden Fell is exceptionally careful. Price always understands his role, but here he seems actually to be possessed by it.

The plot of the film is only vaguely like that of Poe's short story. There is Verden Fell, the sensitive husband (not named in Poe) who is grief stricken at the death of his wife, Ligeia. The camera, peering into her coffin, lets us see that Ligeia's eyes have flickered. A while later, we see that a black cat, perched on the tomb, has become a silent sentinel, guarding it.

The inconsolable Fell comes upon the beautiful Lady Rowena, who in the course of a fox hunt has been thrown from her horse. He helps her to safety, and before very long he falls in love and marries her. The marriage, we learn, has its macabre elements. By day, though he is abstracted, Verden Fell tries his best to be the husband of the living Rowena. At night, because Ligeia hypnotized him before she died, Fell visits his dead wife in her tomb. When Rowena tries to put an end to this macabre *ménage à trois* she precipitates a catastrophe.

The black cat, borrowed from an altogether different Poe story, has the last word.

THE TOOLBOX MURDERS
Film
1977 (C) U.S.A. 95 min.
Production Company: Cal/Am; ***Director:*** Dennis Donnelly; ***Producer:*** Tony Didio; ***Screenplay:*** Neva Friedenn, Robert Easter, Ann Kindberg; ***Photography:*** Gary Graver; ***Editor:*** Nunzio Darpino; ***Music:*** George Deaton. *Cast:* Cameron Mitchell (Kingsley), Nicholas Beauvy (Joey Ballard), Tim Donnelly (Detective Jamison), Aneta Corsaut (Joanne Ballard), Pamelyn Ferdyn (Laurie Ballard), Wesley Eure (Kent).

The Toolbox Murders belongs to the comparatively new genre of slice-and-dice or splatter films, but if one may risk the pun, it is a cut above the usual films in its class.

In its opening sequence we see a car moving through darkened streets. A hand reaches for a toolbox. We are then in an apartment where the same hand plucks flowers from a flower pot. The camera then watches feet in black shoes, then it slants a look at the green toolbox. A woman greets the as-yet unseen man, "I called you Monday. You show up on Thursday." With that, the owner of the toolbox knocks her out, then he activates his drill and we see the bit cutting through her dress. And more.

There is no need to summarize the details of his subsequent murders. They are what one would expect in a splatter film. What makes this one more interesting is the way it shifts abruptly and becomes for a little while a psychological thriller.

The murderer, whose name is Kinsley, kidnaps a teenager named Laurie and keeps her tied up in a bed in an apartment he owns. There, under the insane illusion that she is his daughter who died in an automobile accident, he brings her lollipops, brushes her hair, and confides to her the motive for his murders: "It's such a bad world. It's evil. Full of evil. If you get rid of the evil, all that's left is good." He feeds Laurie tenderly and, calling her Kathy, he reassures her: "That will never happen to you. The others. They were all committing unnatural acts with each other."

The entire conversation between him and Laurie-Kathy has an insane verve as Laurie pretends to participate in his fantasies so that she can get him to loosen her bonds a bit. He talks to her about her own death, "Tell me, did it hurt much when God took you away from me?" "No," Laurie replies. "No. No. Dying is easy. It's over in a second. But this [indicating her bonds] hurts worse."

As the film ends, we get a gratuitous twist in the plot that, nevertheless, brings us to some of its best moments. A clean-cut youngster named Kent Miller, who is the murderer's nephew, suddenly turns out to be as mad as his uncle. With his entry into the plot, the pace of the film's violence turns hysterical. He drenches Joey, Laurie's brother, in gasoline and throws lighted matches at him. Later, as Kent lies beside her in an anguished parody of bridal night pillow talk, Laurie, to free herself, makes bloody use of a pair of shears.

Then Laurie escapes and we enter fully and finally into the haggard nightmare of the city. Here the filmmakers, as if to redeem the essential shabbiness of their venture, reach for a moment toward excellence, as Laurie, in a blue nightgown, moves through the evening streets of a blue Los Angeles toward the film credits. A perfect hallucinatory ending for an utterly mad film.

TOUSSEL'S PALE BRIDE
Short Story
W.B. Seabrook
U.S.A.
1929, in *The Magic Island,* New York, Harcourt Brace; reprinted 1974 (1931) in Montague Summers' (ed.) *The Supernatural Omnibus,* New York, Causeway.

Here is a clammy death-and-the-maiden story with a Haitian setting that W.B. Seabrook uses effectively to introduce voodoo folklore.

At first, "Toussel's Pale Bride" is a traditional January-May story. The beautiful young Camille, a "fair-skinned octoroon girl . . ." from a family that cannot afford to give her a dowry, is given in marriage to:

Matthieu Toussel, a rich coffee-grower from Morne . . . He was dark and more than twice her age, but rich, suave, and well educated.

The trouble is that Toussel is rumored to be affiliated in some way with voodoo, but at first that, seems not to affect the marriage in any way. Then on the evening of their anniversary, Camille wakes at midnight to find her husband at her bedside. "Put on your wedding dress and make yourself beautiful," he tells her. "We are going to a party."

At the party there are four guests in a room that has:

an elegantly set table with damask cloth, flowers, glittering silver. Four men . . . in evening clothes but badly fitting, were already seated at this table. The seated men did not rise when the girl in her bride-clothes entered on her husband's arm. They sat slumped down in their chairs and did not even turn their heads to greet her.

Toussel, oddly constrained and hesitant, urges Camille to forgive the rudeness of his guests. He tells her that:

"presently . . . they will drink with you. Yes, lift . . . their arms, as I lift mine . . . clink glasses with you . . . more . . . they will arise and . . . dance with you . . . more . . . they will . . ."

What follows is the purest of horrors as Seabrook tightly braids innocent beauty with death and madness. What we are not told, and curiously enough do not mind not knowing, is precisely what Toussel had been planning for his bride when he designed his grim banquet. What we do know is bad enough.

TRILOGY OF TERROR   TV Film
1975 (C) U.S.A. 72 min.
Production Company: American Broadcasting Company; *Director:* Dan Curtis; *Producer:* Dan Curtis; *Screenplay:* W.F. Nolan ("Julie" and "Milicent and Therese") and Richard Matheson ("Amelia"), all based on stories by Richard Matheson; *Photography:* Paul Lomann; *Editor:* Les Green; *Special Effects:* Richard Alraine, (puppet master) Erik von Buelow; *Music:* Robert Cobert.
Cast: Robert Burton (Chad), George Gaynes (Dr. Ramsey), Karen Black (Julie, Milicent, Therese, Amelia).

This three-part made-for-television film is two-thirds fine entertainment and one-third sheer genius.

What we have are three stories whose title roles are all played by Karen Black. "Julie" is a repressed-looking, dowdy young instructor whom an egocentric student named Chad decides it might be kinky fun to seduce. Since he is handsome, glib, confident and unscrupulous enough to drug his victim, he has his way with Julie and takes the kind of photographs of the event that only a blackmailer would contrive. He confronts Julie with the pictures, only to discover too late whose idea the entire scenario really was. When, as he is losing consciousness, he says, "You've drugged me," Julie replies, "No dear. I've killed you." And indeed, she has.

"Milicent and Therese," the least successful of the three tales, is a pretty predictable, if grim, two-faces, economy version of *The Three Faces of Eve.* As "Milicent and Therese" ends, we hear Doctor Ramsey intoning, "I knew her very well. She had the most advanced case of dual personality ever encountered . . ."

The third tale, "Amelia," is absolutely stunning. This time Karen Black surpasses herself in the role of a somewhat mousey New York woman in her late twenties who, we are given to understand, has finally had the courage to move out of her mother's home and into a sub-leased apartment. We see her coming home to this apartment early Friday evening with an old wooden case from which she takes out a fierce-looking doll representing a Zuni warrior. The doll, identified in the scroll that has come with it as "He-who-kills," is intended as a birthday present for the anthropology professor whom Amelia is dating.

Amelia sets the doll down on a coffee table and then lifts the phone to confront her devouring mother. In the three or four minutes of painfully accurate dialogue that follow the unheard mother and Amelia exchange guilt, guilt-provocations, love and not so skillfully disguised animosities as the mother lets Amelia know how irresponsible and unfeeling she is for wanting to break their usual Friday date because Amelia has promised to celebrate her anthropologist's birthday with him. The mother, of course, wins the unequal battle, and it is then that Amelia, having hung up the telephone, looks for, but cannot find, "He-who-kills."

A moment later, they find each other and the shrieking, screeching, bloody, frenzied and furious battle that follows between the suddenly animated and viciously armed Zuni doll and the already more than half defeated woman is one of the great achievements in the history of the horror film. Amelia is ingenious and spunky as she defends herself against her impossible antagonist. She traps it in a suitcase from which it whittles its way out; she locks herself away from it in her bathroom; she drowns it in her bathtub; when it sinks its rows of razor-sharp teeth into her arm she smashes it against a lamp. All the while that the battle rages, its teeth are in continual motion and from its throat there emerge perfectly imagined malevolent sounds. And as it chitters and chatters, its wicked little knife whirls away at her until, in a leap that requires both dexterity and wit, she traps it in her glass-fronted oven where we finally see it, still mouthing its horrible sounds, enveloped in flames.

But the story is not yet over. When it ends, there is a transformation and a promise of poetic justice soon to come.

Trilogy of Terror, especially the "Amelia" segment, is surprising TV fare. A sophisticated film for adults, it is a three-fold triumph that displays Richard Matheson's imagination, Dan Curtis' directorial skill and Karen Black's versatility. The film, however, would not be quite the tour de force that it is without the furious life that puppet master Erik von Buelow has imparted to the Zuni warrior.

THE TURN OF THE SCREW   Novella
Henry James
U.S.A.
1898, in *The Two Magics,* London, Heinemann; reprinted 1970 in *The Turn of the Screw and Other Stories* by Henry James, New York, Penguin.

Henry James's classic ghost story (if it is one) continues to be one of the more intriguing as well as genuinely frightening stories even written. This, despite the famous laminated prose style that as James defines and refines his ideas and language, demands a reader's undivided attention. The effort, of course, is worth it. James, working with the tiniest increments of fear, slowly builds a catastrophic design. When, finally, the climax of the tale does come—an event delayed and delayed until almost the final couple of paragraphs—the reader is left shaken by what has been suddenly revealed . . . and perhaps even more shaken by what the narrator, with apparent artlessness, has concealed.

James's story has two narrators, the first, presumably James himself, who merely introduces the tale by describing how on a leisurely English countryhouse weekend he came to hear the story that will soon follow. Preliminary though these pages are, they are by no means unimportant since they establish a long chain of sympathies and curiosity about the second narrator that have a considerable effect on us when we come to the tale itself.

That story purports to be an account, written years after the events it describes, by a governess employed to supervise the education of a couple of orphaned children, Flora and Miles, who are eight and ten, respectively. The children's uncle, young, wealthy, charming, attractive and, the main thing, clearly irresponsible, gives the 20-year-old governess free rein in the supervision and education of the children. All he asks is that he get "no reports." He wants absolutely never to be bothered by any of the details or problems that overtake real children in the real world. Dazzled by her employer's charm (and, no doubt, by his person), the governess accepts the cruel charge in the spirit of an emotionally untutored young woman who has dreamed of seizing heroic opportunities and who believes she has one now before her.

At her employer's Essex countryhouse, the governess meets Mrs. Grose, the comforting and deferential, illiterate housekeeper, and then her two charges, Flora and Miles, who as James describes them are altogether more beautiful and apparently good than human children are ever likely to be. At the same time, we learn that Miles, for reasons that are fiercely unspecified, has been dismissed from the boarding school to which he had been sent.

And now the uncanny enters the tale. The governess one warm afternoon catches sight of a man standing in a tower of the old house. Later, she glimpses the same man staring into the schoolroom window. Mrs. Grose, when she hears the man described, identifies him as Peter Quint, her master's valet. The trouble is that Quint is dead, killed while stumbling home drunkenly from a pub.

Mary (left) and Madeleine Collinson are the **Twins of Evil.** © Hammer Films

Some while later, the governess catches a glimpse of another stranger, a woman. She is identified as Miss Jessel, the children's former governess, who was notorious for having lowered herself by having an affair with Peter Quint. But Miss Jessel, we learn, is also dead.

From this point on, the narrator conceives herself to be locked in a deadly struggle with the two ghosts. As she understands it, the ghosts want to corrupt the souls of the children and the governess, heroically, single-mindedly wants to prevent them from succeeding, though occasionally she has flashes of recognition that the children are already deeply compromised.

What James wants is for the struggle to transcend the somewhat limited bounds of the ghost story and to take on moral, spiritual and psychological dimensions. Eventually, what James wants he gets. What is wonderful in the enterprise is that the *frisson*, the shudder, which is after all the point of a terror tale, remains.

The Innocents, a film version of ''The Turn of the Screw,'' appeared in 1960.

TWINS OF EVIL   Film
(Alternate release titles: **THE GEMINI TWINS, VIRGIN VAMPIRE, TWINS OF DRACULA**)
1971   (C)   Great Britain   87 min.
Production Company: Hammer; *Director:* John Hough; *Producer:* Harry Fine, Michael Style; *Screenplay:* Tudor Gates; *Photography:* Dick Bush; *Editor:* Spencer Reeve; *Special Effects:* Bert Luxford; *Music:* Harry Robinson.
Cast: Peter Cushing (Gustav), Mary Collinson (Maria), Madeleine Collinson (Frieda), Dennis Price (Dietrich), Kathleen Byron (Katy Weil), Damien Thomas (Count Karnstein), David Warbeck (Anton).

It is sometime in the 17th century. In the town of Karnstein, whose chief nobleman is the wicked and vampiric Count Karnstein, Gustav Weil is a stern witchfinder, a member of a brotherhood that scours the countryside for attractive young women to burn at the stake. A pair of well-endowed and recently orphaned nieces from Venice come to live with Gustav and his wife. One of the twins, Maria, is good and proper; her twin, Frieda, is fit for a whole gamut of sins and crimes to which, very soon, she is led by Count Karnstein.

There is a gentle and upright young man named Anton, who, with his sister, teaches in a school for young women. Anton falls in love with Maria; Count Karnstein vampirizes Frieda; and Gustav is shaken by the discovery that one of his nieces is a vampire. All sorts of terrible things are about to happen, but Anton, who has been studying vampirism, finally persuades Gustav that beheading and the stake, not fire, are the only ways to destroy vampires. Gustav leads an aroused mob to Karnstein castle where first Frieda and then Count Karnstein meet the doom they have richly earned, the first at Gustav's hands and the second at Anton's.

Hammer Films' particular contributions to the horror film genre are deep-bosomed young women in décolleté, men on horseback riding through woods on moonlit nights, heavy emphasis on the Freudian implications of sex, truly luxurious color and highly literate film scripts. *Twins of Evil* runs true to Hammer form with the distinction that this time, instead of one deep-bosomed young woman in décolleté as a protagonist we have two. The presence of the twins, one of whom is good while the other is evil, puts a bit of snap into an otherwise well-worn plot.

U

THE UNDYING MONSTER   Film
(Alternate release title: **THE HAMMOND
MYSTERY**)
1942 (B&W) U.S.A. 63 min.
Production Company: 20th Century-Fox; ***Director:*** John
Brahm; ***Producer:*** Bryan Foy; ***Screenplay:*** Lillie Hayward,
Michel Jacoby; ***Photography:*** Lucien Ballard; ***Editor:*** Harry
Reynolds; ***Music:*** Emil Newman, David Raksin.
Cast: James Ellison (detective), John Howard (the heir),
Heather Angel (heir's sister), Heather Thatcher (Dr. Watson).

The Undying Monster is a family curse film that is set on the
Cornwall coast in England in the dark and rambling Hammond family mansion. As the story begins, Walter, an old
family retainer, is looking out at the night and worrying: ''It's
cold and bright outside. I only hope Mr. Oliver doesn't come
through the lane tonight.'' And then we hear the warning
that goes with the family curse:

> When stars are bright
> On a frosty night
> Beware thy bane
> On a rocky lane.

Shortly after this, there is the howling of what may be a
dog. Then a flurry of action in the course of which we learn
that Oliver Hammond has left the laboratory of his friend and
physician Doctor Jeff Cove and that Oliver's dog has been
killed and a young woman named Kate O'Malley has been
horribly mutilated. Oliver says that he saw ''something coming at us from all sides at once. It closed in on me like a blast
from a furnace . . . The monster is never satisfied . . . Unless
we destroy it, it will destroy us.''

A scientist, Robert Curtis, and his colleague, Cornelia
Christopher, who work for Scotland Yard are assigned to the
case. Their presence introduces familiar horror film questions:
Does the evil that has overtaken the house have an occult
source, as family legend suggests, or is there a scientific

explanation for the murders that, over several generations,
have occurred in the family on bright and frosty nights?

The film, when it ends, comes down on the side of science
and the curse turns out to be an inherited disease of the blood
that transforms its victim into a werewolf on bright, cold
nights. But it's only the plot that takes us to this conclusion.
John Brahm, the director of *The Undying Monster*, as if he was
aware of how trivial his film would be if left only to its plot,
has all the while been performing a curious and altogether
admirable directorial sleight of hand with tone and atmosphere.

The trick, which is extremely subtle, consists of an interplay
between the events in which the people are involved and the
nervous activity of the physical world in which they are set.
Brahm, as if meaning to fight the rationalist plot he was
given, moves our eyes toward the craggy coast below the
house so that moonlight and darkness, the drifting of clouds,
the restlessly pounding sea and the jagged rocks resisting it
will, with their natural grandeur, elicit respect for powers so
vast that finally we will experience them, despite the plot, as
supernatural. As a result, we do not feel as cheated by the
glib scientific explanation of the film's lycanthropy as we
might otherwise be.

THE UNEARTHLY   Film
1957 (B&W) U.S.A. 73 min.
Production Company: Republic; ***Director:*** Daniel Hall; ***Pro-
ducer:*** Brook L. Peters; ***Screenplay:*** Geoffrey Dennis, Jane
Mann; ***Photography:*** Merle Connell; ***Music:*** Henry Varse,
Michael Terr.
Cast: John Carradine (Professor Charles Conway), Allison
Hayes (Grace Thomas), Myron Healy (Mark Houston), Mar-
ilyn Buferd (Doctor Gilchrist), Tor Johnson (Lobo), Sally
Todd (Natalie).

Charles Conway is a mad doctor who collects people who
have no relatives so that he can perform experimental surgery
on them. By implanting a 17th gland into the bodies of his

victims, he hopes to produce permanently youthful immortals. For the time being, he has succeeded only in bungling and there is a someone named Jedro who sits in the basement and does absolutely nothing at all. Dr. Conway is aided in his work by a woman doctor who is passionately, and jealously, in love with him, as well as by a massive cretin named Lobo.

One virtue of this film is that it lets us see John Carradine at work exploiting the dry, sinister good looks, thin to the point of gauntness, that helped make his career. Its second virtue is that it has one of the most bizarre endings ever filmed.

UNICORN TAPESTRY   Short Story

Suzy McKee Charnas
U.S.A.
1981, in *Vampire Tapestry,* New York, Timescape; reprinted 1987 in Alan Ryan's (ed.) *Vampires,* New York, Doubleday.

"Unicorn Tapestry" is easily the most intriguing, most complex and, finally, the most pleasing vampire short story to have been published in recent decades. Firmly placed within that most contemporary of modern settings, the psychotherapeutic 50-minute hour, the story terrifies precisely because the therapist-patient relationship has hostility (among other feelings) deeply rooted in it. When this patient, who is tall, muscular and good looking, announces "I seem to have fallen victim to a delusion of being a vampire" and the therapist who is a woman in her mid-forties, has vulnerabilities of her own that leave her anything but secure, we have, one way or another, clear and present danger.

The therapist is named Floria. She is divorced, the mother of a grown daughter who has a child of her own. Professionally, she is at or near the height of her career, with two good books to her credit and a flourishing practice. She is, however, at a crisis point in her own life at which she is reconsidering, to use the jargon of her profession, both her commitments and her options.

Weyland, her vampire patient, whom she at first jokingly calls Dracula, is a "gaunt but graceful figure . . . impressive. Wiry gray hair, worn short, emphasized the massiveness of his face with its long jaw, high cheekbones, and granite cheeks grooved as if by winters of hard weather." He has been sent to her for therapy as a condition for being rehired as a professor of anthropology at Cayslin College where a woman, defending herself against one of his vampiric attacks, shot and severely wounded him. Cayslin College, in a spasm of bureaucratic rationality, wants a note from a therapist asserting that he is cured before it will let him come back to his teaching position.

What Weyland does have, and what proves unsettling to his therapist, is an absolutely focused conviction that he is what he is—a vampire, a unique, perhaps non-human figure whose goal is survival, whose means are his hunting skills and whose food is human blood.

What makes "Unicorn Tapestry" a triumph is that, very quickly, we understand that Weyland's blood drinking is relevant without being essential to the story. We never do have incontrovertible proof that he is the blood drinker he claims to be, though both the reader and Floria feel the erotic force of his descriptions of his blood-hunting expeditions. No, what matters is the effect that therapist and patient have

Suzy McKee Charnas.

on each other and what they do with and to each other before the story ends.

As in any great horror tale, the horror does not fully manifest itself until very near the end. When it does, more than life and death are at stake.

Suave, subtle, elegant and scary as the story is, it is marred just a little by the intrusion into its otherwise effective plot of an unnecessary detail whose implications are not further developed. Weyland, describing his past to Floria talks about having been taken prisoner in New York by a group headed by a certain Alan Reese who, knowing what Weyland was, exhibited him privately for money. The Reese episode is merely mentioned and serves neither plot nor character. I suspect that it is a detail left over from an earlier draft of the story.

The bottom line, however, is magnificent writing, complex characterization and a truly visionary understanding of the vampire theme.

THE UNINVITED   Film

1944 (B&W) U.S.A. 98 min.
Production Company: Paramount; ***Director:*** Lewis Allen; ***Producer:*** Charles Brackett; ***Screenplay:*** Frank Partos and Dodie Smith; ***Photography:*** Charles Lang; ***Editor:*** Doane Harrison; ***Special Effects:*** Farciot Edouart; ***Music:*** Victor Young.
Cast: Ray Milland (Roderick Fitzgerald), Ruth Hussey (Pamela Fitzgerald), Donald Crisp (Commander Bench), Corne-

lia Otis Skinner (Miss Holloway), Dorothy Stickney (Miss Hird), Barbara Everest (Lizzie Flynn), Alan Napier (Dr. Scott), Gail Russell (Stella Meredith).

A composer, Roderick Fitzgerald, and his sister Pamela fall in love with a beautiful, secluded house on the "haunted shores" of Cornwall, but as they settle in to lead lives of quiet rustication they discover that a spacious upstairs room with a sweeping view of the sea is uncannily cold and produces deep depression in anyone who spends time in it. More than that, at night they can clearly hear a woman sobbing.

When they ask the former owner of the house, Commander Bench, to tell them something of the history of the place, he tells them as little as possible. But the two Fitzgeralds with the help of local gossips and what they get from Commander Bench's granddaughter, Stella Meredith, and Dr. Scott, the local doctor, piece together the intriguing story of the house's former inhabitants.

What they learn is that Stella's father was a painter who lived in the house with his wife Mary and with his mistress, a French woman named Carmel. Carmel died mysteriously in France, whence the Merediths returned to the house bringing Mary Meredith's baby, Stella, with them.

What becomes clear is that wife and mistress are still battling each other beyond the grave. One of them is a malign spirit who means to harm Stella. The other one, Stella's mother, is benign. Whenever the malign spirit manifests itself, the room gets cold, dogs and cats turn tail and run. The benign spirit gives off an odor of mimosa and makes Stella feel warm and protected.

It isn't easy to explain just why this creaky old film should entice so much admiration. Partly it has to do with Charles Lang's photography. There are individual scenes that have the ominous look of a Fuselli painting, notably the one in which Stella, alone in the dark old house, is being herded by one of the ghosts out of the house and toward the dangerous edge of the cliff not far away. And there is the occasional light touch in which a comic tone lightens the mood for a few minutes, as in the scene in which Bobby the dog chases a squirrel through the long empty house. Or it may be that the power of the film derives from the way that the family-centered plot rouses our anxieties. The very cliches on which the film is overlaid have archetypal power: a straying father, a coldly beautiful wife, a warm and yet betrayed mistress, and a child whose life and soul are the stakes over which the ghosts of the women battle.

Among the film's other pleasures, one ought to cite the impeccable performances of Ray Milland, Donald Crisp and Gail Russell. Cornelia Otis Skinner, famous in her day as a great actress, hams up her part in a way that reminds one of Jack Nicholson's performance, decades later, in *The Shining.* That small deficit to one side, *The Uninvited* does honor to a genre, the ghost movie, that I have always had trouble taking seriously.

Ray Milland and Gail Russell in **The Uninvited.**

THE UPPER BERTH

Short Story

F. Marion Crawford

U.S.A.

1894, in *The Upper Berth*, London, Unwin; reprinted 1975 in *Classic Ghost Stories by Charles Dickens and Others*, New York, Dover

Here is another in that very British, very male tradition of stories that pretend to be told in a smoke suffused room as a way of breaking a postprandial boredom too crushing to be endured. In this case, the man who rescues the evening is a tall, broad-shouldered, 35-year-old former seaman named Brisbane and what he opens with as he lights his cigar is, ''It is a very singular thing . . .''

And indeed it is. Brisbane describes a transatlantic crossing he made on the steamer *Kamchatka*, in stateroom number 105, whose three previous occupants went overboard in mysterious circumstances. When the initially skeptical Brisbane hears something moving in the cabin, he tears the curtain of the upper berth aside and reaches in to see:

. . . if anyone were there. There was someone.

I remember that the sensation as I put my hands forward was as though I were plunging them into the air of a damp cellar, and from behind the curtains came a gust of wind that smelled horribly of stagnant sea-water. I laid hold of something that had the shape of a man's arm, but was smooth, and wet, and icy cold. But suddenly, as I pulled, the creature sprang violently forward against me, a clammy, oozy mass, as it seemed to me, heavy and wet, yet endowed with supernatural strength.

Brisbane, who is almost idiotically courageous, undertakes with the help of the ship's captain to trap the creature or whatever it is. They maintain a vigil in the cabin. Then, to their consternation, it appears.

It was something ghastly, terrible beyond words . . . It was like the body of a man long drowned, and yet it moved, and had the strength of ten men living . . .

Bad as it is, the narrator never loses his cool. Though a contemporary reader may be tempted to give ''The Upper Berth'' a psychoanalytic reading, the Victorian Brisbane's final, understated judgment of it all is that, ''It was a very disagreeable experience, and I was very badly frightened, which is a thing I do not like.''

Curiously enough, it is that laconic, almost indifferent tone that gives ''The Upper Berth'' its distinctive power because we know Brisbane's experience was well beyond ''disagreeable.'' The horror is unforgettable precisely because it is framed by the equable civility with which Crawford begins and ends his tale. Beneath and behind the amenities we get a strong whiff of the dank mysteries of the sea.

VAMPIR: EIN VERWILDETER ROMAN   Novel

Hanns Heinz Ewers
Germany
1921, Munich, George Muller Verlag; 1934 (as ''Vampire''), New York, John Day.

Ewers, who was born in 1872, lived long enough into the 20th century to become a darling of the Nazi regime in Germany—until he fell out of favor. In the light of his later politics his 1921 novel, *Vampir*, which develops the theme of a non-supernatural vampire and his relationship to his Jewish mistress, takes on especially sinister psychological and political overtones.

In *Vampir* Ewers carries forward the story of Frank Braun, whom we have seen earlier in *Alraune*. This time, he is presented to us as a patriotic German citizen who, before America's entry into World War I, moves to New York where he devotes himself to the German cause by making spectacularly successful fund-raising speeches. But his eloquence (and, therefore, the sums of money he can raise for an embattled Germany) depends on the drafts of blood which he takes entirely unconsciously from the throat of his mistress. That young woman, who is Jewish, offers herself as a willing victim to his thirst because she believes that she is serving the cause of a united destiny for Germans and Jews.

Lotte, the Jewish mistress, reassuring a penitent Braun, tells him, ''You look more German . . . German. You are going down the path I made for you—the way to the Homeland. You are following it—with me—for me . . . my blood flows in you . . . You have done only what the world does.''

After the goosestepping, the brown shirts, after the dive bombers and the death camps, Ewers' 1921 novel, crammed as it is with astrology, expensive sexual decadence and Ewers' ''redeeming'' vision of a joined German-Jewish destiny in which Jewish blood animates the German soul, is particularly unnerving to read.

THE VAMPIRE BAT   Film

1933   (B&W)   U.S.A.   63 min.
Production Company: Majestic Films; ***Director:*** Frank Strayer; ***Producer:*** Phil Goldstone; ***Screenplay:*** Edward T. Lowe; ***Photography:*** Ira Morgan; ***Editor:*** Otis Garrett.
Cast: Lionel Atwill (Dr. Otto von Niemann), Fay Wray (Ruth Bertin), Melvyn Douglas (Karl Breetschnieder), Maude Eburn (Gussie Schnappman), George E. Stone (Kringen), Dwight Frye (Herman Glieb), Robert Fraser (Emil Borst), Lionel Belmore (Gustav Schoen).

The Vampire Bat cheerfully merges three film genres: It is at intervals a vampire film, a mad-scientist-creating-life film and a detective story. It manages just the same to be coherent and unified, largely because its actors give the film the authority of folklore by being so comfortable with their stereotyped roles.

Our story takes place in the village of Kleinschloss, presumably somewhere in Germany, where people with tiny twin wounds in their throats are found dead. Two schools of opinion very quickly form to explain the deaths: the wisdom of the villagers, who blame the deaths on vampires, and the rationalist skepticism of Karl Breetschnieder, the chief of police, and research scientist Dr. Otto von Niemann. Niemann lives in a castle that he shares, for no reason that I can make out, with the hypochondriacal Gussie Schnappman and her beautiful niece, Ruth Bertin, whom Karl loves.

The film, then, like countless horror films that followed it, turns on one more variation of Hamlet's remark to Horatio: ''There are more things in Heaven and earth, Horatio, than are dreamed of in your philosophy.'' As restated by Dr. von Niemann, we have: ''There are many mysteries beyond the power of the human mind to comprehend.'' Though even as he speaks, he is busy doing research into one of those mysteries.

For a while it would seem that the villagers have guessed right, as the evidence mounts against a local half-wit, Herman, who has vampire bats for pets and who is suspiciously present at the crime scenes. Finally, the villagers take the law into their own hands and hunt Herman to his death at precisely the moment that Ruth Bertin discovers who the murderer really is.

In the last few moments of the film, almost everyone's life is suddenly at risk, or is ended. But finally love emerges triumphant.

The Vampire Bat is by no means a masterpiece. It is, however, one of those workmanlike horror films of the thirties in which the villain is meticulously villainous, the mad man ravingly mad and humankind, which clearly is capable of error upon error, is suitably saved by the devoted behavior of good-looking people who are fully entitled to kiss each other as the film comes to its end.

One thing more: Dwight Frye, who as Renfield in *Dracula* got off the most sinister laugh in the history of the horror film, tries it again here. It's not too bad, but one masterful laugh in a lifetime seems to have been his limit.

VAMPYR
Film

1931 (B&W) France/Germany 82/70 min.
Production Company: Dreyer Filmproduktion; *Director:* Carl Theodore Dreyer; *Producer:* Carl Theodore Dreyer and Nicholas de Gunzburg; *Screenplay:* Carl Theodore Dreyer, Christian Jul; *Photography:* Rudolph Mate, Louis Nee; *Music:* Wolfgang Zeller.

Cast: Julian West, pseudonym of Baron Nicholas de Gunzburg (David Gray), Henriette Gerard (old woman in the churchyard/the vampire), Jan Hieronimko (doctor), Maurice Schutz (chatelain), Rena Mandel (Gisele), Sybille Schmitz (Leone).

This profoundly beautiful film does not yield its sombre splendors easily or soon. A hasty viewer can find him- or herself exasperated or baffled or confused by its slow pace or by such primitive matters as who is doing what to whom— and why. But Carl Theodore Dreyer, whose unique vision created *Vampyr*, built these difficulties into it with great deliberation.

Carlos Clarens, in *An Illustrated History of the Horror Film* (p. 107), reports that Dreyer, explaining to his crew what sort of film he had in mind, said:

"Imagine that we are sitting in an ordinary room. Suddenly we are told that there is a corpse behind the door. In an instant the room we are sitting in is completely altered; everything in it has taken on another look; the light, the atmosphere have changed, though they are physically the same. This is because we have changed and the objects are as we conceive them. That is the effect I want to get in my film."

Jan Hieronimko as the Doctor in **Vampyr.**

The point for Dreyer, then, was to make a film which led each of its viewers to participate on his or her own terms in the events unfolding on the screen. His intent was to preserve the inchoate aspects of real experience even as he gave his viewers glimpses of design in the chaotic mists. To that end, he made *Vampyr* deliberately soft-edged, vague. The characters speak rarely and then they are hard to understand. Furthermore, to sustain the dreamlike quality of the action, most of the movie was filmed through gauze held three feet away from the lense of the camera.

There is a story that can be discerned. It begins with a prologue in which we are told:

> There exist certain beings whose very lives seem bound by invisible chains to the supernatural. They crave solitude. To be alone and dream . . . their imaginations are so developed that their vision reaches beyond that of most men. David Gray's personality was thus mysterious.

Then we see Gray as he comes to the inn in the village of Courtenpierre where in the course of the night a strange old man comes to his room and utters the words, "She must not die," after which he hands Gray a packet containing a book then he urges him to read in case he, the old man, should die. Then he takes his leave.

David, or an aspect of his mind, then leaves the inn and follows the shadow of a one-legged gamekeeper through strangely vaulted corridors and comes upon what seems to be a dance of shadows. Later, he sees a sinister white-haired woman handing a doctor a packet containing poison.

David meets the old man who visited him at the inn and learns that he is the chatelain of the nearby chateau and the father of two daughters, one of whom, Leone, the older one, is mysteriously ill. Just then a shot rings out and the old man dies in the arms of Gisele, the younger daughter.

Now that the chatelain is dead, David reads *Strange Tales of the Vampires,* the book he had been given. Then, putting Leone's illness together with what he has seen of the old woman and the doctor and what he has learned from his book, David deduces that the old woman is a vampire who has Leone in thrall.

When Leone is suddenly severely weakened, the doctor asks David to give her a blood transfusion. Weakened by his loss of blood, David, in a trance, sees himself as in a coffin being taken to the cemetery for burial. Most critics agree that this sequence, in which David looks up out of his coffin through a narrow window built into it, is one of the most terrifying in horror film history for the uncanny precision with which it captures dream immobility and the nightmare of being buried alive.

When David comes out of that trance, he is in the cemetery and a servant tells him that he (the servant) has found the vampire's tomb. The two of them go there and drive an iron stake into her heart whereupon her body crumbles into dust. Meanwhile, the doctor is driven either by the spirits of his victims or by the shadows of his guilt, to take refuge in an old mill. In another magnificently staged sequence, we see him trapped in the flour bin where he is buried, slowly, softly, whitely by the steadily sifting flour.

I have called attention to two of the most terrifying sequences in the film. There is a third that is at once subtle and horrifying. I cannot better Carlos Clarens' description of it in *An Illustrated History of the Horror Film* (p. 108). He writes:

The other climactic moment is the essence of the film captured in a few seconds. As Gisele watches over her sister, the lethargic Leone seems to awaken in the grip of demonic possession. Her lips part in a smile that bares her strong, white teeth, already thirsting for blood. She fixes her sister with a stare almost obscene in its craving. The nun in attendance spirits the terrified Gisele away and the smile in Leone's face disappears, giving way to a hard, threatening look.

The "essence of the film," as Clarens realizes, is that Dreyer has found the filmic means to show how thin is the barrier between the nightmare that we dream and the one we live. When that barrier comes down, as it almost does in *Vampyr,* the single hope of the dreamer—that he or she will wake up—is filched away.

THE VAMPYRE: A TALE   Novel
John Polidori
Great Britain
1819, London, Sherwood, Neeley and Jones; reprinted 1966, New York, Dover.

There is a literary evening well known in the history of the Gothic tale, when Byron, Percy Shelley and Mary Godwin, and Dr. John Polidori, Byron's physician and erstwhile lover, were gathered together at Byron's home, the Villa Diodati. In the course of the evening, Byron proposed that each of them undertake to make a scary tale. Only one of the group, Mary Shelley, fulfilled the immediate assignment. Mary Shelley gave the world the classic *Frankenstein*. Two years later Polidori concocted *The Vampyre: A Tale,* which, while hardly a classic, has considerable interest for us as the first major appearance in English literature, of the vampire type: that is, a nobleman, aloof, brilliant, chilling, fascinating to women and suavely evil.

In Polidori's novel, the vampire is Lord Ruthven who is a friend of a gentleman named Aubrey. Aubrey is good-looking, virtuous, honorable, rich and innocent enough not to spurn Ruthven's friendship. Indeed, they set out on the Contintental grand tour together, in the course of which Aubrey learns that Lord Ruthven has a penchant for ruining decent people at the gaming table and for succoring the wicked poor.

In Athens where Aubrey goes to study the inscriptions on ancient tombs, he meets the beautiful Ianthe who tells him about "the living vampyre, who . . . passed years amidst his friends, and dearest ties, forced every year, by feeding upon the life of a lovely female to prolong his existence . . ." The story seems incredible to Aubrey until one day he comes upon a ravished Ianthe: "upon her neck and breast was blood, and upon her throat were the marks of teeth having opened the vein . . ." The sight sends him into shock. When he recovers, he finds himself being tended by Ruthven, who "no longer appeared that apathetic being" he had known. Ruthven, it is clear, is the vampire. Some while later, Ruthven is killed in an encounter with bandits, but with his dying breath he conjures his young friend to keep the terrible truth secret for one year after his death. Aubrey gives his oath, then Ruthven asks to be left lying in a position where his body "should be exposed to the first cold ray of the moon that rose after his death."

When Aubrey returns to England some months later, he is horrified to discover a resurrected Ruthven in London. We come now to the heart of the matter, Aubrey learns that Ruthven has wooed and won Aubrey's sister to a promise of marriage. Aubrey's dilemma is what to do about his oath of silence. On the one hand, his sister's life is in danger. On the other, Aubrey is a gentleman who has sworn an oath.

The trouble with Polidori's novel is that he writes neither out of necessity nor conviction. Even the tone of the fiction, an affected world-weariness, seems borrowed. If we read it today it is simply because of its interest as the first vampire tale in English. Otherwise it would deserve oblivion.

VARNEY, THE VAMPIRE
Novel
or The Feast of Blood
Thomas Preskett Prest
Great Britain
1847, London, E. Lloyd; reprinted 1971, New York, Arno.

Varney, the Vampire is Grand Guignol writing at its childlike best. Perhaps only an old lecher could surpass Prest's enthusiasm for maidens who gaze "upon the face of Varney with . . . the strange glassy looking eyes [that had] glared upon her on that awful night of the storm, when she was visited by the vampyre . . ." To the maiden Flora, Varney says, "You are beautiful. The most cunning statuary might well model some rare work of art from those rounded limbs . . . Your skin rivals the driven snow . . ."

Eight hundred and sixty-eight pages! Glaring, blaring, staring prose. From the very sound of the title to the last shriek as Varney "disappeared into the mountain," Prest adores the horror he is mouthing. The title alone—*Varney, the Vampire: or The Feast of Blood*—is (and was) worth its weight in gold. And the melodrama that follows is just as splendid. There is tinsel thunder, cellophane lightning. Death, blood, gore, pistol shots, stabbings, caves, moonlight resurrections. Indeed, Varney is resurrected so frequently that the idea of dying takes on a thoroughly ludicrous aspect. Varney is shot, hanged, staked, drowned. It doesn't matter. All he requires is a little bit of moonlight to make his corpse twitch and jerk. Before long, he is among the living again, feeling the revival of an old thirst:

> "I was . . . ruminating what I should do, until a strange feeling crept over me that I should like—what? Blood!—raw blood, reeking and hot, bubbling and juicy, from the veins of some gasping victim."

The critic, Sir Devendra P. Varma, believes that, "The impact of *Varney the Vampire* upon our literature is still felt through its reverberations in *Dracula.*" Though it is likely that Stoker read it, *Varney* is on a quite different plane of achievement from *Dracula*. *Varney* is penny-a-line fiction at the very top of its bent. But there is nothing in *Varney,* nothing at all, that is capable of sounding the chords of dark understanding that reverberate in page after page of *Dracula.*

THE VELVET VAMPIRE
Film
1971 (C) U.S.A. 80 min.
Production Company: New World Pictures; ***Director:*** Stephanie Rothman; ***Producer:*** Charles S. Swartz; ***Screenplay:*** Maurice Jules, Charles S. Swartz, Stephanie Rothman; ***Photography:*** Daniel Lacambre; ***Editor:*** Teddi Petersen; ***Music:*** Clancy B. Grass III.
Cast: Michael Blodgett (Lee Ritter), Sherry Miles (Susan Rit-

VARNEY, THE VAMPYRE;
OR,
THE FEAST OF BLOOD
A Romance.

CHAPTER I.
——" How graves give up their dead,
And how the night air hideous grows
With shrieks !"

MIDNIGHT. — THE HAIL-STORM. — THE DREADFUL VISITOR.—THE VAMPYRE.

THE solemn tones of an old cathedral clock have announced midnight—the air is thick and heavy—a strange, death-like stillness pervades all nature. Like the ominous calm which precedes some more than usually terrific outbreak of the elements, they seem to have paused even in their ordinary fluctuations, to gather a terrific strength for the great effort. A faint peal of thunder now comes from far off. Like a signal gun for the battle of the winds to begin, it appeared to awaken them from their lethargy, and one awful, warring hurricane swept over a whole city, producing more devastation in the four or five minutes it lasted, than would a half century of ordinary phenomena.

It was as if some giant had blown upon some toy town, and scattered many of the buildings before the hot blast of his terrific

The first page of text in **Varney the Vampire.**

ter), Celeste Yarnall (Diane), Jerry Daniels (servant), Gene Shane (gallery owner), Paul Prokop (mechanic).

The Velvet Vampire, an otherwise so-so soft porn vampire film, is notable for a dream sequence whose visual beauty and strangeness might creditably have been borrowed from Salvador Dali and whose tone and texture are rarities of female sensibility in a genre dominated by male filmmakers.

The film opens with the camera following a young woman. Suddenly, she glimpses a motorcycle. A moment later, she is seized from behind and rape seems inevitable, but in a quick reversal of roles the would-be rapist becomes the film vampire's first victim.

The scene shifts to an opening in the Stoker Gallery where the same young woman, whose name is Diane, picks up a young couple, Lee Ritter and his wife Susan, and invites them to visit her at her home somewhere in "the desert." The couple accept the invitation.

In their intriguing new friend's home, sexual and vampiric hanky panky soon begin. There are dune buggy escapades and a great deal of heavy breathing. Peering through a two-way mirror Diane watches Lee and Susan making love. Susan is bitten by a rattler and Diane sucks the venom from the wound. Later Diane makes love to Lee.

But none of the events so far are as persuasive or compelling as the sequence in which we see Lee and Susan each simultaneously dreaming the same dream. They keep starting out of sleep only to fall back into it again to dream that they are lying on a Victorian bed set down in a golden desert. There, they see their hostess, Diane, in a diaphanous red gown coming to the bed and leading Lee away from it. The whole sequence is so simple, sensuous and elegant and so deeply threatening that despite the film's exploitative bent we are seized by the conviction that in Stephanie Rothman there is a first-rate directorial talent waiting to come into its own.

THE VILLAGE OF THE DAMNED   Film

1960   (B&W)   Great Britain   78 min.
Production Company: MGM; *Director:* Wolf Rilla; *Producer:* Ronald Kinnoch; *Screenplay:* Stirling Silliphant; *Photography:* Geoffrey Faithful; *Editor:* Gordon Hales; *Photo Effects:* Tom Howard; *Music:* Ron Goodwin.
Cast: George Sanders (Gordon Zellerby), Barbara Shelley (Anthea Zellerby), Michael Gwynn (Allan Zellerby), Laurence Naismith (Dr. Willet).

This film version of John Wyndham's *The Midwich Cuckoos* opens splendidly with a scene in which a shepherd and his dog are driving a flock of sheep across a pasture. Suddenly, sheep, shepherd and dog keel over. The camera then moves to the nearby village of Midwich where we see various of the local citizenry, one by one keeling over in a similar fashion.

We learn very soon that everyone within a certain radius of the town of Midwich fell into a deep sleep at the same time from which, a few hours later, they all woke up. At first, the strange sleep seems not to have produced any ill effects. But a few weeks later, it develops that every woman of childbearing age in the town of Midwich is pregnant. The children born to those women are all extraordinarily well formed, healthy and singularly beautiful. Without exception, they all have strange eyes and they are all telepathic. Their one desire is to be left alone. When they are provoked, their eyes take on the look of a pair of incandescent bull's eyes in

a target and the power they wield as they defend themselves is deadly. To the dismay of their putative parents, they never display any emotion. As David tells his "father," Gordon Zellerby (George Sanders): "If you didn't suffer from emotions, from feelings, you could be as strong as us."

Eventually, we learn that the Midwich children are the only survivors of other children like them born in various parts of the world and that they are a sort of advance guard of a race of extraterrestrials who, of course, mean to take over the world.

For a while, Gordon Zellerby persuades the authorities to spare the children so that he can study them. But when he learns from his own "son" David what their particular agenda is on earth, he is finally persuaded to act against them.

The deeply buried hostility between parents and children—such bewildered parents and such beautiful children—is the emotion this film exploits. Each side gets to see the other as "they" and the result is both poignant and disastrous.

THE VISITOR   Short Story

Roald Dahl
Great Britain
1974, in *Switch Bitch,* New York, Knopf; collection reprinted 1983 New York, Ballantine.

A sly, mean, witty and lethal tale told by an effete but sensuous first-person narrator named Cornelius, a self-described, past master seducer in the tradition of Don Juan and Casanova. Enticed to a house in the Sinai Desert an hour out of Ismailia, Cornelius is introduced to his host's wife and daughter, both of whom are ravishingly beautiful. "By the end of the evening," writes the narrator, "I knew for certain I had done my work well. The old magic had not let me down. Either of the two ladies, should circumstance permit, was mine for the asking."

That night, though Cornelius begs us to forgive him for sparing us the details, he tells us that, "of the many thousands and thousands of women I have known none has transported me to greater extremes of ecstasy than this lady of the Sinai Desert." The mystery is, was it the mother or the daughter? And the answer, when it finally comes on the second to last page of the story, will put a smile on the reader's face even as it curdles his blood.

W

WAIT UNTIL DARK Film
1967 (C) U.S.A. 108 min.
Production Company: Warner-Seven Arts/Mel Ferrer; ***Director:*** Terence Young; ***Producer:*** Mel Ferrer; ***Screenplay:*** Robert and Jane-Howard Carrington; ***Photography:*** Charles Lang; ***Editor:*** Gene Milford; ***Music:*** Henry Mancini.
Cast: Audrey Hepburn (Suzie Hendrix), Alan Arkin (Harry Roat, Jr.), Efrem Zimbalist, Jr. (Sam Hendrix), Richard Crenna (Mike Talman).

Based on the play by Frederick Knott, this film is superlatively frightening because of its central situation. A blind woman, whose husband has inadvertently become a "mule" for a shipment of heroin, is besieged by the crooks who want the drugs that, unbeknownst to her, are in a doll her husband has brought her as a souvenir of his journey.

The odds against the blind woman (Suzie Hendrix) are staggering. In addition to being blind, she is handicapped in dealing with the cruel villains because she is decent, kind and trusting. But, because she is also brilliant, sensitive, quick-witted, brave and ingenious, she can make use of the dark and of the light from an open refrigerator in ways that baffle her sighted tormentors and allow her to triumph in a situation that comes close to being an absolute nightmare.

Alan Arkin is wonderful as the coldly insane chief villain and Audrey Hepburn, with her vulnerable good looks and her extraordinary theatrical intelligence, is magnificently cast as "the world's champion blind lady."

WANDERING WILLIE'S TALE Short Story
Sir Walter Scott
Great Britain
1824, in *Redgauntlet*, Edinburgh, Constable; reprinted 1975 in *Classic Ghost Stories*, New York, Dover.

Blind Willie tells this tale of his grandfather, Steenie Steenson, who was something of a toper as well as much in demand as a bagpipe player in the days of the Civil Wars in 17th-century Great Britain. Steenie is a tenant farmer of the harsh Laird Robert Redgauntlet, a scourge to the rebellious Whigs and Covenanters in the course of those wars. Finding himself in danger of being in arrears with his rent to the laird, Steenie, after much pleading and searching, borrows the money needed and delivers it to the laird whom he finds suffering from an attack of the gout. The laird, however, dies before he can acknowledge, in writing, that he has received Steenies's money, and Sir John, the heir to the property, justly asks for proof that the money was paid.

Steenie, exasperated because neither the money nor the receipt can be found, utters some injudicious words about Laird Redgauntlet, then flies from Sir John's presence. Riding through Pitmurkie Wood, Steenie meets the devil, who hears Steenie's complaints and invites him to visit Hell where he can find Sir Robert and get from him the necessary receipt.

Steenie in Hell is warned by the ghost of Sir Robert's butler, Dougal MacCallum, "to tak naething frae ony body here, neither meat, drink, or siller, except just the receipt that is your ain."

The rest of the tale describes Steenie's fearful dealings with the shade of Laird Robert, his return to the land of the living and how the quarrel between himself and Sir John is resolved in a way to save everyone's reputation.

In the 19th century, Scott, before Dickens, was the irresistible story teller. "Wandering Willie's Tale" is so cunningly crafted, and so beautifully served by the Scots dialect in which it is mostly told, that it seems to be a folktale that has been polished to a fine gloss by centuries of retelling. The story is funnier than it is scary, though Scott, who is always the master of small detail, churns up considerable fear as he describes Willie's experience in hell: Here, as he is handed a bagpipe to play, a nudge from the well-intentioned butler, MacCallum, alerts him to the fact that the chanter, the pipe that produces the melody, is smoking hot.

WE HAVE ALWAYS LIVED IN THE CASTLE

Novel

Shirley Jackson
U.S.A.
1962, New York, Knopf; reprinted 1984, New York, Penguin.

We Have Always Lived in the Castle is one of those rare works, like Tryon's *The Other*, in which the terror is an inextricable part of the work's loveliness. Shirley Jackson has transformed a simple tale of mass poisoning into a story that, because it is rooted in the complexities of family life, turns mythic under her hand.

The narrator of *We Have Always Lived in the Castle*, Mary Catherine Blackwood, describes the idyllic life she leads with her sister Constance, her wheelchair-bound Uncle Julian, and her cat Jonas in the Blackwood family home—six years after all the rest of her family (father, mother, aunt and brother) were all killed by arsenic. Though sister Constance was tried for the murders, she was acquitted, and now the survivors, with plenty of money at their disposal, live a comfortable, if isolated, existence. Constance cooks and cleans. Merrycat, as she is called, leads a fey life, burying magic objects in the soil, dreaming of living on the moon; and Uncle Julian is endlessly writing his memoirs of the day on which the murders were committed.

Then, cousin Charles Blackwood intrudes into the happy garden. Charles is crude, boorish, money-grubbing and attractive to Constance. He offends Merrycat and Uncle Julian. Finally, Merrycat is forced to take strong action and the book comes to a splendid climax.

We Have Always Lived in the Castle is both a find and a treasure.

THE WERE-WOLF

Novel

Clemence Housman
Great Britain
1896, London, John Lane; reprinted 1976, New York, Arno.

Here is a chilly little tale whose mood recalls the Erckmann-Chatrian *Man-Wolf* story that appeared in 1876.

The Were-wolf is an intensely romantic story that Housman, somewhat simplistically, intends to be read as a Christian allegory. Christian and Sweyn are twin brothers who, with their little brother, Rol, live with their mother. Trella, in a farm cabin set among snowy wastes. There one day, they are visited by White Fell, a beautiful young woman swathed in furs. White Fell profoundly attracts Sweyn to her, but Christian very quickly guesses that she is a werewolf. Soon his guess is confirmed as first little Rol, then Trella, each of whom has been kissed by White Fell, disappear. Christian, who has seen how White Fell's delicate, maiden footprints in the snow turned into those of a wolf, tries to warn Sweyn, but Sweyn refuses to believe him and the brothers quarrel. Before the story is done, Christian dies defending Sweyn from the deadly fangs of the werewolf.

Clemence Housman's little novel is essentially slight, but it is swiftly paced and marvelously atmospheric. Her descriptions of the snow-covered mountains in which the tale is set impart a bright, hard edge to the story as if framing it in the light of stars looking down on a frosty night.

THE WEREWOLF OF PARIS

Novel

Guy S. Endore
U.S.A.
1933, New York, Farrar & Rinehart; reprinted 1974, London, Sphere.

This overambitious novel, which creates a fictional life for the 19th-century French murderer and ghoul Sergeant Bertrand, is a landmark horror fiction because it is an early endeavor to link werewolf lore to the mental illness that is called lycanthropy.

Endore opens his story with a prefatory chapter in which we meet two noble families, the Pitavals and the Pitamonts, who have been carrying on a feud for centuries. Jehan Pitamont, in the guise of a monk, sneaks into the Pitaval castle and is caught red-handed murdering a couple of the Pitavals. For his crime, he is immured in a dry well where for 50 years he is fed three times a week. At intervals over the years, wolf howls are heard coming from the well. When the 50 years are up, both the noble families have lost their property and, as the last of the Pitavals leaves the castle, Jehan Pitamont is presumed dead.

We move now into the 19th century where we meet Aymar Galliez and his aunt Mme. Didier, who has a country-bred servant girl named Josephine. Josephine, sent to the church for holy water, is there raped by Father Pitamont. When Josephine's son, Bertrand is born (on Christmas day—

White Fell and Christian run a deadly race.

a very bad sign) it is notable that his eyebrows meet in the middle of his forehead and that he has hair in the palms of his hands. Chaucer readers will recognize that the joined eyebrows are a sign that he has an erotic nature; *Dracula* readers will know that the hair in the palms is the mark of the vampire. Endore, however, means us to understand both marks as signs of the werewolf.

Aymar, his aunt and Josephine form Bertrand's family. Aymar, the scholar, very soon perceives that Bertrand is not normal. Throughout his boyhood, howls come from his room. Then local villagers, discovering the bodies of ravaged lambs and ducks in the neighborhood, blame the deaths on a wolf. One of the villagers, Bramond, suspecting a werewolf, makes a silver bullet with which he shoots "the wolf." It is that silver bullet that Aymar takes from the wounded Bertrand's leg.

Just as Aymar has to face what Bertrand is, the young man: (a) rapes (or at least sleeps with) his not quite unwilling mother, and (b) commits a werewolf murder on his flight to Paris. There his career as a ghoul and werewolf properly begins.

It is at this point that Endore interpolates a most unsettling subplot. We meet Sophie de Blumenberg, a wealthy young Jewish woman who "cures" Bertrand of his werewolf seizures by permitting him to cut wounds in her flesh from which he drinks her oozing blood. Whether, as I think, Endore is influenced here by a similar relationship between a vampire and his Jewish mistress in Hanns Heinz Ewers' *Vampir* or whether the details of that love affair occurred to him independently, it remains a disturbing sequence that has anti-Semitic or at least bizarre Christian-Jewish innuendos. Given what we now know about the Holocaust in Europe, Endore's subplot seems especially macabre.

The Werewolf of Paris has its fascinations. Although Endore's prose style lacks distinction, he is an imaginative plot maker who invents wonderful minor scenes. One that is particularly memorable is a scene in a house of prostitution to which the young Bertrand is inveigled. The prostitute with whom he spends the night (and whom he murders) has a guest album in which she collects the signatures of her customers. Since she cannot read, she does not know that they have written the names of famous men—Victor Hugo, Horace Vernet, Adolph Thiers—in her souvenir book.

The book's major weakness is that Endore trivializes his werewolf theme by linking it at the end to larger profundities. As the violence of the Revolution of 1870 sweeps Paris, Aymar Galliez thinks:

> "What was a werewolf who had killed a couple of prostitutes, who had dug up a few corpses, compared with these bands of tigers slashing at each other . . ."

It is, as profundities go, rather shallow. Endore does much better when he keeps his mind and his eye on his werewolf.

WHAT WAS IT?   Short Story
Fitz-James O'Brien
U.S.A.
March 1859, in *Harper's*; reprinted 1976 in R. Reginald and Douglas Menville's (eds.) *A Stable for Nightmares*, New York, Arno.

"Opium and nightmares," the first-person narrator of this tale tells us, "should never be brought together." With that as an opening, opium and nightmare are promptly brought together in this neat, brief and terrifying story.

The narrator, we learn, has fallen asleep one day after an opium session. He wakes to find that something has its hands at his throat. Whatever it may be is invisible and it is trying to throttle him. Because our narrator is a man of action, he resists. In a battle that is as silent as it is macabre, he finally overcomes the unknown creature and with the help of a friend, he binds it. Then, the question is: What to do with it-him-her.

What the two ingenious friends do is to cause a clay cast to be made of the creature so that they can see what it looks like. They learn that:

> It was shaped like a man—distorted, uncouth, and horrible, but still a man. It was small, not over four feet and some inches in height, and its limbs revealed a muscular development that was unparalleled. Its face surpassed in hideousness anything I had ever seen . . . It was the physiognomy of what I should fancy a ghoul might be. It looked as if it was capable of feeding on human flesh.

Meanwhile, the horror continues, because, though they know what it looks like, they still cannot see it.

And now the tale turns pathetic as well as grim. Try as its captors will, they cannot get the creature to eat anything. And though it is invisible, they can sense that it is losing strength and, in a word, is dying. When finally it is dead, we have the spectacle of the two friends digging a grave into which they deposit what to any bystander would appear to be a quantity of empty air. At this point, a reader is left uncertain whether to shudder or laugh or cry. In any case, what lingers is a sense that the two friends have wrestled with something other-worldly that was at once pathetic and malign.

WHATEVER HAPPENED TO BABY   Film
JANE?
1962   (B&W)   U.S.A.   133 min.
Production Company: Warner Brothers; *Director:* Robert Aldrich; *Producer:* Robert Aldrich; *Screenplay:* Lukas Heller; *Photography:* Ernest Haller; *Special Effects:* Don Steward; *Music:* Frank de Vol.
Cast: Bette Davis (Jane), Joan Crawford (Blanche), Victor Buono (the accompanist).

This incredibly long film has held up remarkably well in the more than 25 years since it was made. There are at least two good reasons why: first, the performances by Joan Crawford and, especially Bette Davis, are superb; and second, the film's focus on the family as a source of monstrosity.

Jane and Blanche Hudson are a couple of aging sisters who live in a creepy old house in Los Angeles. Jane, who was once a child movie star and the apple of her father's eye, looks sullenly after her wheelchair-bound sister, Blanche, who had a brilliant, adult career as a movie star until she was crippled in an accident when she was struck by a car driven by Jane. Both sisters have had their professional hopes blasted and both of them nurture their lifelong sibling rivalry.

The leaden, and guilt-ridden, lives these two lead take a

On the set of **Whatever Happened to Baby Jane:** *Director Robert Aldrich with Bette Davis (standing) and Joan Crawford.* © Seven Arts Associates

sudden departure from routine when Jane, now well into her sixties, has the harebrained notion to revive her career as a child star. To that end, she hires an unscrupulous and wonderfully repellent accompanist to help her refresh her musical routines. Then, lest the helpless Blanche interfere with her plans, Jane undertakes to starve her sister to death. As an added fillip of cruelty, she lifts the lid of a silver serving dish and offers Blanche a dead rat to eat. When a suspicious black cleaning woman seems about to discover what is happening to Blanche, Jane kills her.

The horror of the film, which has been beating more or less mutedly against a viewer's consciousness thus far, blossoms now into full-scale nightmare as a panicked Jane drags Blanche with her in a flight from the house. The concluding scenes, as Jane and the dying Blanche become part of a crowd of sunbathers at the beach, are unbearable. And the anguish is compounded when Jane, who ever since Blanche's accident has believed that it was she who drove the car that crippled her sister, learns from her that it was Blanche who was driving the car and that she was hurt trying to run Jane down with it.

This film is about waste. About the expense of spirit and the waste of shame. About how the strains of family life can knot and cramp burgeoning young lives. Despite its slow-moving pace, *Whatever Happened to Baby Jane?* stands high on the list of psychological horror films.

WHEN A STRANGER CALLS   Film

1979 (C) U.S.A. 96 min.
Production Company: Columbia; ***Director:*** Fred Walton; ***Screenplay:*** Steve Feke and Fred Walton; ***Photography:*** Don Peterman; ***Editor:*** Sam Vitale; ***Special Effects:*** B & D Special Effects; ***Music:*** Dana Kaproff.
Cast: Carol Kane (baby-sitter, Jill Johnson), Charles Durning (private detective, John Clifford), Colleen Dewhurst (Tracy Fuller), Tony Beckley (psycho-killer, Curt Duncan), Rachel Roberts (Doctor Monk), Ron O'Neal (Lieutenant Charlie Garber).

This is an authentic chiller.

A baby-sitter in an affluent home is doing her homework. The telephone rings. The baby-sitter answers the phone and hears an anonymous male voice saying, "Have you checked on the children?" The call is repeated several times in the course of the evening. Finally, the baby-sitter calls the police. The mysterious calls are traced and the sitter learns that the caller is in the house.

From here on, the nightmare moves to a crescendo pitch. The mysterious caller is a psychotic who has destroyed the sleeping children with his bare hands and in a fashion so atrocious that the coroner can hardly put the bodies into presentable shape. The killer is locked away in a mental hospital from which, seven years later, he escapes.

The father of the victims hires a private detective to find the killer; and the film, for breathing space, turns into a more or less ordinary manhunt. When the killer is located in New York City, the audience has some hope that it will be spared more horror. The audience is mistaken. The killer evades the detective.

The scene shifts: The baby-sitter, now a young mother of two herself, is going out with her husband for the evening. At the restaurant, she gets a phone call—from the killer who asks the same question he asked years ago: "Have you checked on the children?" And once again, shrieking fear invades the film, which, after some further bloodcurdling moments, comes to a satisfying end.

What makes this film feel so dreadful is the way that it quietly insinuates the notion that in the real world there is no end to terror; that the wheel of misfortune can turn round and round again; that a nightmare can be redreamed and relived. That, finally, evil can seem—and may even be—immortal.

WHITE ZOMBIE   Film
1932   (B&W)   U.S.A.   73 min.
Production Company: Amusement Securities/United Artists; **Director:** Victor Halperin; **Producer:** Edward Halperin; **Screenplay:** Garnett Weston; **Photography:** Arthur Martinelli; **Editor:** Harold McLernon; **Special Effects:** (makeup) Jack Pierce; **Musical Director:** Abe Meyer.
Cast: Lugosi (Murder Legendre), Madge Bellamy (Madeleine), Joseph Cawthorn (Doctor Bruner), Robert Fraser (Beaumont), John Harron (Neil).

Bela Lugosi, who left his indelible mark on the film image of Dracula in 1931, stalks through this one, the prototype of all subsequent zombie movies, in nearly as authoritative a manner.

Beaumont, a wealthy plantation owner in Haiti, has persuaded a beautiful young woman named Madeleine and her fiancé to come to Haiti to be married at his home. He promises that after their wedding, he will employ the young man as his New York agent. But all of this is merely a plot. The truth is that Beaumont has fallen madly in love with Madeleine and is desperately scheming, down to the last moment, to find a way to make her his.

Besotted by love, he goes for help to the wicked Legendre, the zombie maker, who supplies him with the living-dead men who work his plantation and sugar mill. Legendre tells Beaumont, "I have looked deeply into her eyes. She is in love, but not with you."

Beaumont says: "But there must be a way."

Legendre: "There is a way.

Beaumont: "You give me what I want and you may ask anything."

Legendre promptly strikes an unholy bargain. He will contrive to get Madeleine for Beaumont, but Beaumont, in return, will give him the body of Madeleine's fiancé.

From here on, White Zombie is part horror movie and part scenes from *Romeo and Juliet* as Legendre contrives Madeleine's spurious death in fulfillment of his part of the bargain with Beaumont.

White Zombie has a rather wonderful semi-comic figure, the missionary, Dr. Bruner, who in the most petrifying moments of the plot habitually turns to one or another of the characters to ask for a match with which to light his pipe. Dr. Bruner serves as the film's "chorus," explaining what voodoo is and something of the history and the nature of zombies. His low-key presence is very welcome as it serves to keep a somewhat hyper-fanciful plot rooted in what we think of as the real world.

What makes this slow-paced (nearly sluggish) film work is that its deliberation is in keeping with the pace of the worst kind of nightmare, the one in which things take so long to happen that one gives up all hope of waking when whatever the awful thing is that has been building up finally happens. The pace conforms, too, to our expectations of how zombies must move. We see them in the fields and in Beaumont's sugar mill, eyes glazed, looking straight ahead, their limbs loose so that they seem to flow instead of walk. When one of them falls into the machinery of the sugar mill, the work does not stop. There is no outcry. The machinery is turned by a zombie, and the other zombies keep on with whatever they were doing.

Two final points. First, the sets of *White Zombie* are stunning: curved stairways, precipitous heights from which awful things or people fall into soundless weirs, and bizarre structures that frame action so that it is seen as through a keyhole. The general effect of the sets is to make shadows seem to be carved out of blocks of darkness. And second, we have Lugosi, slim as a rail, using hands and eyes, and even his curiously bifurcated tiny chin whiskers like beautifully constructed implements of evil. He is the true death master, elegant, graceful and as cold as ice at the North Pole.

THE WICKER MAN   Film
1973   (C)   Great Britain   86 min.
Production Company: British Lion; **Director:** Robin Hardy; **Producer:** Peter Snell; **Screenplay:** Anthony Shaffer; **Photography:** Harry Waxman; **Editor:** Eric Boyd-Perkins; **Music:** Paul Giovanni.
Cast: Edward Woodward (Sergeant Neil Howie), Britt Ekland (Willow MacGregor), Diane Cilento (Miss Rose), Ingrid Pitt (librarian), Christopher Lee (Lord Summerisle).

The Wicker Man is another film in which the theme is the survival into modern times of certain deadly primitive religions. It is instructive to compare it to *The Secret of Harvest Home*, *Children of the Corn* and *The Eye of the Devil*.

Before turning to the film itself, one ought to note that *The Wicker Man* is remarkable for, among other things, the presence in it of Christopher Lee, looking more normal and happier than in any of his previous decade's roles.

Sergeant Neil Howie, a British policeman, is sent to an island off the coast of Scotland to investigate a complaint that May Morrison's daughter is missing. The police officer stays at The Green Man inn and notices that people clam up in his presence.

The next morning, he becomes aware that preparations are being made for a May Day celebration and little by little he

Christopher Lee as Lord Summerisle in **The Wicker Man.** © British Lion

Diane Cilento as Miss Rose in **The Wicker Man.** © British Lion

picks up other signs that the island population has beliefs that are different from those of a proper British community. Eventually, the local religion, which is not Christianity, is made clear to him. The island is blessed by the Gulf Stream so that, despite its northern latitude, a wide range of crops can be grown. As a consequence the populace has so elaborated a respect for the fertility of the soil that it believes that an annual human sacrifice is needed to preserve it.

It takes Sergeant Howie a while to understand who the next sacrificial victim is meant to be. By that time, the film audience, and Sergeant Howie, have equal reason to be horrified.

The film is notable for the way that its lighthearted mood actually works to prepare us for the horror to come. The paganism of the island population is, for a long time, seen only in a congenial light. Even the idea of human sacrifice is handled so gracefully that it does not become horrifying until the identity of the victim and the manner of the sacrifice are made clear. Then, *The Wicker Man* becomes the subtle and horrifying film it was intended to be.

WIELAND Novel
or The Transformation
Charles Brockden Brown
U.S.A.
1798, New York, T. & J. Swords, for H. Caritat; reprinted 1977, Kent, Ohio, Kent State University Press, 1977.

This sprawling Greek tragedy-cum-Gothic novel, written by the so-called "father of American literature," is so poorly constructed that its author had to append a tortured postscript to the work to clear up what happened to several of his characters who had somehow been mislaid in the course of depicting more interesting events.

In the tradition of the epistolary 18th-century romance, *Wieland* is presented as a very long letter written by Clara Wieland and addressed "to a small number of friends" whom she intends to inform about the details of her astonishing recent experiences.

She and her brother, Theodore Wieland, we learn, are the children of a man descended from German nobility. Their father, a native of Saxony, became in his youth a passionate convert to the Protestant sect of Camissards. So wholly was he drawn to the religious life that he was moved to preach his new beliefs to the North American Indians, for which reason he moved to Mettingen, near Philadelphia. Here, he eventually became a prosperous but still profoundly religious landowner; as the years went by, Wieland acquired the conviction that he was doomed to die a violent death.

And indeed, one midnight when he was at his prayers in a rocky temple of his own design, there was the sound of an explosion and he was found mortally burned, the victim of spontaneous combustion. His wife, overwhelmed by grief, died not long afterward, and their two children, Clara and Theodore, inherited their not inconsiderable wealth.

With so much as background, Clara introduces those who will henceforth be the chief characters in her story: Theodore

Wieland, her brother, Catherine, his childhood sweetheart and then wife, and Pleyel, Catherine's brother, to whom Clara is drawn. Into the harmonious lives of these four intrudes Carwin, like the serpent into the Garden of Eden.

Carwin, one of Gothic fiction's more interesting (and ambiguous) villains, is described as follows:

> His cheeks were pallid and lank, his eyes sunken, his forehead overshadowed by coarse, straggling hairs, his teeth large and irregular . . . And yet his forehead, so far as shaggy locks would allow it to be seen, his eyes lustrously black, and possessing, in the midst of haggardness, a radiance inexpressibly serene and potent, and something in the rest of his features which it would be in vain to describe, but which served to betoken a mind of the highest order, were essential ingredients of the portrait.

He has, moreover, an extraordinarily beautiful voice. So beautiful that Clara, despite her prepossession in favor of Pleyel, finds herself being drawn to him. Not long after he appears on the scene, first Theodore and then Clara hear mysterious warning voices apparently coming out of thin air. Later, Pleyel seems to hear Clara's voice in a situation that compromises her reputation. Finally, Theodore Wieland hears God's voice commanding him to acts so horrible that the reader of the fiction is utterly nonplussed when he discovers that Wieland has actually committed them.

Petrifying as individual scenes of this fiction are, it should be said that Brown does not play fair. He keeps his readers on tenterhooks by creating a really vivid moment of mystery, then, just as we pine to know what actually happened, he shifts the talk to something else so that one is left uninformed and confounded until much later. Equally irritating is the way that Brown, imitating Ann Radcliffe, steals the wonder

Charles Brockden Brown.

from his terror by explaining its non-supernatural origins. Still, *Wieland* has moments that are so intensely ominous and a climax so atrocious and bloody that it maintains honorably enough its place as a minor Gothic classic.

THE WIFE OF USHER'S WELL
Verse
Anonymous
Great Britain
No date; reprinted in 1979 in Leonard Wolf's (ed.) *Wolf's Complete Book of Terror,* New York, Clarkson N. Potter.

This folk ballad has not one but three ghosts returning to their mortal haunts. The ballad consists of 12 stark four-line stanzas and moves forward in a series of swift starts and stops that, in their visual intensity, would do credit to a film director.

The "carlin[1] wife" we learn has sent her "three stout and stalwart sons" on a sea voyage. Within a week, she gets news "that her three sons are gone" and, later, that "her sons she'd never see." Nevertheless, her fierce unwillingness to believe them dead and the strength of her great desire brings the shades of her sons home and she welcomes them with proper country hospitality:

> Blow up the fire, my maidens,
>   Bring water from the well;
> For a' my house shall feast this night,
>   Since my three sons are well.

But dismay drifts into the narrative with the first rooster's crow:

> The cock he hadna crawed but once,
>   And clapped his wings at a',
> When the youngest to the eldest said,
>   Brother, we must awa'.

This stanza is followed by a quatrain that is a lyric marvel, four lines that suggest with spirited melody and diction what we may have already guessed about the relationship between life and death, this world and the next:

> The cock doth craw, the day doth daw,
>   The channerin'[2] worm doth chide;
> Gin[3] we be missed out o' our place,
>   A sair pain we maun[4] bide.

As the spirits take their leave, there is a heart-twisting moment as they hark back one final time to the comforts of hearth and home:

> Fare ye weel, my mother dear!
>   Fareweel to barn and byre![5]
> And fare ye weel, the bonny lass,
>   That kindles my mother's fire!

WILLARD
Novel
Stephen Gilbert
Great Britain
1968 (as **RATMAN'S NOTEBOOKS**), London, Michael Joseph; New York, Viking, 1969.

Willard is a revenge fantasy novel. The protagonist of the fiction (not named in the book) is a junior clerk in a British company that his father founded but that now belongs to Mr. Jones, a former employee of the company. Ratman (as the

---

[1] old
[2] muttering
[3] if
[4] must
[5] cottage

book styles the main character) lives with his dying mother in a house that begins to be infested by rats. Instructed by his mother to do something, the young man sets out to kill the rats but instead becomes attached to a particular tribe of the creatures, and especially to a wise sort of rat he has named Socrates.

Eventually, Ratman trains Socrates and other bright rats to do his bidding. This includes serving as Ratman's hench-rats in robberies, in the course of which the rats terrorize storekeepers, merchants and other folk who get in their way. The original rat gang is joined by a new rat named Ben who is so smart he seems actually to be able to read.

From here on, things get progressively more terrifying for the Londoners in whose town all this is taking place. Finally, when Ratman decides he can do without his rat allies, the rats, led by Ben, make their own decision about what must be done.

Willard, as one reviewer put it, is "grotesque, bizarre and believable." But what makes *Willard* work for me is the way its author links his protagonist's loneliness to anger. It is an insightful link and it adds considerable meaning to the Ratman's choice of darkly scuttling rats as his allies.

The film version of *Willard* starring Bruce Davison was a 1971 box office success. It was followed in 1972 by a sequel called *Ben.*

WILLIAM WILSON
Short Story

Edgar Allan Poe
U.S.A.
1839, in *The Gift;* reprinted 1981 in Stephen Peithman's (ed.) *The Annotated Tales of Edgar Allan Poe,* New York, Doubleday.

I have suggested in the Introduction to this book that doubles, dummies and dolls are especially terrifying subjects for horror literature because they so directly touch on the question of one's own identity. In "William Wilson" we get an early study of the divided self that influenced such later, and greater, fictions as Stevenson's *Strange Story of Dr. Jekyll and Mr. Hyde,* Oscar Wilde's *The Picture of Dorian Gray* and Joseph Conrad's *The Secret Sharer.*

In Poe's tale, the narrator is named William Wilson. Early in the story, he tells us that he has led a life of

> unspeakable misery and unpardonable crime . . . Men usually grow base by degrees. From me, in an instant, all virtue dropped bodily as a mantle.

He tells us that he is the, "descendent of a race whose imaginative and easily excitable temperament has at all times rendered them remarkable," and goes on to describe his early education at a school where:

> the ardor, the enthusiasm, and the imperiousness of my disposition, soon rendered me a marked character among my schoolmates, and by slow, but natural gradations, gave me an ascendancy over all not greatly older than myself . . .

Over all but one! And that was a youth who, singularly enough, bore the same name as the narrator. That "other" William Wilson refused to submit his will to that of the narrator's. More than that, the protagonist confesses that he secretly feared the rebellious William Wilson.

From here on, we get an account of the narrator's later profligacies, extravagances and debaucheries, interspersed with accounts of how the "other" William Wilson shows up to chide or to warn him. Once, for instance, at Oxford, at a gaming table, just as the narrator has ruined a young man named Glendinning, the door of the room opens and the "other" William Wilson, dressed in a precise imitation of the narrator, appears and tells the company that they are:

> ". . . uninformed of the true character of the person who has tonight won at écarté . . . Please to examine, at your leisure, the inner linings of the cuff of his left sleeve, and the several little packages which may be found in the somewhat capacious pockets of his embroidered morning wrapper."

Over and over again, the "other" William Wilson appears to spoil the narrator's fun or his schemes or, simply, to excoriate him for his follies until one day, maddened because his semblable is interrupting an especially glittering seduction, the narrator William Wilson confronts his double and sheds his blood. The knowledge he acquires at that moment is what the story—and the horror—are all about.

In "William Wilson" Poe's prose is at a lower pitch than in his more famous tales. This may be because this tale is meant to be an exercise in psychological and moral introspection, rather than an account of action. Though the narrator tells us that he had led a life of great wickedness, we get very little detail about his revelries, his mad infatuations, and the story moves, somewhat abruptly, to its unambiguously moral end. That moral, baldly stated, is that anyone who murders the best aspects of himself is also, "dead—dead to the World, to Heaven and to Hope!"

It is a true truism, no doubt. But for this reader, Poe's moral is far less interesting than his frightful conception of an intrusive *doppelganger* leering superiority at his other self throughout the entire length of a misspent life.

THE WISH
Short Story

Roald Dahl
Great Britain
1953, in *Someone Like You,* New York, Knopf; collection reprinted 1983, Knopf.

"The Wish" is as nearly like a distilled shriek of terror as fiction ever gets to be.

Dahl's protagonist is a small, wildly imaginative little boy who, like most of his kind, invests the whole universe with overwhelming dangers and then invents magic formulas to deal with them. In this case, the boy looks at a vast carpet and says to himself:

> I know how it is. The red parts of the carpet are red hot lumps of coal. What I must do is this: I must walk all the way along it to the front door without touching them. If I touch the red I will be burnt. As a matter of fact, I will be burnt up completely. And the black part of the carpet . . . yes, the black parts are snakes, poisonous snakes, adders mostly, and cobras, thick like tree trunks round the middle, and if I touch one of them I'll be bitten and I'll die before tea time. And if I get across safely without being burnt and without being bitten, I will be given a puppy for my birthday tomorrow.

The boy then decides that the only safe color in the carpet is yellow and gives himself the task of crossing the room stepping only on the yellow.

Thus a child's contract, familiar to anyone who has ever played the sidewalk game guided by the rhyme, "Step on a crack/Break your mother's back," is the order of the day.

With the danger clearly defined, the boy's adventure lies before him and he starts slowly across. The trouble is that this time the universe has heard him and has accepted the boy's definition of what is real. Which leaves the reader with nothing to do but join the story as it shrieks.

THE WITCH OF COOS   Verse

Robert Frost
U.S.A.
1923; reprinted 1973 in Richard Ellman and Robert O'Clare's (eds.) *The Norton Anthology of Modern Poetry,* New York, W.W. Norton.

In Robert Frost's laconic blank verse tale, a narrator tells us that he spent the night on a New Hampshire farm where his hosts were a strange mother and her son. In the course of an evening chat, the narrator learns from the son that the mother has spiritualist powers, and the mother herself seems willing to be thought a witch.

When the son coyly says, ''You wouldn't want to tell him [the narrator] what we have/Up attic, mother?'' she, in a strangely confidential mood, reveals a family secret that has been kept for 40 years: There are bones, a skeleton, nailed up in the attic. Bones that left their grave those many years ago to mount the stairs from the cellar to the bedroom to the attic where her husband, urged on by his wife, nailed the door shut. And there the bones still are though:

> . . . . they sometimes
> Come down the stairs at night and stand perplexed
> Behind the door and headboard of the bed,
> Brushing their chalky skull with chalky fingers,
> With sounds like the dry rattling of a shutter . . .

When the son tells the narrator, ''We never could find out whose bones they were,'' his mother contradicts him, ''Yes, we could, too, son. Tell the truth for once.''

The truth, which the mother insists on telling, is pretty grim. Grimmer still for being told in an absolutely deadpan way and in a blank verse so carefully honed to imitate ordinary New England speech that an unwary reader may fail to notice how lovely its music is.

THE WITCH OF PRAGUE   Novel

F. Marion Crawford
U.S.A.
1891, New York, Macmillan.

Hypnotism, Faustian evil and the embalming of the living instead of the dead are the intertwined threads in the plot of this romantic novel. The ''witch'' of Prague is the beautiful Unorna whose name, in Czech, means ''belonging to February.'' Unorna, who has one gray and one brown eye, is a skilled hypnotist who, in addition to being hopelessly in love with a man known only as The Wanderer, has embarked on an experiment to preserve alive the fame and the mind of a failed intellectual who, at the time the reader makes his acquaintance, is 107 years old. Unorna is aided in her experiment by a Mephistophelian dwarf, wonderfully named Keyork Arabian, who is an adept of the dark arts. The love story touches the occult story in several places but, though Unorna is armed with remarkable powers, her rival, the unremarkable but good Beatrice, triumphs in the end.

The Witch of Prague is more curious than it is powerful. Still, it may be that the picture of the inert old man who is the center of Unorna and Arabian's experiment stirred Bram Stoker's imagination when, some years later, he turned his attention to *Dracula.*

THE WOLF MAN   Film

1941   (B&W)   U.S.A.   71 min.
Production Company: Universal; ***Director:*** George Waggner; ***Producer:*** George Waggner; ***Screenplay:*** Curt Siodmak; ***Photography:*** Joe Valentine; ***Editor:*** Ted Kent; ***Special Effects:*** John P. Fulton, (makeup) Jack Pierce; ***Music:*** Hans J. Salter.
Cast: Lon Chaney, Jr. (Lawrence Talbot), Claude Rains (Sir John Talbot), Evelyn Ankers (Gwen Conliffe), Warren William (Dr. Lloyd), Ralph Bellamy (Captain Paul Montford), Bela Lugosi (Bela the Gypsy), Maria Ouspenskaya (Maleva).

Each of the monsters in Universal Pictures' three great horror films, *Dracula, Frankenstein* and *The Wolf Man,* has his unique relationship to evil. Dracula is the consummate villain, specifically identified as satanic. The Frankenstein creature is wicked only because he is provoked. Only the Wolf Man is both reluctant before his crimes and remorseful afterward. Which means, if we look closely, that he is the new look in monsters: a villain for the Age of Freud.

Larry Talbot, who is handy with tools, comes back after 18 years in America to his family home in Wales where his father, Sir John, is the lord of the manor. Larry meets Gwen, a lovely young woman who is the daughter of a local shopkeeper. Though Gwen is engaged to marry Frank Andrews, Sir John's gamekeeper, she and Larry fall in love.

Lon Chaney, Jr., and Evelyn Ankers in **The Wolf Man.**

Meanwhile, the Gypsies come to town. One of them, Bela, tells fortunes, but when the moon is full, he turns into a werewolf. Larry Talbot, trying to save Gwen's friend Jenny from Bela's attack, clubs the werewolf to death with a walking stick that has a silver handle in the form of wolf's head. But in the course of the struggle he is bitten by the werewolf and, as the wise Gypsy woman, Maleva tells him, anyone bitten by a werewolf will turn into a werewolf himself.

Maleva is, of course, right and Larry Talbot is soon loping through the underbrush panting for and finding victims. But Larry, knowing that Gwen is destined to be his next victim, gives his walking stick with its silver wolf's head to his father. Later, when Larry attacks Gwen, Sir John beats the werewolf to death with the silverhandled stick. In death, Larry resumes his human shape quickly enough so that no one, except his father, needs to know the horrid truth.

The Wolf Man, despite its simpleminded story line and in spite of Lon Chaney, Jr.'s wooden-face performance in the title role, remains a memorable film. First, because Claude Rains and Maria Ouspenskaya give perfect performances and then, because Siodmak and Waggner, by surrounding their werewolf story with a fairy tale atmosphere, have managed to domesticate (and thereby intensify) its ominous sexual and family implications. Gwen, Frank and Larry represent the age-old eternal triangle; and another ancient dynamic is at work when we see Sir John beating his son Larry to death to keep him from the wilder temptations of his instincts.

Myth, then, is the source of the film's strengths. And none of the characters better exemplifies the power of myth than Maria Ouspenskaya's Maleva, who is the bearer of the film's werewolf lore and who, enchantingly, recites verses that young filmgoers are likely to remember forever. When Maleva warns Talbot she says:

> Even the man who is pure at heart
> And who says his prayers at night
> May become a wolf when the wolfbane blooms
> And the autumn moon is bright.

And when she mourns a dead werewolf she intones:

> The way you walked was thorny
> Through no fault of your own,
> But as the rain enters the soil
> And the river enters the sea
> So tears come to their predestined end.

Not great poetry, no doubt, but uttered in her wonderful accent and in the context of the events of which she is timelessly aware they have the ring of prophecy.

THE WOLFEN   Film
1981 (C) U.S.A. 115 min.
Production Company: Orion; *Director:* Michael Wadleigh; *Producer:* Rupert Hitzig; *Screenplay:* David Eyre and Michael Wadleigh, based on the novel by Whitley Strieber; *Photography:* Gerry Fisher; *Editors:* Chris Lebenzon, Dennis Dolan, Martin Bram, Marshall Borden; *Special Effects:* Robert Blalack, Ronnie Otteson, Conrad Brink; *Music:* James Horner. *Cast:* Albert Finney (Detective Dewey Wilson), Diane Venora (Rebekka Neff), Edward James Olmos (Eddie Holt), Gregory Hines (Whittington), Tom Noonan (Ferguson).

Based on a flimsy novel by Whitley Strieber, *The Wolfen* achieves some distinction—indeed, it is something of a tour de force—for its camera work. The first 20 minutes of the film are devoted to striking views of New York City—a cold angular scrutiny, replete with intricate architectural details. These are sharp, bright frames that recall the paintings of Charles Sheeler. The camera seems to be in a rush to see. It rises and swoops; it skips and leaps.

The story of *The Wolfen* is more or less as follows: There are suddenly a number of strange and ghastly deaths taking place in various parts of the city. Before the film is over, various explanations for the deaths will be offered: "something to do with voodoo"; radical international terrorism; or, simply, "There's some weird shit happening." Detective Dewey Wilson, who is investigating the murders, remarks, "What's really interesting is what we haven't got. We haven't got a trace of metal." There is a clue, however—wolf hair, found on the mangled remains.

Finally, Detective Wilson and a psychologist named Rebekka are led to Eddie, a Native American who works "on the steel," constructing skyscrapers. Eddie, who often spends the night high in the girders of the Brooklyn Bridge talking to his ancestors, knows what is happening because, among other things, he is capable (by means of an amulet or drug) of shape-shifting. And the shape he shifts into is, presumably, his totemic animal, the wolf.

With Eddie's help, and some mute hints the action provides us, we are reminded that wolves in the wild serve as nature's housekeepers by preying on the weak animals of a herd, thereby improving the gene pool of the coming generations. And we are given to understand that now an intelligent race of wolves, deprived by mankind's rape of the environment of their natural food, have moved to New York City where they are adapting themselves to urban life and where, as in the wild, they will cull the weakest from the herd. "The smartest [wolves]," says Eddie, "went underground into the new wilderness, your cities. . . . You got your technology, but you lost. You lost your senses. . . . You don't have the eyes of the hunter, you have the eyes of the dead."

As *The Wolfen* comes to its close, we hear that what has been happening in Manhattan has also begun to happen in New Orleans.

The ecology tract that, clearly, the filmmakers thought they were creating is, finally, less engaging than the superb moments when the camera seems to live inside the eyes of a wolf stalking its prey through the urban wilderness. It is in those scenes, filmed by Steadicam cameras in infrared and in ultraviolet, that we experience swiftness, vitality, intentness and, what the rest of the film sadly lacks, absolute coherence and focus.

X

"X" THE MAN WITH THE X-RAY EYES   Film
(Alternate release title: **THE MAN WITH THE X-RAY EYES**)

1963   (C)   U.S.A.   86 min.

Production Company: American International; ***Director:*** Roger Corman; ***Producer:*** Roger Corman; ***Screenplay:*** Robert Dillon and Ray Russell; ***Director:*** *Roger Corman;* ***Photography:*** Floyd Crosby; ***Editor:*** Anthony Carras; ***Special Effects:*** Butler-Glouner, Inc., (makeup) Ted Coodley; ***Music:*** Lex Baxter.

Cast: Ray Milland (Dr. James Xavier), Diana Van Der Vlis (Dr. Diane Fairfax), Harold J. Stone (Dr. Sam Brant), John Hoyt (Dr. Willard Benson), Don Rickles (Crane).

Here is another of those phenomenal Roger Corman films in which his genius, assailed by a tight budget ($300,000) and insufficient time (three weeks), has exerted itself to transcend those limitations.

The theme of *"X" The Man With the X-Ray Eyes* is hardly unusual. It is one more reiteration of the caution uttered in innumerable science fiction stories and films that, "There are some things mankind ought not to know." But Corman, with the magnificent help of the screenplay by Robert Dillon and Ray Russell, has managed to turn that commonplace theme into a pain-filled and frequently grand allegory of human pride properly humbled by the Creator of the Universe.

Ray Milland is the pride-filled Dr. James Xavier, a research scientist who has been studying the human eye and has been seized by the ambition to extend the limits of sight. "What," he asks, "could we really see if we had access to the other ninety percent [of the spectrum]." When his friend Dr. Sam Brant cautions, "Only the gods see everything," Xavier replies, "I'm closing in on the gods."

And for a while it seems that he may be right as he develops a solution that allows the eye to expand its visual capabilities many times. Eventually, Xavier, obsessed by his research, begins to use the solution on his own eyes, but the more he uses it, the clearer it becomes that its effects, which enable him to see through objects—"to see more light than I've ever seen"—are both cumulative and irreversible. Meanwhile, goaded by his ambition and frustrated because a scientific foundation will not renew his funds, he is driven further and further down the road to madness. Far enough, anyway, to kill his friend Sam Brant who has tried to restrain him.

Now a fugitive from the law, Xavier, using his chemically induced powers, becomes Mentalo, "the man who sees all," in a carnival where he is under the thumb of the blackmailing and very wicked Crane. By the time Xavier has been rescued from Crane by the beautiful young Dr. Diane Fairfax, he is physically and emotionally at the end of his tether.

In its concluding five or six minutes, the film acquires both its dramatic and spiritual grandeur. In them, we follow a bleeding, dazed Xavier whose eyes, seen now as twin, glowing rubies, are so filled with light that he can hardly see. Utterly exhausted, he stumbles across the Nevada desert until he comes to a revivalist tent meeting. There, when the preacher calls upon the sinners in his flock to come up to repent, Xavier weaves his way forward with the others. The preacher speaks sternly to him, "Do you wish to be saved?"

"No," he replies. "I've come to tell you what I see. There are great darknesses, farther than time itself. And beyond the darkness is a light that glows. That changes. And at the center of the universe there is the Eye that sees us all."

And Xavier, having stared into that Eye, now pays the dreadful penalty. The last glimpse we have of him, masterfully timed to create a red glare of comprehension, is, for pity's sake, followed by a series of neutral but color-distorted shots of buildings as the camera itself, after such knowledge, seems to be searching for someplace to hide.

Y

YABU NO NAKA KURONEKO
Film

(Alternate release title: **KURONEKO,** or **THE BLACK CAT**)

1968 (B&W) Japan 99 min.

Production Company: Kindai Eiga Kyokai/Nihon Eiga Shinsha; *Director:* Kaneto Shindo; *Producer:* Nobuyo Horiaba; *Screenplay:* Kaneto Shindo; *Photography:* Kyomi Kuroda; *Makeup:* Shigeo Kobayashi; *Music:* Hikaru Hayashi.

Cast: Nobuko Otowa (the mother-in-law), Kiwako Taichi (the daughter-in-law), Kichiemon Nakamura (the Samurai).

This haunting tale of transformation is cruelly specific in its acts of violence at the same time as it is an atmospheric, even lyric allegory about the responsibilities and abuses that go with sexual power.

The story, set in the 12th century, has a mother and a daughter-in-law who are raped and killed by Samurai. After the deaths, the women are transformed into cats who, as agents of vengeance, are dedicated to the destruction of passing Samurai.

When the Samurai sent to destroy the spirits turns out to be the husband of the younger woman, the allegory of sexual power becomes a study in family relationships as well. When the cat spirit realizes who the man is, she spares his life, for which act she is condemned to take up her place in hell. The Samurai, however, does battle with the cat who was his mother-in-law. Though he manages to cut off one of her paws, the matter does not end there.

The Black Cat (the title the film had when I saw it) gives us a fascinating glimpse of how the Japanese mind treats the were-animal theme. Unlike the werewolves that come loping out of Hollywood, the image of the animal here is not meant to stand for some unevolved bestial element in our nature. Instead, these cats are the graceful and proper agents of vengeance. This single fact raises, as it were, the level of discourse, and makes the film both denser and darker.

Having said so much, one must add that *The Black Cat* is one of those productions that is more beautiful than it is

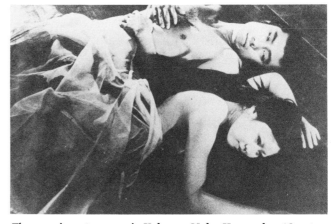

The vampire cat woman in **Yabu no Naka Kuroneko.** (Courtesy of the New York Public Library Picture Collection)

satisfying. Partly, the problem is that a western viewer feels that he or she is missing any number of purely Japanese nuances of speech and character. Partly, too, it is because the film is raggedly edited. Either way, this is a movie that must be seen because even a flawed Kaneto Shindo film deserves attention.

THE YELLOW WALLPAPER
Short Story

Charlotte Perkins Gilman

U.S.A.

1899, Boston, Small Maynard; reprinted 1979 in Leonard Wolf's (ed.) *Wolf's Complete Book of Terror*, New York, Clarkson N. Potter Inc.

''The Yellow Wallpaper'' is a story that is widely perceived as feminist protest fiction. Certainly, it is one of the finest studies of the way thoughtless men can oppress the women they love by relegating them to the status of dandled dependents.

The first-person narrator tells us that she and her husband,

John, have taken a house for the summer. It is, "A colonial mansion, a hereditary estate. I would say a haunted house . . ." And the reason for taking the house is to give the narrator, who seems to be something of a neurasthenic, a chance to rest, to breathe deeply of the invigorating summer air.

Immediately, however, we learn certain ominous details. The narrator hates her bedroom at the top of the house. It appears once to have been a children's nursery, but the children in it must have been singularly unhappy. There are bars on the windows. The bed is nailed into place. But worst of all is the hideous wall paper whose, "color is repellent, almost revolting; a smouldering unclean yellow strangely faded by the slow-turning sunlight." While the narrator would rather have the downstairs bedroom that, "opened on the piazza and had roses all over the window . . .," John would not hear of it, and John is "very careful and loving, and hardly lets me stir without special direction."

As the weeks pass and the narrator continues to live in the room with the horrid wallpaper certain things become clear: first, that she is virtually a prisoner, her every move watched and reported by her husband's sister; second, that she is being both debilitated and driven mad by her confinement; and third, that she sees the yellow wallpaper as the sinister agent of her torment.

> There is a recurrent spot where the pattern lolls like a broken neck and two bulbous eyes stare at you upside down.

> I get positively angry with the impertinence of it and the everlastingness. Up and down and sideways they crawl, and those absurd, unblinking eyes are everywhere.

Then one day she notices that, "in the places where [the wallpaper] isn't faded and where the sun is just so—I can see a strange, provoking sort of figure, that seems to skulk about behind that silly and conspicuous front design." Over the days, that figure becomes more and more distinct. "It is always the same shape, only very numerous. And it is like a woman stooping down and creeping about behind that pattern." As the story approaches its climax, the woman behind the pattern and the narrator form a silent bond. Finally, the narrator is certain that:

> The front pattern does move—and no wonder! The woman behind shakes it! . . . And she is all the time trying to climb through. But nobody could climb through that pattern—it strangles so . . .

Eventually the woman behind the pattern gets out but who she is and just what her escape really means to the narrator is shrouded in the richest kind of ambiguity. The story's ending, too, manages to be precisely horrifying without being clear.

The Yellow Wallpaper is a pioneering work. Written while English Victorianism was still very much alive, it is nevertheless a fully realized modernist fiction that continues to illuminate the tyrannies (in this case, masculine) of love.

YOUNG FRANKENSTEIN   Film
1974 (B&W) U.S.A. 108 min.

Production Company: Gruskoff Ventures Films/20th Century-Fox; ***Director:*** Mel Brooks; ***Producer:*** Michael Gruskoff; ***Screenplay:*** Gene Wilder and Mel Brooks; ***Photography:*** Gerald Hirshfield; ***Editor:*** John C. Howard; ***Special Effects:*** Henry Millar, Jr., and Hal Millar; ***Music:*** John Morris.
Cast: Gene Wilder (Frankenstein), Peter Boyle (The Creature), Marty Feldman (Igor), Madeline Kahn (Elizabeth), Cloris Leachman (Frau Blücher), Terri Garr (Inga), Kenneth Mars (Inspector Kemp) and Gene Hackman (the blind man).

This is a memorable comic gloss of the Frankenstein legend as it was established in Hollywood in the thirties. Alert viewers will see frequent, if slightly cockeyed, replays of scenes in *Frankenstein* (1931), *The Bride of Frankenstein* (1935) and *The Son of Frankenstein* (1939). Mostly the fun of *Young Frankenstein* comes from the way that Wilder and Brooks handle the old classics with gingerly respect even as they turn them on their ears; and from the stylish, literate and perfectly timed clowning of the cast.

Friedrich Frankenstein (pronounced Frahnken*steen*) is teaching in an American medical school when he is informed that the last Baron Frankenstein, in Transylvania, has died and that he, Friedrich, has inherited the castle and the title.

He bids a fond, if difficult, farewell to his fiancee, Elizabeth, who cannot be kissed (it would smear her lipstick) or touched (it would rumple her taffeta dress). Moments later, via the magic of swift film editing, Friedrich leans out of a window to ask, "Pardon me, boy. Is this the Transylvania Station?" A German-speaking boy replies, "Ja, ja. Track 29."

Friedrich at once meets Igor (pronounced Eye-gore), his saucer-eyed, humpbacked servant who introduces him to Inga, the bosomy blonde who is to be his lab assistant. Then he is driven off to the castle where he meets Frau Blücher whose name, each time that it is spoken, produces whinnies from the horses in the stable.

Now that the cast is more or less in place, the story of *Young Frankenstein* makes its parodic way through one or another of the great old scenes in the great old films. Friedrich, who begins by believing that his grandfather's researches were "doo doo," is finally persuaded to replicate the work of creation. "Destiny," he cries. "There is no escaping destiny." Igor, of course, drops the brain of the "scientist and saint" he was asked to get and brings an "abnormal brain" to his master. Later we get Gene Wilder's somewhat noisy version of the famous, "It's alive, it's alive" scene. Eventually, the Creature, by the connivance of Frau Blücher is permitted to escape and we follow its adventures for a time. Again (as in *Frankenstein*) it meets the little girl; again (as in *The Bride of Frankenstein*) there is a scene in a hut with a blind man. Invariably, the Creature, marvelously made up and marvelously played by Peter Boyle, is a sort of long-suffering Candide whom other people invariably torment with their kindness.

When the film leaves the track of its predecessors and we see both Friedrich Frankenstein and the Creature in top hat and tails on stage doing a vaudeville turn, an uneasy sexist humor, which has always been present in subdued form, takes over. That humor, which earlier had been flip and genial, becomes raunchy and cruel as the size and the effect of the Creature's "*schwannenstecker*" provide Wilder and Brooks with opportunity for the sort of jokes that nowadays make sensitive people wince.

YUKI-ONNA

Short Story

Lafcadio Hearn
Japan
1904, in *Kwaidan*, New York, Harpers; collection reprinted 1968. New York, Dover.

"Yuki-Onna," like the other tales Lafcadio Hearn retold and collected in his volume *Kwaidan* is memorable for its unstrained prose style that seems to breathe the tale without artifice. It becomes that much more horrible because it is so very much a part of the commonplace.

Lafcadio Hearn tells us that a couple of woodcutters, Mosaku, an old man, and Minokichi, his 18-year-old apprentice, are on their way home from a forest where they have been chopping wood. They are overtaken by a snowstorm and take refuge in a primitive hut where they lie down to sleep. In the course of the night, the young man, Minokichi, wakes and sees a white form bending over Mosaku, "blowing her breath upon him—and her breath was like a bright white smoke."

Minokichi sees that the figure is a beautiful woman all in white and when she notices that she has been observed she says to him, "I intended to treat you like the other man. But I cannot help feeling some pity for you, because you are so young." She spares his life but warns him, "if you ever tell anybody—even your own mother—about what you have seen this night, I shall know it; and then I will kill you . . ."

The next morning, Minokichi finds that Mosaku is dead.

Time passes and Minokichi, in the winter of the following year, meets an attractive young damsel who calls herself O-Yuki, which signifies snow. It does not take long for the young people to discover that each of them is single and not much longer before they fall in love and are married. Years pass and O-Yuki bears Minokichi 10 children, but it is notable that, "O-Yuki, even after having become the mother of ten children, looked as young and fresh as on the day when she had first come to the village."

Then one night, in one of those comfortable moments when husbands and wives share memories of their pasts, Minokichi makes the mistake of confiding to O-Yuki the story of the Woman in the Snow and suddenly the charm of his marriage is shattered.

It should be said that O-Yuki is not an atypical Oriental demon. Both Japanese and Chinese folklore have tales in which nonhuman spirits fall in love with or marry humans and the marriages can work just so long as the human remembers to obey the rules the spirit has laid down.

Z

ZOLTAN, HOUND OF DRACULA
Film

(Alternate release title: **DRACULA'S DOG**)

1977 (C) U.S.A. 88 min.

Production Company: Vic Productions; *Director:* Albert Band; *Producer:* Albert Band, Frank Ray Perilli; *Screenplay:* Frank Ray Perilli; *Photography:* Ron Johnson; *Editor:* Harry Keramidas; *Special Effects:* Sam Shaw; *Music:* Andrew Belling.

Cast: Michael Pataki (Michael Drake)/Count Dracula), Jan Shutan (Marla Drake), Libbie Chase (Linda Drake), John Levin (Steve Drake), Reggie Nalder (Veidt Smit), Jose Ferrer (Inspector Branco).

This is a surprisingly watchable, inexpensive addition to the film lore of Dracula.

Somewhere in the Soviet Union a team of soldiers comes upon a number of tombs in which bodies are found with stakes driven through their hearts. When a soldier pulls a stake out of one of the bodies, it comes to life and kills the soldier for his pains. The resuscitated creature then promptly pulls the stake from a second body and what leaps from the coffin is Zoltan, the hound of Dracula, a Doberman pinscher with blazing white eyes that have no pupils.

Enter now Inspector Branco (Jose Ferrer) who understands at once why two of the Dracula family coffins are empty. Branco informs a photogenic young woman army major that the missing creatures are quasi-vampires who do not have a vampire's bloodthirst but who must serve a vampire or die. Though Branco does not know that one of the vampires is a dog, he shrewdly suspects that they will search for a living Dracula to serve. With the major's permission, Branco goes off to Los Angeles where Michael Drake, the last of the Draculas, is leading a solid suburban life, and where the vampires are sure to go.

Branco turns out to be right. Veidt Smit, the quasi-vampire, and Zoltan, the hound of Dracula, have indeed gone to California as we learn in a quite funny scene in which American customs officers inspect the dog's coffin. Once past customs, the two servants of evil, man and dog, drive off in a hearse to find Michael Drake. Smit's scheme is for Zoltan to vampirize Drake so that man and dog may acquire the sort of master they are destined to serve.

Drake, his wife, their small son and slightly older daughter as well as two police dogs and a puppy have just gone off for a camping trip in their huge and luxurious recreation vehicle.

Drake is an unexceptional American paterfamilias who has nothing of the vampire in him. But soon he and his family are subjected to night attacks, first from Zoltan, and then later from Zoltan and other dogs he has vampirized. Things get pretty hairy until Inspector Branco shows up to explain what is really happening. Michael Drake then sends his wife and children back home while he and the inspector stay on to battle the devil dog and his master. There is a lot of fine yelping, growling, howling, scratching, biting, clawing and sinister risings and settings of a full moon before good almost triumphs. As the film ends, Michael heaves a sigh of relief and says, ''Well, we got the last of them,'' but the camera moves away from the scene to show us a vampirized puppy staring up at the full moon with eyes that have no pupils.

Zoltan is one of those horror films that endears itself to the viewer because it makes such imaginative use of the few assets a skimpy production budget provides. In this case those are, first, Jose Ferrer, who is relaxed and cheerful even as he stays in character as a vampire hunter, second, an ingenious screenplay and finally, the dogs who commit their wickedness with a zest that is altogether admirable and does credit to their trainers.

BIBLIOGRAPHY

Addis, Stephen, ed., *Japanese Ghosts & Demons: Art of the Supernatural*. New York: George Braziller, 1985.

Aickman, Robert, *Cold Hand in Mine: Strange Stories*. New York: Scribner, 1977.

Ainsworth, William Harrison, Esq. The Lancashire Witches, a Romance of Pendle Forest. London: Colburn, 1849.

Alexa, *The Spectre Bridegroom*. London: Dean and Munday, 1890.

Andrews, Nigel, *Horror Films*. New York: Gallery Books, 1985.

Anson, Jay, *The Amityville Horror*. Englewood Cliffs, N.J.: Prentice-Hall, 1977.

Apuleius Madaurensis. *The Golden Ass*. Cambridge, Mass.: Harvard University Press, 1915.

Arthur, Robert, comp., *Davy Jones' Haunted Locker; Great Ghost Stories of the Sea*. New York: Random House, 1965.

Asquith, Cynthia, *This Mortal Coil*. Sauk City, Wis.: Arkham House, 1947.

Asquith, Cynthia, ed., *The Ghost Book*. London: Hutchinson, 1927.

———, ed., *The Second Ghost Book*. London: Barrie, 1952.

———, ed., *Shudders*. New York: Scribner, 1929.

———, ed., *The Third Ghost Book*. London: Barrie, 1956.

Barchilon, Jacques, *Le Conte Merveilleux Français de 1690 à 1790*, 7th ed. Paris: Libraireonoré Champion, 1975.

Baring-Gould, Sabine. *A Book of Ghosts*. London: Methuen, 1904; Freeport, N.Y.: Libraries Press, 1969.

Barker, Clive, *In The Flesh*. New York: Poseidon Press, 1986.

Bataille, Georges, *Death and Sensuality*. Salem, N.H.: Ayer, 1977.

Beck, L. Adams, *The Ghost Plays of Japan*. New York: The Japan Society, 1933.

Benchley, Peter, *Jaws*. Garden City, N.Y.: Doubleday, 1974.

Benedict, Stewart H., ed., *Tales of Terror and Suspense*. New York: Dell, 1963.

Benson, A.C., *The Hill of Trouble and Other Stories*. London: Isbister, 1903.

Benson, E.F., *The Room in the Tower*. London: Mills & Boon, 1912.

———, *Spook Stories*. London: Hutchinson, 1928.

Bierce, Ambrose, *Can Such Things Be?* New York: Cassell, 1893.

———, *Collected Writings*. New York: Citadel, 1946.

———, *Ghost and Horror Stories of Ambrose Bierce*, ed. E.F. Bleiler. New York: Dover, 1964.

Blackwood, Algernon, *Best Ghost Stories of Algernon Blackwood*, ed. E.F. Bleiler. New York: Dover, 1973.

———, *The Best Supernatural Tales of Algernon Blackwood*, New York: Causeway, 1973.

———, *Tales of Terror and the Unknown*. New York: Dutton, 1965.

———, *Tales of the Mysterious and Macabre*. London: Spring Books, 1967.

———, *Tales of the Uncanny and Supernatural*. London: P. Nevil, 1949.

———, *The Doll and One Other*. Sauk City, Wis.: Arkham House, 1946.

Blatty, William Peter, *The Exorcist*. New York: Harper & Row, 1971.

Blavatsky, Helena Petrovna, *Nightmare Tales*. London: Theosophical Publishing Society, 1892. In A. Trevor Barker, ed., *The Complete Works of Helena Petrovna Blavatsky*. London: Rider, 1933–36.

Bleiler, E.F., *Supernatural Fiction Writers*, 2 vols. New York: Scribner, 1985.

Bleiler, E.F., ed., *Five Victorian Ghost Novels*. New York: Dover, 1971.

Bloch, Robert, *Blood Runs Cold*. New York: Simon & Schuster, 1961.

———, *Pleasant Dreams-Nightmares*. Sauk City, Wis.: Arkham House, 1962.

———, *Psycho*. New York: Simon and Shuster, 1959.

Bontly, Thomas, *Celestial Chess*. New York: Harper and Row, 1979.

Borges, Jorge Luis, *A Personal Anthology*. New York: Grove Press, 1976.

Boucher, Anthony, *Far and Away*. New York: Ballantine, 1953.

Boucher, Anthony, ed., *A Treasury of Great Science Fiction*. Garden City, N.Y.: Doubleday, 1959.

Bowen, Marjorie (pseud. Gabrielle Margaret Vere), *Kecksies and Other Twilight Tales*. Sauk City, Wis.: Arkham House, 1973.

————, *Black Magic: A Tale of the Rise and Fall of Antichrist*. London: Alston Rivers, 1909.

Bradbury, Ray, *The Vintage Bradbury*. New York: Vintage/Random House, 1965.

Brandner, Gary, *The Howling*. New York: Fawcett, 1977.

Broster, Dorothy Kathleen, *Couching at the Door*. London: Heinemann, 1942; New York: Arno, 1976.

Brown, Charles Brockden, *Wieland; or the Transformation. An American Tale*. New York: T. & J. Swords, for H. Caritat, 1798. Bicentennial edition, Kent, Ohio: Kent State University Press, 1977.

Bullen, A.H., ed., *The Works of Christopher Marlowe*. New York: AMS Press, 1970.

Bulwer-Lytton, Lord Edward G., "The Haunted and the Haunters; or The House and the Brain," in *Minor Classics of Nineteenth Century Fiction*, ed. William E. Buckler, 2 vols. Boston: Riverside, 1967.

————, *A Strange Story*. London: Sampson Low, 1862.

Burgess, Anthony, *Clockwork Orange*. New York: Ballantine, 1963.

Butler, Ivan, *The Horror Film*. Cranbury, N.J.: A.S. Barnes, 1967.

Caillois, Roger, ed., *Anthologies du Fantastique*. Paris: Gallimard, 1966.

Campbell, Leroy A., *Mithraic Iconography and Ideology*. Leiden: E.J. Brill, 1968.

Campbell, Ramsey, *Demons by Daylight*. Sauk City, Wis.: Arkham House, 1973.

Cerf, Bennett, ed., *Famous Ghost Stories*. New York: Random House, 1944.

Chambers, R.W., *The King in Yellow*. New York and Chicago: Neely, 1895; contents revised, expanded, edited by E.F. Bleiler, New York: Dover, 1970.

Clarens, Carlos, *An Illustrated History of the Horror Film*. New York: Putnam, 1967.

Cline, Terry C., *Damon*. New York: Putnam, 1975.

Cohen, Daniel, *A Modern Look at Monsters*. New York: Dodd, Mead, 1970.

Collins, Charles M., *A Feast of Blood*. New York: Avon, 1967.

Collins, Wilkie, *The Haunted Hotel: A Mystery of Modern Venice*. New York: Dover, 1982.

————, *Tales of Terror and the Supernatural*. New York: Dover, 1972.

Congdon, Don, ed., *Stories for the Dead of Night*. New York: Dell, 1957.

Conklin, Groff, ed., *The Supernatural Reader*. New York: Collier, 1962.

Coppard, A.E., *The Collected Tales of A.E. Coppard*. New York: Knopf, 1951.

Crane, Stephen, *The Complete Short Stories and Sketches of Stephen Crane*. Garden City, N.Y.: Doubleday, 1963.

Crawford, F. Marion, *Wandering Ghosts*. London: Unwin, 1911.

————, *The Witch of Prague, a Fantastic Tale*. London & New York: Macmillan, 1891.

Cross, John K., ed., *Best Horror Stories*. London: Faber and Faber, 1963.

Cuddon, J.A., ed., *The Penguin Book of Ghost Stories*. New York: Penguin, 1984.

Dahl, Roald, *Roald Dahl's Book of Ghost Stories*. New York: Farrar, Straus & Giroux, 1983.

————, *Kiss Kiss*. 1953; republished in New York: Dell, 1961.

————, *Someone Like You*. New York: Knopf, 1953; New York: Dell, 1961.

————, *Switch Bitch*. New York: Warner Books, 1965.

Daniel, Howard, *Devils, Monsters and Nightmares*. New York: Abelard-Schuman, 1964.

Daniels, Lee, ed., *Dying of Fright*. New York: Scribner, 1976.

Davenport, Basil, ed., *Deals with the Devil*. New York: Dodd, Mead, 1958.

De La Mare, Walter, *The Connoisseur and Other Stories*. New York: Knopf, 1926.

————, *The Return*. London: Putnam, 1910; New York: Arno, 1976.

De Ludes, Count Ignatius, *The Tourist's Guide To Transylvania: A Traveller's Handbook of Count Dracula's Kingdom*. London: Octopus, 1981.

Derleth, August, *The Mask of Cthulhu*. Sauk City, Wis.: Arkham House, 1964.

————, *The Trail of Cthulhu*. Sauk City, Wis.: Arkham House, 1969.

Derleth, August, ed., *Tales of the Cthulhu Mythos*. Sauk City, Wis.: Arkham House, 1969.

De Sade, Marquis, *Three Complete Novels*, tr. Richard Seaver and Austryn Wainhouse. New York: Grove Press, 1968.

Dickens, Charles, et al., *Classic Ghost Stories by Charles Dickens and Others*. New York: Dover Publications. 1975.

Diderot, Denis, *La Religieuse* ("Memoirs of a Nun"). Paris: Buisson, 1796; republished Paris: A. Colin, 1961.

Douglas, Drake, *Horror!* New York: Macmillan, 1966.

Douglas, George Brisbane, ed., *Scottish Fairy and Folk Tales*. London: Arno Press, 1901.

Doyle, Arthur Conan, *The Best Supernatural Tales of Arthur Conan Doyle*, ed. E.F. Bleiler. New York: Dover, 1979.

————, *The Complete Adventures and Memoirs of Sherlock Holmes*. New York: Clarkson N. Potter, 1975.

————, *Tales of Terror and Mystery*. Garden City, N.Y.: Doubleday, 1977.

Du Maurier, Daphne, *Kiss Me Again, Stranger*. Garden City, N.Y.: Doubleday, 1952.

Ducasse, Isidore, *Maldoror*, tr. Guy Wernham. New York: New Directions, 1946.

Dunsany, Lord, *Gods, Men, and Ghosts: The Best Supernatural Fiction of Lord Dunsany*, ed. E.F. Bleiler. New York: Dover, 1972.

Ellison, Harlan, *Alone Against Tomorrow*. New York: Macmillan, 1971.

————, *Deathbird Stories: A Pantheon of Modern Gods*. New York: Harper & Row, 1975.

Etchison, Dennis, ed., *Cutting Edge*. Garden City, N.Y.: Doubleday, 1986.

Ewers, Hanns Heinz, *Alraune*. New York: John Day, 1929; New York: Arno, 1976.

Eyries, Jean Baptiste Benoit, *Fantasmagoriana*. Paris: Chez F. Schoell, 1812.

Farson, Daniel, *The Man Who Wrote Dracula: A Biography of Bram Stoker*. London: M. Joseph, 1975.

Fiedler, Leslie A., ed., *In Dreams Awake*. New York: Dell, 1975.

Frank, Alan, *The Horror Film Handbook*. Totowa, N.J.: Barnes & Noble, 1982.

Freeman, Mary E. Wilkins, *The Collected Ghost Stories of Mary Wilkins-Freeman*, intro. Edward Wagenknecht. Sauk City, Wis.: Arkham House, 1974.

Fuseli, Henry, *Johann Heinrich Fuseli*. Zurich: Gemalde und Zeichnungen, Kunsthaus, 1969.

Gifford, Denis, *The British Film Catalogue, 1895–1985: A Reference Guide*. New York: Facts On File, 1986.

Gilman, Charlotte Perkins, *The Yellow Wallpaper*. Boston: Small Maynard, 1899; Old Westbury, N.Y.: The Feminist Press, 1973, afterword by Elaine R. Hedges.

Glatser, Nahum, ed., *Twenty-one Stories*. New York: Schocken, 1970.

Goethe, Johann Wolfgang von, *Faust: A Tragedy*. 1808, 1832; Boston: Houghton Mifflin, 1911, tr. Bayard Taylor; New York: Farrar, Straus & Giroux, 1976, tr. Randall Jarrell.

Green, William Child, *The Abbot of Montserrat, or The Pool of Blood*, 2 vols. London: A.K. Newman, 1826; republished New York: Arno, 1977.

Hadfield, John, ed., *A Chamber of Horrors Unlocked*. Boston: Little, Brown, 1965.

Haggard, H. Rider, *Ayesha: The Return of She*. London: Ward Lock, 1905; New York: Dover, 1978.

Haining, Peter, ed., *The Fantastic Pulps*. New York: St. Martin's Press, 1975.

———, ed., *The Gentlewomen of Evil: An Anthology of Rare Supernatural Stories from the Pens of Victorian Ladies*. New York: Taplinger, 1967.

———, ed., *The Ghouls*. New York: Stein and Day, 1971.

———, ed., *Gothic Tales of Terror*. New York: Taplinger, 1972.

———, ed., *Great British Tales of Terror*, vol. 1. London: Gollancz, 1972.

———, ed., *The Midnight People*. New York: Popular Library, 1968.

———, ed., *The Unspeakable People*. New York: Popular Library, 1969.

Harvey, W.F., *The Beast with Five Fingers and Other Tales*. London: Dent, 1928; New York: Dutton, 1947 (expanded ed.).

———, *Midnight Tales*. London: Dent, 1946.

Hawthorne, Nathaniel, *Hawthorne's Short Stories*. New York: Vintage, 1946.

———, *Complete Short Stories*. Garden City, N.Y.: Hanover House, 1959.

Hearn, Lafcadio, *Kwaidan: Stories and Studies of Strange Things*. Boston: Houghton Mifflin, 1904; New York: Dover, 1968.

———, *Some Chinese Ghosts*. Boston: Roberts Bros., 1887; republished New York: Modern Library, 1927.

Hecht, Ben, *Collected Stories of Ben Hecht*. New York: Crown, 1943.

Hemming, Roy, ed., *Video Review's Movies on Video*. New York: Viare Publishing Co., 1980.

Hitchcock, Alfred, ed., *Alfred Hitchcock Presents My Favorites in Suspense*. New York: Random House, 1959.

———, ed., *Alfred Hitchcock Presents Stories They Wouldn't Let Me Do on TV*. New York: Simon & Schuster, 1957.

———, ed., *Monster Museum: Twelve Shuddery Stories for Daring Young Readers*. New York: Random House, 1965.

Hoffman, Martin, *The Gay World: Male Homosexuality and the Social Creation of Evil*. New York: Basic Books, 1968.

Hoffmann, Ernst T.A., *The Best Tales of Hoffmann*, ed. E.F. Bleiler. New York: Dover, 1967.

———, *Weird Tales*, tr. J.T. Bealby. New York: Scribner, 1885; Freeport, N.Y.: Books for Libraries Press, 1970.

Hogg, Garry, *Cannibalism and Human Sacrifice*. New York: Citadel Press, 1966.

Housman, Clemence, *The Were-Wolf*. New York: Arno, 1976.

Howe, Florence & Bass, Ellen, eds., *An Anthology of Poems by Women*. New York: Doubleday/Anchor, 1973.

Hugo, Victor, *La Légende des Siècles; La fin de Satan*. Bruxelles: Edition Hetzel, Meline, Cans, 1859; Paris: Librairie Gallimard, 1950.

Huysmans, J.K., *Down There [Là-bas]: A Study in Satanism*, tr. Keene Wallis. 1884; New York: University Books, 1958.

Hyde, H. Montgomery, *The Annotated Oscar Wilde*. New York: Clarkson N. Potter, 1982.

Irving, Washington, *The Legend of Sleepy Hollow; and other selections*, ed. Austin Fox. New York: Pocket Books, 1962.

Jackson, Shirley, *The Haunting of Hill House*. New York: Viking, 1959.

———, *The Lottery, or the Adventures of James Harris*. New York: Farrar, Strauss, 1959; New York: Avon, 1969.

———, *We Have Always Lived in the Castle*. New York: Viking, 1962; New York: Popular Library, 1963.

Jacobs, Joseph, ed., *Celtic Fairy Tales*. London: D. Nutt, 1892; New York: Dover, 1968.

James, Henry, *The Ghostly Gales of Henry James*, ed. Leon Edel. New Brunswick, N.J.: Rutgers University Press, 1949.

James, M.R., *The Collected Ghost Stories of M.R. James*. London: Edward Arnold, 1931; republished New York: St. Martin's, 1974.

———, *Ghost Stories of an Antiquary*. London: E. Arnold, 1904; New York: Dover, 1971. (See also the 1974 Penguin edition, which includes *More Ghost Stories of an Antiquary* under the same title.)

Johnson, Pamela Hansford, *On Iniquity*. New York: Scribner, 1967.

Jones, Ernest, *On the Nightmare*. New York: Liveright, 1951.

Jerome, Jerome K., *Told After Supper*. New York: Scribner, 1891.

Kassem, Ceza & Hashem, Malak, eds., *Flights of Fantasy: Arabic Short Stories*. Cairo, Egypt: Elias Modern Publishing House, 1985.

Keay, Carolyn, ed., *Henry Fuseli*. New York: St. Martin's Press, 1974.

Kelly, Isabella, *The Abbey of St. Asaph*, 3 vols. London: Minerva Press, 1795; New York: Arno, 1977.

Kersh, Gerald, *Men Without Bones* New York: Paperback Library, 1962.

Kieji, Nikolas, *Japanese Grotesqueries*, intro. Terrence Barron. Rutland, Vt.: Charles E. Tuttle, 1973.

King, Stephen, *Carrie*. Garden City, N.Y.: Doubleday, 1974.

———, *It*. New York: Viking-Penguin, 1986.

———, *The Shining.* Garden City, N.Y.: Doubleday, 1977.

Kipling, Rudyard, *The Phantom Rickshaw and Other Stories.* Allahabad: Wheeler, 1888; New York: Standard Classics, 1930.

———, *Phantoms and Fantasies.* Garden City, N.Y.: Doubleday, 1965.

Konvitz, Jeffrey, *The Sentinel.* New York: Simon & Schuster, 1976.

Krafft-Ebing, Richard von, M.D., *Psychopathia Sexualis.* New York: Pioneer Publication, 1950.

Kramer, Noah Samuel, ed., *Mythologies of the Ancient World.* New York: Doubleday/Anchor, 1961.

Lambert, R.S., *Exploring the Supernatural and the Weird in Canadian Folklore.* Toronto: McClelland & Stewart, 1955.

Larkin, David, *The English Dreamers,* intro. Rowland Elzea. Toronto: Peacock Press, 1975.

Lawrence, D.H., *The Complete Short Stories of D.H. Lawrence.* New York: Penguin, 1976–77.

Lazare, Christopher, ed., *Tales of Hoffmann.* New York: Grove Press, 1946.

Le Guin, Ursula, *The Left Hand of Darkness.* New York: Ace, 1959.

———, *Orsinian Tales.* New York: Harper & Row, 1976.

———, *Wild Angels.* Santa Barbara: Capra Press, 1975.

———, *The Wind's Twelve Quarters.* New York: Harper & Row, 1975.

Lecky, W.E.H., *History of European Morals.* New York: Appleton, 1917.

Lederer, Wolfgang, *The Fear of Women.* New York: Grune and Stratton, 1968.

Lee, Vernon (pseud. of Violet Paget), *For Maurice: Five Unlikely Stories.* London: J. Lane, 1927.

———, *Hauntings: Fantastic Stories.* London: John Lane, 1906.

———, *Pope Jacynth and More Supernatural Tales.* London: Peter Owen, 1956.

———, *The Snake Lady and Other Stories,* ed. E.F. Bleiler. New York: Dover, 1964.

Le Fanu, J.S., *Best Ghost Stories,* ed. E.F. Bleiler. New York: Dover, 1964.

———, *Ghost Stories and Mysteries,* ed. E.F. Bleiler. New York: Dover, 1975.

———, *The Hours after Midnight: Tales of Terror and the Supernatural,* ed. Des Hickey. London: Leslie Frewin, 1975.

———, et al., *A Stable for Nightmares; or Weird Tales.* New York: New Amsterdam Book Company, 1896; New York: Arno, 1976.

Leiber, Fritz, ed., *H.P. Lovecraft: A Symposium.* Regina, Canada: Riverside Quarterly, 1970.

Lewis, Matthew G., *The Monk.* London: J. Bell, 1796; republished, ed. John Berryman, New York: Grove Press, 1952.

Lieberman, Herbert, *The Eighth Square.* New York: Pocket Books, 1978.

Long, Frank Belknap, *The Horror from the Hills.* Sauk City, Wis.: Arkham House, 1963.

Lovecraft, H.P., *At the Mountains of Madness and Other Novels.* ed. August Derleth. Sauk City, Wis.: Arkham House, 1964.

———, *Dagon and Other Macabre Tales,* ed. August Derleth. Sauk City, Wis.: Arkham House, 1965.

———, *The Dark Brotherhood and Other Pieces.* Sauk City, Wis.: Arkham House, 1970.

———, *The Dunwich Horror,* ed. August Derleth. Sauk City, Wis.: Arkham House, 1963.

———, *The Horror in the Museum and Other Revisions.* Sauk City, Wis.: Arkham House, 1970.

———, *Supernatural Horror in Literature.* New York: Ben Abramson, 1927; New York: Dover, 1973.

Lytton, Edward Bulwer. See Bulwer-Lytton.

MacDougall, James, comp., *Folk Tales and Fairy Lore in Gaelic and English.* Edinburgh: J. Grant, 1910.

Machen, Arthur, *The Strange World of Arthur Machen.* New York: Juniper Press, 1960.

———, *Tales of Horror and the Supernatural.* New York: Knopf, 1948; New York: Pinnacle, 1971.

Manley, Seon, comp., *Ladies of Horror: Two Centuries of Supernatural Stories by the Gentle Sex.* New York: Lothrop, Lee & Shephard, 1971.

Mann, Thomas, *Doctor Faustus; the Life of the German Composer,* tr. H.T. Lowe-Porter. New York: Knopf, 1948; New York: Vintage, 1971.

———, *Last Essays.* New York: Knopf, 1959.

Mare, Walter de la. See De La Mare.

Masterton, Graham, *The Sphinx.* New York: Pinnacle, 1978.

Maturin, Charles R., *The Fatal Revenge; or, The Family of Montorio,* 3 vols. New York: Arno, 1974.

———, *Melmoth the Wanderer.* Edinburgh: A. Constable, 1820; republished Lincoln: Univ. of Nebraska Press, 1961.

———, *The Wild Irish Boy.* New York: Arno, 1977.

McCarthy, John, *Splatter Movies: Breaking the Last Taboo of the Screen.* New York: St. Martin's Press, 1984.

McCauley, Kirby, ed., *Night Chills.* New York: Avon, 1975.

McDowell, Michael, *The Amulet.* New York: Avon, 1979.

McNally, Raymond, *A Clutch of Vampires.* New York: Bell Publishing Co., 1974.

McSherry, Frank D., Jr., et al., eds., *A Treasury of American Horror Stories.* New York: Bonanza, 1985.

Menville, Douglas, *A Historical and Critical Survey of the Science Fiction Film.* London: Arno Press, 1974.

Menville, Douglas and Reginald, R., eds., *Phantasmagoria.* New York: Arno, 1976.

Mérimée, Prosper, *La Guzla.* Paris: Heitz, 1926.

Merritt, Abraham and Hannes Bok, *The Black Wheel.* New York: New Collectors Group, 1947; New York: Arno, 1976.

———, *The Fox Woman and the Blue Pagoda.* New York: New Collectors Group, 1946; New York: Arno, 1976.

Meyers, Richard, *For One Week Only: The World of Exploitation Films.* Piscataway, N.J.: New Century Publishers, 1983.

Monaco, James, *The Connoisseur's Guide to the Movies.* New York: Facts on File, 1985.

Moore, Darrell (and the editors of *Consumer Guide*), *The Best, Worst, and Most Unusual: Horror Films.* New York: Beekman House, 1983.

Munro, Dana Carleton, *The Middle Ages.* New York: Century, 1922.

Munro, Hector H. (aka Saki), *The Short Stories of Saki.* New York: Viking, 1930.

Naha, Ed, *The Films of Roger Corman: Brilliance on a Budget.* New York: Arco, 1982.

Nietzsche, Friedrich, *The Birth of Tragedy and the Genealogy of Morals.* Garden City, N.Y.: Doubleday, 1956.

Oates, Joyce Carol, *Night-Side: Eighteen Tales.* New York: Vanguard, 1977.

O'Flaherty, Wendy, *The Origins of Evil in Hindu Mythology*. Berkeley: University of California Press, 1976.

Oliphant, Margaret O., *Stories of the Seen and the Unseen*. Freeport, N.Y.: Books for Libraries Press, 1970.

Onions, Oliver, *Collected Ghost Stories of Oliver Onions*. London: Ivor Nicholson and Watson, 1935; New York: Dover, 1978.

———, *Collected Ghost Stories of Oliver Onions*. New York: Dover, 1971.

Page, Thomas, *The Hephaestus Plague*. New York: Putnam, 1973; republished New York: Bantam, 1975.

Paget, Violet. See Lee, Vernon.

Parker, Henry, *Village Folk-Tales of Ceylon*, 3 vols. London: Arno Press, 1941; reprinted 1978.

Parry, Michel, ed., *Beware of the Cat*. New York: Taplinger, 1973.

Peacock, Thomas Love, *Nightmare Abbey*. London: T. Hookham, Jr. and Baldwin, Cradock & Joy, 1818; republished New York: Holt, Rinehart & Winston, 1971.

Peithman, Stephen, *The Annotated Tales of Edgar Allan Poe*. New York: Avenel, 1981; republished New York: Crown, 1986.

Pirie, David, *A Heritage of Horror: The English Gothic Cinema, 1946–1972*. New York: Avon, 1973.

———, *The Vampire Cinema*. New York: Crescent Publications, 1977.

Poe, Edgar Allan, *Complete Tales and Poems*. New York: Random House, 1938.

Polidori, John, *The Vampyre, A Tale*. London: Sherwood, Neely, and Jones, 1819; republished Pasadena, Calif.: Grant Dahlstrom, 1968.

Prest, Thomas Preskett, *Varney the Vampire, or The Feast of Blood*. London: E. Lloyd, 1847; republished New York: Arno, 1971.

Pritchett, V.S., ed., *Novels and Stories by Robert Louis Stevenson*. New York: Duell, Sloan and Pearce, 1946.

Pronzini, Bill, et al., eds., *Great Tales of Horror & The Supernatural*. Secaucus, N.J.: Castle, 1981.

———, eds., *Tales of the Dead*. New York: Bonanza, 1981.

P'u Sung-Ling, *Chinese Ghost and Love Stories*. New York: Pantheon, 1946.

Rabkin, Eric S., *The Fantasatic in Literature*. Princeton, N.J.: Princeton University Press, 1976.

Radcliffe, Ann, *The Italian; or The Confessional of the Black Penitents*, ed. Frederick Garber. New York: Oxford University Press, 1981.

Ralston, William R.S., *Russian Folk Tales*. New York: Arno, 1977 (1873).

Randall, Bob, The Fan. New York: Random House, 1977.

Renard, Maurice, *Les Mains D'Orlac*. Paris: Editions Pierre Belfond, 1970.

Reginald, R. and Menville, Douglas, eds., *The Spectre Bridegroom and Other Stories*. New York: Arno, 1976.

Rhodes, Henry Taylor-Fowkes, *The Satanic Mass: A Sociological and Criminological Study*. London: Rider and Co., 1954.

Rice, Anne, *Interview with the Vampire*. New York: Knopf, 1976.

Riddell, Mrs. J.H., *The Collected Ghost Stories*, ed. E.F. Bleiler. New York: Dover, 1977.

Roberts, Bette B., *The Gothic Romance: Its Appeal to Women Writers and Readers in Late Eighteenth-Century England*. New York: Arno, 1980.

Rosetti, Christina G., *Goblin Market and Other Poems*. London: Macmillan, 1862; republished New York: Dover, 1983.

Roy, Claude, *Les Arts fantastiques*. Paris: Encyclopédie Essentielle, 1960.

Russell, John, *Where the Pavement Ends*. London: Eyre and Spottiswoode, 1921.

Sade, Marquis de. See De Sade, Marquis.

Saki. See Munro, Hector H.

Saty, Wilfried, ed., *The Illustrated Edgar Allan Poe*. New York: Clarkson N. Potter, 1976.

Scarborough, Dorothy, *The Supernatural in Modern Fiction*. New York: Putnam, 1917; New York: Octagon, 1967.

Scheuer, Steven H., *Movies On TV*, rev. ed. New York: Bell Publishing Co., 1984.

Scott, Sir Walter, *The Bride of Lammermoor*. London: A. Constable, 1819; republished New York: Dutton, 1973.

Seabrook, William, *Witchcraft*. London: Sphere, 1942.

Siddons, Anne Rivers, *The House Next Door*. New York: Simon and Schuster, 1978.

Siegel, Joel E., *Val Lewton: the Reality of Terror*. New York: Viking, 1973.

Smith, Clark Ashton, *The Abominations of Yondo*. London: Neville Spearman, 1972.

———, *Lost Worlds*. Sauk City, Wis.: Arkham House, 1944; republished London: Neville Spearman, 1971 (2 vols.).

Stanley, John, *John Stanley's Creature Features Movie Guide*. Pacifica, Calif.: Creatures at Large, 1981.

Stephen, Gilbert, *Willard* (original title, *Ratman's Journal*). London: Lancer, 1968; New York: Viking, 1968.

Stevenson, Robert Louis, *The Merry Men and Other Tales*. London: Chatto & Windus, 1887; republished New York: Scribner, 1925.

———, *The Strange Case of Doctor Jekyll and Mr. Hyde*. London: Longmans, 1886; republished London: Thomas Nelson and Sons Ltd., 1956.

Stoker, Bram, *The Bram Stoker Bedside Companion*, ed. Charles Horne. New York: Taplinger, 1973.

———, *Dracula*. London: Constable, 1897; republished in Leonard Wolf's (ed.), *The Annotated Dracula*, New York, Ballantine, 1975.

Sturgeon, Theodore, *Some of Your Blood*. New York: Ballantine, 1961.

Sullivan, Jack, ed., *The Penguin Encyclopedia of Horror and the Supernatural*. New York: Viking-Penguin, 1986.

Summers, Montague, ed., *The Supernatural Omnibus*. London: Gollanez, 1931; New York: Causeway, 1974.

———, ed., *Victorian Ghost Stories*. London: Fortune, 1933.

Taylor, Al & Roy, Sue, *Making a Monster: The Creation of Screen Characters by the Great Makeup Artists*. New York: Crown, 1980.

Tessier, Thomas, *The Nightwalker*. New York: Atheneum, 1979.

Thompson, Richard Lowe, *History of the Devil*. London: K. Paul, Trench, Trubner, and Co., Ltd., 1929.

Todorov, Tzetvan, *The Fantastic*. Ithaca, N.Y.: Cornell University Press, 1970.

Trachtenberg, Joshua, *The Devil and the Jews*. New Haven, Conn.: Yale University Press, 1943.

Tracy, Ann Blaisdell, *Patterns of Fear in the Gothic Novel, 1790–1830*. New York: Arno, 1980.

Tryon, Thomas, *The Other*. New York: Knopf, 1971.

Turgenev, Ivan, *The Two Friends and Other Stories,* tr. Constance Garnett. London: Heinemann, 1921.

Twitchell, James B., *Dreadful Pleasures: An Anatomy of Modern Horror.* New York: Oxford University Press, 1985.

Tymm, Marshall B., *Horror Literature: A Core Collection and Reference Guide.* New York: R.R. Bowker, 1981.

Vermaseren, M.J., *Mithras The Secret God.* New York: Barnes and Noble, 1959.

Viereck, George Sylvester, *The House of the Vampire.* New York: Yard and Co., 1970; republished New York: Arno, 1976.

Walpole, Horace (aka Onuphrio Muralto), *The Castle of Ontranto.* London: Thomas Lownds, 1765; ed. W.S. Lewis, New York: Oxford University Press, 1982.

Wells, H.G., *The Short Stories of H.G. Wells.* London: Ernest Benn, 1927; New York: St. Martin, 1974.

Wharton, Edith, *The Ghost Stories of Edith Wharton.* New York: Scribner, 1973.

Wheatley, Dennis, *To the Devil a Daughter.* London: Hutchinson, 1953.

Willoughby, Harold R., *Pagan Regeneration.* Chicago: University of Chicago Press, 1929.

Wise, Hergert & Fraser, Phyllis, eds., *Great Tales of Terror and the Supernatural.* New York: Random House, 1944; reprinted in the "Modern Library."

Wolf, Leonard, *The Annotated Dracula.* New York: Clarkson N. Potter, 1975.

———, *The Annotated Frankenstein.* New York: Clarkson N. Potter, 1977.

———, *A Dream of Dracula.* New York: Popular Library, 1972.

———, *Monsters; Twenty Terrible and Wonderful Beasts from the Classic Dragon and Colossal Minotaur to King Kong and the Great Godzilla.* San Francisco: Straight Arrow Books, 1974.

Wolf, Leonard, ed., *Wolf's Complete Book of Terror.* New York: Clarkson N. Potter, 1979.

Wollheim, Donald A., ed., *The Girl with the Hungry Eyes.* New York: Avon, 1949.

Woolf, Virginia, "Henry James's Ghosts," in *The Turn of the Screw: Backgrounds and Sources,* ed. Robert Kimbrough. New York: Norton Critical, 1966.

Wright, Gene, *Horrorshows: The A-to-Z of Horror in Film, TV, Radio and Theater.* New York: Facts On File, 1986.

Wyndham, John, *The John Wyndham Omnibus.* New York: Simon and Schuster, 1951.

INDEX